MCSE

Self-Paced Training Kit

Microsoft

2

Second Edition

Microsoft

WINDOWS 2000
ACTIVE DIRECTORY
SERVICES

Exam 70-217

PUBLISHED BY
Microsoft Press
A Division of Microsoft Corporation
One Microsoft Way
Redmond, Washington 98052-6399

Copyright © 2003 by Microsoft Corporation

Library of Congress Cataloging-in-Publication Data
MCSE Self-Paced Training Kit : Microsoft Windows 2000 Active Directory Services
(Exam 70-217) / Microsoft Corporation.-- 2nd ed.
        p. cm.
        Includes index.
    ISBN 0-7356-1759-7
    1. Electronic data processing personnel--Certification. 2. Microsoft
software--Examinations--Study guides. 3. Directory services (Computer network
technology) 4. Microsoft Windows (Computer file) I. Microsoft Corporation.

QA76.3 .M33255 2002
005.7'13769--dc21

                                                    2002023534

Printed and bound in the United States of America.

2 3 4 5 6 7 8 9   QWT   7 6 5 4 3

Distributed in Canada by H.B. Fenn and Company Ltd.

A CIP catalogue record for this book is available from the British Library.

Microsoft Press books are available through booksellers and distributors worldwide. For further information about international editions, contact your local Microsoft Corporation office or contact Microsoft
Press International directly at fax (425) 936-7329. Visit our Web site at www.microsoft.com/mspress. Send
comments to *tkinput@microsoft.com.*

Active Directory, ActiveX, BackOffice, FrontPage, JScript, Microsoft, Microsoft Press, MS-DOS, Visual
Basic, Win32, Windows, and Windows NT are either registered trademarks or trademarks of Microsoft
Corporation in the United States and/or other countries. Other product and company names mentioned
herein may be the trademarks of their respective owners.

The example companies, organizations, products, domain names, e-mail addresses, logos, people, places,
and events depicted herein are fictitious. No association with any real company, organization, product,
domain name, e-mail address, logo, person, place, or event is intended or should be inferred.

Program Manager: Jeff Madden
Project Editor: Michael Bolinger

Author: Jill Spealman

Body Part No. X08-76693

Contents

Part 1   Self-Paced Training for Microsoft Windows 2000 Active Directory Services

Part 2   Preparation for MCP Exam 70-217

About This Book

Welcome to the *MCSE Training Kit—Microsoft Windows 2000 Active Directory Services*. This book is organized in two parts. Part 1 is a self-paced training course designed to prepare you to install, configure, administer, monitor, and troubleshoot Microsoft Windows 2000 Active Directory, and prepare you for the related Microsoft Certified Professional exam 70-217: Implementing and Administering a Microsoft Windows 2000 Directory Services Infrastructure. Part 2 is designed to give you a focused, timesaving way to identify the information you need to know to pass the Microsoft Certified Professional (MCP) exam, and is accompanied by a realistic electronic assessment tool to help you become familiar with the types of questions that you will encounter on MCP exam 70-217. By reviewing the objectives and sample questions in Part 2, you can focus on the specific skills you need to improve before taking the exam.

Before You Begin Part 1

Part 1 introduces you to Windows 2000 Active Directory and prepares you to plan, configure, and administer your Active Directory infrastructure. You will learn to configure Domain Name System (DNS) to manage name resolution, schema, and replication. You will also learn to use Active Directory to centrally manage users, groups, shared folders, and network resources, and to administer the user environment and software with group policy. This kit shows you how to implement and troubleshoot security in a directory services infrastructure and monitor and optimize Active Directory performance. You also learn to deploy Windows 2000 remotely using Remote Installation Services (RIS).

This course supports the Microsoft Certified Systems Engineer program.

Note   For more information on becoming a Microsoft Certified Systems Engineer, see the section of this chapter titled "The Microsoft Certified Professional Program."

Each chapter in Part 1 is divided into lessons. Most lessons include hands-on procedures that allow you to practice or demonstrate a particular concept or skill. Each chapter ends with a short summary of all chapter lessons and a set of review questions to test your knowledge of the chapter material.

The "Getting Started" section of this chapter provides important setup instructions that describe the hardware and software requirements to complete the procedures in this course. It also provides information about the networking configuration necessary to complete some of the hands-on procedures. Read through this section thoroughly before you start the lessons.

Intended Audience

This book has been developed for information system (IS) professionals who need to install, configure, administer, monitor, and troubleshoot Microsoft Windows 2000 Active Directory, or who plan to take the related Microsoft Certified Professional exam 70-217, *Implementing and Administering a Microsoft Windows 2000 Directory Services Infrastructure*.

Prerequisites

This course requires that students meet the following prerequisites:

- A knowledge of the fundamentals of current networking technology is required.
- Successful completion of the *MCSE Training Kit—Microsoft Windows 2000 Server* is recommended.

Reference Materials

You might find the following reference materials useful:

- Windows 2000 white papers and case studies, available online at *http://www.microsoft.com/windows/server/*
- Windows 2000 Server Help, available on the Start Menu when Windows 2000 Server is installed
- Windows 2000 Support Tools Help, available on the Start, Programs, Windows 2000 Support Tools Menu when Windows 2000 Support Tools are installed
- Windows 2000 Server Resource Kit, in print format or on CD-ROM

Features of This Book

Each chapter opens with a "Before You Begin" section, which prepares you for completing the chapter.

▶ Each chapter is divided into lessons. Whenever possible, the lessons contain practices that give you an opportunity to use the skills being presented or to explore the part of the application being described. These practices are placed at the end of lessons and consist of one or more exercises containing procedures. Each procedure is marked with a bullet symbol like the one to the left of this paragraph.

Important The additional procedures that are not included within the practice sections are intended as general information to advance your knowledge of Windows 2000 Active Directory. Because many of the practices build on procedures you do in earlier practices, if you work through the additional procedures in the general text of the book you may alter the state of your test machine and may not be able to carry out subsequent practices exactly as they are presented.

The "Review" section at the end of the chapter allows you to test what you have learned in the chapter's lessons.

Appendix A, "Questions and Answers," contains all of the book's questions and corresponding answers.

Notes

Several types of Notes appear throughout the lessons.

- Notes marked **Note** contain supplemental information.
- Notes marked **Important** contain information that is essential to completing a task.
- Notes marked **Caution** contain warnings about possible loss of data.
- Notes marked **Tip** contain explanations of possible results or alternative methods.

Conventions

The following conventions are used throughout this book.

Notational Conventions

- Characters or commands that you type appear in **bold lowercase** type.
- *Italic* in syntax statements indicates placeholders for variable information. *Italic* is also used for book titles.
- Names of files appear in Title Caps, except when you are to type them directly. Unless otherwise indicated, you can use all lowercase letters when you type a filename in a dialog box or at a command prompt.

- Filename extensions appear in all lowercase.

- Acronyms appear in all uppercase.

- Monospace type represents code samples, examples of screen text, or entries that you might type at a command prompt or in initialization files.

- Square brackets [ ] are used in syntax statements to enclose optional items. For example, [*filename*] in command syntax indicates that you can choose to type a file name with the command. Type only the information within the brackets, not the brackets themselves.

- Braces { } are used in syntax statements to enclose required items. Type only the information within the braces, not the braces themselves.

- Icons represent specific sections in the book as follows:

Icon	Represents
	A hands-on practice. You should perform the practice to give yourself an opportunity to use the skills being presented in the lesson.
	Chapter review questions. These questions at the end of each chapter allow you to test what you have learned in the lessons. You will find the answers to the review questions in the Questions and Answers section at the end of the book.

Keyboard Conventions

- A plus sign (+) between two key names means that you must press those keys at the same time. For example, "Press Alt+Tab" means that you hold down Alt while you press Tab.

- A comma (,) between two or more key names means that you must press each of the keys consecutively, not together. For example, "Press Alt, F, X" means that you press and release each key in sequence. "Press Alt+W, L" means that you first press Alt and W together, and then release them and press L.

- You can choose menu commands with the keyboard. Press the Alt key to activate the menu bar, and then sequentially press the keys that correspond to the highlighted or underlined letter of the menu name and the command name. For some commands, you can also press a key combination listed in the menu.

- You can select or clear check boxes or option buttons in dialog boxes with the keyboard. Press Tab until the option is highlighted, and then press the space-bar to select or clear the check box or option button.

- You can cancel the display of a dialog box by pressing the Esc key.

Chapter and Appendix Overview

This self-paced training course combines notes, hands-on procedures, and review questions to teach you how to install, configure, administer, monitor, and troubleshoot Windows 2000 Active Directory. It is designed to be completed from beginning to end, but you can choose a customized track and complete only the sections that interest you. (See the next section, "Finding the Best Starting Point for You," for more information.) If you choose the customized track option, see the "Before You Begin" section in each chapter. Any hands-on procedures that require preliminary work from preceding chapters refer to the appropriate chapters.

Part 1 is divided into the following chapters:

- The "About This Book" section contains a self-paced training overview and introduces the components of this training. Read this section thoroughly to get the greatest educational value from this self-paced training and to plan which lessons you will complete.

- Chapter 1, "Introduction to Microsoft Windows 2000," introduces Windows 2000. It includes overviews of the Windows 2000 operating system, Windows 2000 architecture, and Windows 2000 Directory Services.

- Chapter 2, "Introduction to Active Directory," introduces you to Active Directory components, including objects, domains, organizational units (OUs), trees, and forests. It also introduces you to Active Directory concepts, including the global catalog, replication, trust relationships, DNS namespaces, and naming conventions.

- Chapter 3, "Active Directory Administration Tasks and Tools," introduces you to the primary Active Directory administration tasks, including configuring Active Directory, administering users and groups, securing network resources, administering the desktop computing environment, auditing resources and events, and monitoring resources and events. It also introduces you to the Active Directory administration tools, including Microsoft Management Consoles (MMCs) and the Task Scheduler.

- Chapter 4, "Implementing Active Directory," walks you through the steps of implementing Active Directory, including planning, installation, determining operations master roles, and implementing an OU structure.

- Chapter 5, "DNS and Active Directory Integration," introduces you to DNS name resolution and zones. It also provides practice in configuring zones and discusses zone replication and transfer. The chapter concludes with information on troubleshooting an Active Directory DNS configuration.

- Chapter 6, "Configuring Sites," shows you how to configure site settings and inter-site replication. It provides troubleshooting information for problems you may encounter that relate to inter-site replication. This chapter also discusses the tasks necessary for configuring server settings.

- Chapter 7, "User Account Administration," introduces you to user accounts and how to plan them. You learn the procedures for creating domain and local user accounts and setting their properties, as well as for setting up user profiles and home directories. This chapter also covers user account maintenance, including disabling, enabling, renaming, deleting, and unlocking user accounts and resetting user passwords.

- Chapter 8, "Group Account Administration," provides you with a group planning strategy and procedures for creating groups. You learn about the default groups provided by Microsoft Windows 2000 and the groups to which administrators should be assigned.

- Chapter 9, "Securing Network Resources," introduces you to Microsoft Windows 2000 file system (NTFS) folder and file permissions. You learn how to assign NTFS folder and file permissions to user accounts and groups and how moving or copying files and folders affects NTFS file and folder permissions. The chapter concludes with information on troubleshooting common resource access problems.

- Chapter 10, "Administering Shared Folders," introduces you to shared folders and to how to plan them. You learn the procedures for sharing folder resources, securing them with permissions, and providing access to them. The chapter concludes with information on setting up the Microsoft distributed file system (Dfs) to provide users with convenient access to shared folders that are distributed throughout a network.

- Chapter 11, "Administering Active Directory," provides instruction on Active Directory administration tasks, including locating objects, assigning permissions to objects, publishing resources, moving objects within and between domains, delegating administrative control to OUs, backing up and restoring, and troubleshooting Active Directory.

- Chapter 12, "Administering Group Policy," introduces you to group policy concepts and implementation planning. You learn the procedures for implementing group policy. You also learn how to manage software and special folders using group policy. The chapter concludes with information on troubleshooting common group policy problems.

- Chapter 13, "Administering a Security Configuration," discusses the use of security settings to determine a system's security configuration, including auditing, using security logs, user rights, using security templates, and the Security Configuration and Analysis tool. The chapter concludes with information on troubleshooting a security configuration.

- Chapter 14, "Managing Active Directory Performance," provides details on the performance monitoring tools, support tools, and shared folder monitoring tools available to help you to manage Active Directory performance.

- Chapter 15, "Deploying Windows 2000 Using RIS," introduces you to RIS. Procedures walk you through the steps for implementing and administering RIS. The chapter concludes with answers to frequently asked RIS questions and information on troubleshooting RIS problems.

Following Part 2 you will find

- Appendix A, "Questions and Answers," lists all of the practice and review questions from the book, showing suggested answers.

- Appendix B, "Installing and Configuring the DHCP Service," contains basic instructions for installing and configuring the Dynamic Host Configuration Protocol (DHCP) service in preparation for the use of RIS.

- The Glossary lists and defines the terms associated with your study of Windows 2000 Active Directory.

Finding the Best Starting Point for You

Because Part 1 is self-paced, you can skip some lessons and revisit them later. But note that you must complete the setup instructions in this chapter before you can perform procedures in the other chapters. Use the following table to find the best starting point for you. For sample questions to help you gauge your readiness for Exam 70-217, see Part 2, "Preparation for MCP Exam 70-217."

If You	Follow This Learning Path
Are preparing to take the Microsoft Certified Professional exam 70-217, Implementing and Administering a Microsoft Windows 2000 Directory Services Infrastructure	Read the "Getting Started" section and follow the setup procedure in the "Setup Instructions" section. Then work through Chapters 1 through 15, in order.
Want to review information about specific topics from the exam	Use the "Where to Find Specific Skills in This Book" section that follows this table.

Where to Find Specific Skills in This Book

The following tables provide a list of the skills measured on certification exam 70-217, *Implementing and Administering a Microsoft Windows 2000 Directory Services Infrastructure*. The table provides the skill and where in this book you will find the lesson relating to that skill.

Note   Exam skills are subject to change without prior notice and at the sole discretion of Microsoft.

Installing and Configuring Active Directory

Skill Being Measured	Location in Book
Install, Configure, and Troubleshoot the Components of Active Directory	
Install Active Directory	Chapter 4, Lesson 2
Create sites	Chapter 6, Lesson 1
Create subnets	Chapter 6, Lesson 1
Create site links	Chapter 6, Lesson 1
Create site link bridges	Chapter 6, Lesson 2
Create connection objects	Chapter 6, Lesson 2
Create global catalog servers	Chapter 6, Lesson 4
Move server objects between sites	Chapter 6, Lesson 4
Transfer Operations Master roles	Chapter 4, Lesson 3
Verify Active Directory installation	Chapter 4, Lesson 2
Implement an OU structure	Chapter 4, Lesson 4
Back Up and Restore Active Directory	
Perform an authoritative restore of Active Directory	Chapter 11, Lesson 6
Recover from a system failure	Chapter 11, Lesson 7

Installing, Configuring, Managing, Monitoring, and Troubleshooting DNS for Active Directory

Skill Being Measured	Location in Book
Install and Configure DNS for Active Directory	
Integrate an Active Directory DNS with a non-Active Directory DNS	Chapter 5, Lessons 2 and 4
Configure zones for dynamic updates	Chapter 5, Lessons 2 and 4
Manage, Monitor, and Troubleshoot DNS	
Manage replication of DNS data	Chapter 5, Lessons 3 and 4

Configuring, Managing, Monitoring, Optimizing, and Troubleshooting Change and Configuration Management

Skill Being Measured	Location in Book
Implement and Troubleshoot Group Policy	
Create a group policy object (GPO)	Chapter 12, Lessons 3 and 6
Link an existing GPO	Chapter 12, Lessons 3 and 6
Delegate administrative control of group policy	Chapter 12, Lessons 3 and 6
Modify group policy inheritance	Chapter 12, Lessons 3 and 6
Filter group policy settings by associating security groups to GPOs	Chapter 12, Lessons 3 and 6
Modify group policy	Chapter 12, Lessons 3 and 6
Manage and Troubleshoot User Environments by Using Group Policy	
Control user environments by using Administrative Templates	Chapter 12, Lessons 3 and 6
Assign script policies to users and computers	Chapter 12, Lessons 3 and 6
Install, Configure, Manage, and Troubleshoot Software by Using Group Policy	
Deploy software by using group policy	Chapter 12, Lesson 4
Maintain software by using group policy	Chapter 12, Lesson 4
Configure deployment options	Chapter 12, Lesson 4
Troubleshoot common problems that occur during software deployment	Chapter 12, Lesson 6
Manage Network Configuration by Using Group Policy	Chapter 12, Lesson 5
Deploy Windows 2000 by Using RIS	
Install an image on an RIS client computer	Chapter 15, Lesson 2
Create an RIS boot disk	Chapter 15, Lesson 2
Configure remote installation options	Chapter 15, Lesson 2
Troubleshoot RIS problems	Chapter 15, Lesson 4
Manage images for performing remote installations	Chapter 15, Lesson 3
Configure RIS Security	
Authorize an RIS server	Chapter 15, Lesson 3
Grant computer account creation rights	Chapter 15, Lesson 3
Prestage RIS client computers for added security and load balancing	Chapter 15, Lesson 3

Managing, Monitoring, and Optimizing the Components of Active Directory

Skill Being Measured	Location in Book
Manage Active Directory Objects	
Move Active Directory objects	Chapter 11, Lesson 4
Publish resources in Active Directory	Chapter 11, Lesson 3
Locate objects in Active Directory	Chapter 11, Lesson 1
Create and manage accounts manually or by scripting	Chapter 7, Lessons 3, 4, and 5 Chapter 8, Lessons 3, 4, and 5
Control access to Active Directory objects	Chapter 11, Lesson 2
Delegate administrative control of objects in Active Directory	Chapter 11, Lesson 5
Manage Active Directory Performance	
Monitor, maintain, and troubleshoot domain controller performance	Chapter 14, Lessons 1, 2, and 3
Monitor, maintain, and troubleshoot Active Directory components	Chapter 14, Lessons 1, 2, and 3
Manage and Troubleshoot Active Directory Replication	
Manage inter-site replication	Chapter 6, Lessons 1, 2, and 3
Manage intra-site replication	Chapter 6, Lessons 1 and 3

Configuring, Managing, Monitoring, and Troubleshooting Security in a Directory Services Infrastructure

Skill Being Measured	Location in Book
Configure and Troubleshoot Security in a Directory Services Infrastructure	
Apply security policies by using group policy	Chapter 13, Lessons 1, 3, 4, and 7
Create, analyze, and modify security configurations by using Security Configuration and Analysis and Security Templates	Chapter 13, Lessons 5, 6, and 7
Implement an audit policy	Chapter 13, Lessons 2 and 7
Monitor and Analyze Security Events	Chapter 13, Lesson 3

Getting Started

This self-paced training course contains hands-on procedures to help you learn about Windows 2000 Active Directory. To complete these procedures, you must have the following:

- One computer running Windows 2000 Server

There are a few optional practices and exercises in Part 1 that require two computers. Using a second computer is optional; it is not required to meet the lesson objectives. If you have only one computer, read through the steps and familiarize yourself with the procedure as best you can.

It is recommended that you set up the server on its own network specifically for this self-paced training because, to complete the lessons in Part 1, you will need to set up a domain controller and make changes to the domain controller that can affect other network users. However, you can use a domain controller on an existing network.

Caution   Several exercises may require you to make changes to your servers. This may have undesirable results if you are connected to a larger network. Check with your network administrator before attempting these exercises.

Hardware Requirements

Each computer must have the following minimum configuration. All hardware should be on the Microsoft Windows 2000 Hardware Compatibility List (HCL). The latest version of the HCL can be downloaded from the Hardware Compatibility List Web page at *http://www.microsoft.com/hwtest/hcl/*.

- 133-MHz or higher Pentium-compatible CPU
- 128 MB memory minimum
- 2 GB hard disk
- 12X or faster CD-ROM drive
- SVGA monitor capable of 800 × 600 resolution (1024 × 768 recommended)
- High-density 3.5-inch disk drive, unless your CD-ROM is bootable and supports starting the setup program from a CD-ROM
- Microsoft Mouse or compatible pointing device

Software Requirements

The following software is required to complete the procedures in this course:

☐ Windows 2000 Server CD-ROM or

☐ Windows 2000 Server 120-day evaluation version CD-ROM.

Setup Procedures

The following information is a checklist of the tasks that you need to perform to prepare your computer for the lessons in Part 1. If you do not have experience installing Windows 2000 or another network operating system, you may need help from an experienced network administrator. As you complete a task, mark it off in the check box. Step-by-step instructions for each task follow.

☐ Create Windows 2000 Server setup diskettes

☐ Run the Windows 2000 Server Pre-Copy and Text Mode Setup Routine

☐ Run the GUI mode and gathering information phase of Windows 2000 Server Setup

☐ Complete the Installing Windows Networking Components phase of Windows 2000 Server Setup

☐ Complete the hardware installation phase of Windows 2000 Server Setup

---

Note   The installation information provided will help you prepare a computer for use with Part 1. It is not intended to teach you installation. For comprehensive information on installing Windows 2000 Server, see the *MCSE Training Kit—Microsoft Windows 2000 Server*, also available from Microsoft Press.

Installing Windows 2000 Server

To complete the exercises in this course, you should install Windows 2000 Server on a computer with no formatted partitions. During installation, you can use the Windows 2000 Server Setup program to create a partition on your hard disk, on which you install Windows 2000 Server as a stand-alone server in a workgroup.

▶ **To create Windows 2000 Server Setup Diskettes**

- Complete this procedure on a computer running MS-DOS or any version of Windows with access to the Bootdisk directory on the Windows 2000 Server installation CD-ROM. If your computer is configured with a bootable CD-ROM drive, you can install Windows 2000 without using the Setup disks. To complete this exercise as outlined, bootable CD-ROM support must be disabled in the BIOS.

Important   This procedure requires four formatted 1.44-MB disks. If you use diskettes that contain data, the data will be overwritten without warning.

---

1. Label the four blank, formatted 1.44-MB diskettes as follows:
   - Windows 2000 Server Setup Disk #1
   - Windows 2000 Server Setup Disk #2
   - Windows 2000 Server Setup Disk #3
   - Windows 2000 Server Setup Disk #4
2. Insert the Microsoft Windows 2000 Server CD-ROM into the CD-ROM drive.
3. If the Windows 2000 CD-ROM dialog box appears prompting you to install or upgrade to Windows 2000, click No.
4. Open a command prompt.
5. At the command prompt, change to your CD-ROM drive. For example, if your CD-ROM drive name is E, type **e:** and press Enter.
6. At the command prompt, change to the Bootdisk directory by typing **cd bootdisk** and pressing Enter.
7. If you are creating the setup boot diskettes from a computer running MS-DOS, a Windows 16-bit operating system, Windows 95, or Windows 98, type **makeboot a:** (where A: is the name of your floppy disk drive), then press Enter. If you are creating the setup boot diskettes from a computer running Windows NT or Windows 2000, type **makebt32 a:** (where A: is the name of your floppy disk drive), then press Enter. Windows 2000 displays a message indicating that this program creates the four setup disks for installing Windows 2000. It also indicates that four blank, formatted, high-density floppy disks are required. Windows 2000 then prompts you to insert the disk that will become the Windows 2000 Setup Boot Disk.

8. Insert the blank formatted diskette labeled Windows 2000 Server Setup Disk #1 into the floppy disk drive and press any key to continue. After Windows 2000 creates the disk image, it displays a message prompting you to insert the diskette labeled Windows 2000 Setup Disk #2.

9. Remove Disk #1, insert the blank formatted diskette labeled Windows 2000 Server Setup Disk #2 into the floppy disk drive, and press any key to continue. After Windows 2000 creates the disk image, it displays a message prompting you to insert the diskette labeled Windows 2000 Setup Disk #3.

10. Remove Disk #2, insert the blank formatted diskette labeled Windows 2000 Server Setup Disk #3 into the floppy disk drive, and press any key to continue. After Windows 2000 creates the disk image, it displays a message prompting you to insert the diskette labeled Windows 2000 Setup Disk #4.

11. Remove Disk #3, insert the blank formatted diskette labeled Windows 2000 Server Setup Disk #4 into the floppy disk drive, and press any key to continue. After Windows 2000 creates the disk image, it displays a message indicating that the imaging process is done.

12. At the command prompt, type **exit** and then press Enter.

13. Remove the disk from the floppy disk drive and the CD-ROM from the CD-ROM drive.

▶ **Running the Windows 2000 Server Pre-Copy and Text Mode Setup Routine**

It is assumed for this procedure that your computer has no operating system installed, the disk is not partitioned, and bootable CD-ROM support, if available, is disabled.

1. Insert the disk labeled Windows 2000 Server Setup Disk #1 into the floppy disk drive, insert the Windows 2000 Server CD-ROM into the CD-ROM drive, and restart your computer.

   After the computer starts, Windows 2000 Setup displays a brief message that your system configuration is being checked, and then the Windows 2000 Setup screen appears.

   Notice that the gray bar at the bottom of the screen indicates that the computer is being inspected and that the Windows 2000 Executive is loading, which is a minimal version of the Windows 2000 kernel.

2. When prompted, insert Setup Disk #2 into the floppy disk drive and press Enter.

   Notice that Setup indicates that it is loading the HAL, fonts, local specific data, bus drivers, and other software components to support your computer's motherboard, bus, and other hardware. Setup also loads the Windows 2000 Setup program files.

3. When prompted, insert Setup Disk #3 into the floppy disk drive and press Enter.

   Notice that Setup indicates that it is loading disk drive controller drivers. After the drive controllers load, the setup program initializes drivers appropriate to support access to your disk drives. Setup might pause several times during this process.

4. When prompted, insert Setup Disk #4 into the floppy disk drive and press Enter.

   Setup loads peripheral support drivers, like the floppy disk driver and file systems, and then it initializes the Windows 2000 Executive and loads the rest of the Windows 2000 Setup program.

   Setup then displays the Welcome To Setup screen. Notice that, in addition to the initial installation of Windows 2000, you can use Windows 2000 Setup to repair or recover a damaged Windows 2000 installation. If you are installing the evaluation version of Windows 2000, a Setup Notification screen appears informing you that you are about to install an evaluation version of Windows 2000.

5. If you are installing the evaluation version of Windows 2000, read the Setup Notification message and press Enter to continue; otherwise, skip this step.

6. Read the Welcome To Setup message and press Enter to begin the installation phase of Windows 2000 Setup. Setup displays the License Agreement screen.

7. Read the license agreement, pressing Page Down to scroll down to the bottom of the screen.

8. Select I Accept The Agreement by pressing F8.

   Setup displays the Windows 2000 Server Setup screen, prompting you to select an area of free space or an existing partition on which to install Windows 2000. This stage of setup provides a way for you to create and delete partitions on your hard disk.

   If your computer does not contain any disk partitions (as required for this exercise), you will notice that the hard disk listed on the screen contains an existing unformatted partition.

9. Make sure that the Unpartitioned space partition is highlighted and then type **c.**

   Setup displays the Windows 2000 Setup screen, confirming that you've chosen to create a new partition in the unpartitioned space and informing you of the minimum and maximum sizes of the partition you might create.

10. Specify the size of the partition you want to create (at least 2 GB) and press Enter to continue.

    Setup displays the Windows 2000 Setup screen, showing the new partition as C: New (Unformatted).

Note Although you can create additional partitions from the remaining unpartitioned space during setup, it is recommended that you perform additional partitioning tasks after you install Windows 2000. To partition hard disks after installation, use the Disk Management console.

---

11. Make sure the new partition is highlighted and press Enter.

    You are prompted to select a file system for the partition.

12. Use the arrow keys to select Format The Partition Using The NTFS File System and press Enter.

    The Setup program formats the partition with NTFS. After it formats the partition, Setup examines the hard disk for physical errors that might cause Setup to fail and then copies files to the hard disk. This process will take several minutes.

    Eventually, Setup displays the Windows 2000 Server Setup screen. A red status bar counts down for 15 seconds before Setup restarts the computer.

13. Remove the Setup disk from the floppy disk drive.

Important If your computer supports booting from the CD-ROM drive and this feature was not disabled in the BIOS, the computer will boot from the Windows 2000 Server installation CD-ROM after Windows 2000 Setup restarts. This will cause Setup to start again from the beginning. If this happens, remove the CD-ROM and then restart the computer.

---

14. Setup copies additional files and then restarts your machine and loads the Windows 2000 Setup Wizard.

▶ **Running the GUI mode and gathering information phase of Windows 2000 Server Setup**

This procedure begins the graphical portion of setup on your computer.

1. On the Welcome To The Windows 2000 Setup Wizard page, click Next to begin gathering information about your computer.

   Setup configures NTFS folder and file permissions for the operating system files, detects the hardware devices in the computer, and then installs and configures device drivers to support the detected hardware. This process takes several minutes.

2. On the Regional Settings page, make sure that the system locale, user locale, and keyboard layout are correct for your language and location, then click Next.

Note   You can modify regional settings after you install Windows 2000 by using Regional Options in Control Panel.

   Setup displays the Personalize Your Software page, prompting you for your name and organization name. Setup uses your organization name to generate the default computer name. Many applications that you install later will use this information for product registration and document identification.

3. In the Name field, type your name; in the Organization field, type the name of an organization; then click Next.

Note   If the Your Product Key screen appears, enter the product key, located on the yellow sticker on the back of your Windows 2000 Server CD-ROM case.

   Setup displays the Licensing Modes page, prompting you to select a licensing mode. By default, the Per Server licensing mode is selected. Setup prompts you to enter the number of licenses you have purchased for this server.

4. Select the Per Server Number of concurrent connections button, type **5** for the number of concurrent connections, then click Next.

Important   Per Server Number of concurrent connections and 5 concurrent connections are suggested values to be used to complete your self-study. You should use a legal number of concurrent connections based on the actual licenses that you own. You can also choose to use Per Seat instead of Per Server.

Setup displays the Computer Name And Administrator Password page.

Notice that Setup uses your organization name to generate a suggested name for the computer.

5. In the Computer Name field, type **server1**.

Windows 2000 displays the computer name in all capital letters regardless of how it is entered.

Warning   If your computer is on a network, check with the network administrator before assigning a name to your computer.

Throughout the rest of this self-paced training kit, the practices and exercises will refer to Server1. If you do not name your computer Server1, everywhere the materials reference Server1, you will have to substitute the name of your server.

6. In the Administrator Password field and the Confirm Password field, type **password** (all lowercase) and click Next. Passwords are case-sensitive, so make sure you type **password** in all lowercase letters.

For the labs in this self-paced training kit, you will use password for the Administrator account. In a production environment, you should always use a complex password for the Administrator account (one that others cannot easily guess). Microsoft recommends mixing uppercase and lowercase letters, numbers, and symbols (for example, Lp6*g9).

Setup displays the Windows 2000 Components page, indicating which Windows 2000 system components Setup will install.

7. On the Windows 2000 Components page, click Next.

You can install additional components after you install Windows 2000 by using Add/Remove Programs in Control Panel. Make sure to install only the components selected by default during setup. Later in your training, you will be installing additional components.

If a modem is detected in the computer during setup, Setup displays the Modem Dialing Information page.

8. If the Modem Dialing Information page appears, enter an area code or city code and click Next.

   The Date And Time Settings page appears.

Important   Windows 2000 services perform many tasks whose successful completion depends on the computer's time and date settings. Be sure to select the correct time zone for your location to avoid problems in later labs.

---

9. Enter the correct Date and Time and Time Zone settings, then click Next.

   The Networking Settings page appears and Setup installs networking components.

▶ **Completing the Installing Windows Networking Components phase of Windows 2000 Server Setup**

Networking is an integral part of Windows 2000 Server. There are many selections and configurations available. In this procedure, basic networking is configured. In a later exercise, you will install additional network components.

1. On the Networking Settings page, make sure that Typical Settings is selected, then click Next to begin installing Windows networking components.

   This setting installs networking components that are used to gain access to and share resources on a network and configures Transmission Control Protocol/Internet Protocol (TCP/IP) to automatically obtain an IP address from a DHCP server on the network.

   Setup displays the Workgroup Or Computer Domain page, prompting you to join either a workgroup or a domain.

2. On the Workgroup Or Computer Domain page, make sure that the button No, This Computer Is Not On A Network Or Is On A Network Without A Domain is selected, and that the workgroup name is WORKGROUP, then click Next.

   Setup displays the Installing Components page, displaying the status as Setup installs and configures the remaining operating system components according to the options you specified. This will take several minutes.

   Setup then displays the Performing Final Tasks page, which shows the status as Setup finishes copying files, making and saving configuration changes, and deleting temporary files. Computers that do not exceed the minimum hardware requirements might take 30 minutes or more to complete this phase of installation.

   Setup then displays the Completing The Windows 2000 Setup Wizard page.

3. Remove the Windows 2000 Server CD-ROM from the CD-ROM drive, then click Finish.

Important   If your computer supports booting from the CD-ROM drive and you did not remove the installation CD-ROM, and if you disable this feature in the BIOS, the computer will run Setup again soon after Setup restarts the computer. If this happens, remove the CD-ROM and then restart the computer.

Windows 2000 restarts and runs the newly installed version of Windows 2000 Server.

▶ **Completing the hardware installation phase of Windows 2000 Server Setup**

During this final phase of installation, any Plug and Play hardware not detected in the previous phases of Setup will be detected.

1. At the completion of the startup phase, log on by pressing Ctrl+Alt+Delete.
2. In the Enter Password dialog box, type **administrator** in the User Name field and type **password** in the Password field.
3. Click OK.

   If Windows 2000 detects hardware that was not detected during Setup, the Found New Hardware Wizard screen displays, indicating that Windows 2000 is installing the appropriate drivers.

4. If the Found New Hardware Wizard screen appears, verify that the Restart The Computer When I Click Finish check box is cleared and click Finish to complete the Found New Hardware Wizard.

   Windows 2000 displays the Microsoft Windows 2000 Configure Your Server dialog box. From this dialog box, you can configure a variety of advanced options and services.

5. Select I Will Configure This Server Later, then click Next.
6. From the next screen that appears, clear the Show This Screen At Startup check box.
7. Close the Configure Your Server screen.

   You have now completed the Windows 2000 Server installation and are logged on as Administrator.

Note To properly shutdown Windows NT Server, click Start, choose Shut Down, then follow the directions that appear.

For the exercises that require networked computers, you need to make sure the computers can communicate with each other. The first computer will be designated as a domain controller in Chapter 4. The domain controller will be assigned the computer account name Server1 and the domain name microsoft.com. This computer will act as a domain controller in microsoft.com.

The second computer will be assigned the computer account name Server2 and the domain name microsoft.com. This computer will act as a member server in the microsoft.com domain for most of the optional practices in this course.

Caution If your computers are part of a larger network, you *must* verify with your network administrator that the computer names, domain name, and other information used in setting up Windows 2000 Server as described in this chapter do not conflict with network operations. If they do conflict, ask your network administrator to provide alternative values and use those values throughout all of the exercises in this book.

About the eBook

The Supplemental Course Materials CD-ROM includes an online version of the book that you can view on screen using Microsoft Internet Explorer 5.01 or later. For installation information, see the README.TXT file included in the root directory of the Supplemental Course Materials CD-ROM.

Note You must have the CD inserted in your CD-ROM drive for the online version of the book to run properly.

Before You Begin Part 2

Part 2 will help you evaluate your readiness for the MCP Exam 70-217: Implementing and Administering a Microsoft Windows 2000 Directory Services Infrastructure. When you pass this exam, you earn core credit toward Microsoft Certified Systems Engineer (MCSE) certification. In addition, when you pass this exam you achieve Microsoft Certified Professional status.

Note You can find a complete list of MCP exams and their related objectives on the Microsoft Certified Professional Web site at *http://www.microsoft.com/mcp/*.

The Components of Part 2

An electronic assessment program for Exam 70-217 is provided on the Supplemental Course Materials CD. This program is a practice certification test that helps you evaluate your skills. It provides instant scoring feedback, so you can determine areas in which additional study may be helpful before you take the certification exam. Although your score on the electronic assessment does not necessarily indicate what your score will be on the certification exam, it does give you the opportunity to answer questions that are similar to those on the actual certification exam.

Part 2 is organized by the exam's objectives. Each chapter covers one of the five primary groups of objectives on the actual exam, called the *Objective Domains*. Each Objective Domain lists the tested skills you need to master to answer the exam questions. Because the certification exams focus on real-world skills, the Tested Skills and Suggested Practices sections emphasize the practical application of the exam objectives. Each Objective includes a list of Further Readings to help you understand the objectives and increase your ability to perform the task or skills specified by the objectives.

Within each Objective Domain, you will find the related objectives that are covered on the exam. Each objective provides you with the following:

- **Key terms** you must know to understand the objective. Knowing these terms can help you answer the objective's questions correctly.
- Several sample exam questions with the correct answers. The answers are accompanied by explanations of each correct and incorrect answer. (These questions match the questions on the electronic assessment.)

Take the electronic assessment first to determine which exam objectives you need to study; then use Part 2 of the book to learn more about those particular objectives. You can also use Part 2 to research the answers to specific sample test questions. Keep in mind that to pass the exam, you should understand not only the answer to the question, but also the concepts on which the correct answer is based.

MCP Exam Prerequisites

No exams or classes are required before you take the Implementing and Administering a Microsoft Windows 2000 Directory Services Infrastructure exam. However, in addition to the skills tested by the exam, you should have a working knowledge of the operation and support of hardware and software in standalone computers. This knowledge should include:

- Using an operating system with a graphical user interface, such as Microsoft Windows 95, Microsoft Windows 98, Microsoft Windows NT 4.0, or Microsoft Windows 2000.

- Current networking technology.
- Successful completion of Part 1, "Self-Paced Training for Microsoft Windows 2000 Active Directory Services" is recommended.

Note After you have determined that you are ready for the exam, use the Get More MCP Information link provided in the home page of the electronic assessment tool for information on scheduling for the exam. You can schedule exams up to six weeks in advance, or as late as one working day before the exam date.

Know the Products

Microsoft's certification program relies on exams that measure your ability to perform a specific job function or set of tasks. Microsoft develops the exams by analyzing the tasks performed by people who are currently working in the field. Therefore, the specific knowledge, skills, and abilities relating to the job are reflected in the certification exam.

Because the certification exams are based on real-world tasks, you need to gain hands-on experience with the applicable technology in order to master the exam. You should consider hands-on experience a prerequisite for passing an MCP exam. Many of the questions relate directly to Microsoft products or technology, so use opportunities at your organization or home to practice using the relevant tools.

Using the Electronic Assessment and Part 2

Although you can use Part 2 in a number of ways, you might start your studies by taking the electronic assessment as a pretest. After completing the exam, review your results for each Objective Domain and focus your study first on the Objective Domains for which you received the lowest scores. The electronic assessment allows you to print your results, and a printed report of how you fared can be useful when reviewing the exam material in this book.

After you have taken the electronic assessment, use Part 2 to learn more about the Objective Domains that you find difficult and to find listings of appropriate study materials that may supplement your knowledge. By reviewing why the answers are correct or incorrect, you can determine whether you need to study the objective topics more.

You can also use Part 2 to focus on the exact objectives that you need to master. Each objective in the book contains several questions that help you determine whether you understand the information related to that particular skill. The book is also designed to allow you to answer each question before turning the page to review the correct answer.

The best method to prepare for the MCP exam is to use Part 2 in conjunction with the electronic assessment and other study material. A thorough study of the material combined with substantial real-world experience is the best preparation for the MCP exam.

Understanding the Conventions for Part 2

Before you begin Part 2, it is important that you understand the terms and conventions used in the electronic assessment and book.

Question Numbering System

The electronic assessment and Part 2 contain reference numbers for each question. Understanding the numbering format will help you use the training kit more effectively. When Microsoft creates the exams, the questions are grouped by job skills called *Objectives*. These Objectives are then organized by sections known as *Objective Domains*. Each question can be identified by the Objective Domain and the Objective it covers. The question numbers follow this format:

Test Number.Objective Domain.Objective.Question Number

For example, question number 70-217.02.01.003 means this is question three (003) for the first Objective (01) in the second Objective Domain (02) of the Implementing and Administering a Microsoft Windows 2000 Directory Services Infrastructure exam (70-217). Each question is numbered based on its presentation in the printed book. You can use this numbering system to reference questions on the electronic assessment or in Part 2 of the book. Even though the questions in the book are organized by objective, questions in the electronic assessment and actual certification exam are presented in random order.

Notational Conventions

- Characters or commands that you type appear in **bold lowercase** type. Bold type is also used to identify **Key Terms** in the text.
- Variable information and URLs are *italicized*. Italic is also used for book titles.
- Acronyms, filenames, and names of utilities appear in FULL CAPITALS.

Notes

Notes appear throughout the book.

- Notes marked *Caution* contain information you will want to know before continuing with the book's material.
- Notes marked *Note* contain supplemental information.
- Notes marked *Tip* contain helpful process hints.

Using the Electronic Assessment

The electronic assessment is designed to provide you with an experience that simulates that of the actual MCP exam. The electronic assessment questions are similar to those you will see on the certification exam. Furthermore, the electronic assessment format approximates the certification exam format and includes additional features to help you prepare for the real examination.

Each iteration of the electronic assessment consists of 50 questions covering all the objectives for the Implementing and Administering a Microsoft Windows 2000 Directory Services Infrastructure exam. (The actual certification exams generally consist of 50 to 70 questions.) Just as on a real certification exam, you see questions from the objectives in random order during the practice test. Similar to the certification exam, the electronic assessment allows you to mark questions and review them after you finish the test.

To increase its value as a study aid, you can take the electronic assessment multiple times. Each time, you are presented with a different set of questions in a revised order; however, some questions may be repeated.

If you have used one of the certification exam preparation tests available from Microsoft, the electronic assessment should look familiar. The difference is that the electronic assessment provides you with the opportunity to learn as you take the exam.

Installing and Running the Electronic Assessment Software

Before you begin using the electronic assessment, you need to install the software. You need a computer with the following minimum configuration:

- Multimedia PC with a 75MHz Pentium or higher processor
- Microsoft Internet Explorer 5.01 or later
- If you do not have Internet Explorer 5.01, you can download it for free from *http://www.microsoft.com/ie.*
- 16 MB RAM for Windows 95 or Windows 98, or
- 32 MB RAM for Windows NT, or
- 64 MB RAM for Windows 2000
- 17 MB of available hard disk space
- A double-speed CD-ROM drive or better
- Super VGA display with at least 256 colors
- Microsoft Mouse or compatible pointing device (recommended)

▶ **To install the electronic assessment**

1. Insert the Supplemental Course Materials compact disc into your CD-ROM drive.

   A starting menu will display automatically, with links to the resources included on the CD-ROM. Click the link to the exam you want to install.

2. Click Next.

   The License Agreement dialog box appears.

3. To continue with the installation of the electronic assessment engine, you must accept the License Agreement by clicking Yes.

4. The Choose Destination Location dialog box appears showing a default installation directory. Either accept the default or change the installation directory if needed. Click Next to copy the files to your hard drive.

5. A Question dialog box appears asking whether you would like Setup to create a desktop shortcut for this program. If you click Yes, an icon will be placed on your desktop.

6. The Setup Complete dialog box appears. Select whether you want to view the Readme.txt file after closing the Setup program, and then click Finish.

   The electronic assessment software is completely installed. If you chose to view the Readme.txt file, it will launch in a new window. For optimal viewing, enable word wrap.

▶ **To start the electronic assessment**

1. From the Start menu, point to Programs, point to MCSE Readiness Review, and then click MCSE RR Exam 70-217.

   The electronic assessment program starts.

2. Click Start Test.

   Information about the electronic assessment program appears.

3. Click OK.

Note The electronic assessment programs are designed to run one at a time. Other Readiness Review electronic assessment programs will not run simultaneously.

Taking the Electronic Assessment

The electronic assessment consists of 50 multiple-choice questions, and as in the certification exam, you can skip questions or mark them for later review. Each exam question contains a question number that you can use to refer back to Part 2 of the book.

Before you end the electronic assessment, you should make sure to answer all the questions. When the exam is graded, unanswered questions are counted as incorrect and will lower your score. Similarly, on the actual certification exam you should complete all questions or they will be counted as incorrect. No trick questions appear on the exam. The correct answer will always be among the list of choices. Some questions may have more than one correct answer, and this will be indicated in the question. A good strategy is to eliminate the most obvious incorrect answers first to make it easier for you to select the correct answer.

You have 75 minutes to complete the electronic assessment. During the exam, you will see a timer indicating the amount of time you have remaining. This will help you to gauge the amount of time you should use to answer each question and to complete the exam. The amount of time you are given on the actual certification exam varies with each exam. Generally, certification exams take approximately 90 minutes to complete.

Ending and Grading the Electronic Assessment

When you click the Score Test button, you have the opportunity to review the questions you marked or left incomplete. (This format is not similar to the one used on the actual certification exam, where you can verify whether you are satisfied with your answers, and then click the Grade Test button.) The electronic assessment is graded when you click the Score Test button, and the software presents your section scores and your total score.

Note You can always end a test without grading your electronic assessment by clicking the Home button.

After your electronic assessment is graded, you can view the correct and incorrect answers by clicking the Review Questions button.

Interpreting the Electronic Assessment Results

The Score screen shows you the number of questions in each Objective Domain section, the number of questions you answered correctly, and a percentage grade for each section. You can use the Score screen to determine where to spend additional time studying. On the actual certification exam, the number of questions and passing score will depend on the exam you are taking. The electronic assessment records your score each time you grade an exam so that you can track your progress over time.

▶ **To view your progress and exam records**

1. From the electronic assessment Main menu, click View History. Your scores will appear.

2. Click on a test attempt date/time to view your score for each objective domain.

   The section score for each attempt appears. You can review the section score information to determine which Objective Domains you should study further. You can also use the scores to determine your progress as you continue to study and prepare for the real exam.

Ordering More Questions

Self Test Software offers practice tests to help you prepare for a variety of MCP certification exams. These practice tests contain hundreds of additional questions and are similar to the electronic assessment. For a fee, you can order exam practice tests for this exam and other Microsoft certification exams. Click on the Order More Questions link on the electronic assessment home page for more information.

Using Part 2 of this Book

You can use Part 2 of this book as a supplement to the electronic assessment, or as a standalone study aid. If you decide to use the book as a standalone study aid, review the Table of Contents to find topics of interest or an appropriate starting point for you. To get the greatest benefit from the book, use the electronic assessment as a pretest to determine which Objective Domains to study. Or, if you would like to research specific questions while taking the electronic assessment, you can use the question number located on the question screen to reference the question number in the book.

One way to determine areas where additional study may be helpful is to carefully review your individual section scores from the electronic assessment and note objective areas where your score could be improved. The section scores correlate to the Objective Domains listed in the book.

Reviewing the Objectives

Each Objective Domain in the book contains an introduction and a list of practice skills. Each list of practice skills describes suggested tasks you can perform to help you understand the objectives. Some of the tasks suggest reading additional material, while others are hands-on practices using software or hardware. You should pay particular attention to the hands-on suggestions, as the certification exam reflects real-world knowledge you can gain only by working with the technology. Increasing your real-world experience will improve your performance on the exam.

Once you have determined the objectives you would like to study, you can use the Table of Contents to locate the objectives in the book. When reviewing a specific objective, you should make sure you understand the purpose of the objective and the skill or knowledge it is measuring on the certification exam. You can study each objective separately, but you may need to understand the concepts explained in other objectives.

Make sure you understand the key terms in each objective. You will need a thorough understanding of these terms to answer the objective's questions correctly. Key term definitions are located in the glossary of the electronic assessment on the Supplemental Course Materials CD-ROM.

Reviewing the Questions

Each odd-numbered page contains one or two questions followed by the possible answers. After you review the question and select a probable answer, you can turn to the following page to determine whether you answered the question correctly. (For information about the question numbering format, see "Question Numbering System," earlier in this introduction.)

Part 2 briefly discusses each possible answer and provides a specific reason why each answer is correct or incorrect. You should review the answer explanations to help you understand why the correct answer is the best answer among the choices given. You should understand not only the answer to the question, but the concepts that the correct answer is based on. If you feel you need more information about a topic or you do not understand the answer, use the Further Readings section to learn where you can find more information.

The answers to the questions in Part 2 are based on current industry specifications and standards. However, the information provided by the answers is subject to change as technology improves and changes.

The Microsoft Certified Professional Program

The Microsoft Certified Professional (MCP) program provides the best method to prove your command of current Microsoft products and technologies. Microsoft, an industry leader in certification, is on the forefront of testing methodology. Our exams and corresponding certifications are developed to validate your mastery of critical competencies as you design and develop or implement and support solutions with Microsoft products and technologies. Computer professionals who become Microsoft certified are recognized as experts and are sought after industry-wide.

The Microsoft Certified Professional program offers multiple certifications, based on specific areas of technical expertise:

- **Microsoft Certified Professional (MCP)** Demonstrated in-depth knowledge of at least one Microsoft operating system. Candidates may pass additional Microsoft certification exams to further qualify their skills with Microsoft BackOffice products, development tools, or desktop programs.

- **Microsoft Certified Professional + Internet** MCPs with a specialty in the Internet are qualified to plan security, install and configure server products, manage server resources, extend servers to run scripts, monitor and analyze performance, and troubleshoot problems.

- **Microsoft Certified Professional + Site Building** Demonstrated what it takes to plan, build, maintain, and manage Web sites using Microsoft technologies and products.

- **Microsoft Certified Systems Administrator (MCSA)** on Microsoft Windows 2000. Individuals who implement, manage, and troubleshoot existing network and system environments based on the Microsoft Windows 2000 and Windows .NET Server operating systems.

- **Microsoft Certified Systems Engineer (MCSE)**   Qualified to effectively plan, implement, maintain, and support IS in a wide range of computing environments with Microsoft Windows NT Server and the Microsoft BackOffice integrated family of server software.

- **Microsoft Certified Systems Engineer + Internet**   MCSEs with an advanced qualification to enhance, deploy, and manage sophisticated intranet and Internet solutions that include a browser, proxy server, host servers, database, and messaging and commerce components. In addition, an MCSE + Internet-certified professional is able to manage and analyze Web sites.

- **Microsoft Certified Database Administrator (MCDBA)**   Individuals who derive physical database designs, develop logical data models, create physical databases, create data services by using Transact-SQL, manage and maintain databases, configure and manage security, monitor and optimize databases, and install and configure Microsoft SQL Server.

- **Microsoft Certified Solution Developer (MCSD)**   Qualified to design and develop custom business solutions with Microsoft development tools, technologies, and platforms, including Microsoft Office and Microsoft BackOffice.

- **Microsoft Certified Trainer (MCT)**   Instructionally and technically qualified to deliver Microsoft Official Curriculum through a Microsoft Certified Technical Education Center (CTEC).

Microsoft Certification Benefits

Microsoft certification, one of the most comprehensive certification programs available for assessing and maintaining software-related skills, is a valuable measure of an individual's knowledge and expertise. Microsoft certification is awarded to individuals who have successfully demonstrated their ability to perform specific tasks and implement solutions with Microsoft products. Not only does this provide an objective measure for employers to consider; it also provides guidance for what an individual should know to be proficient. As with any skills-assessment and benchmarking measure, certification brings a variety of benefits to the individual and to employers and organizations.

Microsoft Certification Benefits for Individuals

As a Microsoft Certified Professional, you receive many benefits, including the following:

- Industry recognition of your knowledge and proficiency with Microsoft products and technologies.

- Access to technical and product information directly from Microsoft through a secured area of the MCP Web site.

- MSDN Online Certified Membership that helps you tap into the best technical resources, connect to the MCP community, and gain access to valuable resources and services. (Some MSDN Online benefits may be available in English only or may not be available in all countries.) See the MSDN Web site for a growing list of certified member benefits.

- Logos to enable you to identify your Microsoft Certified Professional status to colleagues or clients.

- Invitations to Microsoft conferences, technical training sessions, and special events.

- A Microsoft Certified Professional certificate.

- Subscription to *Microsoft Certified Professional Magazine* (North America only), a career and professional development magazine.

Additional benefits, depending on your certification and geography, include the following:

- A complimentary 1-year subscription to the Microsoft TechNet Technical Plus, providing valuable information on monthly CD-ROMs.

- A 1-year subscription to the Microsoft Beta Evaluation program. This benefit provides you with up to 12 free monthly CD-ROMs containing beta software (English only) for many of Microsoft's newest software products.

Microsoft Certification Benefits for Employers and Organizations

Through certification, computer professionals can maximize the return on investment in Microsoft technology. Research shows that Microsoft certification provides organizations with the following:

- Excellent return on training and certification investments by providing a standard method of determining training needs and measuring results

- Increased customer satisfaction and decreased support costs through improved service, increased productivity, and greater technical self-sufficiency

- A reliable benchmark for hiring, promoting, and career planning
- Recognition and rewards for productive employees by validating their expertise
- Retraining options for existing employees so they can work effectively with new technologies
- Assurance of quality when outsourcing computer services

Requirements for Becoming a Microsoft Certified Professional

The certification requirements differ for each certification and are specific to the products and job functions addressed by the certification.

To become a Microsoft Certified Professional, you must pass rigorous certification exams that provide a valid and reliable measure of technical proficiency and expertise. These exams are designed to test your expertise and ability to perform a role or task with a product, and they are developed with the input of professionals in the industry. Questions on the exams reflect how Microsoft products are used in actual organizations, giving them real-world relevance.

Microsoft Certified Product Specialists are required to pass one operating system exam. Candidates may pass additional Microsoft certification exams to further qualify their skills with Microsoft BackOffice products, development tools, or desktop applications.

Microsoft Certified Professional + Internet specialists are required to pass the prescribed Microsoft Windows NT Server 4.0, TCP/IP, and Microsoft Internet Information System exam series.

Microsoft Certified Professionals with a specialty in site building are required to pass two exams covering Microsoft FrontPage, Microsoft Site Server, and Microsoft Visual InterDev technologies to provide a valid and reliable measure of technical proficiency and expertise.

Microsoft Certified Systems Engineers are required to pass a series of core Microsoft Windows operating system and networking exams and BackOffice technology elective exams.

Microsoft Certified Systems Engineers + Internet specialists are required to pass seven operating system exams and two elective exams that provide a valid and reliable measure of technical proficiency and expertise.

Microsoft Certified Database Administrators are required to pass three core exams and one elective exam that provide a valid and reliable measure of technical proficiency and expertise.

Microsoft Certified Solution Developers are required to pass two core Microsoft Windows operating system technology exams and two BackOffice technology elective exams.

Microsoft Certified Trainers are required to meet instructional and technical requirements specific to each Microsoft Official Curriculum course they are certified to deliver. In the United States and Canada, call Microsoft at (800) 636-7544 for more information on becoming a Microsoft Certified Trainer or visit *http://www.microsoft.com/traincert/mcp/*. Outside the United States and Canada, contact your local Microsoft subsidiary.

Technical Training for Computer Professionals

Technical training is available in a variety of ways, with instructor-led classes, online instruction, or self-paced training available at thousands of locations worldwide.

Self-Paced Training

For motivated learners who are ready for the challenge, self-paced instruction is the most flexible, cost-effective way to increase your knowledge and skills.

A full line of self-paced print and computer-based training materials is available direct from the source—Microsoft Press. Microsoft Official Curriculum courseware kits from Microsoft Press are designed for advanced computer system professionals. These resources are available from Microsoft Press and the Microsoft Developer Division. Self-paced training kits from Microsoft Press feature print-based instructional materials, along with CD-ROM-based product software, multimedia presentations, lab exercises, and practice files. The Mastering Series provides in-depth, interactive training on CD-ROM for experienced developers. They're both great ways to prepare for Microsoft Certified Professional exams.

Online Training

For a more flexible alternative to instructor-led classes, turn to online instruction. It's as near as the Internet and it's ready whenever you are. Learn at your own pace and on your own schedule in a virtual classroom, often with easy access to an online instructor. Without ever leaving your desk, you can gain the expertise you need. Online instruction covers a variety of Microsoft products and technologies. It includes options ranging from Microsoft Official Curriculum to choices available nowhere else. It's training on demand, with access to learning resources 24 hours a day. Online training is available through Microsoft Certified Technical Education Centers.

Microsoft Certified Technical Education Centers

Microsoft Certified Technical Education Centers (CTECs) are the best source for instructor-led training that can help you prepare to become a Microsoft Certified Professional. The Microsoft CTEC program is a worldwide network of qualified technical training organizations that provide authorized delivery of Microsoft Official Curriculum courses by Microsoft Certified Trainers to computer professionals.

For a listing of CTEC locations in the United States and Canada, visit *http://www.microsoft.com/traincert/CTEC/*.

Technical Support

Every effort has been made to ensure the accuracy of this book. If you have comments, questions, or ideas regarding this book, please send them to Microsoft Press using either of the following methods:

E-mail:
TKINPUT@MICROSOFT.COM

Postal Mail:
Microsoft Press
Attn: *MCSE Training Kit—Microsoft Windows 2000*
Active Directory Services Editor
One Microsoft Way
Redmond, WA 98052–6399

Microsoft Press provides corrections for books through the World Wide Web at the following address:

http://www.microsoft.com/mspress/support/

Please note that product support is not offered through the above mail addresses. For further information regarding Microsoft software support options, please connect to *http://www.microsoft.com/support/* or call Microsoft Support Network Sales at (800) 936-3500.

For information about ordering the full version of any Microsoft software, please call Microsoft Sales at (800) 426-9400 or visit *www.microsoft.com*.

P A R T   1

Self-Paced Training for Microsoft Windows 2000 Active Directory Services

CHAPTER 1

Introduction to Microsoft Windows 2000

About This Chapter

This chapter introduces the Microsoft Windows 2000 operating system. It includes an overview of the products that comprise the Windows 2000 operating system, the roles they play, and a description of the administrative differences between them in a workgroup and a domain. Overviews of the Microsoft Windows 2000 architecture and Windows 2000 Directory Services are also provided. Hands-on practices guide you through the basic procedures of logging on and performing key tasks from the Windows Security dialog box.

Before You Begin

To complete the lessons in this chapter, you must have completed the Setup procedures located in "About This Book."

Lesson 1: Windows 2000 Overview

This lesson introduces you to the Windows 2000 family of products, including their features and benefits. It explains the key administrative differences between these products and the environment for which each product is designed.

After this lesson, you will be able to

- Describe Windows 2000
- Explain the key differences between Microsoft Windows 2000 Professional and Windows 2000 Server
- Describe the features and benefits of Windows 2000
- Describe the difference between a workgroup model and a domain model in a network environment

Estimated lesson time: 15 minutes

Overview of Windows 2000

Windows 2000 is a multipurpose operating system with integrated support for client/server and peer-to-peer networks. It incorporates technologies that reduce the total cost of ownership and provides for scalability from a small network to a large enterprise network. *Total cost of ownership (TCO)* is the total amount of money and time associated with purchasing computer hardware and software and deploying, configuring, and maintaining the hardware and software. TCO includes hardware and software updates, training, maintenance and administration, and technical support. One other major factor in TCO is lost productivity. Lost productivity can occur because of user errors, hardware problems, or software upgrades and retraining.

This training kit focuses on the following two versions of the Windows 2000 operating system:

- **Windows 2000 Professional.**   This product is a high-performance, secure network client computer and corporate desktop operating system that includes the best features of Microsoft Windows 98 and significantly extends the manageability, reliability, security, and performance of Microsoft Windows NT Workstation 4.0. Windows 2000 Professional can be used alone as a desktop operating system, networked in a peer-to-peer workgroup environment, or used as a workstation in a Windows 2000 Server or Windows NT domain environment. Windows 2000 Professional can be used with the Microsoft BackOffice family of products to access resources from all the BackOffice products. This product is the main Microsoft desktop operating system for businesses of all sizes.

- **Windows 2000 Server.**   This product is a file, print, terminal, and applications server, as well as a Web-server platform that contains all of the features of Windows 2000 Professional plus many new server-specific functions. This product is ideal for small- to medium-sized enterprise application deployments, Web servers, workgroups, and branch offices.

The Windows 2000 family also includes the following two products:

- **Windows 2000 Advanced Server.**   This product is a powerful departmental and application server and provides rich network operations system (NOS) and Internet services. Advanced Server supports large physical memories, clustering, and load balancing. This product is beyond the scope of this training kit; features unique to Advanced Server will not be covered in this kit.

- **Windows 2000 Datacenter Server.**   This product is the most powerful and functional server operating system in the Windows 2000 family. It is optimized for large data warehouses, econometric analysis, large-scale simulations in science and engineering, and server consolidation projects. This product is beyond the scope of this training kit; features unique to Datacenter Server will not be covered in this kit.

Table 1.1 describes the new features included in Windows 2000.

Table 1.1   New Features Included in Windows 2000

Feature	Description
Active Directory	Active Directory is an enterprise-class directory service that is scalable, built from the ground up using Internet-standard technologies, and fully integrated at the operating-system level. Active Directory simplifies administration and makes it easier for users to find resources. Active Directory provides a wide range of features and capabilities, including group policy, scalability without complexity, support for multiple authentication protocols, and the use of Internet standards.
Active Directory Service Interfaces (ADSI)	ADSI is a directory service model and a set of Component Object Model (COM) interfaces. It enables Windows 95, Windows 98, Windows NT, and Windows 2000 applications to access several network directory services, including Active Directory. It is supplied as a Software Development Kit (SDK).
Asynchronous Transfer Mode (ATM)	ATM is a high-speed, connection-oriented protocol designed to transport multiple types of traffic across a network. It is applicable to both local area networks (LANs) and wide area networks (WANs). Using ATM, your network can simultaneously transport a wide variety of network traffic: voice, data, image, and video.

Table 1.1   New Features Included in Windows 2000   *(continued)*

Feature	Description
Certificate Services	Using Certificate Services and the certificate management tools in Windows 2000, you can deploy your own public key infrastructure. With a public key infrastructure, you can implement standards-based technologies such as smart card logon capabilities, client authentication (through Secure Sockets Layer and Transport Layer Security), secure e-mail, digital signatures, and secure connectivity (using Internet Protocol Security).
Component Services	Component Services is a set of services based on extensions of the COM and on Microsoft Transaction Server (an earlier release of a component-based transaction processing system). Component Services provides improved threading and security, transaction management, object pooling, queued components, and application administration and packaging.
Disk quota support	You can use disk quotas on volumes formatted with the NTFS file system to monitor and limit the amount of disk space available to individual users. You can define the responses that result when users exceed your specified thresholds.
Dynamic Host Configuration Protocol (DHCP) with Domain Name System (DNS) and Active Directory	DHCP works with DNS and Active Directory on Internet Protocol (IP) networks, freeing you from assigning and tracking static IP addresses. DHCP dynamically assigns IP addresses to computers or other resources connected to an IP network.
Encrypting File System (EFS)	The EFS in Windows 2000 complements existing access controls and adds a new level of protection for your data. The Encrypting File System runs as an integrated system service, making it easy to manage, difficult to attack, and transparent to the user.
Graphical Disk Management	Disk Management is a graphical tool for managing disk storage that includes many new features, such as support for new dynamic volumes, online disk management, local and remote drive management, and Volume Mount Points.
Group Policy (part of Active Directory)	Policies can define the allowed actions and the settings for users and computers. In contrast with local policy, you can use group policy to set policies that apply across a given site, domain, or organizational unit in Active Directory. Policy-based management simplifies such tasks as operating system updates, application installation, user profiles, and desktop-system lock down.
Indexing Service	Indexing Service provides a fast, easy, and secure way for users to search for information locally or on the network. Users can use powerful queries to search in files in different formats and languages, either through the Start menu Search command or through Hypertext Markup Language (HTML) pages that they view in a browser.

Feature	Description
IntelliMirror	IntelliMirror provides high levels of control on client systems running Windows 2000 Professional. You can use IntelliMirror to define policies based on the respective user's business roles, group memberships, and locations. Using these policies, Windows 2000 Professional desktops are automatically reconfigured to meet a specific user's requirements each time that user logs on to the network, no matter where the user logs on.
Internet Authentication Service (IAS)	IAS provides you with a central point for managing authentication, authorization, accounting, and auditing of dial-up or Virtual Private Network users. IAS uses the Internet Engineering Task Force (IETF) protocol called Remote Authentication Dial-In User Service (RADIUS).
Internet Connection Sharing	With the Internet connection sharing feature of Network and Dial-Up Connections, you can use Windows 2000 to connect your home network or small office network to the Internet. For example, you might have a home network that connects to the Internet by using a dial-up connection. By enabling Internet connection sharing on the computer that uses the dial-up connection, you are providing network address translation, addressing, and name resolution services for all computers on your network.
Internet Information Services (IIS) 5.0	The powerful features in Internet Information Services (IIS), a part of Microsoft Windows 2000 Server, make it easy to share documents and information across a company intranet or the Internet. Using IIS, you can deploy scalable and reliable Web-based applications, and you can bring existing data and applications to the Web. IIS includes Active Server Pages and other features.
Internet Security (IPSec) support	Use IPSec to secure communications within an intranet and to Protocol create secure Virtual Private Network solutions across the Internet. IPSec was designed by the IETF and is an industry standard for encrypting Transmission Control Protocol/Internet Protocol (TCP/IP) traffic.
Kerberos V5 Protocol support	Kerberos V5 is a mature, industry-standard network authentication protocol. With Kerberos V5 support, a fast, single logon process gives users the access they need to Windows 2000 Server-based enterprise resources, as well as to other environments that support this protocol. Support for Kerberos V5 includes additional benefits such as mutual authentication (client and server must both provide authentication) and delegated authentication (the user's credential is tracked end-to-end).
Layer 2 Tunneling Protocol (L2TP) support	L2TP is a more secure version of Point-to-Point Tunneling Protocol (PPTP) and is used for tunneling, address assignment, and authentication.

Table 1.1   New Features Included in Windows 2000   *(continued)*

Feature	Description
Lightweight Directory Access Protocol (LDAP) support	LDAP, an industry standard, is the primary access protocol for Active Directory. LDAP version 3 was defined by the IETF.
Message queuing	Integrated message-queuing functionality in Windows 2000 helps developers build and deploy applications that run more reliably over networks, including the Internet. These applications can interoperate with applications running on different platforms such as mainframes and UNIX-based systems.
Microsoft Management Console (MMC)	Use MMC to arrange the administrative tools and processes you need within a single interface. You can also delegate tasks to specific users by creating preconfigured MMC consoles for them. The console will provide the user with the tools you select.
Network Address Translation (NAT)	NAT hides internally managed IP addresses from external networks by translating private internal addresses to public external addresses. This reduces IP address registration costs by letting you use unregistered IP addresses internally, with translation to a small number of registered IP addresses externally. It also hides the internal network structure, reducing the risk of attacks against internal systems.
Operating system migration, support, and integration	Windows 2000 integrates seamlessly with existing systems and contains support for earlier Windows operating systems, as well as new features for supporting other popular operating systems. Windows 2000 offers: Interoperability with Windows NT Server 3.51 and 4.0; support for clients running a variety of operating systems including Windows 3.x, Windows 95, Windows 98, and Windows NT Workstation 4.0; mainframe and midrange connectivity, using S/390 and AS/400 transaction and queuing gateways through Systems Network Architecture (SNA) Server; File Server for Macintosh, allowing Macintosh clients to use the TCP/IP protocol (AppleTalk File Protocol (AFP) over IP) to share files and to access shares on a Windows 2000 server.
Plug and Play	With Plug and Play, a combination of hardware and software support, the server can recognize and adapt to hardware configuration changes automatically, without your intervention and without restarting.
Public key infrastructure (PKI) and smart card infrastructure	Using Certificate Services and the certificate management tools in Windows 2000, you can deploy your own public key infrastructure. With a public key infrastructure, you can implement standards-based technologies such as smart card logon capabilities, client authentication (through Secure Sockets Layer and Transport Layer Security), secure e-mail, digital signatures, and secure connectivity (using Internet Protocol Security). Using Certificate Services, you can set up and manage certification authorities that issue and revoke X.509V3 certificates. This means that you don't have to depend on commercial client authentication services, although you can integrate commercial client authentication into your public key infrastructure if you choose.

Feature	Description
Quality of Service (QoS)	Using QoS, you can control how applications are allotted network bandwidth. You can give important applications more bandwidth, and less important applications less bandwidth. QoS-based services and protocols provide a guaranteed, end-to-end, express delivery system for information across the network.
Remote Installation Services (RIS)	With Remote Installation Services, you can install Windows 2000 Professional remotely, without the need to visit each client. The target clients must either support remote booting with the Pre-Boot eXecution Environment (PXE) ROM, or else must be started with a remote-startup floppy disk. Installation of multiple clients becomes much simpler.
Removable Storage and Remote Storage	Removable Storage makes it easy to track your removable storage media (tapes and optical discs) and to manage the hardware libraries, such as changers and jukeboxes, that contain them. Remote Storage uses criteria you specify to automatically copy little-used files to removable media. If hard-disk space drops below specified levels, Remote Storage removes the (cached) file content from the disk. If the file is needed later, the content is automatically recalled from storage. Since removable optical discs and tapes are less expensive per megabyte (MB) than hard disks, Removable Storage and Remote Storage can decrease your costs.
Routing and Remote Access service	Routing and Remote Access service is a single integrated service that terminates connections from either dial-up or Virtual Private Network (VPN) clients, or provides routing (IP, IPX, and AppleTalk), or both. With Routing and Remote Access, your Windows 2000 server can function as a remote access server, a VPN server, a gateway, or a branch-office router.
Safe mode startup	With safe mode, you can start Windows 2000 with a minimal set of drivers and services, and then view a log showing the sequence of events at startup. Using safe mode, you can diagnose problems with drivers and other components that might be preventing normal startup.
Smart card infrastructure	Using Certificate Services and the certificate management tools in Windows 2000, you can deploy your own public key infrastructure. With a public key infrastructure, you can implement standards-based technologies such as smart card logon capabilities, client authentication (through Secure Sockets Layer and Transport Layer Security), secure e-mail, digital signatures, and secure connectivity (using Internet Protocol Security).
TAPI 3.0	TAPI 3.0 unifies IP and traditional telephony to enable developers to create a new generation of powerful computer telephony applications that work as effectively over the Internet or an intranet as over the traditional telephone network.

Table 1.1 **New Features Included in Windows 2000** *(continued)*

Feature	Description
Terminal Services	The Windows 2000 Server family offers the only server operating systems that integrate terminal emulation services. Using Terminal Services, a user can access programs running on the server from a variety of older devices. For example, a user could access a virtual Windows 2000 Professional desktop and 32-bit Windows-based applications from hardware that couldn't run the software locally. Terminal Services provides this capability for both Windows and non-Windows-based client devices. (Non-Windows devices require add-on software by Citrix Systems.)
Virtual Private Network (VPN)	You can allow users ready access to the network even when they're out of the office, and reduce the cost of this access, by implementing a VPN. Using VPNs, users can easily and securely connect to the corporate network. The connection is through a local Internet Service Provider (ISP), which reduces connect-time charges. With Windows 2000 Server, you can use several new, more secure protocols for creating Virtual Private Networks, including: L2TP, a more secure version of PPTP (L2TP is used for tunneling, address assignment, and authentication) and IPSec, a standard-based protocol that provides the highest levels of VPN security. Using IPSec, virtually everything above the networking layer can be encrypted.
Windows Media Services	Using Windows Media Services, you can deliver high-quality streaming multimedia to users on the Internet and intranets.
Windows Script Host (WSH)	Using WSH, you can automate actions such as creating a shortcut and connecting to and disconnecting from a network server. WSH is language-independent. You can write scripts in common scripting languages such as VBScript and JScript.

Windows 2000 Network Environments

A Windows 2000-based network environment can be set up using either a workgroup model or a domain model. Both Windows 2000 Professional and Windows 2000 Server can participate in either of these two models. The administrative differences between the two products depend on the network environmental model.

Windows 2000 Workgroup Model

A Windows 2000 *workgroup* is a logical grouping of networked computers that share resources, such as files and printers. A workgroup is referred to as a *peer-to-peer* network because all computers in the workgroup can share resources as equals, or as peers, without a dedicated server. Each computer in the workgroup, running either Windows 2000 Server or Windows 2000 Professional, maintains a local security database, as shown in Figure 1.1. A *local security database* is a list of user accounts and resource security information for the computer on which it resides. Therefore, the administration of user accounts and resource security in a workgroup is decentralized.

Figure 1.1   An example of a Windows 2000 workgroup

The following are disadvantages of using workgroup mode:

- A user must have a user account on each computer to which he or she wants to gain access.

- Any changes to user accounts, such as changing a user's password or adding a new user account, must be made on each computer in the workgroup. If you forget to add a new user account to a computer in your workgroup, the new user will not be able to log on to that computer and will be unable to access resources on it.

- Device and file sharing is handled by individual computers, and only for the users that have accounts on each individual computer.

A Windows 2000 workgroup provides the following advantages:

- A workgroup does not require a computer running Windows 2000 Server to hold centralized security information.

- A workgroup is simple to design and implement. A workgroup does not require the extensive planning and administration that a domain requires.

- A workgroup is convenient for a limited number of computers in close proximity. (A workgroup becomes impractical in environments with more than 10 computers.)

Note   In a workgroup, a computer running Windows 2000 Server that is not a member of a Windows 2000 domain is called a *stand-alone server*.

Windows 2000 Domain Model

A Windows 2000 *domain* is a logical grouping of network computers that share a central directory database (see Figure 1.2). A *directory database* contains user accounts and security information for the domain. This directory database is known as the directory and is the database portion of Active Directory, which is the Windows 2000 directory service. Active Directory replaces all previous "domain" information storage containers, including multiple domains. Active Directory also contains information about services and other resources, organizations, and more.

Figure 1.2   An example of a Windows 2000 domain

In a domain, the directory resides on computers that are configured as domain controllers. A *domain controller* is a server that manages all security-related aspects of user-domain interactions. Security and administration are centralized. Only computers running Windows 2000 Server may be designated as domain controllers.

A domain does not refer to a single location or specific type of network configuration. The computers in a domain can share physical proximity on a small LAN or can be located in different corners of the world, communicating over any number of physical connections, including dial-up lines, Integrated Services Digital Network (ISDN) lines, fiber lines, Ethernet lines, token ring connections, frame relay connections, satellite connections, and leased lines. You can learn more about domains in Chapter 2, "Introduction to Active Directory."

The benefits of a Windows 2000 domain are as follows:

- A domain allows centralized administration because all user information is stored centrally. If a user changes his or her password, the change is automatically replicated throughout the domain.

- A domain provides a single logon process for users to gain access to network resources, such as file, print, and application resources for which they have permissions. In other words, a user can log on to one computer and use resources on another computer in the network as long as he or she has appropriate privileges to the resource.

- A domain provides scalability so that an administrator can create very large networks.

A typical Windows 2000 domain will have the following types of computers:

- **Domain controllers running Windows 2000 Server.**   Each domain controller stores and maintains a copy of the directory. In a domain, you create a user account once, which Windows 2000 records in the directory. When a user logs on to a computer in the domain, a domain controller checks the directory for the user name, password, and logon restrictions to authenticate the user. When there are multiple domain controllers, they periodically replicate their directory information.

- **Member servers running Windows 2000 Server.**   A *member server* is a server that is not configured as a domain controller. A member server does not store directory information and cannot authenticate domain users. Member servers provide shared resources such as shared folders or printers.

- **Client computers running Windows 2000 Professional.**   Client computers run a user's desktop environment and allow the user to gain access to resources in the domain.

Lesson Summary

In this lesson you learned that Windows 2000 is a multipurpose operating system with integrated support for client/server and peer-to-peer networks. Windows 2000 consists of a family of four products: Windows 2000 Professional, Windows 2000 Server, Windows 2000 Advanced Server, and Windows 2000 Datacenter Server. Windows 2000 Professional is optimized for use alone as a desktop operating system, as a networked computer in a peer-to-peer workgroup environment, or as a workstation in a Windows 2000 Server domain environment. Windows 2000 Server is optimized for use as a file, print, and application server, as well as a Web-server platform.

A Windows 2000 workgroup is a logical grouping of networked computers that share resources, such as files and printers. A workgroup does not have a Windows 2000 Server domain controller. Security and administration for Windows 2000 Professional and Windows 2000 Server member servers are not centralized in a workgroup because each computer maintains a list of user accounts and resource security information for that computer.

A Windows 2000 domain is a logical grouping of networked computers that share a central directory database containing security and user account information. This directory database is known as the directory and is the database portion of Active Directory, the Windows 2000 directory service. In a domain, security and administration are centralized because the directory resides on domain controllers, which manage all security-related aspects of user-domain interactions.

Lesson 2: Windows 2000 Architecture Overview

Windows 2000 is a modular operating system—a collection of small, self-contained software components that work together to perform operating system tasks. Each component provides a set of functions that act as an interface to the rest of the system.

After this lesson, you will be able to

- Identify the layers and layer components in the Windows 2000 operating system architecture

Estimated lesson time: 15 minutes

Windows 2000 Layers, Subsystems, and Managers

The Windows 2000 architecture contains two major layers: user mode and kernel mode, as illustrated in Figure 1.3. This lesson provides an overview of the Windows 2000 architecture layers and their respective components.

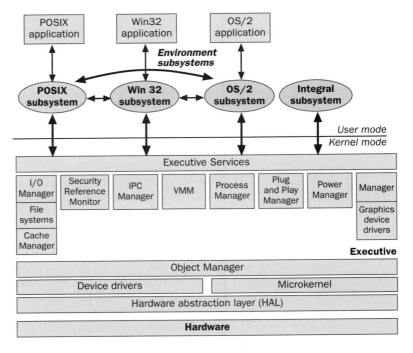

Figure 1.3   Windows 2000 architecture layers

User Mode

Windows 2000 has two different types of user mode components: *environment subsystems* and *integral subsystems*.

Environment Subsystems

One of the features of Windows 2000 is the ability to run applications written for different operating systems. Windows 2000 accomplishes this through the use of environment subsystems. *Environment subsystems* emulate different operating systems by presenting the application programming interfaces (APIs) that the applications expect to be available. The environment subsystems accept the API calls made by the application, convert the API calls into a format understood by Windows 2000, and then pass the converted API to the Executive Services for processing.

Table 1.2 lists the environment subsystems included with Windows 2000.

Table 1.2   Environment Subsystems Included with Windows 2000

Environment Subsystem	Function
Windows 2000 32-bit Windows-based subsystem (Win32)	Responsible for controlling Win32-based applications, as well as for providing an environment for Win16 and Microsoft MS-DOS-based applications. Controls all screen-oriented input/output (I/O) between subsystems. This ensures a consistent user interface, regardless of the application a user runs.
OS/2 subsystem	Provides a set of APIs for 16-bit, character mode OS/2 applications.
Portable Operating System Interface for UNIX (POSIX) subsystem	Provides APIs for POSIX-based applications.

The environment subsystems and the applications that run within them are subject to the following limitations and restrictions:

- They have no direct access to hardware.
- They have no direct access to device drivers.
- They have no access to the certain Clipboard API operations.
- They have no access to certain Microsoft CD-ROM Extensions (MSCDEX).
- They have no access to task-switching APIs.
- They are limited to an assigned address space.
- They are forced to use hard disk space as virtual random access memory (RAM) whenever the system needs memory.
- They run at a lower priority level than kernel mode processes.
- Because they run at a lower priority level than the kernel mode processes, they have less access to central processing unit (CPU) cycles than processes that run in kernel mode.

Integral Subsystems

Many different integral subsystems perform essential operating system functions. In Figure 1.3, there is a generic subsystem on the far right of the figure labeled *integral subsystem*. This integral subsystem represents any of the various integral subsystems. To introduce you to some of the more important integral subsystems, Table 1.3 lists some examples.

Table 1.3   Windows 2000 Integral Subsystems

Integral Subsystem	Function
Security subsystem	Tracks rights and permissions associated with user accounts. Tracks which system resources are audited. Accepts user logon requests. Initiates logon authentication.
Workstation service	Networking integral subsystem that provides an API to access the network redirector. Allows a user running Windows 2000 to access the network.
Server service	Networking integral subsystem that provides an API to access the network server. Allows a computer running Windows 2000 to provide network resources.

Kernel Mode

The kernel mode layer has access to system data and hardware. Kernel mode provides direct access to memory and executes in an isolated memory area. Kernel mode consists of four components: Windows 2000 Executive, Device Drivers, the Microkernel, and the Hardware Abstraction Layer (HAL).

Windows 2000 Executive

This component performs most of the I/O and object management, including security. It does not perform screen and keyboard I/O; the Microsoft Win32 subsystem performs these functions. The Windows 2000 Executive contains the Windows 2000 kernel mode components. Each of these components provides the following two distinct sets of services and routines:

- **System services** are available to both the user mode subsystems and to other Executive components.

- **Internal routines** are available only to other components within the Executive.

The Executive consists of the kernel mode components listed in Table 1.4.

Table 1.4   Windows 2000 Executive Components

Component	Function
I/O Manager	Manages input from and the delivery of output to different devices. The components that make up the I/O Manager include the following: *File systems* accept the oriented I/O requests and translate these requests into device-specific calls. The network redirector and the network server are both implemented as file system drivers. *Device drivers* are low-level drivers that directly manipulate hardware to accept input or to write output. *Cache Manager* improves disk I/O by storing disk reads in system memory. Cache Manager also improves write performance by caching write requests and writes to disk in the background.
Security Reference Monitor	Enforces security policies on the local computer.
Interprocess Communication (IPC) Manager	Manages communications between clients and servers, for example, between an environment subsystem (which would be acting like a client requesting information) and an Executive Services component (which would be acting like a server and satisfying the request for information). The IPC Manager consists of the following two components: *Local procedure call (LPC) facility* manages communications when clients and servers exist on the same computer. *Remote procedure call (RPC) facility* manages communications when clients and servers exist on separate computers.
Virtual Memory Manager (VMM)	Implements and controls *virtual memory*, a memory management system that provides and protects the private address space for each process. The VMM also controls demand paging. *Demand paging* allows the use of disk space as a storage area to move code and data in and out of physical RAM.
Process Manager	Creates and terminates processes and threads. (A *process* is a program or part of a program. A *thread* is a specific set of commands within a program.)
Plug and Play	Maintains central control of the Plug and Play process. Communicates with device drivers, directing the drivers to add and start devices.
Power Manager	Controls power management APIs, coordinates power events, and generates power management requests.
Window Manager and Graphical Device Interface (GDI)	These two components, implemented as a single device driver named Win32k.sys, manage the display system. They perform the following functions: *Window Manager* controls window displays and manages screen output. This component is also responsible for receiving input from devices such as the keyboard and the mouse and then passing the input messages to applications. *GDI* contains the functions that are required for drawing and manipulating graphics.
Object Manager	Creates, manages, and deletes objects that represent operating system resources, such as processes, threads, and data structures.

Device Drivers

This component translates driver calls into hardware manipulation.

Microkernel

This component manages the microprocessor only. The kernel coordinates all I/O functions and synchronizes the activities of the Executive Services.

Hardware Abstraction Layer (HAL)

This component virtualizes, or hides, the hardware interface details, making Windows 2000 more portable across different hardware architectures. The HAL contains the hardware-specific code that handles I/O interfaces, interrupt controllers, and multiprocessor communication mechanisms. This layer was originally designed to allow Windows 2000 to run on both Intel-based and Alpha-based systems without having to maintain two separate versions of Windows 2000 Executive.

Lesson Summary

This lesson introduced you to the Windows 2000 architecture. The Windows 2000 architecture contains two major layers: user mode and kernel mode. User mode has two different types of components: environment subsystems, which allow Windows 2000 to run applications written for different operating systems, and integral subsystems, which perform essential operating system functions. The kernel mode layer has access to system data and hardware, provides direct access to memory, and executes in an isolated memory area.

Lesson 3: Windows 2000 Directory Services Overview

You use a directory service to uniquely identify users and resources on a network. Windows 2000 uses Active Directory to provide directory services. It is important to understand the overall purpose of Active Directory and the key features it provides. Understanding the interactions of Active Directory architectural components provides the basis for understanding how Active Directory stores and retrieves data. This lesson introduces you to Active Directory functions, features, and architecture.

After this lesson, you will be able to

- Explain the function of a directory service
- Explain the purpose of Active Directory
- Identify the features of Active Directory
- Identify the layers in the Active Directory architecture

Estimated lesson time: 20 minutes

What Is a Directory Service?

A *directory* is a stored collection of information about objects that are related to one another in some way. For example, a telephone directory stores names of entities and their corresponding telephone numbers. The telephone directory listing may also contain an address or other information about the entity.

In a distributed computing system or a public computer network such as the Internet, there are many objects, such as file servers, printers, fax servers, applications, databases, and users. Users must be able to locate and use these objects. Administrators must be able to manage how these objects are used. A directory service stores all the information needed to use and manage these objects in a centralized location, simplifying the process of locating and managing these resources.

In this course, the terms *directory* and *directory service* refer to the directories found in public and private networks. A *directory* provides a means of storing information related to the network resources to facilitate locating and managing these resources. A *directory service* is a network service that identifies all resources on a network and makes them accessible to users and applications. A directory service differs from a directory in that it is both the source of the information and the services making the information available to the users.

A directory service acts as the main switchboard of the network operating system. It is the central authority that manages the identities and brokers the relationships between distributed resources, enabling them to work together. Because a directory service supplies these fundamental operating system functions, it must be tightly coupled with the management and security mechanisms of the operating system to ensure the integrity and privacy of the network. It also plays a critical role in an organization's ability to define and maintain the network infrastructure, perform system administration, and control the overall user experience of a company's information systems.

Why Have a Directory Service?

A directory service provides the means to organize and simplify access to resources of a networked computer system. Users and administrators may not know the exact name of the objects they need. However, they may know one or more attributes of the objects in question. As illustrated in Figure 1.4, they can use a directory service to query the directory for a list of objects that match known attributes. For example, "Find all color printers on the third floor" queries the directory for all color printer objects with the attributes of color and third floor (or maybe a location attribute that has been set to "third floor"). A directory service makes it possible to find an object based on one or more of its attributes.

Figure 1.4   Using a directory service

Other functions of the directory service are:

- Enforcing security to protect the objects in its database from outside intruders or from internal users who do not have permission to access those objects.

- Distributing a directory across many computers in a network.

- Replicating a directory to make it available to more users and resistant to failure.

- Partitioning a directory into multiple stores that are located on different computers across the network. This makes more space available to the directory as a whole and allows the storage of a large number of objects.

A directory service is both an administration tool and an end user tool. As a network becomes larger, more resource objects must be managed and the directory service becomes a necessity.

Windows 2000 Directory Services

Active Directory is the directory service included in Windows 2000 Server. Active Directory includes the directory, which stores information about network resources, as well as all the services that make the information available and useful. The resources stored in the directory, such as user data, printers, servers, databases, groups, services, computers, and security policies, are known as *objects*.

Active Directory is integrated within Windows 2000 Server and offers:

- Simplified administration
- Scalability
- Open standards support
- Support for standard name formats

Simplified Administration

Active Directory organizes resources hierarchically in domains. A *domain* is a logical grouping of servers and other network resources under a single domain name. The domain is the basic unit of replication and security in a Windows 2000 network.

Each domain includes one or more domain controllers. A *domain controller* is a computer running Windows 2000 Server that manages user access to a network, which includes logging on, authentication, and access to the directory and shared resources. To simplify administration, all domain controllers in the domain are equal. You can make changes to any domain controller, and the updates are replicated to all other domain controllers in the domain.

Active Directory further simplifies administration by providing a single point of administration for all objects on the network. Because Active Directory provides a single point of logon for all network resources, an administrator can log on to one computer and administer objects on any computer in the network.

Scalability

In Active Directory, the directory stores information by organizing the directory into sections that permit storage for a very large number of objects. As a result, the directory can expand as an organization grows, allowing users to scale from a small installation with a few hundred objects to a large installation with millions of objects.

Note   You can distribute directory information across several computers in a network.

Open Standards Support

Active Directory integrates the Internet concept of a name space with the Windows 2000 directory services. This allows you to unify and manage the multiple name spaces that now exist in the heterogeneous software and hardware environments of corporate networks. Active Directory uses DNS for its name system and can exchange information with any application or directory that uses LDAP or Hypertext Transfer Protocol (HTTP).

Important   Active Directory also shares information with other directory services that support LDAP version 2 and version 3, such as Novell Directory Services (NDS).

DNS

Because Active Directory uses DNS as its domain naming and location service, Windows 2000 domain names are also DNS names. Windows 2000 Server uses Dynamic DNS (DDNS), which enables clients with dynamically assigned addresses to register directly with a server running the DNS service and update the DNS table dynamically. DDNS eliminates the need for other Internet naming services, such as Windows Internet Name Service (WINS), in a homogeneous environment.

Important   For Active Directory and associated client software to function correctly, you must have installed and configured the DNS service.

Support for LDAP and HTTP

Active Directory further embraces Internet standards by directly supporting LDAP and HTTP. LDAP is a version of the X.500 directory access protocol, which was developed as a simpler alternative to the Directory Access Protocol (DAP). Active Directory supports both LDAP version 2 and version 3. HTTP is the standard protocol for displaying pages on the World Wide Web. A user can display every object in Active Directory as an HTML page in a Web browser. Thus, users receive the benefit of the familiar Web browsing model when querying and viewing objects in Active Directory.

Note   Active Directory uses LDAP to exchange information between directories and applications.

More Info   For more information about LDAP, use your Web browser to search for **RFC 1777** and retrieve the text of this Request for Comment.

Support for Standard Name Formats

Active Directory supports several common name formats. Consequently, users and applications can access Active Directory using the format with which they are most familiar. Table 1.5 describes some standard name formats supported by Active Directory.

Table 1.5   Standard Name Formats Supported by Active Directory

Format	Description
RFC 822	Takes the form of someone@domain and is familiar to most users as an Internet e-mail address.
HTTP Uniform Resource Locator (URL)	Takes the form of *http://domain/path-to-page* and is familiar to users with Web browsers.
Universal Naming Convention (UNC)	Takes the form of *\\microsoft.com\xl\BUDGET.XLS* and is used in Windows 2000 Server-based networks to refer to shared volumes, printers, and files.
LDAP URL	Active Directory supports a draft to RFC 1779 and uses the attributes in the following example: LDAP://someserver.microsoft.com/CN=FirstnameLastname, OU=sys, OU=product, OU=division, DC=devel Where CN represents Common Name OU represents Organizational Unit Name DC represents Domain Component Name An LDAP URL specifies the server on which the Active Directory services reside and the attributed name of the object.

Active Directory in the Windows 2000 Architecture

As you learned in the previous lesson, Windows 2000 uses modules and modes that combine to provide operating system services to applications. Two processor access modes, *kernel* and *user*, divide the low-level, platform-specific processes from the upper level processes, respectively, to shield applications from platform differences and to prevent direct access to system code and data by applications. Each application, including service applications, runs in a separate *module* in user mode, from which it requests system services through an API that gains limited access to system data. An application process begins in user mode and is transferred to kernel mode, where the actual service is provided in a protected environment. The process is then transferred back to user mode. Active Directory runs in the security subsystem in user mode. The *security reference monitor*, which runs in kernel mode, is the primary authority for enforcing the security rules of the security subsystem. Figure 1.5 shows the location of Active Directory within Windows 2000.

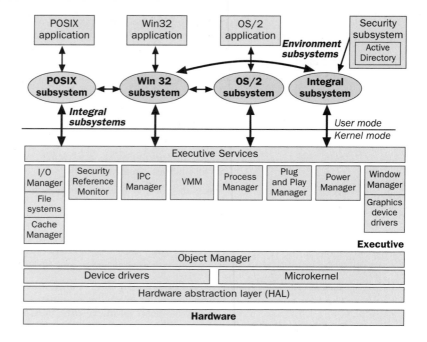

Figure 1.5   Location of Active Directory within Windows 2000

The tight integration of the directory service and security subsystem services is key to the implementation of Windows 2000 distributed systems. Access to all directory objects first requires proof of identity (authentication), which is performed by components of the security subsystem, and then validation of access permissions (authorization), which is performed by the security subsystem in conjunction with the security reference monitor. The security reference monitor enforces the access control applied to Active Directory objects.

Active Directory Architecture

Active Directory functionality can be illustrated as a layered architecture in which the layers represent the server processes that provide directory services to client applications. Active Directory consists of three service layers and several interfaces and protocols that work together to provide directory services. The three service layers accommodate the different types of information required to locate records in the directory database. Above the service layers in this architecture are the protocols and APIs that enable communication between clients and directory services.

Figure 1.6 shows the Active Directory service layers and their respective interfaces and protocols. The direction of the arrows indicates how different clients gain access to Active Directory through the interfaces.

Figure 1.6 Active Directory architecture

The key service components include the following:

- **Directory System Agent (DSA)** builds a hierarchy from the parent-child relationships stored in the directory. Provides APIs for directory access calls.

- **Database Layer** provides an abstraction layer between applications and the database. Calls from applications are never made directly to the database; they go through the database layer.

- **Extensible Storage Engine** communicates directly with individual records in the directory data store on the basis of the object's relative distinguished name attribute.

- **Data store (the database file NTDS.DIT)** is manipulated only by the Extensible Storage Engine database engine, stored in the \Winnt\NTDS folder on the domain controller. You can administer the file by using the NTDSUTIL tool, located in the \Winnt\system32 folder on the domain controller.

Clients obtain access to Active Directory by using one of the following mechanisms that is supported by the DSA:

- **LDAP/ADSI.** Clients that support LDAP use it to connect to the DSA. Active Directory supports LDAP version 3 (defined by RFC 2251) and LDAP version 2 (defined by RFC 1777). Windows 2000 clients, as well as Windows 98 and Windows 95 clients that have the Active Directory client components installed, use LDAP version 3 to connect to the DSA. ADSI is a means of abstracting LDAP API; however, Active Directory uses only LDAP.

- **Messaging API (MAPI).** Legacy MAPI clients, such as Microsoft Outlook, connect to the DSA by using the MAPI RPC address book provider interface.

- **Security Accounts Manager (SAM).**   Windows clients that use Windows NT 4.0 or earlier use the SAM interface to connect to the DSA. Replication from backup domain controllers in a mixed-mode domain goes through the SAM interface as well.

- **Replication (REPL).**   When they are performing directory replication, Active Directory DSAs connect to each other by using a proprietary RPC interface.

Lesson Summary

In this lesson you learned that a directory service is a network service that identifies all resources on a network and makes them accessible to users and applications. A directory service differs from a directory in that it is both the source of the information and the services making the information available to the users.

You also learned that Active Directory is the directory service included in Windows 2000 Server. Active Directory includes the directory, which stores information about network resources such as user data, printers, servers, data-bases, groups, computers, and security policies. The directory can scale from a small installation with a few hundred objects to a large installation with millions of objects. Active Directory offers simplified administration, scalability, open standards support, and support for standard name formats.

Finally, you learned that Active Directory runs in the security subsystem in the user mode in the Windows 2000 architecture. The security reference monitor, which runs in kernel mode, is the primary authority for enforcing the security rules of the security subsystem. Active Directory functionality can be illustrated as a layered architecture in which the layers represent the server processes that provide directory services to client applications. Active Directory consists of three service layers and several interfaces and protocols that work together to provide directory services.

Lesson 4: Logging On to Windows 2000

This lesson explains the process of logging on to the domain or local computer using the Log On To Windows dialog box. It also explains how Windows 2000 authenticates a user during the logon process to verify the identity of the user. This mandatory process ensures that only valid users can gain access to resources and data on a computer or the network.

After this lesson, you will be able to

- Identify the features of the Log On To Windows dialog box
- Identify how Windows 2000 authenticates a user when the user logs on to a domain or logs on locally
- Log on to a stand-alone server

Estimated lesson time: 10 minutes

Logging On to a Domain

To log on to a computer running Windows 2000, you must provide a user name and password. Windows 2000 authenticates the user during the logon process to verify the user identity. Only valid users can gain access to resources and data on a computer or the network. Windows 2000 authenticates users who log on to either the domain or a local computer.

When you start a computer running Windows 2000, the Welcome To Windows window prompts you to press Ctrl+Alt+Delete to log on (see Figure 1.7). By pressing Ctrl+Alt+Delete you guarantee that you are providing your user name and password to only the Windows 2000 operating system. Windows 2000 then displays the Log On To Windows dialog box (see Figure 1.7).

Figure 1.7   The Welcome To Windows window and the Log On To Windows dialog box

Table 1.6 describes the default options on the Log On To Windows dialog box.

Table 1.6   Log On To Windows Dialog Box Options

Option	Description
User Name box	A unique user logon name that is assigned by an administrator. To log on to a domain with the user name, the user account must reside in the directory.
Password box	Passwords are case-sensitive. The password components appear on the screen as asterisks (*) to maintain privacy. To prevent unauthorized access to resources and data, you must keep passwords secret.
Log On To list	Select the domain that contains your user account. This list contains all of the domains in a domain tree.
Log On Using Dial-Up Connection check box	Permits a user to connect to a domain server by using dial-up networking, which allows a user to log on and perform work from a remote location.
Shutdown button	Closes all files, saves all operating system data, and prepares the computer so that a user can safely turn it off. On a computer running Windows 2000 Server, the Shutdown button is unavailable by default. This prevents an unauthorized person from using this dialog box to shut down the server. To shut down a server, a user must be able to log on to it.
Options button	Toggles on and off the Log On To list and the Log On Using Dial-Up Connection check box.

Important   A user cannot log on to either the domain or the local computer from any computer running Windows 2000 Server unless that user is assigned the *Log On Locally* user right by an administrator or has administrative privileges for the server. This feature helps to secure the server.

Logging On to a Local Computer

A user can log on locally to either of the following:

- A computer that is a member of a workgroup.
- A computer that is a member of a domain but is not a domain controller. The user selects the computer name in the Log On To list in the Log On To Windows dialog box.

Note   Domain controllers do not maintain a local security database. Therefore, local user accounts are not available on domain controllers, and a user cannot log on locally to a domain controller.

Windows 2000 Authentication Process

To gain access to a computer running Windows 2000 or to any resource on that computer, a user must provide a user name and password. The way Windows 2000 authenticates a user varies based on whether the user is logging on to a domain or logging on locally to a computer (see Figure 1.8).

Figure 1.8   Windows 2000 authentication process at logon

The steps in the authentication process are as follows:

1. The user logs on by providing logon information, including user name and password.
   - If the user is logging on to a domain, Windows 2000 forwards this information to a domain controller.
   - If the user is logging on locally, Windows 2000 forwards this information to the security subsystem of that local computer.

2. Windows 2000 compares the logon information with the user information that is stored in the appropriate database.
   - If the user is logging on to a domain, the domain controller contains a copy of the directory that Windows 2000 uses to validate the logon information.
   - If the user is logging on locally, the security subsystem of the local computer contains the local security database that Windows 2000 uses to validate the logon information.

3. If the information matches and the user account is enabled, Windows 2000 creates an access token for the user. An *access token* is the user's identification for the computers in the domain or for that local computer, and it contains the user's security settings, including the user's security ID (SID). These security settings allow the user to gain access to the appropriate resources and

to perform specific system tasks. The SID is a unique number that identifies user, group, and computer accounts.

4. If the logon information does not match or the user account is not validated, access to the domain or local computer is denied.

Note   In addition to the logon process, any time a user makes a connection to a computer or to other resources, that computer or resource authenticates the user and returns an access token. This authentication process is invisible to the user.

Practice: Logging On to a Stand-Alone Server

After completing this practice, you will be able to

- Log on to a stand-alone server in a workgroup

In this practice, you will use the Log On To Windows dialog box to log on to a stand-alone server in a workgroup.

▶ **To log on to a stand-alone server**

1. Press Ctrl+Alt+Delete.

   The Log On To Windows dialog box appears.

2. In the User Name box, type **administrator** (the administrator account you configured during Setup described in "About This Book"). By default, the account name that was last used to log on appears in this box. If this is the first time logging on, the default administrator account appears in this box.

3. In the Password box, type **password** (the password you assigned to the administrator account during Setup). Keep in mind that passwords are case-sensitive, and note that for security reasons, the password appears as asterisks to shield the password from onlookers.

4. Click OK.

Lesson Summary

In this lesson you learned that when a user starts a computer running Windows 2000, the user is prompted to press Ctrl+Alt+Delete to log on. Windows 2000 then displays the Log On To Windows dialog box, and the user must enter a valid user name and password to log on. You also learned about the various options available in the Log On To Windows dialog box. In the practice portion of this lesson, you logged on to a stand-alone server in a workgroup.

When a user logs on, he or she can log on to the local computer or, if the computer is a member of a domain, the user can log on to the domain. If a user supplies a valid domain user account, the directory in the domain controller validates the user name and password. If a user supplies a valid local user account, the user name and password are validated by the security database in the local computer.

Lesson 5: The Windows Security Dialog Box

This lesson explains the options and functionality of the Windows Security dialog box.

After this lesson, you will be able to

- Use the functions of the Windows Security dialog box

Estimated lesson time: 20 minutes

Using the Windows Security Dialog Box

The Windows Security dialog box provides easy access to important security functions. You will need to educate your users about these functions.

The Windows Security dialog box displays the user account currently logged on, the domain or computer to which the user is logged on, and the date and time at which the user logged on. This information is important for users with multiple user accounts, such as an individual who has a regular user account as well as a user account with administrative privileges. You access the Windows Security dialog box by pressing Ctrl+Alt+Delete (see Figure 1.9).

Figure 1.9   Windows Security dialog box

Table 1.7 describes the Windows Security dialog box buttons.

Table 1.7   Buttons on the Windows Security Dialog Box

Button	Description
Lock Computer	Allows you to secure the computer without logging off. All programs remain running. You should lock your computer if you leave it for a short period of time. The user who locks the computer can unlock it by pressing Ctrl+Alt+Delete and entering the valid password. An administrator can also unlock a locked computer by logging off the current user; however, this is a forced logoff and data may be lost.
Log Off	Allows you to log off as the current user and close all running programs, but leaves Windows 2000 running.
Shut Down	Allows you to close all files, save all operating system data, and prepare the computer so that you can safely turn it off.
Change Password	Allows you to change your user account password. You must know the old password to create a new one. This is the only way you can change your own password. Administrators should require users to change their passwords regularly and should set password restrictions as part of account policy.
Task Manager	Provides a list of the current programs that are running, a summary of overall CPU and memory usage, and a quick view of how each program, program component, or system process is using the CPU and memory resources. You can also use Task Manager to switch between programs and to stop a program that is not responding.
Cancel	Closes the Windows Security dialog box.

Practice: Using the Windows Security Dialog Box

After completing this practice, you will be able to

- Lock a computer
- Change your password
- Close a program using Task Manager
- Log off Windows 2000
- Shut down a computer

In this practice, you'll use the Windows Security dialog box to perform various security functions.

Exercise 1: Locking a Computer

▶   **To lock a computer**

1. Press Ctrl+Alt+Delete.

   The Windows Security dialog box appears.

2. Click Lock Computer.

The Computer Locked window appears, indicating that the computer is in use, but locked, and can only be opened by an administrator or by the authenticated user.

3. Press Ctrl+Alt+Delete.

The Unlock Computer dialog box appears.

4. In the Password box, enter your password, and then click OK to unlock your computer.

Exercise 2: Changing Your Password

► **To change your password**

1. Press Ctrl+Alt+Delete.

The Windows Security dialog box appears.

2. Click Change Password.

The Change Password dialog box appears. Notice that the User Name box and the Log On To list show the current user account and domain or computer name.

3. In the Old Password box, enter the current password.

4. In the New Password and Confirm New Password boxes, enter the new password and then click OK.

Your password change is confirmed.

5. Click OK to return to the Windows Security dialog box.

6. Click Cancel.

Exercise 3: Closing a Program Using Task Manager

In this procedure, you open WordPad and then close it using Task Manager. Use this procedure when a program has stopped responding and you need to close it.

► **To close a program using Task Manager**

1. Click the Start button, point to Programs, point to Accessories, and then click WordPad.

WordPad opens.

2. Type in a few miscellaneous letters or words.

3. Press Ctrl+Alt+Delete.

The Windows Security dialog box appears.

4. Click Task Manager.

The Windows Task Manager dialog box appears.

5. Click the Applications tab if it is not already the default.

A list of open programs appears.

6. Under Task, click WordPad, and then click End Task.

When WordPad has stopped responding, the message in Figure 1.10 appears.

Figure 1.10 End Program message

Note If a program stops responding on its own (without invoking End Task), the Wait button appears, allowing you to wait for the application to respond.

If you want to return to WordPad to save changes made to a document before WordPad stops responding, click Cancel. If you want to end WordPad without saving changes, click End Now to end the WordPad session.

Note When Task Manager closes a program, all unsaved data is lost.

7. Exit Task Manager.

Exercise 4: Logging Off

▶ **To log off**

1. Press Ctrl+Alt+Delete.

The Windows Security dialog box appears.

2. Click Log Off.

A message appears, asking if you're sure you want to log off.

3. Click Yes.

Note Another method to log off is to click the Start button, click Shut Down, and then select Log Off Administrator.

Exercise 5: Shutting Down Your Computer

▶ **To shut down your computer**

1. Press Ctrl+Alt+Delete.

   The Windows Security dialog box appears.

2. Click Shut Down.

   The Shut Down Windows dialog box appears. The default is Shut Down.

3. Click OK to shut down or click Cancel to return to the Windows Security dialog box.

Note   Another method to shut down the computer is to click the Start button, click Shut Down, and then select Shut Down.

Lesson Summary

In this lesson you learned that you access the Windows Security dialog box by pressing Ctrl+Alt+Delete and that this dialog box provides information such as the user account currently logged on, and the domain or computer to which the user is logged on. In the practice portion of this lesson, you used the Windows Security dialog box to lock your computer, to change your password, to access Task Manager, to log off your computer while leaving Windows 2000 running, and to shut down your computer.

Review

The following questions are intended to reinforce key information presented in the chapter. If you are unable to answer a question, review the appropriate lesson and then try the question again. Answers to the questions can be found in Appendix A, "Questions and Answers."

1. What is the primary difference between Windows 2000 Professional and Windows 2000 Server?

2. What is the major difference between a workgroup and a domain?

3. Which of the integral subsystems is responsible for running Active Directory?

4. What is the purpose of Active Directory?

5. What happens when a user logs on to a domain?

6. How would you use the Windows Security dialog box?

C H A P T E R   2

Introduction to Active Directory

About This Chapter

You use a directory service to uniquely identify users and resources on a network. Active Directory in Microsoft Windows 2000 is a significant enhancement over the directory services provided in previous versions of Windows. Active Directory provides a single point of network management, allowing you to add, remove, and relocate users and resources easily. This chapter introduces you to Active Directory.

Before You Begin

There are no special requirements to complete this chapter.

Lesson 1: Active Directory Overview

Active Directory provides a method for designing a directory structure that meets the needs of your organization. This lesson introduces the use of objects in Active Directory and the function of each of its components.

After this lesson, you will be able to

- Explain the purpose of object attributes and the schema in Active Directory
- Identify the components of Active Directory
- Describe the function of Active Directory components

Estimated lesson time: 30 minutes

Active Directory Objects

In Chapter 1 you learned that Active Directory stores information about network resources, as well as all the services that make the information available and useful. The resources stored in the directory, such as user data, printers, servers, databases, groups, computers, and security policies, are known as *objects*.

An object is a distinct named set of attributes that represents a network resource. Object *attributes* are characteristics of objects in the directory. For example, the attributes of a user account might include the user's first and last names, department, and e-mail address (see Figure 2.1).

Figure 2.1   Active Directory objects and attributes

In Active Directory, you can organize objects in *classes*, which are logical group-ings of objects. Examples of object classes are those representing user accounts, groups, computers, domains, or organizational units (OUs).

Note Some objects, known as *containers*, can contain other objects. For example, a domain is a container object that can contain users, computers, and other objects.

The Active Directory schema defines objects that can be stored in Active Directory.

Active Directory Schema

The Active Directory schema is the list of definitions that defines the kinds of objects and the types of information about those objects that can be stored in Active Directory. The definitions are themselves stored as objects so that Active Directory can manage the schema objects with the same object management operations used for managing the rest of the objects in Active Directory.

There are two types of definitions in the schema: *attributes* and *classes*. Attributes and classes are also referred to as *schema objects* or *metadata*.

Attributes are defined separately from classes. Each attribute is defined only once and can be used in multiple classes. For example, the Description attribute is used in many classes, but is defined once in the schema, assuring consistency.

Classes, also referred to as *object classes,* describe the possible Active Directory objects that can be created. Each class is a collection of attributes. When you create an object, the attributes store the information that describes the object. The User class, for example, is composed of many attributes, including Network Address, Home Directory, and so on. Every object in Active Directory is an instance of an object class.

A set of basic classes and attributes is shipped with Windows 2000 Server. Experienced developers and network administrators may dynamically extend the schema by defining new classes and attributes for existing classes. For example, if you need to provide information about users not currently defined in the schema, you must extend the schema for the Users class. However, extending the schema is an advanced operation with possible serious consequences. Because a schema cannot be deleted, but only deactivated, and a schema is automatically replicated, you must plan and prepare before extending the schema.

Active Directory Components

Active Directory uses components to build a directory structure that meets the needs of your organization. The logical structures of your organization are represented by the following Active Directory components: domains, organizational units, trees, and forests. The physical structure of your organization is represented by the following Active Directory components: sites (physical subnets) and domain controllers. Active Directory completely separates the logical structure from the physical structure.

Logical Structures

In Active Directory, you organize resources in a logical structure that mirrors the logical structure of your organization. Grouping resources logically enables you to find a resource by its name rather than by its physical location. Because you group resources logically, Active Directory makes the network's physical structure transparent to users. Figure 2.2 illustrates the relationship of the Active Directory components.

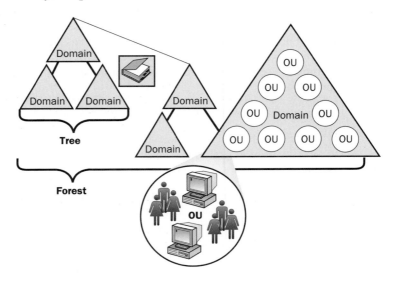

Figure 2.2   Resources organized in a logical hierarchical structure

Domains

The core unit of logical structure in Active Directory is the domain, which can store millions of objects. Objects stored in a domain are those considered "interesting" to the network. "Interesting" objects are items the networked community members need to do their jobs: printers, documents, e-mail addresses, databases, users, distributed components, and other resources. All network objects exist within a domain, and each domain stores information only about the objects it contains. Active Directory is made up of one or more domains. A domain can span more than one physical location.

Grouping objects into one or more domains allows your network to reflect your company's organization. Domains share these characteristics:

- All network objects exist within a domain, and each domain stores information only about the objects that it contains. Theoretically, a domain directory can contain up to 10 million objects, but 1 million objects per domain is a more practical number.

■ A domain is a security boundary. *Access control lists* (ACLs) control access to domain objects. ACLs contain the permissions associated with objects that control which users can gain access to an object and what type of access users can gain to the objects. In Windows 2000, objects include files, folders, shares, printers, and other Active Directory objects. All security policies and settings—such as administrative rights, security policies, and ACLs—do not cross from one domain to another. The domain administrator has absolute rights to set policies only within that domain.

Organizational Units

An *organizational unit* (*OU*) is a container used to organize objects within a domain into logical administrative groups that mirror your organization's functional or business structure. An OU can contain objects such as user accounts, groups, computers, printers, applications, file shares, and other OUs from the same domain. The OU hierarchy within a domain is independent of the OU hierarchy structure of other domains—each domain can implement its own OU hierarchy.

OUs can provide a means for handling administrative tasks, as they are the smallest scope to which you can delegate administrative authority. This provides a way to delegate administration of users and resources.

In Figure 2.3, the domain.com domain contains three OUs: US, ORDERS, and DISP. In the summer months, the number of orders taken for shipping increases and management has requested the addition of a subadministrator for the Orders department. The subadministrator must only have the capability to create user accounts and provide users with access to Orders department files and shared printers. Rather than creating another domain, the request can be met by assigning the subadministrator the appropriate permissions within the ORDERS OU.

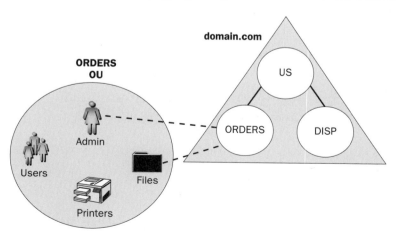

Figure 2.3   Using an organizational unit to handle administrative tasks

If the subadministrator was later required to create user accounts in the US, ORDERS, and DISP OUs, you could grant the appropriate permissions separately within each OU. However, a more efficient method would be to assign permissions once in the US OU and allow them to be inherited by the ORDERS and DISP OUs. By default, all child objects (ORDERS and DISP) within the Active Directory inherit permissions from their parents (US). Granting permissions at a higher level and using inheritance capabilities can reduce administrative tasks.

Trees

A *tree* is a grouping or hierarchical arrangement of one or more Windows 2000 domains that you create by adding one or more child domains to an existing parent domain. Domains in a tree share a contiguous namespace and a hierarchical naming structure. Namespaces are covered in detail in the next lesson. Trees share these characteristics:

- Following Domain Name System (DNS) standards, the domain name of a child domain is the relative name of that child domain appended with the name of the parent domain. In Figure 2.4, microsoft.com is the parent domain and us.microsoft.com and uk.microsoft.com are its child domains. The child domain of uk.microsoft.com is sls.uk.microsoft.com.

- All domains within a single tree share a common schema, which is a formal definition of all object types that you can store in an Active Directory deployment.

- All domains within a single tree share a common *global catalog*, which is the central repository of information about objects in a tree. The global catalog is covered in detail in the next lesson.

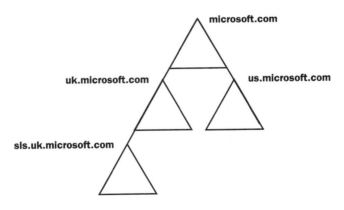

Figure 2.4   A domain tree

By creating a hierarchy of domains in a tree, you can retain security and allow for administration within an OU or within a single domain of a tree. Permissions can flow down the tree by granting permissions to the user on an OU basis. This tree structure easily accommodates organizational changes.

Forests

A *forest* is a grouping or hierarchical arrangement of one or more separate, completely independent domain trees. As such, forests have the following characteristics:

- All trees in a forest share a common schema.

- Trees in a forest have different naming structures, according to their domains.

- All domains in a forest share a common global catalog.

- Domains in a forest operate independently, but the forest enables communication across the entire organization.

- Implicit two-way transitive trusts exist between domains and domain trees.

In Figure 2.5, the trees microsoft.com and msn.com form a forest. The namespace is contiguous only within each tree.

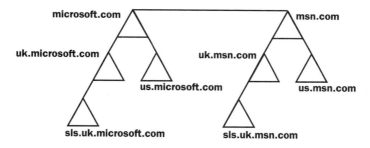

Figure 2.5   A forest of trees

Physical Structure

The physical components of Active Directory are sites and domain controllers. You will use these components to develop a directory structure that mirrors the physical structure of your organization.

Sites

A *site* is a combination of one or more Internet Protocol (IP) subnets connected by a highly reliable and fast link to localize as much network traffic as possible. Typically, a site has the same boundaries as a local area network (LAN). When you group subnets on your network, you should combine only those subnets that have fast, cheap, and reliable network connections with one another. "Fast" network connections are at least 512 kilobits per second (Kbps). An available bandwidth of 128 Kbps and higher is sufficient.

With Active Directory, sites are not part of the namespace. When you browse the logical namespace, you see computers and users grouped into domains and OUs, not sites. Sites contain only computer objects and connection objects used to configure replication between sites.

Note   A single domain can span multiple geographical sites, and a single site can include user accounts and computers belonging to multiple domains.

Domain Controllers

A domain controller is a computer running Windows 2000 Server that stores a replica of the domain directory (local domain database). Because a domain can contain one or more domain controllers, all domain controllers in a domain have a complete replica of the domain's portion of the directory.

The following list describes the functions of domain controllers:

- Each domain controller stores a complete copy of all Active Directory information for that domain, manages changes to that information, and replicates those changes to other domain controllers in the same domain.

- Domain controllers in a domain automatically replicate all objects in the domain to each other. When you perform an action that causes an update to Active Directory, you are actually making the change at one of the domain controllers. That domain controller then replicates the change to all other domain controllers within the domain. You can control replication of traffic between domain controllers in the network by specifying how often replication occurs and the amount of data that Windows 2000 replicates at one time.

- Domain controllers immediately replicate certain important updates, such as the disabling of a user account.

- Active Directory uses multimaster replication, in which no one domain controller is the master domain controller. Instead, all domain controllers within a domain are peers, and each domain controller contains a copy of the directory database that can be written to. Domain controllers may hold different information for short periods of time until all domain controllers have synchronized changes to Active Directory.

- Having more than one domain controller in a domain provides fault tolerance. If one domain controller is offline, another domain controller can provide all required functions, such as recording changes to Active Directory.

- Domain controllers manage all aspects of users' domain interaction, such as locating Active Directory objects and validating user logon attempts.

Lesson Summary

In this lesson you learned that an object is a distinct named set of attributes that represents a network resource in Active Directory. Objects' attributes describe the characteristics of a specific resource in the directory. In Active Directory, you can organize objects in classes, which are logical definitions of objects. You also learned that the Active Directory schema contains a formal definition of the contents and structure of Active Directory, including all attributes and object classes.

You also learned that Active Directory offers you a method for designing a directory structure to meet the needs of your organization's business structure and operations. Active Directory completely separates the logical structure of the domain hierarchy from the physical structure.

In Active Directory, grouping resources logically enables you to find a resource by its name rather than by its physical location. The core unit of logical structure in Active Directory is the domain, which stores information only about the objects that it contains. An OU is a container used to organize objects within a domain into logical administrative groups. A tree is a grouping or hierarchical arrangement of one or more Windows 2000 domains that share a contiguous namespace. A forest is a grouping or hierarchical arrangement of one or more trees that form a disjointed namespace.

The physical structure of Active Directory is based on sites and domain controllers. A site is a combination of one or more IP subnets connected by a high-speed link. A domain controller is a computer running Windows 2000 Server that stores a replica of the domain directory.

Lesson 2: Understanding Active Directory Concepts

There are several new concepts introduced with Active Directory, including the global catalog, replication, trust relationships, DNS namespaces, and naming conventions. It is important that you understand the meaning of these concepts as applied to Active Directory.

After this lesson, you will be able to

- Explain the purpose of the global catalog in Active Directory
- Explain Active Directory replication
- Explain the security relationships between domains in a tree (trusts)
- Describe the DNS namespace used by Active Directory
- Describe the naming conventions used by Active Directory

Estimated lesson time: 20 minutes

Global Catalog

The global catalog is the central repository of information about objects in a tree or forest, as shown in Figure 2.6. By default, a global catalog is created automatically on the initial domain controller in the forest, known as the *global catalog server*. It stores a full replica of all object attributes in the directory for its host domain and a partial replica for all object attributes contained in the directory of every domain in the forest. The partial replica stores attributes most frequently used in search operations (such as a user's first and last names, logon name, and so on). Object attributes replicated to the global catalog inherit the same permissions as in source domains, ensuring that data in the global catalog is secure.

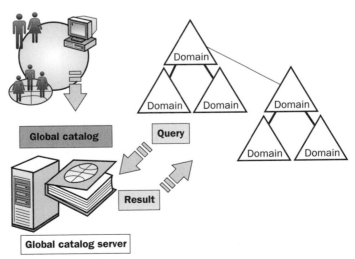

Figure 2.6   The global catalog is the central repository of information

The global catalog performs two key directory roles:

- It enables network logon by providing universal group membership information to a domain controller when a logon process is initiated.
- It enables finding directory information regardless of which domain in the forest actually contains the data.

When a user logs on to the network, the global catalog provides universal group membership information for the account to the domain controller processing the user logon information. If there is only one domain controller in the domain, the domain controller and the global catalog are the same server. If there are multiple domain controllers in the network, the global catalog is the domain controller configured as such. If a global catalog is not available when a user initiates a network logon process, the user is only able to log on to the local computer.

Important   If the domain controller cannot contact a Global Catalog server, the user is not able to log on. An exception is made only for the administrator account in the domain. This account is allowed to log on even without a Global Catalog, so that in an emergency situation a Global Catalog can be configured.

The global catalog is designed to respond to user and programmatic queries about objects anywhere in the domain tree or forest with maximum speed and minimum network traffic. Because a single global catalog contains information about all objects in all domains in the forest, a query about an object can be resolved by a global catalog in the domain in which the query is initiated. Thus, finding information in the directory does not produce unnecessary query traffic across domain boundaries.

You can optionally configure any domain controller or designate additional domain controllers as global catalog servers. When considering which domain controllers to designate as global catalog servers, base your decision on the ability of your network structure to handle replication and query traffic. However, the availability of additional servers can provide quicker responses to user inquiries, as well as redundancy. It is recommended that every major site in your enterprise have at least one global catalog server.

Replication

Users and services should be able to access directory information at any time from any computer in the domain tree or forest. Replication ensures that changes to a domain controller are reflected in all domain controllers within a domain. Directory information is replicated to domain controllers both within and among sites.

What Information Is Replicated?

The information stored in the directory is partitioned into three categories. Each of these information categories is referred to as a *directory partition*. These directory partitions are the units of replication. The following information is contained in each directory:

- **Schema information.**   This defines the objects that can be created in the directory and what attributes those objects can have. This information is common to all domains in the domain tree or forest.

- **Configuration information.**   This describes the logical structure of your deployment, containing information such as domain structure or replication topology. This information is common to all domains in the domain tree or forest.

- **Domain data.**   This describes all of the objects in a domain. This data is domain-specific and is not distributed to any other domains. For the purpose of finding information throughout the domain tree or forest, a subset of the properties for all objects in all domains is stored in the global catalog.

Schema and configuration information is replicated to all domain controllers in the domain tree or forest. All of the domain data for a particular domain is replicated to every domain controller in that domain. All of the objects in every domain, and a subset of the properties of all objects in a forest, are replicated to the global catalog.

A domain controller stores and replicates:

- The schema information for the domain tree or forest.

- The configuration information for all domains in the domain tree or forest.

- All directory objects and properties for its domain. This data is replicated to any additional domain controllers in the domain. For the purpose of finding information, a subset of the properties of all objects in the domain is replicated to the global catalog.

A global catalog stores and replicates:

- The schema information for a forest

- The configuration information for all domains in a forest

- A subset of the properties for all directory objects in the forest (replicated between global catalog servers only)

- All directory objects and all their properties for the domain in which the global catalog is located

Caution   Specific schema changes can cause all global catalog servers in the forest to rebuild the partial attribute set. This can result in a significant amount of replication traffic.

How Replication Works

Active Directory replicates information within a site more frequently than across sites, balancing the need for up-to-date directory information with the limitations imposed by available network bandwidth.

Replication Within a Site

Within a site, Active Directory automatically generates a topology for replication among domain controllers in the same domain using a ring structure. The topology defines the path for directory updates to flow from one domain controller to another until all domain controllers receive the directory updates (see Figure 2.7).

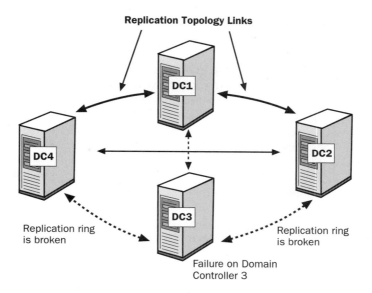

Figure 2.7   Replication topology

The ring structure ensures that there are at least two replication paths from one domain controller to another; if one domain controller is down temporarily, replication still continues to all other domain controllers.

Active Directory periodically analyzes the replication topology within a site to ensure that it is still efficient. If you add or remove a domain controller from the network or a site, Active Directory reconfigures the topology to reflect the change.

Replication Between Sites

To ensure replication between sites, you must customize how Active Directory replicates information using site links to represent network connections. Active Directory uses the network connection information to generate connection objects that provide efficient replication and fault tolerance.

You provide information about the replication protocol used, cost of a site link, times when the link is available for use, and how often the link should be used. Active Directory uses this information to determine which site link will be used to replicate information. Customizing replication schedules so replication occurs during specific times, such as when network traffic is light, will make replication more efficient.

Note   When operating in Native Mode, Windows 2000 domain controllers do not replicate with pre-Windows 2000 domain controllers.

Trust Relationships

A *trust relationship* is a link between two domains in which the trusting domain honors the logon authentication of the trusted domain. Active Directory supports two forms of trust relationships:

- **Implicit two-way transitive trust.**   A relationship between parent and child domains within a tree and between the top-level domains in a forest. This is the default; trust relationships among domains in a tree are established and maintained implicitly (automatically). Transitive trust is a feature of the Kerberos authentication protocol, which provides the distributed authentication and authorization in Windows 2000.

  For example, in Figure 2.8 a Kerberos transitive trust simply means that if Domain A trusts Domain B, and Domain B trusts Domain C, then Domain A trusts Domain C. As a result, a domain joining a tree immediately has trust relationships established with every domain in the tree. These trust relationships make all objects in the domains of the tree available to all other domains in the tree.

  Transitive trust between domains eliminates the management of interdomain trust accounts. Domains that are members of the same tree automatically participate in a transitive, bidirectional trust relationship with the parent domain. As a result, users in one domain can access resources to which they have been granted permission in all other domains in a tree.

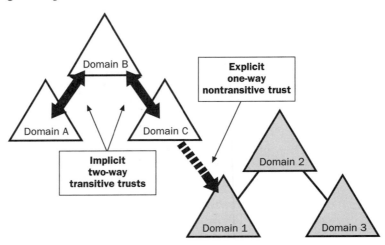

Figure 2.8   Active Directory supports two types of trust relationships

- **Explicit one-way nontransitive trust.**   A relationship between domains that are not part of the same tree. A nontransitive trust is bounded by the two domains in the trust relationship and does not flow to any other domains in the forest. In most cases, you must explicitly (manually) create nontransitive trusts. For example, in Figure 2.8, a one-way, nontransitive trust is shown where Domain C trusts Domain 1, so users in Domain 1 can access resources in Domain C. Explicit one-way nontransitive trusts are the only form of trust possible with

  - A Windows 2000 domain and a Windows NT domain

  - A Windows 2000 domain in one forest and a Windows 2000 domain in another forest

  - A Windows 2000 domain and an MIT Kerberos V5 realm, allowing a client in a Kerberos realm to authenticate to an Active Directory domain in order to access network resources in that domain

DNS Namespace

Active Directory, like all directory services, is primarily a namespace. A *namespace* is any bounded area in which a name can be resolved. *Name resolution* is the process of translating a name into some object or information that the name represents. The Active Directory namespace is based on the DNS naming scheme, which allows for interoperability with Internet technologies. Private networks use DNS extensively to resolve computer names and to locate computers within their local networks and the Internet. DNS provides the following benefits:

- DNS names are user-friendly, which means they are easier to remember than IP addresses.

- DNS names remain more constant than IP addresses. An IP address for a server can change, but the server name remains the same.

- DNS allows users to connect to local servers using the same naming convention as the Internet.

Note   For more information on DNS, see RFCs 1034 and 1035. To read the text of these Requests for Comment (RFCs), use your Web browser to search for **RFC 1034** and **RFC 1035**.

Because Active Directory uses DNS as its domain naming and location service, Windows 2000 domain names are also DNS names. Windows 2000 Server uses Dynamic DNS (DDNS), which enables clients with dynamically assigned addresses to register directly with a server running the DNS service and update the DNS table dynamically. DDNS eliminates the need for other Internet naming services, such as Windows Internet Name Service (WINS), in a homogeneous environment.

Important   For Active Directory and associated client software to function correctly, you must have installed and configured the DNS service.

Domain Namespace

The *domain namespace* is the naming scheme that provides the hierarchical structure for the DNS database. Each node represents a partition of the DNS database. These nodes are referred to as *domains*.

The DNS database is indexed by name; therefore, each domain must have a name. As you add domains to the hierarchy, the name of the parent domain is appended to its child domain (called a *subdomain*). Consequently, a domain's name identifies its position in the hierarchy. For example, in Figure 2.9, the domain name *sales.microsoft.com* identifies the sales domain as a subdomain of the *microsoft.com* domain and *microsoft* as a subdomain of the *com* domain.

Figure 2.9   Hierarchical structure of a domain namespace

The hierarchical structure of the domain namespace typically consists of a root domain, top-level domains, second-level domains, and host names.

There are two types of namespaces:

- **Contiguous namespace.**   The name of the child object in an object hierarchy always contains the name of the parent domain. A tree is a contiguous namespace.

- **Disjointed namespace.** The names of a parent object and a child of the same parent object are not directly related to one another. A forest is a disjointed namespace. For example, consider the domain names

  - www.microsoft.com

  - msdn.microsoft.com

  - www.msn.com

The first two domain names create a contiguous namespace within microsoft.com, but the third domain is part of a disjointed namespace.

Note The term *domain,* in the context of DNS, is not related to domain as used in Windows 2000 directory services. A Windows 2000 domain is a group of computers and devices that are administered as a unit.

Root Domain

The root domain is at the top of the hierarchy and is represented as a period (.). The Internet root domain is managed by several organizations, including Network Solutions, Inc.

Top-Level Domains

Top-level domains are organized by organization type or geographic location. Table 2.1 provides some examples of top-level domain names.

Table 2.1   Examples of Top-Level Domains

Top-Level Domain	Description
gov	Government organizations
com	Commercial organizations
edu	Educational institutions
org	Noncommercial organizations
net	Commercial sites or networks

Note Individual country names may also be a part of top-level domains. Examples of country domain names are "au" for Australia or "fr" for France.

Top-level domains can contain second-level domains and host names.

Second-Level Domains

Organizations, such as Network Solutions, Inc. and others, assign and register second-level domains to individuals and organizations for the Internet. A second-level name has two name parts: a top-level name and a unique second-level name. Table 2.2 provides some examples of second-level domains.

Table 2.2   Examples of Second-Level Domains

Second-Level Domain	Description
ed.gov	United States Department of Education
microsoft.com	Microsoft Corporation
stanford.edu	Stanford University
w3.org	World Wide Web Consortium
pm.gov.au	Prime Minister of Australia

Note   In the case of country names, "gov.au", "edu.au", and "com.au" are top-level domains. If the name is structured as "company.au", however (and in this case only), ".au" is top-level.

Host Names

Host names refer to specific computers on the Internet or a private network. For example, in Figure 2.9, Computer1 is a host name. A host name is the leftmost portion of a *fully qualified domain name (FQDN)*, which describes the exact position of a host within the domain hierarchy. In Figure 2.9, Computer1.sales. microsoft.com. (including the end period, which represents the root domain) is an FQDN.

Note   The host name does not have to be the same as the computer name, NetBIOS, or any other naming protocol.

Zones

A zone represents a discrete portion of the domain namespace. Zones provide a way to partition the domain namespace into manageable sections.

Multiple zones in a domain namespace are used to distribute administrative tasks to different groups. For example, Figure 2.10 depicts the microsoft.com domain namespace divided into two zones. The two zones allow one administrator to manage the microsoft and sales domains and another administrator to manage the development domain.

A zone must encompass a contiguous domain namespace. For example, in Figure 2.10, you could not create a zone that consists of only the sales.microsoft.com and development.microsoft.com domains because the sales and development domains are not contiguous.

The name-to-IP-address mappings for a zone are stored in the zone database file. Each zone is anchored to a specific domain, referred to as the zone's *root domain*. The zone database file does not necessarily contain information for all subdomains of the zone's root domain, only those subdomains within the zone.

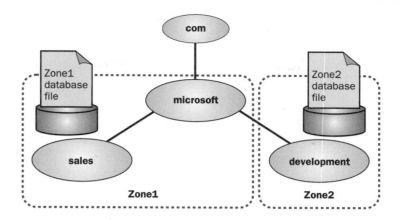

Figure 2.10   Domain namespace divided into zones

In Figure 2.10, the root domain for Zone1 is microsoft.com and its zone file contains the name-to-IP-address mappings for the microsoft and sales domains. The root domain for Zone2 is development, and its zone file contains the name-to-IP-address mappings for the development domain only. The zone file for Zone1 does not contain the name-to-IP-address mappings for the development domain, although development is a subdomain of the microsoft domain.

Name Servers

A DNS name server stores the zone database file. Name servers can store data for one zone or multiple zones. A name server is said to have authority for the domain namespace that the zone encompasses.

One name server contains the master zone database file, referred to as the *primary zone database file,* for the specified zone. As a result, there must be at least one name server for a zone. Changes to a zone, such as adding domains or hosts, are performed on the server that contains the primary zone database file.

Multiple name servers act as a backup to the name server containing the primary zone database file. Multiple name servers provide the following advantages:

- They perform zone transfers. The additional name servers obtain a copy of the zone database file from the name server that contains the primary database zone file. This is called a *zone transfer.* These name servers periodically query the name server containing the primary zone database file for updated zone data.

- They provide redundancy. If the name server containing the primary zone database file fails, the additional name servers can provide service.

- They improve access speed for remote locations. If there are a number of clients in remote locations, use additional name servers to reduce query traffic across slow wide area network (WAN) links.
- They reduce the load on the name server containing the primary zone database file.

Note You can find information on configuring DNS for Active Directory in Chapter 5, "DNS and Active Directory Integration."

Naming Conventions

Every object in Active Directory is identified by a name. Active Directory uses a variety of naming conventions: distinguished names, relative distinguished names, globally unique identifiers, and user principal names.

Distinguished Name

Every object in Active Directory has a distinguished name (DN) that uniquely identifies an object and contains sufficient information for a client to retrieve the object from the directory. The DN includes the name of the domain that holds the object, as well as the complete path through the container hierarchy to the object.

For example, the following DN identifies the Firstname Lastname user object in the microsoft.com domain (where *Firstname* and *Lastname* represent the actual first and last name of a user account):

/DC=COM/DC=microsoft/OU=dev/CN=Users/CN=*Firstname Lastname*

Table 2.3 describes the attributes in the example.

Table 2.3   Distinguished Name Attributes

Attribute	Description
DC	Domain Component Name
OU	Organizational Unit Name
CN	Common Name

DNs must be unique. Active Directory does not allow duplicate DNs.

Note For more information on distinguished names, see RFC 1779. To read the text of this Request for Comment (RFC), use your Web browser to search for **RFC 1779**.

Relative Distinguished Name

Active Directory supports querying by attributes, so you can locate an object even if the exact DN is unknown or has changed. The *relative distinguished name* (RDN) of an object is the part of the name that is an attribute of the object itself. In the preceding example, the RDN of the *Firstname Lastname* user object is Firstname Lastname. The RDN of the parent object is Users.

You can have duplicate RDNs for Active Directory objects, but you cannot have two objects with the same RDN in the same OU. For example, if a user account is named Jane Doe, you cannot have another user account called Jane Doe in the same OU. However, objects with duplicate RDN names can exist in separate OUs because they have different DNs (see Figure 2.11).

Figure 2.11   Distinguished names and relative distinguished names

Globally Unique Identifier

A *globally unique identifier* (GUID) is a 128-bit number that is guaranteed to be unique. GUIDs are assigned to objects when the objects are created. The GUID never changes, even if you move or rename the object. Applications can store the GUID of an object and use the GUID to retrieve that object regardless of its current DN.

In earlier versions of Windows NT, domain resources were associated to a security identifier (SID) that was generated within the domain. This meant that the SID was only guaranteed to be unique within the domain. A GUID is unique across all domains, meaning that you can move objects from domain to domain and they will still have a unique identifier.

User Principal Name

User accounts have a "friendly" name, the *user principal name* (UPN). The UPN is composed of a "shorthand" name for the user account and the DNS name of the tree where the user account object resides. For example, *Firstname Lastname* (substitute the first and last names of the actual user) in the microsoft.com tree might have a UPN of FirstnameL@microsoft.com (using the full first name and the first letter of the last name).

Lesson Summary

In this lesson you learned about several new concepts introduced with Active Directory, including the global catalog, replication, trust relationships, DNS namespaces, and naming conventions.

You learned that the global catalog is a service and a physical storage location that contains a replica of selected attributes for every object in Active Directory. You can use the global catalog to locate objects anywhere in the network without replication of all domain information between domain controllers.

Active Directory includes replication to ensure that changes to a domain controller are reflected in all domain controllers within a domain. Within a site, Active Directory automatically generates a ring topology for replication among domain controllers in the same domain. Between sites, you must customize how Active Directory replicates information using site links to specify how your sites are connected.

A trust relationship is a link between two domains in which the trusting domain honors the logon authentication of the trusted domain. Active Directory supports two forms of trust relationships: implicit two-way transitive trusts and explicit one-way nontransitive trusts.

In this lesson you also learned that Active Directory uses DNS as its domain naming and location service; therefore, Windows 2000 domain names are also DNS names. Windows 2000 Server uses DDNS, so clients with dynamically assigned addresses can register directly with a server running the DNS service and dynamically update the DNS table. There are contiguous namespaces and disjointed namespaces.

Finally, you learned about the naming conventions employed by Active Directory: DNs, RDNs, GUIDs, and UPNs.

Review

The following questions are intended to reinforce key information presented in the chapter. If you are unable to answer a question, review the appropriate lesson and then try the question again. Answers to the questions can be found in Appendix A, "Questions and Answers."

1. What is the Active Directory schema?

2. What is the purpose of an organizational unit (OU)?

3. What are sites and domains and how are they different?

4. What is the difference between implicit two-way transitive trusts and explicit one-way nontransitive trusts?

C H A P T E R   3

Active Directory Administration Tasks and Tools

About This Chapter

This chapter introduces you to the Microsoft Windows 2000 Active Directory administration tasks and administrative tools. The primary Active Directory administration tasks are configuring and administering Active Directory, administering users and groups, securing network resources, administering the desktop computing environment, securing Active Directory, Managing Active Directory performance, and installing Windows 2000 remotely. The primary Windows 2000 Active Directory administration tools are the Active Directory administrative tools, Microsoft Management Consoles (available in the *Administrative Tools* Start Group), and the Task Scheduler (available in the *Control Panel*).

Before You Begin

To complete the lessons in this chapter, you must have

- Completed the Setup procedures located in "About This Book"
- Experience logging on and off Windows 2000

Lesson 1: Active Directory Administration Tasks

This lesson presents an overview of Windows 2000 Active Directory administration tasks.

After this lesson, you will be able to

- Describe the tasks required for Windows 2000 Active Directory administration

Estimated lesson time: 5 minutes

Windows 2000 Active Directory Administration Tasks

Administering Windows 2000 Active Directory involves both configuration and day-to-day maintenance tasks. Administrative tasks can be grouped into the six categories described in Table 3.1.

Table 3.1   Active Directory Administration Tasks

Administrative Category	Specific Tasks
Configuring Active Directory	Plan, deploy, manage, monitor, optimize, and troubleshoot Active Directory, including the domain structure, organizational unit (OU) structure, and site structure. Determine an efficient site topology.
Administering users and groups	Plan, create, and maintain user and group accounts to ensure that each user can log on to the network and gain access to necessary resources.
Securing network resources	Administer, monitor, and troubleshoot authentication services. Plan, implement, and enforce a security policy to ensure protection of data and shared network resources, including folders, files, and printers.
Administering Active Directory	Manage the location and control of Active Directory objects. Plan and implement Active Directory backup and restore operations.
Administering the desktop computing environment	Deploy, install, and configure the desktop computing environment using group policy.
Securing Active Directory	Administer, monitor, and troubleshoot a security configuration. Plan and implement a policy to audit network events so that you can find security breaches.
Managing Active Directory performance	Monitor, maintain, and troubleshoot domain controller performance and Active Directory components using performance monitoring and diagnostic tools.
Installing Windows 2000 remotely	Use Remote Installation Services to deploy Windows 2000 remotely.

The structure of this self-paced training course maps to these categories. The tasks in each category are described in detail in the corresponding chapters of this book.

Lesson Summary

In this lesson you learned about Active Directory administration tasks, which include configuring Active Directory, administering users and groups, securing network resources, administering Active Directory, administering the desktop computing environment, securing Active Directory, managing Active Directory performance, and installing Windows 2000 remotely.

Lesson 2: Active Directory Administrative Tools

The powerful and flexible Active Directory administrative tools that are included with Windows 2000 Server simplify directory service administration. You can use the standard consoles or, using Microsoft Management Console (MMC), you can create custom consoles that focus on single management tasks. This lesson introduces the Active Directory administrative tools and the MMC.

After this lesson, you will be able to

- Describe the function of the Active Directory Users and Computers administrative console
- Describe the function of the Active Directory Sites and Services administrative console
- Describe the function of the Active Directory Domains and Trusts administrative console
- Describe the function and components of MMC, including console trees, details panes, snap-ins, extensions, and console modes

Estimated lesson time: 20 minutes

Active Directory Administrative Tools

The Active Directory administrative tools are installed automatically on computers configured as Windows 2000 domain controllers. The administrative tools are also available with the optional Administrative Tools package. This package can be installed on other versions of Windows 2000 to allow you to administer Active Directory from a computer that is not a domain controller. The following Active Directory standard administrative tools are available on the Administrative Tools menu of all Windows 2000 domain controllers:

- Active Directory Domains and Trusts console
- Active Directory Sites and Services console
- Active Directory Users and Computers console

Active Directory Domains and Trusts Console

The Active Directory Domains and Trusts console helps you manage trust relationships between domains. These domains can be Windows 2000 domains in the same forest, Windows 2000 domains in different forests, pre-Windows 2000 domains, and even Kerberos V5 realms.

Using Active Directory Domains and Trusts, you can

- Provide interoperability with other domains (such as pre-Windows 2000 domains or domains in other Windows 2000 forests) by managing explicit domain trusts

- Change the mode of operation of a Windows 2000 domain from mixed mode to native mode
- Add and remove alternate user principal name (UPN) suffixes used to create user logon names
- Transfer the domain naming operations master role from one domain controller to another
- Provide information about domain management

Active Directory Sites and Services Console

You provide information about the physical structure of your network by publishing sites to Active Directory using the Active Directory Sites and Services console. Active Directory uses this information to determine how to replicate directory information and handle service requests.

Active Directory Users and Computers Console

The Active Directory Users and Computers console allows you to add, modify, delete, and organize Windows 2000 user accounts, computer accounts, security and distribution groups, and published resources in your organization's directory. It also allows you to manage domain controllers and OUs.

Other Active Directory Administrative Tools

In addition to the Active Directory consoles provided on the Administrative Tools menu, there are several other tools provided for administering Active Directory.

Active Directory Schema Snap-In

The Active Directory Schema snap-in allows you to view and modify Active Directory schema. This snap-in is not available by default on the Administrative Tools menu. You must install it, and all of the Windows 2000 Administration Tools, using Add/Remove Programs in the Control Panel. Do not use the ADMINPAK.MSI file on the Windows 2000 Server CD-ROM to perform these operations.

▶ **To install the Active Directory Schema snap-in on a domain controller**

1. Log on as an Administrator.
2. Click Start, point to Settings, then click Control Panel.
3. Double-click Add/Remove Programs.
4. On the Add/Remove Programs dialog box, click Change Or Remove Programs, click Windows 2000 Administration Tools, then click Change.
5. On the Welcome To The Windows 2000 Administration Tools Setup Wizard page, click Next.
6. On the Setup Options page, click Install All Of The Administrative Tools, then click Next.

7. The wizard installs the Windows 2000 Administration Tools. When it finishes, click Finish.

8. Close the Add/Remove Programs dialog box, then close the Control Panel.

9. Click Start, and then click Run.

10. In the Open box, type **mmc** and then click OK.

11. On the Console menu, click Add/Remove Snap-In.

12. In the Add/Remove Snap-In dialog box, click Add.

13. In the Add Standalone Snap-In dialog box, in the Snap-In column, double-click Active Directory Schema, click Close, then click OK.

14. To save this console, from the Console menu, click Save.

Important   Modifying the Active Directory schema is an advanced operation that is best performed programmatically by experienced programmers or system administrators. For detailed information about modifying the Active Directory schema, see the *Microsoft Active Directory Programmer's Guide*.

Active Directory Support Tools

Several additional tools that can be used to configure, manage, and debug Active Directory are available in the Windows 2000 Support Tools. The Windows 2000 Support Tools are included on the Windows 2000 CD in the \Support\Tools folder. These tools are intended for use by Microsoft support personnel and experienced users.

To use Active Directory support tools you must first install the Windows 2000 Support Tools on your computer.

▶ **To install the Windows 2000 Support Tools**

1. Start Windows 2000. You must log on as a member of the Administrator group to install these tools.

2. Insert the Windows 2000 CD into your CD-ROM drive.

3. When the Microsoft Windows 2000 CD screen appears, click Browse This CD.

4. Browse to the \SUPPORT\TOOLS directory.

5. Click SETUP.EXE.

6. Follow the instructions that appear on your screen.

The Setup program installs all Windows 2000 Support Tools files onto your hard disk and requires a maximum of 19 megabytes (MB) of free space.

Setup creates a Windows 2000 Support Tools folder within the Programs folder on the Start menu. For detailed information about individual tools, click the Tools Help menu item. Graphical User Interface (GUI) tools can be selected from the Tools menu.

Setup also adds the \Program Files\Resource Kit directory (or the directory name you choose for installing the tools) to your computer's PATH statement.

Table 3.2 describes the support tools that pertain to Active Directory.

Table 3.2   Active Directory Support Tools

Tool	Used To
ACLDIAG.EXE: ACL Diagnostics[1]	Determine whether a user has been granted or denied access to an Active Directory object. It can also be used to reset access control lists to their default state. See Chapter 14, "Managing Active Directory Performance," for more information.
ADSI Edit[3]	View all objects in the directory (including schema and configuration naming contexts), modify objects, and set access control lists on objects.
DFSUTIL.EXE: Distributed File System Utility[1]	Manage all aspects of distributed file system (Dfs), check the configuration concurrency of Dfs servers, and display the Dfs topology.
DNSCMD.EXE: DNS Server Troubleshooting Tool[1]	Check dynamic registration of DNS resource records including secure DNS update, as well as deregister resource records.
DSACLS.EXE[1]	View or modify the access control lists of objects in Active Directory. See Chapter 14, "Managing Active Directory Performance," for more information.
DSASTAT.EXE: Active Directory Diagnostic Tool[1]	Compare naming contexts on domain controllers and detect differences. See Chapter 14, "Managing Active Directory Performance," for more information.
LDP.EXE: Active Directory Administration Tool[2]	Allow Lightweight Directory Access Protocol (LDAP) operations to be performed against the Active Directory. See Chapter 14, "Managing Active Directory Performance," for more information.
MOVETREE.EXE: Active Directory Object Manager[1]	Move Active Directory objects such as OUs and users between domains in a single forest. See Chapter 11, "Administering Active Directory," for more information.
NETDOM.EXE: Windows 2000 Domain Manager[1]	Manage Windows 2000 domains and trust relationships.
NLTEST.EXE[1]	Provide a list of primary domain controllers, force a shutdown, provide information about trusts and replication. See Chapter 14, "Managing Active Directory Performance," for more information.
REPADMIN.EXE: Replication Diagnostics Tool[1]	Check replication consistency between replication partners, monitor replication status, display replication metadata, force replication events and knowledge consistency checker recalculation. See Chapter 14, "Managing Active Directory Performance," for more information.

Table 3.2   Active Directory Support Tools (*continued*)

Tool	Used To
REPLMON.EXE: Active Directory Replication Monitor[2]	Graphically display replication topology, monitor replication status (including Policies), force replication events and knowledge consistency checker recalculation. See Chapter 14, "Managing Active Directory Performance," for more information.
SDCHECK.EXE: Security Descriptor Check Utility[1]	Check access control list propagation and replication for specified objects in the directory. This tool enables an administrator to determine if access control lists are being inherited correctly and if access control list changes are being replicated from one domain controller to another. See Chapter 14, "Managing Active Directory Performance," for more information.
SIDwalker: Security Administration Tools	Manage access control policies on Windows 2000 and Windows NT systems. SIDwalker consists of three separate programs: SHOWACCS.EXE[1] and SIDWALK.EXE[1] for examining and changing access control entries, and Security Migration Editor[3] for editing mapping between old and new security IDs (SIDs).

[1]   command-line tool

[2]   graphical user interface tool

[3]   Microsoft Management Console snap-in

For more information about the Active Directory support tools, see the *Microsoft Windows Server 2000 Resource Kit*.

Active Directory Service Interfaces

Active Directory Service Interfaces (ADSI) provides a simple, powerful, object-oriented interface to Active Directory. ADSI makes it easy for programmers and administrators to create programs utilizing directory services by using high-level tools such as Microsoft Visual Basic, Java, C, or Visual C++, as well as ActiveX Scripting Languages, such as VBScript, JScript, or PerlScript, without having to worry about the underlying differences between the different namespaces. ADSI is a fully programmable automation object for use by administrators.

ADSI enables you to build or buy programs that give you a single point of access to multiple directories in your network environment, whether those directories are based on LDAP or another protocol.

The Microsoft Management Console (MMC)

The MMC is a tool used to create, save, and open collections of administrative tools, which are called *consoles*. When you access the Active Directory administrative tools, you are accessing the MMC for that tool. The Active Directory Domains and Trusts, Active Directory Sites and Services, and Active Directory Users and Computers administrative tools are each a console. The console does not provide management functions itself, but is the program that hosts management applications called *snap-ins*. You use snap-ins to perform one or more administrative tasks.

There are two types of MMCs: preconfigured and custom. Preconfigured MMCs contain commonly used snap-ins, and they appear on the Administrative Tools menu. You create custom MMCs to perform a unique set of administrative tasks. You can use both preconfigured and custom MMCs for remote administration.

Preconfigured MMCs

Preconfigured MMCs contain snap-ins that you use to perform the most common administrative tasks. Windows 2000 installs a number of preconfigured MMCs during installation. Preconfigured MMCs

- Contain one or more snap-ins that provide the functionality to perform a related set of administrative tasks.

- Function in User mode. Because preconfigured MMCs are in User mode, you cannot modify them, save them, or add additional snap-ins. However, when you create custom consoles, you can add as many preconfigured consoles as you want as snap-ins to your custom console.

- Vary, depending on the operating system that the computer is running and the installed Windows 2000 components. Windows 2000 Server and Windows 2000 Professional have different preconfigured MMCs.

- Might be added by Windows 2000 when you install additional components. Optional Windows 2000 components might include additional preconfigured MMCs that Windows 2000 adds when you install a component. For example, when you install the Domain Name System (DNS) service, Windows 2000 also installs the DNS console.

Table 3.3 lists the typical preconfigured MMCs in Windows 2000 and their function.

Table 3.3   Preconfigured MMCs

Preconfigured MMC	Function
Active Directory Domains and Trusts [1,2]	Manages the trust relationships between domains
Active Directory Sites and Services [1,2]	Creates sites to manage the replication of Active Directory information
Active Directory Users and Computers [1,2]	Manages users, computers, security groups, and other objects in Active Directory
Component Services	Configures and manages COM+ applications
Computer Management	Manages disks and provides access to other tools to manage local and remote computers
Configure Your Server [1]	Sets up and configures Windows services for your network
Data Sources (ODBC)	Adds, removes, and configures Open Database Connectivity (ODBC) data sources and drivers
DHCP [1,2]	Used to configure and manage the Dynamic Host Configuration Protocol (DHCP) service

Table 3.3   Preconfigured MMCs *(continued)*

Preconfigured MMC	Function
Distributed File System [1]	Creates and manages DFSs that connect shared folders from different computers
DNS [1,2]	Manages the DNS service, which translates DNS computer names to IP addresses
Domain Controller Security Policy [1,2]	Used to view and modify security policy for the Domain Controllers organizational unit
Domain Security Policy [1,2]	Used to view and modify security policy for the domain, such as user rights and audit policies
Event Viewer	Displays monitoring and troubleshooting messages from Windows and other programs
Internet Services Manager [1]	Manages Internet Information Services (IIS), the Web server for Internet and intranet Web sites
Licensing [1]	Manages client access licensing for a server product
Local Security Policy [3]	Used to view and modify local security policy, such as user rights and audit policies
Performance	Displays graphs of system performance and configures data logs and alerts
Routing and Remote Access [1]	Used to configure and manage the Routing and Remote Access service
Server Extensions Administrator [1]	Used to administer Microsoft FrontPage Server Extensions and FrontPage extended webs
Services	Starts and stops services
Telnet Server Administration [1]	Used to view and modify telnet server settings and connections

[1]   MMC not available on Windows 2000 Professional.

[2]   MMC not available on Windows 2000 Server stand-alone server.

[3]   MMC not available on Windows 2000 Server domain controller.

Custom MMCs

You can use many of the preconfigured MMCs for administrative tasks. However, there will be times when you need to create your own custom MMCs. Although you can't modify preconfigured consoles, you can combine multiple preconfigured snap-ins with third-party snap-ins that perform related tasks to create custom MMCs. You can then do the following:

- Save the custom MMCs to use again.
- Distribute the custom MMCs to other administrators.
- Use the custom MMCs from any computer to centralize and unify administrative tasks.

Creating custom MMCs allows you to meet your administrative requirements by combining snap-ins that you use to perform common administrative tasks. By creating a custom MMC, you do not have to switch between different programs or different preconfigured MMCs because all of the snap-ins that you need to perform your job are located in the custom MMC.

Consoles are saved as files and have an .msc extension. All the settings for the snap-ins contained in the console are saved and restored when the file is opened, even if the console file is opened on a different computer or network.

Console Tree and Details Pane

Every MMC has a console tree. A *console tree* displays the hierarchical organization of the snap-ins contained with an MMC. As you can see in Figure 3.1, this MMC contains the Device Manager on the local computer and the Disk Defragmenter snap-ins.

Figure 3.1   A sample MMC

The console tree organizes snap-ins that are part of an MMC. This allows you to easily locate a specific snap-in. Items that you add to the console tree appear under the console root. The *details pane* lists the contents of the active snap-in.

Every MMC contains the Action menu and the View menu. The choices on these menus are context-sensitive, depending on the current selection in the console tree.

Snap-Ins

Snap-ins are applications that are designed to work in an MMC. Use snap-ins to perform administrative tasks. There are two types of snap-ins: standalone snap-ins and extension snap-ins.

Standalone Snap-Ins

Standalone snap-ins are usually referred to simply as *snap-ins*. Use standalone snap-ins to perform Windows 2000 administrative tasks. Each snap-in provides one function or a related set of functions. Windows 2000 Server comes with standard snap-ins. Windows 2000 Professional includes a smaller set of standard snap-ins.

Extension Snap-Ins

Extension snap-ins are usually referred to simply as *extensions*. They are snap-ins that provide additional administrative functionality to another snap-in. The following are characteristics of extensions:

- Extensions are designed to work with one or more standalone snap-ins, based on the function of the standalone snap-in. For example, the Software Installation extension is available in the Group Policy snap-in; however, it is not available in the Disk Defragmenter snap-in, because Software Installation does not relate to the administrative task of disk defragmentation.

- When you add an extension, Windows 2000 displays only extensions that are compatible with the standalone snap-in. Windows 2000 places the extensions into the appropriate location within the standalone snap-in.

- When you add a snap-in to a console, MMC adds all available extensions by default. You can remove any extension from the snap-in.

- You can add an extension to multiple snap-ins.

Figure 3.2 demonstrates the concept of snap-ins and extensions. A toolbox (an MMC) holds a drill (a snap-in). You can use a drill with its standard drill bit, and you can perform additional functions with different drill bits (extensions).

■ **Snap-ins are administrative tools.**
■ **Extensions provide additional functionality to snap-ins.**
  · Extensions are preassigned to snap-ins.
  · Multiple snap-ins may use the same extensions.

Figure 3.2   Snap-ins and extensions

Some standalone snap-ins can use extensions that provide additional functionality, for example, Computer Management. However, some snap-ins, like Event Viewer, can act as a snap-in or an extension.

Console Options

Use console options to determine how each MMC operates by selecting the appropriate console mode. The console mode determines the MMC functionality for the person who is using a saved MMC. The two available console modes are Author mode and User mode.

Note   Additional console options can be set using group policy. For information on setting group policies, see Chapter 12, "Administering a Group Policy."

Author Mode

When you save an MMC in Author mode, you enable full access to all MMC functionality, which includes modifying the MMC. Save the MMC using Author mode to allow those using it to do the following:

- Add or remove snap-ins
- Create new windows
- View all portions of the console tree
- Save MMCs

Note   By default, all new MMCs are saved in Author mode.

User Mode

Usually, if you plan to distribute an MMC to other administrators, you save the MMC in User mode. When you set an MMC to User mode, users cannot add snap-ins to, remove snap-ins from, or save the MMC.

There are three types of User modes that allow different levels of access and functionality. Table 3.4 describes when to use each User mode.

Table 3.4   MMC Console User Modes

User Mode	Use When
Full Access	You want to allow users to navigate between snap-ins, open new windows, and gain access to all portions of the console tree.
Limited Access, Multiple Windows	You do not want to allow users to open new windows or gain access to a portion of the console tree. You want to allow users to view multiple windows in the console.
Limited Access, Single Window	You do not want to allow users to open new windows or gain access to a portion of the console tree. You want to allow users to view only one window in the console.

Lesson Summary

In this lesson you learned about the Active Directory administrative tools. The Active Directory Domains and Trusts console manages the trust relationships between domains. The Active Directory Sites and Services console creates sites to manage the replication of Active Directory information. The Active Directory Users and Computers console manages users, computers, security groups, and other objects in Active Directory.

The MMC is a tool used to create, save, and open collections of administrative tools, called consoles. MMCs hold one or more management applications, called snap-ins, which you use to perform administrative tasks. Preconfigured MMCs contain commonly used snap-ins, and they appear on the Administrative Tools menu. You create custom MMCs to perform a unique set of administrative tasks. You can use both preconfigured and custom MMCs for remote administration.

You learned that every MMC has a console tree. The console tree displays the hierarchical organization of the snap-ins that are contained within that MMC. This allows you to easily locate a specific snap-in. The details pane lists the contents of the active snap-in. You also learned that there are two types of snap-ins: standalone snap-ins and extension snap-ins.

Finally, in this lesson you learned about console options. You use console options to determine how each MMC operates by selecting the appropriate console mode. The two available console modes are Author mode and User mode. When you save an MMC in Author mode, you enable full access to all MMC functionality, which includes modifying the MMC. When you set an MMC to User mode, users cannot add snap-ins to, remove snap-ins from, or save the MMC.

Lesson 3: Using Microsoft Management Consoles

This lesson explains how you can use preconfigured consoles and how you can create, use, and modify custom MMCs.

After this lesson, you will be able to

- Use preconfigured MMCs
- Create and use customized MMCs
- Create custom MMCs for remote administration

Estimated lesson time: 30 minutes

Using Preconfigured MMCs

To select preconfigured MMCs, click Start, point to Programs, and then click Administrative Tools. The Computer Management preconfigured console is also available by right-clicking My Computer and selecting Manage.

Using Custom MMCs

To create a custom MMC you must open an empty console and then add the snap-ins needed to perform the desired administrative tasks.

▶ **To start MMC and open an empty console**

1. Click Start.
2. Click Run.
3. Type **mmc** in the Open box, and then click OK.

   An MMC console window opens, titled Console1 and containing a window titled Console Root. This is an empty MMC console and you must decide what to do.

Table 3.5 describes when to use the different options on the Console menu.

Table 3.5   Using Options on the Console Menu

Option	Use When
New	You want to create a new custom MMC console
Open	You want to use a saved MMC console
Save or Save As	You want to use the MMC console later
Add/Remove Snap-In	You want to add or remove one or more snap-ins and their associated extensions to or from an MMC console
Options	You want to configure the console mode and create a custom MMC console

4. Close MMC.

Using MMCs for Remote Administration

When you create custom MMCs, you can set up a snap-in for remote administration. Remote administration allows you to perform administrative tasks from any location. For example, you can use a computer running Windows 2000 Professional to perform administrative tasks on a computer running Windows 2000 Server. You cannot use all snap-ins for remote administration; the design of each snap-in dictates whether or not you can use it for remote administration.

To perform remote administration

- You can use snap-ins from computers running with different versions of Windows 2000.

- You must use specific snap-ins designed for remote administration. If the snap-in is available for remote administration, Windows 2000 prompts you to choose the target computer to administer.

Suppose you need to administer Windows 2000 Server from a Windows 2000 Professional desktop. Because Windows 2000 Professional does not provide the same level of administrative tools as Windows 2000 Server, you will need to install a more complete set of tools on the Professional desktop. By accessing the server through My Network Places and launching the Windows 2000 Administration Tools Setup Wizard using Add/Remove Programs in the Control Panel, you can copy the administrative tools onto the Professional desktop. Then configure each tool for use with the server. Note that some tools may be installed that are not actually running on the server; the Windows 2000 Administration Tools Setup Wizard is simply a means for loading administrative tools to a remote machine.

Practice: Using Microsoft Management Console

After completing this practice, you will be able to

- Use preconfigured consoles
- Customize a console
- Organize and add MMC snap-ins

Exercise 1: Using a Preconfigured MMC

▶ **To use a preconfigured MMC**

1. Log on as Administrator.
2. Click Start, point to Programs, point to Administrative Tools, and then click Event Viewer.

   Windows 2000 displays the Event Viewer console, which gives you access to the contents of the event log files on your computer. You use Event Viewer to monitor various hardware and software activities.

Looking at the console tree, what three logs are listed?

Can you add snap-ins to this console? Why or why not?

3. Close Event Viewer.

Exercise 2: Creating a Custom Microsoft Management Console

In this exercise, you create and customize an MMC. You position this console for easy access and use this console to confirm the last time that your computer was started. You also add a snap-in with extensions.

▶ **To create a custom MMC**

1. Click Start and then click Run.

   The Run dialog box appears.

2. Type **mmc** in the Open box and click OK.

   An MMC window opens, titled Console1 and containing a window titled Console Root. This is an empty MMC and you must determine which snap-ins you need to create a customized MMC.

3. Maximize the Console1 window.

4. Maximize the Console Root window.

5. To view the currently configured options, click Options on the Console menu.

   MMC displays the Options dialog box with the Console tab active. The Console tab allows you to configure the console mode.

   How does a console that is saved in User mode differ from one that is saved in Author mode?

6. In the Console Mode list, make sure that Author Mode is selected, and then click OK.

7. On the Console menu, click Save As.

   MMC displays the Save As dialog box.

8. In the File Name box, type **All Events** and then click Save.

   The name of your console appears in the MMC title bar.

9. On the Console menu, click Exit.

   You have now created and saved a customized console named All Events.

▶ **To access a customized console**

1. Click Start, point to Programs, point to Administrative Tools, then click All Events. The All Events console is visible. Windows 2000 opens the All Events console that you saved previously.

▶ **To add the Event Viewer snap-in to a console**

1. On the Console menu of the All Events console, click Add/Remove Snap-In.

   MMC displays the Add/Remove Snap-In dialog box with the Standalone tab active. Notice that there are currently no loaded snap-ins. You will add a snap-in to the console root.

2. In the Add/Remove Snap-In dialog box, click Add.

   MMC displays the Add Standalone Snap-In dialog box, as shown in Figure 3.3.

Figure 3.3   Add Standalone Snap-In dialog box

Notice the available snap-ins. MMC allows you to add one or more snap-ins to a console, enabling you to create your own customized management tools.

3. In the Add Standalone Snap-In dialog box, select Event Viewer, and then click Add.

   MMC displays the Select Computer dialog box, allowing you to specify which computer you want to administer.

   Notice that you can add Event Viewer for the local computer on which you are working, or if your local computer is a part of the network, you can also add Event Viewer for a remote computer.

Note   To add Event Viewer for a remote computer, click Another Computer and then click Browse. In the Select Computer dialog box, click the remote computer for which you would like to add Event Viewer and then click OK.

---

4. In the Select Computer dialog box, make sure that Local Computer is selected and click Finish.

5. In the Add Standalone Snap-In dialog box, click Close and in the Add/Remove Snap-In dialog box click OK.

    The Event Viewer (Local) snap-in now appears in the console tree and in the details pane.

Tip   To see the entire folder name, drag the border between the console panes to the right.

▶ **To determine the last time that the computer was started**

1. In the console tree of the All Events console, expand the Event Viewer (Local) folder and click System.

    MMC displays the most recent system events in the details pane.

2. Double-click the most recent information event listed as eventlog in the Source column.

    The Event Properties dialog box appears. The Event Log service started as part of your system startup. The date and time represent the approximate time that your system was started.

3. To close the Event Properties dialog box, click OK.

4. On the Console menu, click Exit to close the All Events console.

    The Microsoft Management Console message box appears, asking if you want to save the console settings to All Events.

5. Click No.

▶ **To remove extensions from a snap-in**

1. Click Start and then click Run.

    The Run dialog box appears.

2. Type **mmc** in the Open box and click OK.

    MMC displays an empty console.

3. Maximize the Console1 and Console Root windows.

4. On the Console menu, click Add/Remove Snap-In.

    MMC displays the Add/Remove Snap-In dialog box with the Standalone tab active. You will add a snap-in to the console root.

5. Click Add.

The Add Standalone Snap-In dialog box appears. All snap-ins listed here are standalone snap-ins.

6. Select Computer Management and then click Add.

MMC displays the Computer Management dialog box, allowing you to specify which computer you want to administer. In this procedure, you will add the Computer Management snap-in for your own computer.

7. Verify that Local Computer is selected and then click Finish.

8. Click Close.

Computer Management appears in the list of snap-ins that have been added.

9. In the Add/Remove Snap-In dialog box, click OK.

MMC displays the Computer Management snap-in in the console tree below Console Root. Console Root acts as a container for several categories of administrative functions.

10. Expand Computer Management and review the available functions, and then expand System Tools.

Note   Do not use any of the tools at this point.

Notice that several extensions are available, including System Information and Device Manager. You can restrict the functionality of a snap-in by removing extensions.

11. On the Console menu, click Add/Remove Snap-In.

MMC displays the Add/Remove Snap-In dialog box with the Standalone tab active.

12. Click Computer Management (Local), and then click the Extensions tab.

MMC displays a list of available extensions for the Computer Management snap-in.

What determines which extensions MMC displays in this dialog box?

13. Clear the Add All Extensions check box, and then, in the Available Extensions box, clear the Device Manager Extension check box and the System Information Extension check box.

14. Click OK.

MMC displays the console window again.

15. Expand Computer Management and then expand System Tools to confirm that System Information and Device Manager have been removed.

Note   Do not use any of the tools at this point.

When should you remove extensions from a console?

16. Close the console.

The Microsoft Management Console message box appears, asking if you want to save the console settings.

17. Click No.

Lesson Summary

In this lesson you learned that preconfigured MMCs contain commonly used snap-ins. In the practice portion of this lesson, you viewed the preconfigured MMCs and started the preconfigured MMC containing Event Viewer.

You also learned that you can create custom MMCs to perform a unique set of administrative tasks. They can be easily accessed from the Start menu. In the practice portion of this lesson, you created two customized MMCs. The first console contained the Event Viewer snap-in, which you used to determine the last time your computer was started. The second custom MMC you created contained the Computer Management snap-in. After you created the second customized console, you learned how to restrict the functionality of a console by removing two of the extensions normally available with the Computer Management snap-in. Finally, in this lesson you learned how to create custom MMC consoles for remote administration.

Lesson 4: Using Task Scheduler

Use Task Scheduler to schedule programs and batch files to run once, at regular intervals, or at specific times. You can use Task Scheduler to schedule any script, program, or document to start at a specified time and interval or when certain operating system events occur. You can use Task Scheduler to complete many administrative tasks for you.

After this lesson, you will be able to

- Use Task Scheduler to schedule tasks

Estimated lesson time: 25 minutes

Introduction to Task Scheduler

Windows 2000 saves scheduled tasks in the Scheduled Tasks folder, which is in the Control Panel folder in My Computer and on the Accessories, System Tools menu. In addition, you can access Scheduled Tasks on another computer by browsing that computer's resources using My Network Places. This allows you to move tasks from one computer to another. For example, you can create task files for maintenance and then add them to a user's computer as needed.

Use Task Scheduler to

- Run maintenance utilities at specific intervals
- Run programs when there is less demand for computer resources

Options

Use the Scheduled Task Wizard to schedule tasks. You access the wizard in the Scheduled Tasks folder by double-clicking Add Scheduled Task. Table 3.6 describes the options that you can configure in the Scheduled Task Wizard.

Table 3.6   Scheduled Task Wizard Options

Option	Description
Program to run	The applications to schedule. Select the applications to schedule from a list of applications that are registered with Windows 2000, or click Browse to specify any program, script, or batch file.
Task name	A descriptive name for the task.
Frequency	How often Windows 2000 will perform the task. You can select daily, weekly, monthly, one time only, when the computer starts, or when you log on.
Time and date	The start time and start date for the task to occur. If applicable, you can enter the context-sensitive date information on which to repeat the task.

Option	Description
Name and password	A user name and password. You can enter your user name and password or another user name and password to have the application run under the security settings for that user account.
	If the user account that you used to log on does not have the rights that are required by the scheduled task, you can use another user account that does have the required rights. For example, you can run a scheduled backup by using a user account that has the required rights to back up data but does not have other administrative privileges.
Advanced properties	Select this check box if you want the wizard to display the Advanced Properties dialog box so that you can configure additional properties after you click Finish.

Advanced Properties

In addition to the options that are available in the Scheduled Task Wizard, you can set several additional options for tasks. You can change options that you set with the Scheduled Task Wizard or set additional advanced options by configuring advanced properties for the task.

Table 3.7 describes the tabs in the Advanced Properties dialog box for the scheduled task.

Table 3.7   Scheduled Task Wizard Advanced Preperties Dialog Box Tabs

Tab	Description
Task	Change the scheduled task, add parameters required by the task, or change the user account that is used to run the task. You can also turn the task on and off.
Schedule	Set and display multiple schedules for the same task. You can set the date, time, and number of repeat occurrences for the task. For example, you can set up a task to run every Friday at 10:00 P.M.
Settings	Set options that can delete or stop a task, start or stop a task based on idle or non-idle time, start or stop a task if the computer is running on batteries, and wake the computer to run a task.
Security	Change the list of users and groups that have permission to perform the task, or change the permissions for a specific user or group.

Practice: Using Task Scheduler

After completing this practice, you will be able to

- Schedule tasks to start automatically
- Configure Task Scheduler options

In this practice, you schedule Disk Defragmenter to start at a predetermined time. You also configure Task Scheduler options.

▶ **To schedule a task to start automatically**

1. Double-click My Computer, double-click Control Panel, and then double-click Scheduled Tasks.

    Windows 2000 opens the Scheduled Tasks folder. Because no tasks are currently scheduled, only the Add Scheduled Task entry appears.

2. Double-click Add Scheduled Task.

    The Scheduled Task Wizard appears.

3. Click Next.

    Windows 2000 displays a list of currently installed programs. To schedule a program that is not registered with Windows 2000, you would click Browse to locate the program.

4. Click Browse.

    The Select Program To Schedule dialog box appears.

5. Double-click WINNT, and then double-click system32.

6. Double-click DFRG.MSC.

7. In the name box, type **Launch Disk Defragmenter**, as shown in Figure 3.4.

    The Name box allows you to enter a description that is more intuitive than the program name. Windows 2000 displays this name in the Scheduled Tasks folder when you finish the wizard.

Figure 3.4   Using the Scheduled Task Wizard

8. Click One Time Only and then click Next.

9. In the Start Time box, set the time to 4 minutes after the current system time and make a note of this time.

   To confirm the current system time, look at the taskbar. Do not change the entry in the Start Date box.

10. Click Next.

    The wizard requires you to enter the name and password of a user account. When Task Scheduler runs the scheduled task, the program receives all of the rights and permissions of the user account that you enter here. The program is also bound by any restrictions on the user account. Notice that your user name, SERVER1\Administrator, is already filled in as the default. (If your computer name is not SERVER1, SERVER1 will be replaced by your computer's name.) You must type the correct password for the user account in both password boxes before you can continue.

    You will schedule the console to run with your administrative privileges.

11. In both the Enter The Password box and the Confirm Password box, type **password**.

12. Click Next.

    Do not check the box to open the Advanced Properties dialog box for this task. You will review these properties in the next procedure.

13. Click Finish.

    Notice that the wizard added the task to the list of scheduled tasks.

14. To confirm that you scheduled the task successfully, wait for the time that you configured in Step 9. Disk Defragmenter will start.

15. Close Disk Defragmenter.

▶   **To configure advanced Task Scheduler options**

1. In the Scheduled Tasks folder, double-click Launch Disk Defragmenter.

   Windows 2000 displays the Launch Disk Defragmenter dialog box. Notice the tabs and review the options on the tabs. These are the same options that are available if you select the check box for setting advanced options on the last page of the Scheduled Task Wizard. Do not change any of the settings.

2. Click the Settings tab.

   Review the options that are available on the Settings tab.

3. Select the Delete The Task If It Is Not Scheduled To Run Again check box.

4. Click the Schedule tab, and then set the start time for 2 minutes after the current system time.

   Make a note of this time.

5. Click OK.

   To confirm that you scheduled the task successfully, wait for the time that you set in Step 4 of this procedure. Disk Defragmenter will start.

6. Close Disk Defragmenter.

   Notice that the scheduled event is no longer in the Scheduled Tasks folder. The option to automatically delete a task after it finished is useful for cleaning up after tasks that only need to run once.

7. Close the Scheduled Tasks folder.

8. Log off Windows 2000.

Lesson Summary

In this lesson you learned that you can use the Task Scheduler to schedule programs and batch files to run once, at regular intervals, at specific times, or when certain operating system events occur. Windows 2000 saves scheduled tasks in the Scheduled Tasks folder, which is in the Control Panel folder in My Computer. Once you have scheduled a task to run, you can modify any of the options or advanced features for the task, including the program to be run.

In addition, you learned that you can access Scheduled Tasks on another computer by browsing that computer's resources using My Network Places. This allows you to move tasks from one computer to another. For example, you can create task files for maintenance and then add them to a user's computer as needed. In the practice portion of this lesson, you used the Scheduled Task Wizard to schedule Disk Defragmenter to launch at a specified time.

Review

The following questions are intended to reinforce key information presented in the chapter. If you are unable to answer a question, review the appropriate lesson and then try the question again. Answers to the questions can be found in Appendix A, "Questions and Answers."

1. What are the functions of the Active Directory Domains and Trusts, the Active Directory Sites and Services, and the Active Directory Users and Computers consoles?

2. What is the purpose of creating custom MMCs?

3. When and why would you use an extension?

4. You need to create a custom MMC for an administrator who only needs to use the Computer Management and Active Directory Users and Computers consoles. The administrator

   ▪ Must not be able to add any additional consoles or snap-ins

   ▪ Needs full access to both consoles

   ▪ Must be able to navigate between consoles

   What console mode would you use to configure the custom MMC?

5. What do you need to do to remotely administer a computer running Windows 2000 Server from a computer running Windows 2000 Professional?

6. You need to schedule a maintenance utility to run once a week on a computer running Windows 2000 Server. What do you use to accomplish this?

C H A P T E R   4

Implementing Active Directory

About This Chapter

The success of your Microsoft Windows 2000 implementation depends on your Active Directory plan. This chapter assists you in planning your Active Directory implementation. It also walks you through the steps of installing Active Directory using the Active Directory Installation Wizard. Finally, this chapter shows you how to implement an OU structure and provides procedures for setting OU properties.

Before You Begin

To complete the lessons in this chapter, you must have

- Completed the Setup procedures located in "About This Book"
- Knowledge about the difference between a workgroup and a domain
- Knowledge about the difference between a domain controller and a member server
- Experience using Microsoft Management Consoles (MMCs)

Lesson 1: Planning Active Directory Implementation

Active Directory provides methods for designing a directory structure that meet the needs of your organization. Before implementing Active Directory you must examine your organization's business structure and operations and plan the domain structure, domain namespace, OU structure, and site structure needed by your organization. With the flexibility of Active Directory, you can create the network structure that best fits your company's needs. This lesson walks you through the steps of planning an Active Directory implementation.

After this lesson, you will be able to

- Plan a domain structure
- Plan a domain namespace
- Plan an OU structure
- Plan a site structure

Estimated lesson time: 35 minutes

Planning a Domain Structure

Because the core unit of logical structure in Active Directory is the domain, which can store millions of objects, it is essential to plan the domain structure for your company carefully. When planning a domain structure, you must assess your company's

1. Logical and physical environment structure
2. Administrative requirements
3. Domain requirements
4. Domain organization needs

Assessing the Logical Environment

You must understand how your company conducts daily operations to determine the logical structure of your organization. Consider how the company operates functionally and geographically. For example, Figure 4.1 shows fictitious functional and geographical divisions for Microsoft. Functionally, Microsoft operates through its Administration, Purchasing, Sales, and Distribution departments. Geographically, Microsoft has offices in Kansas City, St. Paul, Chicago, and Columbus.

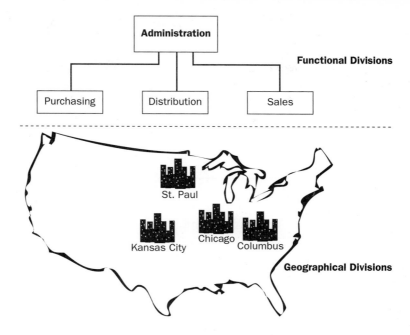

Figure 4.1 Functional and geographical divisions for Microsoft

Assessing the Physical Environment

By assessing your company's physical environment, you can determine the technical requirements for implementing Active Directory. Although you've already examined geographical locations, you must now consider your company's user and network requirements so you can determine the logical requirements for implementing Active Directory.

To assess user requirements, for each functional and geographical division determine

- The number of employees
- The growth rate
- Plans for expansion

To assess network requirements, for each geographical division determine

- How network connections are organized
- Network connection speed
- How network connections are utilized
- TCP/IP subnets

For example, Figure 4.2 shows the physical environment for Microsoft. Employees are distributed fairly evenly among the four locations. However, among the functional divisions, more employees are employed in the Administration department. In the next five years, growth for all locations and all departments is estimated at 3 percent. The Chicago office is the hub of the Microsoft wide area network (WAN). Network connections are utilized moderately; however, the Kansas City-to-Chicago connection has a high degree of utilization.

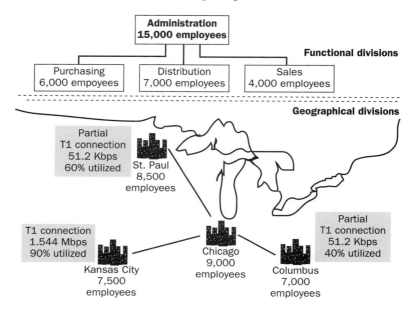

Figure 4.2   Physical environment for Microsoft

Assessing Administrative Requirements

Assessing how your company's network resources are managed also helps you to plan your domain structure. Identify the method of network administration used by your company:

- **Centralized administration.**   A single administrative team provides network services. Smaller companies with fewer locations or business functions often use this method.

- **Decentralized administration.**   A number of administrators or administrative teams provide network services. Teams may be divided by location or business function.

- **Customized administration.**   The administration of some resources is centralized and it is decentralized for others, depending on business needs.

In the example, Microsoft requires decentralized administration methods. Each location requires its own team of administrators to provide network services for all four functional divisions.

After you've determined the logical and physical environment structure and the administrative requirements for your company, you can begin to determine the need for a domain in your organization.

Domain Requirements

The easiest domain structure to administer is a single domain. When planning, you should start with a single domain and only add domains when the single domain model no longer meets your needs.

One domain can span multiple sites and contain millions of objects. Keep in mind that site and domain structures are separate and flexible. A single domain can span multiple geographical sites, and a single site can include users and computers belonging to multiple domains. Planning your site structure is covered later in this lesson.

You do not need to create separate domains merely to reflect your company's organization of divisions and departments. Within each domain, you can model your organization's management hierarchy for delegation or administration using OUs for this purpose, which will act as logical containers for other objects. You can then assign group policy and place users, groups, and computers into the OUs. Planning OU structure is covered later in this lesson.

The following are some reasons to create more than one domain:

- Decentralized network administration
- Replication control
- Different password requirements between organizations
- Massive numbers of objects
- Different Internet domain names
- International requirements
- Internal political requirements

In the example, Microsoft requires multiple domains for the following reasons:

- Stricter password requirements exist at the Chicago office.
- There is a need to control replication on the highly utilized Chicago-to-Kansas City network connection.
- There are plans for adding a new office in Fargo, North Dakota within two years.

Assessing Domain Organization Needs

If you've determined that your company requires more than one domain, you must organize the domains into a hierarchy that fits the needs of your organization. You can arrange domains into a tree or a forest depending on the company's business needs. Recall that domains in trees and forests share the same configuration, schema, and global catalog. As domains are placed in a tree or forest hierarchy, the two-way transitive trust relationship allows the domains to share resources.

The primary difference between domain trees and forests is in their Domain Name Service (DNS) name structure. All domains in a domain tree have a contiguous DNS namespace. Unless your organization operates as a group of several entities, such as a partnership or conglomerate, your network probably lends itself to a contiguous DNS namespace, and you should set up multiple domains in a single domain tree. If you need to combine organizations with unique domain names, create a forest. You can also use a forest to separate DNS zones. Each tree in the forest has its own unique namespace.

In the example, the Microsoft organizational structure maps to a group of domains in a domain tree. Microsoft is not a part of any other entity, nor are there any known plans for creating multiple entities in the future.

Planning a Domain Namespace

In Windows 2000 Active Directory, domains are named with DNS names. But before you begin using DNS on your network, you must plan your DNS namespace. You must make some decisions about how you intend to use DNS naming and what goals you are trying to accomplish using DNS. For instance:

- Have you previously chosen and registered a DNS domain name for use on the Internet?
- Will your company's internal Active Directory namespace be the same or different from its external Internet namespace?
- What naming requirements and guidelines must you follow when choosing DNS domain names?

Choosing a DNS Domain Name

When setting up DNS servers, it is recommended that you first choose and register a unique parent DNS name that can be used for hosting your organization on the Internet. For example, Microsoft uses microsoft.com. This name is a second-level domain within one of the top-level domains used on the Internet.

Before you decide on a parent DNS name for your organization to use on the Internet, perform a search to see if the name is already registered to another entity. The Internet DNS namespace is currently managed by Network Solutions, Inc., though other domain name registrars are also available.

Once you have chosen your parent DNS name, you can combine this name with a location or organizational name used within your organization to form other subdomain names. For example, a subdomain added to the Microsoft second-level domain might be chicago, forming the namespace chicago.microsoft.com.

Internal and External Namespaces

To implement Active Directory, there are two choices for namespace design. The Active Directory namespace can either be the same or separate from the established, registered DNS namespace.

Same Internal and External Namespaces

In this scenario, the company uses the same name for the internal and external namespaces as shown in Figure 4.3. Microsoft.com is used both inside and outside of the company. To implement this scenario, the following requirements must be met:

- Users on the company's internal, private network must be able to access both internal and external servers (both sides of the firewall).

- Clients accessing resources from the outside must not be able to access internal company resources or resolve names to protect company data.

Figure 4.3   Same internal and external namespaces

For this scenario to work, two separate DNS zones must exist. One zone will exist outside the firewall, providing name resolution for public resources. This zone is not configured to resolve internal resources, thereby making internal company resources nonaccessible to external clients.

The challenge in this configuration is making publicly available resources accessible to internal clients, as the external DNS zone is not configured to resolve internal resources. One suggestion is to duplicate the external zone on an internal DNS for internal clients to resolve resources. If a proxy server is being used, the proxy client should be configured to treat microsoft.com as an internal resource.

The advantages to using the same internal and external namespaces are as follows:

- The tree name, microsoft.com, is consistent both on the internal private network and on the external public Internet.
- This scenario extends the idea of a single logon name to the public Internet, allowing users to use the same logon name both internally and externally. For example, jsmith@microsoft.com would serve as both the logon and e-mail ID.

The disadvantages to using the same internal and external namespaces are as follows:

- It results in a more complex proxy configuration. Proxy clients must be configured to know the difference between internal and external resources.
- Care must be taken not to publish internal resources on the external public Internet.
- There will be duplication of efforts in managing resources; for example, maintaining duplicate zone records for internal and external name resolution.
- Even though the namespace is the same, users will get a different view of internal and external resources.

Separate Internal and External Namespaces

In this scenario, the company uses separate internal and external namespaces as shown in Figure 4.4. Basically, the names will be different on either side of the firewall. Microsoft.com is the name that is used outside the firewall and msn.com is the name used inside the firewall.

Figure 4.4   Separate internal and external namespaces

Separate names are used inside and outside the corporation. Microsoft.com is the name that the Internet community sees and uses. Msn.com is the name that the private network sees and uses. To do this, two namespaces must be registered with the Internet DNS. The purpose of registering both names is to prevent duplication of the internal name by another public network. If the name were not reserved, internal clients would not be able to distinguish between the internal name and the publicly registered DNS namespace.

Two zones will be established. One zone will resolve microsoft.com and the other DNS zone will resolve msn.com on the inside of the firewall. Users can clearly distinguish between internal and external resources.

The advantages to using the separate internal and external namespaces are as follows:

- Based on different domain names, the difference between internal and external resources is clear.

- There is no overlap or duplication of effort, resulting in a more easily managed environment.

- Configuration of proxy clients is simpler because exclusion lists only need to contain microsoft.com when identifying external resources.

The disadvantages to using the separate internal and external namespaces are as follows:

- Logon names are different from e-mail names. For example, John Smith would log on as jsmith@msn.com and his e-mail address would be jsmith@microsoft.com.

- Multiple names must be registered with an Internet DNS.

Note   In this scenario, logon names are different by default. An administrator can use the MMC to change the user principal name (UPN) suffix properties of users so that the user logon will match the user e-mail address. However, this requires additional intervention.

Domain Naming Requirements and Guidelines

When you plan your company's domain namespace, consider the following domain naming requirements and guidelines for root domains and subdomains:

- Select a root domain name that will remain static. Changing a root domain name may be impossible or costly in the future.

- Use simple names. Simple and precise domain names are easier for users to remember and they enable users to search intuitively for resources.

- Use standard DNS characters and Unicode characters. Windows 2000 supports the following standard DNS characters: A-Z, a-z, 0-9, and the hyphen (-), as defined in Request for Comment (RFC) 1035. The Unicode character set includes additional characters not found in the American Standard Code for Information Exchange (ASCII) character set, which are required for some languages other than English.

Note   Use Unicode characters only if all servers running DNS service in your environment support Unicode. For more information on the Unicode character set, read RFC 2044, by searching for **RFC 2044** with your Web browser.

- Limit the number of domain levels. Typically, DNS host entries should be three or four levels down the DNS hierarchy and no more than five levels down the hierarchy. Multiple levels increase administrative tasks.

- Use unique names. Each subdomain must have a unique name within its parent domain to ensure that the name is unique throughout the DNS namespace.

- Avoid lengthy domain names. Domain names can be up to 63 characters, including the periods. The total length of the name cannot exceed 255 characters. Case-sensitive naming is not supported.

Taking into account the logical, physical, and administrative requirements, as well as the need for domains and domain organization, Figure 4.5 shows the domain structure for Microsoft. The company's root domain, microsoft.com, contains subdomains for its four offices.

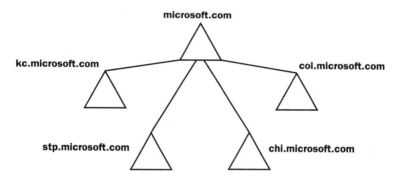

Figure 4.5   Microsoft domain structure and domain names

Planning an OU Structure

After you determine your company's domain structure and plan its domain namespace, you must plan its OU structure. You can create a hierarchy of OUs in a domain. In a single domain, organize users and resources by using a hierarchy of OUs to reflect the structure of the company. OUs allow you to model your organization in a meaningful and manageable way and to assign an appropriate local authority as administrator at any hierarchical level.

Each domain can implement its own OU hierarchy. If your enterprise contains several domains, you can create OU structures within each domain, independent of the structures in the other domains.

Consider creating an OU if you want to do the following:

- Reflect your company's structure and organization within a domain. Without OUs, all users are maintained and displayed in a single list, regardless of a user's department, location, or role.

- Delegate administrative control over network resources, but maintain the ability to manage them. You can grant administrative permissions to users or groups of users at the OU level.

- Accommodate potential changes in your company's organizational structure. You can reorganize users between OUs easily, whereas reorganizing users between domains generally requires more time and effort.

- Group objects to allow administrators to locate similar network resources easily, to simplify security, and to perform any administrative tasks. For example, you could group all user accounts for temporary employees into an OU called TempEmployees.

- Restrict visibility of network resources in Active Directory. Users can view only the objects for which they have access.

Planning an OU Hierarchy

When planning an OU hierarchy, it's important to consider two main guidelines:

1. Although there are no restrictions on the depth of the OU hierarchy, a shallow hierarchy performs better than a deep one.

2. OUs should represent business structures that are not subject to change.

There are many ways to structure OUs for your company. It is important to determine what model will be used as a base for the OU hierarchy. Consider the following models for classifying OUs in the OU hierarchy:

Business function-based OUs can be created based on various business functions within the organization. A business function-based OU hierarchy for domain.com is shown in Figure 4.6. The top level of OUs—ADMIN, DEVELOPMENT (DEVEL), and SALES—corresponds to the company's business divisions. The second level of OUs represents the functional divisions within the business divisions.

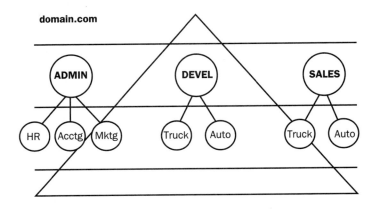

Figure 4.6   A business function-based OU structure

Geographical-based OUs can be created based on the location of company offices. A geographical-based OU hierarchy for domain.com is shown in Figure 4.7. The top level of OUs—WEST, CENTRAL, and EAST— corresponds to the regions set up for the organization. The second level of OUs represents the physical locations of the company's eight offices.

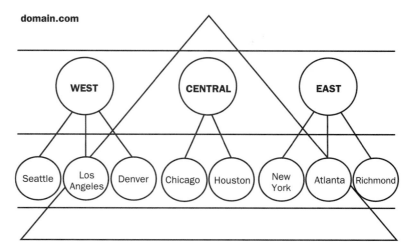

Figure 4.7   A geographical-based OU structure

Business function and geographical-based OUs can be created based on both business function and the location of company offices. A business function and geographical-based OU hierarchy for domain.com is shown in Figure 4.8. The top level of OUs—NORTH AMERICA and EUROPE—corresponds to the continents on which the company has offices. The second level of OUs represents the functional divisions within the company.

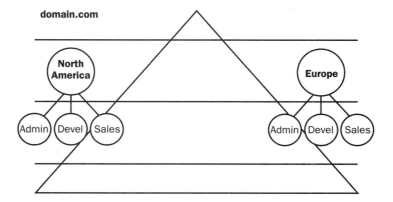

Figure 4.8   A business and geographical-based OU structure

Planning a Site Structure

Recall that a site is part of the Active Directory physical structure and is a combination of one or more Internet Protocol (IP) subnets connected by a highly reliable and fast network connection. In Active Directory, site structure is concerned with the physical environment and is maintained separately from the logical environment, the domain structure. A single domain can include multiple sites, and a single site can include multiple domains or parts of multiple domains. The main role of a site is to provide good network connectivity.

The way in which you set up your sites affects Windows 2000 in two ways:

- **Workstation logon and authentication.**   When a user logs on, Windows 2000 will try to find a domain controller in the same site as the user's computer to service the user's logon request and subsequent requests for network information.
- **Directory replication.**   You can configure the schedule and path for replication of a domain's directory differently for inter-site replication, as opposed to replication within a site. Generally, you should set replication between sites to be less frequent than replication within a site.

Optimizing Workstation Logon Traffic

When planning sites, consider which domain controller(s) the workstations on a given subnet should use. To have a particular workstation only log on to a specific set of domain controllers, define the sites so that only those domain controllers are in the same subnet as that workstation.

Optimizing Directory Replication

When planning sites, consider where the domain controllers and the network connections between the domain controllers will be located. Because each domain controller must participate in directory replication with the other domain controllers in its domain, configure sites so that replication occurs at times and intervals that will not interfere with network performance. Consider establishing a bridgehead server to provide criteria for choosing which domain controller should be preferred as the recipient for inter-site replication.

Designing a Site Structure

Designing a site structure for a network that consists of a single local area network (LAN) is simple. Because local area connections are typically fast, the entire network can be a single site. Establish a separate site with its own domain controllers when you feel domain controllers are not responding fast enough to meet the needs of your users. Determining what is fast enough depends on your criteria for network performance. Inadequate performance is more common when deployments span a wide geographic range. Other inadequacies may be attributed to poor network design and implementation.

Follow these steps to design a site structure for an organization with multiple physical locations:

1. **Assess the physical environment.**   Review the information you gathered when determining domain structure, including site locations, network speed, how network connections are organized, network connection speed, how network connections are utilized, and TCP/IP subnets.

2. **Determine the physical locations that form domains.**   Determine which physical locations are involved in each domain.

3. **Determine which areas of the network should be sites.**   If the network area requires workstation logon controls or directory replication, the area should be set up as a site.

4. **Identify the physical links connecting sites.**   Identify the link types, speeds, and utilization that exist so the links can be determined as site link objects. A *site link object* contains the schedule that determines when replication can occur between the sites that it connects.

5. **For each site link object, determine the cost and schedule.**   The lowest cost site link performs replication; determine the priority of each link by setting the cost (default cost is 100; lower cost provides a higher priority). Replication occurs every 3 hours by default; set the schedule according to your needs.

6. **Provide redundancy by configuring a site link bridge.**   A *site link bridge* provides fault tolerance for replication.

Note   For detailed information on configuring sites and inter-site replication, see Chapter 6, "Configuring Sites."

Lesson Summary

In this lesson you learned that before implementing Active Directory you must examine your organization's business structure and operations and plan the domain structure, domain namespace, OU structure, and site structure needed by your organization.

When planning a domain structure, you must assess your company's logical and physical environment structure, administrative requirements, need for multiple domains, and domain organization needs.

You also learned that you must make some decisions about how you intend to use DNS naming, including the use of previously chosen DNS domain names, and whether your company's internal Active Directory namespace will be the same or different from its external Internet namespace. You learned the naming requirements and guidelines you must follow when choosing DNS domain names.

You learned how OUs allow you to model your organization in a meaningful and manageable way and assign an appropriate local authority as administrator at any hierarchical level. You explored various ways to structure OUs for your company.

Finally, you learned how setting up sites affects Windows 2000 Professional logon traffic and directory replication. You learned about the steps necessary to design a site structure for an organization with multiple physical locations.

Lesson 2: Installing Active Directory

This lesson presents information on installing and removing Active Directory including using the Active Directory Installation Wizard. In addition, the lesson addresses the database and shared system volume that Active Directory creates during installation and setting up DNS for Active Directory. Finally, the lesson discusses domain modes.

After this lesson, you will be able to

- Install Active Directory
- Remove Active Directory from a domain controller

Estimated lesson time: 25 minutes

The Active Directory Installation Wizard

The Active Directory Installation Wizard can perform the following tasks:

- Add a domain controller to an existing domain
- Create the first domain controller of a new domain
- Create a new child domain
- Create a new domain tree
- Install a DNS server
- Create the database and database log files
- Create the shared system volume
- Remove Active Directory services from a domain controller

To launch the Active Directory Installation Wizard, run Configure Your Server on the Administrative Tools menu of the Start menu, or run DCPROMO from the command prompt. These two methods will run the Active Directory Installation Wizard on a stand-alone server and help you through the process of installing Active Directory on the computer and creating a new domain controller.

As you install Active Directory, you can choose whether to add the new domain controller to an existing domain or create the first domain controller for a new domain.

Adding a Domain Controller to an Existing Domain

If you choose to add a domain controller to an existing domain, you create a peer domain controller. You create peer domain controllers for redundancy and to reduce the load on the existing domain controllers.

Creating the First Domain Controller for a New Domain

If you choose to create the first domain controller for a new domain, you create a new domain. You create domains on your network to partition your information, which enables you to scale Active Directory to meet the needs of your organization. When you create a new domain, you can create a new child domain or a new tree. Table 4.1 describes creating a new child domain and creating a new domain tree.

Table 4.1 Creating New Domains

Creating a New Domain	Description
New child domain	When you create a child domain, the new domain is a child domain in an existing domain.
New domain tree	When you create a new tree, the new domain is not part of an existing domain. You can create a new tree in an existing forest, or you can create a new forest.

Configuring DNS for Active Directory

Active Directory uses DNS as its location service, enabling computers to find the location of domain controllers. To find a domain controller in a particular domain, a client queries DNS for resource records that provide the names and IP addresses of the Lightweight Directory Access Protocol (LDAP) servers for the domain. LDAP is the protocol used to query and update Active Directory, and all domain controllers run the LDAP service. You cannot install Active Directory without having DNS on your network, because Active Directory uses DNS as its location service. However, you can install DNS separately without Active Directory.

You can configure your Windows 2000 DNS server automatically using the Active Directory Installation Wizard. Unless you are using a DNS server other than Windows 2000 or you want to perform a special configuration, you do not need to manually configure DNS to support Active Directory. However, if you want to set up a configuration other than the default configuration that the Active Directory Installation Wizard sets up, you can manually configure DNS using the DNS console. Manually configuring DNS is beyond the scope of this course; refer to the *MCSE Training Kit—Microsoft Windows 2000 Network Infrastructure Administration*, for more information on this topic.

Note   For detailed information on configuring DNS for Active Directory, see Chapter 5, "DNS and Active Directory Integration."

The Database and Shared System Volume

Installing Active Directory creates the database and database log files, as well as the shared system volume. Table 4.2 describes these files.

Table 4.2 Types of Files Created by Installing Active Directory

Type of File Created	Description
Database and database log files	The database is the directory for the new domain. The default location for the database and database log files is *systemroot*\NTDS, where *systemroot* is the Windows 2000 directory. For best performance, place the database and the log file on separate hard disks.
Shared system volume	The shared system volume is a folder structure that exists on all Windows 2000 domain controllers. It stores scripts and some of the group policy objects for both the current domain and the enterprise. The default location for the shared system volume is *systemroot*\SYSVOL. The shared system volume must be located on a partition or volume formatted with Microsoft Windows NT file system (NTFS) 5.0.

Replication of the shared system volume occurs on the same schedule as replication of the Active Directory. As a result, you may not notice file replication to or from the newly created system volume until two replication periods have elapsed (typically, 10 minutes). This is because the first file replication period updates the configuration of other system volumes so that they are aware of the newly created system volume.

Domain Modes

There are two domain modes: mixed mode and native mode.

Mixed Mode

When you first install or upgrade a domain controller to Windows 2000 Server, the domain controller is set to run in *mixed mode*. Mixed mode allows the domain controller to interact with any domain controllers in the domain that are running previous versions of Windows NT.

Native Mode

When all the domain controllers in the domain run Windows 2000 Server, and you do not plan to add any more pre-Windows 2000 domain controllers to the domain, you can switch the domain from mixed mode to *native mode*.

During the conversion from mixed mode to native mode

- Support for pre-Windows 2000 replication ceases. Because pre-Windows 2000 replication is gone, you can no longer have any domain controllers in your domain that are not running Windows 2000 Server.

- You can no longer add new pre-Windows 2000 domain controllers to the domain.

- The server that served as the primary domain controller during migration is no longer the domain master; all domain controllers begin acting as peers.

Note   The change from mixed mode to native mode is one-way only; you cannot change from native mode to mixed mode.

▶ **To change the domain mode to native mode**

1. Click Start, point to Programs, point to Administrative Tools, and then click Active Directory Domains And Trusts.
2. Right-click the domain and then click Properties.
3. On the General tab, click Change Mode.
4. In the Active Directory message box, click Yes, then click OK.
5. Restart your computer.

Removing Active Directory Services from a Domain Controller

Running DCPROMO from the Run dialog box on an existing domain controller allows you to remove Active Directory from the domain controller, thus demoting it to a member server. If the domain controller is the last domain controller in the domain, it will become a stand-alone server. If you remove Active Directory from all domain controllers in a domain, you also delete the directory database for the domain, and the domain no longer exists. Computers joined to this domain can no longer log on to the domain or use domain services.

▶ **To remove Active Directory from a domain controller**

1. Log on as Administrator.
2. Click Start, click Run, and then type **dcpromo** in the Open box and click OK.

   The Active Directory Installation Wizard appears.
3. Click Next on the Welcome To The Active Directory Installation Wizard page.
4. If the server is the last domain controller in the domain, select the check box, then click Next.
5. Enter a user name and password with Enterprise Administrator privileges for the domain, then click Next.
6. Enter and confirm the password to be assigned to the server Administrator account, then click Next.
7. Click Next on the Summary page.
8. Click Finish to complete the removal of Active Directory from the computer.

Practice: Installing Active Directory

In this practice you install Active Directory on your stand-alone server, which will make it a domain controller of a new domain. In Exercise 1 you use the DCPROMO program and Active Directory Installation Wizard to install Active Directory. In Exercise 2 you view the domain you have created. In Exercise 3 you are introduced to the Active Directory Users and Computers console. In Exercise 4 you confirm that the DNS service is working.

Exercise 1: Promoting a Stand-Alone Server to a Domain Controller

In this exercise, you run DCPROMO to install the Active Directory service on your stand-alone server, making it a domain controller in a new domain, in a new tree, and in a forest.

▶ **To install the Active Directory service on a stand-alone server**

1. Restart your computer and log on as Administrator.

2. If the Windows 2000 Configure Your Server page opens, close it because the DCPROMO program will be used instead to accomplish the tasks in this practice.

3. Click Start and then click Run.

   The Run dialog box appears.

4. Type **dcpromo** in the Open box and click OK.

   The Active Directory Installation Wizard appears.

5. Click Next.

   The Domain Controller Type page appears.

6. Select Domain Controller For A New Domain, then click Next.

   The Create Tree Or Child Domain page appears.

7. Ensure that Create A New Domain Tree is selected, then click Next.

   The Create Or Join Forest page appears.

8. Select Create A New Forest Of Domain Trees, then click Next.

   The New Domain Name page appears.

9. In the Full DNS Name For New Domain box, type **microsoft.com** and click Next.

   (If you are not using microsoft.com as your DNS domain name, type the name you are using for your DNS domain name.)

   After a few moments, the NetBIOS Domain Name page appears.

10. Ensure that MICROSOFT (or a shortened form of the DNS name you have chosen) appears in the Domain NetBIOS Name box, then click Next.

   The Database and Log Locations page appears.

11. Ensure that *systemroot*\NTDS is the location of both the database and the log and click Next. (If you did not install Windows 2000 in the WINNT directory, both locations should default to the NTDS folder in the folder where you did install Windows 2000.)

    The Shared System Volume page appears.

12. Ensure that the SYSVOL folder location is *systemroot*\SYSVOL. (If you did not install Windows 2000 in the WINNT directory, the SYSVOL location should default to a SYSVOL folder in the folder where you installed Windows 2000.)

    What is the one SYSVOL location requirement?

    What is the function of SYSVOL?

13. Click Next to accept *systemroot*\SYSVOL (or the path where you installed Windows 2000) as the path for SYSVOL.

    The Active Directory Installation Wizard message box appears, reminding you to install and configure a DNS server. Click OK. The Configure DNS page appears.

14. Select Yes, Install And Configure DNS On This Computer, then click Next.

    The Permissions page appears.

15. Unless your network administrator tells you to do otherwise, select Permissions Compatible Only With Windows 2000 Servers, then click Next.

    The Directory Services Restore Mode Administrator Password page appears.

16. Type the password you want to assign to this server's Administrator account in the event the computer is started in Directory Services Restore mode, then click Next.

    The Summary page appears, listing the options that you selected.

17. Review the contents of the Summary page, then click Next.

    The Configuring Active Directory progress indicator appears as the Active Directory service is installed on the server. This process will take several minutes, during which you are prompted to place the Windows 2000 Server CD-ROM in your CD-ROM drive.

18. When the Completing The Active Directory Installation Wizard page appears, click Finish, then click Restart Now.

Exercise 2: Viewing Your Domain Using My Network Places

In this exercise, you view your domain to verify Active Directory installation.

▶ **To view a domain using My Network Places**

1. Log on as Administrator.

2. If the Windows 2000 Configure Your Server page appears, close it.

3. Double-click My Network Places.

   The My Network Places window appears.

   What selections do you see?

4. Double-click Entire Network, and then double-click Microsoft Windows Network.

   What do you see?

5. Close the Microsoft Windows Network window.

Exercise 3: Viewing a Domain Using the Active Directory Users and Computers Console

In this exercise, you use the Active Directory Users and Computers console to view your domain.

▶ **To view a domain using the Active Directory Users and Computers console**

1. Click Start, point to Programs, point to Administrative Tools, then click Active Directory Users And Computers.

   Windows 2000 displays the Active Directory Users and Computers console.

2. In the console tree, double-click microsoft.com (or the name of your domain).

   What selections are listed under microsoft?

3. In the console tree, click Domain Controllers.

   Notice that SERVER1 appears in the details pane. If you did not use SERVER1 as your server name, the DNS name of your server appears in the details pane.

4. Close the Active Directory Users and Computers console.

Exercise 4: Testing Your DNS Server

In this exercise, you confirm that your DNS service is working.

▶ **To test your DNS service using the DNS console**

1. Click Start, point to Programs, point to Administrative Tools, and then click DNS.

2. The DNS console appears. In the DNS console tree, right-click SERVER1 (or the name of your server), then click Properties.

   The SERVER1 Properties dialog box appears. (If you did not use SERVER1 as your server name, the dialog box will reflect your server name.)

3. Click the Monitoring tab.

4. Under Select A Test Type, select the A Simple Query Against This DNS Server check box and the A Recursive Query To Other DNS Servers check box, then click Test Now.

On the SERVER1 Properties dialog box, under Test Results, you should see PASS in the Simple Query and Recursive Query columns.

5. Click OK.

6. Close the DNS console.

Lesson Summary

In this lesson you learned about installing Active Directory, including running Windows 2000 Configure Your Server to start the Active Directory Installation Wizard. You can also go to a command prompt and type DCPROMO to launch the Active Directory Installation Wizard. You can use the Active Directory Installation Wizard to add a domain controller to an existing domain, to create the first domain controller of a new domain, to create a new child domain, and to create a new domain tree. You also learned how the Active Directory Installation Wizard can be used to remove Active Directory from a domain controller.

In addition, you learned about the Active Directory database, which is the directory for the new domain, and the database log files. The default location for the database and database log files is *systemroot*\NTDS. You also learned about the shared system volume that Active Directory creates during installation. The shared system volume is a folder structure that exists on all Windows 2000 domain controllers. It stores scripts and some of the group policy objects for both the current domain and the enterprise. The default location for the shared system volume is *systemroot*\SYSVOL.

You learned how Active Directory uses DNS as its location service, enabling computers to find the location of domain controllers. You cannot install Active Directory without having DNS on your network, because Active Directory uses DNS as its location service. You can configure your Windows 2000 DNS server automatically by using the Active Directory Installation Wizard. Unless you are using a DNS server other than Windows 2000 or you want to perform a special configuration, you do not need to manually configure DNS to support Active Directory.

You also learned about mixed and native domain modes. Mixed mode allows compatibility with previous versions of Windows NT. Native mode is only used when all domain controllers in the domain are running Windows 2000 Server.

In the practice portion of this lesson, you used the Active Directory Installation Wizard to install Active Directory on your computer, to promote your computer to a domain controller, and to create a domain. You then viewed your domain using My Network Places and the Active Directory Users and Computers console. Finally, you used the DNS console to confirm that your DNS service is working.

Lesson 3: Operations Master Roles

Operations master roles are special roles assigned to one or more domain controllers in an Active Directory domain. The domain controllers assigned these roles perform single-master replication. This lesson introduces you to operations master roles and the tasks involved with master role assignments.

After this lesson, you will be able to

- Describe the forest-wide operations master roles
- Describe the domain-wide operations master roles
- Plan operations master locations
- View operations master role assignments
- Transfer operations master role assignments

Estimated lesson time: 15 minutes

Operations Master Roles

As discussed in Chapter 2, Active Directory supports multimaster replication of the Active Directory database between all domain controllers in the domain. However, some changes are impractical to perform in multimaster fashion, so one or more domain controllers can be assigned to perform operations that are single-master (not permitted to occur at different places in a network at the same time). *Operations master roles* are assigned to domain controllers to perform single-master operations.

In any Active Directory forest, five operations master roles must be assigned to one or more domain controllers. Some roles must appear in every forest. Other roles must appear in every domain in the forest. You can change the assignment of operations master roles after setup, but in most cases this will not be necessary. You must be aware of operations master roles assigned to a domain controller if problems develop on the domain controller or if you plan to take it out of service.

Forest-Wide Operations Master Roles

Every Active Directory forest must have the following roles:

- Schema master
- Domain naming master

These roles must be unique in the forest. This means that throughout the entire forest there can be only one schema master and one domain naming master.

Schema Master Role

The schema master domain controller controls all updates and modifications to the schema. To update the schema of a forest, you must have access to the schema master. At any time, there can be only one schema master in the entire forest.

Domain Naming Master Role

The domain controller holding the domain naming master role controls the addition or removal of domains in the forest. There can be only one domain naming master in the entire forest at any time.

Domain-Wide Operations Master Roles

Every domain in the forest must have the following roles:

- Relative ID master
- Primary domain controller (PDC) emulator
- Infrastructure master

These roles must be unique in each domain. This means that each domain in the forest can have only one relative ID master, PDC emulator, and infrastructure master.

Relative ID Master Role

The relative ID master allocates sequences of relative IDs to each of the various domain controllers in its domain. At any time, there can be only one domain controller acting as the relative ID master in each domain in the forest.

Whenever a domain controller creates a user, group, or computer object, it assigns the object a unique security ID. The security ID consists of a domain security ID (which is the same for all security IDs created in the domain), and a relative ID that is unique for each security ID created in the domain.

To move an object between domains (using MOVETREE.EXE: Active Directory Object Manager), you must initiate the move on the domain controller acting as the relative ID master of the domain that currently contains the object.

PDC Emulator Role

If the domain contains computers operating without Windows 2000 client software or if it contains Windows NT backup domain controllers (BDCs), the PDC emulator acts as a Windows NT primary domain controller. It processes password changes from clients and replicates updates to the BDCs. At any time, there can be only one domain controller acting as the PDC emulator in each domain in the forest.

Even after all systems are upgraded to Windows 2000, and the Windows 2000 domain is operating in native mode, the PDC emulator receives preferential replication of password changes performed by other domain controllers in the domain. If a password was recently changed, that change takes time to replicate to every domain controller in the domain. If a logon authentication fails at another domain controller due to a bad password, that domain controller will forward the authentication request to the PDC emulator before rejecting the logon attempt.

Infrastructure Master Role

The infrastructure master is responsible for updating the group-to-user references whenever the members of groups are renamed or changed. At any time, there can be only one domain controller acting as the infrastructure master in each domain.

When you rename or move a member of a group (and that member resides in a different domain from the group), the group may temporarily appear not to contain that member. The infrastructure master of the group's domain is responsible for updating the group so it knows the new name or location of the member. The infrastructure master distributes the update via multimaster replication.

There is no compromise to security during the time between the member rename and the group update. Only an administrator looking at that particular group membership would notice the temporary inconsistency.

Planning Operations Master Locations

In a small Active Directory forest with only one domain and one domain controller, that domain controller is assigned all the operations master roles. When you create the first domain in a new forest, all of the operations master roles are automatically assigned to the first domain controller in that domain.

When you create a new child domain or the root domain of a new domain tree in an existing forest, the first domain controller in the new domain is automatically assigned the following roles:

- Relative identifier master
- Primary domain controller (PDC) emulator
- Infrastructure master

Because there can be only one schema master and one domain naming master in the forest, these roles remain in the first domain created in the forest.

Figure 4.9 shows how the operations master roles are distributed throughout a forest by default.

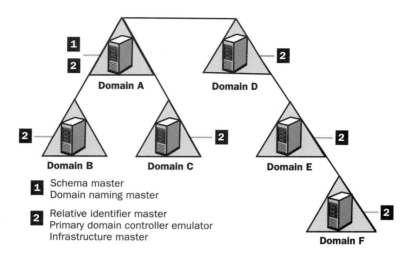

Schema master
Domain naming master

Relative identifier master
Primary domain controller emulator
Infrastructure master

Figure 4.9   Operations master role default distribution in a forest

In Figure 4.9, Domain A was the first domain created in the forest (also called the forest root domain). It holds both of the forest-wide operations master roles. The first domain controller in each of the other domains is assigned the three domain-specific roles.

The default operations master locations work well for a forest deployed on a few domain controllers in a single site. In a forest with more domain controllers, or in a forest that spans multiple sites, you might want to transfer the default operations master role assignments to other domain controllers in the domain or forest.

Planning the Operations Master Role Assignments by Domain

If a domain has only one domain controller, that domain controller will hold all of the domain roles. Otherwise, choose two well-connected domain controllers that are direct replication partners. Make one of the domain controllers the operations master domain controller. Make the other the *standby* operations master domain controller. The standby operations master domain controller is used in case of failure of the operations master domain controller.

In typical domains, you assign both the relative identifier master and PDC emulator roles to the operations master domain controller. In a very large domain, you can reduce the peak load on the PDC emulator by placing these roles on separate domain controllers, both of which are direct replication partners of the standby operations master domain controller. Keep the two roles together unless the load on the operations master domain controller justifies separating the roles.

Unless there is only one domain controller in the domain, the infrastructure master role should not be assigned to the domain controller that is hosting the global catalog. However, you should assign the infrastructure master role to any domain controller that is well connected to a global catalog (from any domain) in the same site. If the operations master domain controller meets these requirements, use it unless the load justifies the extra management burden of separating the roles.

If the infrastructure master and global catalog are on the same domain controller, the infrastructure master will not function. The infrastructure master will never find data that is out of date, so it will never replicate any changes to the other domain controllers in the domain. If all of the domain controllers in a domain are also hosting the global catalog, all of the domain controllers will have the current data and it does not matter which domain controller holds the infrastructure master role.

Planning the Operations Master Roles for the Forest

Once you have planned all of the domain roles for each domain, consider the forest roles. The schema master and the domain naming master roles should always be assigned to the same domain controller. For best performance, assign them to a domain controller that is well connected to the computers used by the administrator or group responsible for schema updates and the creation of new domains. The load of these operations master roles is very light, so, to simplify management, place these roles on the operations master domain controller of one of the domains in the forest.

Planning for Growth

Normally, as your forest grows, you will not need to change the locations of the various operations master roles. But when you are planning to decommission a domain controller, change the global catalog status of a domain controller, or reduce the connectivity of parts of your network, you should review your plan and revise the operations master role assignments, as necessary.

Identifying Operations Master Role Assignments

Before you can revise operations master role assignments, you need to view the current operations master role assignments for your domain.

▶ **To identify the relative ID master, the PDC emulator, or the infrastructure master role assignments**

1. Open the Active Directory Users and Computers console.

2. In the console tree, right-click the Active Directory Users And Computers node, then click Operations Masters.

3. In the Operations Master dialog box, select one of the following:

   ▪ Click the RID tab, and the name of the relative ID master appears in the Operations Master box.

   ▪ Click the PDC tab, and the name of the PDC emulator appears in the Operations Master box.

- Click the Infrastructure tab, and the name of the infrastructure master appears in the Operations Master box.

4. Click Cancel to close the Operations Master dialog box.

▶ **To identify the domain naming master role assignment**

1. Open the Active Directory Domains and Trusts console.

2. In the console tree, right-click the Active Directory Domains And Trusts node, then click Operations Master.

   In the Change Operations Master dialog box, the name of the current domain naming master appears in the Domain Naming Operations Master box.

3. Click Close to close the Change Operations Master dialog box.

▶ **To identify the schema master role assignment**

1. Open the Active Directory Schema snap-in.

Note   The Active Directory Schema snap-in must be installed with the Windows 2000 Administration Tools using Add/Remove Programs in the Control Panel. See Chapter 3 for details on installing the Active Directory Schema console.

---

2. In the console tree, right-click Active Directory Schema, then click Operations Master.

3. In the Change Schema Master dialog box, the name of the current schema master appears in the Current Operations Master box.

Transferring Operations Master Role Assignments

Transferring an operations master role assignment means moving it from one domain controller to another, with the cooperation of the original role holder. Depending upon the operations master role to be transferred, you perform the role transfer using one of the three Active Directory consoles.

▶ **To transfer the relative ID master, the PDC emulator, or the infrastructure master role assignments**

1. Open the Active Directory Users and Computers console.

2. In the console tree, right-click the domain node that will become the new relative ID master, PDC emulator, or infrastructure master, then click Connect To Domain.

3. In the Connect To Domain dialog box, type the domain name or click Browse to select the domain from the list, then click OK.

4. In the console tree, right-click the Active Directory Users And Computers node, then click Operations Masters.

5. In the Operations Master dialog box, select one of the following:

   ▪ Click the RID tab, then click Change.

   ▪ Click the PDC tab, then click Change.

   ▪ Click the Infrastructure tab, then click Change.

6. Click OK to close the Operations Master dialog box.

▶ **To transfer the domain naming master role assignment**

1. Open the Active Directory Domains and Trusts console.

2. In the Console tree, right-click the domain controller node that will become the new domain naming master, then click Connect To Domain.

3. In the Connect To Domain dialog box, type the domain name or click Browse to select the domain from the list, then click OK.

4. In the console tree, right-click the Active Directory Domains And Trusts node, then click Operations Master.

5. In the Change Operations Master dialog box, click Change.

6. Click OK to close the Change Operations Master dialog box.

▶ **To transfer the schema master role assignment**

1. Open the Active Directory Schema snap-in.

Note   The Active Directory Schema snap-in must be installed with the Windows 2000 Administration Tools Using Add/Remove Programs in the Control Panel. See Chapter 3 for details on installing the Active Directory Schema console.

---

2. In the console tree, right-click Active Directory Schema, then click Change Domain Controller.

3. In the Change Domain Controller dialog box, click one of the following:

   ▪ Any DC to let Active Directory select the new schema operations master.

   ▪ Specify Name and type the name of the new schema master to specify the new schema operations master.

4. Click OK.

5. In the console tree, right-click Active Directory Schema, then click Operations Master.

6. In the Change Schema Master dialog box, click Change.

7. Click OK to close the Change Schema Master dialog box.

Responding to Operations Master Failures

Some of the operations master roles are crucial to the operation of your network. Others can be unavailable for quite some time before their absence becomes a problem. Generally, you will notice that a single master operations role holder is unavailable when you try to perform some function controlled by the particular operations master.

If an operations master is not available due to computer failure or network problems, you can *seize* the operations master role. This is also referred to as forcing the transfer of the operations master role.

Before forcing the transfer, first determine the cause and expected duration of the computer or network failure. If the cause is a networking problem or a server failure that will be resolved soon, wait for the role holder to become available again. If the domain controller that currently holds the role has failed, you must determine if it can be recovered and brought back online.

In general, seizing an operations master role is a drastic step that should be considered only if the current operations master will never be available again. The decision depends upon the role and how long the particular role holder will be unavailable. The impact of various role holder failures is discussed in the following topics.

Important   A domain controller whose schema, domain naming, or relative identifier master role has been seized must *never* be brought back online without first reformatting the drives and reloading Windows 2000.

Schema Master Failure

Temporary loss of the schema operations master is not visible to network users. It will not be visible to network administrators either, unless they are trying to modify the schema or install an application that modifies the schema during installation.

If the schema master will be unavailable for an unacceptable length of time, you can seize the role to the standby operations master. However, seizing this role is a step that you should take only when the failure of the schema master is permanent.

Domain Naming Master Failure

Temporary loss of the domain naming master is not visible to network users. It will not be visible to network administrators either, unless they are trying to add a domain to the forest or remove a domain from the forest.

If the domain naming master will be unavailable for an unacceptable length of time, you can seize the role to the standby operations master. However, seizing this role is a step that you should take only when the failure of the domain naming master is permanent.

Relative ID Master Failure

Temporary loss of the relative identifier operations master is not visible to network users. It will not be visible to network administrators either, unless they are creating objects and the domain in which they are creating the objects runs out of relative identifiers.

If the relative identifier master will be unavailable for an unacceptable length of time, you can seize the role to the standby operations master. However, seizing this role is a step that you should take only when the failure of the relative identifier master is permanent.

PDC Emulator Failure

The loss of the primary domain controller (PDC) emulator affects network users. Therefore, when the PDC emulator is not available, you may need to immediately seize the role.

If the current PDC emulator master will be unavailable for an unacceptable length of time and its domain has clients without Windows 2000 client software, or if it contains Windows NT backup domain controllers, seize the PDC emulator master role to the standby operations master. When the original PDC emulator master is returned to service, you can return the role to the original domain controller.

Infrastructure Master Failure

Temporary loss of the infrastructure master is not visible to network users. It will not be visible to network administrators either, unless they have recently moved or renamed a large number of accounts.

If the infrastructure master will be unavailable for an unacceptable length of time, you can seize the role to a domain controller that is not a global catalog but is well connected to a global catalog (from any domain), ideally in the same site as the current global catalog. When the original infrastructure master is returned to service, you can transfer the role back to the original domain controller.

Lesson Summary

In this lesson you learned about the two forest-wide operations master roles, the schema master, and the domain naming master. You also learned about the three domain-wide operations master roles, the relative ID master, the PDC emulator, and the infrastructure master.

You learned the default operations master locations and some strategies for planning locations. You also learned how to view operations master role assignments and how to transfer operations master role assignments if necessary.

Lesson 4: Implementing an Organizational Unit Structure

You should create OUs that mirror your organization's functional or business structure. Each domain can implement its own OU hierarchy. If your enterprise contains several domains, you can create OU structures within each domain, independent of the structures in the other domains. This lesson walks you through the steps for creating an OU structure.

After this lesson, you will be able to

- Create OUs

Estimated lesson time: 10 minutes

Creating OUs

Use the Active Directory Users and Computers console to create OUs. When you create an OU, it is always created on the first available domain controller that is contacted by MMC, and then the OU is replicated to all domain controllers.

▶ **To create OUs**

1. Log on as Administrator.
2. Click Start, point to Programs, point to Administrative Tools, and then click Active Directory Users And Computers.
3. Click the location where you want to create this OU, either a domain (such as microsoft.com) or another OU.
4. On the Action menu, point to New, and then click Organizational Unit.
5. In the New Object-Organizational Unit dialog box, in the Name box, type the name of the new OU, then click OK.

Setting OU Properties

A set of default properties is associated with each OU that you create. These properties equate to the object attributes.

You can use the properties that you define for an OU to search for OUs in the directory. For this reason, you should provide detailed property definitions for each OU that you create. For example, you can search for the OU's description or address.

The tabs in the Organizational Unit Properties dialog box contain information about each OU. The tabs are General, Managed By, and Group Policy, as shown in Figure 4.10. For example, if all the properties on the General tab are complete, you can locate the OU using the OU description or another field.

Figure 4.10   General tab of the OU properties dialog box

Table 4.3 describes the tabs in the Organizational Unit Properties dialog box.

Table 4.3 Tabs on the Organizational Unit Properties Dialog Box

Tab	Description
General	Documents the OU's description, street address, city, state or province, zip or postal code, and country or region
Managed By	Documents the OU manager's name, office location, street address, city, state or province, country or region, telephone number, and fax number
Group Policy	Documents the OU's group policy links

▶ **To set OU properties**

1. Click Start, point to Programs, point to Administrative Tools, and then click Active Directory Users And Computers.

2. Expand the domain.

3. Right-click the appropriate OU, then click Properties.

4. Click the appropriate tab for the OU properties that you want to enter or change, then enter values for each property.

Practice: Creating an OU

In this practice, you create part of the organizational structure of a domain by creating three OUs.

▶ **To create an OU**

1. Log on as Administrator.

2. Click Start, point to Programs, point to Administrative Tools, and then click Active Directory Users And Computers.

   Windows 2000 displays the Active Directory Users and Computers console.

3. Expand the microsoft.com domain (or the domain you set up).

   The OUs appear as folders with a directory book icon under the domain. Plain folders are specialized containers.

   What are the default OUs in your domain?

   To ensure that you are creating a new OU in the correct location, you must first select the location where you want to create this OU.

4. In the console tree, click your domain (such as microsoft.com).

5. On the Action menu, point to New, then click Organizational Unit.

   The New Object-Organizational Unit dialog box appears. Notice that the only required information is the name of the OU. The dialog box indicates the location where the object will be created. This should be your domain.

6. In the Name box, type **Sales**, and then click OK.

   Active Directory Users and Computers displays the newly created Sales OU in addition to the default OUs in your domain.

7. In the console tree, click the Sales OU.

8. On the Action menu, point to New, and then click Organizational Unit.

   The New Object-Organizational Unit dialog box appears.

9. In the name box, type **Trucks**, and then click OK.

   Active Directory Users and Computers displays the newly created Trucks OU under the Sales OU in addition to the default OUs in your domain.

10. Under the Sales OU, create another OU called Autos.

    Active Directory Users and Computers displays the newly created Autos OU under the Sales OU in addition to the Trucks OU and the default OUs in your domain (see Figure 4.11).

Figure 4.11   An OU structure

Lesson Summary

In this lesson you learned that you use the Active Directory Users and Computers console to create a new OU. When you create an OU, it is always created on the first available domain controller that is contacted by MMC, and then replicated to all domain controllers.

You also learned that there is a set of default properties associated with each OU that you create. You learned that these properties equate to object attributes, so you can use these properties to search for OUs in the directory.

Review

The following questions are intended to reinforce key information presented in the chapter. If you are unable to answer a question, review the appropriate lesson and then try the question again. Answers to the questions can be found in Appendix A, "Questions and Answers."

1. What are some reasons for creating more than one domain?

2. Your company has an external Internet namespace reserved with a DNS registration authority. As you plan the Active Directory implementation for your company, you decide to recommend extending the namespace for the internal network. What benefits does this option provide?

3. In what two ways does your site configuration affect Windows 2000?

4. What is the shared system volume, what purpose does it serve, where is it located, and what is its name?

5. What is the purpose of the operations master roles?

6. What administrative tool is used to create OUs?

C H A P T E R   5

DNS and Active Directory Integration

About This Chapter

For Microsoft Windows 2000 Server, the Domain Name System (DNS) service has been carefully integrated into the design and implementation of Active Directory. When deploying Active Directory and Windows 2000 Server together:

- DNS name resolution is needed to locate Windows 2000 domain controllers. The Netlogon service uses DNS server support for the service (SRV) resource record to provide registration of domain controllers in your DNS domain namespace.
- Active Directory can be used to store, integrate, and replicate zones.

This chapter introduces you to DNS name resolution and zones. It also explores the benefits of using Active Directory integrated zones and provides practice in configuring zones. Finally, this chapter discusses zone replication and transfer and provides information on troubleshooting an Active Directory DNS configuration.

Before You Begin

To complete the lessons in this chapter, you must have

- Completed the Setup procedures located in "About This Book."
- Installed Active Directory following the procedures in Chapter 4.
- Experience using Microsoft Management Consoles (MMCs).

Lesson 1: Understanding DNS Name Resolution

The DNS service provides name resolution for clients running Windows 2000. With name resolution, users can access servers by name rather than having to use IP addresses that are difficult to remember. This lesson introduces you to the name resolution process.

After this lesson, you will be able to

- Explain the name resolution process

Estimated lesson time: 10 minutes

Name Resolution

Name resolution is the process of resolving DNS names to IP addresses. Name resolution is similar to looking up a name in a telephone book, where the name is associated with a telephone number. For example, when you connect to the Microsoft Web site, you use the name *www.microsoft.com*. DNS resolves *www.microsoft.com* to its associated IP address, 207.46.130.149. The mapping of names to IP addresses is stored in the DNS distributed database.

IP Addressing

An IP address identifies each host that communicates by using TCP/IP. Each 32-bit IP address is separated internally into two parts—a network ID and a host ID.

- The network ID, also known as a network address, identifies a single network segment within a larger TCP/IP internetwork (a network of networks). All the systems that attach and share access to the same network have a common network ID within their full IP address. This ID is also used to uniquely identify each network within the larger internetwork.

- The host ID, also known as a host address, identifies a TCP/IP node (a workstation, server, router, or other TCP/IP device) within each network. The host ID for each device identifies a single system uniquely within its own network.

Here is an example of a 32-bit IP address:

```
10000011 01101011 00010000 11001000
```

To make IP addressing easier, IP addresses are expressed in dotted decimal notation. The 32-bit IP address is segmented into four 8-bit octets. The octets are converted to decimal (base-10 numbering system) and separated by periods. Therefore, the previous IP address example is 131.107.16.200 when converted to dotted decimal notation.

Continuing with the sample IP address (131.107.16.200), if the network ID portion (131.107) is indicated by the first two numbers of the IP address, then the host ID portion (16.200) is indicated by the last two numbers of the IP address.

Lookup Queries

DNS name servers resolve forward and reverse lookup queries. A *forward lookup query* resolves a name to an IP address. A *reverse lookup query* resolves an IP address to a name. A name server can only resolve a query for a zone for which it has authority. If a name server cannot resolve the query, it passes the query to other name servers that can resolve the query. The name server caches the query results to reduce the DNS traffic on the network.

Forward Lookup Query

The DNS service uses a client/server model for name resolution. To resolve a forward lookup query, a client passes a query to a local name server. The local name server either resolves a query or queries another name server for resolution.

Figure 5.1 represents a client from outside of the microsoft.com zone, querying the name server for an IP address of *www.microsoft.com*.

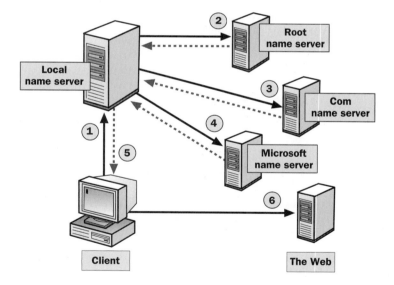

Figure 5.1 Resolving a forward lookup query

The numbers in the figure depict the following activities:

1. The client passes a forward lookup query for *www.microsoft.com* to its local name server.

2. The local name server checks its zone database file to determine whether it contains the name-to-IP-address mapping for the client query. The local name server does not have authority for the micrososft.com domain, so it passes the query to one of the DNS root servers, requesting resolution of the host name. The root name server sends back a referral to the com name servers.

3. The local name server sends a request to a com name server, which responds with a referral to the Microsoft name servers.

4. The local name server sends a request to the Microsoft name server. The Microsoft name server receives the request. Because the Microsoft name server has authority for that portion of the domain namespace, it returns the IP address for *www.microsoft.com* to the local name server.

5. The name server sends the IP address for *www.microsoft.com* to the client.

6. The name resolution is complete, and the client can access *www.microsoft.com*.

Name Server Caching

When a name server is processing a query, it might be required to send out several queries to find the answer. With each query, the name server discovers other name servers that have authority for a portion of the domain namespace. The name server caches these query results to reduce network traffic (see Figure 5.2).

Figure 5.2   Caching query results

When a name server receives a query result the following actions take place:

1. The name server caches the query result for a specified amount of time, referred to as Time To Live (TTL).

Note   The zone that provided the query results specifies the TTL. TTL is configured using the DNS console. The default TTL value is 60 minutes.

---

2. Once the name server caches the query result, TTL starts counting down from its original value.

3. When TTL expires, the name server deletes the query result from its cache.

Caching query results enables the name server to resolve other queries to the same portion of the domain namespace quickly.

Note   Use shorter TTL values to help ensure that data about the domain namespace is more current across the network. Shorter TTL values, however, *increase* the load on name servers. A longer TTL value decreases the time required to resolve information. However, if a change does occur (for example, a change in the subnet), the client will not receive the updated information until the TTL expires and a new query to that portion of the domain namespace is resolved.

Reverse Lookup Query

A reverse lookup query maps an IP address to a name. Troubleshooting tools, such as the NSLOOKUP command-line utility, use reverse lookup queries to report back host names. Additionally, certain applications implement security based on the ability to connect to names, not IP addresses.

Because the DNS distributed database is indexed by name and not by IP address, a reverse lookup query would require an exhaustive search of every domain name. To solve this problem, a special second-level domain called *in-addr.arpa* was created.

The in-addr.arpa domain follows the same hierarchical naming scheme as the rest of the domain namespace; however, it is based on IP addresses, not domain names:

- Subdomains are named after the numbers in the dotted-decimal representation of IP addresses.

- The order of the IP address octets is reversed.

- Companies administer subdomains of the in-addr.arpa domain based on their assigned IP addresses and subnet mask.

For example, Figure 5.3 shows the in-addr.arpa domain representation of the IP address 169.254.16.200. A company that has an assigned IP address range of 169.254.16.0 to 169.254.16.255 with a subnet mask of 255.255.255.0 will have authority over the 16.254.169.in-addr.arpa domain.

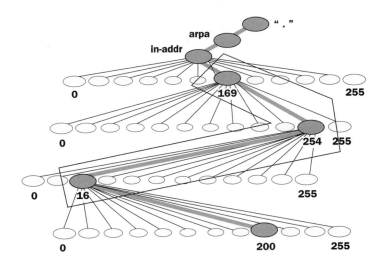

Figure 5.3   The in-addr.arpa domain

Lesson Summary

In this lesson you learned that name resolution is the process of resolving names to IP addresses and that mapping of names to IP addresses is stored in the DNS distributed database. You learned that DNS name servers resolve forward lookup queries, and what actually happens when a client queries the name server for an IP address. You also learned about name server caching and that the name server caches the query results to reduce the DNS traffic on the network.

In addition to forward lookup queries, DNS name servers resolve reverse lookup queries. A reverse lookup query resolves an IP address to a name. Because the DNS distributed database is indexed by name and not by IP address, a special second-level domain called in-addr.arpa was created. The in-addr.arpa domain follows the same hierarchical naming scheme as the rest of the domain namespace; however, it is based on IP addresses instead of domain names.

Lesson 2: Understanding and Configuring Zones

The DNS service allows a DNS namespace to be divided up into zones that store name information about one or more DNS domains. The zone becomes the authoritative source for information about each DNS domain name included in a zone. This lesson introduces you to DNS zones and how they are configured.

After this lesson, you will be able to

- Identify zone types
- List the benefits of Active Directory integrated zones
- Explain zone delegation
- Configure zones
- Configure Dynamic Domain Name Service (DDNS) for a zone

Estimated lesson time: 30 minutes

Zones

The DNS service provides the option of dividing up the namespace into one or more zones, which can then be stored, distributed, and replicated to other DNS servers. The DNS namespace represents the logical structure of your network resources, and DNS zones provide physical storage for these resources.

Zone Planning

When deciding whether or not to divide your DNS namespace to make additional zones, consider the following reasons to use additional zones:

- Is there a need to delegate management of part of your DNS namespace to another location or department within your organization?
- Is there a need to divide one large zone into smaller zones for distributing traffic loads among multiple servers, improve DNS name resolution performance, or create a more fault-tolerant DNS environment?
- Is there a need to extend the namespace by adding numerous subdomains at once, such as to accommodate the opening of a new branch or site?

If you can answer "yes" to one of these questions, it may be useful to add or restructure your namespace into additional zones. When choosing how to structure zones, you should use a plan that meets the needs of your organization.

There are two zone lookup types: forward lookup zones and reverse lookup zones.

Forward Lookup Zones

A *forward lookup zone* enables forward lookup queries. On name servers, you must configure at least one forward lookup zone for the DNS service to work. When you install Active Directory using the Active Directory Installation Wizard and allow the wizard to install and configure your DNS server, the wizard automatically creates a forward lookup zone based on the DNS name you specified for the server.

▶ **To create a new forward lookup zone**

1. Click Start, point to Programs, point to Administrative Tools, and then click DNS.

2. Expand the DNS server.

3. Right-click the Forward Lookup Zone folder and click New Zone. The New Zone Wizard guides you through the process of setting up a forward lookup zone. The wizard presents the following configuration options: Zone Type, Zone Name, Zone File, and Master DNS Servers.

Zone Type

There are three types of zones that you can configure:

- **Active Directory-integrated.**   An Active Directory-integrated zone is the master copy of a new zone. The zone uses Active Directory to store and replicate zone files.

- **Standard primary.**   A standard primary zone is the master copy of a new zone stored in a standard text file. You administer and maintain a primary zone on the computer on which you create the zone.

- **Standard secondary.**   A standard secondary zone is a replica of an existing zone. Secondary zones are read-only and are stored in standard text files. A primary zone must be configured to create a secondary zone. When creating a secondary zone, you must specify the DNS server, called the master server, that will transfer zone information to the name server containing the standard secondary zone. You create a secondary zone to provide redundancy and to reduce the load on the name server containing the primary zone database file.

Benefits of Active Directory-Integrated Zones

For networks deploying DNS to support Active Directory, directory-integrated primary zones are strongly recommended and provide the following benefits:

- Multimaster update and enhanced security based on the capabilities of Active Directory.

In a standard zone storage model, DNS updates are conducted based on a single-master update model. In this model, a single authoritative DNS server for a zone is designated as the primary source for the zone. This server maintains the master copy of the zone in a local file. With this model, the primary server for the zone represents a single fixed point of failure. If this server is not available, update requests from DNS clients are not processed for the zone.

With directory-integrated storage, dynamic updates to DNS are conducted based on a multimaster update model. In this model, any authoritative DNS server (such as a domain controller running the DNS service) is designated as a primary source for the zone. Because the master copy of the zone is maintained in the Active Directory database, which is fully replicated to all domain controllers, the zone can be updated by the DNS service at any domain controller in the domain. With the multimaster update model of Active Directory, any of the primary servers for the directory-integrated zone can process requests from DNS clients to update the zone as long as a domain controller is available and reachable on the network.

Also, when using directory-integrated zones, you can use access control list (ACL) editing to provide granulated access to either the zone or a specified resource record in the zone. For example, an ACL for a specific domain name in the zone can be restricted so that dynamic updates are only allowed for specified DNS clients or to authorize only a secure group such as domain administrators with permissions for updating zone or record properties for it. This security feature is not available with standard primary zones.

- Zones are replicated and synchronized to new domain controllers automatically whenever a new zone is added to an Active Directory domain.

Although DNS service can be selectively removed from a domain controller, directory-integrated zones are already stored at each domain controller, so zone storage and management are not additional resources. Also, the methods used to synchronize directory-stored information offer performance improvement over standard zone update methods, which can potentially require transfer of the entire zone.

- By integrating storage of your DNS namespace in Active Directory, you simplify planning and administration for both DNS and Active Directory.

When namespaces are stored and replicated separately (for example, one for DNS storage and replication and another for Active Directory), an additional administrative complexity is added to planning and designing your network and allowing for its eventual growth. By integrating DNS storage, you can unify managing of storage and replication for both DNS and Active Directory information as a single administrative entity.

- Directory replication is faster and more efficient than standard DNS replication.

Because Active Directory replication processing is performed on a per-property basis, only relevant changes are propagated. This allows less data to be used and submitted in updates for directory-stored zones.

Zone Name

Typically, a zone is named after the highest domain in the hierarchy that the zone encompasses—that is, the root domain for the zone. For example, for a zone that encompasses both microsoft.com and sales.microsoft.com, the zone name would be microsoft.com. For further information on zone naming, see Chapter 2, "Introduction to Active Directory."

Zone File

For the standard primary reverse lookup zone type you must specify a zone file. The zone file is the zone database file name, which defaults to the zone name with a .dns extension. For example, if your zone name is microsoft.com, the default zone database file name is MICROSOFT.COM.DNS.

When migrating a zone from another server, you can import the existing zone file. You must place the existing file in the *systemroot*\System32\DNS directory on the target computer before creating the new zone, where systemroot indicates the Windows 2000 installation folder, typically C:\Winnt.

Master DNS Servers

For the standard secondary forward lookup zone type you must specify the DNS server(s) from which you want to copy the zone. You must enter the IP address of one or more DNS servers.

Reverse Lookup Zones

A *reverse lookup zone* enables reverse lookup queries. Reverse lookup zones are not required. However, a reverse lookup zone is required to run troubleshooting tools, such as NSLOOKUP, and to record a name instead of an IP address in Internet Information Services (IIS) log files.

▶   **To create a new reverse lookup zone**

1. Click Start, point to Programs, point to Administrative Tools, and then click DNS.

2. Expand the DNS server.

3. Right-click the Reverse Lookup Zone folder and click New Zone. The New Zone Wizard guides you through the process of setting up a reverse lookup zone. The wizard presents the following configuration options: Zone Type, Reverse Lookup Zone, Zone File, and Master DNS Servers.

Zone Type

For the zone type, select Active Directory-integrated, Standard Primary, or Standard Secondary, as defined previously.

Reverse Lookup Zone

To identify the reverse lookup zone, type the network ID or the name of the zone. For example, a network ID with an IP address of 169.254.16.200 would result in a network ID of 169.254. All reverse lookup queries within the 169.254 network are resolved in this new zone.

Zone File

For the standard primary reverse lookup zone type, you must specify a zone file. The network ID and subnet mask determine the default zone file name. DNS reverses the IP octets and adds the in-addr.arpa suffix. For example, the reverse lookup zone for the 169.254 network becomes 254.169.in-addr.arpa.dns.

When migrating a zone from another server, you can import the existing zone file. You must place the existing file in the *systemroot*\System32\DNS directory on the target computer before creating the new zone.

Master DNS Servers

For the standard secondary reverse lookup zone type you must specify the DNS server(s) from which you want to copy the zone. You must enter the IP address of one or more DNS servers.

Resource Records

Resource records are entries in the zone database file that associate DNS domain names to related data for a given network resource, such as an IP address. There are many different types of resource records. When a zone is created, DNS automatically adds two resource records: the Start of Authority (SOA) and the Name Server (NS) records. Table 5.1 describes these resource record types, along with the most frequently used resource records.

Table 5.1   Frequently Used Resource Record Types

Resource Record Type	Description
Host (A)	Lists the host name-to-IP-address mappings for a forward lookup zone.
Alias (CNAME)	Creates an alias, or alternate name, for the specified host name. You can use a Canonical Name (CNAME) record to use more than one name to point to a single IP address. For example, you can host a File Transfer Protocol (FTP) server, such as *ftp.microsoft.com,* and a Web server, such as *www.microsoft.com*, on the same computer.
Host Information (HINFO)	Identifies the CPU and operating system used by the host. Use this record as a low-cost resource-tracking tool.

Table 5.1   Frequently Used Resource Record Types *(continued)*

Resource Record Type	Description
Mail Exchanger (MX)	Identifies which mail exchanger to contact for a specified domain and in what order to use each mail host.
Name Server (NS)	Lists the name servers that are assigned to a particular domain.
Pointer (PTR)	Points to another part of the domain namespace. For example, in a reverse lookup zone, it lists the IP-address-to-name mapping.
Service (SRV)	Identifies which servers are hosting a particular service. For example, if a client needs to find a server to validate logon requests, the client can send a query to the DNS server to obtain a list of domain controllers and their associated IP addresses.
Start of Authority (SOA)	Identifies which name server is the authoritative source of information for data within this domain. The first record in the zone database file must be the SOA record.

Note   For more information on resource records, use your Web browser to search for **RFC 1035**, **RFC 1183**, **RFC 1886**, and **RFC 2052** to retrieve the contents of these Requests for Comment (RFCs).

▶ **To view a resource record**

1. In the DNS console tree, click the zone for which you want to view a resource record.

2. In the details pane, click the record you want to view.

3. On the Action menu, click Properties.

4. On the Properties dialog box, view the properties specific to the record you selected.

5. When you have finished viewing the record, click OK.

▶ **To add a resource record**

1. Right-click the zone to which you want to add the record, then select the type of record that you want to add, for example New Host or New Mail Exchanger.

Delegating Zones

A zone starts as a storage database for a single DNS domain name. If other domains are added below the domain used to create the zone, these domains can either be part of the same zone or part of another zone. Once a subdomain is added, it can then be

- Managed and included as part of the original zone records
- Delegated away to another zone created to support the subdomain

For example, Figure 5.4 shows the microsoft.com domain, which contains domain names for Microsoft. When the microsoft.com domain is first created at a single server, it is configured as a single zone for all of the Microsoft DNS namespace. If, however, the microsoft.com domain needs to use subdomains, those subdomains must be included in the zone or delegated away to another zone. In Figure 5.4, the *example* subdomain was added to the microsoft.com domain. The example.microsoft.com zone was created to support the example.microsoft.com subdomain.

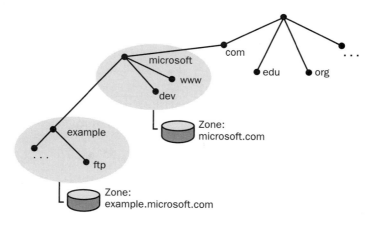

Figure 5.4   Delegating a new subdomain to a new zone

When you delegate zones within a namespace, you must also create SOA resource records to point to the authoritative DNS server for the new zone. This is necessary both to transfer authority and to provide correct referral to other DNS servers and clients of the new servers being made authoritative for the new zone. The New Delegation Wizard is available to assist in delegation of zones.

▶ **To create a zone delegation**

1. In the DNS console tree, click the subdomain for which you want to create a zone delegation.
2. On the Action menu, click New Delegation.
3. On the New Delegation Wizard welcome page, click Next.
4. On the Delegated Domain Name page, specify the name of the domain you want to create, then click Next.

5. On the Name Servers page, specify the servers to host the delegated zone, then click Next.

6. Review your settings on the Completing The New Delegation Wizard page, then click Finish.

Note   All domains (or subdomains) that appear as part of the applicable zone delegation must be created in the current zone prior to performing delegation.

Configuring Dynamic DNS

The DNS service includes a dynamic update capability, called Dynamic DNS (DDNS). With DNS, when there are changes to the domain for which a name server has authority, you must manually update the zone database file on the primary name server. With DDNS, name servers and clients within a network automatically update the zone database files, as shown in Figure 5.5.

Figure 5.5   DDNS updates the zone database when IP addresses change

Dynamic Updates

You can configure a list of authorized servers to initiate dynamic updates. This list can include secondary name servers, domain controllers, and other servers that perform network registration for clients, such as servers running the Dynamic Host Configuration Protocol (DHCP) service or Microsoft Windows Internet Name Service (WINS).

DDNS and DHCP

DDNS interacts with the DHCP service to maintain synchronized name-to-IP mappings for network hosts. By default, the DHCP service allows clients to add their own A (Host) records to the zone, and the DHCP service adds the PTR resource record to the zone. The DHCP service cleans up both the A and PTR resource records in the zone when the lease expires.

Important   To send dynamic updates, you must configure the DHCP server to point to the appropriate DNS servers. Configuring DHCP is beyond the scope of this course; refer to *MCSE Training Kit—Microsoft Windows 2000 Network Infrastructure Administration* for more information on this topic.

▶   **To configure a zone for DDNS**

1. From the DNS console, right-click the forward or reverse lookup zone that you want to configure, and then click Properties.

2. On the General tab, in the Allow Dynamic Updates? list, choose one of the following options:

   ▪ **No.**   Does not allow dynamic updates for this zone.

   ▪ **Yes.**   Allows all dynamic DNS update requests for this zone.

   ▪ **Only Secure Updates.**   Allows only dynamic DNS updates that use secure DNS for this zone. This is the preferred option.

The Only Secure Updates option only appears if the zone type is Active Directory-integrated. If you select the Only Secure Updates option, the requester's permission to update the records in the zone database is tested using mechanisms specified in a subsequent secure DNS update protocol.

Note   For more information on DDNS, use your Web browser to search for **RFC 2136** and **RFC 2137**.

Practice: Configuring Zones

In this practice, you configure zones. In Exercise 1 you create a forward and a reverse lookup zone for the DNS service. In Exercise 2 you configure the zones you created in Exercise 1 for DDNS. In Exercise 3 you add a PTR resource record for a reverse lookup zone.

Exercise 1: Creating Zones

In this exercise, you create a forward lookup zone and a reverse lookup zone.

▶   **To create a forward lookup zone**

1. Click Start, point to Programs, point to Administrative Tools, and then click DNS.

   The DNS console window appears.

2. Double-click SERVER1 (or the name of your computer).

The Forward Lookup Zones and Reverse Lookup Zones folders appear.

3. Right-click SERVER1, then click New Zone.

The New Zone Wizard appears.

4. Click Next to continue.

The Zone Type page appears.

5. Ensure that Standard Primary is selected, and then click Next.

The Forward or Reverse Lookup Zone page appears.

6. Ensure that Forward Lookup Zone is selected, and then click Next.

The Zone Name page appears.

7. Type **training.microsoft.com** and click Next. (If you are on a network, check with your network administrator to make sure it is OK to use this as your DNS domain name.)

The Zone File page appears.

8. Ensure that Create A New File With This File Name is selected and that the name of the file to be created is TRAINING.MICROSOFT.COM.DNS. (If you did not use training.microsoft.com as the domain name in Step 7, this will be the domain name you typed in Step 7 with a .dns extension.)

9. Click Next.

The Completing the New Zone Wizard page appears.

10. Click Finish.

▶ **To create a reverse lookup zone**

1. Right-click SERVER1, and then click New Zone.

The New Zone Wizard appears.

2. Click Next to continue.

The Zone Type page appears.

3. Ensure that Standard Primary is selected, and then click Next.

The Forward or Reverse Lookup Zone page appears.

4. Ensure that Reverse Lookup Zone is selected, and then click Next.

The Reverse Lookup Zone page appears.

5. Ensure that Network ID is selected, and type **10.10.1** in the Network ID box. (If you are on a network and did not use 10.10.1.1 as your static IP address, type in the octets identifying your network ID.)

Note   In the Name box at the bottom of the screen, notice that the in-addr.arpa name is typed in and is 1.10.10.in-addr.arpa. If you did not use 10.10.1.1, your name will match the IP address that you are using.

---

6. Click Next.

   The Zone File page appears.

7. Ensure that Create A New File With This File Name is selected and that the name of the file to be created is 1.10.10.in-addr.arpa.dns. (If you did not use 10.10.1 as your Network ID in Step 5, the file name will match the IP address that you used.)

8. Click Next.

   The Completing the New Zone Wizard page appears.

9. Review the information on the Completing the New Zone Wizard page, then click Finish.

Exercise 2: Configuring DDNS Service

In this exercise, you configure the DNS service to allow dynamic updates for forward and reverse lookup zones.

▶   **To configure DDNS**

1. In the DNS console tree, double-click SERVER1 (or the name of your server).

2. Double-click Forward Lookup Zones, and then double-click training.microsoft.com. (If you did not use training.microsoft.com as your DNS domain name, double-click your DNS domain name.)

3. Right-click training.microsoft.com (or your DNS domain name), and then click Properties.

   The training.microsoft.com Properties dialog box appears. (If you did not use training.microsoft.com as your DNS domain name, the name of the dialog box will reflect your DNS domain name.)

4. In the Allow Dynamic Updates? list on the General tab, select Yes, and click OK.

   This configures DDNS for the forward lookup zone.

5. Double-click Reverse Lookup Zones, then click 10.10.1.x Subnet or the reverse lookup zone you created in Exercise 1.

6. Right-click 10.10.1.x Subnet, then click Properties.

   The 10.10.1.x Subnet Properties dialog box appears.

7. In the Allow Dynamic Updates? list on the General tab, select Yes, then click OK.

   This configures DDNS for the reverse lookup zone.

Exercise 3: Adding a Resource Record

In this exercise, you practice adding a PTR resource record for a zone.

▶ **To add a PTR resource record for a zone**

1. In the console tree, click Reverse Lookup Zones.

2. Click 10.10.1.x Subnet. (If you did not use 10.10.1.1 as the static IP address for your server name, click the appropriate subnet.)

   What types of resource records exist in the reverse lookup zone?

3. In the console tree, right-click 10.10.1.x Subnet (if you did not use 10.10.1.1 as the static IP address for your server name, click the appropriate subnet), then click New Pointer.

4. In the Host IP Number box, type **1** in the highlighted octet of your IP address (if you did not use 10.10.1.1 as the static IP address for your server name, then enter the appropriate octet value from the IP address that you used).

5. In the Host Name box, type the fully qualified domain name of your computer, followed by a period.

   You can also "browse" though existing DNS records using Browse. For example, if your computer name is SERVER1, type **server1.microsoft.com.** Remember to include the trailing period.

6. Click OK.

   A Pointer record appears in the details pane.

7. Close the DNS console.

Lesson Summary

In this lesson you learned that the DNS service provides the option of dividing up the namespace into one or more zones, which can then be stored, distributed, and replicated to other DNS servers. The DNS namespace represents the logical structure of your network resources, and DNS zones provide physical storage for these resources.

You also learned how to configure forward and reverse lookup zones and that directory-integrated primary zones are strongly recommended and provide the following benefits: multimaster update and enhanced security, automatic zone replication when new domain controllers are added, simplified administration with integrated namespace storage, and faster replication.

You learned how to add resource records and delegate zones when new subdomains are added. You also learned that the DNS service includes a dynamic update capability called DDNS, by which name servers and clients within a network automatically update the zone database files.

In the practice portion of this lesson, you created a forward and a reverse lookup zone for the DNS service, configured the zones for DDNS, and added a PTR resource record for a reverse lookup zone.

Lesson 3: Zone Replication and Transfer

This lesson introduces zone replication and transfer. *Zone transfer* is the process by which DNS servers interact to maintain and synchronize authoritative name data.

After this lesson, you will be able to

- Explain the purpose of zone transfers
- Configure zone transfers

Estimated lesson time: 10 minutes

Zone Replication and Zone Transfers

Because of the important role that zones play in DNS, it is intended that they be available from more than one DNS server on the network to provide availability and fault tolerance when resolving name queries. Otherwise, if a single server is used and that server is not responding, queries for names in the zone can fail. For additional servers to host a zone, zone transfers are required to replicate and synchronize all copies of the zone used at each server configured to host the zone.

When structuring your zones, there are several good reasons to use additional DNS servers for zone replication:

- Added DNS servers provide zone redundancy, enabling DNS names in the zone to be resolved for clients if a primary server for the zone stops responding.
- Added DNS servers can be placed to reduce DNS network traffic. For example, adding a DNS server to the opposing side of a low-speed wide area network (WAN) link can be useful in managing and reducing network traffic.
- Additional secondary servers can be used to reduce loads on a primary server for a zone.

When a new DNS server is added to the network and is configured as a new secondary server for an existing zone, it performs a *full zone transfer (AXFR)* to obtain and replicate a full copy of resource records for the zone. For earlier DNS server implementations, this same method of full transfer for a zone is also used when the zone requires updating after changes are made to the zone. For Windows 2000 Server, the DNS service supports *incremental zone transfer (IXFR)*, a revised DNS zone transfer process for intermediate changes.

Incremental Zone Transfers

IXFR is described in RFC 1995 as an additional DNS standard for replicating DNS zones. IXFRs provide a more efficient method of propagating zone changes and updates.

In earlier DNS implementations, any request for an update of zone data required a full transfer of the entire zone database using an AXFR query. With incremental transfer, an IXFR query is used instead. IXFR allows the secondary server to pull only those zone changes it needs to synchronize its copy of the zone with its source, either a primary or secondary copy of the zone maintained by another DNS server.

With IXFR zone transfers, differences between the source and replicated versions of the zone are first determined. If the zones are identified to be the same version—as indicated by the serial number field in the SOA resource record of each zone—no transfer is made.

If the serial number for the zone at the source is greater than at the requesting secondary server, a transfer is made of only those changes to resource records for each incremental version of the zone. For an IXFR query to succeed and changes to be sent, the source DNS server for the zone must keep a history of incremental zone changes to use when answering these queries. The incremental transfer process requires substantially less traffic on a network and zone transfers are completed much faster.

Example: Zone Transfer

In addition to a manual initiation, a zone transfer occurs during any of the following scenarios:

- When starting the DNS service on the secondary server for a zone
- When the refresh interval time expires for the zone
- When changes are made to the primary zone and a notify list is configured

Zone transfers are always initiated by the secondary server for a zone and sent to the DNS server configured as its source for the zone. This DNS server can be any other DNS server that loads the zone, either a primary or another secondary server. When the source server receives the request for the zone, it can reply with either a partial or full transfer of the zone.

As shown in Figure 5.6, zone transfers between servers follow an ordered process. This process varies depending on whether a zone has been previously replicated or if initial replication of a new zone is being performed.

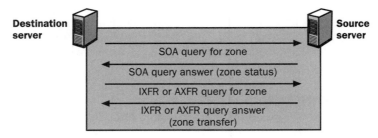

Figure 5.6   Zone transfer process

In this example, the following sequence is performed for a requesting secondary server—the destination server—for a zone and its source server, another DNS server that hosts the zone.

1. During new configuration, the destination server sends an initial (AXFR) transfer request for the zone to the DNS server configured as its source for the zone.

2. The source server responds and fully transfers the zone to the destination server.

   The zone is delivered to the server requesting the transfer with its version established by use of a serial number field in the properties for the SOA resource record. The SOA record also contains a stated refresh interval in seconds (by default, 15 minutes) to indicate when the destination server should next request renewal of the zone with the source server.

3. When the refresh interval expires, the destination server requests renewal of the zone from the source server with an SOA query.

4. The source server answers the query for its SOA record.

   This response contains the serial number for the zone in its current state at the source server.

5. The destination server checks the serial number of the SOA record in the response and determines how to renew the zone.

   If the value of the serial number in the SOA response is equal to its current local serial number, it concludes the zone is the same at both servers and a zone transfer is not needed. The destination server then renews the zone by resetting its refresh interval based on the value of this field in the SOA response from its source server.

   If the value of the serial number in the SOA response is higher than its current local serial number, it concludes that the zone has been updated and a transfer is needed.

6. If the destination server concludes the zone has changed, it sends an IXFR query to the source server containing its current local value for the serial number in the SOA record for the zone.

7. The source server responds with either an incremental or full transfer of the zone.

   If the source server supports incremental transfer by maintaining a history of recent and incremental zone changes for modified resource records, it can answer with an incremental (IXFR) transfer of the zone.

   If the source server does not support incremental transfer or does not have a history of zone changes, it can, alternatively, answer with a full (AXFR) transfer of the zone instead.

Note For Windows 2000 Server, incremental zone transfer through IXFR query is supported. For earlier versions of the DNS service running in Windows NT Server 4.0, and for many other DNS server implementations, incremental zone transfer is not available and only full-zone (AXFR) queries and transfers are used to replicate zones.

Zone Transfer Security

The DNS console permits you to specify the servers allowed to participate in zone transfers. This can help prevent an undesired attempt by an unknown or unapproved DNS server to pull, or request, zone updates.

▶ **To specify servers allowed to participate in zone transfers**

1. Click Start, point to Programs, point to Administrative Tools, then click DNS.
2. In the DNS console tree, right-click the zone for which you want to set up zone transfers, and then click Properties.
3. Select the Zone Transfers tab (see Figure 5.7).

Figure 5.7 The Zone Transfers tab

4. Specify the servers for which you want to allow zone transfers, then click OK.

DNS Notification

The DNS service supports DNS notification, which is an updated revision to the DNS standard specification (RFC 1996). DNS notification implements a push mechanism for notifying a select set of secondary servers for a zone when a zone is updated. The notified servers can then initiate the zone transfer process and pull changes from the notifying server to update the zone.

Use DNS notification only to notify DNS servers that are operating as secondary servers for a zone. For replication of directory-integrated zones, DNS notification is not needed. This is because any DNS servers that load a zone from Active Directory automatically poll the directory approximately once every 15 minutes (depending on the SOA refresh interval setting) to update and refresh the zone. In these cases, configuring a notification list can actually degrade system performance by causing unnecessary additional transfer requests for the updated zone.

▶ **To specify servers to be notified**

1. Click Start, point to Programs, point to Administrative Tools, and then click DNS.

2. In the DNS console tree, right-click the zone for which you want to set up zone transfers, and then click Properties.

3. Select the Zone Transfers tab, then click Notify.

4. In the Notify dialog box (see Figure 5.8), specify the secondary servers to be notified when the zone changes, then click OK.

Figure 5.8   The Notify dialog box

The DNS Notify Process

The following is a brief summary of the typical DNS Notify process:

1. The local zone on a DNS server acting as a source for the zone to other servers is updated. When the zone is updated at the source, the serial number field in the SOA record also updates, indicating a new local version of the zone.

2. The source server sends a notify message to other servers specified on the Notify screen.

3. All secondary servers that receive the notification message can then respond by initiating a zone transfer request back to the notifying server. The normal zone transfer process can then continue as described in the previous section.

Lesson Summary

In this lesson you learned how zone transfers are required to replicate and synchronize all copies of the zone used at each server configured to host the zone. For earlier DNS server implementations, when a new DNS server is added to the network and is configured as a new secondary server for an existing zone, it performs a full initial transfer of the zone to obtain and replicate a full copy of resource records for the zone. For Windows 2000 Server, the DNS service supports incremental zone transfer, a revised, more efficient DNS zone transfer process for intermediate changes.

You also learned how the DNS console permits you to specify the servers allowed to participate in zone transfers. Finally, you learned how DNS notification implements a push mechanism for notifying a select set of secondary servers for a zone when a zone is updated. The notified servers can then initiate the zone transfer process and pull changes from the notifying server to update the zone. The DNS console allows you to specify the secondary servers for notification; for replication of directory-integrated zones, DNS notification is not needed.

Lesson 4: Monitoring and Troubleshooting DNS for Active Directory

This lesson explains the monitoring options available for DNS servers. It also describes problems you may encounter that relate to configuring DNS for Active Directory and possible solutions to these problems.

After this lesson, you will be able to

- Monitor DNS server
- Troubleshoot DNS configuration for Active Directory

Estimated lesson time: 10 minutes

Monitoring DNS Servers

Windows 2000 Server includes two options for monitoring DNS servers:

- Default logging of DNS server event messages to the DNS server log
- Optional debug options for trace logging to a text file on the DNS server computer

DNS Server Event Logging

For Windows 2000 Server, DNS server event messages are kept separate from events raised by other applications and services in the DNS server log, which can be viewed using Event Viewer. The DNS server log contains basic predetermined events logged by the DNS server service, such as when the DNS server starts and stops.

You can also use Event Viewer to view and monitor client-related DNS events. These events appear in the system log and are written by the DNS client service at any computers running Windows 2000 (all versions).

Note For details on using the Event Viewer, see Chapter 14, "Managing Active Directory Performance."

Debug Options

The DNS console allows you to set additional logging options to create a temporary trace log as a text-based file of DNS server activity. The file created and used for this feature, DNS.LOG, is stored in the *systemroot*\System32\Dns folder. For Windows 2000 DNS servers, the debug logging options described in Table 5.2 are supported for use.

Table 5.2   DNS Server Debug Logging Options

Logging Option	Description
Query	Logs queries received by the DNS server service from clients
Notify	Logs notification messages received by the DNS server service from other servers
Update	Logs dynamic updates received by the DNS server service from other computers
Questions	Logs the contents of the question section for each DNS query message processed by the DNS server service
Answers	Logs the contents of the answer section for each DNS query message processed by the DNS server service
Send	Logs the number of DNS query messages sent by the DNS server service
Receive	Logs the number of DNS query messages received by the DNS server service
UDP	Logs the number of DNS requests received by the DNS server service over a UDP port
TCP	Logs the number of DNS requests received by the DNS server service over a TCP port
Full Packets	Logs the number of full packets written and sent by the DNS server service
Write Through	Logs the number of packets written through by the DNS server service and back to the zone

By default, all debug logging options are disabled. When selectively enabled, the DNS server service can perform additional trace-level logging of selected types of events or messages for general troubleshooting and debugging of the server.

Debug logging can be resource-intensive, affecting overall server performance and consuming disk space. Therefore, it should only be used temporarily when more detailed information about server performance is needed.

► **To set DNS Server debug options**

1. In the DNS console tree, right-click the name server, then click Properties.

2. On the Logging tab, select the debug options you want to log, then click OK.

DNS Troubleshooting Scenarios

Table 5.3 describes some zone problems you may encounter and possible solutions to these problems.

Table 5.3   Troubleshooting Scenarios for Zone Problems

Symptom: A problem related to zone transfers

Cause	Solution
The DNS server service is stopped or the zone is paused.	Verify that the master (source) and secondary (destination) DNS servers involved in completing transfer of the zone are both started and that the zone is not paused at either server.
The DNS servers used during a transfer do not have network connectivity with each other.	Eliminate the possibility of a basic network connectivity problem between the two servers. Using the PING command, ping each DNS server by its IP address from its remote counterpart. Both ping tests should succeed. If not, investigate and resolve intermediate network connectivity issues.
The serial number is the same at both the source and destination servers. Because the value is the same at both servers, no zone transfer occurs between the servers.	Using the DNS console, perform the following tasks: On the Start of Authority (SOA) tab, increase the value of the serial number for the zone at the master server (source) to a number greater than the value at the applicable secondary server (destination). Initiate zone transfer at the secondary server.
The master server (source) and its targeted secondary server (destination) are having interoperability-related problems.	Investigate possible causes for any problems related to interoperability between Windows 2000 DNS servers and other DNS servers running different implementations, such as an older version of the Berkeley Internet Name Domain (BIND) distribution.
The zone has resource records or other data that cannot be interpreted by the DNS server.	Verify that the zone does not contain incompatible data, such as unsupported resource record types or data errors. Also, verify that the server has not been configured in advance to prevent loading a zone when bad data is found and investigate its method for checking names. These settings can be configured using DNS console.
Authoritative zone data is incorrect.	If a zone transfer continues to fail, ensure that the zone does not contain nonstandard data. To determine if erroneous zone data is a likely source for a failed zone transfer, look in the DNS server event log for messages.

Symptom: Zone delegation appears to be broken

Cause	Solution
Zone delegations are not configured correctly.	Review how zone delegations are used and revise your zone configurations as needed.

Table 5.4 describes some problems you may encounter with dynamic updates and possible solutions to these problems.

Table 5.4   Troubleshooting Scenarios for Dynamic Updates

Symptom: The client is not performing dynamic updates

Cause	Solution
The client (or its DHCP server) does not support the use of the DNS dynamic update protocol.	Verify that your clients or servers support the DNS dynamic update protocol using the options for dynamic update support provided in Windows 2000. In order for client computers to be registered and updated dynamically with a DNS server, either: Install or upgrade client computers to Windows 2000 or install and use a Windows 2000 DHCP server on your network to lease client computers.
The client was not able to register and update with the DNS server because of missing or incomplete DNS configuration.	Verify that the client is fully and correctly configured for DNS, and update its configuration as needed. To update the DNS configuration for a client, either: Configure a primary DNS suffix at the client computer for static TCP/IP clients or configure a connection-specific DNS suffix for use at one of the installed network connections at the client computer.
The DNS client attempted to update its information with the DNS server but failed because of a problem related to the server.	If a client can reach its preferred and alternate DNS servers as configured, it is likely that the cause of its failed updates can be found elsewhere. At Windows 2000 client computers, use Event Viewer to check the System log for any event messages that explain why attempts by the client to dynamically update its host (A) or pointer (PTR) resource records failed.
The DNS server does not support dynamic updates.	Verify that the DNS server used by the client can support the DNS dynamic update protocol, as described in RFC 2136. For Windows DNS servers, only Windows 2000 DNS servers support dynamic updates. The DNS server provided with Windows NT Server 4.0 does not.
The DNS server supports dynamic updates but is not configured to accept them.	Verify that the primary zone where clients require updates is configured to allow dynamic updates. For Windows 2000 DNS servers, the default for a new primary zone is to not accept dynamic updates. At the DNS server that loads the applicable primary zone, modify zone properties to allow updates.
The zone database is not available.	Verify that the zone exists. Verify that the zone is available for update. For a standard primary zone, verify that the zone file exists at the server and that the zone is not paused. Secondary zones do not support dynamic updates. For Active Directory-integrated zones, verify that the DNS server is running as a domain controller and has access to the Active Directory database where zone data is stored.

Lesson Summary

In this lesson you learned about the monitoring options available for DNS servers. You also examined some DNS configuration problems you may encounter and possible solutions to these problems.

Review

The following questions are intended to reinforce key information presented in the chapter. If you are unable to answer a question, review the appropriate lesson and then try the question again. Answers to the questions can be found in Appendix A, "Questions and Answers."

1. What is the function of a forward lookup query? A reverse lookup query?

2. What are the advantages of using the Active Directory-integrated zone type?

3. What is the purpose of the SOA resource record?

4. What must be done when you delegate zones within a namespace?

5. Why is an IXFR query more efficient than an AXFR query?

C H A P T E R   6

Configuring Sites

About This Chapter

How you set up your sites affects Microsoft Windows 2000 in two ways:

- Workstation logon and authentication
- Directory replication

Note   Your site configuration will also affect any applications that will take advantage of the Active Directory, such as Exchange 2000 or Site Server's Personalization and Membership services.

This chapter introduces you to configuring site settings and inter-site replication. It provides troubleshooting information for problems you may encounter that relate to inter-site replication. This chapter also discusses the tasks necessary for configuring server settings.

Before You Begin

To complete the lessons in this chapter, you must have

- Completed the Setup procedures located in "About This Book"
- Installed Active Directory using the exercises in Chapter 4
- Experience using Microsoft Management Consoles (MMCs)

Lesson 1: Configuring Site Settings

This lesson walks you through the steps for configuring site settings, including creating a site, associating a subnet with a site, connecting a site using site links, and selecting a site license server.

After this lesson, you will be able to

- Configure site settings

Estimated lesson time: 20 minutes

Configuring Site Settings

To configure site settings you must complete the following tasks:

1. Create a site
2. Associate a subnet with the site
3. Connect the site using site links
4. Select a site license server

Sites

Sites define sets of domain controllers that are well-connected in terms of speed and cost. Domain controllers in the same site replicate on the basis of notification: When a domain controller has changes, it notifies its replication partners. Then the notified partner requests the changes and replication takes place. Because there is no concern about replication speed or cost, replication within sites occurs as needed rather than as scheduled. Replication between sites occurs according to a schedule; you can use the schedule to determine the most beneficial time for replication to occur on the basis of network traffic and cost. A site is the equivalent of a set of one or more IP subnets.

When you install Active Directory on the first domain controller in the site, an object named Default-First-Site-Name is created in the Sites container. It is necessary to install the first domain controller into this site. Subsequent domain controllers are either installed into the site of the source domain controller (assuming the IP address maps to the site) or an existing site. When your first domain controller has been installed, you can rename Default-First-Site-Name to the name you want to use for the site.

When you install Active Directory on subsequent servers, if alternate sites have been defined in Active Directory and the IP address of the installation computer matches an existing subnet in a defined site, the domain controller is added to that site. Otherwise, it is added to the site of the source domain controller.

▶ **To create a new site**

1. Click Start, point to Programs, point to Administrative Tools, then click Active Directory Sites And Services.

2. Right-click the Sites folder, then click New Site.

3. In the New Object-Site dialog box, shown in Figure 6.1, type the name of the new site in the Name box. Select a site link object, then click OK.

Figure 6.1   New Object-Site dialog box

4. On the Active Directory message box, click OK.

▶ **To rename a site**

1. Click Start, point to Programs, point to Administrative Tools, then click Active Directory Sites And Services.

2. Click on the Sites folder.

3. Click the site you want to rename twice, slowly, or right-click the site you want to rename, then click Rename.

4. Type the new site name over the existing site name. Click in an empty part of the console tree.

Subnets

Computers on TCP/IP networks are assigned to sites based on their location in a subnet or a set of subnets. Subnets group computers in a way that identifies their feasible physical proximity on the network. Subnet information is used to find a domain controller in the same site as the computer that is authenticated during logon, and is used during Active Directory replication to determine the best routes between domain controllers.

▶ **To create a subnet**

1. Click Start, point to Programs, point to Administrative Tools, then click Active Directory Sites And Services.

2. Double-click the Sites folder.

3. Right-click the Subnets folder, and click New Subnet.

4. In the New Object-Subnet dialog box, shown in Figure 6.2, enter the subnet address in the Address box. In the Mask box enter the subnet mask that describes the range of addresses included in this site's subnet. Choose a site to associate this subnet with, then click OK.

Figure 6.2   New Object-Subnet dialog box

▶ **To associate an existing subnet with a site**

1. Click Start, point to Programs, point to Administrative Tools, then click Active Directory Sites And Services.

2. Open the Subnets folder, right-click the subnet, then click Properties.

3. In the Properties dialog box for the subnet, shown in Figure 6.3, select a site with which to associate this subnet from the choices available in the Site list, then click OK.

Figure 6.3   Properties dialog box for a subnet

Site Links

For replication to occur between two sites, a link must be established between the sites. Site links are not generated automatically and must be created in Active Directory Sites and Services. Unless a site link is in place, connections cannot be made between computers in the two sites and replication between the sites cannot take place. Each site link contains the schedule that determines when replication can occur between the sites that it connects. The Active Directory Sites and Services console guarantees that every site is placed in at least one site link. A site link can contain more than two sites, in which case all the sites are equally well connected.

When you install Active Directory on the first domain controller in the site, the Active Directory Installation Wizard automatically creates an object named DEFAULTIPSITELINK in the IP container. It is necessary to create this site link for the first default site, also created by the Active Directory Installation Wizard. Subsequent site links are created separately. When your first domain controller has been installed, you can rename the DEFAULTIPSITELINK to the name you want to use for the site link.

Replication Protocols

Directory information can be exchanged over site links using different network protocols such as IP or SMTP:

- **IP replication** uses remote procedure calls (RPCs) for replication over site links (inter-site) and within a site (intra-site). By default, inter-site IP replication does adhere to replication schedules, although you may configure Active

Directory to ignore schedules. IP replication does not require a certificate authority (CA).

- **SMTP replication** is only used for replication over site links (inter-site), and not for replication within a site (intra-site). Because SMTP is asynchronous, it typically ignores all schedules.

If you choose to use SMTP over site links, you must complete the process of installing and configuring a certification authority (CA). The CA signs SMTP messages that are exchanged between domain controllers, ensuring the authenticity of directory updates. Installing and configuring a CA is beyond the scope of this course; refer to the *MCSE Training Kit—Microsoft Windows 2000 Network Infrastructure Administration* for more information on this topic.

▶ **To create a site link**

1. Click Start, point to Programs, point to Administrative Tools, then click Active Directory Sites And Services.
2. Open the Inter-Site Transports folder and right-click on either the IP or SMTP folder, depending on which protocol you want the site to use. Select New Site Link.

Caution   If you create a site link that uses SMTP, you must have an Enterprise CA available and SMTP must be installed on all domain controllers that will use the site link.

---

3. In the New Object-Site Link dialog box, shown in Figure 6.4, type the name to be given to the site link in the Name field.

Figure 6.4   New Object-Site Link dialog box

4. Click two or more sites to connect, then click Add.

5. Click OK.

▶ **To add a site to an existing site link**

1. Click Start, point to Programs, point to Administrative Tools, then click Active Directory Sites And Services.

2. Open the Inter-Site Transports folder and either the IP or SMTP folder, and right-click on the site link to which you want to add the site. Click Properties.

3. In the Properties dialog box for the site link, in the Sites Not In This Site Link box in the General Tab, click the site you want to add to this site link, then click Add.

4. Click OK.

Site Licensing

An administrator can ensure an organization's legal compliance with Microsoft BackOffice software license agreements by monitoring license purchases, deletions, and usage. This licensing information is collected on a server by the License Logging service in Windows 2000 Server.

The License Logging service on each server in a site replicates this licensing information to a centralized database on a server called the site license server for the site. A site administrator or administrator for the site license server can then use the Licensing utility in Administrative Tools to view the licensing history for the entire site stored on the site license server.

The default site license server is the first domain controller created for the site; however, the site license server does not have to be a domain controller. For optimal performance, however, the site license server and domain controller should be in the same site. In a large organization with multiple sites, licensing information for each site is collected separately by the site license server in each site.

▶ **To select a site license server**

1. Click Start, point to Programs, point to Administrative Tools, then click Active Directory Sites And Services.

2. Click on the site for which you want to assign a site license server.

3. In the details pane, right-click Licensing Site Settings, then click Properties.

4. In the Licensing Site Settings Properties dialog box, click Change in the Licensing Computer box.

5. In the Select Computer dialog box, select the computer you want to designate as the site license server, then click OK.

6. In the Licensing Site Settings Properties dialog box, click OK.

▶ **To view licensing for a site**

1. Click Start, point to Programs, point to Administrative Tools, and click Licensing.

2. On the License menu, choose Select Domain to connect to the site license server for the domain.

3. In the Select Domain dialog box, enter the name of the site license server in the Domain box, then click OK.

Practice: Configuring a Site

In this practice you configure a site. To configure a site you must first create a site. Then you must associate a subnet with the site, and connect the site using site links. Finally, you must select a site license server.

▶ **To rename a site**

1. Click Start, point to Programs, point to Administrative Tools, then click Active Directory Sites And Services.

   The Active Directory Sites and Services console appears.

2. Click on the Sites folder.

   What objects appear in the details pane?

3. Right-click the Default-First-Site-Name site, then click Rename.

4. Type the new site name, **Redmond**, over Default-First-Site-Name. Click in an empty part of the console tree.

   The Default-First-Site-Name site has been renamed Redmond.

▶ **To create a new site**

1. Right-click the Sites folder, then click New Site.

   The New Object-Site dialog box appears.

2. In the Name box, type **Chicago**. Select DEFAULTIPSITELINK for the Chicago site's site link, then click OK.

   The Active Directory message box appears reminding you that to finish configuring the site Chicago you must:

   ▪ Ensure that the site is linked to other sites with site links as appropriate

   ▪ Add subnets for the site to the subnets container

   ▪ Install one or more domain controllers in the site or move existing domain controllers into the site

   ▪ Select the licensing for the site

3. Click OK.

▶ **To create a subnet**

1. Double-click the Sites folder.

2. Right-click the Subnets folder, and click New Subnet.

   The New Object-Subnet dialog box appears.

3. In the Address box, type **10.10.1.1** for the subnet address. In the Mask box type **255.0.0.0** for the subnet mask that describes the range of addresses included in this site's subnet. Choose the Chicago site to associate to this subnet, then click OK.

   The 10.0.0.0/8 subnet is created and the Chicago site is associated to the subnet.

▶ **To associate an existing subnet with a site**

1. Open the Subnets folder, right-click the 10.0.0.0/8 subnet, then click Properties.

   The Properties dialog box for the 10.0.0.0/8 subnet appears with the Subnet tab chosen.

2. In the Sites list, select the Redmond site to associate to this subnet, then click OK.

▶ **To create a site link**

1. Open the Inter-Site Transports folder and click the IP folder.

   What object appears in the details pane?

2. Right-click the IP folder, then select New Site Link.

   The New Object-Site Link dialog box appears.

3. In the Name box, type **Redmond to Chicago**.

4. Ensure that the Chicago and Redmond sites are in the Sites In This Site Link box, then click OK.

▶ **To select a site license server**

1. Click on the Chicago site.

2. In the details pane, right-click Licensing Site Settings, then click Properties.

   The Licensing Site Settings Properties dialog box appears.

3. In the Licensing Computer box, click Change.

   The Select Computer dialog box appears.

4. Select the SERVER1 (or the name you selected for your computer), then click OK.

   You return to the Licensing Site Settings Properties dialog box. The computer is SERVER1 and the domain is microsoft.com (or the computer and domain you selected) for the site license server in the Licensing Computer box.

5. Click OK.

6. Close Active Directory Sites and Services.

▶ **To view licensing for a site**

1. Click Start, point to Programs, point to Administrative Tools, then click Licensing.

   The MICROSOFT.COM-Licensing utility appears. You can view licensing information using the Products View tab.

Lesson Summary

In this lesson you learned how to configure sites. After you create a site, you must add subnets for the site to the subnets container, ensure that the site is linked to other sites with site links as appropriate, and select the licensing for the site. Subnets group computers in a way that identifies their physical proximity on the network. Site links contain the cost and schedule for replication traffic and allow replication to occur between two sites.

You also learned how the License Logging service on each server in a site replicates this licensing information to a centralized database on a server called the site license server for the site. A site administrator or administrator for the site license server can then use the Licensing utility in Administrative Tools to view the licensing history for the entire site stored on the site license server.

In the practice portion of this lesson you created a site, associated a subnet with the site, connected a site using site links, and selected a site license server.

Lesson 2: Configuring Inter-Site Replication

Network connections are represented by site links. By creating site links and configuring their cost, replication frequency, and replication availability, you provide the directory service with information about how to use these connections to replicate directory data. You can improve site link connectivity by linking overlapping existing site links together into site link bridges, or you can bridge all site links and maximize connectivity. You can also designate a server, known as a bridgehead server, to serve as a contact point for the exchange of directory information between sites. This lesson explains how to configure inter-site replication.

After this lesson, you will be able to

- Configure inter-site replication

Estimated lesson time: 25 minutes

Configuring Inter-Site Replication

To configure inter-site replication you must complete the following tasks:

1. Create site links (see Lesson 1)
2. Configure site link attributes
3. Create site link bridges
4. Configure connection objects (optional)
5. Designate a preferred bridgehead server (optional)

Site Link Attributes

You should provide site link cost, replication frequency, and replication availability information for all site links as part of the process of configuring inter-site replication.

Site Link Cost

Configure site link cost to assign a value for the cost of each available connection used for inter-site replication. If you have multiple redundant network connections, establish site links for each connection, and then assign costs to these site links that reflect their relative bandwidth. For example, if you have a high-speed T1 line and a dial-up network connection in case the T1 line is unavailable, configure a lower cost for the T1 line and a higher cost for the dial-up network connection. Active Directory always chooses the connection on a per-cost basis, so the cheaper connection will be used as long as it is available.

▶ **To configure site link cost**

1. Click Start, point to Programs, point to Administrative Tools, then click Active Directory Sites And Services.

2. Open the Inter-Site Transports folder and either the IP or SMTP folder, and right-click on the site link for which you want to configure site link cost. Click Properties.

3. On the Properties dialog box for the site link, shown in Figure 6.5, enter a value for the cost of replication in the Cost box. The default cost is 100; the lower the value, the higher the priority. For example, the cost of a T1 link might be 100, while the cost of a dial-up link might be 120.

Figure 6.5   Properties dialog box for a site link

4. Click OK.

Replication Frequency

Configure site link replication frequency for site links by providing an integer value that tells Active Directory how many minutes it should wait before using a connection to check for replication updates. The replication interval must be at least 15 and no more than 10,080 minutes (equal to one week). A site link must be available for any replication to occur, so if a site link is scheduled as unavailable when the number of minutes between replication updates has passed, no replication will occur.

▶ **To configure site link replication frequency**

1. Click Start, point to Programs, point to Administrative Tools, then click Active Directory Sites And Services.

2. Open the Inter-Site Transports folder and either the IP or SMTP folder, and right-click on the site link for which you want to configure site replication frequency. Click Properties.

3. On the Properties dialog box for the site link, enter the number of minutes between replications in the Replicate Every box. The default time is 180; the value is processed as the nearest multiple of 15, ranging from a minimum of 15 to a maximum of 10,080 minutes (one week).

4. Click OK.

Replication Availability

Configure site link replication availability to determine when a site link will be available for replication. Because SMTP is asynchronous, it typically ignores all schedules. Therefore, do not configure site link replication availability on SMTP site links unless

- The site links use scheduled connections
- The SMTP queue is not on a schedule
- Information is being exchanged directly from one server to another, and not through intermediaries, as is the case, for example, on a network backbone

▶ **To configure site link replication availability**

1. Click Start, point to Programs, point to Administrative Tools, then click Active Directory Sites And Services.

2. Open the Inter-Site Transports folder and either the IP or SMTP folder, and right-click on the site link for which you want to configure site link replication availability. Click Properties.

3. In the Properties dialog box for the site link, click Change Schedule.

4. On the Schedule For dialog box for the site link, shown in Figure 6.6, select the block of time when this connection is or is not available to replicate directory information, then click OK.

5. In the Properties dialog box for the site link, click OK.

Note   This procedure will have no effect if you have enabled Ignore Schedules on the Properties dialog box for the inter-site transport.

Figure 6.6   Schedule for dialog box for a site link

▶ **To ignore schedules for an inter-site transport**

1. Click Start, point to Programs, point to Administrative Tools, then click Active Directory Sites And Services.

2. Open the Inter-Site Transports folder and right-click either the IP or SMTP folder, then click Properties.

3. In the IP or SMTP Properties dialog box, on the General tab, click the Ignore Schedules check box.

4. Click OK.

Site Link Bridges

When more than two sites are linked for replication and use the same transport, by default, all of the site links are "bridged" in terms of cost, assuming the site links have common sites. When site links are bridged, they are *transitive*. That is, all site links for a specific transport implicitly belong to a single site link bridge for that transport. So in the common case of a fully routed IP network (all sites can communicate with each other via IP), you do not have to configure any site link bridges. If your IP network is not fully routed, you can turn off the transitive site link feature for the IP transport, in which case all IP site links are considered intransitive and you configure site link bridges. A site link bridge is the equivalent of a disjoint network; all site links within the bridge can route transitively, but they do not route outside of the bridge.

▶ **To create a site link bridge**

1. Click Start, point to Programs, point to Administrative Tools, then click Active Directory Sites And Services.

2. Open the Inter-Site Transports folder and right-click either the IP or SMTP folder, and then click New Site Link Bridge.

3. In the New Object-Site Link Bridge dialog box, shown in Figure 6.7, type a name for the site link bridge in the Name box.

Figure 6.7   New Object-Site Link Bridge dialog box

4. Click two or more sites to connect, then click Add.
5. Click OK.

Note   This procedure is redundant and will have no effect if you have enabled Bridge All Site Links on the Properties dialog box for the inter-site transport.

▶ **To bridge all site links for an inter-site transport**

1. Click Start, point to Programs, point to Administrative Tools, then click Active Directory Sites And Services.
2. Open the Inter-Site Transports folder and right-click either the IP or SMTP folder, then click Properties.
3. In the IP or SMTP Properties dialog box, on the General tab, click the Bridge All Site Links check box.
4. Click OK.

Manually Configuring Connections

Active Directory automatically creates and deletes connections under normal conditions. Although you can manually add or configure connections or force replication over a particular connection, normally you should allow replication to be automatically optimized based on information you provide to Active Directory

Sites and Services about your deployment. Only create connections manually if you are certain the connection is required, and you want the connection to persist until manually removed.

▶ **To manually configure connections**

1. Click Start, point to Programs, point to Administrative Tools, then click Active Directory Sites And Services.

2. Double-click the site that contains the domain controller for which you want to manually add or configure a connection.

3. Open the Servers folder, open the domain controller, right-click NTDS Settings, and then click New Active Directory Connection.

4. In the Find Domain Controllers dialog box, click the domain controller that you want to include in the connection object and click OK.

5. In the New Object-Connection dialog box, enter a name for the new Connection object in the Name field and click OK.

▶ **To force replication over a connection**

1. Click Start, point to Programs, point to Administrative Tools, then click Active Directory Sites And Services.

2. Double-click the site that contains the connection over which you want to replicate directory information.

3. Open the Servers folder, select the domain controller, then open NTDS Settings.

4. Right-click the connection over which you want to replicate directory information, and click Replicate Now (see Figure 6.8).

Figure 6.8   Forcing replication over a connection

Designating a Preferred Bridgehead Server

Ordinarily, all domain controllers are used to exchange information between sites, but you can further control replication behavior by specifying a bridgehead server for inter-site replicated information. Establishing a bridgehead server provides some ranking or criteria for choosing which domain controller should be preferred as the recipient for inter-site replication. This bridgehead server then subsequently distributes the directory information via intra-site replication.

Bridgehead servers are the contact point for exchange of directory information between sites. You can specify a preferred bridgehead server if you have a computer with appropriate bandwidth to transmit and receive information. If there's typically a high level of directory information exchange, a computer with more bandwidth can ensure these exchanges are handled promptly. Matching the demands of your Active Directory deployment with a domain controller having the capacity to handle those demands will enable efficient updates of directory information.

You can specify multiple preferred bridgehead servers, but only one will be the active preferred bridgehead server at any time at a single site. If the active preferred bridgehead server fails, Active Directory will select another preferred bridgehead server to be the active preferred bridgehead server from the set you designate. If no active preferred bridgehead server is available and there are no other preferred bridgehead servers available for Active Directory to select, it will select another domain controller in the site to be the preferred bridgehead server. This can be a problem if the domain controller Active Directory selects does not have the bandwidth to efficiently handle the increased requirements posed by being a preferred bridgehead server.

You must specify a preferred bridgehead server if your deployment uses a firewall to protect a site. Establish your firewall proxy server as the preferred bridgehead server, making it the contact point for exchanging information with servers outside the firewall. If you do not do this, directory information may not be successfully exchanged.

Establishing a preferred bridgehead server designates that server as the preeminent server for information exchange over the protocol for which the site link is established. Other domain controllers could still exchange directory information if a need arises, but under normal conditions, the bridgehead server will be used as the first choice to receive and send all directory traffic.

▶ **To designate a preferred bridgehead server**

1. Click Start, point to Programs, point to Administrative Tools, then click Active Directory Sites And Services.

2. In the AD Sites and Services console tree, right-click the domain controller that you want to make a bridgehead server, then click Properties.

3. On the Properties dialog box for the domain controller, in the Transports Available For Inter-Site Data Transfer box, click the inter-site transport or

transports for which this computer will be a preferred bridgehead server, then click Add.

4. Click OK.

Practice: Configuring Inter-Site Replication

In this practice you configure site link cost, replication availability, and replication frequency. Then you configure a site link bridge.

▶ **To configure site link cost**

1. Click Start, point to Programs, point to Administrative Tools, then click Active Directory Sites And Services.

   The Active Directory Sites and Services console appears.

2. Open the Inter-Site Transports folder and the IP folder, and right-click the Redmond To Chicago site link you configured in the previous lesson. Click Properties.

   The Redmond To Chicago Properties dialog box appears.

3. In the Cost box, type **20** for the cost of replication.

▶ **To configure site link replication frequency**

1. In the Replicate Every box, type **120** for the number of minutes between replications.

▶ **To configure site link replication availability**

1. Click Change Schedule.

   The Schedule For Redmond To Chicago dialog box appears.

2. Make the connection available at all times except Monday through Friday from 8 AM to 9 AM and from 4 PM to 5 PM, then click OK.

3. On the Redmond To Chicago Properties dialog box, click OK.

▶ **To create a site link bridge**

1. Open the Inter-Site Transports folder, right-click the IP folder, then click New Site Link Bridge.

   The New Object-Site Link Bridge dialog box appears.

2. In the Name box, type **Redmond to Chicago Bridge**.

3. Ensure that the DEFAULTIPSITELINK and Redmond to Chicago site links are in the Site Links In This Site Link Bridge box, then click OK.

Lesson Summary

In this lesson you learned that you should provide site link cost, replication frequency, and replication availability information for all site links as part of the process of configuring inter-site replication. Active Directory always chooses the connection on a per-cost basis so the cheaper connection will be used as long as it is available. You can improve site link connectivity by linking overlapping existing site links together into site link bridges, or you can bridge all site links and maximize connectivity. You also learned that you can designate a domain controller as a bridgehead server to specify which domain controller should be preferred as the recipient for inter-site replication.

In the practice portion of this lesson you configured site link cost, replication availability, and replication frequency. Then you configured a site link bridge.

Lesson 3: Troubleshooting Replication

This lesson describes problems you may encounter that relate to replication. Most problems that can be remedied with Active Directory Sites and Services involve poor directory information. This can mean that

- New directory information is not distributed in a timely fashion
- Service requests are not handled in a timely fashion

This lesson also describes how to check replication topology.

After this lesson, you will be able to

- Troubleshoot replication

Estimated lesson time: 5 minutes

Troubleshooting Replication

Ineffective replication can result in declining Active Directory performance, such as new users not being recognized. Ineffective replication or request handling primarily results in out-of-date directory information or unavailable domain controllers. Each problem (cause) has one or more possible solutions. Replication troubleshooting scenarios are discussed in Table 6.1.

Table 6.1   Replication Troubleshooting Scenarios

Symptom: Replication of directory information has stopped

Cause	Solution
The sites containing the clients and domain controllers are not connected by site links to domain controllers in other sites in the network. This results in a failure to exchange directory information between sites.	Create a site link from the current site to a site that is connected to the rest of the sites in the network.

Symptom: Replication has slowed but not stopped

Cause	Solution
Although all sites are connected by site links, your inter-site replication structure is not as complete as it might be. Directory information is replicated to all domain controllers if they are all connected by site links, but this is not optimal. If there are site links but no site link bridges, changes made to domain controllers may take an un-acceptably long time to be distributed to other domain controllers that are not closely linked.	Make sure Active Directory has been configured properly. To span the multiple site links that need more efficient replication, consider creating a site link bridge or consider bridging all site links.

Symptom: Replication has slowed but not stopped

Cause	Solution
The current network resources are insufficient to handle the amount of replication traffic. This can affect services unrelated to Active Directory, because the exchange of directory information is consuming an inordinate amount of network resources.	Increase the proportion of available network resources relative to directory traffic. Decrease the frequency of the replication schedule. Configure site link costs. To achieve network connections with more bandwidth, create site links or site link bridges.
Directory information changed at domain controllers in one site is not being updated in domain controllers in other sites in a timely fashion because inter-site replication is scheduled too infrequently.	Increase the frequency of replication. If the replication is occurring over a site link bridge, check which site link is restricting replication. Increase the time range during which replication can occur or the frequency of replication within the time frame for that site link.
Clients are having to request authentication, information, and services from a domain controller with a low-bandwidth connection. This may result in clients receiving a slow response for authentication, directory information, or other services.	Check if there is a site that will better serve the client's subnet. If a client who is experiencing poor service is isolated from domain controllers, consider creating another site with its own domain controller that will include the client. Install a connection with more bandwidth.

Checking Replication Topology

Active Directory runs a process that considers the cost of inter-site connections, checks if any previously available domain controllers are no longer available, checks if new domain controllers have been added, and then uses this information to add or remove connection objects to create an efficient replication topology. This process does not affect manually created connection objects.

► **To check the replication topology**

1. Click Start, point to Programs, point to Administrative Tools, then click Active Directory Sites And Services.

2. In the AD Sites and Services console tree, double-click the server that you want to use to check replication topology.

3. Right-click NTDS Settings, point to All Tasks, and then click Check Replication Topology.

Lesson Summary

In this lesson you examined some replication problems you may encounter and possible solutions to these problems.

Lesson 4: Maintaining Server Settings

To meet changing business needs, you may need to maintain server settings for a site. This lesson examines some tasks for maintaining server settings to meet the changing needs of your organization. The tasks include: creating a server object in a site, moving a server object between sites, enabling or disabling a global catalog, and removing an inoperative server object from a site.

After this lesson, you will be able to

- Maintain server settings for a site

Estimated lesson time: 10 minutes

Maintaining Server Settings

As a site changes and grows based on business needs, you may find it necessary to meet these changing needs by maintaining server settings for the site. The tasks you may need to perform to maintain server settings are

- Creating a server object in a site
- Moving a server object between sites
- Enabling or disabling a global catalog
- Removing an inoperative server object from a site

Creating a Server Object in a Site

This procedure can be used to create member servers and domain controllers in a site. Creating a server object is not the same as installing a domain controller using the Active Directory Installation Wizard.

▶ **To create a server object in a site**

1. Click Start, point to Programs, point to Administrative Tools, then click Active Directory Sites And Services.

2. In the AD Sites and Services console tree, double-click the site that you want to contain the new domain controller server object.

3. Right-click the Servers folder, point to New, then click Server.

4. On the New Object-Server dialog box, enter the name for the new server object in the Name box, then click OK.

Moving Server Objects Between Sites

This procedure can be used to move member servers and domain controllers between sites.

1. Click Start, point to Programs, point to Administrative Tools, then click Active Directory Sites And Services.
2. In the AD Sites and Services console tree, right-click the server object that you want to move to a different site, then click Move.
3. In the Move Server dialog box, click the site to which you want to move the server object, then click OK.

Enabling or Disabling a Global Catalog

Clients must have access to a global catalog to log on, so you should have at least one global catalog in every site to receive the benefits of containing network traffic provided by using sites.

▶ **To enable or disable a global catalog**

1. Click Start, point to Programs, point to Administrative Tools, then click Active Directory Sites And Services.
2. In the AD Sites and Services console tree, double-click the domain controller hosting the global catalog.
3. Right-click NTDS Settings, then click Properties.
4. Do one of the following:
   ▪ To enable a global catalog, select the Global Catalog check box, then click OK.
   ▪ To disable a global catalog, clear the Global Catalog check box, then click OK.

Removing an Inoperative Server Object from a Site

Use this procedure only if you want to permanently remove a server object from a site. If you plan to reactivate the server, delete the NTDS Settings object for the server, rather than the server object itself. When you bring the server back online, Active Directory will automatically create a new NTDS Settings object, inserting the server into the replication topology as appropriate.

▶ **To remove an inoperative server object from a site**

1. Click Start, point to Programs, point to Administrative Tools, then click Active Directory Sites And Services.
2. In the AD Sites and Services console tree, right-click the server object to be removed, then click Delete.
3. On the Active Directory message box, click Yes.

Lesson Summary

In this lesson you learned tasks for maintaining server settings to meet the changing needs of your organization. The tasks included: creating a server object in a site, moving a server object between sites, enabling or disabling a global catalog, and removing an inoperative server object from a site.

Review

The following questions are intended to reinforce key information presented in the chapter. If you are unable to answer a question, review the appropriate lesson and then try the question again. Answers to the questions can be found in Appendix A, "Questions and Answers."

1. What four tasks must be completed to configure a site?

2. What two site configuration objects does the Active Directory Installation Wizard create automatically?

3. Which replication protocol uses RPCs for replication over site links (inter-site) and within a site (intra-site)?

4. What three tasks must be completed to configure inter-site replication?

5. What is the difference between replication frequency and replication availability?

6. What is the function of a bridgehead server?

C H A P T E R   7

User Account Administration

About This Chapter

This chapter introduces you to user accounts and to how to plan them. It also presents the skills and knowledge necessary to create domain and local user accounts and to set their properties, as well as to set up user profiles and home directories. Finally, this chapter covers user account maintenance, including disabling, enabling, renaming, deleting, and unlocking user accounts and resetting user passwords.

Before You Begin

To complete the lessons in this chapter, you must have

- Knowledge about the difference between a workgroup and a domain
- Knowledge about the difference between a domain controller and a member server
- Experience logging on and off Microsoft Windows 2000
- Knowledge about the Active Directory naming conventions

Lesson 1: Introduction to User Accounts

A user account provides a user with the ability to log on to the domain to gain access to network resources or to log on to a computer to gain access to resources on that computer. Each person who regularly uses the network should have a unique user account.

Windows 2000 provides different types of user accounts: local user accounts, domain user accounts, and built-in user accounts. With a *local user account,* a user logs on to a specific computer to gain access to resources on that computer. With a *domain user account,* a user can log on to the domain to gain access to network resources. *Built-in user accounts* are used to perform administrative tasks or to gain access to network resources. This lesson introduces user accounts and the differences between account types.

After this lesson, you will be able to

- Describe the difference between a local user account and a domain user account
- Describe the purpose of a built-in account

Estimated lesson time: 10 minutes

Local User Accounts

Local user accounts allow users to log on at and gain access to resources on only the computer where you create the local user account.

When you create a local user account, Windows 2000 creates the account only in that computer's security database, which is called the local security database, as shown in Figure 7.1. Windows 2000 does not replicate local user account information to domain controllers. After the local user account exists, the computer uses its local security database to authenticate the local user account, which allows the user to log on to that computer.

Do not create local user accounts on computers that require access to domain resources, because the domain does not recognize local user accounts. Therefore, the user is unable to gain access to resources in the domain. Also, the domain administrator is unable to administer the local user account properties or assign access permissions for domain resources unless he or she connects to the local computer using the Action menu on the Computer Management console.

Local user accounts
- Provide access to resources on the local computer
- Are created in the local security database

Figure 7.1   Local user accounts

Domain User Accounts

Domain user accounts allow users to log on to the domain and gain access to resources anywhere on the network. The user provides his or her user name and password during the logon process. By using this information, Windows 2000 authenticates the user and then builds an access token that contains information about the user and security settings. The access token identifies the user to computers running Windows 2000 and pre-Windows 2000 computers on which the user tries to gain access to resources. Windows 2000 provides the access token for the duration of the logon session.

You create a domain user account in a container or an organizational unit (OU) in the copy of the Active Directory database (called the directory) on a domain controller, as shown in Figure 7.2. The domain controller replicates the new user account information to all domain controllers in the domain.

After Windows 2000 replicates the new user account information, all of the domain controllers in the domain tree can authenticate the user during the logon process.

Note   It can take a few minutes to replicate the domain user account information to all of the domain controllers. This delay might prevent a user from immediately logging on using the newly created domain user account. By default, replication of directory information occurs every five minutes.

Domain user accounts
- Provide access to network resources
- Provide the access token for authentication
- Are created in Active Directory on a domain controller

Figure 7.2   Domain user account

Built-In User Accounts

Windows 2000 automatically creates accounts called built-in accounts. Two commonly used built-in accounts are Administrator and Guest.

Note   The IUSR_*computername* and IWAM_*computername* built-in accounts are automatically created when Internet Information Services are installed on the domain controller. IUSR_*computername* is an account for anonymous access to IIS. IWAM_*computername* is an account for anonymous access to IIS out-of-process applications.

The TsInternetUser account is automatically created when Terminal Services are installed on the domain controller. TsInternetUser is an account used by Terminal Services.

Administrator

Use the built-in Administrator account to manage the overall computer and domain configuration for such tasks as creating and modifying user accounts and groups, managing security policies, creating printers, and assigning permissions and rights to user accounts to gain access to resources.

If you are the administrator, you should create a user account that you use to perform nonadministrative tasks. Log on by using the Administrator account only when you perform administrative tasks. For information on setting up user accounts for performing nonadministrative tasks, see Chapter 8, "Group Account Administration."

Note   You can rename the Administrator account, but you cannot delete it. As a best practice, you should always rename the built-in Administrator account to provide a greater degree of security. Use a name that does not identify it as the Administrator account. This makes it difficult for unauthorized users to break into the Administrator account because they do not know which user account it is.

Guest

Use the built-in Guest account to give occasional users the ability to log on and gain access to resources. For example, an employee who needs access to resources for a short time can use the Guest account.

Note   The Guest account is disabled by default. Enable the Guest account only in low-security networks, and always assign it a password. You can rename and disable the Guest account, but you cannot delete it.

Lesson Summary

In this lesson you learned that Microsoft Windows 2000 provides different types of user accounts: domain user accounts and local user accounts. With a domain user account, a user can log on to the domain to gain access to network resources. With a local user account, a user logs on to a specific computer to gain access to resources on that computer. There are also built-in user accounts, which can be either domain user accounts or local user accounts. With built-in user accounts, you can perform administrative tasks or gain access to network resources.

When you create a domain user account, Windows 2000 creates the account in the copy of the Active Directory database (called the directory) on a domain controller. The domain controller then replicates the new user account information to all domain controllers in the domain. When you create a local user account, Windows 2000 creates the account only in that computer's security database, which is called the local security database. Windows 2000 does not replicate local user account information to domain controllers. You do not create built-in user accounts; Windows 2000 automatically creates them.

Lesson 2: Planning New User Accounts

You can streamline the process of creating user accounts by planning or organizing the information for user accounts. This lesson introduces you to planning the following items for user accounts:

- Naming conventions for user accounts
- Requirements for passwords
- Account options, such as logon hours, the computers from which users can log on, and account expiration

After this lesson, you will be able to

- Plan a strategy for creating new user accounts
- Explain how password requirements affect security levels

Estimated lesson time: 10 minutes

Naming Conventions

The naming convention establishes how users are identified in the domain. A consistent naming convention will help you and your users remember user logon names and locate them in lists.

Table 7.1 summarizes some points you might want to consider in determining a naming convention for your organization.

Table 7.1   Naming Convention Considerations

Consideration	Explanation
Local user accounts	Local user account names must be unique on the computer where you create the local user account.
Domain user accounts	The user's logon name (DN) must be unique to the directory. The user's full name (also referred to as display name or account name) (RDN) must be unique within the OU where you create the domain user account.
20 characters maximum	User logon names can contain up to 20 uppercase or lowercase characters. Although the field accepts more than 20 characters, Windows 2000 recognizes only the first 20.
Invalid characters	The following characters are invalid: " / \ [ ] : ; l = , + * ? < >
User logon names are not case-sensitive	You can use a combination of special and alphanumeric characters to help uniquely identify user accounts. User logon names are not case-sensitive, but Windows 2000 preserves the case.

Consideration	Explanation
Accommodate employees with duplicate names	If two users were named John Doe, you could use the first name and the last initial, and then add letters from the last name to differentiate the duplicate names. In this example, one user account logon name could be Johnd and the other Johndo. Another possibility would be to number each user logon name—for example, Johnd1 and Johnd2.
Identify the type of employee	In some organizations, it is useful to identify temporary employees by their user account. To identify temporary employees, you can use a T and a dash in front of the user's logon name—for example, T-Johnd. Alternatively, use parentheses in the name—for example, John Doe (Temp).
E-mail compatibility	Some e-mail systems may not accept characters, such as spaces and "()" brackets.

Password Requirements

To protect access to the domain or a computer, every user account should have a password. Consider the following guidelines for passwords:

- Always assign a password for the Administrator account to prevent unauthorized access to the account.

- Determine whether the Administrator or the users will control passwords. You can assign unique passwords for the user account and prevent users from changing them, or you can allow users to enter their own passwords the first time that they log on. In most cases, users should control their passwords.

- Use passwords that are hard to guess. For example, avoid using passwords with an obvious association, such as a family member's name.

- Passwords can be up to 127 characters; a minimum length of eight characters is recommended.

- Use characters from each of the following three groups: uppercase and lowercase letters, numerals, and nonalphanumeric characters.

- Have at least one symbol character in the second through sixth positions.

- Make them significantly different from prior passwords.

- They must not contain the user's name or user name.

- They must not be a common word or name.

Note Windows 2000 group policies can also affect passwords. For further information on using group policy, see Chapter 12, "Administering Group Policy."

Account Options

You should assess the hours when a user can log on to the network and the computers from which a user can log on, and you should determine if temporary user accounts need to expire. To determine account options, consider the following information.

Logon Hours

Set logon hours for users who only require access at specific times. For example, allow night-shift workers to log on only during their working hours.

Computers from Which Users Can Log On

Determine the computers from which users can log on. By default, users can log on to the domain by using any computer in the domain. For security reasons, require users to log on to the domain only from their computer. This prevents users from gaining access to sensitive information that is stored on other computers.

Caution   If you have disabled NetBIOS over TCP/IP, Windows 2000 is unable to determine which computer you are logging on from and therefore you cannot restrict users to specific computers.

Account Expiration

Determine whether a user account should expire. If so, set an expiration date on the user account to ensure that the account is disabled when the user would no longer have access to the network. As a good security practice, you should set user accounts for temporary employees to expire when their contracts end.

Practice: Planning New User Accounts

In this practice, you plan how to implement user accounts for employees on the new hire list.

Scenario

As the Windows 2000 administrator for your corporate network, you need to set up the user accounts for new employees. Ten employees have recently been hired. You need to determine the following:

- A naming convention that will easily accommodate employees with duplicate or similar names and temporary contract personnel
- The hours during which users can log on
- The computers at which a user can log on

Criteria

Use the following criteria to make your decisions:

- All employees require a user account.
- Permanent employees should control their passwords.
- For security reasons, an administrator should control passwords for temporary employees.
- Day-shift hours are from 8 AM through 5 PM and night-shift hours are from 6 PM through 6 AM.
- Permanent employees require access to the network 24 hours a day, seven days a week.
- Temporary employees log on at only their assigned computers and only during their shifts. The computer names for computers that temporary employees use are Temp1 and Temp2.

New Hire List

Table 7.2 provides fictitious names and hiring information for the new employees.

Table 7.2   New Hire List for Practice

User Name	Title	Department	Status	Shift
Don Hall	Representative	Sales	Temporary	Day
Donna Hall	Manager	Product Support	Permanent	Night
James Smith	Vice President	Training	Permanent	Day
James Smith	Representative	Sales	Permanent	Day
Jon Morris	Developer	Product Development	Temporary	Night
Judy Lew	Developer	Product Development	Temporary	Day
Kim Yoshida	President	Training	Permanent	Day
Laurent Vernhes	Engineer	Product Support	Temporary	Night
Sandra Martinez	Engineer	Product Support	Permanent	Day

Planning Questions

Complete Table 7.3 to determine a naming convention for the users in the new hire list by considering the information that is provided in the sections "Scenario," "Criteria," and "New Hire List" in this practice.

Table 7.3   New Hire Naming Convention Plan for Practice

User Name	Full Name	User Logon Name
Don Hall		
Donna Hall		
James Smith		

Table 7.3   New Hire Naming Convention Plan for Practice *(continued)*

User Name	Full Name	User Logon Name
Jon Morris		
Judy Lew		
Kim Yoshida		
Laurent Vernhes		
Sandra Martinez		

Complete Table 7.4 to determine logon hours and computer use for the users in the new hire list by considering the information that is provided in the sections "Scenario," "Criteria," and "New Hire List" in this practice.

Table 7.4   New Hire Scheduling Plan for Practice

User Name	When Can the User Log On?	Where Can the User Log On?
Don Hall		
Donna Hall		
James Smith		
James Smith		
Jon Morris		
Judy Lew		
Kim Yoshida		
Laurent Vernhes		
Sandra Martinez		

Select the appropriate password setting for each user in Table 7.5 to determine who controls the user's password.

Table 7.5   New Hire Password Settings Plan for Practice

User Name	User Must Change Password the Next Time He or She Logs On	User Cannot Change Password
Don Hall		
Donna Hall		
James Smith		
James Smith		
Jon Morris		
Judy Lew		
Kim Yoshida		
Laurent Vernhes		
Sandra Martinez		

Lesson Summary

In this lesson you learned that in planning user accounts, you should determine naming conventions for user accounts, requirements for passwords, and account options such as logon hours, the computers from which users can log on, and account expiration. You learned that domain user accounts can be up to 20 characters in length and must be unique within the OU where you create the domain user account. The user's logon name (DN) must be unique to the directory. The user's full name (also referred to as display name or account name) (RDN) must be unique within the OU where you create the domain user account. Local user account names can also be up to 20 characters in length and must be unique on the computer where you create the local user account. Making these decisions before you start creating user accounts will reduce the amount of time it takes to create the needed user accounts and will simplify managing these accounts.

In the practice portion of this lesson, you were presented with a fictitious scenario and planned a naming convention that easily accommodated employees with duplicate or similar names and temporary contract personnel. You also had to plan the hours during which users could log on and the computers at which a user could log on, based on the scenario and criteria you were supplied.

Lesson 3: Creating User Accounts

Local user accounts are created using the Local Users and Groups snap-in within the Computer Management console. Domain user accounts are created using the Active Directory Users and Computers console. To use either tool, you must have administrator privileges. This lesson takes you step-by-step through creating user accounts and setting user account properties.

After this lesson, you will be able to

- Create local user accounts
- Create domain user accounts
- Set user account properties

Estimated lesson time: 45 minutes

Creating Local User Accounts

Using the Local Users and Groups snap-in (illustrated in Figure 7.3), you create, delete, or disable local user accounts on the local computer in a workgroup. You cannot create local user accounts on a domain controller.

Figure 7.3   Local Users and Groups snap-in and the New User dialog box

▶ **To create local user accounts**

1. Click Start, point to Programs, point to Administrative Tools, and then click Computer Management.

2. Expand the Local Users and Groups snap-in, right-click Users, and select New User.

3. In the New User dialog box (see Figure 7.3), set the local user account options described in Table 7.6.

Table 7.6   Local User Account Options

Option	Description
User Name	A unique name based on your naming convention. An entry in this box is required.
Full Name	The complete name of the user, to determine which person belongs to an account. An entry in this box is optional.
Description	A description that is useful for identifying users—for example, a department or an office location. An entry in this box is optional.
User Must Change Password At Next Logon	Requires the user to change his or her password the first time that he or she logs on.
User Cannot Change Password	Only administrators are allowed to control passwords.
Password Never Expires	Password will never change. The User Must Change Password at Next Logon option overrides the Password Never Expires option.
Account Is Disabled	Prevents use of the user's account—for example, for a new employee who has not yet started.

Creating Domain User Accounts

Using the Active Directory Users and Computers console (illustrated in Figure 7.4), you create, delete, or disable domain user accounts on the domain controller, or local user accounts on any computer in the domain.

When you create the domain user account, the user logon name defaults to the domain in which you are creating the domain user account. However, you can select any domain in which you have permissions to create domain user accounts. You must select the container in which to create the new account. You can create the domain user account in the default Users container or in a container that you create to hold domain user accounts.

▶ **To create domain user accounts**

1. Click Start, point to Programs, point to Administrative Tools, then click Active Directory Users And Computers.

2. Click the domain, right-click the Users container, point to New, and click User.

Note In a live system environment, the Users container is merely a default container. Actual users should be added to a custom OU rather than the Users container.

Figure 7.4   Active Directory Users and Computers console and the New Object User
dialog box

3. In the New Object-User dialog box (see Figure 7.4), set the domain user name
options described in Table 7.7.

Table 7.7   User Name Options on the New Object-User Dialog Box

Option	Description
First Name	The user's first name. An entry in the First Name, the Last Name, or the Full Name box is required.
Initials	The User's initials. An entry in this, the First Name, the Last Name, or the Full Name box is required.
Last Name	The user's first name. An entry in the First Name, the Last Name, or the Full Name box is required.
Full Name	The user's complete name. The name must be unique within the container where you create the user account. Windows 2000 completes this option if you enter information in the First Name, Initials, or Last Name boxes. The Create-In field displays this name in the DN path of the container where the user account is located in the directory.
User Logon	The User Logon Name contains a box and a list that uniquely Name identify the user throughout the entire network. The box (on the left) is the user's unique logon name, based on your naming conventions. An entry is required and must be unique within the domain. The list (on the right) is the domain name.
User Logon Name (Pre-Windows 2000)	The user's unique logon name that is used to log on from earlier versions of Windows, such as Windows NT 4.0 or Windows NT 3.5.1. An entry is required and must be unique within the domain.

Setting Password Options

In the New Object-User dialog box, shown in Figure 7.4, click Next to open a second New Object-User dialog box, shown in Figure 7.5, which contains password settings. In this dialog box, you set the password requirements for the domain user account.

Figure 7.5   New Object-User dialog box

Table 7.8 describes the password options in the New Object-User dialog box.

Table 7.8   Password Options on the New Object-User Dialog Box

Option	Description
Password	The password that is used to authenticate the user. For greater security, you should always assign a password.
Confirm Password	Confirm the password by typing it a second time to make sure that you typed the password correctly. An entry is required if you assign a password.
User Must Change Password At Next Logon	Requires the user to change his or her password the first time that he or she logs on. This ensures that the user is the only person who knows the password.
User Cannot Change Password	Only administrators are allowed to control passwords. Select this check box if you have more than one person using the same domain user account (such as Guest) or to maintain control over user account passwords.
Password Never Expires	Password will never change. Possible use: for a domain user account that will be used by a program or a Windows 2000 service. The Password Never Expires option overrides the User Must Change Password At Next Logon option.
Account Is Disabled	Prevents use of the user's account—for example, for a new employee who has not yet started.

Note   Always require new users to change their passwords the first time that they log on. This prevents a user account from existing without a password, and once the user logs on and changes his or her password, only the user knows the password.

Tip   For added security on networks, create unrelated initial passwords for all new user accounts by using a random combination of letters and numbers. Creating an unrelated initial password will help keep the user account secure.

Practice: Creating Domain User Accounts

In this practice, you create the domain user accounts shown in Table 7.9.

Table 7.9   Domain User Accounts for Practice

First Name	Last Name	User Logon Name	Password	Change Password
User	One	User1	(blank)	Must
User	Three	User3	(blank)	Must
User	Five	User5	User5	Must
User	Seven	User7	User7	Must
User	Nine	User9	User9	Cannot

The following procedure outlines the steps that are required to create the first user account using the Active Directory Users and Computers console. After you have created the first user account, follow the same steps to create the remaining user accounts.

▶ **To create a domain user account**

1. Log on as Administrator.

2. Click Start, point to Programs, point to Administrative Tools, then click Active Directory Users And Computers.

   Windows 2000 displays the Active Directory Users and Computers console.

3. Expand microsoft.com (if you did not use Microsoft as your domain name, expand your domain), and then double-click Users.

   In the details pane, notice the default user accounts.

   Which user accounts does the Active Directory Installation Wizard create by default?

4. Right-click Users, point to New, then click User.

   Windows 2000 displays the New Object-User dialog box.

   Where in the Active Directory will the new user account be created?

5. Type **User** in the First Name box.

6. Type **One** in the Last Name box.

   Notice that Windows 2000 completes the Full Name box for you.

7. Type **user1** in the User Logon Name box.

8. In the list to the right of the User Logon Name box, select @microsoft.com. (The domain name will vary if you did not use microsoft.com as your DNS domain name.)

   The user logon name, combined with the domain name in the box that appears to the right of the User Logon Name box, is the user's full Internet logon name. This name uniquely identifies the user throughout the directory (for example, user1@microsoft.com).

   Notice that Windows 2000 completes the pre-Windows 2000 logon name box for you.

   When is the pre-Windows 2000 logon name used?

9. Click Next to continue.

   Windows 2000 displays the New Object-User dialog box, prompting you to supply password options and restrictions.

10. In the Password box and the Confirm Password box, type the password or leave these boxes blank if you are not assigning a password.

    If you enter a password, notice that the password is displayed as asterisks as you type. This prevents onlookers from viewing the password as it is entered.

11. Specify whether or not the user can change his or her password.

    What are the results of selecting both the User Must Change Password At Next Logon check box and the User Cannot Change Password check box? Explain.

    Under what circumstances would you select the Account Is Disabled check box when creating a new user account?

12. After you have selected the appropriate password options, click Next.

    Windows 2000 displays the New Object-User dialog box, displaying the options and restrictions that you have configured for this user account.

13. Verify that the user account options are correct, then click Finish.

Note If the user account options are incorrect, click Back to modify the user account options.

In the details pane of the Active Directory Users and Computers console, notice that the user account that you just created now appears.

14. Complete Steps 4-13 for the remaining user accounts.

User Account Properties

A set of default properties is associated with each user account that you create. After you create a user account you can configure personal and account properties, logon options, and dial-in settings. For domain users, these account properties equate to object attributes.

You can use the properties that you define for a domain user account to search for users in the directory or for use in other applications as objects' attributes. For this reason, you should provide detailed definitions for each domain user account that you create.

The tabs in the Properties dialog box (see Figure 7.6) contain information about each user account. Table 7.10 describes the tabs in the Properties dialog box.

Table 7.10   Tabs in the Properties Dialog Box

Tab	Description
General	Documents the user's first name, last name, display name, description, office location, telephone number(s), e-mail address, home page, and additional Web pages
Address	Documents the user's street address, post office box, city, state or province, zip or postal code, and country or region
Account	Documents the user's account properties, including the following: user logon name, logon hours, computers permitted to log on to, account options, account expiration
Profile	Sets a profile path, logon script path, home directory, and shared document folder
Telephones	Documents the user's home, pager, mobile, fax, and Internet Protocol (IP) telephone numbers, and contains space for comments
Organization	Documents the user's title, department, company, manager, and direct reports
Remote Control	Configures Terminal Services remote control settings
Terminal Services Profile	Configures the Terminal Services user profile
Member Of	Documents the groups to which the user belongs
Dial-In	Documents the dial-in properties for the user
Environment	Configures the Terminal Services startup environment
Sessions	Sets the Terminal Services timeout and reconnection settings

Note   For a local user account, the Properties dialog box contains only the General, Member Of, and Profile tabs, as local users are not user objects in Active Directory.

Setting Personal Properties

Four of the tabs in the Properties dialog box contain personal information about each user account. These tabs are General, Address, Telephones, and Organization. Completing the properties of each of these tabs allows you to locate domain user accounts in the directory. For example, if all of the properties on the Address tab are complete, as shown in Figure 7.6, you can locate that person by using the street address or another field.

Figure 7.6   Address tab of the Properties dialog box

▶ **To set personal properties**

1. On the Administrative Tools menu, click Active Directory Users And Computers, then click the domain.

2. Click the appropriate container to view available domain user accounts.

3. Right-click the appropriate domain user account and click Properties.

4. Click the appropriate tab for the personal properties that you want to enter or change and then enter values for each property.

5. Click OK.

Setting Account Properties

Use the Account tab in the Properties dialog box (see Figure 7.7) to set options for a domain user account.

Some of the domain user account options are the same for both the Account tab and the New Object-User dialog box. Table 7.11 describes the additional account properties that are not available when you create a domain user account.

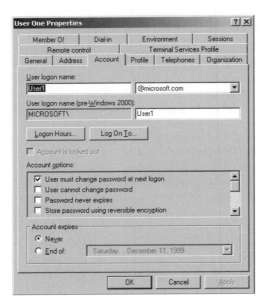

Figure 7.7   Account tab of the Properties dialog box

Table 7.11   Additional Account Options

Option	Description
Store Password Using Reversible Encryption	Enables Macintosh users to log on. Macintosh computers only send this type of command.
Smart Card Is Required For Interactive Logon	Allows a user to log on with a smart card. Additional hardware is required.
Account Is Trusted For Delegation	Allows a user to assign responsibility for management and administration of a portion of the namespace to another user, group, or organization.
Account Is Sensitive And Cannot Be Delegated	Prevents the account from being assigned for delegation by another account.
Use DES Encryption Types For This Account	Provides the Data Encryption Standard (DES).
Do Not Require Kerberos Preauthentication	Removes Kerberos preauthentication for accounts using another implementation of Kerberos. Not all implementations or deployments of Kerberos use the preauthentication feature.
Account Expires	Sets account expiration dates. Select Never if you do not want the account to expire. Select End Of and then enter a date in the adjoining text box if you want Windows 2000 to automatically disable the user account on the date you specify.

Setting Logon Hours

Set logon hours to control when a user can log on to the domain. Restricting logon hours limits the hours that users can explore the network. By default, Windows 2000 permits access for all hours on all days. You might want to allow users to log on only during working hours. Setting logon hours reduces the amount of time that the account is open to unauthorized access.

▶ **To set logon hours**

1. In the Properties dialog box, on the Account tab, click Logon Hours.

   On the Logon Hours dialog box for the user, a blue box indicates that the user can log on during the hour. A white box indicates that the user cannot log on (see Figure 7.8).

2. To allow or deny access, do one of the following:
   - Select the rectangles on the days and hours for which you want to allow access, click the start time, drag to the end time, and then click Logon Permitted.
   - Select the rectangles on the days and hours for which you want to deny access, click the start time, drag to the end time, and then click Logon Denied.

Note The days and hours for which you have allowed access are now shown in blue.

---

3. Click OK.

   It is important that you remember that any connections to network resources on the domain are not disconnected when the user's logon hours run out. However, the user will not be able to make any new connections.

Figure 7.8 Logon Hours dialog box

Setting the Computers from Which Users Can Log On

Setting logon options for a domain user account allows you to control the computers from which a user can log on to the domain. By default, each user can log on from all computers in the domain. Setting the computers from which a user can log on prevents users from accessing another user's data that is stored on that user's computer.

Note To control the computers from which a user can log on to a domain, NetBIOS must be enabled over TCP/IP.

▶ **To set logon workstations**

1. In the Properties dialog box, on the Account tab, click Log On To.

2. On the Logon Workstations dialog box (see Figure 7.9), select the option that specifies from which computers a user can log on.

3. Add the computers from which a user can log on.

   Use the computer name that you specified when you installed Windows 2000, which is the name of the computer account in the directory.

4. If necessary, delete or edit the name of a computer from which the user can log on.

5. Click OK.

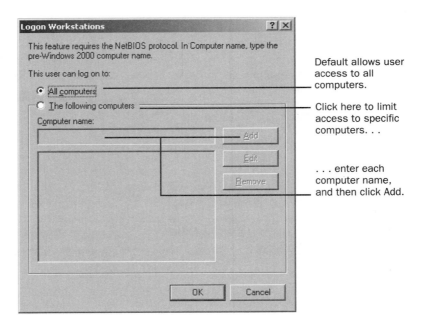

Figure 7.9 Logon Workstations dialog box

Configuring Dial-In Settings

Configuring dial-in settings for a user account permits you to control how a user can make a dial-in connection to the network from a remote location. To gain access to the network, the user dials in to a computer running the Windows 2000 Remote Access Server (RAS).

Note   In addition to configuring dial-in settings and having RAS on the server to which the user is dialing in, you must also set up a dial-up connection for the server on the client computer. Set up a dial-up connection by using the Network Connection Wizard, which you can access from Network Connections in My Computer.

Configure dial-in settings on the Dial-In tab of the Properties dialog box. Table 7.12 describes the required options for setting up security for a dial-up connection.

Table 7.12   Options on the Dial-In Tab in the Properties Dialog Box

Option	Description
Allow Access	Turns on dial-in or virtual private network (VPN) remote access for the user.
Deny Access	Turns off dial-in or VPN remote access for the user.
Control Access Through Remote Access Policy	Specifies that remote access permission for this user is controlled through a remote access policy.
Verify Caller-ID	Indicates the telephone number that the user must use to dial in.
Callback Options	The callback methods, including: *No Callback.* The RAS server will not call the user back and the user pays the telephone charges. This is the default. *Set By Caller (Routing and Remote Access Service Only).* The user provides the telephone number for the RAS server to call back. The company pays the telephone charges for the session. *Always Callback To.* The RAS server uses the specified telephone number to call back the user. The user must be at the specified telephone number to make a connection to the server. This reduces the risk of an unauthorized person dialing in because the number is preconfigured. Use this option in a high-security environment.
Assign A Static IP Address	Specifies whether to disregard group dial-in profile settings and assign a static TCP/IP address to this user.
Apply Static Routes	Specifies whether to configure predefined routes for one-way initiated demand-dial routed connections.
Static Routes	Allows the definition of static routes.

Practice: Modifying User Account Properties

In this practice, you modify user account properties. You configure the logon hours and account expiration settings for several of the user accounts that you created in the previous practice. You add these user accounts to the Print Operators group so that the accounts can log on to the domain controller. Then you test the logon hours restrictions, the password restrictions that you set up when you created the accounts, and the account expiration settings.

Exercise 1: Configuring Logon Hours and Account Expiration

In this exercise you configure the hours during which User3 and User5 can log on to the computer, and for User5 you also set a date for the account to expire.

Scenario

Modify the following user accounts with the properties specified in Table 7.13.

Table 7.13   User Account Properties for Exercise 1

User Account	Logon Hours	Account Expires
User3	6 PM-6AM, Monday-Friday	
User5		Today

Important   Complete the following procedure while you are logged on as Administrator with the Active Directory Users and Computers console running and your domain expanded in the console tree.

▶   **To specify logon hours**

1. In the console tree of the Active Directory Users and Computers console, expand Users.

2. In the details pane, right-click User Three, then click Properties.

   Windows 2000 displays the User Three Properties dialog box with the General tab active.

   In the General tab, what information can you specify for the user account in addition to the first and last name? How would this information be useful?

3. Click the Account tab, and then click Logon Hours.

   Windows 2000 displays the Logon Hours For User Three dialog box.

   Currently, when can User Three log on?

4. To restrict the user's logon hours, click the start time of the first period during which you want to prevent the user from logging on and then drag the pointer to the end time for the period.

   A frame outlines the blocks for all of the selected hours.

Note   To select the same block of time for all days in the week, above the Sunday row, click the gray block that represents the start time, and then drag the pointer to the end time. To select an entire day, click the gray block that is labeled with the name of the day.

5. Click Logon Denied.

   The outlined area is now a white block, indicating that the user will not be permitted to log on during those hours.

6. Repeat Steps 4 and 5 as necessary until only the correct logon hours are allowed.

7. Click OK to close the Logon Hours For User Three dialog box.

8. In the User Three Properties dialog box, click OK to apply your settings and return to the Active Directory Users and Computers console.

▶ **To set account expiration for a user account**

1. In the console tree of the Active Directory Users and Computers console, click Users.

2. In the details pane, right-click User Five and click Properties.

   Windows 2000 displays the User Five Properties dialog box with the General tab active.

3. Click the Account tab.

   When will the account expire?

4. Click End Of and then set the date to today's date.

5. Click OK to apply your changes and return to the Active Directory Users and Computers console.

6. Close the Active Directory Users and Computers console and log off Windows 2000.

Exercise 2: Testing User Accounts

In this exercise you log on each of the user accounts that you created in the previous exercises and then test the effects of the account settings.

▶ **To test logon capabilities of user accounts**

1. Attempt to log on as User1 with no password.

   Windows 2000 displays the Logon Message message box, indicating that you must change your password.

2. In the Change Password dialog box, leave the Old Password box blank, type **student** in the New Password box and the Confirm New Password box, and click OK.

Windows 2000 displays the Change Password message box indicating that your password was changed.

3. Click OK to close the Change Password message box.

Were you able to successfully log on? Why or why not?

There are several ways to allow regular users to log on at a domain controller. In the next procedure you add the users to the Print Operators group, because this group has the right to log on to a domain controller. Only users belonging to certain administrative groups may log on interactively onto a domain controller. A group is a collection of user accounts. Groups simplify administration by allowing you to assign permissions to a group of users rather than having to assign permissions to each individual user account. For more information on groups, see Chapter 8, "Group Account Administration."

▶ **To add users to the Print Operators group**

1. Log on as Administrator.

2. In the console tree of the Active Directory Users and Computers console, expand Users.

3. In the details pane, right-click User One, then click Properties.

Windows 2000 displays the User One Properties dialog box with the General tab active.

4. Click the Member Of tab.

5. Click Add.

Windows 2000 displays the Select Groups dialog box.

6. Select Print Operators, click Add, then click OK.

7. Click OK to close the User One Properties window.

8. Repeat Steps 3-7 for User3, User5, User7, and User9.

9. Close the Active Directory Users and Computers console and log off Windows 2000.

▶ **To test restrictions on logon hours**

1. Attempt to log on as User1 with a password of student.

Were you able to successfully log on? Why or why not?

2. Log off Windows 2000 and attempt to log on as User3 with no password.

3. When prompted, change the password to student.

Were you able to successfully log on? Why or why not?

▶ **To test password restrictions**

1. Attempt to log on as User7 with no password.

Were you able to successfully log on? Why or why not?

2. Attempt to log on as User7 with a password of User7.

3. When prompted, change the password to student.

Were you able to log on? Why or why not?

4. Log off Windows 2000.

5. Attempt to log on as User9 with a password of User9.

Were you able to successfully log on? Why or why not?

▶ **To test password restrictions by attempting to change a password**

1. Press Ctrl+Alt+Delete.

Windows 2000 displays the Windows Security dialog box.

2. Click Change Password.

Windows 2000 displays the Change Password dialog box.

3. In the Old Password box, type the password for the User9 user account; in the New Password and Confirm New Password boxes, type **student**, then click OK.

Were you able to change the password? Why or why not?

4. Click OK to close the Change Password message box, then click Cancel to return to the Windows Security dialog box.

5. Click Log Off.

Windows 2000 displays the Log Off Windows dialog box, prompting you to verify that you want to log off.

6. Click Yes to log off.

▶ **To test account expiration**

1. Attempt to log on as User5.

2. When prompted, change your password to student.

Were you successful? Why or why not?

3. Log off Windows 2000.

▶ **To change the system time**

1. Log on to your domain as Administrator, click Start, point to Settings, then click Control Panel.

2. In Control Panel, double-click Date/Time.

Windows 2000 displays the Date/Time Properties dialog box.

3. Under Date, enter tomorrow's date, then click OK to apply your changes and return to Control Panel.

4. Close Control Panel and log off Windows 2000.

▶ **To test account expiration**

1. Attempt to log on as User5 with a password of student.

   Were you successful? Why or why not?

▶ **To change the system time**

1. Log on to your domain as Administrator, click Start, point to Settings, then click Control Panel.

2. In Control Panel, double-click Date/Time.

   Windows 2000 displays the Date/Time Properties dialog box.

3. Under Date, enter today's date, then click OK to apply your changes and return to Control Panel.

4. Close Control Panel and log off Windows 2000.

Lesson Summary

In this lesson you learned that local user accounts are created using the Local Users and Groups snap-in built into the Computer Management console, and domain user accounts are created using the Active Directory Users and Computers console. When you create a domain user account, it is always created on the first available domain controller that is contacted by Microsoft Management Console (MMC), and then the account is replicated to all domain controllers.

You also learned that there is a set of default properties associated with each user account that you create. You learned that for domain user accounts, these properties equate to object attributes, so you can use these properties to search for domain users in the directory.

In the practice portion of this lesson, you created five domain user accounts. You then configured account properties including modifying the logon hours, setting account expiration, and determining when and if a user can change his or her password. Finally, you tested these properties to verify that they worked as expected.

Lesson 4: Creating User Profiles

A *user profile* is a collection of folders and data that stores the user's current desktop environment, application settings, and personal data. A user profile also contains all of the network connections that are established when a user logs on to a computer, such as Start menu items and mapped drives to network servers. User profiles maintain consistency for users in their desktop environments by providing each user with the same desktop environment that he or she had the last time that he or she logged on to the computer. This lesson introduces user profiles and explains the differences between local user profiles, roaming user profiles, and mandatory user profiles.

After this lesson, you will be able to

- Explain the difference between a local user profile, a roaming user profile, and a mandatory user profile
- Configure a local user profile
- Create a roaming user profile
- Create a mandatory user profile

Estimated lesson time: 45 minutes

User Profiles

On computers running Windows 2000, user profiles automatically create and maintain the desktop settings for each user's work environment on the local computer. A user profile is created for each user when he or she logs on to a computer for the first time.

User profiles provide several advantages to users:

- More than one user can use the same computer, and each receives desktop settings when he or she logs on.
- When users log on to their workstation, they receive the desktop settings as they existed when they logged off.
- Customization of the desktop environment by one user does not affect another user's settings.
- User profiles can be stored on a server so that they can follow users to any computer running Windows NT 4.0 or Windows 2000 on the network. These are called *roaming user profiles*.
- Application settings are retained for applications that are Windows 2000-certified.

As an administrative tool, user profiles provide these options:

- You can create a default user profile that is appropriate for the user's tasks.

- You can set up a *mandatory user profile*, a profile that does not save changes made by the user to the desktop settings. Users can modify the desktop settings of the computer while they are logged on, but none of these changes is saved when they log off. The mandatory profile settings are downloaded to the local computer each time the user logs on.

- You can specify the default user settings that will be included in all of the individual user profiles.

Profile Types

There are three types of user profiles:

- **Local user profile.** A local user profile is created the first time you log on to a computer and is stored on a computer's local hard disk. Any changes made to your local user profile are specific to the computer on which you make the changes.

- **Roaming user profile.** A roaming user profile is created by your system administrator and is stored on a server. This profile is available every time you log on to any computer on the network. Changes made to your roaming user profile are updated on the server.

- **Mandatory user profile.** A mandatory user profile is a roaming profile that can be used to specify particular settings for individuals or an entire group of users. Only system administrators can make changes to mandatory user profiles.

Settings Saved in a User Profile

A user profile contains configuration preferences and options for each user—a snapshot of a user's desktop environment.

Table 7.14 shows the settings contained in a user profile.

Table 7.14   Settings Contained in a User Profile

Parameters Saved	Source
All user-definable settings for Windows Explorer	Windows Explorer
User-stored documents	My Documents
User-stored picture items	My Pictures
Shortcuts to favorite locations on the Internet	Favorites
Any user-created mapped network drives	Mapped network drive
Links to other computers on the network	My Network Places
Items stored on the Desktop and Shortcut elements	Desktop contents
All user-definable computer screen colors and display text settings	Screen colors and fonts

Parameters Saved	Source
Application data and user-defined configuration settings	Application data and registry hive
Network printer connections	Printer settings
All user-defined settings made in Control Panel	Control Panel
All user-specific program settings affecting the user's Windows environment, including Calculator, Clock, Notepad, and Paint	Accessories
Per-user program settings for programs written specifically for Windows 2000 and designed to track program settings	Windows 2000-based programs
Any bookmarks placed in the Windows 2000 Help system	Online user education bookmarks

Contents of a User Profile

Local user profiles are stored in C:\Documents and Settings*user_ logon_name* folder, where C:\ is the name of your system drive and *user_ logon_name* is the name the user enters when logging on to the system. Roaming user profiles are stored in a shared folder on the server. Table 7.15 lists the contents of a sample user profile folder.

Table 7.15   Contents of a Sample User Profile Folder

Item	Description
Application data folder*	Program-specific data—for example, a custom dictionary. Program vendors decide what data to store in the user profile folder.
Cookies folder	User information and preferences.
Desktop folder	Desktop items including files, shortcuts, and folders.
Favorites folder	Shortcuts to favorite locations on the Internet.
FrontPageTempDir folder	Temporary folder used by Microsoft Front Page.
Local Settings folder*	Application data, History, and Temporary files. Application data roams with the user by way of roaming user profiles.
My Documents folder	User documents.
My Pictures folder	User picture items.
NetHood folder*	Shortcuts to My Network Places items.
PrintHood folder*	Shortcuts to printer folder items.
Recent folder*	Shortcuts to the most recently used documents and accessed folders.
SendTo folder*	Shortcuts to document-handling utilities.
Start Menu folder	Shortcuts to program items.
Templates folder	User template items.
NTUSER.DAT file*	Stores user registry settings.

*Indicates item is hidden.

Using the My Documents folder centralizes all user settings and personal documents into a single folder that is part of the user profile. Windows 2000 automatically sets up the My Documents folder and it is the default location for storing users' data for Microsoft applications. Home directories can also contain files and programs for a user. Home directories are covered in the next lesson.

Local User Profiles

Windows 2000 creates a local user profile the first time that a user logs on at a computer, storing the profile on that computer. The local user profile is stored in the C:\Documents and Settings*user_logon_name* folder, where C:\ is the name of your system drive and *user_logon_name* is the name the user enters when logging on to the system. When a user logs on to the client computer running Windows 2000, the user always receives his or her individual desktop settings and connections, regardless of how many users share the same client computer.

A user changes his or her local user profile by changing desktop settings. For example, a user may make a new network connection or add a file to My Documents. Then, when a user logs off, Windows 2000 incorporates the changes into the user profile stored on the computer. The next time that the user logs on, the new network connection and the file are present.

Roaming User Profiles

To support users who work at multiple computers, you can set up roaming user profiles. A roaming user profile is a user profile that you set up on a network server so that the profile is available to the user no matter where the user logs on in the domain. The user always receives his or her individual desktop settings and connections, in contrast to a local user profile, which only resides on one client computer.

When a user logs on, Windows 2000 copies the roaming user profile from the network server to the client computer and applies the roaming user profile settings to that computer. The first time that a user logs on at a computer, Windows 2000 copies all documents to the local computer. Thereafter, when the user logs on to the computer, Windows 2000 compares the locally stored user profile files and the roaming user profile files. It copies only the files that have changed since the last time that the user logged on at the computer, which makes the logon process shorter.

When a user logs off, Windows 2000 copies changes that were made to the local copy of the roaming user profile back to the server where the profile is stored.

Standard Roaming User Profiles

You can create a standard roaming user profile for a group of users by configuring the desired desktop environment and then copying the standard profile to the user's roaming user profile location.

You use standard roaming user profiles for the following reasons:

- To provide a standard desktop environment for multiple users with similar job responsibilities. These users require the same network resources.
- To provide users with the work environment that they need to perform their jobs and to remove connections and applications that they do not require.
- To simplify troubleshooting. Technical support would know the exact baseline setup of the desktops and could easily find a deviation or a problem.

Creating Roaming User Profiles

You should create roaming user profiles on a file server that you frequently back up, so that you have copies of the latest roaming user profiles. To improve logon performance for a busy network, place the roaming user profile folder on a member server instead of a domain controller. The copying of roaming user profiles between the server and client computers can use a lot of system resources, such as bandwidth and computer processing. If the profiles are on the domain controller, this can delay the authentication of users by the domain controller.

Note   To successfully create roaming user profiles and assign home directories for user accounts, you must have permission to administer the object in which the user accounts reside.

▶ **To set up a roaming user profile**

1. On a server, create a shared folder and use a path with the following format: *server_name**shared_folder_name*
2. On the Profile tab in the Properties dialog box (see Figure 7.10) for the user account, provide the path to the shared folder in the Profile Path box (such as *server_name**shared_folder_name**logon_name*).

You can type the variable *%username%* instead of the user's logon name. When you use this variable, Windows 2000 automatically replaces the variable with the user account name for the roaming user profile, which is useful when copying template accounts.

Figure 7.10   Profile path for a roaming user profile

Creating a Standard Roaming User Profile

The following checklist provides an overview of the tasks required to implement a standard roaming user profile for a group of users.

1. Create a user profile template with the appropriate configuration. Do this by creating a user account using the Active Directory Users and Computers console and then configuring the appropriate desktop settings.

2. Create a shared folder on the server, which will be used to allow users to access the profile template from a remote computer.

3. Copy the user profile template to the shared folder on the server and specify the users who are permitted to use the profile in the User Profile tab in the System Properties dialog box in the Control Panel (see Figure 7.11).

4. Specify the path to the profile template in the Profile tab in the User Properties dialog box (see Figure 7.10).

Figure 7.11   Copying a user profile template

Mandatory User Profiles

A mandatory user profile is a read-only roaming user profile. Users can modify the desktop settings of the computer while they are logged on, but none of these changes is saved when they log off. The next time that the user logs on, the profile is the same as the last time that he or she logged on. The mandatory profile settings are downloaded to the local computer each time the user logs on.

You can assign one mandatory profile to multiple users who require the same desktop settings, such as bank tellers. By changing only one profile, you can change the desktop environment for several users.

Creating a Mandatory User Profile

A hidden file in the profile (for example, \\SERVER1*share**user_logon_name*) called NTUSER.DAT contains that section of the Windows 2000 system settings that applies to the individual user account and contains the user environment settings, such as desktop appearance. This is the file that you make read-only by changing its name to NTUSER.MAN.

Practice: Managing User Profiles

In this practice you configure and test a local user profile. Then you create and test a standard roaming user profile.

Exercise 1: Configuring a Local User Profile

In this exercise you create a local user account and profile and then view, define, and test the profile.

▶ **To create a user account**

1. Log on to your domain as Administrator.
2. Use the Active Directory Users and Computers console to create the puser account listed in Table 7.16. In the list to the right of the User Logon Name box, select @microsoft.com. Add puser to the Print Operators group so that he or she can log on to the domain controller.

   Table 7.16   Puser Account Information for Exercise 1

First Name	Last Name	User Logon Name	Password	Member Of
Profile	User	puser	None	Print Operators

3. Log off Windows 2000.

▶ **To create a local user profile**

1. Log on to your domain as puser.

   The first time that you log on to Windows 2000, a local user profile is created for you with default settings. Logging on as puser creates a local user profile.

2. Log off Windows 2000.

▶ **To view existing profiles**

1. Log on to your domain as Administrator.
2. Click Start, point to Settings, click Control Panel, and then double-click System.

   Windows 2000 displays the System Properties dialog box.

3. Click the User Profiles tab.

   Which users' profiles are stored on your computer?

4. Click OK to close the System Properties dialog box, then close Control Panel.
5. Log off Windows 2000.

▶ **To define and test a local profile**

1. Log on to your domain as puser.

2. Right-click anywhere on the desktop, then click Properties.

   The Display Properties dialog box appears.

3. Click the Appearance tab.

   Notice the current color scheme.

4. In the Scheme list, select a different color scheme, then click OK.

   This change takes effect immediately.

5. Log off and log on as the same user, puser.

   Were screen colors saved? Why or why not?

6. Log off Windows 2000.

Exercise 2: Defining a Standard Roaming User Profile

In this exercise you create a shared folder in which a standard roaming user profile can reside. You create a user account named Profile Template, which will be the model for a standard roaming user profile. You configure the settings for the template profile. Then, you copy the Profile Template user profile to the shared folder for User2. Finally, you specify the path to the profile for User2. Optionally, you can test the standard roaming profile if you have access to two computers on the same network.

▶ **To create a shared folder in which to store roaming user profiles**

Note   Shared folders are covered in detail in Chapter 11. For now, you are walked through the steps for creating a shared folder for the purpose of sharing user profiles.

1. Log on to your domain as Administrator, at your domain controller.

2. In the C:\ folder (where C:\ is the name of your system drive), create a folder named Profiles.

3. Right-click the Profiles folder, then click Properties.

4. In the Profiles Properties dialog box, select the Sharing tab.

5. Click Share This Folder, then click Permissions.

6. In the Permissions For Profiles dialog box, ensure that the Everyone group is selected and that Full Control-Allow is checked, then click OK.

7. On the Profiles Properties dialog box, click OK.

▶ **To create a user profile template**

1. Click Start, point to Programs, point to Administrative Tools, then click Active Directory Users And Computers.

2. Use the Active Directory Users and Computers console to create the ptemplate account listed in Table 7.17. In the list to the right of the User Logon Name box, select @microsoft.com. Add ptemplate to the Print Operators group so that he or she can log on to the domain controller.

Table 7.17   Ptemplate Account Information for Exercise 2

First Name	Last Name	User Logon Name	Password	Member Of
Profile	Template	ptemplate	None	Print Operators

3. Log off Windows 2000.

4. Log on as ptemplate.

   A local user profile is automatically created for the Profile Template users on the local computer in the C:\Documents and Settings*user_logon_name* folder (where C:\ is the name of your system drive).

5. Right-click anywhere on the desktop, then click Properties.

   The Display Properties dialog box appears.

6. Click the Appearance tab.

   Notice the current color scheme.

7. In the Scheme list, select a different color scheme, then click OK.

   This change takes effect immediately.

8. Log off and log on as the same user, ptemplate.

   Notice that the screen colors are saved in the user's profile.

9. Log off Windows 2000.

▶ **To copy the user profile template to a shared folder on a network server**

1. Log on to your domain as Administrator.

2. Use the Active Directory Users and Computers console to create the User2 account listed in Table 7.18. In the list to the right of the User Logon Name box, select @microsoft.com. Add User2 to the Print Operators group so that he or she can log on to the domain controller.

Table 7.18   User2 Account Information for Exercise 2

First Name	Last Name	User Logon Name	Password	Member Of
User	Two	User2	None	Print Operators

3. Click Start, point to Settings, then click Control Panel.

4. In Control Panel, double-click System.

 The System Properties dialog box appears.

5. Click the User Profiles tab.

 Notice that a user profile has been created for all users who have previously logged on to the computer, including a user profile named MICROSOFT\ptemplate.

6. Under Profiles Stored On This Computer, click MICROSOFT\ptemplate, then click Copy To.

 The Copy To dialog box appears.

7. In the Copy Profile To box, type ***computer_name*\profiles\user2** (where *computer_name* is SERVER1 or the name of your computer). This is the location of the shared folder where the profile template will be stored.

▶ **To specify the users who are permitted to use the profile**

1. In the Copy To dialog box, under Permitted To Use, click Change.

 The Select User Or Group dialog box appears.

2. In the Name column, click User Two, then click OK.

 MICROSOFT\user2 appears in the Permitted To Use box in the Copy To dialog box.

3. Click OK.

 A folder named user2 is created in the Profiles folder with all the desktop settings configured for the Profile Template user account.

4. In Windows Explorer, view Profiles\user2. Notice the folders for the desktop settings that are stored in the Profiles folder.

▶ **To specify a path to the roaming user profile**

1. In the Active Directory Users and Computers console, double-click User Two.

 The User Two Properties dialog box appears.

2. Click the Profile tab.

3. In the Profile path box, type ***computer_name*\profiles*user2*** (where *computer_name* is SERVER1 or the name of your computer).

4. Click OK.

5. Exit the Active Directory Users and Computers console.

Note   To make the Profile Template mandatory, type the actual profile name, for example: **\\server1\profiles\user2\ntuser.man**.

- If users will log on to computers running Windows NT or Windows 2000, but not to computers running Windows 3.1, then the user profile path does not need a filename.

- If users will log on to computers running Windows NT 3.1, as well as to computers running Windows NT 4.0 or Windows 2000, then the user profile path must contain a filename.

- If users will log on only to computers running Windows 2000, the user profile path should be to a folder name and should not include an extension of .man. If the folder specified in the user profile path does not exist, it is automatically created the first time the user logs on.

▶ **To test the roaming profile**

1. Log off and log on as User2.

   Are the screen colors and desktop the same or different from those set in the Profile Template? Why or why not?

▶ **To determine the type of profile assigned to a user**

1. Log off and log on as Administrator, and start Control Panel.

2. Double-click System, then click the User Profiles tab.

   What type of profile is listed for the User2 account?

3. Exit all programs and log off Windows 2000.

Note   If you have access to two computers on the same network, complete this procedure from the second computer.

▶ **To test the roaming profile from another computer**

1. Log on to the second computer as User2.

2. If a dialog box appears that provides profile options, click Download.

   Notice that the screen colors are the same as those set on the first computer because the roaming profile for the template user account is downloaded from the server and applied to the computer that the template logs on to.

3. Log off the second computer.

▶ **To delete the Profile Template user profile**

1. In the User Profiles tab, under Profiles Stored On This Computer, click the MICROSOFT\ptemplate profile and click Delete.

   A Confirm Delete message appears.

2. Click Yes to delete the local profile.

The Profile Template user profile is deleted from the local computer.

Lesson Summary

In this lesson you learned that a user profile is a collection of folders and data that stores the user's current desktop environment and application settings, as well as personal data. A user profile also contains all of the network connections that are established when a user logs on to a computer, such as Start menu items and mapped drives to network servers.

You learned that there are three types of user profiles: local user profiles, roaming user profiles, and mandatory user profiles. A local user profile is created the first time you log on to a computer and is stored on a computer's local hard disk. Any changes made to your local user profile are specific to the computer on which you make the changes. A roaming user profile is created by your system administrator and is stored on a server. This profile is available every time you log on to any computer on the network. Changes made to your roaming user profile are updated on the server. A mandatory user profile is a roaming profile that can be used to specify particular settings for individuals or an entire group of users. Only system administrators can make changes to mandatory user profiles.

In the practice portion of this lesson, you created a local user account and profile and then viewed, defined, and tested the profile. You also created a standard roaming user profile, which included creating a user account model for use as a profile template, copying the profile template to a shared folder in the server, and specifying the path to the profile for the user.

Lesson 5: Creating Home Directories

Although the My Documents folder is the default location for users to store their personal documents, Windows 2000 provides another location for storage. This additional location is the user's home directory.

After this lesson, you will be able to

- Manage home directories

Estimated lesson time: 5 minutes

Introducing Home Directories

A *home directory* is an additional folder that you can provide for users to store personal documents, and, for older applications, it is sometimes the default folder for saving documents. You can store a home directory on a client computer or in a shared folder on a file server. Because a home directory is not part of a roaming user profile, its size does not affect network traffic during the logon process. You can locate all users' home directories in a central location on a network server.

Storing all home directories on a file server provides the following advantages:

- Users can gain access to their home directories from any client computer on the network.
- The backing up and administration of user documents is centralized.
- The home directories are accessible from a client computer running any Microsoft operating system (including MS-DOS, Windows 95, Windows 98, and Windows 2000).

Note   You should store home directories on a Windows NT file system (NTFS) volume so that you can use NTFS permissions to secure user documents. If you store home directories on a file allocation table (FAT) volume, you can only restrict home directory access by using shared folder permissions.

Creating Home Directories on a Server

To successfully complete the tasks for creating home directories, you must have permission to administer the object in which the user accounts reside. To create a home directory on a network file server, you must perform the following tasks:

1. Create and share a folder in which to store all home directories on a network server. The home directory for each user will reside in this shared folder.
2. For the shared folder, remove the default permission Full Control from the Everyone group and assign Full Control to the Users group. This ensures that only users with domain user accounts can gain access to the shared folder.

3. Provide the path to the user's home directory folder in the shared home directory folder in the Profile tab of the Properties dialog box (see Figure 7.12) for the user account. Because the home directory is on a network server, click Connect and specify a drive letter to use to connect. In the To box, specify a UNC name, for example, *server_name**shared_folder_ name**user_ logon_name*. Type the *%username%* variable as the user's logon name to automatically name each user's home directory as the user logon name. For example, type **\\server_name\Users\%username%**.

Figure 7.12 Specifying a path to a home directory folder

If you use *%username%* to name a folder on an NTFS volume, the user is assigned the NTFS Full Control permission and all other permissions are removed for the folder, including those for the Administrator account.

Lesson Summary

In addition to the My Documents folder, Windows 2000 provides you with the means to create a home directory for users to store their personal documents. You can create a home directory on a client computer or in a shared folder on a file server. Because a home directory is not part of a roaming user profile, its size does not affect network traffic during the logon process.

Storing all home directories on a file server provides several advantages. The first advantage is that users can gain access to their home directories from any client computer on the network. The second advantage is that backup and administration of user documents is centralized. Another advantage is that home directories are accessible from client computers running any Microsoft operating system (including MS-DOS, Windows 95, Windows 98, and Windows 2000).

Lesson 6: Maintaining User Accounts

The needs of your organization may require you to modify user accounts. Other modifications are based on personnel changes or personal information. These include disabling, enabling, and deleting a user account. You may also need to unlock a user account or reset a user's password. This lesson takes you step-by-step through disabling, enabling, deleting, and unlocking user accounts and resetting user passwords.

Note To modify a user account, you make changes to the user account object in Active Directory. To successfully complete the tasks for modifying user accounts you must have permission to administer the object in which the user accounts reside.

After this lesson, you will be able to

- Disable, enable, rename, and delete user accounts
- Reset user passwords
- Unlock user accounts

Estimated lesson time: 30 minutes

Disabling, Enabling, Renaming, and Deleting User Accounts

Modifications that you make to user accounts that affect the functionality of the user accounts include the following:

- **Disabling and enabling a user account.** You disable a user account when a user does not need an account for an extended period, but will need it again. For example, if John takes a two-month leave of absence, you would disable his user account when he leaves. When he returns, you would enable his user account so that he could log on to the network again.

- **Renaming a user account.** You rename a user account when you want to retain all rights, permissions, and group memberships for the user account and reassign it to a different user. For example, if there is a new company accountant replacing an accountant who has left the company, rename the account by changing the first, last, and user logon names to those of the new accountant.

- **Deleting a user account.** Delete a user account when an employee leaves the company and you are not going to rename the user account. By deleting these user accounts, you do not have unused accounts in Active Directory.

The procedures for disabling, enabling, renaming, and deleting user accounts are very similar.

► **To disable, enable, rename, and delete user accounts**

1. In the Active Directory Users and Computers console, expand the console tree until the appropriate user account is visible, and then select the user account.

2. On the Action menu, click the command for the type of modification that you want to make (see Figure 7.13).

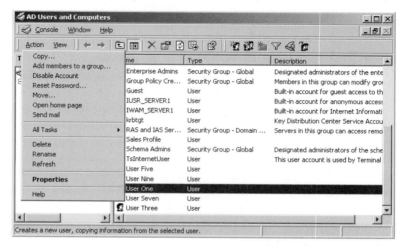

Figure 7.13   Disabling, enabling, deleting, or renaming user accounts

---

Note   If a user account is enabled, the Action menu displays the Disable Account command. If a user account is disabled, the Action menu displays the Enable Account command.

Resetting Passwords and Unlocking User Accounts

If a user cannot log on to the domain or to a local computer because of a password problem, you might need to reset the user's password or unlock the user's account. To perform these tasks, you must have administrative privileges for the object in which the user account resides.

Resetting Passwords

If a user's password expires before he or she can change it, or if a user forgets his or her password, you need to reset the password. You do not need to know the old password to reset a password.

After the password has been set for a user account, either by the administrator or by the user, the password is not visible to any user, including the administrator. This improves security by preventing users, including the administrator, from learning another user's password. If passwords were readable, an administrator could look up a user's password, reset the password, and then log on as that user. After the administrator was through impersonating the user, the administrator could log back on and change the user's password back to what it was.

▶ **To reset user passwords**

1. In the Active Directory Users and Computers console, expand the console tree until the appropriate user account is visible, and then select the user account.

2. On the Action menu, click Reset Password.

   The Reset Password dialog box appears.

3. Enter a new password for the user, confirm the password, and click OK.

In the Reset Password dialog box, you should always select User Must Change Password At Next Logon to force the user to change his or her password the next time he or she logs on.

Note   If a user logs on through the Internet only, do not select the User Must Change Password At Next Logon option.

Unlocking User Accounts

A Windows 2000 group policy locks out a user account when the user violates the policy—for example, if the user exceeds the limit that a group policy allows for bad logon attempts. When a user account is locked out, Windows 2000 displays an error message. For further information on using group policy, see Chapter 12, "Administering Group Policy."

▶ **To unlock a user's account**

1. In the Active Directory Users and Computers console, expand the console tree until the appropriate user account is visible, and then select the user account, designated with a red "X."

2. On the Action menu, click Properties, and then in the Properties dialog box, click the Account tab.

   Notice that the Account Lock Out check box is selected.

3. Clear the check box and click OK.

Practice: Administering User Accounts

In this practice you work with disabling and enabling a user account and learn how to reset the password for a user account.

Exercise 1: Enabling a User Account

In this exercise you disable a user account so that it can no longer be used to log on to the domain. You then enable the same account.

▶ **To disable a user account**

1. Log on to your domain as Administrator.
2. Start the Active Directory Users and Computers console.
3. Expand Microsoft.com domain and click Users.
4. In the details pane, right-click the Profile User account you created in Lesson 5, then click Disable Account.

   The Active Directory message box appears, stating that the account has been disabled. The account is also marked with a red "X."

5. Click OK to return to the Active Directory Users and Computers console.
6. In the details pane of the Active Directory Users and Computers console, right-click the user account that you just disabled to display the shortcut menu.

   How can you tell that the user account is disabled?

7. Log off Windows 2000.
8. Attempt to log on as puser.

   Were you successful? Why or why not?

▶ **To enable a user account**

1. Log on to your domain as Administrator.
2. Start the Active Directory Users and Computers console.
3. Expand Microsoft.com domain and click Users.
4. In the details pane, right-click the Profile User account you created, and then click Enable Account.

   The Active Directory message box appears, confirming that the account has been enabled.

5. Click OK to return to the Active Directory Users and Computers console.
6. In the details pane of the Active Directory Users and Computers console, right-click the user account that you just enabled to display the shortcut menu.

   How can you tell that the user account is enabled?

7. Log off Windows 2000.

▶ **To test account enabling and to change the password for a user account**

1. Log on as puser.

   Were you successful? Why or why not?

2. Change your password to **student**.
3. Log off Windows 2000.

Exercise 2: Resetting the Password for a User Account

In this exercise you reset the password for a user account.

▶ **To reset the password for a user account**

1. Log on to your domain as Administrator.
2. Start the Active Directory Users and Computers console.
3. Expand Microsoft.com domain and click Users.
4. In the details pane, right-click the Profile User account, then click Reset Password.

   The Reset Password dialog box appears, prompting you for the new password for this account. Notice that the Administrator account is not able to view the current password.

5. In the New Password box and the Confirm Password box, type **password** and check the box labeled User Must Change Password At Next Logon. Click OK.

   Windows 2000 displays the Active Directory message confirming that the password has been changed.

6. Click OK to return to the Active Directory Users and Computers console.
7. Log off Windows 2000.

▶ **To test password resetting**

1. Log on as puser and type **password** as the password.

   Were you successful? Why or why not?

2. Log off Windows 2000.

Lesson Summary

In this lesson you learned about disabling and enabling user accounts. You disable a user account when a user does not need a user account for an extended period, but will need it again. You enable the account when it is needed again.

You also learned about renaming user accounts and deleting user accounts. You rename a user account when you want to retain all rights, permissions, and group memberships for the user account and reassign it to a different user. You delete a user account when it is no longer needed.

Finally, in this lesson you learned about resetting the password for a user account and enabling a user account that is locked. If a user's password expires before he or she can change it, or if a user forgets his or her password, you need to reset the password so that the user can log on to the domain. You also learned that if a user forgets his or her password and gets locked out of the system, you can log on as Administrator and unlock the account.

In the practice portion of this lesson, you disabled and enabled a user account and reset the password for a user account.

Review

The following questions are intended to reinforce key information presented in the chapter. If you are unable to answer a question, review the appropriate lesson and then try the question again. Answers to the questions can be found in Appendix A, "Questions and Answers."

1. What different capabilities do local user accounts and domain user accounts provide to users?

2. What should you consider when you plan new user accounts?

3. What information is required to create a domain user account?

4. A user wants to gain access to network resources remotely from home. The user does not want to pay the long-distance charges for the telephone call. How would you set up the user account to accomplish this?

5. What is the difference between a local user profile and a roaming user profile?

6. What do you do to ensure that a user on a client computer running Windows 2000 has a roaming user profile?

7. How can you ensure that a user has a centrally located home directory?

8. Why would you rename a user account and what is the advantage of doing so?

CHAPTER 8

Group Account Administration

About This Chapter

Groups simplify administration by organizing user accounts into manageable units. This chapter provides you with a group planning strategy and procedures for creating groups. The hands-on procedures give you an opportunity to plan and implement global and domain local groups for a network. You learn about the default groups provided by Microsoft Windows 2000. Finally, this chapter discusses the groups to which administrators should be assigned and the benefits of using the Run As program to start a program as an administrator while logged on as a user.

Before You Begin

To complete the lessons in this chapter, you must have

- Completed the Setup procedures located in "About This Book"
- The knowledge and skills covered in Chapter 7, "User Account Administration"
- Knowledge about the difference between a workgroup and a domain, and between a domain controller and a member server
- Created the User1, User5, and User9 accounts as directed in Chapter 7

Lesson 1: Introduction to Groups

In this lesson you will learn what groups are and how groups are used to simplify administration tasks. You will also learn the group types and the group scopes you can create in Windows 2000 and how these group types and scopes are used, along with the rules for group membership. Finally, you will learn the purpose of using local groups.

After this lesson, you will be able to

- Explain the purpose of groups
- Explain the purpose of security and distribution group types
- Explain the purpose of domain local, global, and universal group scopes
- Explain the purpose of local groups

Estimated lesson time: 15 minutes

Groups and Permissions

A *group* is a collection of user accounts. Groups simplify administration by allowing you to assign permissions and rights to a group of users rather than having to assign permissions and rights to each individual user account (see Figure 8.1).

Permissions control what users can do with a resource, such as a folder, file, or printer. When you assign permissions, you give users the capability to gain access to a resource and define the type of access that they have. For example, if several users need to read the same file, you would add their user accounts to a group. Then, you would give the group permission to read the file. *Rights* allow users to perform system tasks, such as changing the time on a computer, backing up or restoring files, or logging on locally.

- Groups are a collection of user accounts.
- Members receive permissions given to groups.
- Users can be members of multiple groups.
- Groups can be members of other groups.

Figure 8.1   Groups simplify administration

Note For detailed information about Permissions, see Chapter 9, "Securing Network Resources." For detailed information about rights, see Chapter 13, "Administering a Security Configuration."

In addition to user accounts, you can add other groups, contacts, and computers to groups. You add groups to other groups to create a consolidated group and reduce the number of times that you need to assign permissions. You add computers to groups to simplify giving a system task on one computer access to a resource on another computer.

Group Types

Sometimes you create groups for security-related purposes, such as assigning permissions. Other times you use them for nonsecurity purposes, such as sending e-mail messages. To facilitate this, Windows 2000 includes two group types: *security* and *distribution*. The group type determines how you use the group. Both types of groups are stored in the database component of Active Directory, which allows you to use them anywhere in your network.

Security Groups

Windows 2000 uses only security groups, which you use to assign permissions to gain access to resources. Programs that are designed to search Active Directory can also use security groups for nonsecurity-related purposes, such as retrieving user information for use in a Web application. A security group also has all the capabilities of a distribution group. Because Windows 2000 uses only security groups, this chapter focuses on security groups.

Distribution Groups

Applications use distribution groups as lists for nonsecurity-related functions. Use distribution groups when the only function of the group is nonsecurity-related, such as sending e-mail messages to a group of users at the same time. You cannot use distribution groups to assign permissions.

Note Only programs that are designed to work with Active Directory can use distribution groups. For example, future versions of Microsoft Exchange server will be able to use distribution groups as distribution lists for sending e-mail messages.

Group Scopes

When you create a group you must select a group type and a group scope. *Group scopes* allow you to use groups in different ways to assign permissions. The scope of a group determines where in the network you are able to use the group to assign permissions to the group. The three group scopes are global, domain local, and universal, as shown in Figure 8.2.

Figure 8.2   Group scopes

Global Groups

Global security groups are most often used to organize users who share similar network access requirements. A global group has the following characteristics:

- **Limited membership.**   You can add members only from the domain in which you create the global group.

- **Access to resources in any domain.**   You can use a global group to assign permissions to gain access to resources that are located in any domain in the domain tree or forest.

Domain Local Groups

Domain local security groups are most often used to assign permissions to resources. A domain local group has the following characteristics:

- **Open membership.**   You can add members from any domain.

- **Access to resources in one domain.**   You can use a domain local group to assign permissions to gain access to resources that are located only in the same domain where you create the domain local group.

Universal Groups

Universal security groups are most often used to assign permissions to related resources in multiple domains. A universal security group has the following characteristics:

- **Open membership.**   You can add members from any domain.

- **Access to resources in any domain.**   You can use a universal group to assign permissions to gain access to resources that are located in any domain.

- **Only available in native mode.**   Universal security groups are not available in mixed mode. The full feature set of Windows 2000 is only available in native mode.

Group Nesting

Adding groups to other groups, or *nesting*, creates a consolidated group and can reduce network traffic between domains and simplify administration in a domain tree. For example, you could add the managers in each region to a group that is specific to the group that represents managers in their region. Then, you could add all of the regional manager groups to a worldwide managers group. When all managers need access to resources, you assign permissions only to the world-wide managers group.

Guidelines for group nesting include the following:

- **Minimize levels of nesting.**   Tracking permissions and troubleshooting becomes more complex with multiple levels of nesting. One level of nesting is the most effective to use.

- **Document group membership to keep track of permissions assignments.**   Providing documentation of group membership can eliminate the redundant assignment of user accounts to groups and reduce the likelihood of accidental group assignments.

To efficiently use nesting it is important to understand the membership rules of groups.

Rules for Group Membership

The group scope determines the membership of a group. Membership rules determine the members that a group can contain. Group members can be user accounts and other groups. To assign the correct members to groups and to use nesting, it is important to understand group membership rules.

Table 8.1 describes group membership rules, including what each group scope can contain in native and mixed mode.

Table 8.1   Group Scope Membership Rules

Group Scope	In Native Mode, Scope Can Contain	In Mixed Mode, Scope Can Contain
Global	User accounts and global groups from the same domain	Users from the same domain
Domain local	User accounts, universal groups, and global groups from any domain; domain local groups from the same domain	User accounts and global groups from any domain
Universal	User accounts, other universal groups, and global groups from any domain	Not applicable; universal groups cannot be created in mixed mode

Local Groups

A *local group* is a collection of user accounts on a computer. Use local groups to assign permissions to resources residing on the computer on which the local group is created. Windows 2000 creates local groups in the local security database.

Caution   Because Active Directory groups with a "domain local" scope are sometimes referred to as "local groups," it is important to distinguish between a local group and a group with a domain local scope.

Using Local Groups

The following are guidelines for using local groups:

- You can use local groups only on the computer where you create the local groups. Local group permissions provide access to only the resources on the computer where you created the local group.

- You can use local groups on computers running Windows 2000 Professional and member servers running Windows 2000 Server. Local groups cannot be created on domain controllers because domain controllers cannot have a security database that is independent of the database in Active Directory.

- Use local groups to limit the ability of local users and groups to gain access to network resources without creating domain groups, such as in an Internet Information Server environment.

Membership rules for local groups include the following:

- Local groups can contain local user accounts from the computer where you create the local group.

- Local groups cannot be members of any other group.

Lesson Summary

In this lesson you learned that a group is a collection of user accounts. Groups can also contain other groups. Groups simplify administration by allowing you to assign permissions and rights to a group of users rather than having to assign permissions to each individual user account.

You also learned that when you create a group, you must choose a group type and a group scope. Windows 2000 includes two group types, security groups and distribution groups, but uses only security groups. Applications designed to work with Active Directory can use distribution groups as lists for nonsecurity-related functions, such as e-mail. Windows 2000 includes three group scopes: global, domain local, and universal.

You learned that there are rules for group membership. These rules determine the members that a global security group, a domain local security group, and a universal security group can contain.

Finally, you learned how local groups are used to assign permissions to resources residing on the computer on which the local group is created.

Lesson 2: Planning a Group Strategy

To use groups effectively, you need a strategy for using the different group scopes. This lesson presents a strategy for implementing global, domain local, and universal groups.

After this lesson, you will be able to

- Describe the steps of a sound implementation strategy
- Plan a group strategy

Estimated lesson time: 30 minutes

Planning Global and Domain Local Groups

It is important to have a group strategy in place before you create groups. The recommended method is to use global and domain local groups. When you plan to use global and domain local groups, use the following strategy:

1. **Assign users with common job responsibilities to global groups.**   Identify users with common job responsibilities and add the user accounts to a global group. For example, in an accounting department, add user accounts for all accountants to a global group called Accounting.

2. **Create a domain local group for resources to be shared.**   Identify the resources or group of resources, such as related files or printers, to which users need access and then create a domain local group for that resource. For example, if you have a number of color printers in your company, create a domain local group called Color Printers.

3. **Add global groups that need access to the resources to the domain local group.**   Identify all global groups that share the same access needs for resources and make them members of the appropriate domain local group. For example, add the global groups Accounting, Sales, and Management to the domain local group Color Printers.

4. **Assign resource permissions to the domain local group.**   Assign the required permissions for the resource to the domain local group. For example, assign the necessary permissions to use color printers to the Color Printers group. Users in the Accounting, Sales, and Management global groups receive the required permissions because their global group is a member of the domain local group Color Printers.

Figure 8.3 illustrates the strategy for using groups: Place user accounts into global groups, create a domain local group for a group of resources to be shared in common, place the global groups into the domain local group, and then assign permissions to the domain local group. This strategy gives you the most flexibility for growth and reduces permissions assignments.

Figure 8.3   Planning a group strategy

Some of the possible limitations of other strategies include the following:

- **Placing user accounts in domain local groups and assigning permissions to the domain local groups.**   This strategy does not allow you to assign permissions for resources outside of the domain. This strategy reduces the flexibility when your network grows.
- **Placing user accounts in global groups and assigning permissions to the global groups.**   This strategy can complicate administration when you are using multiple domains. If global groups from multiple domains require the same permissions, you have to assign permissions for each global group.

Using Universal Groups

When you plan to use universal groups, follow these guidelines:

- Use universal groups to give users access to resources that are located in more than one domain. Unlike domain local groups, you can assign permissions to universal groups for resources in any domain in your network. For example, if executives need access to printers throughout your network, you can create a universal group for this purpose and assign it permissions for using printers on print servers in all domains.
- Use universal groups only when their membership is static. In a domain tree, universal groups can cause excessive network traffic between domain controllers whenever you change membership for the universal group because changes to the membership of universal groups may be replicated to a larger number of domain controllers.
- Add global groups from several domains to a universal group, and then assign permissions for access to a resource to the universal group. This allows you to use a universal group in the same way as domain local groups to assign permissions for resources. However, unlike a domain local group, you can assign permissions to a universal group to give users access to a resource that is located in any domain.

Practice: Planning New Group Accounts

In this practice you plan the groups that are required for a business scenario.

Scenario

You are an administrator for the customer service division of a manufacturing company. You administer a domain that is part of your company's domain tree. You do not administer other domains, but you may have to give selected user accounts from other domains access to resources in your domain. Users at the company use several shared network resources. The company is also planning to implement an e-mail program that uses Active Directory.

As the administrator, you must determine the following:

- Which groups are needed.
- The membership of each group. This can be user accounts or other groups.
- The type and scope for each group.

Record your planning strategies on the Group Planning Worksheet. Follow these instructions to complete the worksheet:

1. On the worksheet, provide a name for each group. Record each name in the Group Name column.
2. Specify type and scope of the group.
3. List the members of the group.

After completing the exercise, turn to Appendix A, Chapter 8 and compare your worksheet to the sample provided. The sample presents only one set of possible answers. You may have planned your accounts differently.

Table 8.2 provides the job function and number of employees in each job function in the customer service division.

Table 8.2   Customer Service Division Employee Information

Job Function	Number of Employees
Product tester	20
Customer service representative	250
Maintenance worker	5
Manager	5
Sales representative	5
Network administrator	2

Table 8.3 lists the information access requirements for the classes of employees.

Table 8.3   Employee Information Access Requirements

Employee	Need Access To
Customer service representatives and managers	Customer database, full access
Sales representatives	Customer database, read-only access
All employees	Company policies, read-only access
All employees	Receive company announcements through e-mail
Any employees in any domain who are interested in these topics	Receive periodic announcements through e-mail about manufacturing topics
All employees, except maintenance workers	Shared installation of Microsoft Office
Network administrators	Full access to all resources in the company
Sales representatives from your domain and all other domains	Sales reports

Group Accounts Planning Worksheet

Group Name	Type and Scope	Members

1. Does your network require local groups?

2. Does your network require universal groups?

3. Sales representatives at the company frequently visit the company headquarters and other divisions. Therefore, you need to give sales representatives with user accounts in other domains the same permissions for resources that sales representatives in your domain have. You also want to make it easy for administrators in other domains to assign permissions to sales representatives in your domain. How can you accomplish this?

Lesson Summary

In this lesson you learned a couple of common group strategies. The group strategy you choose depends on your Windows 2000 network environment. In a single domain, the best strategy is to use global and domain local groups to assign permissions to network resources, and this is Microsoft's recommendation for most Windows 2000 installations.

You also learned that the strategy for using global and domain local groups is to place user accounts into global groups. You then create a domain local group for a group of resources to be shared in common, and place the global groups into the domain local group. Finally, you assign permissions to the domain local group. This strategy gives you the most flexibility for growth and reduces permissions assignments.

Lesson 3: Creating Groups

After you assess user needs and have a group plan in place, you are ready to create your groups. To implement your group plan, you should be familiar with the guidelines for creating groups. This lesson shows you how to create groups, delete groups, add members to groups, and change the group type and scope.

After this lesson, you will be able to

- Create and delete groups
- Add members to groups
- Change group type and scope

Estimated lesson time: 25 minutes

Creating and Deleting Groups

Use the Active Directory Users and Computers console to create and delete groups. When you create groups, create them in the Users container or in another container or an organizational unit (OU) that you have created specifically for groups. As your organization grows and changes, you may discover that there are groups that you no longer need. Be sure that you delete groups when you no longer need them. This will help you maintain security so that you do not accidentally assign permissions for accessing resources to groups that you no longer need.

▶ **To create a group**

1. Click Start, point to Programs, point to Administrative Tools, then click Active Directory Users And Computers.

2. Click the domain, right-click the Users container, point to New, and click Group.

3. Complete the New Object-Group dialog box (shown in Figure 8.4) and click OK.

Table 8.4 describes the options in the New Object-Group dialog box in the Active Directory Users and Computers console.

Table 8.4   Options in the New Object-Group Dialog Box

Option	Description
Group Name	The name of the new group. The object name must be unique in the domain where you create the group.
Group Name (pre-Windows 2000)	The name of the group from prior versions of Windows, such as Microsoft Windows NT 4.0 or Microsoft Windows NT 3.5.1. This is filled in automatically for you based on the group name you type in.
Group Scope	The group scope. Click Domain Local, Global, or Universal.
Group Type	The type of group. Click Security or Distribution.

Figure 8.4   New Object-Group dialog box

Deleting a Group

Each group that you create has a unique, nonreusable identifier called the security identifier (SID). Windows 2000 uses the SID to identify the group and the permissions that are assigned to it. When you delete a group, Windows 2000 does not use the SID for that group again, even if you create a new group with the same name as the group that you deleted. Therefore, you cannot restore access to resources by recreating the group.

When you delete a group, you delete only the group and remove the permissions and rights that are associated with it. Deleting a group does not delete the user accounts that are members of the group.

Note   You cannot delete a group if one of the group's members has the group set as his or her primary group.

▶ **To delete a group**

1. Right-click the group, then click Delete.
2. Click Yes on the Active Directory message box.

Adding Members to a Group

After you create a group, you add members. Members of groups can include user accounts, contacts, other groups, and computers. You can add a computer to a group to give one computer access to a shared resource on another computer—for example, for remote backup. To add members, use the Active Directory Users and Computers console.

▶ **To add members to a group**

1. Start the Active Directory Users and Computers console and expand Users.

2. Right-click the appropriate group, then click Properties.

3. In the Properties dialog box, click the Members tab, then click Add.

4. The Select Users, Contacts, Computers, Or Groups dialog box appears, as shown in Figure 8.5.

Figure 8.5   The Select Users, Contacts, Computers, Or Groups dialog box

5. In the Look In list you can select a domain from which to display user accounts and groups, or you can select Entire Directory to view user accounts and groups from anywhere in Active Directory. In the Name column, select an object that you want to add and click Add.

   The accounts you have selected are listed in the box at the bottom of the Select Users, Contacts, Computers, Or Groups dialog box.

Note   If there are multiple user accounts or groups that you want to add, you can repeat the process of selecting them one at a time and then click Add, or you can hold down the Shift or Ctrl key to select multiple user accounts or groups at a time. The Shift key allows you to select a consecutive range of accounts and the Ctrl key allows you to select specific accounts that you wish to add.

6. Review the accounts to make sure that they are the accounts you wish to add to the group and click OK to add the members.

7. On the Properties dialog box, click OK.

Note   You can also add a user account or group by using the Member Of tab in the Properties dialog box for that user account or group. Use this method to quickly add the same user or group to multiple groups.

Changing the Group Type

As group functions change, you may need to change a group type. For example, suppose a distribution group contains members from multiple departments working on the same project for the purpose of sending e-mail. As the project progresses, it becomes necessary for the members to access a common database. By converting the distribution group to a security group and assigning permissions to the group, you can provide the project members with access to the common database. Group types may be changed only when Windows 2000 is operating in native mode.

▶ **To change group type**

1. Right-click the group, then click Properties.

2. Change the group type in the General tab of the Properties dialog box for the group.

Changing the Group Scope to Universal

As your network changes, you may need to change a global or domain local group scope to universal. For example, you may want to change an existing domain local group to a universal group when you need to assign permissions to allow users to gain access to resources in other domains. Group scopes may be changed to universal only when Windows 2000 is operating in native mode.

The following group scopes can be changed:

■ A global group to a universal group, but only if the global group is not a member of another global group

■ A domain local group to a universal group, but only if the domain local group does not contain another domain local group

Note   Windows 2000 does not allow changing the scope of a universal group because usage and membership rules for other groups are more restrictive.

▶ **To change the scope of a group**

1. Right-click the group, then click Properties.

2. Change the group scope in the General tab of the Properties dialog box for the group.

Creating Local Groups

Use the Local Users and Groups snap-in within the Computer Management console to create local groups. You create local groups in the Groups folder.

▶ **To create a local group**

1. Click Start, point to Programs, point to Administrative Tools, and then click Computer Management. For Windows 2000 Professional, click Start, point to Settings, and open the Control Panel.

2. Expand the Local Users and Groups snap-in, right-click Groups, and select New Group.

3. Complete the New Group dialog box (shown in Figure 8.6), then click OK.

Figure 8.6   New Group dialog box

Table 8.5 describes the options presented in the New Group dialog box in the Local Users and Groups snap-in.

Table 8.5   Options in the New Group Dialog Box

Option	Description
Group Name	A unique name for the local group. This is the only required entry. Use any character except for the backslash (\). The name can contain up to 256 characters; however, very long names may not display in some windows.
Description	A description of the group.
Members	Members of the local group.
Add	Adds a user or global group to the list of members.

Table 8.5   Options in the New Group Dialog Box *(continued)*

Option	Description
Remove	Removes a user or global group from the list of members.
Create	Creates the group.

You can add members to a local group when you create the group or after you create the local group.

▶ **To delete a local group**

1. Right-click the group, then click Delete.

2. Click Yes on the Local Users and Groups message box.

▶ **To add members to a local group**

1. Expand the Local Users and Groups snap-in, then expand Groups.

2. Right-click the appropriate group, then click Properties.

3. In the Properties dialog box, click Add.

4. The Select Users Or Groups dialog box appears, as shown in Figure 8.7.

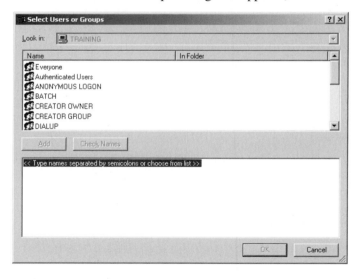

Figure 8.7   The Select Users Or Groups dialog box

5. The Look In list shows the computer for which you are creating a group. Select the user account that you want to add, then click Add.

6. Review the accounts to make sure that they are the accounts you wish to add to the group, then click OK to add the members.

7. On the Properties dialog box, click OK.

Practice: Creating Groups

In this practice you create a global security group. You then add members to the group. To add members to the group, you add two user accounts, User1 and User5, which you created previously. Next you create a domain local security group that you use to assign permissions to gain access to the sales reports. Finally, you provide access to the sales reports for the members of the security global group by adding the global group to the domain local group.

Exercise 1: Creating a Global Group and Adding Members

In this exercise you create a global security group and add members to the group.

▶ **To create a global group in a domain**

1. Log on to your domain as Administrator.
2. Click Start, point to Programs, point to Administrative Tools, then click Active Directory Users And Computers.
3. Expand your domain and double-click Users.

   In the details pane, Active Directory Users and Computers displays a list of current user accounts and built-in global groups.
4. Right-click the Users container, point to New, then click Group.

   The New Object-Group dialog box appears. Notice the different group scopes and types that are available. You use global security groups to group user accounts.
5. Type **Sales** in the Group Name box.
6. Select Global under Group Scope and select Security under Group Type.
7. Click OK.

   Windows 2000 creates the group and adds it to the Users container.

▶ **To add members to a global group**

1. In the details pane of Active Directory Users and Computers, double-click Sales.

   The Sales Properties dialog box displays the properties of the group.
2. To view the members of the group, click the Members tab.

   The Sales Properties dialog box displays a list of group members. This list is currently empty.
3. To add a member to a group, click Add.
4. In the Select Users, Contacts, Or Computers dialog box, in the Look In list, ensure that your domain is selected.
5. In the list, select User One, then click Add.
6. In the list, select User Five, then click Add.

7. Click OK.

    User One and User Five are now members of the Sales security global group.

8. Click OK to close the Sales Properties dialog box.

Exercise 2: Creating a Domain Local Group and Adding Members

In this exercise you create a domain local group that you use to assign permissions to gain access to sales reports. Because you use the group to assign permissions, you make it a domain local group. You then add members to the group by adding the security global group you created in Exercise 1.

▶ **To create a domain local group in a domain**

1. Make sure that Active Directory Users and Computers is open with the Users container selected in the console tree.

2. Right-click the Users container, point to New, then click Group.

    The New Object-Group dialog box appears.

3. In the Group Name box, type **Reports**.

4. Select Domain Local under Group Scope and select Security under Group Type.

5. Click OK.

    Windows 2000 creates the domain local group and adds it to the Users container.

▶ **To add members to a domain local group**

1. In the details pane of Active Directory Users and Computers, double-click Reports.

    The Reports Properties dialog box displays the properties of the Reports group.

2. To view the members of the group, click the Members tab.

    The Reports Properties dialog box displays a list of group members. This list is currently empty.

3. To add a member to the group, click Add.

4. In the Select Users, Contacts, Computers, Or Groups dialog box, in the Look In list, select Entire Directory.

    The Select Users, Contacts, Computers, Or Groups dialog box displays available objects that can be part of the group and shows the location of each object as *domain*/Users.

5. Above the list of user accounts, groups, and computers, click Name.

    Active Directory Users and Computers sorts all entries in the list alphabetically by name.

6. Click the Sales group, click Add, then click OK.

   The Sales global group is now a member of the Reports domain local group.

7. Click OK to close the Reports Properties dialog box.

Lesson Summary

In this lesson you learned some important guidelines for creating groups. First you should determine the required group scope based on how you want to use the group. Then you should determine if you have the necessary permissions to create a group in the appropriate domain. By default, in a domain, members of the Administrators group or the Account Operators group have the necessary permissions to create groups. An administrator can give a user the permission to create groups in the domain or in a single container or OU.

You also learned that you use the Active Directory Users and Computers console to create, delete, add members to, and change the group scope and type for global, domain local, and universal groups. You use the Local Users and Groups snap-in in the Computer Management console to create, delete, and add members to local groups.

In the practice portion of this lesson, you created a global security group and added members to it. You then created a domain local security group and added members by adding the global security group you created.

Lesson 4: Understanding Default Groups

Windows 2000 has four categories of default groups: predefined, built-in, built-in local, and special identity. Default groups have a predetermined set of user rights or group membership. User rights determine the system tasks that a user or member of a default group can perform. This lesson explains how default groups are used.

After this lesson, you will be able to

- Describe the Windows 2000 default groups

Estimated lesson time: 15 minutes

Predefined Groups

Windows 2000 creates predefined groups with a global scope to group common types of user accounts. By default, Windows 2000 automatically adds members to some predefined global groups. You can add user accounts to these predefined groups to provide additional users with the privileges and permissions that you assign to the group.

When you create a domain, Windows 2000 creates predefined global groups in the Users folder in Active Directory. By default, these predefined groups do not have any inherent rights. You assign rights by either adding the global groups to domain local groups or explicitly assigning user rights or permissions to the predefined global groups.

The Users container contains the predefined global groups in a domain. Table 8.6 describes the default membership of the most commonly used predefined global groups.

Table 8.6   Default Membership of Commonly Used Predefined Global Groups

Predefined Global Group	Description
Domain Admins	Windows 2000 automatically adds Domain Admins to the Administrators built-in domain local group so that members of Domain Admins can perform administrative tasks on any computer anywhere in the domain. By default, the Administrator account is a member.
Domain Guests	Windows 2000 automatically adds Domain Guests to the Guests built-in domain local group. By default, the Guest account is a member.
Domain Users	Windows 2000 automatically adds Domain Users to the Users built-in domain local group. By default, the Administrator, Guest IUSR_*computername*, IWAM_*computername*, Krbtgt, and TsInternetUser accounts are initially members, and each new domain user account is automatically a member.

Predefined Global Group	Description
Enterprise Admins	You can add user accounts to Enterprise Admins for users who should have administrative control for the entire network. Then, add Enterprise Admins to the Administrators domain local group in each domain. By default, the Administrator account is a member.

Built-In Groups

Windows 2000 creates built-in groups with a domain local scope in the Builtin folder in Active Directory. These groups provide users with user rights and permissions to perform tasks on domain controllers and in Active Directory. Built-in domain local groups give predefined rights and permissions to user accounts when you add user accounts or global groups as members.

The Builtin container holds the built-in domain local groups in a domain. Table 8.7 describes the most commonly used built-in domain local groups and the capabilities that the members have.

Table 8.7   Commonly Used Built-In Domain Local Global Groups

Built-In Domain Local Group	Description
Account Operators	Members can create, delete, and modify user accounts and groups; members cannot modify the Administrators group or any of the operators groups.
Administrators	Members can perform all administrative tasks on all domain controllers and the domain itself. By default, the Administrator user account and the Domain Admins and Enterprise Admins predefined global groups are members.
Backup Operators	Members can back up and restore all domain controllers by using Windows Backup.
Guests	Members can perform only tasks for which you have granted rights; members can gain access only to resources for which you have assigned permissions; members cannot make permanent changes to their desktop environment. By default, the Guest, IUSR_*computername*, IWAM_*computername*, and TsInternetUser user accounts and the Domain Guests predefined global group are members.
Pre-Windows 2000 Compatible Access	A backward compatibility group that allows read access for all users and groups in the domain. By default, only the Everyone pre-Windows 2000 system group is a member.
Print Operators	Members can set up and manage network printers on domain controllers.
Replicator	Supports directory replication functions. The only member should be a domain user account used to log on to the Replicator services of the domain controller. Do not add the accounts of actual users to this group.

Table 8.7   Commonly Used Built-In Domain Local Global Groups *(continued)*

Built-In Domain Local Group	Description
Server Operators	Members can share disk resources and back up and restore files on a domain controller.
Users	Members can perform only tasks for which you have granted rights, and gain access only to resources for which you have assigned permissions. By default, the Authenticated Users and INTERACTIVE pre-Windows 2000 groups and the Domain Users pre-defined global group are members. Use this group to assign permissions and rights that every user with a user account in your domain should have.

Built-In Local Groups

All stand-alone servers, member servers, and computers running Windows 2000 Professional have built-in local groups. Built-in local groups give users the rights to perform system tasks on a single computer, such as backing up and restoring files, changing the system time, and administering system resources. Windows 2000 places the built-in local groups into the Groups folder in the Local User Manager snap-in.

Table 8.8 describes the capabilities that members of the most commonly used built-in local groups have. Except where noted, there are no initial members in these groups.

Table 8.8   Commonly Used Built-In Local Groups

Built-In Local Group	Description
Administrators	Members can perform all administrative tasks on the computer. By default, the built-in Administrator user account for the computer is a member. When a member server or computer running Windows 2000 Professional joins a domain, Windows 2000 adds the Domain Admins predefined global group to the local Administrators group.
Backup Operators	Members can use Windows Backup to back up and restore the computer.
Guests	Members can perform only tasks for which you have specifically granted rights, and can gain access only to resources for which you have assigned permissions; members cannot make permanent changes to their desktop environment. By default, the built-in Guest account for the computer is a member. When a member server or a computer running Windows 2000 Professional joins a domain, Windows 2000 adds the Domain Guests predefined global group to the local guests group.
Power Users	Members can create and modify local user accounts on the computer and share resources.

Built-In Local Group	Description
Replicator	Supports directory replication functions. The only member should be a domain user account used to log on to the Replicator services of the domain controller. Do not add the accounts of actual users to this group.
Users	Members can perform only tasks for which you have specifically granted rights, and can gain access only to resources for which you have assigned permissions. By default, Windows 2000 adds local user accounts that you create on the computer to the Users group. When a member server or a computer running Windows 2000 Professional joins a domain, Windows 2000 adds the Domain Users predefined global group to the local Users group.

Special Identity Groups

Special identity groups exist on all computers running Windows 2000. These groups do not have specific memberships that you can modify, but they can represent different users at different times, depending on how a user gains access to a computer or resource. You do not see special identity groups when you administer groups, but they are available for use when you assign rights and permissions to resources. Windows 2000 bases special identity group membership on how the computer is accessed, not on who uses the computer. Table 8.9 describes the most commonly used special identity groups.

Table 8.9   Commonly Used Special Identity Groups

Special Identity Group	Description
Anonymous Logon	Includes any user account that Windows 2000 did not authenticate.
Authenticated Users	Includes all users with a valid user account on the computer or in Active Directory. Use the Authenticated Users group instead of the Everyone group to prevent anonymous access to a resource.
Creator Owner	Includes the user account for the user who created or took ownership of a resource. If a member of the Administrators group creates a resource, the Administrators group is owner of the resource.
Dialup	Includes any user who currently has a dial-up connection.
Everyone	Includes all users who access the computer. Be careful if you assign permissions to the Everyone group and enable the Guest account. Windows 2000 will authenticate a user who does not have a valid user account as Guest. The user automatically gets all rights and permissions that you have assigned to the Everyone group. The Everyone group is assigned full control to many resources by default.

Table 8.9   Commonly Used Special Identity Groups *(continued)*

Special Identity Group	Description
Interactive	Includes the user account for the user who is logged on at the computer. Members of the Interactive group gain access to resources on the computer at which they are physically located. They log on and gain access to resources by "interacting" with the computer.
Network	Includes any user with a current connection from another computer on the network to a shared resource on the computer.

Lesson Summary

In this lesson you learned that Windows 2000 has four categories of default groups: predefined, built-in, built-in local, and special identity. You also learned that default groups have a predetermined set of user rights or group membership. Windows 2000 creates these groups for you so you don't have to create groups and assign rights and permissions for commonly used functions.

Lesson 5: Groups for Administrators

For optimum security, Microsoft recommends that you do not assign administrators to the Administrators group and that you avoid running your computer while logged on as an administrator. This lesson examines reasons why you should not run your computer as an administrator, and the actions you should take to ensure security for administrators.

After this lesson, you will be able to

- Explain why you should not run your computer as an administrator
- Explain the groups administrators should use to log on
- Explain how to use Run As to start a program as an administrator

Estimated lesson time: 15 minutes

Why You Should Not Run Your Computer as an Administrator

Running Windows 2000 as an administrator or a member of one of the administrative groups makes the network vulnerable to Trojan horse attacks and other security risks. The simple act of visiting an Internet site can be extremely damaging to the system. An unfamiliar Internet site may contain Trojan horse code that can be downloaded to the system and executed. If you are logged on with administrator privileges, a Trojan horse could possibly reformat your hard drive, delete all files, create a new user account with administrative access, and so on.

Therefore, you should not assign yourself to the Administrators group and you should avoid running nonadministrative tasks on your computer while logged on as an administrator. For most computer activity, you should assign yourself to the Users or Power Users group. Then, if you need to perform an administrator-only task, you should log on as an administrator, or run the program as the administrator, perform the task, and then log off.

Administrators as Members of the Users and Power Users Groups

When you log on as a member of the Users group, you can perform routine tasks, including running programs and visiting Internet sites, without exposing your computer to unnecessary risk. As a member of the Power Users group, you can perform routine tasks and install programs, add printers, and use most Control Panel items. If you need to perform administrative tasks such as upgrading the operating system or configuring system parameters, then log off and log back on as an administrator.

If you frequently need to log on as an administrator, for certain administrative tasks you can use Run As to start a program as an administrator.

Using Run As to Start a Program

To run a program that requires you to be logged on as an administrator, you can use the Run As program. This program allows you to run administrative tools with either local or domain administrator rights and permissions while logged on as a normal user.

The Run As program can be used to start any program, program shortcut, saved MMC console, or Control Panel item, as long as

- You provide the appropriate user account and password information
- The user account has the ability to log on to the computer
- The program, MMC tool, or Control Panel item is available on the system and to the user account

Some applications, such as Windows Explorer, the Printers folder, and desktop items are started indirectly by Windows 2000 and therefore cannot be started with the Run As program.

▶ **To use Run As to start a program as an administrator**

1. In Windows Explorer, click the program or its shortcut, MMC console, or Control Panel item you want to open.

2. Press Shift and right-click the program, tool, or item; then click Run As.

3. On the Run As Other User dialog box (see Figure 8.8), click Run The Program As The Following User.

Figure 8.8   Run As Other User dialog box

4. In the User Name and Password boxes, type the user name and password of the administrator account you want to use.

5. In the Domain box:

   ▪ If you want to use the local administrator account on your computer, type the name of your computer.

   ▪ If you want to use the domain administrator account on your computer, type the name of the domain.

6. Click OK.

If you attempt to start a program, MMC console, or Control Panel item from a network location using the Run As program, it may fail if the credentials used to connect to the network share are different from the credentials used to start the program. The credentials used to run the program may not be able to gain access to the same network share.

If the Run As program fails, the RunAs service may not be running. You can set the RunAs service to start automatically when the system starts using the RunAs Service option in the Services console.

Note Run As is usually used to run programs as an administrator, although it is not limited to administrator accounts. Any user with multiple accounts can use Run As to run a program, MMC tool, or Control Panel item with alternate credentials.

You can also set a property on shortcuts to programs and MMC tools so that you will always be prompted for alternate credentials when you use the shortcut. To set the property, right-click the shortcut, click Properties, and then click the Run As Different User check box. When you start the shortcut, the Run As Other User dialog box appears, prompting you for the alternate user name, password, and domain as described previously.

RUNAS Command

The RUNAS command performs the same functions as the Run As program. The syntax for the RUNAS command is as follows:

```
runas [/profile] [/env] [/netonly] /user:UserAccountName program
```

where:

- **/profile** specifies the name of the user's profile, if it needs to be loaded.

- **/env** specifies that the current network environment be used instead of the user's local environment.

- **/netonly** indicates that the user information specified is for remote access only.

- **/user:***UserAccountName* specifies the name of the user account under which to run the program. The user account format should be *user@domain* or *domain\user*. If you want to use the Administrator account on your computer, for the **/user:** parameter, type **/user:***AdministratorAccountName@ComputerName* or **/user:***ComputerName\AdministratorAccountName*.
  If you want to use this command as a domain administrator, type **/user:***AdministratorAccountName@DomainName* or **/user:***DomainName\AdministratorAccountName*.

- **/program** specifies the program or command to run using the account specified in /user.

RUNAS Examples

- To start an instance of the Windows 2000 command prompt as an administrator on the local computer, type:

```
runas /user:localmachinename\administrator cmd
```

When prompted, type the administrator password.

- To start an instance of the Computer Management snap-in using a domain administrator account called companydomain\domainadmin, type:

```
runas /user:companydomain\domainadmin
"mmc %windir%\system32\compmgmt.msc"
```

When prompted, type the account password.

- To start an instance of Notepad using a domain administrator account called user in a domain called domain.microsoft.com, type:

```
runas /user:user@domain.microsoft.com "notepad my_file.txt"
```

When prompted, type the account password.

- To start an instance of a command prompt window, saved MMC console, Control Panel item, or program that will administer a server in another forest, type:

```
runas /netonly /user:domain\username "command"
```

domain\username must be a user with sufficient permissions to administer the server. When prompted, type the account password. In this same situation, you can also type:

```
runas /user:username@domain.mycompany.com program.exe
```

Practice: Using Run As
to Start a Program as an Administrator

In this practice you log on as User9, created in the previous chapter. Then, using Run As, you start the Active Directory Users and Computers console as a domain administrator.

▶ **To use Run As to start a program as an administrator**

1. Log on as User9.

2. Click Start, point to Programs, point to Administrative Tools, and point to (do not click on) Active Directory Users And Computers.

3. Press Shift and right-click Active Directory Users And Computers; then click Run As.

4. On the Run As Other User dialog box, click Run The Program As The Following User.

5. In the User Name box, ensure that Administrator appears.

6. In the Password box, type your administrator password.

7. In the Domain box, type **microsoft.com** (or the name of your domain).

8. Click OK.

You can now use Active Directory Users and Computers as a domain administrator.

Lesson Summary

In this lesson you learned why you should not run your computer as an administrator. Running Windows 2000 as an administrator makes the system vulnerable to Trojan horse attacks and other security risks. For most computer activity, you should assign yourself to the Users or Power Users group. Then, if you need to perform an administrator-only task, you should log on as an administrator, perform the task, and then log off. If you frequently need to log on as an administrator, you can use the Run As program or command.

You learned how the Run As program or command allows you to run administrative tools with either local or domain administrator rights and permissions while logged on as a normal user.

In the practice portion of this lesson, you logged on as a regular user and used the Run As program to start the Active Directory Users and Computers console as a domain administrator.

Review

The following questions are intended to reinforce key information presented in the chapter. If you are unable to answer a question, review the appropriate lesson and then try the question again. Answers to the questions can be found in Appendix A, "Questions and Answers."

1. Why should you use groups?

2. What is the purpose of adding a group to another group?

3. When should you use security groups instead of distribution groups?

4. What strategy should you apply when you use domain local and global groups?

5. Why should you not use local groups on a computer after it becomes a member of a domain?

6. What is the easiest way to give a user complete control over all computers in a domain?

7. Why shouldn't you run your computer as an administrator? What action should you take instead?

8. Suppose the headquarters for this chapter's imaginary manufacturing company has a single domain that is located in Paris. The company has managers who need to access the inventory database to perform their jobs. What would you do to ensure that the managers have the required access to the inventory database?

9. Now suppose the company has a three-domain environment with the root domain in Paris and the other two domains in Australia and North America. Managers from all three domains need access to the inventory database in Paris to perform their jobs. What would you do to ensure that the managers have the required access and that there is a minimum of administration?

C H A P T E R   9

Securing Network Resources

About This Chapter

This chapter introduces you to Microsoft Windows 2000 file system (NTFS) folder and file permissions. You will learn how to assign NTFS folder and file permissions to user accounts and groups, and how moving or copying files and folders affects NTFS file and folder permissions. You will also learn how to troubleshoot common resource access problems.

Before You Begin

To complete the lessons in this chapter, you must have

- Completed the Setup procedures located in "About This Book"
- Completed the exercises and obtained the knowledge and skills covered in Chapter 7, "User Account Administration" and Chapter 8, "Group Account Administration"
- Configured the computer as a domain controller in a domain

Lesson 1: Understanding NTFS Permissions

NTFS permissions are rules associated with objects that regulate which users can gain access to an object and in what manner. This lesson introduces standard NTFS folder and file permissions. It also explores the effects of combining user account and group permissions with file and folder permissions.

After this lesson, you will be able to

- Define standard NTFS folder and file permissions
- Describe the result when multiple NTFS permissions are applied to a resource
- Describe the result when you combine user account and group permissions for a resource

Estimated lesson time: 10 minutes

NTFS Permissions

Use NTFS permissions to specify which users and groups can gain access to files and folders, and what they can do with the contents of the file or folder. NTFS permissions are only available on NTFS volumes. NTFS permissions are not available on volumes that are formatted with the file allocation table (FAT) or FAT32 file systems. NTFS security is effective whether a user gains access to the file or folder at the computer or over the network. The permissions you assign for folders are different from the permissions you assign for files.

NTFS Folder Permissions

You assign folder permissions to control the access that users have to folders and to the files and subfolders that are contained within the folder.

Table 9.1 lists the standard NTFS folder permissions that you can assign and the type of access that each provides.

Table 9.1   NTFS Folder Permissions

NTFS Folder Permission	Allows the User To
Full Control	Change permissions, take ownership, and delete subfolders and files, plus perform actions permitted by all other NTFS folder permissions
Modify	Delete the folder plus perform actions permitted by the Write permission and the Read & Execute permission
Read & Execute	Move through folders to reach other files and folders, even if the users do not have permission for those folders, and perform actions permitted by the Read permission and the List Folder Contents permission

NTFS Folder Permission	Allows the User To
List Folder Contents	See the names of files and subfolders in the folder
Read	See files and subfolders in the folder and view folder ownership, permissions, and attributes (such as Read-only, Hidden, Archive, and System)
Write	Create new files and subfolders within the folder, change folder attributes, and view folder ownership and permissions

You can deny folder permission to a user account or group. To deny all access to a user account or group for a folder, deny the Full Control permission.

NTFS File Permissions

You assign file permissions to control the access that users have to files. Table 9.2 lists the standard NTFS file permissions that you can assign and the type of access that each provides.

Table 9.2   NTFS File Permissions

NTFS File Permission	Allows the User To
Full Control	Change permissions and take ownership, plus perform the actions permitted by all other NTFS file permissions
Modify	Modify and delete the file plus perform the actions permitted by the Write permission and the Read & Execute permission
Read & Execute	Run applications plus perform the actions permitted by the Read permission
Read	Read the file, and view file attributes, ownership, and permissions
Write	Overwrite the file, change file attributes, and view file ownership and permissions

Access Control List

NTFS stores an *access control list* (ACL) with every file and folder on an NTFS volume. The ACL contains a list of all user accounts and groups that have been granted access for the file or folder, as well as the type of access that they have been granted. When a user attempts to gain access to a resource, the ACL must contain an entry, called an *access control entry* (ACE), for the user account or a group to which the user belongs. The entry must allow the type of access that is requested (for example, Read access) for the user to gain access. If no ACE exists in the ACL, the user cannot gain access to the resource.

Multiple NTFS Permissions

You can assign multiple permissions to a user account by assigning permissions for a resource to an individual user account and to each group of which the user is a member. You need to understand the rules and priorities that are associated with how NTFS assigns and combines multiple permissions. You also need to understand NTFS permission inheritance.

Permissions Are Cumulative

A user's *effective permissions* for a resource are the sum of the NTFS permissions that you assign to the individual user account and to all of the groups to which the user belongs. If a user has Read permission for a folder and is a member of a group with Write permission for the same folder, the user has both Read and Write permission for that folder.

File Permissions Override Folder Permissions

NTFS file permissions take priority over NTFS folder permissions. A user with access to a file will be able to gain access to the file even if he or she does not have access to the folder containing the file. A user can gain access to the files for which he or she has permissions by using the full Universal Naming Convention (UNC) or local path to open the file from its respective application, even though the folder in which it resides will be invisible if the user has no corresponding folder permission. In other words, if you do not have permission to access the folder containing the file you want to access, you must know the full path to the file to access it. Without permission to access the folder, you cannot see the folder, so you cannot browse for the file you want to access.

Note The Traverse Folder/Execute File special permission allows or denies moving through folders to reach other files or folders, even if the user has no permissions for the traversed folders. This permission takes effect only when the group or user is not granted the Bypass Traverse Checking user right in the Group Policy snap-in. For more information on special permissions, see Lesson 3. For more information on user rights, see Chapter 13, "Administering a Security Configuration."

Deny Overrides Other Permissions

You can deny permission to a user account or group for a specific file, although this is not the recommended way to control access to resources. Denying permission overrides all instances where that permission is allowed. Even if a user has permission to gain access to the file or folder as a member of a group, denying permission to the user blocks any other permission that the user might have (see Figure 9.1).

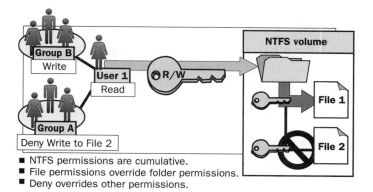

Figure 9.1   Multiple NTFS permissions

In Figure 9.1, User1 has Read permission for FolderA and is a member of Group A and Group B. Group B has Write permission for FolderA. Group A has been denied Write permission for File2.

User1 can read and write to File1. The user can also read File2, but she cannot write to File2 because she is a member of Group A, which has been denied Write permission for File2.

NTFS Permissions Inheritance

By default, permissions that you assign to the parent folder are inherited by and propagated to the subfolders and files that are contained in the parent folder. However, you can prevent permissions inheritance, as shown in Figure 9.2.

Figure 9.2   Permissions inheritance

Understanding Permissions Inheritance

Files and subfolders can inherit permissions from their parent folder. Whatever permissions you assign to the parent folder can also apply to subfolders and files that are contained within the parent folder, depending on the inheritance option set for a given object. When you assign NTFS permissions to give access to a folder, you assign permissions for the folder and for any existing files and sub folders, as well as any new files and subfolders that are created in the folder.

Preventing Permissions Inheritance

You can prevent permissions that are assigned to a parent folder from being inherited by subfolders and files that are contained within the folder by setting an inheritance option set for a given object. That is, the subfolders and files will not inherit permissions that have been assigned to the parent folder containing them.

If you prevent permissions inheritance for a folder, that folder becomes the top parent folder. Permissions assigned to this folder will be inherited by the sub folders and files that it contains.

Lesson Summary

In this lesson you learned how NTFS permissions are used to specify which users and groups can gain access to files and folders, and what these permissions allow users to do with the contents of the files or folders. NTFS permissions are only available on NTFS volumes. You also learned that the folder permissions are Full Control, Modify, Read & Execute, List Folder Contents, Read, and Write. The file permissions are similar to the folder permissions. The file permissions are Full Control, Modify, Read & Execute, Read, and Write.

You learned about applying NTFS permissions. NTFS stores an ACL with every file and folder on an NTFS volume. The ACL contains a list of all user accounts and groups that have been granted access for the file or folder, as well as the type of access that they have been granted.

You also learned that you can assign multiple permissions to a user account by assigning permissions to the individual user account and to each group of which the user is a member. You learned that NTFS file permissions take priority over NTFS folder permissions.

Finally, you learned how permissions that you assign to the parent folder are inherited by and propagated to the subfolders and files that are contained in the parent folder by setting an inheritance option set for a given object. When per missions inheritance is prevented for a folder, the folder at which you prevent inheritance becomes the new parent folder. Permissions assigned to this folder will be inherited by the subfolders and files that are contained within it. Permissions inheritance can also be prevented for a file.

Lesson 2: Assigning NTFS Permissions

There are certain guidelines you should follow for assigning NTFS permissions. Assign permissions according to group and user needs; this includes allowing or preventing permissions inheritance from parent folders to subfolders and files that are contained in the parent folder. This lesson presents guidelines for planning NTFS permissions and then walks you through the steps of assigning NTFS permissions.

After this lesson, you will be able to

- Plan what permissions to assign to users or groups for applications and data folders
- Assign NTFS folder and file permissions to user accounts and groups

Estimated lesson time: 60 minutes

Planning NTFS Permissions

If you take the time to plan your NTFS permissions and follow a few guidelines, you will find that NTFS permissions are easy to manage. Use the following guidelines when you assign NTFS permissions:

1. To simplify administration, group files into application, data, and home folders. Centralize home and public folders on a volume that is separate from applications and the operating system. Doing so provides the following benefits:

    - You assign permissions only to folders, not to individual files.
    - Backup is less complex because there is no need to back up application files, and all home and public folders are in one location.

2. Allow users only the level of access that they require. If a user only needs to read a file, assign the Read permission to his or her user account for the file. This reduces the possibility of users accidentally modifying or deleting important documents and application files.

3. Create groups according to the access that the group members require for resources, and then assign the appropriate permissions to the group. Assign permissions to individual user accounts only when necessary.

4. When you assign permissions for working with data or application folders, assign the Read & Execute permission to the Users group and the Administrators group. This prevents application files from being accidentally deleted or damaged by users or viruses.

5. Turn off the permissions inheritance option at the home directory level. This allows the user to consider permissions for each file or folder in the home directory.

6. When you assign permissions for public data folders, assign the Read & Execute permission and the Write permission to the Users group, and the Full Control permission to CREATOR OWNER identity group. The user who creates a file is by default the creator and owner of the file. After you create a file, you may grant another user permission to take ownership of the file. The person who takes ownership would then become the owner of the file. If you assign the Read & Execute permission and the Write permission to the Users group, and the Full Control permission to CREATOR OWNER, users have the ability to read and modify documents that other users create and the ability to read, modify, and delete the files and folders that they create.

7. Deny permissions only when it is essential to deny specific access to a specific user account or group.

8. Encourage users to assign permissions to the files and folders that they create and educate them about how to do so.

Setting NTFS Permissions

By default, when you format a volume with NTFS, the Full Control permission is assigned to the Everyone group. You should change this default permission and assign other appropriate NTFS permissions to control the access that users have to resources. Be careful if you assign permissions to the Everyone group and enable the Guest account. Windows 2000 will authenticate a user who does not have a valid user account as Guest. The user automatically gets all rights and permissions that you have assigned to the Everyone group.

Assigning or Modifying Permissions

Administrators, users with the Full Control permission, and the owners of files and folders (Creator Owner) can assign permissions to user accounts and groups.

▶ **To assign or modify NTFS permissions for a file or a folder**

1. Right-click the file or folder for which you want to assign permissions, then click Properties.

2. In the Security tab (see Figure 9.3) of the Properties dialog box for the file or folder, configure the options that are described in Table 9.3.

Figure 9.3   Security tab of the Properties dialog box for the Data folder

Table 9.3   Security Tab Options

Option	Description
Name	Select the user account, group, or special entity for which you want to change permissions or that you want to remove from the list.
Permission	To allow a permission, select the Allow check box. To deny a permission, select the Deny check box.
Add	Opens the Select Users, Computers, Or Groups dialog box, which you use to select user accounts and groups to add to the Name list.
Remove	Removes the selected user account, group, or special entity and the associated permissions for the file or folder.
Advanced	Opens the Access Control Settings For dialog box, which you use to add, remove, view, or edit special permissions for selected user accounts and groups.
Allow Inheritable Permissions From Parent To Propogate To This Object	Specifies whether permissions for this object will be affected by inheritance.

Preventing Permissions Inheritance

By default, subfolders and files inherit permissions that you assign to their parent folder. This is indicated in the Security tab in the Properties dialog box by a check in the Allow Inheritable Permissions From Parent To Propagate To This Object check box. If the check boxes under Permissions are shaded, then the file or folder has inherited permissions from the parent folder. To prevent a subfolder or file from inheriting permissions from a parent folder, clear the Allow Inheritable Permissions From Parent To Propagate To This Object check box. If you clear this check box, you are prompted to select one of the options described in Table 9.4.

Table 9.4   Preventing Permissions Inheritance Options

Option	Description
Copy	Copy the permissions from the parent folder to the current folder and then deny subsequent permissions inheritance from the parent folder.
Remove	Remove the permissions that are assigned to the parent folder and retain only the permissions that you explicitly assign to the file or folder.
Cancel	Cancel the dialog box and restore the check mark in the Allow Inheritable Permissions From Parent To Propagate To This Object check box.

Practice: Planning and Assigning NTFS Permissions

In this practice you plan NTFS permissions for folders and files based on a business scenario. Then you apply NTFS permissions for folders and files on your computer based on a second scenario. Finally, you test the NTFS permissions that you set up to make sure that they are working properly.

Exercise 1: Planning NTFS Permissions

In this exercise you plan how to assign NTFS permissions to folders and files on a computer running Windows 2000 Server, based on the scenario described in the next section.

Scenario

The default NTFS folder and file permissions are Full Control for the Everyone group. Figure 9.4 shows the folder and file structure used for this practice. You need to review the following security criteria and record the changes that you should make to the NTFS folder and file permissions to meet the security criteria.

Figure 9.4   Folder and file structure for practice

To plan NTFS permissions, you must determine the following:

- What groups to create and what built-in groups to use
- What permissions users will require to gain access to folders and files
- Whether or not to clear the Allow Inheritable Permissions From Parent To Propagate To This Object check box for the folder or file for which you are assigning permissions

Keep the following general guidelines in mind:

- NTFS permissions that are assigned to a folder are inherited by all of the folders and files that it contains. To assign permissions for all of the folders and files in the Apps folder, you need only assign NTFS permissions to the Apps folder.
- To assign more restrictive permissions to a folder or file that is inheriting permissions, you must either deny the unwanted permissions or block inheritance by clearing the Allow Inheritable Permissions From Parent To Propagate To This Object check box.

The decisions that you make are based on the following criteria:

- In addition to the default built-in groups, the following groups have been created in the domain:
  - Accounting
  - Managers
  - Executives
- Administrators require the Full Control permission for all folders and files.
- All users will run programs in the WordProc folder, but they should not be able to modify the files in the WordProc folder.
- Only members of the Accounting, Managers, and Executives groups should be able to read documents in the Spreadsh and Database application folders by running the associated spreadsheet and database applications, but they should not be able to modify the files in those folders.
- All users should be able to read and create files in the Public folder.
- All users should be prevented from modifying files in the Public\Library folder.
- Only User81 should be able to modify and delete files in the Public\Manuals folder.

When you apply custom permissions to a folder or file, which default permission entry should you remove?

Complete Table 9.5 to plan and record your permissions.

Table 9.5   Permissions Planning Table for Exercise 1

Path	User Account or Group	NTFS Permissions	Block Inheritance (Yes/No)
Apps			
Apps\WordProc			
Apps\Spreadsh			
Apps\Database			
Public			
Public\Library			
Public\Manuals			

Exercise 2: Assigning NTFS Permissions for the Data Folder

In this exercise you assign NTFS permissions for the C:\Data folder (where C:\ is the name of your system drive) based on the scenario described next.

Before beginning the following exercises, create the users and groups listed in Table 9.6.

Table 9.6   Users and Groups for Exercise 2

Group	User Account
Managers	User81 (member of Print Operators)
Sales	User82 (member of Sales and Print Operators)
Sales	User83 (member of Managers and Print Operators)

Create the following folders (where C:\ is the name of your system drive):

- C:\Data
- C:\Data\Managers
- C:\Data\Managers\Reports
- C:\Data\Sales

Scenario

The permissions that you assign are based on the following criteria:

- All users in the domain should be able to read documents and files in the Data folder.
- All users in the domain should be able to create documents in the Data folder.

- All users in the domain should be able to modify the contents, properties, and permissions of the documents that they create in the Data folder.

▶ **To remove permissions from the Everyone group**

1. Log on to your domain as Administrator.

2. Right-click My Computer, then click Explore.

3. Expand the Local Disk (C:), right-click the C:\Data folder, then click Properties.

   Windows 2000 displays the Data Properties dialog box with the General tab active.

4. Click the Security tab to display the permissions for the Data folder.

   Windows 2000 displays the Data Properties dialog box with the Security tab active.

   What are the existing folder permissions?

   Notice that the current allowed permissions cannot be modified.

5. Under Name, select the Everyone group, then click Remove.

   What do you see?

6. Click OK to close the message box.

7. Clear the Allow Inheritable Permissions From Parent To Propagate To This Object check box to block permissions from being inherited.

   Windows 2000 displays the Security message box, prompting you to copy the currently inherited permissions to the folder or remove all permissions for the folder except those that you explicitly specify.

8. Click Remove.

   What are the existing folder permissions?

▶ **To assign permissions to the Users group for the Data folder**

1. In the Data Properties dialog box, click Add.

   Windows 2000 displays the Select Users, Computers, Or Groups dialog box.

2. In the Look In list at the top of the Select Users, Computers, Or Groups dialog box, select your domain.

   The Look In list allows you to select the computer or domain from which to select user accounts, groups, or computers when you assign permissions. You should specify your domain to select from the user accounts and groups that you created.

3. In the Name column, select Users, then click Add.

   Users is listed in the box at the bottom of the Select Users, Computers, Or Groups dialog box.

In the box at the bottom of the Select Users, Computers, Or Groups dialog box, you can also type the name of the object you want. You can type multiple names by separating them with semicolons. If the object exists in a Windows 2000 domain or global catalog, you can type the first few characters of the name and then click Check Names. Windows 2000 either completes the name if there are no similar names, or prompts you to choose a name from a list of similar names.

4. Click OK to return to the Data Properties dialog box.

   What are the existing allowed folder permissions?

5. Make sure that Users is selected, and then next to Write, select the Allow check box.

6. Click Apply to save your changes.

▶ **To assign permissions to the CREATOR OWNER group for the Data folder**

1. In the Security tab of the Data Properties dialog box, click Add.

   Windows 2000 displays the Select Users, Computers, Or Groups dialog box.

2. In the Look In list at the top of the Select Users, Computers, Or Groups dialog box, select your domain.

3. In the Name list, select CREATOR OWNER, then click Add.

   CREATOR OWNER is listed in the box at the bottom of the Select Users, Computers, Or Groups dialog box.

4. Click OK to return to the Data Properties dialog box.

   What are the existing allowed folder permissions?

5. Make sure that CREATOR OWNER is selected, and next to Full Control, select the Allow check box, then click Apply to save your changes.

   What do you see?

6. Click Advanced to display the additional permissions.

   Windows 2000 displays the Access Control Settings For Data dialog box.

7. Under Name, select CREATOR OWNER.

   What permissions are assigned to the CREATOR OWNER group and where do these permissions apply? Why?

8. Click OK.

9. On the Data Properties dialog box, click OK, then log off your domain.

▶ **To test the folder permissions that you assigned for the Data folder**

1. Log on to your domain as User81, then start Windows Explorer.

2. Expand the C:\Data directory.

3. In the Data folder, attempt to create a text file named USER81.TXT.

   Were you successful? Why or why not?

4. Attempt to perform the following tasks for the file that you just created, and then record those tasks that you are able to complete.

   - Open the file
   - Modify the file
   - Delete the file

5. Close all applications, then log off Windows 2000.

Exercise 3: Assigning NTFS Permissions

In this exercise you assign NTFS permissions to the Data, Managers, Reports, and Sales folders based on the scenario described in the following section.

Scenario

Assign the appropriate permissions to folders as listed in Table 9.7.

Table 9.7   Folder Permissions for Exercise 3

Folder Name	User Account or Group	Permissions
C:\Data	Users group Administrators group	Read & Execute Full Control
C:\Data\Managers	Users group Managers group Administrators group	Read & Execute Full Control Modify
C:\Data\Managers\ Reports	Users group Administrators group User82	Read & Execute Full Control Modify
C:\Data\Sales	Users group Administrators group Sales group	Read & Execute Full Control Modify

▶ **To assign NTFS permissions for a folder**

1. Log on to your domain as Administrator, then start Windows Explorer.

2. Expand the Local Disk (C:).

3. Right-click the folder for which you are modifying permissions, then click Properties.

   Windows 2000 displays the Properties dialog box for the folder with the General tab active.

4. In the Properties dialog box for the folder, click the Security tab.

5. In the Security tab, if you need to modify the inherited permissions for a user account or group, clear the Allow Inheritable Permissions From Parent To Propagate To This Object check box, and then when prompted to copy or remove inherited permissions, click Copy.

6. To add permissions to user accounts or groups for the folder, click Add.

Windows 2000 displays the Select User, Computer, Or Group dialog box.

7. Make sure that your domain appears in the Look In list at the top of the Select Users, Computers, Or Groups dialog box.

8. In the Name column, type the name of the appropriate user account or group, based on the preceding scenario, then click Add.

   Windows 2000 displays the user account or group under Name at the bottom of the dialog box.

9. Repeat Step 8 for each user account or group that is listed for the folder in the preceding scenario.

10. Click OK to return to the Properties dialog box for the folder.

11. If the Properties dialog box for the folder contains user accounts and groups that are not listed in the preceding scenario, select the user account or group, then click Remove.

12. For all user accounts and groups that are listed for the folder in the preceding scenario, under Name, select the user account or group, and then under Permissions, select the Allow check box or the Deny check box next to the appropriate permissions that are listed for the folder in the preceding scenario.

13. Click OK to apply your changes, and close the Properties dialog box for the folder.

14. Repeat this procedure for each folder for which you are assigning permissions as specified in the preceding scenario.

15. Log off Windows 2000.

Exercise 4: Testing NTFS Permissions

In this exercise you log on using various user accounts and test NTFS permissions.

▶ **To test permissions for the Reports folder while logged on as User81**

1. Log on as User81, then start Windows Explorer.

2. In Windows Explorer, expand the C:\Data\Managers\Reports directory.

3. Attempt to create a file in the Reports folder.

   Were you successful? Why or why not?

4. Log off Windows 2000.

▶ **To test permissions for the Reports folder while logged on as User82**

1. Log on as User82, then start Windows Explorer.

2. Expand the C:\Data\Managers\Reports directory.

3. Attempt to create a file in the Reports folder.

   Were you successful? Why or why not?

4. Log off Windows 2000.

▶ **To test permissions for the Sales folder while logged on as Administrator**

1. Log on to your domain as Administrator, then start Windows Explorer.

2. Expand the C:\Data\Sales directory.

3. Attempt to create a file in the Sales folder.

   Were you successful? Why or why not?

4. Close Windows Explorer, and then log off Windows 2000.

▶ **To test permissions for the Sales folder while logged on as User81**

1. Log on as User81, then start Windows Explorer.

2. Expand the C:\Data\Sales directory.

3. Attempt to create a file in the Sales folder.

   Were you successful? Why or why not?

▶ **To test permissions for the Sales folder while logged on as User82**

1. Log on as User82, then start Windows Explorer.

2. Expand the C:\Data\Sales directory.

3. Attempt to create a file in the Sales folder.

   Were you successful? Why or why not?

4. Close all applications, then log off Windows 2000.

Lesson Summary

In this lesson you learned that by default, when you format a volume with NTFS, the Full Control permission is assigned to the Everyone group. You learned that you should change this default permission and assign other appropriate NTFS permissions to control the access that users have to resources. You learned that Administrators, the owners of files or folders, and users with Full Control permission can assign NTFS permissions to users and groups to control access to files and folders. You learned how to assign or modify NTFS permissions for a file or a folder by using the Security tab of the Properties dialog box for the file or folder.

You also learned that by default, subfolders and files inherit permissions that you assign to their parent folder, and you learned how to disable this feature so that subfolders and files do not inherit the permissions assigned to their parents. In the practice exercises, you created some folders, assigned NTFS permissions, and then tested the permissions you set up to determine if you set them up correctly.

Lesson 3: Assigning Special Permissions

The standard NTFS permissions generally provide all of the access control that you need to secure your resources. However, there are instances in which the standard NTFS permissions do not provide the specific level of access that you may want to assign to users. To create a specific level of access, you can assign NTFS special permissions. This lesson introduces the NTFS special permissions. It then outlines the requirements and procedures for taking ownership of a folder or file.

After this lesson, you will be able to

- Define special permissions
- Give users the ability to change permissions on files or folders
- Give users the ability to take ownership of files and folders
- Explain the concept of taking ownership of a file or folder
- Take ownership of a file or folder

Estimated lesson time: 20 minutes

Special Permissions

Special permissions provide an additional level of access to assign to users. Table 9.8 lists the special permissions that can be assigned to files and folders.

Table 9.8   Special File and Folder Permissions

Special Permission	Function
Traverse Folder/Execute File	Traverse Folder allows or denies moving through folders that the user does not have permission to access, to reach files or folders that the user does have permission to access (applies to folders only). Traverse Folder takes effect only when the group or user is not granted the Bypass Traverse Checking user right in group policy. (By default, the Everyone group is given the Bypass Traverse Checking user right.) Setting the Traverse Folder permission on a folder does not automatically set the Execute File permission on all files within that folder. Execute File allows or denies running program files (applies to files only).
List Folder/Read Data	List Folder allows or denies viewing file names and subfolder names within the folder (applies to folders only). Read Data allows or denies viewing data in files (applies to files only).

Special Permission	Function
Read Attributes	Allows or denies viewing the attributes of a file or folder, such as read-only and hidden. Attributes are defined by NTFS.
Read Extended Attributes	Allows or denies viewing the extended attributes of a file or folder. Extended attributes are defined by programs and may vary.
Create Files/Write Data	Create Files allows or denies creating files within the folder (applies to folders only). Write Data allows or denies making changes to the file and overwriting existing content (applies to files only).
Create Folders/Append Data	Create Folders allows or denies creating folders within a folder (applies to folders only). Append Data allows or denies making changes to the end of the file but not changing, deleting, or overwriting existing data (applies to files only).
Write Attributes	Allows or denies changing the attributes of a file or folder, such as read-only or hidden. Attributes are defined by NTFS.
Write Extended Attributes	Allows or denies changing the extended attributes of a file or folder. Extended attributes are defined by programs and may vary.
Delete Subfolders and Files	Allows or denies deleting subfolders and files, even if the Delete permission has not been granted on the subfolder or file.
Delete	Allows or denies deleting the file or folder. If you don't have Delete permission on a file or folder, you can still delete it if you have been granted the Delete Subfolders and Files permission on the parent folder.
Read Permissions	Allows or denies reading permissions for the file or folder, such as Full Control, Read, and Write.
Change Permissions	Allows or denies changing permissions for the file or folder, such as Full Control, Read, and Write.
Take Ownership	Allows or denies taking ownership of the file or folder. The owner of a file or folder can always change permissions on it, regardless of any existing permissions that protect the file or folder.
Synchronize	Allows or denies different threads to wait on the handle for the file or folder and synchronize with another thread that may signal it. This permission applies only to multithreaded, multiprocess programs.

Special permissions are set on the Permission Entry For dialog box for the file or folder. This dialog box is accessed by selecting Advanced on the Security tab of the Properties dialog box for the file or folder, and then selecting View/Edit for a Permission Entry on the Access Control Setting For dialog box for the file or folder.

Each of the standard file and folder permissions consists of a logical group of special permissions. Table 9.9 lists each standard file or folder permission and specifies which special permissions are associated with the standard permission.

Table 9.9   Special Permissions Associated with Standard File and Folder Permissions

Special Permission	Full Control	Modify	Read & Execute	List Folder Contents	Read	Write
Traverse Folder/ Execute File	x	x	x	x		
List Folder/ Read Data	x	x	x	x	x	
Read Attributes	x	x	x	x	x	
Read Extended Attributes	x	x	x	x	x	
Create Files/ Write Data	x	x				x
Create Folders/ Append Data	x	x				x
Write Attributes	x	x				x
Write Extended Attributes	x	x				x
Delete Subfolders and Files	x					
Delete	x	x				
Read Permissions	x	x	x	x	x	x
Change Permissions	x					
Take Ownership	x					
Synchronize	x	x	x	x	x	x

Note   Although the List Folder Contents and Read & Execute standard permissions appear to have the same special permissions, these special permissions are inherited differently. List Folder Contents is inherited by folders but not files, and it only appears when you view folder permissions. Read & Execute is inherited by both files and folders and is always present when you view file or folder permissions.

When you assign special permissions to folders, you can choose where to apply the permissions down the tree to subfolders and files.

The Change Permissions and Take Ownership special permissions are particularly useful for controlling access to resources.

Change Permissions

Using the Change Permissions special permission, you can give other administrators and users the ability to change permissions for a file or folder without giving them the Full Control permission over the file or folder. In this way, the administrator or user cannot delete or write to the file or folder but can assign permissions to the file or folder.

To give administrators the ability to change permissions, assign Change Permissions to the Administrators group for the file or folder.

Take Ownership

Using the Take Ownership special permission, you can give users or groups the ability to take ownership of files or folders. As an administrator, you can take ownership of a file or folder.

The following rules apply for taking ownership of a file or folder:

- The current owner or any user with Full Control permission can assign the Full Control standard permission or the Take Ownership special permission to another user account or group, allowing the user account or a member of the group to take ownership.

- An administrator can take ownership of a file or folder, regardless of assigned permissions. If an administrator takes ownership, the Administrators group becomes the owner and any member of the Administrators group can change the permissions for the file or folder and assign the Take Ownership permission to another user account or group.

   For example, if an employee leaves the company, an administrator can take ownership of the employee's files, assign the Take Ownership permission to another employee, and then that employee can take ownership of the former employee's files.

Important   You cannot *assign* anyone ownership of a file or folder. The owner of a file, an administrator, or anyone with Full Control permission can assign Take Ownership permission to a user account or group, allowing that user to take ownership. To become the owner of a file or folder, a user or group member with Take Ownership permission must explicitly take ownership of the file or folder, as explained later in this chapter.

Setting Special Permissions

You can assign the Change Permissions or Take Ownership special permissions to enable users to change permissions and take ownership of files and folders.

▶ **To set Change Permissions or Take Ownership permissions**

1. Locate the file or folder for which you want to apply special permissions. Right-click the file or folder, click Properties, then click the Security tab.

2. Click Advanced.

3. In the Access Control Settings For dialog box (see Figure 9.5) for a file or folder, in the Permissions tab, select the user account or group for which you want to apply special permissions.

Figure 9.5   Access Control Settings For dialog box for the Program Files folder

On the Access Control Settings For dialog box, you can view the permissions that are applied to the file or folder, the owner, and where the permissions apply.

4. For the Allow Inheritable Permissions From Parent To Propagate To This Object check box:

   ▪ Check the box to specify that this object will inherit permissions from the parent folder.

   ▪ Clear the box to specify that this object will not inherit any permissions from the parent folder.

5. For the Reset Permissions On All Child Objects And Enable Propagation Of Inheritable Permissions check box:

   ▪ Check the box to reset any existing permissions on child objects so that the child objects will inherit permissions from the parent object.

- Clear the box to not reset any existing permissions on child objects so that the child objects will not inherit permissions from the parent object.

6. Click View/Edit to open the Permission Entry For dialog box for the file or folder (see Figure 9.6).

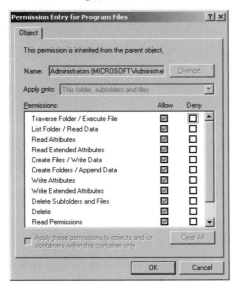

Figure 9.6 Permission Entry For dialog box for the Program Files folder

The options in the Permission Entry For dialog box are described in Table 9.10.

Table 9.10   Options in the Permission Entry For Dialog Box

Option	Description
Name	The user account or group name. To select a different user account or group, click Change.
Apply Onto	The level of the folder hierarchy at which the special NTFS permissions are inherited. The default is This folder, subfolders, and files.
Permissions	The special permissions. To allow the Change Permissions permission or Take Ownership permission, select the Allow check box.
Apply These Permissions To Objects And/Or Containers Within This Container Only	Specify whether subfolders and files within a folder inherit the special permissions from the folder. Select this check box to propagate the special permissions to files and subfolders. Clear this check box to prevent permissions inheritance.
Clear All	Click this button to clear all selected permissions.

Taking Ownership of a File or Folder

To take ownership of a file or folder, the user or a group member with Take Ownership permission must explicitly take ownership of the file or folder.

▶ **To take ownership of a file or folder**

1. In the Access Control Settings For dialog box for the file or folder, in the Owner tab, in the Change Owner To list, select your name.

2. Select the Replace Owner On Subcontainers And Objects check box to take ownership of all objects and subcontainers within the folder.

3. Click OK.

Practice: Taking Ownership of a File

In this practice you observe the effects of taking ownership of a file. To do this, you determine permissions for a file, assign the Take Ownership permission to a user account, and then take ownership as that user.

▶ **To determine the permissions for a file**

1. Log on to your domain as Administrator, then start Windows Explorer.

2. In the C:\Data directory (where C:\ is the name of your system drive), create a text file named OWNER.TXT.

3. Right-click OWNER.TXT, then click Properties.

   Microsoft Windows 2000 displays the OWNER.TXT Properties dialog box with the General tab active.

4. Click the Security tab to display the permissions for the OWNER.TXT file.

   What are the current allowed permissions for OWNER.TXT?

5. Click Advanced.

   Windows 2000 displays the Access Control Settings For OWNER.TXT dialog box with the Permissions tab active.

6. Click the Owner tab.

   Who is the current owner of the OWNER.TXT file?

▶ **To assign permission to a user to take ownership**

1. In the Access Control Settings For OWNER.TXT dialog box, click the Permissions tab.

2. Click Add.

   Windows 2000 displays the Select User, Computer, Or Group dialog box.

3. In the Look In list at the top of the dialog box, select your domain.

4. Under Name, click User83, then click OK.

   Windows 2000 displays the Permission Entry For OWNER.TXT dialog box.

   Notice that all of the permission entries for User83 are blank.

5. Under Permissions, select the Allow check box next to Take Ownership.

6. Click OK.

   Windows 2000 displays the Access Control Settings For OWNER.TXT dialog box with the Permissions tab active.

7. Click OK to return to the OWNER.TXT Properties dialog box.

8. Click OK to apply your changes and close the OWNER.TXT Properties dialog box.

9. Close all applications, then log off Windows 2000.

▶ **To take ownership of a file**

1. Log on to your domain as User83, then start Windows Explorer.

2. Expand the C:\Data directory.

3. Right-click OWNER.TXT, then click Properties.

   Windows 2000 displays the OWNER.TXT Properties dialog box with the General tab active.

4. Click the Security tab to display the permissions for OWNER.TXT.

   Windows 2000 displays the Security message box, indicating that you can only view the current permission information on OWNER.TXT.

5. Click OK.

   Windows 2000 displays the OWNER.TXT Properties dialog box with the Security tab active.

6. Click Advanced to display the Access Control Settings For OWNER.TXT dialog box, then click the Owner tab.

   Who is the current owner of OWNER.TXT?

7. Under Name, select User83, then click Apply.

   Who is the current owner of OWNER.TXT?

8. Click OK to close the Access Control Settings For OWNER.TXT dialog box.

   Windows 2000 displays the OWNER.TXT Properties dialog box with the Security tab active.

9. Click OK to close the OWNER.TXT Properties dialog box.

▶ **To test permissions for a file as the owner**

1. While you are logged on as User83, assign User83 the Full Control permission for the OWNER.TXT file, then click Apply.

2. Clear the Allow Inheritable Permissions From Parent To Propagate To This Object check box.

3. In the Security dialog box, click Remove to remove permissions from the Users group and the Administrators group for the OWNER.TXT file.

   Were you successful? Why or why not?

4. Click OK to close the OWNER.TXT Properties dialog box.

5. Delete the OWNER.TXT file.

6. Close all applications.

Lesson Summary

In this lesson you learned about special permissions. You learned specifically about two of them: Change Permissions and Take Ownership. You can give administrators and other users the ability to change permissions for a file or folder without giving them the Full Control permission over the file or folder. This prevents the administrator or user from deleting or writing to the file or folder, but it allows them to assign permissions to the file or folder.

You also learned how to use the Take Ownership special permission to give users or groups the ability to take ownership of files or folders. The current owner or any user with Full Control permission can assign the Full Control standard permission or the Take Ownership special permission to another user account or group, allowing the user account or a member of the group to take ownership. You cannot assign anyone ownership of a file or folder. To become the owner of a file or folder, a user or group member with Take Ownership permission must explicitly take ownership of the file or folder.

An administrator can take ownership of a folder or file, regardless of assigned permissions. When an administrator takes ownership of a file or folder, the Administrators group becomes the owner and any member of the Administrators group can change the permissions for the file or folder and assign the Take Ownership permission to another user account or group.

In the practice portion of this lesson you determined the permissions for a file, assigned the Take Ownership permission to a user account, and then took ownership as that user.

Lesson 4: Copying and Moving Files and Folders

When you copy or move files and folders, the permissions you set on the files or folders might change. There are rules that control how and when permissions change. It is important that you understand how and when permissions change during a copy or move. This lesson explains what happens to permissions when a folder or file is copied or moved.

After this lesson, you will be able to

- Describe the effect on NTFS file and folder permissions when files and folders are copied
- Describe the effect on NTFS file and folder permissions when files and folders are moved
- List the required permissions for copying or moving files and folders

Estimated lesson time: 15 minutes

Copying Files and Folders

When you copy files or folders from one folder to another folder, or from one volume to another volume, permissions change, as shown in Figure 9.7.

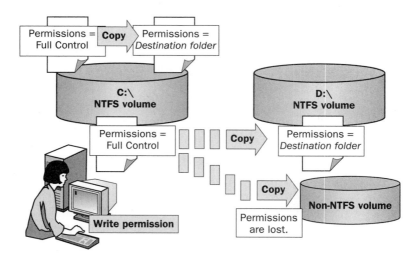

Figure 9.7.   Copying files or folders between folders or volumes

When you copy a file within a single NTFS volume or between NTFS volumes

- Windows 2000 treats it as a new file. As a new file, it takes on the permissions of the destination folder or volume.

- You must have Write permission for the destination folder to copy files and folders.

- You become the Creator Owner.

Note   When you copy files or folders to non-NTFS volumes, the folders and files lose their NTFS permissions because FAT volumes do not support NTFS permissions.

Moving Files and Folders

When you move a file or folder, permissions might or might not change, depending on where you move the file or folder (see Figure 9.8).

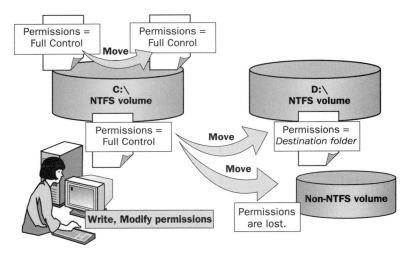

Figure 9.8   Moving files or folders between folders or volumes

Moving Within a Single NTFS Volume

When you move a file or folder within a single NTFS volume

- The folder or file retains the original permissions.

- You must have the Write permission for the destination folder to move files and folders into it.

- You must have the Modify permission for the source folder or file. The Modify permission is required to move a folder or file because Windows 2000 deletes the folder or file from the source folder after it is copied to the destination folder.

- You become the Creator Owner.

Moving Between NTFS Volumes

When you move a file or folder between NTFS volumes

- The folder or file inherits the permissions of the destination folder.

- You must have the Write permission for the destination folder to move files and folders into it.

- You must have the Modify permission for the source folder or file. The Modify permission is required to move a folder or file because Windows 2000 deletes the folder or file from the source folder after it is copied to the destination folder.

- You become the Creator Owner.

Note When you move files or folders to FAT volumes, the folders and files lose their NTFS permissions because FAT volumes do not support NTFS permissions.

Practice: Copying and Moving Folders

In this practice you see the effects of permissions and ownership when you copy and move folders.

▶ **To create a folder while logged on as a user**

1. While you are logged on as User83, in Windows Explorer, in C:\ (where C:\ is the name of your system drive), create a folder named Temp1.

   What are the permissions that are assigned to the folder?

   Who is the owner? Why?

2. Close all applications, then log off Windows 2000.

▶ **To create a folder while logged on as Administrator**

1. Log on to your domain as Administrator, then start Windows Explorer.

2. In C:\ (where C:\ is the name of your system drive), create the following two folders: Temp2 and Temp3.

   What are the permissions for the folders that you just created?

   Who is the owner of the Temp2 and Temp3 folders? Why?

3. Remove the Everyone group, then assign the permissions shown in Table 9.11 to the Temp2 and Temp3 folders. You will have to clear the Allow Inheritable Permissions From Parent To Propagate To This Object check box. To assign permissions for a group, click Add, select the group(s) from the Select Users, Computers, Or Groups dialog box, click Add, then click OK. Set the appropriate permissions for the group(s) on the Properties dialog box.

Table 9.11   Folder Permissions for Practice

Folder	Assign These Permissions
C:\Temp2	Administrators: Full Control Users: Read & Execute
C:\Temp3	Backup Operators: Read & Execute Users: Full Control

▶ **To copy a folder to another folder within a Windows 2000 NTFS volume**

1. Copy C:\Temp2 to C:\Temp1.

2. Select C:\Temp1\Temp2, then compare the permissions and ownership with C:\Temp2.

   Who is the owner of C:\Temp1\Temp2 and what are the permissions? Why?

3. Close all applications, then log off Windows 2000.

▶ **To move a folder within the same NTFS volume**

1. Log on to your domain as User83.

2. Select C:\Temp3, then move it to C:\Temp1.

   What happens to the permissions and ownership for C:\Temp1\Temp3? Why?

3. Close all applications, then log off Windows 2000.

Lesson Summary

In this lesson you learned that when you copy or move files and folders, the permissions you set on the files or folders might change. You also learned that there are rules that control how and when permissions change. For example, when you copy files or folders from one folder to another folder, or from one volume to another volume, permissions change. Windows 2000 treats the file or folder as a new file or folder, and therefore it takes on the permissions of the destination folder. You must have Write permission for the destination folder to copy files and folders. When you copy a file, you become the Creator Owner of the file. When you move a file or folder within a single NTFS volume, the file or folder retains the original permissions. However, when you move a file or folder between NTFS volumes, the file or folder inherits the permissions of the destination folder.

In the practice portion of this lesson you observed the effects of permissions and ownership when you copy and move folders.

Lesson 5: Troubleshooting Permissions Problems

When you assign or modify NTFS permissions to files and folders, problems might arise. Troubleshooting these problems is important to keep resources available to users. This lesson describes common permission-related problems and their solutions.

After this lesson, you will be able to

- Recognize common reasons why users cannot gain access to resources
- Solve common permission-related problems

Estimated lesson time: 5 minutes

Troubleshooting Permissions Problems

Table 9.12 describes some common permissions problems that you might encounter and provides solutions that you can try to resolve these problems.

Table 9.12   Permissions Problems and Solutions

Problem	Solution
A user cannot gain access to a file or folder.	If the file or folder was copied, or if it was moved to another NTFS volume, the permissions might have changed. Check the permissions that are assigned to the user account and to groups of which the user is a member. The user might not have permission or might be denied access either individually or as a member of a group.
You add a user account to a group to give that user access to a file or folder, but the user still cannot gain access.	For access permissions to be updated to include the new group to which you have added the user account, the user must either log off and then log on again or close all network connections to the computer on which the file or folder resides and then make new connections.
A user with Full Control permission to a folder deletes a file in the folder although that user does not have permission to delete the file itself. You want to stop the user from being able to delete more files.	Clear the special permission Delete Subfolders And Files check box on the folder to prevent users with Full Control of the folder from being able to delete files in the folder.

Note Windows 2000 supports Portable Operating System Interface for UNIX (POSIX) applications that are designed to run on UNIX. On UNIX systems, Full Control permission allows you to delete files in a folder. In Windows 2000, the Full Control permission includes the Delete Subfolders and Files special permission, allowing you the same ability to delete files in that folder regardless of the permissions that you have for the files in the folder.

Avoiding Permissions Problems

The following list provides best practices for implementing NTFS permissions. These guidelines will help you avoid permission problems.

- Assign the most restrictive NTFS permissions that still enable users and groups to accomplish necessary tasks.

- Assign all permissions at the folder level, not at the file level. Group files in a separate folder for which you want to restrict user access, and then assign that folder restricted access.

- For all application executable files, assign Read & Execute and Change Permissions to the Administrators group, and assign Read & Execute to the Users group. Damage to application files is usually a result of accidents and viruses. By assigning Read & Execute to Users and Read & Execute and Change Permissions to Administrators, you can prevent users or viruses from modifying or deleting executable files. To update files, members of the Administrators group can assign Full Control to their user account to make changes and then reassign Read & Execute and Change Permissions to their user account.

- Assign Full Control to Creator Owner for public data folders so that users can delete and modify files and folders that they create. Doing so gives the user who creates the file or folder (Creator Owner) full access to only the files or folders that he or she creates in the public data folder.

- For public folders, assign Full Control to Creator Owner and Read and Write to the Everyone group. This gives users full access to the files that they create, but members of the Everyone group can only read files in the folder and add files to the folder.

- Use long, descriptive names if the resource will be accessed only at the computer. If a folder will eventually be shared, use folder and file names that are accessible by all client computers.

- Allow permissions rather than deny permissions. If you do not want a user or group to gain access to a particular folder or file, do not assign permissions. Denying permissions should be an exception, not a common practice.

Practice: Deleting a File with All Permissions Denied

In this exercise you simulate the third problem described in Table 9.12. You grant a user Full Control permission to a folder, but deny all permissions to a file in the folder. You then observe what happens when the user attempts to delete that file.

▶ **To assign the Full Control permission for a folder**

1. Log on to your domain as Administrator, then start Windows Explorer.
2. Expand C:\ (where C:\ is the name of your system drive), then create a folder named Fullaccess.
3. Verify that the Everyone group has the Full Control permission for the C:\Fullaccess folder.

▶ **To create a file and deny access to it**

1. In C:\Fullaccess, create a text file named NOACCESS.TXT.
2. Clear the Allow Inheritable Permissions From Parent To Propagate To This Object check box. Deny the Everyone group the Full Control permission for the NOACCESS.TXT, then click OK.

   Windows 2000 displays the Security dialog box with the following message:

   ```
   You have denied everyone access to noaccess.txt. No one will be able
   to access noaccess.txt and only the owner will be able to change
   permissions.

   Do you wish to continue?
   ```

3. Click Yes to apply your changes and close the Security dialog box.

▶ **To view the result of denying the Full Control permission for a folder**

1. In Windows Explorer, double-click NOACCESS.TXT in C:\Fullaccess to open the file.

   Were you successful? Why or why not?

2. Click Start, point to Programs, point to Accessories, then click Command Prompt.
3. Type **cd fullaccess** to change the directory to C:\Fullaccess.
4. Delete NOACCESS.TXT by typing **del noaccess.txt**.

   Were you successful? Why or why not?

   How would you prevent users with Full Control permission for a folder from deleting a file in that folder for which they have been denied the Full Control permission?

Lesson Summary

When you assign or modify NTFS permissions for files and folders, problems might arise. Troubleshooting these problems is important to keep resources available to users. In this lesson you learned about some common permissions problems and some possible solutions to resolve these problems.

In the practice portion of this lesson you observed how users can delete a file with all permissions denied.

Review

Here are some questions to help you determine if you have learned enough to move on to the next chapter. If you have difficulty answering these questions, please go back and review the material in this chapter before beginning the next chapter. The answers for these questions are located in Appendix A, "Questions and Answers."

1. What is the default permission when a volume is formatted with NTFS? Who has access to the volume?

2. If a user has Write permission for a folder and is also a member of a group with Read permission for the folder, what are the user's effective permissions for the folder?

3. If you assign the Modify permission to a user account for a folder and the Read permission for a file, and then copy the file to that folder, what permission does the user have for the file?

4. What happens to permissions that are assigned to a file when the file is moved from one folder to another folder on the same NTFS volume? What happens when the file is moved to a folder on another NTFS volume?

5. If an employee leaves the company, what must you do to transfer ownership of his or her files and folders to another employee?

6. What three things should you check when a user cannot gain access to a resource?

C H A P T E R   1 0

Administering Shared Folders

About This Chapter

In Chapter 9, "Securing Network Resources," you learned about Microsoft Windows 2000 file system (NTFS) permissions. You use NTFS permissions to specify which users and groups can gain access to files and folders and what these permissions allow users to do with the contents of the files or folders. NTFS permissions are only available on NTFS volumes. NTFS security is effective whether a user gains access to the file or folder at the computer or over the network. In this chapter you will learn how to make folders accessible over the network. You can only access a computer's folders and their contents by physically sitting at the computer and logging on to it or by accessing a shared folder on a remote computer. Sharing folders is the only way to make folders and their contents available over the network. Shared folders also provide another way to secure file resources, one that can be used on file allocation table (FAT) or FAT32 partitions. In this chapter you will learn how to share folder resources, secure them with permissions, and provide access to them.

Before You Begin

To complete this chapter, you must have

- Completed the Setup procedures located in "About This Book"
- Completed the exercises and obtained the knowledge and skills covered in Chapter 7, "User Account Administration," Chapter 8, "Group Account Administration," and Chapter 9, "Securing Network Resources"
- Configured the computer as a domain controller in a domain

Lesson 1: Understanding Shared Folders

Microsoft Windows 2000 allows you to designate folders to share with others. For example, when a folder is shared, authorized users can make connections to the folder (and access its files) from their own computers. This lesson introduces shared folders and shared folder permissions.

After this lesson, you will be able to

- Use shared folders to provide access to network resources
- Describe how permissions affect access to shared folders

Estimated lesson time: 15 minutes

Shared Folders

Shared folders provide network users centralized access to network files. When a folder is shared, all users by default can connect to the shared folder and gain access to the folder's content. A shared folder can contain applications, data, or a user's personal data in a home directory. Each type of data requires different shared folder permissions.

Shared Folder Permissions

You can assign shared folder permissions to user and group accounts to control what users can do with the content of a shared folder. The following are characteristics of shared folder permissions:

- Shared folder permissions apply to folders, not individual files. Because you can only apply shared folder permissions to the entire shared folder, and not to individual files or subfolders in the shared folder, shared folder permissions provide less detailed security than NTFS permissions.

- Shared folder permissions do not restrict access to users who gain access to the folder at the computer where the folder is stored. They only apply to users who connect to the folder over the network.

- Shared folder permissions are the only way to secure network resources on a FAT volume. NTFS permissions are not available on FAT volumes.

- The default shared folder permission is Full Control, and it is assigned to the Everyone group when you share the folder.

Note By default, a shared folder appears in Microsoft Windows Explorer as an icon of a hand holding the shared folder (Figure 10.1 shows the default sharing icon).

To control how users gain access to a shared folder, you assign shared folder permissions.

Figure 10.1   Shared Folders in Windows Explorer

Table 10.1 explains what each of the shared folder permissions allows a client to do. Permissions are presented in order from the most restrictive to the least restrictive.

Table 10.1   Shared Folder Permissions

Shared Folder Permission	Allows the User To
Read	View file names and subfolder names, view data in files, traverse to subfolders, and run programs
Change	Add files and subfolders to the shared folder, change data in files, delete subfolders and files, plus perform actions permitted by the Read permission
Full Control	Change file permissions (NTFS only), take ownership of files (NTFS only), and perform all tasks permitted by the Change permission

You can allow or deny shared folder permissions. Generally, it is best to allow permissions and to assign permissions to a group rather than to individual users. Deny permissions only when it is necessary to override permissions that are otherwise applied. In most cases, you should deny permissions only when it is necessary to deny permission to a specific user who belongs to a group to which you have given the permission. If you deny a shared folder permission to a user, the user will not have that permission. For example, to deny all access to a shared folder, deny Full Control permission.

How Shared Folder Permissions Are Applied

Applying shared permissions to user accounts and groups affects access to a shared folder. Denying permission takes precedence over the permissions that you allow.

Multiple Permissions Combine for Effective Permissions

A user can be a member of multiple groups, each with different permissions that provide different levels of access to a shared folder. When you assign permission to a user for a shared folder, and that user is a member of a group to which you assigned a different permission, the user's *effective permissions* are the combination of the user and group permissions. For example, if a user has Read permission and is a member of a group with Change permission, the user's effective permission is Change, which includes Read.

Deny Overrides Other Permissions

Denied permissions take precedence over any permissions that you otherwise allow for user accounts and groups. If you deny a shared folder permission to a user, the user will not have that permission, even if you allow the permission for a group of which the user is a member.

NTFS Permissions Are Required on NTFS Volumes

Shared folder permissions are sufficient to gain access to files and folders on a FAT volume, but not on an NTFS volume. On a FAT volume, users can gain access to a shared folder for which they have permissions, as well as all of the folder's contents. When users gain access to a shared folder on an NTFS volume, they need the shared folder permission and also the appropriate NTFS permissions for each file and folder to which they gain access.

Copied, Moved, or Renamed Shared Folders Are No Longer Shared

When you copy a shared folder, the original shared folder is still shared, but the copy is not shared. When you move or rename a shared folder, it is no longer shared.

Guidelines for Shared Folder Permissions

The following list provides some general guidelines for managing your shared folders and assigning shared folder permissions:

- Determine which groups need access to each resource and the level of access that they require. Document the groups and their permissions for each resource.

- Assign permissions to groups instead of user accounts to simplify access administration.

- Assign to a resource the most restrictive permissions that still allow users to perform required tasks. For example, if users need only to read information in a folder and they will never delete or create files, assign the Read permission.

- Organize resources so that folders with the same security requirements are located within a folder. For example, if users require Read permission for several application folders, store the application folders within the same folder. Then share this folder instead of sharing each individual application folder.

- Use intuitive share names so that users can easily recognize and locate resources. For example, for the Applications folder, use Apps for the share name. You should also use share names that all client operating systems can use.

Table 10.2 describes share and folder naming conventions for different client computer operating systems.

Table 10.2   Shared Folder Naming Conventions

Client Computer Operating System	Share Name Length	Folder Name Length
Windows 2000, Windows NT, Windows 98, and Windows 95	80 characters	255 characters
MS-DOS, Windows 3.1, and Windows for Workgroups	8.3 characters	8.3 characters

Windows 2000 provides 8.3-character equivalent names, but the resulting names might not be intuitive to users. For example, a Windows 2000 folder named Accountants Database would appear as Account~1 on client computers running MS-DOS, Windows 3.1, and Windows for Workgroups.

Practice: Applied Permissions

In the following practice User1 has local access to files and has been assigned permissions to gain access to resources as an individual and as a member of a group, as shown in Figure 10.2. Determine what effective permissions User1 has in each situation:

1. User1 is a member of Group1, Group2, and Group3. Group1 has Read permission and Group3 has Full Control permission for FolderA. Group2 has no permissions for FolderA. What are User1's effective permissions for FolderA?

2. User1 is also a member of the Sales group, which has Read permission for FolderB. User1 has been denied the shared folder permission Full Control for FolderB as an individual user. What are User1's effective permissions for FolderB?

Figure 10.2   Applied permissions

Lesson Summary

In this lesson you learned that you can make a folder and its contents available to other users over a network by sharing the folder. Shared folder permissions are the only way to secure file resources on FAT volumes. Shared folder permissions apply to folders, not individual files. You also learned that shared folder permissions do not restrict access to users who gain access to the folder at the computer where the folder is stored. They only apply to users who connect to the folder over the network.

The shared folder permissions are Read, Change, and Full Control. Read permission allows users to view file names and subfolder names and view data in files. Read permission also allows users to run programs and to traverse to subfolders. Change permission allows users to add files and folders to the shared folder, change data in files, and delete subfolders and files. It also allows the user to perform actions permitted by the Read permission. Full Control permission allows users to change file permissions and take ownership of files on NTFS volumes, and to perform all tasks permitted by the Change permission. The default shared folder permission is Full Control, and it is assigned to the Everyone group when you share the folder.

Lesson 2: Planning Shared Folders

When you plan shared folders, you can reduce administrative overhead and ease user access. To plan shared folders, you must determine which resources you want shared, and then organize resources according to function, use, and administration needs.

Shared folders can contain applications and data. Use shared application folders to centralize administration. Use shared data folders to provide a central location for users to store and gain access to common files. This lesson outlines the points you must consider when sharing application and data folders.

After this lesson, you will be able to

- Plan which shared folder permissions to assign to user accounts and groups for application and data folders

Estimated lesson time: 5 minutes

Application Folders

Shared application folders are used for applications that are installed on a network server and they can be used from client computers. The main advantage of shared applications is that you do not need to install and maintain most components of the applications on each computer. Whereas program files for applications can be stored on a server, configuration information for most network applications is often stored on each workstation. The exact way in which you share application folders will vary depending on the application, your particular network environment, and your organization.

When you share application folders, consider the points in Figure 10.3, explained in more detail as follows:

- Create one shared folder for applications and organize all of your applications under this folder. When you combine all applications under one shared folder, you designate one location for installing and upgrading software.

- Assign the Administrators group the Full Control permission for the applications folder so that administrators can manage the application software and control user permissions.

- Remove the Full Control permission from the Everyone group and assign Read permission to the Users group. This provides more security because the Users group includes only user accounts that you created, whereas the Everyone group includes anyone who has access to network resources, including the Guest account.

- Assign the Change permission to groups that are responsible for upgrading and troubleshooting applications.

- Create a separate shared folder outside your application folder hierarchy for any application for which you need to assign different permissions. Then assign the appropriate permissions to that folder.

- Create a shared folder for applications.

- Assign Full Control to Administrators.

- Remove Full Control from Everyone and assign Read to Users.

- Assign Change to groups that upgrade and troubleshoot.

- Create a separate shared folder for each set of permissions.

Figure 10.3   Creating and sharing application folders

Data Folders

Users on a network use data folders to exchange public and working data. Working data folders are used by members of a team who need access to shared files. Public data folders are used by larger groups of users who all need access to common data.

When you use data folders, create and share common data folders on a volume that is separate from the operating system and applications. Data files should be backed up frequently, and with data folders on a separate volume, you can conveniently back them up. If the operating system requires reinstallation, the volume containing the data folder remains intact.

Public Data

When you share a common public data folder, do the following:

- Use centralized data folders so that data can be easily backed up.
- Assign the Change permission to the Users group for the common data folder (see Figure 10.4). This will provide users with a central, publicly accessible location for storing data files that they want to share with other users. Users will be able to gain access to the folder and read, create, or change files in it.

- Back up centralized data folders consistently.
- Share lower-level folders.

Figure 10.4   Public data and working data shared folders

Working Data

When you share a data folder for working files, do the following:

- Assign the Full Control permission to the Administrators group for a central data folder so that administrators can perform maintenance more easily.
- Share lower-level data folders below the central folder with the Change permission for the appropriate groups when you need to restrict access to those folders.

For an example, see Figure 10.4. To protect data in the Accountants folder, which is a subfolder of the Data folder, share the Accountants folder and assign the Change permission only to the Accountants group so that only members of the Accountants group can gain access to the Accountants folder.

Note   Because an administrator will always be able to take ownership of a file, your organization may find it necessary to encrypt files and folders to meet security requirements. You can find more information about encryption in the "File encryption overview" topic in system help and by researching on your own.

Lesson Summary

In this lesson you learned that you use shared application folders to centralize administration and make it easier to upgrade application software. When you use shared application folders, you should assign the Administrators group the Full Control permission for the applications folder so that members of this group can manage the application software and control user permissions. You should also remove the Full Control permission from the Everyone group and assign Read permission to the Users group. This provides more security because the Users group includes only user accounts that you created, whereas the Everyone group includes anyone who has access to network resources, including the Guest account.

You also learned that you use shared data folders to provide a central location for users to store and gain access to common files. When you use data folders, you should create and share common data folders on a volume that is separate from the operating system and applications. Data files should be backed up frequently, and with data folders on a separate volume, you can conveniently back them up.

Lesson 3: Sharing Folders

You can share resources with others by sharing folders containing those resources. To share a folder, you must be a member of one of several groups, depending on the role of the computer where the shared folder resides. When you share a folder, you can control access to the folder by limiting the number of users who can simultaneously gain access to it, and you can also control access to the folder and its contents by assigning permissions to selected users and groups. After a shared folder is created, you may need to modify folder sharing properties. You can stop sharing a folder, change its share name, and change user and group permissions to gain access to it. To access a shared folder, users must first have appropriate permissions and then make a connection to it. This lesson explains how to create and modify shared folders and how to connect to a shared folder.

After this lesson, you will be able to

- Create and modify shared folders
- Make a connection to a shared folder

Estimated lesson time: 20 minutes

Requirements for Sharing Folders

In Windows 2000, members of the built-in Administrators, Server Operators, and Power Users groups are able to share folders. The groups that can share folders and the machines on which they can share folders depend on the following requirements:

- In a Windows 2000 domain, the Administrators and Server Operators groups can share folders residing on any machines in the domain. The Power Users group is a local group and can only share folders residing on the stand-alone server or computer running Windows 2000 Professional where the group is located.

- In a Windows 2000 workgroup, the Administrators and Power Users groups can share folders on the stand-alone server or the computer running Windows 2000 Professional on which the group exists.

Note   If the folder to be shared resides on an NTFS volume, users must also have at least the Read permission for that folder to be able to share it.

Administrative Shared Folders

Windows 2000 automatically shares certain folders for administrative purposes. These shares are appended with a dollar sign ($). The $ hides the shared folder from users who browse the computer. The root of each volume, the system root folder, and the location of the printer drivers are all hidden shared folders that you can access from across the network.

Table 10.3 describes the purpose of the administrative shared folders that Windows 2000 automatically provides.

Table 10.3   Windows 2000 Administrative Shared Folders

Share	Purpose
C$, D$, E$, and so on	The root of each volume on a hard disk is automatically shared, and the share name is the drive letter appended with a dollar sign ($). When you connect to this folder, you have access to the entire volume. You use the administrative shares to remotely connect to the computer to perform administrative tasks. Windows 2000 assigns the Full Control permission to the Administrators group. Windows 2000 also automatically shares CD-ROM drives and creates the share name by appending the $ to the CD-ROM drive letter.
Admin$	The systemroot folder, which is C:\Winnt by default, is shared as Admin$. Administrators can gain access to this shared folder to administer Windows 2000 without knowing the folder in which it is installed. Only members of the Administrators group have access to this share. Windows 2000 assigns the Full Control permission to the Administrators group.
Print$	When you install the first shared printer, the *systemroot*\System32\Spool\Drivers folder is shared as Print$. This folder provides access to printer driver files for clients. Only members of the Administrators, Server Operators, and Print Operators groups have the Full Control permission. The Everyone group has the Read permission.

Hidden shared folders are not limited to those that the system automatically creates. You can share additional folders and append a $ to the end of the share name. Then, only users who know the folder name and posess proper permissions can gain access to the folder.

Sharing a Folder

When you share a folder, you can give it a share name, provide comments to describe the folder and its content, limit the number of users who have access to the folder, assign permissions, and share the same folder multiple times.

▶ **To share a folder**

1. Right-click the folder that you want to share, then click Sharing.

2. In the Sharing tab of the Properties dialog box (see Figure 10.5), click Share This Folder.

Figure 10.5   The Sharing tab of the properties dialog box for a folder

3. Type the name that users from remote locations use to make a connection to the shared folder in the Share Name box.

4. Optionally, type a description for the share name in the Comment box. The comment appears in addition to the share name when users at client computers browse the server for shared folders, and can be used to identify contents of the shared folder.

5. In the User Limit area, enter the number of users who can concurrently connect to the shared folder. If you click Maximum Allowed as the user limit, Windows 2000 Professional supports up to 10 connections total for all shares, services, etc. Windows 2000 Server can support an unlimited number of connections, but the number of client access licenses that you purchased limits the connections.

6. Click OK.

Assigning Shared Folder Permissions

After you share a folder, the next step is to specify which users have access to the shared folder by assigning shared folder permissions to selected user accounts and groups.

▶   **To assign permissions to user accounts and groups for a shared folder**

1. In the Sharing tab of the Properties dialog box for the shared folder, click Permissions.

2. In the Permissions For dialog box for the shared folder (see Figure 10.6), ensure that the Everyone group is selected and then click Remove.

Figure 10.6   Permissions For dialog box for a shared folder

3. In the Permissions dialog box, click Add.
4. In the Select Users, Computers, Or Groups dialog box (see Figure 10.7), click the user accounts and groups to which you want to assign permissions.

Figure 10.7   Select Users, Computers, Or Groups dialog box

5. Click Add to add the user account or group to the shared folder, or double-click on an object. Repeat this step for all user accounts and groups to which you want to assign permissions.

6. Click OK.

7. In the Permissions dialog box for the shared folder, click the user account or group, and then, under Permissions, select the Allow or the Deny check box of the appropriate permissions for the user account or group.

Note   In the Select Users, Computers, Or Groups dialog box, use the Look In list to see other domains or the local computer from which you can select user account and group names for assigning permissions. You can also search Active Directory for user accounts and groups by selecting Entire Directory from the Look In list.

Modifying Shared Folders

You can modify shared folders. You can stop sharing a folder, add or remove the share name, and modify shared folder permissions.

▶   **To modify a shared folder**

1. Click the Sharing tab in the Properties dialog box of the shared folder.

2. To complete the appropriate task, use the steps in Table 10.5.

Table 10.5   Steps to modify a Shared Folder

To	Do This
Stop sharing a folder	Click Do Not Share This Folder. A warning message appears if another user is connected to the shared folder.
Add a share name (share folder multiple times)	Click New Share. This option appears only after the folder has been shared once. Do so to consolidate multiple shared folders into one while allowing users to continue to use the same shared folder name that they used before you consolidated the folders.
Remove a share name	Click Remove Share. This option only appears after the folder has been shared more than once.
Modify shared folder permissions	Click Permissions. In the Permissions For dialog box, click Add or Remove. In the Select Users, Computers, Or Groups dialog box, click the user account or group whose permissions you want to modify.

Note   If you stop sharing a folder while a user has a file open, the user might lose data. If you click Do Not Share This Folder and a user has a connection to the shared folder, Windows 2000 displays a dialog box notifying you that a user has a connection to the shared folder.

Connecting to a Shared Folder

There are four methods for gaining access to a shared folder on another computer:

- Map to a network drive using the Map Network Drive Wizard
- Add a network place using the Add Network Place Wizard
- Connect using the Run command
- Connect using My Network Places

▶ **To connect to a shared folder by using the Map Network Drive Wizard**

1. Right-click the My Network Places icon on your desktop, then click Map Network Drive.

2. In the Map Network Drive Wizard, shown in Figure 10.8, click Folder, then type a Universal Naming Convention (UNC) path to the folder (*server_name**share_name*).

Figure 10.8   Map Network Drive Wizard

3. Enter a drive letter for the shared folder in the Drive list.

4. Select the Reconnect At Logon check box if you want to reconnect to the shared folder each time that you log on.

5. Click the link labeled Connect Using A Different User Name to connect to a shared folder with a different user account, then enter the user name and password in the Connect As dialog box.

▶ **To connect to a shared folder using the Add Network Place Wizard**

1. Double-click the My Network Places icon.

2. Double-click the Add Network Place icon.

3. On the Welcome To The Add Network Place Wizard page, type the location of the shared folder in the Type The Location Of The Network Place box, then click Next.

4. On the Completing The Add Network Place Wizard page, type a name you want to use for the shared folder in the Enter A Name For This Network Place box, then click Finish.

5. Connect to the shared folder by double-clicking the folder in My Network Places.

▶ **To connect to a shared folder by using the Run command**

1. Click Start, click Run, type **\\computer_name** in the Open box, then click OK.

2. On the windows containing the shared folders for the computer, double-click the shared folder to which you want to connect.

▶ **To connect to a shared folder by using My Network Places**

1. Double-click the My Network Places icon.

2. Locate the computer on which the shared folder is located.

3. Double-click the shared folder to which you want to connect.

Lesson Summary

In this lesson you learned that you can share resources with others by sharing folders containing those resources. To share a folder, you must be a member of one of several groups, depending on the role of the computer where the shared folder resides. You can control access to a shared folder by limiting the number of users who can simultaneously gain access to it, and you can also control access to the folder and its contents by assigning permissions to selected users and groups. You also learned that you may modify a shared folder. You can stop sharing it, add or remove its share name, and change user and group permissions to gain access to it. Finally, you learned that in order to access a shared folder, users must connect to it and have the appropriate permissions.

Lesson 4: Combining Shared Folder Permissions and NTFS Permissions

You share folders to provide network users with access to resources. If you are using a FAT volume, the shared folder permissions are all that is available to provide security for the folders you have shared and the folders and files they contain. If you are using an NTFS volume, you can assign NTFS permissions to individual users and groups to better control access to the files and subfolders in the shared folders. When you combine shared folder permissions and NTFS permissions, the more restrictive permission is always the overriding permission. This lesson introduces you to strategies for combining shared folder and NTFS permissions, and provides shared folder management practice.

After this lesson, you will be able to

- Combine shared folder permissions and NTFS permissions

Estimated lesson time: 45 minutes

Strategies for Combining Shared Folder Permissions and NTFS Permissions

One strategy for providing access to resources on an NTFS volume is to share folders with the default shared folder permissions and then control access by assigning NTFS permissions. When you share a folder on an NTFS volume, both shared folder permissions and NTFS permissions combine to secure file resources.

Shared folder permissions provide limited security for resources. You gain the greatest flexibility by using NTFS permissions to control access to shared folders. Also, NTFS permissions apply whether the resource is accessed locally or over the network.

When you use shared folder permissions on an NTFS volume, the following rules apply:

- You can apply NTFS permissions to files and subfolders in the shared folder. You can apply different NTFS permissions to each file and subfolder that a shared folder contains.

- In addition to shared folder permissions, users must have NTFS permissions for the files and subfolders that shared folders contain to gain access to those files and subfolders. This is in contrast to FAT volumes, where permissions for a shared folder are the only permissions protecting files and subfolders in the shared folder.

- When you combine shared folder permissions and NTFS permissions, the more restrictive permission is always the overriding permission.

In Figure 10.9, the Users group has the shared folder Full Control permission for the Public folder and the NTFS Read permission for FileA. The Users group's effective permission for FileA is Read because Read is the more restrictive permission. The effective permission for FileB is Full Control because both the shared folder permission and the NTFS permission allow this level of access.

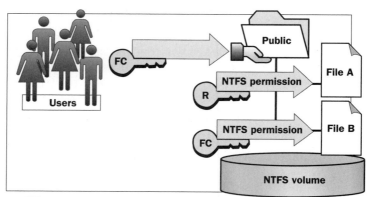

- NTFS permissions are required on NTFS volumes.
- Apply NTFS permissions to files and subfolders.
- Most restrictive permission is the effective permission.

Figure 10.9   Combining shared folder permissions and NTFS permissions

Practice: Managing Shared Folders

In this practice you determine users' effective permissions, plan shared folders, plan permissions, share a folder, assign shared folder permissions, connect to a shared folder, stop sharing a folder, and test the combined effects of shared folder permissions and NTFS permissions.

Important   To complete Optional Exercises 5 and 8, a second computer running as a Windows 2000 member server in the domain is ideal. However, you can still perform the steps if you have one computer.

Exercise 1: Combining Permissions

Figure 10.10 shows examples of shared folders on NTFS volumes. These shared folders contain subfolders that also have been assigned NTFS permissions. Determine a user's effective permissions for each example.

Figure 10.10   Combined permissions

1. In the first example, the Data folder is shared. The Sales group has the shared folder Read permission for the Data folder and the NTFS Full Control permission for the Sales subfolder.

    What are the Sales group's effective permissions for the Sales subfolder when Sales group members gain access to the Sales subfolder by making a connection to the Data shared folder?

2. In the second example, the Users folder contains user home folders. Each user home folder contains data that is only accessible to the user for whom the folder is named. The Users folder has been shared, and the Users group has the shared folder Full Control permission for the Users folder. User1 and User2 have the NTFS Full Control permission for only their home folder and no NTFS permissions for other folders. These users are all members of the Users group.

    What permissions does User1 have when he or she accesses the User1 subfolder by making a connection to the Users shared folder? What are User1's permissions for the User2 subfolder?

Exercise 2: Planning Shared Folders

In this exercise you plan how to share resources on servers in the main office of a manufacturing company. Record your decisions in Table 10.6 at the end of this exercise.

Figure 10.11 illustrates a partial folder structure for the servers at the manufacturing company.

Figure 10.11   Partial folder structure for the servers at a manufacturing Company

You need to make resources on these servers available to network users. To do this, determine which folders to share and what permissions to assign to groups, including the appropriate built-in groups.

Base your planning decisions on the following criteria:

- Members of the Managers group need to read and revise documents in the Management Guidelines folder. Nobody else should have access to this folder.

- Administrators need complete access to all shared folders, except for Management Guidelines.

- The Customer Service department requires its own network location to store working files. All customer service representatives are members of the Customer Service group.

- All employees need a network location to share information with each other.

- All employees need to use the spreadsheet, database, and word processing software.

- Only members of the Managers group should have access to the project management software.

- Members of the CustomerDBFull group need to read and update the customer database.

- Members of the CustomerDBRead group need to read the customer database only.

- Each user needs a private network location to store files. This location must be accessible by that user only.

- Share names must be accessible from Windows 2000, Windows NT, Windows 95, and non-Windows NT-based platforms.

Record your answers in Table 10.6.

Table 10.6   Shared Folders and Permissions for Exercise 2

Folder Name and Location	Shared Name	Groups and Permissions
Example: Management Guidelines	MgmtGd	Managers: Full Control

Exercise 3: Sharing Folders

In this exercise you share a folder.

▶ **To share a folder**

1. Log on to your domain as Administrator.

2. Start Windows Explorer, create a folder named C:\Apps (where C:\ is the name of your system drive), right-click Apps, then click Sharing.

   On the Sharing tab, notice that the folder is currently not shared.

3. Click Share This Folder.

   Notice that Share Name defaults to the name of the folder. If you want the share name to be different from the folder's name, change it here.

4. In the Comment box, type **shared productivity applications**, then click OK.

   How does Windows Explorer change the appearance of the Apps folder to indicate that it is a shared folder?

Exercise 4: Assigning Shared Folder Permissions

In this exercise you determine the current permissions for a shared folder and assign shared folder permissions to groups in your domain.

▶ **To determine the current permissions for the Apps shared folder**

1. Open the Apps Properties dialog box, click the Sharing tab, then click Permissions.

   Windows 2000 displays the Permissions For Apps dialog box.

   What are the default permissions for the Apps shared folder?

▶ **To remove permissions for a group**

1. Verify that the Everyone group is selected.
2. Click Remove.

▶ **To assign Full Control to the Administrators group**

1. Click Add.

   Windows 2000 displays the Select Users, Computers, Or Groups dialog box.

2. In the Look In list, select your domain; in the Name box, click Administrators, then click Add.
3. Click OK.

   Windows 2000 adds Administrators to the list of names with permissions.

   What type of access does Windows 2000 assign to Administrators by default?

4. In the Permissions box, under Allow, click Full Control.

   Why did Windows Explorer also select the Change permission for you?

5. Click OK.
6. Click OK to close the Apps Properties dialog box.

Optional Exercise 5: Connecting to a Shared Folder

In this exercise you use two methods to connect to a shared folder.

Important   To complete Optional Exercise 5, a second computer running as a Windows 2000 member server in the domain is ideal. However, you can still perform the steps if you have one computer.

▶ **To connect to a network drive using the Run command**

1. Log on to your second computer as Administrator.
2. Click Start, then click Run.

3. In the Open box, type **\\server1** (if you did not use SERVER1 as the name of your domain controller, use the appropriate name here and in the following steps), then click OK.

   Windows 2000 displays the Server1 window.

   Notice that only the folders that are shared appear.

   Which shared folders are currently available?

4. Double-click Apps to confirm that you can gain access to its contents.

5. Close the Apps On Server1 window.

▶ **To connect a network drive to a shared folder using the Map Network Drive command**

1. Right-click My Network Places, then click Map Network Drive.

2. In the Map Network Drive Wizard, in the Folder box, type **\\server1\apps** (if you did not use SERVER1 as the name of your domain controller, use the appropriate name here and in the following steps).

3. In the Drive box, select P:.

4. Clear the Reconnect At Logon check box.

   You will gain access to this shared folder only in this exercise. Disabling the option to reconnect will ensure that Windows 2000 will not automatically attempt to reconnect to this shared folder later.

5. To complete the connection, click Finish.

6. Close the Apps On Server1 (P:) window.

7. To confirm that Windows Explorer has successfully completed the drive mapping, on your desktop, double-click My Computer.

   Notice that Windows 2000 has added drive P as Apps On Server1 (P:).

   How does Windows Explorer indicate that this drive points to a remote shared folder?

▶ **To disconnect from a network drive using Windows Explorer**

1. In Windows Explorer, right-click Apps On Server1 (P:), then click Disconnect.

   Windows 2000 removes Apps On Server1 (P:) from the My Computer window.

2. Close the My Computer window.

▶ **To attempt to connect to a shared folder on your domain controller**

1. Log off Windows 2000, then log on to your domain as User81.

2. Click Start, then click Run.

3. In the Open box, type **\\server1\apps** (if you did not use SERVER1 as the name of your domain controller, use the appropriate name), then click OK.

   Windows 2000 displays a message stating that access is denied.

   Why were you denied access to the Apps shared folder?

4. Close all open windows and dialog boxes.

▶ **To connect to a shared folder using another user account**

1. Right-click My Network Places, then click Map Network Drive.

2. In the Map Network Drive Wizard, in the Folder box, type **\\server1\apps** (if you did not use SERVER1 as the name of your domain controller, use the appropriate name).

3. In the Drive box, select J:.

4. Click the link labeled Connect Using A Different User Name.

   The Connect As dialog box appears. This dialog box lets you specify a different user account to use to make a connection to the shared folder. It may also be a way to connect to other domains on the network (pre-Windows 2000). When would you use this option?

5. In the Connect As dialog box, in the User Name box, type **domain1\administrator** (where domain1 is your Windows 2000 domain).

6. In the Password box, type **password**, then click OK.

7. Confirm that the Reconnect At Logon check box is cleared, then click Finish.

   In Windows Explorer, can you gain access to drive J? Why or why not?

8. Close all windows and log off Windows 2000.

Exercise 6: Stopping Folder Sharing

In this exercise you stop sharing a shared folder.

▶ **To stop sharing a folder**

1. Log on to your domain as Administrator at your domain controller, then start Windows Explorer.

2. Right-click C:\Apps, then click Properties.

3. In the Apps Properties dialog box, click the Sharing tab.

4. Click Do Not Share This Folder, then click OK.

   Notice that Windows 2000 no longer displays the hand icon that identifies a shared folder under the Apps folder. You might need to refresh the screen; press F5 to refresh the screen.

5. Close Windows Explorer.

Exercise 7: Assigning NTFS Permissions and Sharing Folders

In this exercise you assign NTFS permissions to the Apps, Wordprocessing, Database, Public, and Manuals folders. Then, you share the Apps and the Public folders.

▶ **To assign NTFS permissions**

Use Windows Explorer to create the necessary folders (where C:\ is the name of your system drive) and to assign the NTFS permissions that are listed in Table 10.7. For each folder, do not allow inherited permissions to propagate to the object and remove any previously existing NTFS permissions.

Table 10.7   Folders and NTFS Permissions for Exercise 7

Path	User Account or Group in the Domain	NTFS Permissions
C:\Apps	Administrators Users	Full Control Read & Execute
C:\Apps\Wordprocessing	Administrators Users	Full Control Read & Execute
C:\Apps\Database	Administrators	Read & Execute
C:\Public	Administrators Users	Full Control Modify
C:\Public\Manuals	Administrators Users User83	Full Control Read & Execute Full Control

▶ **To share folders and assign shared folder permissions**

Share the appropriate application folders and assign permissions to network user accounts based on the information in Table 10.8. Remove all other shared folder permissions.

Table 10.8   Folders and Shared Folder Permissions for Exercise 7

Path and Shared Folder Name	User Account or Group	Shared Folder Permissions
C:\Apps shared as Apps	Administrators Users	Read Read
C:\Public shared as Public	Administrators Users	Full Control Full Control

Optional Exercise 8: Testing NTFS and Shared Folder Permissions

In this exercise you use different user accounts to test the permissions that you assigned in Exercise 1. To answer the questions in this exercise, refer to Tables 10.7 and 10.8 in Exercise 7.

> **Important** To complete Optional Exercise 8, a second computer running as a Windows 2000 member server in the domain is ideal. However, you can still perform the steps if you have one computer.

▶ **To test permissions for the Manuals folder when a user logs on locally as User82**

1. Log on to your domain as User82 at your domain controller.

2. In Windows Explorer, expand C:\Public\Manuals.

3. In the Manuals folder, attempt to create a file.

   Were you successful? Why or why not?

4. Close Windows Explorer.

▶ **To test permissions for the Manuals folder when a user makes a connection over the network**

1. Log on to your domain as User82 at your second computer, not at your domain controller.

2. Click Start, then click Run.

3. In the Open box, type **\\server1\public** (where SERVER1 is your domain controller), then click OK.

4. In the Public On Server1 window, double-click Manuals.

5. In the Manuals folder on your domain controller, attempt to create a file.

   Were you successful? Why or why not?

6. Close all windows and log off Windows 2000.

▶ **To test permissions for the Manuals folder when a user logs on locally as User83**

1. Log on to your domain as User83 at your domain controller.

2. In Windows Explorer, expand C:\Public\Manuals.

3. In the Manuals folder, attempt to create a file.

   Were you successful? Why or why not?

4. Close all windows and log off Windows 2000.

▶ **To test permissions for the Manuals folder when a user logs on as User83 and connects over the network**

1. Log on to your domain as User83 at your second computer, not at your domain controller.

2. Make a connection to the Public shared folder on your second computer.

3. In the Public On Server1 explorer window, double-click Manuals.

4. In the Manuals folder on your domain controller, attempt to create a file.

   Were you successful? Why or why not?

5. Close all windows and log off Windows 2000.

Lesson Summary

In this lesson you learned that you share folders to provide network users with access to resources. On a FAT volume, the shared folder permissions are all that is available to provide security for the folders you have shared and for the folders and files they contain. On an NTFS volume, you can assign NTFS permissions to individual users and groups to better control access to the files and subfolders in the shared folders. You also learned that when you combine shared folder permissions and NTFS permissions, the more restrictive permission is always the overriding permission.

In the practice portion of this lesson, you created and shared folders, stopped sharing a folder, created folders, applied NTFS permissions, and then shared the folders. If you have a second computer, you were able to test how the shared folder permissions and NTFS permissions combined to provide access to resources.

Lesson 5: Configuring Dfs to Gain Access to Network Resources

The Microsoft distributed file system (Dfs) for Windows 2000 Server provides users with convenient access to shared folders that are distributed throughout a network. A single Dfs shared folder serves as an access point to other shared folders in the network. This lesson introduces you to Dfs.

After this lesson, you will be able to

- Configure Dfs for Windows 2000 Server to provide user access to shared folders

Estimated lesson time: 40 minutes

Understanding Dfs

The Microsoft Dfs for Windows 2000 Server allows system administrators to make it easy for users to access and manage files that are physically distributed across a network. With Dfs, you can make files distributed across multiple servers appear to users as if they reside in one place on the network.

Dfs organizes shared folders that can reside on different computers, as shown in Figure 10.12. Dfs provides users with easy navigation to these shared folders. Users do not need to know where a resource is on a network to gain access to it. Dfs facilitates administering multiple shared folders.

Figure 10.12   Overview of Dfs

To share file resources across the network, Dfs does the following:

- **Organizes resources in a hierarchy.**   Dfs uses a hierarchy of server shares called a *Dfs share*. To create a Dfs share, you must first create a Dfs root. A *Dfs root* is a container for files and Dfs links. Each Dfs root can have multiple links beneath it, each of which points to a shared folder. The links of the Dfs root represent shared folders that can be physically located on different file servers. Table 10.9 describes the two types of Dfs roots.

Table 10.9   Types of Dfs Roots

Type of Dfs Root	Description
Domain	Stores the Dfs topology in Active Directory. Allows links to point to multiple identical shared folders for fault tolerance. Supports Domain Name System (DNS), multiple-level Dfs links, and file replication.
Standalone	Stores the Dfs topology on a single computer, not in Active Directory. Provides no fault tolerance if the computer that stores the Dfs topology or any of the shared folders that Dfs uses fails. Supports only one level of Dfs links.

- **Facilitates network navigation.**   A user who navigates a Dfs-managed shared folder does not need to know the name of the server on which the folder is shared. This simplifies network access because users no longer need to locate the network server on which a specific resource is located. After connecting to a Dfs root, users can browse and gain access to all resources below the root, regardless of the location of the server on which the resource is located.

- **Facilitates network administration.**   Dfs also simplifies network administration. If a server fails, you can move a link from one server to another without users being aware of the change. All that is required to move a link is to modify the Dfs folder to refer to the new server location of the shared folders. Users continue to use the same Dfs path for the link.

- **Preserves network permissions.**   A user can gain access to a shared folder through Dfs as long as the user has the required permission to gain access to the shared folder. If further restrictions are necessary, NTFS permissions can be set.

Note   Only client computers with Dfs client software can gain access to Dfs resources. Computers running Windows NT 4.0 and later or Windows 98 include a Dfs client. You must download and install a Dfs client for Windows 95.

Reasons for Using Dfs

You should consider implementing Dfs if

- Users who access shared folders are distributed across a site or sites
- Most users require access to multiple shared folders
- Server load balancing could be improved by redistributing shared folders
- Users require uninterrupted access to shared folders
- Your organization has Web sites for either internal or external use

Dfs Topology

A Dfs topology consists of a Dfs root, one or more Dfs links, and one or more Dfs shared folders (also known as replicas), to which each Dfs link points.

For domain-based Dfs, the domain server on which a Dfs root resides is known as a host server. You can replicate a Dfs root by creating roots on other servers in the domain. This provides file availability if the host server becomes unavailable.

To users, a Dfs topology provides a unified and transparent access to the network resources they need. To system administrators, a Dfs topology is a single DNS namespace. With domain-based Dfs, the DNS names for the Dfs roots resolve to the host servers for the Dfs root.

Because the host server for a domain-based Dfs is a member server within a domain, the Dfs topology is automatically published to Active Directory by default, thus providing synchronization of Dfs topologies across host servers. This in turn provides fault tolerance for the Dfs root and supports optional replication of Dfs shared folders.

Creating a Dfs

The tasks for creating a Dfs are:

1. Create a Dfs root.
2. Create a Dfs link.
3. Add Dfs shared folders (optional).
4. Set replication policy.

Creating a Dfs Root

You can create a Dfs root on Windows 2000 FAT or NTFS partitions. However, the FAT file system does not offer the security advantages of NTFS. When setting up a Dfs root, you have the option of establishing either a domain or a standalone Dfs root.

▶ **To create a Dfs root**

1. Click Start, point to Programs, point to Administrative Tools, then click Distributed File System.

2. In the Action menu, click New Dfs Root to start the New Dfs Root Wizard. Table 10.10 describes the wizard options that you can configure.

Table 10.10   Options on the New Dfs Root Wizard

Option	Description
Select The Dfs Root Type	Specifies either a domain or standalone Dfs root.
Specify The Host Domain For The Dfs Root (domain Dfs root type only)	Specifies the host domain for the domain Dfs root.
Specify The Host Server For The Dfs Root	Specifies the initial connection point for all resources in the Dfs tree or the host server. You can create a Dfs root on any computer running Windows 2000 Server.
Specify The Dfs Root Share	Specifies a shared folder to host the Dfs root. You can choose an existing shared folder or create a new share.
Name The Dfs Root	Specifies a descriptive name for the Dfs root.

Creating a Dfs Link

In a network environment, it might be difficult for users to keep track of the physical locations of shared resources. When you use Dfs, the network and file system structures become transparent to users. This enables you to centralize and optimize access to resources based on a single tree structure. Users can browse the links under a Dfs root without knowing where the referenced resources are physically located.

After you create a Dfs root, you can create Dfs links. Currently, the maximum number of Dfs links that you can assign to a Dfs root is 1000.

▶ **To create a Dfs link**

1. Click Start, point to Programs, point to Administrative Tools, then click Distributed File System.

2. Click the Dfs root to which you will attach a Dfs link. In the Action menu, click New Dfs Link.

3. In the Create A New Dfs Link dialog box (see Figure 10.13), in the Link Name box, type a name that users will see when they connect to Dfs.

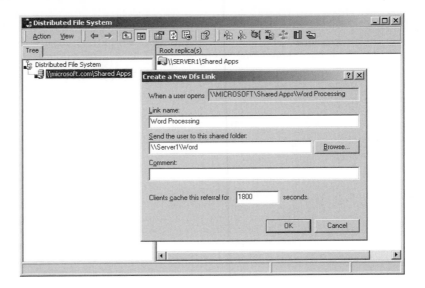

Figure 10.13   Create A New Dfs Link dialog box

4. In the Send The User To This Shared Folder box type or browse for the UNC name for the actual location of the shared folder to which the link refers.

5. In the Comment box, type optional additional information to help keep track of the shared folder (for example, the actual name of the shared folder).

6. In the Clients Cache This Referral For *X* Seconds box, enter the length of time for which clients cache a referral to a Dfs link. After the referral time expires, a client queries the Dfs server about the location of the link, even if the client has previously established a connection with the link.

7. Click OK.

The link appears below the Dfs root volume in the Distributed File System console.

Adding a Dfs Shared Folder

For each Dfs link, you can create a set of Dfs shared folders to which the Dfs link points. Within a set of Dfs shared folders, you add the first folder to the set when you create the Dfs link, using the Distributed File System console. Subsequent folders are added using the console's Add A New Replica dialog box. The maximum number of Dfs shared folders allowed in a set of shared folders is 32.

When you add Dfs shared folders, you can choose which folders will participate in replication. If you set folders to participate in replication, you must then set the replication policy for the shared folders, described later in this lesson.

▶ **To add a Dfs shared folder**

1. Click Start, point to Programs, point to Administrative Tools, then click Distributed File System.

2. In the Dfs console tree, right-click the Dfs link to which you want to assign a shared folder, then click New Replica.

3. In the Add A New Replica dialog box (see Figure 10.14), enter or browse for the name of the new shared folder in the Send The User To This Shared Folder box.

Figure 10.14   Add A New Replica dialog box

4. In the Replication Policy box

   ▪ Click Manual Replication to prevent the files located in the folder from participating in replication.

   ▪ Click Automatic Replication to cause the files located in the folder to participate in replication. Automatic replication is not available for standalone distributed file systems and can only be used for files stored on NTFS volumes on Windows 2000 servers.

5. Click OK.

Setting Replication Policy

You can ensure that the content of folders is always available to users by replicating that content to other roots or Dfs shared folders in the domain. You can replicate both Dfs roots and Dfs shared folders. Replication copies the content of one Dfs root to another, or from one Dfs shared folder to another Dfs shared folder.

Replicating a Dfs Root

Replicating a Dfs root to another server in the domain ensures that if the host server becomes unavailable for any reason, the Dfs associated with that Dfs root is still available to domain users.

▶ **To replicate a Dfs root**

1. Click Start, point to Programs, point to Administrative Tools, then click Distributed File System.
2. In the Dfs console tree, right-click the existing Dfs root that you want to replicate and select New Root Replica.
3. The New Dfs Root Wizard guides you through the process of replicating the Dfs root.

Setting Replication Policy for Dfs Shared Folders

When replicating a Dfs shared folder, Dfs stores a duplicate copy of the contents of the original shared folder in another shared folder.

Replicating a Dfs shared folder is a two-step process. First, you add the Dfs shared folder to a Dfs link, specifying that the folder will participate in replication. Then, you set the replication policy for the set of Dfs shared folders associated with that link. Replication of Dfs shared folders can be done either manually or automatically, as described in the following sections. Do not mix automatic and manual replication within a set of Dfs shared folders. Using one method of replication exclusively ensures that the contents of the Dfs shared folders remain synchronized.

Automatic Replication

For domain Dfs roots only, you can enable Dfs to automatically replicate the contents of a Dfs shared folder to other folders in the set of Dfs shared folders. This keeps the content of the Dfs shared folders synchronized as changes to one or more of the Dfs shared folders occurs. Automatic replication is not available for standalone Dfs and can only be used for files stored on NTFS volumes on Windows 2000 servers. Other types of files, such as FAT files, must be replicated manually.

Although invisible to users and administrators, Dfs uses the File Replication Service (FRS) to perform this function. Within a set of Dfs folders, FRS manages updates across any folders that are targeted for replication. By default, FRS synchronizes the contents of the Dfs shared folders at 15-minute intervals.

When you set replication policy, you select one of your Dfs shared folders as the initial master, which then replicates its contents to the other Dfs shared folders in the set of Dfs shared folders.

Manual Replication

For domain Dfs, if you do not enable FRS management of Dfs shared folders, you must maintain the same content in all of the Dfs shared folders manually.

▶ **To set replication policy for shared folders**

1. Click Start, point to Programs, point to Administrative Tools, then click Distributed File System.

2. In the Dfs console tree, right-click the Dfs link containing the shared folders for which you want to set a replication policy and select Replication Policy.

3. In the Replication Policy dialog box (see Figure 10.15), click a Dfs shared folder that you want to use as the master folder for replication, then click Set Master.

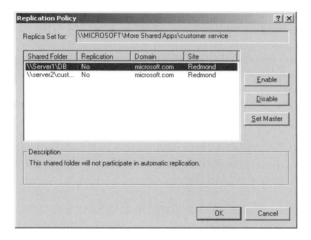

Figure 10.15   Replication Policy dialog box

4. Click each shared folder in the list and click Enable, then click OK.

Note   Do not mix automatic and manual replication within a set of Dfs shared folders. Using one method of replication exclusively ensures that the contents of the Dfs shared folders remain synchronized.

Practice: Using Dfs

In this practice you share some existing folders, and create and share some new folders. Then you create a new Dfs root and create some Dfs links.

Important   To complete the optional procedures in this practice, you must have two computers running Windows 2000 Server. This practice also assumes that one of the two computers is configured as a domain controller and the other computer is configured as a member server in the domain. If you have only one computer, read through the steps in the procedures marked as optional to learn how to perform them in the future.

▶ **To share existing folders**

1. Log on to your domain at your domain controller as Administrator.
2. Start Windows Explorer and share the folders listed in Table 10.12, using all default permissions. You created these folders in Exercise 7 of Lesson 4, earlier in this chapter.

Table 10.12   Shared Folders for Practice

Folder	Share Name
C:\Apps\Database	DB
C:\Apps\Wordprocessing	Word

▶ **To create new shared folders on a remote computer (optional)**

In Windows Explorer, create the folders listed in Table 10.13 (where C:\ is the name of your system drive) on your second (remote) computer and share them, using all default permissions.

Table 10.13   New Shared Folders for Practice

Folder	Share Name
C:\MoreApps\Maintenance	Maint
C:\MoreApps\CustomerService	Custom

▶ **To create a new Dfs root**

1. On your domain controller, click Start, point to Programs, point to Administrative Tools, then click Distributed File System.

   The Distributed File System console opens.

2. On the Action menu, click New Dfs Root.

   Windows starts the New Dfs Root Wizard.

3. Click Next.

   The wizard displays the Select The Dfs Root Type page. In this exercise you will create a domain Dfs root.

4. Click Create A Domain Dfs Root, then click Next.

   The wizard displays the Select The Host Domain For The Dfs Root page.

5. In the Domain Name box, confirm that microsoft.com (or the name of your domain) is displayed, then click Next.

   The wizard displays the Specify The Host Server For The Dfs Root page. You will create a Dfs root on your own server.

6. In the Server Name box, confirm that SERVER1 (or the name of your server) is displayed, then click Next.

   The wizard displays the Specify The Dfs Root Share page. Notice that you can use an existing share for the Dfs root, or the wizard can create a new shared folder for you.

   In this exercise you will let the wizard create a new shared folder for you. You have to provide both the location of the folder on your computer and a share name.

7. Select the Create A New Share option. Type **c:\app-dfs** in the Path To Share box (where C:\ is the name of your system drive), then type **Shared Apps** in the Share Name box.

8. Click Next.

   The Distributed File System message box appears, asking if you want to create the C:\App-Dfs folder.

9. Click Yes.

   The wizard displays the Name The Dfs Root page. The wizard fills in the Dfs Root Name box for you.

10. Click Next.

    The wizard displays the Completing The New Dfs Root Wizard page, which contains a summary of the choices that you made.

11. Confirm that the options that the wizard displays are correct, then click Finish.

    Notice that the *microsoft.com\Shared* Apps Dfs root now appears in the console tree (where microsoft.com is the name of your domain).

In the following two procedures you will create Dfs links according to Table 10.14 (where C:\ is the name of your system drive).

Table 10.14   Dfs Links for Practice

Link	Shared Folder	Folder Name
Database	\\Server1\DB	C:\Apps\Database
Word Processing	\\Server1\Word	C:\Apps\Wordprocessing
Maintenance	*second_computer*\Maint	C:\MoreApps\Maintenance
Customer Service	*second_computer*\Custom	C:\MoreApps\CustomerService

▶ **To add Dfs links on your domain controller**

1. Open the Distributed File System console and in the console tree, click \\microsoft.com\Shared Apps (where microsoft.com is the name of your domain).

2. On the Action menu, click New Dfs Link.

   The Distributed File System console displays the Create A New Dfs Link dialog box.

3. Type **Database** in the Link Name box.

4. In the Send The User To This Shared Folder box, type **\\server1\DB** (where SERVER1 is the name of your domain controller).

5. Click OK.

6. Repeat Steps 1 to 5 to add another link called Word Processing, which points to the shared folder \\Server1\Word (where SERVER1 is the name of your domain controller).

▶ **To add a Dfs link to a remote computer**

1. In the console tree, click \\microsoft.com\Shared Apps (where microsoft.com is the name of your domain).

2. On the Action menu, click New Dfs Link.

   The Distributed File System console displays the Create A New Dfs Link dialog box.

3. Type **Maintenance** in the Link Name box.

4. In the Send The User To This Shared Folder box, type **\\second_computer\maint** (where second_computer is the name of your non-domain-controller computer), then click OK.

5. Repeat Steps 1 to 4 to add another link called Customer Service, which points to the shared folder \\second_computer\Custom (where second_computer is the name of your non-domain-controller computer).

6. Close the Distributed File System console.

▶ **To gain access to a Dfs root**

1. On your domain controller or your second computer, double-click My Network Places, double-click Entire Network, click the Entire Contents link, double-click Microsoft Windows Network, and then double-click Microsoft (where Microsoft is the name of your domain).

2. Double-click SERVER1.

   Windows Explorer displays a list of all shared folders on your domain controller. Notice that one of the shared folders is Shared Apps, your Dfs root.

   Does Windows 2000 provide an indication that Shared Apps is a Dfs root and not an ordinary shared folder?

3. To view the Dfs links, double-click Shared Apps.

   Windows Explorer displays the Shared Apps On Server1 window, which shows all the links of Shared Apps.

   Does Windows 2000 indicate that the folders inside Shared Apps are Dfs links and not ordinary folders?

4. Close all open windows.

Lesson Summary

In this lesson you learned that the Microsoft distributed file system (Dfs) for Windows 2000 Server provides users with convenient access to shared folders that are distributed throughout a network. A Dfs share uses a tree structure containing a root and links. The links of the Dfs root represent shared folders that can be physically located on different file servers.

It might be difficult for users to keep track of the physical locations of shared resources in a network environment. When you use Dfs, the network and file system structures become transparent to users. A user who navigates a Dfs-managed shared folder does not need to know the name of the server on which the folder is shared, or the actual file name.

After connecting to a Dfs root, users can browse and gain access to all resources below the root, regardless of the location of the server on which the resource is located. If a server fails, you can move a link from one server to another without users being aware of the change. All that is required to move a link is a modification of the Dfs folder to refer to the new server location of the shared folders. Users continue to use the same Dfs path for the link.

In the practice portion of this lesson you shared some existing folders, created some new share folders, created a Dfs root, and then created some Dfs links.

Review

Here are some questions to help you determine if you have learned enough to move on to the next chapter. If you have difficulty answering review questions, please go back and review the material in this chapter before beginning the next chapter. The answers for these questions are located in Appendix A, "Questions and Answers."

1. When a folder is shared on a FAT volume, what does a user with the Full Control shared folder permissions for the folder have access to?

2. What are the shared folder permissions?

3. By default, what are the permissions that are assigned to a shared folder?

4. When a folder is shared on an NTFS volume, what does a user with the Full Control shared folder permission for the folder have access to?

5. When you share a public folder, why should you use centralized data folders?

6. What is the best way to secure files and folders that you share on NTFS partitions?

7. How does Dfs facilitate network navigation for users?

C H A P T E R   1 1

Administering Active Directory

About This Chapter

Administering Active Directory goes beyond setup and configuration. It includes locating objects, assigning permissions to objects, publishing resources, moving objects within and between domains, delegating administrative control to organizational units (OUs), backing up and restoring, and troubleshooting Active Directory. This chapter provides details on Active Directory administrative tasks.

Before You Begin

To complete this chapter, you must have

- Completed the Setup procedures located in "About This Book"
- The knowledge and skills covered in Chapter 7, "User Account Administration," Chapter 8, "Group Account Administration," Chapter 9, "Securing Network Resources," and Chapter 10, "Administering Shared Folders"
- Configured the computer as a domain controller in a domain
- Installed the Windows 2000 Support Tools using the procedure in Chapter 3, "Active Directory Administration Tasks and Tools"

Lesson 1: Locating Active Directory Objects

Active Directory stores information about objects on the network. Each object is a distinct, named set of attributes that represents a specific network entity. Active Directory is designed to provide information to queries about directory objects from both users and programs. In this lesson you will learn how to use Find (located in the Active Directory Users and Computers console) to locate Active Directory objects.

After this lesson, you will be able to

- Identify the types of Active Directory objects
- Use Find to locate any type of Active Directory object

Estimated lesson time: 15 minutes

Understanding Common Active Directory Objects

Adding new resources to your network creates new Active Directory objects that represent these resources. You should be familiar with some of the common Active Directory objects. Table 11.1 describes the most common object types that you can add to Active Directory.

Table 11.1   Common Object Types and Their Contents

Object Type	Contents
User account	The information that allows a user to log on to Windows 2000, such as user logon name. This information also has many optional fields including first name, last name, display name, telephone number, e-mail, and home page.
Contact	Information about a person with a connection to the organization. This information also has many optional fields including Telephone Number, E-mail, Address, and Home Page.
Group	A collection of user accounts, groups, or computers that you can create and use to simplify administration.
Shared folder	A pointer to the shared folder on a computer. A *pointer* contains the address of certain data, rather than the data itself. Shared folders and printers exist in the registry of a computer. When you publish a shared folder in Active Directory, you are creating an object that contains a pointer to the shared folder.
Printer	A pointer to a printer on a computer. You must manually publish a printer on a computer that is not in Active Directory. Microsoft Windows 2000 automatically adds printers that you create on domain computers to Active Directory.
Computer	The information about a computer that is a member of the domain.

Table 11.1   Common Object Types and Their Contents *(continued)*

Object Type	Contents
Domain controllers	The information about a domain controller including an optional description, its Domain Name System (DNS) name, its pre-Windows 2000 name, the version of the operating system loaded on the domain controller, the location, and who is responsible for managing the domain controller.
Organizational Unit (OU)	Contains other objects, including other OUs. Used to organize Active Directory objects.

Using Find

To locate Active Directory objects, open the Active Directory Users and Computers console located in the Administrative Tools folder. Then right-click a domain or a container in the console tree and click Find. The Find dialog box provides options that allow you to search the global catalog to locate Active Directory objects (see Figure 11.1). The Find dialog box helps you create an LDAP query that will be executed against the directory or a specific OU. The global catalog contains a partial replica of the Entire Directory, so it stores information about every object in a domain tree or forest. Because the global catalog contains information about every object, a user can find information regardless of which domain in the tree or forest contains the data. Active Directory automatically generates the contents of the global catalog from the domains that make up the directory.

Figure 11.1   Using the Find dialog box to locate objects

Table 11.2 describes the options in the Find dialog box.

Table 11.2   Options in the Find Dialog Box

Element	Description
Find	A list of object types for which you can search, including users, contacts, and groups; computers; printers; shared folders; OUs; and custom search. Custom search builds the Lightweight Directory Access Protocol (LDAP) query or allows you to enter your own LDAP query based on parameters you enter. For example, the LDAP query, OU=*er*, (entered in the Advanced tab) searches for OU names containing "er" in the middle, and returns the Domain Controllers OU.
In	A list of locations in which you can search, including the entire Active Directory, a specific domain, or an OU.
Browse	A button that allows you to select the path of your search.
Advanced	The context-sensitive tab in which you define the search criteria to locate the object that you need. This tab provides an array of choices when you choose to find users, contacts, and groups; computers; printers; shared folders; or OUs. When you choose custom search, the Advanced tab makes you type in the query manually, or create a search through the use of the most common available attributes that are organized by object type on the Custom Search tab. The Custom Search tab provides the same elements that are otherwise found on the Advanced tab.
Field	A context-sensitive list of the attributes for which you can search on the object type that you select; located in the Advanced tab.
Condition	A context-sensitive list of the methods available to further define the search for an attribute; located in the Advanced tab.
Value	A box that allows you to enter the value for the condition of the field (attribute) that you are using to search the Directory; located in the Advanced tab. You can search for an object by using an attribute of the object only if you enter a value for the attribute. For example, if you are looking for users whose first name starts with the letter R, you select First Name in the field list, select Starts With in the condition list, and type R in the Value box.
Search Criteria	A box that lists each search criteria that you have defined; located in the Advanced tab. To define a search criterion you use the Field list, Condition list, and Value box, then click Add. To remove search criteria, select the criteria, then click Remove. You can add or remove search criteria to narrow or widen your search.
Find Now	A button used to begin a search after search criteria are defined.
Stop	A button used to stop a search. Items found up to the point of stopping the search are displayed.
Clear All	A button used to clear the specified search criteria.
Results	A box that opens at the bottom of the Find window and displays the results of your search after you click Find Now.

Practice: Searching Active Directory

In this practice you search Active Directory for objects based on search criteria that you provide. First, you create user accounts for the practice. Then you find a user's account based on his or her primary phone number, and finally you find a printer that is able to staple the pages it prints.

Important   You need to have a local printer installed on your computer. However, you do *not* need a printing device connected to the computer. If you do not have a local printer installed, create one now. Remember that *printing device* refers to the physical machine that prints and that *local printer* refers to the software that Windows 2000 needs to send data to the printing device.

▶ **To create user accounts in a domain**

1. Log on to your domain as Administrator, then open the Active Directory Users and Computers console.

2. In the console tree, click Users.

3. On the Action menu, point to New, then click User.

   Notice that the New Object-User dialog box shows that the new user account is being created in the Users folder of your domain.

4. Create the user accounts shown in Table 11.3.

   Table 11.3   User Accounts for Practice

First Name	Last Name	User Logon Name	Password	Change Password
User	Twenty	User20	Password	Default setting
User	Twentyone	User21	Password	Default setting
User	Twentytwo	User22	Password	Default setting

   Make each user a member of the Print Operators group or another group with the right to log on locally to a domain controller.

5. Edit the properties of the User20 account that you created, and in the General tab of the Properties dialog box, in the Telephone Number box, type **555-1234**.

▶ **To find user accounts in the domain**

1. In the console tree, right-click your domain, then click Find.

   Windows 2000 displays the Find dialog box.

   In the Find dialog box, what object type can you select for a search?

2. Ensure that Users, Contacts, And Groups is selected in the Find box, then click Find Now. What do you see?

   Notice how Windows 2000 can find objects, such as user accounts, regardless of their location.

3. In the Find Users, Contacts, And Groups dialog box, click Clear All, then click OK to acknowledge that you want to clear the search results.

4. In the In list, select your domain.

5. Click the Advanced tab.

6. Click Field, point to User, then scroll down and click Telephone Number.

   Notice that Windows 2000 fills in Starts With in the Condition list.

7. In the Value box, type **555**, then click Add.

8. Click Find Now.

   In the Find Users, Contacts, And Groups dialog box, Windows 2000 displays the User Twenty account for which you typed a telephone number of 555-1234.

9. Close the Find Users, Contacts, And Groups dialog box.

▶ **To view printers in Active Directory Users and Computers**

1. On the View menu, click Users, Groups, And Computers As Containers.

   By default, Active Directory Users and Computers does not show printers. You have to change the view options.

2. In the console tree, expand Domain Controllers to view your computer.

   Active Directory Users and Computers displays your computer in the console tree. Notice that you can expand the computer because it is now shown as a container.

3. In the console tree, click your computer.

   Active Directory Users and Computers displays all printers on your computer as objects that are associated with your computer.

4. To view the properties of a printer, double-click the printer.

5. On the Properties dialog box for the printer, click the Staple check box to identify the printer as one that can staple, then click OK.

6. Minimize Active Directory Users and Computers.

7. Click Start, point to Search, then click For Printers.

8. In the Find Printers dialog box, click the Features tab.

9. Click the Can Staple check box.

10. In the In list, select your domain, then click Find Now.

    Windows 2000 displays the printer that you modified in the list of printers that are capable of stapling.

11. Close the Find Printers dialog box.

Lesson Summary

In this lesson you learned that common Active Directory objects include user accounts, contacts, groups, shared folders, printers, computers, domain controllers, and OUs. You learned to locate objects by starting the Active Directory Users and Computers console, right-clicking an object within a domain in the console tree, and clicking Find. The Find dialog box provides fields that allow you to search for Active Directory objects.

In the practice portion of this lesson you searched Active Directory for objects based on search criteria you specified.

Lesson 2: Controlling Access to Active Directory Objects

Windows 2000 uses an object-based security model to implement access control for all Active Directory objects. This security model is similar to the one that Windows 2000 uses to implement Microsoft Windows NT file system (NTFS) security. Every Active Directory object has a security descriptor that defines who has the permissions to gain access to the object and what type of access is allowed. Windows 2000 uses these security descriptors to control access to objects. This lesson explains how to set permissions for Active Directory objects.

After this lesson, you will be able to

- Set permissions on Active Directory objects to control user access

Estimated lesson time: 20 minutes

Understanding Active Directory Permissions

Active Directory permissions provide security for resources by allowing you to control who can gain access to individual objects or object attributes and the type of access that you will allow.

Active Directory Security

Use Active Directory permissions to determine who has the permissions to gain access to the object and what type of access is allowed. An administrator or the object owner must assign permissions to the object before users can gain access to the object. Windows 2000 stores a list of user access permissions, called the access control list (ACL), for every Active Directory object. The ACL for an object lists who can access the object and the specific actions that each user can perform on the object.

You can use permissions to assign administrative privileges to a specific user or group for an OU, a hierarchy of OUs, or a single object, without assigning administrative permissions for controlling other Active Directory objects.

Object Permissions

The object type determines which permissions you can select. Permissions vary for different object types. For example, you can assign the Reset Password permission for a user object but not for a printer object.

A user can be a member of multiple groups, each with different permissions that provide different levels of access to objects. When you assign a permission to a user for access to an object and that user is a member of a group to which you assigned a different permission, the user's effective permissions are the combination of the user and group permissions. For example, if a user alone has Read permission for an object and is a member of a group with Write permission, the user's effective permission for the object is Read and Write.

You can allow or deny permissions. Denied permissions take precedence over any permissions that you otherwise allow for user accounts and groups. If you deny a user permission to gain access to an object, the user will not have that permission, even if you allow the permission for a group of which the user is a member. You should deny permissions only when it is absolutely necessary to deny permission to a specific user who is a member of a group with allowed permissions.

Note Always ensure that all objects have at least one user with the Full Control permission. Failure to do so might result in some objects being inaccessible to the person using the Active Directory Users and Computers console, even an administrator, unless object ownership is changed.

Standard Permissions and Special Permissions

You can set standard permissions and special permissions on objects. Standard permissions are the most frequently assigned permissions and are composed of special permissions. Special permissions provide you with a finer degree of control for assigning access to objects.

For example, the standard Write permission is composed of the Write All Properties, Add/Remove Self As Member, and Read special permissions.

Table 11.4 lists standard object permissions that are available for most objects (most object types also have special permissions) and the type of access that each standard permission allows.

Table 11.4   Standard Object Permissions and Type of Access Allowed

Object Permission	Allows the User To
Full Control	Change permissions and take ownership, plus perform the tasks that are allowed by all other standard permissions
Read	View objects and object attributes, the object owner, and Active Directory permissions
Write	Change object attributes
Create All Child Objects	Add any type of child object to an OU
Delete All Child Objects	Remove any type of object from an OU

Assigning Active Directory Permissions

You can use the Active Directory Users and Computers console to set standard permissions for objects and attributes of objects. You use the Security tab of the Properties dialog box for the object to assign permissions (see Figure 11.2). The Properties dialog box is different for each object type.

Important   You must select Advanced Features on the View menu to access the Security tab and assign standard permissions for an object.

Figure 11.2   Setting Active Directory permissions

If the check boxes under Permissions are shaded, then the object has inherited permissions from the parent object. To prevent an object from inheriting permissions from a parent folder, clear the Allow Inheritable Permissions From Parent To Propagate To This Object check box.

► **To assign standard permissions for an object**

1. In Active Directory Users and Computers, on the View menu, ensure that Advanced Features is selected.

2. Select an object, click Properties on the Action menu, then click the Security tab in the Properties dialog box for the object.

3. To assign standard permissions:

   ▪ To add a new permission, click Add, click the user account or group to which you want to assign permissions, click Add, then click OK.

   ▪ To change an existing permission, click the user account or group.

4. Under Permissions, select the Allow check box or the Deny check box for each permission you want to add or remove.

Standard permissions are sufficient for most administrative tasks. However, you might need to view the special permissions that constitute a standard permission. Occasionally the Security tab will display a user or a group where none of the standard permissions is allowed or denied; in such a case, the user or group has been given special permissions that are accessible through the Advanced button.

▶ **To view special permissions**

1. In the Security tab in the Properties dialog box for the object, click Advanced.

2. In the Access Control Settings For dialog box for the object (an example is shown in Figure 11.3), in the Permissions tab, click the entry that you want to view in the Permission Entries list, then click View/Edit.

Figure 11.3   Access Control Settings For Users dialog box

3. In the Permission Entry For dialog box (see Figure 11.4) for the object, view the special permissions on the appropriate tab:

   ▪ Object tab, to view special object permissions assigned to the user or group.

   ▪ Properties tab, to view user or group read and write access to specific object properties.

Note   Avoid assigning permissions for specific properties of objects because this can complicate system administration. Errors can result, such as Active Directory objects not being visible, preventing users from completing tasks.

Figure 11.4   Permission Entry For Users dialog box

Using Permissions Inheritance

Similar to file and folder permissions inheritance, permissions inheritance for Active Directory objects minimizes the number of times that you need to assign permissions for objects. When you assign permissions, you can apply the permissions to child objects, which propagates the permissions to all of the child objects for a parent object, as shown in Figure 11.5. To indicate that permissions are inherited, the check boxes for inherited permissions are shown as shaded.

■ Permissions flow down to child objects.

■ Preventing inheritance stops the flow of permissions.

Figure 11.5   Inheriting permissions and blocking inheritance

For example, you can assign Full Control permission to a group for an OU that contains printers and then propogate this permission to all child objects. The result is that all group members can administer all printers in the OU.

You can specify that permissions for a given object are propagated to all child objects. You can also prevent permissions inheritance. When you copy previously inherited permissions, you are starting with exactly the same permissions that the object currently inherits from its parent object. However, any permissions for the parent object that you modify after blocking inheritance no longer apply. When you remove previously inherited permissions, Windows 2000 removes existing permissions and assigns no additional permissions to the object. You have to assign any permissions you want for the object.

Preventing Permissions Inheritance

You can prevent permissions inheritance so that a child object does not inherit permissions from its parent object by clearing the Allow Inheritable Permissions From Parent To Propagate To This Object check box. When you prevent inheritance, only the permissions that you explicitly assign to the object apply. You use the Security tab in the Properties dialog box to prevent permissions inheritance.

When you prevent permissions inheritance, Windows 2000 allows you to

- Copy previously inherited permissions to the object. The new explicit permissions for the object are a copy of the permissions that it previously inherited from its parent object. Then, according to your needs, you can make any necessary changes to the permissions.
- Remove previously inherited permissions from the object. Windows 2000 removes any previously inherited permissions. No permissions exist for the object. Then, according to your needs, you can assign any permissions for the object.

Practice: Controlling Access to Active Directory Objects

In this practice you create an OU with two users and review the default security settings on Active Directory components.

Caution   In this exercise do not change any security settings in Active Directory. Making changes could result in losing access to portions of Active Directory.

▶ **To create an OU containing two user accounts**

1. Log on to your domain as Administrator, then open Active Directory Users and Computers.
2. In the console tree, click your domain.
3. On the Action menu, point to New, then click Organizational Unit.

4. In the New Object-Organizational Unit dialog box, in the Name box, type **security1**, then click OK.

5. In the Security1 OU, create a user account that has the First Name field and the User Logon Name field set to Assistant1. Type **password** as the password and accept the defaults for all other options.

6. In the same OU, create another user account that has the First Name field and the User Logon Name set to Secretary1. Type **password** as the password and accept the defaults for all other options.

7. Grant both users membership in the Print Operators group or another group with the right to log on locally to the domain controller.

▶ **To view default Active Directory permissions for an OU**

1. On the View menu, enable Advanced Features.

   Enabling the viewing of advanced features allows you to review and configure Active Directory permissions.

2. In the console tree, right-click Security1, then click Properties.

3. Click the Security tab.

4. In Table 11.5, list the groups that have permissions for the Security1 OU. You will need to refer to these permissions in Lesson 5.

Table 11.5   Groups that Have Permissions for the Security1 OU

User Account or Group	Assigned Permissions

How can you tell if any of the default permissions are inherited from the domain, which is the parent object?

▶ **To view special permissions for an OU**

1. In the Security1 Properties dialog box, in the Security tab, click Advanced.

   The Access Control Settings For Security1 dialog box appears.

2. To view special permissions for Account Operators, in the Permission Entries box, click each entry for Account Operators, then click View/Edit.

The Permission Entry For Security1 dialog box appears.

What object permissions are assigned to Account Operators? What can Account Operators do in this OU? (Hint: Check each permission entry for Account Operators in the Permission Entries box in the Access Control Settings For Security1 dialog box.)

Do any objects within this OU inherit the permissions assigned to the Account Operators group? Why or why not?

3. Close all open dialog boxes, but do not close Active Directory Users and Computers.

▶ **To view the default Active Directory permissions for a user object**

1. In the Active Directory Users and Computers console tree, click Security1.

2. In the details pane, right-click Secretary1, then click Properties.

3. Click the Security tab.

4. In Table 11.6, list the groups that have permissions for the Secretary1 user account. You will need to refer to these permissions in Lesson 5. If the dialog box indicates that special permissions are present for a group, do not list the special permissions to which you can gain access through the Advanced button.

Table 11.6   Permissions for the Secretary1 User Account

Group	Assigned Permissions

Are the standard permissions for a user object the same as those for an OU object? Why or why not?

Are any of the standard permissions inherited from Security1, the parent object? How can you tell?

What do the permissions of the Account Operators group allow its members to do with the user object?

5. Close all programs and log off Windows 2000.

Lesson Summary

In this lesson you learned that every Active Directory object has a security descriptor that defines who has permission to gain access to the object and what type of access is allowed. An administrator or the object owner must assign permissions to an object before users can gain access to it. Windows 2000 stores a list of user access permissions, called the ACL, for every Active Directory object.

You also learned how to set standard permissions and special permissions on objects. The standard permissions are Full Control, Write, Read, Create All Child Objects, and Delete All Child Objects. Special permissions provide you with a finer degree of control over assigning access to objects. Permissions inheritance in Active Directory minimizes the number of times that you need to assign permissions for objects. When you assign permissions, you can apply the permissions to child objects, which propagates the permissions inheritance for a given parent object. You also learned to how to block permissions inheritance.

In the practice portion of this lesson you created an OU with two users and reviewed the default security settings on Active Directory components.

Lesson 3: Publishing Resources in Active Directory

As an administrator, you need to be able to provide secure and selective publication of network resources to network users and make it easy for users to find information. The directory stores this information for rapid retrieval and integrates Windows 2000 security mechanisms to control access. This lesson explains how to publish resources in Active Directory.

After this lesson, you will be able to

- Publish shared folders
- Publish printers
- Publish network services

Estimated lesson time: 10 minutes

Publishing Resources in Active Directory

Resources that can be published in the directory include objects such as users, computers, printers, folders, files, and network services.

Publishing Users and Computers

User and computer accounts are added to the directory using the Active Directory Users and Computers console. Information about the accounts that is useful for other network users is published automatically. Other information, such as account security information, is made available only to certain administrator groups.

Publishing Shared Resources

Publishing information about shared resources such as printers, folders, and files makes it easy for users to find these resources on the network. Windows 2000 network printers are automatically published in the directory when installed. Information about Windows NT printers and shared folders can be published in the directory using the Active Directory Users and Computers console.

▶   **To publish a shared folder**

1. Click Start, point to Programs, point to Administrative Tools, then click Active Directory Users And Computers.

2. In the console tree, double-click the domain node.

3. Right-click the container in which you want to add the shared folder, point to New, and click Shared Folder.

4. In the New Object-Shared Folder dialog box, type the name of the folder in the Name box.

5. In the Network Path box, type the UNC name (*server**share*\\) that you want to publish in the directory, then click OK.

The shared folder appears in the directory in the container you selected.

▶ **To publish a Windows NT printer**

Note The Windows NT printer must be installed before publishing in Active Directory. To install a Windows NT printer, click Start, point to Settings, and then click Printers.

---

1. Click Start, point to Programs, point to Administrative Tools, then click Active Directory Users And Computers.

2. In the console tree, double-click the domain node.

3. In the console tree, right-click the container where you want to publish the printer, point to New, and then click Printer.

4. In the New Object-Printer dialog box, type the UNC name that you want to publish in the directory in the Network Path Of The Pre-Windows 2000 Print Share box, then click OK.

The Windows NT printer appears in the directory in the folder you selected.

Publishing Network Services

Network-enabled services, such as Certificate Services, can be published in the directory so administrators can find and administer them using the Active Directory Sites and Services console. By publishing a service, rather than computers or servers, administrators can focus on managing the service regardless of which computer is providing the service or where the computer is located. Additional services or applications can be published in the directory using Active Directory programming interfaces.

The following topics describe some types of service information that may be useful to publish to the directory. The qualities that make a service appropriate for publishing may be better understood by understanding how Active Directory uses services.

Categories of Service Information

Binding and configuration information are the two types of information frequently published using Active Directory.

- Binding information allows clients to connect to services that do not have well known bindings and that conform to a service-centric model. By publishing the bindings for these kinds of services, Windows 2000 can automatically establish connections with services. Machine-centric services are typically handled on a service-by-service basis and should not be published to the directory.

- Configuration information can be common across client applications. Publishing this information allows you to distribute current configuration information for these applications to all clients in the domain. The configuration information is accessed by client applications as needed. This eases application configuration for users and gives you more control over application behaviors.

Characteristics of Service Information

Service information that you publish to the directory is most effective if it has the following characteristics:

- **Useful to many clients.**   Information that is useful to a small set of clients or that is useful only in certain areas of the network should not be published. If not widely used, this information wastes network resources, since it is published to every domain controller in the domain.

- **Relatively stable and unchanging.**   Although there may be exceptions to this rule, it generally makes sense to publish only service information that changes less frequently than two replication intervals. For intra-site replication, the maximum replication period is 15 minutes, and for inter-site replication, the maximum replication period is configured based on the replication interval of the site link used for the replication. Object properties that change more frequently create excessive demands on network resources. Property values may be out of date until updates are published, which can take as long as the maximum replication period. Consequently, having properties out of date for that period of time must not create unacceptable conditions. For example, some network services select a valid TCP port for use each time they are started. After selecting the port, the service updates Active Directory with this information, which is stored as the service connection point. Clients access the service connection point when they want to use the service, but if the new service connection point has not been replicated when the client requests it, the client will receive an outdated port, rendering the service temporarily inaccessible.

- **Well-defined, reasonable properties.**   Information that is of a consistent form is easier for services to use. The information should be relatively small in size.

Example of Service Publication

The following is an example of service publication using Active Directory Sites and Services:

▶ **To set security permissions and delegate control of certificate templates**

1. Log on to the system as an Administrator.

2. Click Start, point to Programs, point to Administrative Tools, then click Active Directory Sites And Services.

3. In the console tree, click Active Directory Sites And Services.

4. On the View menu, click Show Services Node.

5. In the console tree, click Active Directory Sites And Services, click Services, click Public Key Services, and click Certificate Templates.

6. For each certificate template for which you want to set security permissions, double-click the certificate template in the details pane to open properties.

7. On the Properties dialog box for the certificate template, click the Security tab and set the security permissions accordingly.

8. Click OK.

These changes apply only to certificate templates in the current domain.

Lesson Summary

In this lesson you learned how to publish shared folders, printers, and network services in Active Directory.

Lesson 4: Moving Active Directory Objects

You move objects from one location to another when organizational or administrative functions change—for example, when an employee moves from one department to another. This lesson shows you how to move Active Directory objects within and between domains.

After this lesson, you will be able to

- Move objects within a domain
- Move objects between domains
- Move workstations or member servers between domains
- Move domain controllers between sites

Estimated lesson time: 20 minutes

Moving Objects

In the logical environment, you can move objects within and between domains in Active Directory. In the physical environment, you can move domain controllers between sites.

Moving Objects Within a Domain

To reduce administrative overhead, you can move objects with identical security requirements into an OU or container within a domain. You can then assign access permissions to the OU or container and all objects in it.

▶ **To move objects within a domain**

1. In Active Directory Users and Computers, select the object to move, then from the Action menu, click Move.

2. In the Move dialog box (see Figure 11.6), select the OU or container to which you want the object to move, then click OK.

The following conditions apply when you move objects between OUs or containers:

- Permissions that are assigned directly to objects remain the same.
- The objects inherit permissions from the new OU or container. Any permissions that were previously inherited from the old OU or container no longer affect the objects.
- You can move multiple objects at the same time.

Figure 11.6   The Move dialog box

Note   To simplify assignment of permissions for printers, move printers on different print servers that require identical permissions to the same OU or container. Printers are located in the Computer object for the print server. To view a printer, click View, then click Users, Groups, And Computers As Containers.

Moving Objects Between Domains

To support domain consolidation or organizational restructuring operations, Windows 2000 allows you to move objects between domains. The MOVETREE command-line utility is used to move Active Directory objects such as organizational units, users, and groups between domains in a single forest, with some exceptions. This tool is available in Windows 2000 Support Tools. The Windows 2000 Support Tools are included on the Windows 2000 CD-ROM in the \SUP-PORT\TOOLS folder. For information on installing the Windows 2000 Support Tools, see Chapter 3, "Active Directory Administration Tasks and Tools."

The procedure for moving an object (whether it be a leaf object or the root object) involves taking an existing object and moving it below an existing parent. The distinguished name of the moved object reflects its new position in the hierarchy. The object's globally unique identifier (GUID) is unchanged by a move or rename.

As users and groups are migrated from one domain to another, they are given a new security identifier (SID). To preserve the security credentials of an account when it is moved from one domain to another, Windows 2000 supports SIDHistory, a security attribute available only in Windows 2000 native mode. As users and groups are moved from one domain to another, to reduce the administrative overhead of resetting ACLs and ownership of resources, the old SID is added to the SIDHistory attribute for the new object. Whenever users log on, any SIDs present in their SID history, or any SIDs present in the SIDHistory of a group of which the users are members, are added to their access token, and they are given permissions and ownership to any resources that they previously had.

MOVETREE allows an OU to be moved to another domain, keeping all of the linked group policy objects (GPOs) in the old domain intact. The GPO link is moved and continues to work, although clients receive their group policy settings from the GPOs located in the old domain. For more information on group policy, see Chapter 12, "Administering Group Policy."

Supported MOVETREE Operations

The following operations are supported with the MOVETREE utility:

- Move an object or a nonempty container to a different domain. Valid only within the same forest.

- Move Domain Local and Global groups *between* domains without members and *within* domains with members. Valid only within the same forest.

- Move Universal groups with members *within* and *between* domains. Valid only within the same forest.

Unsupported MOVETREE Operations

Some objects and information are not moved. Objects that are not moved are classified as *orphaned objects* and are placed in an "orphan" container in the LostAndFound container in the source domain. The LostAndFound container is visible in the Active Directory Users and Computers console in Advanced View. The orphan container is named using the GUID of the parent container being moved and it contains the objects that were selected for the MOVETREE operation. Specifically, objects and information that cannot be moved by using the MOVETREE utility are:

- Local and Domain Global groups that contain members. Universal group memberships remain intact so that security is not compromised.

- The domain join information for computer objects. The MOVETREE utility can move a computer object from one domain to another, along with its subordinate objects. However, the MOVETREE utility does not disjoin a computer from its source domain and rejoin it to the target domain. For this reason, the NETDOM utility is recommended to move computer objects.

- Associated object data. This includes group policies, user profiles, logon scripts, users' personal data, encrypted files, smart cards, and public key certificates. Group policies would need to be applied to the users, groups, or computers. New smart cards and certificates would need to be issued from the Certificate Authority in the new domain. Use additional scripts or management tools, such as the Remote Administration Scripts, in conjunction with MOVETREE, to perform these additional steps.

- System objects. Those objects identified by the objectClass being marked as systemOnly.
- Objects in the configuration or schema naming contexts.
- Objects in the special containers in the domain. Objects in the Builtin, ForeginSecurityPrincipals, System, and LostAndFound containers.
- Domain controllers or any object whose parent is a domain controller.
- Any object with the same name as an object that already exists in the target domain.

MOVETREE may fail due to some of the following error conditions:

- The source domain controller cannot transfer the relative identifier master role owner.
- The source object is locked due to another operation in progress. For example, if another user is currently creating child objects under the source object that is selected for the move operation.
- Either the source or destination domain has invalid credentials.
- The destination knows the source object is deleted but the source does not. For example, the source object has been deleted on a different domain controller, but due to replication latency the source domain controller has not yet received the deletion event.
- There is a failure at the destination domain controller. For example, Disk Full.
- The source and destination have a schema mismatch.

Moving Users

Moving users between domains is supported with the following restrictions:

- If the user object contains any objects, the move operation fails. The user object must be a leaf object.
- If a security accounts manager (SAM) constraint is met, the move operation fails. SAM constraints include when the user's *samAccountName* already exists in the destination domain, or if the user's password length does not meet the password restrictions in the target domain.
- If the user object belongs to a Global group from the source domain, its membership is voided and the move operation fails. This is because a Global group can only have a member in the same domain, thereby preventing movement of any member of a Global group.

However, there is one exception: If the user object belongs to the Domain Users group (without belonging to any other Global groups) and the Domain Users group is this user object's Primary group, then the move operation succeeds. It succeeds because when a user object is created, the system automatically places it into the Domain Users group and assigns the Domain Users group as its Primary group.

Moving Groups

Like users, groups can be moved between domains, with similar restrictions:

- If the group object contains any object, the move operation fails.
- If its membership and its reverse memberships do not fulfill the requirements of its type, the operation fails.
- If the group's *samAccountName* exists on the destination domain, the move operation fails.

Moving Objects Between Domains Using MOVETREE

Before using the MOVETREE utility, verify that you have the necessary privileges to perform this operation. For example, make sure that you are authorized to move and create objects in both the source and destination domains. The MOVETREE utility can be used from the command line and can be called from a batch file to script user and group creation.

▶ **To move objects between domains using MOVETREE**

1. Open a command prompt and type **movetree {/start | /startnocheck | /continue | /check} /s** *SrcDSA* **/d** *DstDSA* **/sdn** *SrcDN* **/ddn** *DstDN* **[/u [***Domain***\]***Username* **/p** *Password***] [/verbose] [{/? | /help}]**

   where:

   - **/start** initiates a MOVETREE operation. This command includes a /check operation by default. To start a MOVETREE operation with no check, use /startnocheck.
   - **/continue** continues the execution of a previously paused or failed MOVETREE operation.
   - **/check** performs a test run of the MOVETREE operation, checking the whole tree without moving any objects.
   - **/s** *SrcDSA* is the source server's fully qualified primary DNS name.
   - **/d** *DstDSA* is the destination server's fully qualified primary DNS name.
   - **/sdn** *SrcDN* is the distinguished name of the leaf, container, or subtree you are moving from the source domain.
   - **/ddn** *DstDN* is the distinguished name of the leaf, container, or subtree you are moving to the destination domain.

- **/u** [*Domain*]*Username* **/p** *Password* runs MOVETREE under the credentials of a valid *Username* and *Password*. Optionally, a *Domain* can be specified as well. If these optional arguments are not provided, MOVETREE uses the credentials of the currently logged-on user.

- **/verbose** runs MOVETREE in verbose mode, which displays more details about the operation as it runs (optional).

- **/?** or **/help** displays syntax information.

MOVETREE Command Example

In the Marketing domain, there is a server called Server1 and an OU called Promotions. In the Sales domain, there is a server called Server2. The desired operation is to move the Promotions OU from Marketing to Sales and rename the new OU Sales Promotions. The MOVETREE command performs a test run, and then, if no errors are encountered, performs the move operation.

```
movetree /start /s Server1.Marketing.Reskit.Com /d
Server2.Sales.Reskit.com /sdn
OU=Promotions,DC=Marketing,DC=Reskit,DC=Com /ddn OU=Sales
Promotions,DC=Sales,DC=Reskit,DC=Com
```

MOVETREE Log Files

The following log files are created after the MOVETREE operation. They are located in the directory where you performed the MOVETREE operation.

- **MOVETREE.ERR** lists any errors encountered during the MOVETREE operation.

- **MOVETREE.LOG** lists statistical results of the MOVETREE operation.

- **MOVETREE.CHK** lists any potential errors or conflicts detected during the move operation's precheck phase (or test phase).

Moving Workstations or Member Servers Between Domains

You can use NETDOM: Windows 2000 Domain Manager support tool to move a workstation or member server from one domain to another. This tool is available in the Windows 2000 Support Tools. The Windows 2000 Support Tools are included on the Windows 2000 CD-ROM in the \SUPPORT\TOOLS folder. For information on installing the Windows 2000 Support Tools, see Chapter 3, "Active Directory Administration Tasks and Tools."

▶ **To move a workstation or member server from one domain to another**

1. Open a command prompt and type **netdom move machine /D:***domain* **[/ OU:***ou_path***] [/Ud:***User* **/Pd:{***Password***|*****}] [/Uo:***User* **/Po:{***Password***|*****}] [/Reboot:[***time_in_seconds***]]**

where:

- **/D:*domain*** is the domain that the workstation or member server should belong to after the operation is completed.

- **/OU:*ou_path*** is the name of a destination OU in /D:*domain*.

- **/Ud:*User*** is the user account used to make the connection with the domain specified by the /D argument. If this option is not specified, the current user account is used.

- **/Pd:{*password*|*}** is the password of the user account specified with /Ud. If *, then the password is prompted for.

- **/Uo:*User*** is the user account used to make the connection with the object on which the action is to be performed. If this option is not specified, the current user account is used.

- **/Po:{*password*|*}** is the password of the user account specified with /Uo. If *, then the password is prompted for.

- **/Reboot:[*time_in_seconds*]** specifies that the computer being moved should be shut down and automatically rebooted after the operation has completed. If the number of seconds is not specified, a default value of 20 seconds is used.

NETDOM Command Example

To move a workstation named **mywksta** from its current domain into the **mydomain** domain, you would enter the following command:

```
netdom move /d:mydomain mywksta /ud:mydomain\admin /pd:password
```

If the destination is a Windows 2000 domain, the SID History for the workstation is updated, retaining the security permissions that the computer account had previously.

Moving Domain Controllers Between Sites

In general, you can install a domain controller into a site that has existing domain controllers. The exception to this rule is the first domain controller installed, which automatically creates the Default-First-Site-Name site. You cannot create a first domain controller in any site but Default-First-Site-Name, but you can create a domain controller in a site that has a previously existing domain controller and then move it to another site. Therefore, after the first domain controller has been installed, creating Default-First-Site-Name, you can create other domain controllers in this site and then move them to alternative sites.

This procedure may also be used to move member servers between sites.

▶ **To move a domain controller between sites**

1. In Active Directory Sites and Services, select the domain controller that you want to move to a different site, then click Move on the Action menu.

2. In the Move Server dialog box (see Figure 11.7), select the site to which you want to move the domain controller, then click OK.

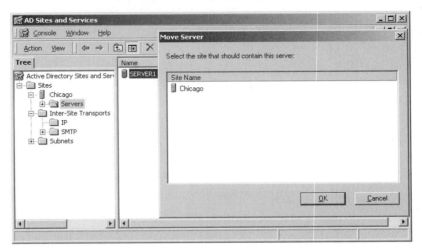

Figure 11.7   The Move Server dialog box

Practice: Moving Objects Within a Domain

In this exercise you move three user accounts from one OU to another. You also attempt to log on using a different account.

▶ **To move objects within the domain**

1. Log on to your domain as Administrator, then open Active Directory Users and Computers.

2. In the console tree, click Users.

3. Select all three user accounts (User20, User21, and User22) that you created in Lesson 1 by clicking one of the user accounts, press Ctrl, and then click the remaining two user accounts.

4. On the Action menu, click Move.

5. In the Move dialog box, to select the new location for the user accounts, expand your domain, click Security1 (the OU you set up in Lesson 2), then click OK.

   Notice that the user accounts that you moved no longer appear in the Users container.

6. To verify that the user accounts were moved to the correct location, in the console tree, click Security1.

   Notice that the user accounts that you moved are now located in the Security1 OU.

7. Close the Active Directory Users and Computers console.

▶   **To log on as a user in a nonstandard OU**

1. Log on to your domain by using the User21 account.

    Did Windows 2000 require you to specify the OU in which your user account is located as part of the logon process? Why or why not?

2. Log off Windows 2000.

Lesson Summary

In this lesson you learned how to move objects within domains in Active Directory using the Move dialog box. You learned how to move objects between domains using the MOVETREE command-line utility. You learned how to move workstations or member servers between domains using the NETDOM command-line utility. You also learned how to move domain controllers between sites using the Move Server dialog box.

In the practice portion of this lesson you used Active Directory Users and Computers to select the object to move within a domain, and the Move dialog box to select the location to which you want to move the object.

Lesson 5: Delegating Administrative Control of Active Directory Objects

In this lesson you will learn that you can delegate administrative control of objects to individuals so that they can perform administrative tasks on the objects. You will learn how to use the Delegation Of Control Wizard to delegate control of objects and the guidelines for delegating control.

After this lesson, you will be able to

- Delegate administrative control of OUs and objects

Estimated lesson time: 20 minutes

Guidelines for Delegating Control

You delegate administrative control of objects by assigning permissions to the object to allow users or groups of users to administer the objects. An administrator can delegate the following types of control:

- Assign a user the permissions to change properties on a particular container
- Assign a user the permissions to create, modify, or delete objects of a specific type in a specific OU or container
- Assign a user the permissions to modify specific properties on objects of a specific type in a specific OU or container

Because tracking permissions at the OU or container level is easier than tracking permissions on objects or object attributes, the most common method of delegating administrative control is to assign permissions at the OU or container level. Assigning permissions at the OU or container level allows you to delegate administrative control for the objects that are contained in the OU or container. Use the Delegation Of Control Wizard to assign permissions at the OU or container level.

For example, you can delegate administrative control by assigning Full Control for an OU to the appropriate manager, only within his or her area of responsibility. By delegating control of the OU to the manager, you can decentralize administrative operations and issues. This reduces your administration time and costs by distributing administrative control closer to its point of service.

To help you delegate administrative control, you may want to follow these suggestions:

- Assign control at the OU or container level whenever possible. Assigning control at the OU or container level allows for easier tracking of permission assignments. Tracking permission assignments becomes more complex for objects and object attributes.

- Use the Delegation Of Control Wizard. The wizard assigns permissions only at the OU or container level. The wizard simplifies the process of assigning object permissions by stepping you through the process.

- Track the delegation of permission assignments. Tracking assignments allows you to maintain records to easily review security settings.

- Follow business requirements. Follow any guidelines that your organization has in place for delegating control.

Delegation Of Control Wizard

The Delegation Of Control Wizard steps you through the process of assigning permissions at the OU or container level. More specialized permissions must be manually assigned.

In Active Directory Users and Computers, click the OU or container for which you want to delegate control, and then on the Action menu, click Delegate Control to start the wizard.

Table 11.7 describes the Delegation Of Control Wizard options.

Table 11.7   Delegation Of Control Wizard Options

Option	Description
Users Or Groups	Select the user accounts or groups to which you want to delegate control.
Tasks To Delegate	Select common tasks from a list or create custom tasks to delegate.
Active Directory Object Type (available only when custom tasks are selected in "Tasks To Delegate")	Select the scope of the tasks you want to delegate, either: This Folder, Existing Objects In This Folder, And Creation Of New Objects In This Folder, or Only The Following Objects In This Folder.
Permissions (available only when custom tasks are selected in "Tasks To Delegate")	Select one of the following permissions to delegate: *General*—the most commonly assigned permissions that are available for the object *Property-Specific*—the permissions that you can assign to the attributes of the object *Creation/Deletion Of Specific Child Objects*—the permissions to create and delete child objects.

Guidelines for Administering Active Directory

The following are best practices for administering Active Directory:

- In larger organizations, coordinate your Active Directory structure with other administrators. You can move objects later, but this might create extra work.

- When you create Active Directory objects, such as user accounts, complete all attributes that are important to your organization. Completing the attributes gives you more flexibility when you search for objects.

- Use deny permissions sparingly. If you assign permissions correctly, you should not need to deny permissions. In most cases, denied permissions indicate mistakes that were made in assigning group membership.

- Always ensure that at least one user has Full Control for each Active Directory object. Failure to do so might result in objects being inaccessible.

- Ensure that delegated users take responsibility and can be held accountable. You gain nothing if you delegate administrative control without ensuring future accountability. As an administrator, you are ultimately responsible for all of the administrative changes that are made. If the users to whom you delegate responsibility are not performing the administrative tasks, you will need to assume responsibility for their failure.

- Provide training for users who have control of objects. Ensure that the users to whom you delegate responsibility understand their responsibilities and know how to perform the administrative tasks.

Practice: Delegating Administrative Control in Active Directory

In this practice you delegate to a user control over objects in an OU. Refer to the tables that you completed in Lesson 2 to answer the questions in this practice.

▶ **To test current permissions**

1. Log on to your domain as Assistant1, and type **password** as the password.

2. Start Active Directory Users and Computers.

3. In the console tree, expand your domain, then click Security1.

   What user objects are visible in the Security1 OU?

   Which permissions allow you to see these objects? (Hint: Refer to your answers in Lesson 2.)

   For the user account with the logon name Secretary1, change the logon hours. Were you successful? Why or why not?

   For the Assistant1 user account, under which you are currently logged on, change the logon hours. Were you successful? Why or why not?

4. Close Active Directory Users and Computers and log off Windows 2000.

▶ **To use the Delegation Of Control Wizard to assign Active Directory permissions**

1. Log on to your domain as Administrator and open Active Directory Users and Computers.

2. In the console tree, expand your domain.

3. Click Security1, and then on the Action menu, click Delegate Control.

4. In the Delegation Of Control Wizard, click Next.

   The Delegation Of Control Wizard displays the Users Or Groups page.

   Notice that the wizard does not display any user accounts or groups. You will add a user account to which to delegate control.

5. Click Add.

   The Select Users, Computers, Or Groups dialog box appears.

6. Select Assistant1, click Add, then click OK.

7. Click Next.

   The Delegation Of Control Wizard displays the Tasks To Delegate page. Here you can choose to delegate common tasks from a list or create custom tasks to delegate.

8. For this exercise, confirm that Delegate The Following Common Tasks is selected, click the Create, Delete, And Manage User Accounts check box, then click Next.

   The Delegation Of Control Wizard displays the Completing The Delegation Of Control Wizard page.

9. Review the Summary page.

   ▪ If all choices reflect the delegation of control on all objects for Assistant1, click Finish.

   ▪ To make changes, click Back.

10. Close Active Directory Users and Computers and log off Windows 2000.

▶   **To test delegated permissions**

1. Log on to your domain as Assistant1, and type **password** as your password.

2. Open Active Directory Users and Computers.

3. In the console tree, expand your domain, then click Security1.

4. Attempt to change the logon hours for the user accounts in the Security1 OU.

   Were you successful? Why or why not?

5. Attempt to change the logon hours for a user account in the Users container.

   Were you successful? Why or why not?

6. Close Active Directory Users and Computers and log off Windows 2000.

Lesson Summary

In this lesson you learned that you can delegate administrative control of objects to individuals so that they can perform administrative tasks on the objects. Assigning permissions at the OU or container level allows you to delegate administrative control for the objects that are contained in the OU or container. You learned how to use the Delegation Of Control Wizard to delegate control of objects and the guidelines for delegating control. In the practice portion of this lesson you used the Delegation Of Control Wizard to delegate to a user control over objects in an OU.

Lesson 6: Backing Up Active Directory

This lesson guides you through the steps required to back up data. When you create a backup, you need to conduct several preliminary tasks, and then perform a number of tasks using the Backup Wizard. You will also learn about scheduling and running an unattended backup.

After this lesson, you will be able to

- Back up Active Directory at a local computer
- Schedule a backup of Active Directory

Estimated lesson time: 20 minutes

Performing Preliminary Tasks

An important part of backing up Active Directory is performing the preliminary tasks. One task that you must do is ensuring that the files that you want to back up are closed. You should send a notification to users to close files before you begin backing up data. Applications using the system or users who cannot be notified (such as users logged on through the Internet) will have their sessions terminated. Windows Backup does not back up files that are locked by applications. You can use e-mail or the Send Console Message dialog box (available in the Computer Management and the Services consoles and the Shared Folders snap-in) to send administrative messages to users.

If you use a removable media device, make sure that the following preliminary tasks occur:

- The backup device is attached to a computer on the network and is turned on. If you are backing up to tape, you must attach the tape device to the computer on which you run Windows Backup.
- The media device is listed on the Windows 2000 Hardware Compatibility List (HCL).
- The media is loaded in the media device. For example, if you are using a tape drive, ensure that a tape is loaded in the tape drive.

The Backup Wizard

After you have completed the preliminary tasks, you can perform the Active Directory backup using the Backup Wizard.

▶ **To start the Backup Wizard**

1. Log on to your domain as Administrator, and then point to Start, point to Programs, point to Accessories, point to System Tools, and select Backup.

2. Select Backup Wizard on the Welcome To The Windows 2000 Backup And Recovery Tools page.

3. Click Next to begin using the Backup Wizard. Proceed through the What To Back Up, Where To Store The Backup, and Advanced Backup Settings pages as needed.

4. On the Completing The Backup Wizard page, click Finish.

What to Back Up

The first phase of using the Backup Wizard to back up Active Directory is to specify that you want to back up only System State data (see Figure 11.8).

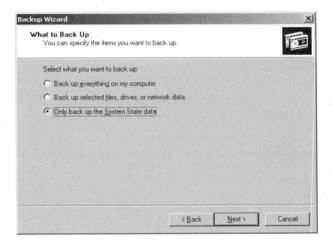

Figure 11.8   Backup Wizard What To Back Up page

For Windows 2000 Server operating systems, the System State data comprises the registry, the COM+ Class Registration database, system boot files, and the Certificate Services database (if the server is a certificate server). If the server is a domain controller, Active Directory and the SYSVOL directory are also contained in the System State data. When you choose to back up System State data, all of the System State data that is relevant to your computer is backed up; you cannot choose to back up individual components of the System State data. This is due to dependencies among the System State components. You can only back up the System State data on a local computer. You cannot back up the System State data on a remote computer.

Where to Store the Backup

After you indicate that you need to back up System State data, you need to provide information about the backup media (see Figure 11.9).

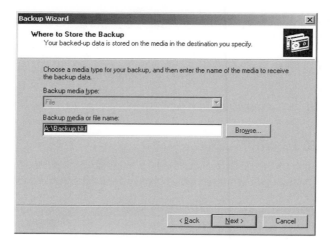

Figure 11.9   Backup Wizard Where To Store The Backup page

Table 11.8 describes the information that you must provide for the backup media options.

Table 11.8   Backup Media Options

Option	Description
Backup Media Type	The target medium to use, such as tape or file. A file can be located on any disk-based medium, including a hard disk, a shared network folder, or a removable disk.
Backup Media Or File Name	The location where Windows Backup will store the data. For a tape, enter the tape name. For a file, enter the path for the backup file.

After you provide the media information, the Backup Wizard displays the wizard settings and provides the opportunity to do either of the following:

- **Start the backup.**   If you click Finish, during the backup process, the Backup Wizard displays status information about the backup job in the Backup Progress dialog box.

- **Specify advanced backup options.**   If you click Advanced, the Backup Wizard allows you to select the advanced backup settings.

Note   When the backup process is complete, you can choose to review the backup report, which is the backup log. A *backup log* is a text file that records backup operations. It is stored on the hard disk of the computer on which you are running Windows Backup.

Specifying Advanced Backup Settings

When you specify advanced backup settings, you are changing the default backup settings for only the current backup job. The advanced settings are listed in Table 11.9.

Table 11.9   Advanced Backup Settings

Advanced Settings Page	Advanced Option	Description
Type Of Backup	Select The Type Of Backup Operation To Perform	A list that allows you to choose the backup type that is used for this backup job. Select one of the following types: Normal, Copy, Incremental, Differential, or Daily.
	Backup Migrated Remote Storage Data	A check box that backs up data that Hierarchical Storage Manager (HSM) has moved to remote storage when checked.
How To Backup	Verify Data After Backup	A check box that confirms that files are correctly backed up. Windows Backup compares the backup data and the source data to verify that they are the same when checked. *Microsoft recommends that you select this option.*
	Use Hardware Compression, If Available	A check box that enables hardware compression for tape devices that support it if checked. If your tape device does not support hardware compression, this check box is unavailable.
Media Options	If The Archive Media Already Contains Backups	Options that specify whether to append or replace the existing backup on the backup media. Choose Append This Backup To Media to store multiple backup jobs on a storage device. Choose Replace The Data On The Media With This Backup if you do not need to save previous backup jobs and you only want to save the most recent backup data.
	Allow Only The Owner And The Administrator Access To The Backup Data And To Any Backups Appended To This Media	A check box that allows you to restrict who can gain access to the completed backup file or tape. This option is only available if you choose to replace an existing backup on a backup medium, rather than appending to the backup medium. If you back up the registry or Active Directory, click this option to prevent others from getting copies of the backup data.

Table 11.9   Advanced Backup Settings *(continued)*

Advanced Settings Page	Advanced Option	Description
Backup Label	Backup Label	A box that allows you to specify a name and description for the backup job. The name and description appear in the backup log. The default set is Set Created *Date* At *Time*. You can change the *name* and description to a more intuitive name (for example, Active Directory backup 09-12-00).
	Media Label	A box that allows you to specify the name of the backup medium (for example, the tape name). The default name is Media Created *Date* At *Time*. The first time that you back up to a new medium or overwrite an existing backup job, you can specify the medium name, such as Active Directory.
When To Back Up	When to back up	Options that allow you to specify Now or Later. If you choose Later, you specify the job name and the start date. You can also set the schedule.
	Job Name	A box that allows you to specify the backup job name.
	Start Date	A box that allows you to set the backup start date.
	Set Schedule	A button that allows you to set the backup schedule.

Depending on whether you chose to back up now or later, the Backup Wizard provides you with the opportunity to do either of the following:

- If you chose to finish the backup process, the Backup Wizard displays the Completing The Backup Wizard settings and then presents the option to finish and immediately start the backup. During the backup, the wizard displays status information about the backup job.

- If you chose to back up later, you are shown additional dialog boxes to schedule the backup process to occur later, as described in the next section.

Scheduling Active Directory Backup Jobs

Scheduling an Active Directory backup job means that you can have an unattended backup job occur later when users are not at work and files are closed. You can also schedule Active Directory backup jobs to occur at regular intervals. To enable this, Windows 2000 integrates Windows Backup with the Task Scheduler service.

▶ **To schedule a backup**

1. Click Later on the When To Back Up page of the Backup Wizard.

   The Task Scheduler service presents the Set Account Information dialog box, prompting you for your password. The user account must have the appropriate user rights and permissions to perform backup jobs.

Note   If the Task Scheduler service is not running or not set to start automatically, Windows 2000 displays a dialog box prompting you to start the service. Click OK, and the Set Account Information dialog box appears.

---

2. Enter your password in the Password box and Confirm Password box, then click OK.

   The When To Back Up page appears. You must provide a name for the backup job, and by default, the wizard displays the present date and time for the start date.

3. Type in the appropriate name in the Job Name box.

4. Click Set Schedule to set a different start date and time. This selection causes Task Scheduler to display the Schedule Job dialog box.

   In the Schedule Job dialog box, you can set the date, time, and number of occurrences for the backup job to repeat, such as every Friday at 10:00 PM. You can also display all of the scheduled tasks for the computer by selecting the Show Multiple Schedules check box. This helps to prevent you from scheduling multiple tasks on the same computer at the same time.

   By clicking the Advanced button, you can also schedule how long the backup can last and for how many days, weeks, months, or years you want this schedule to continue.

After you schedule the backup job and complete the Backup Wizard, Windows Backup places the backup job on the calendar in the Schedule Jobs tab in Windows Backup. The backup job automatically starts at the time that you specified.

Lesson Summary

In this lesson you learned that you must ensure that the files that you want to back up are closed because Windows Backup does not back up files that are locked by applications. You also learned that in using the Backup Wizard, the first phase is to specify what to back up. To back up Active Directory you must back up System State data. After you select System State data, you need to provide the target destination and the backup medium or file name. Then you can finish the backup or you can specify advanced backup options. You also learned how Windows Backup allows you to schedule backup jobs using the Task Scheduler service.

Lesson 7: Restoring Active Directory

There are two ways to restore Active Directory: nonauthoritatively and authoritatively. In this lesson you will learn how to restore Active Directory.

After this lesson, you will be able to

- Explain the difference between nonauthoritative and authoritative restore
- Restore Active Directory

Estimated lesson time: 25 minutes

Preparing to Restore Active Directory

Like the backup process, when you choose to restore Active Directory, you can only restore all of the System State data that was backed up, including the registry, the COM+ Class Registration database, system boot files, the SYSVOL directory, the Active Directory, and the Certificate Services database (if the server is a certificate server). You cannot choose to restore individual components (for example, only the Active Directory) of the System State data.

If you are restoring the System State data to a domain controller, you must choose whether you want to perform a *nonauthoritative restore* or an *authoritative restore*. The default method of restoring the System State data to a domain controller is nonauthoritative.

Nonauthoritative Restore

In nonauthoritative mode, any component of the System State that is replicated with another domain controller, such as Active Directory directory service, will be brought up to date by replication after you restore the data. For example, if the last backup was performed a week ago, and the System State is restored nonauthoritatively, any changes made subsequent to the backup operation will be replicated from the other domain controllers. The Active Directory replication system will update the restored data with newer data from your other servers.

Authoritative Restore

If you do not want to replicate the changes that have been made subsequent to the last backup operation you must perform an authoritative restore. For example, you must perform an authoritative restore if you inadvertently delete users, groups, or OUs from Active Directory and you want to restore the system so that the deleted objects are recovered and replicated.

To authoritatively restore Active Directory data, you must run the NTDSUTIL utility after you have performed a nonauthoritative restore of the System State data but before you restart the domain controller in normal mode. The NTDSUTIL utility allows you to mark objects as authoritative. Marking objects as authoritative changes the update sequence number of an object so it is higher than any other update sequence number in the Active Directory replication system. This ensures that any replicated or distributed data that you have restored is properly replicated or distributed throughout your organization. The NTDSUTIL utility can be found in the *systemroot*\system32 directory and accompanying documentation within the Windows 2000 Help files (available from the Start menu).

For example, suppose you back up the system on Monday, and then create a new user called James Smith on Tuesday, which replicates to other domain controllers in the domain, but on Wednesday, another user, Amy Anderson, is accidentally deleted. To authoritatively restore Amy Anderson without reentering information, you can nonauthoritatively restore the domain controller with the backup created on Monday. Then, using NTDSUTIL, you can mark Amy Anderson as authoritative. The result is that Amy Anderson is restored without any effect on James Smith.

Performing a Nonauthoritative Restore

To restore the System State data on a domain controller, you must first start your computer in a special safe mode called Directory Services Restore Mode. This allows you to restore the SYSVOL directory and Active Directory directory services database. You can only restore System State data on a local computer. You cannot restore the System State data on a remote computer.

Note   If you restore the System State data and you do not designate an alternate location for the restored data, Backup will erase the System State data that is currently on your computer and replace it with the System State data you are restoring. Also, if you restore the System State data to an alternate location, only the registry files, SYSVOL directory files, and system boot files are restored to the alternate location. The Active Directory directory services database, Certificate Services database, and COM+ Class Registration database are not restored if you designate an alternate location.

▶ **To nonauthoritatively restore Active Directory**

1. Restart the computer.

2. During the phase of startup where the operating system is normally selected, press F8.

3. On the Windows 2000 Advanced Options Menu, select Directory Services Restore Mode and press Enter. This ensures that the domain controller is offline and is not connected to the network.

4. At the Please Select The Operating System To Start prompt, select Microsoft Windows 2000 Server and press Enter.

5. Log on as Administrator.

6. On the Desktop message box that warns you that Windows is running in Safe Mode, click OK.

Note   When you restart the computer in Directory Services Restore Mode, you must log on as an Administrator by using a valid Security Accounts Manager (SAM) account name and password, *not* the Active Directory Administrator's name and password. This is because Active Directory is offline, and account verification cannot occur. Rather, the SAM accounts database is used to control access to Active Directory while it is offline. You specified this password when you set up Active Directory.

7. Point to Start, point to Programs, point to Accessories, point to System Tools, then select Backup.

8. On the Welcome To The Windows 2000 Backup And Recovery Tools page, select Restore Wizard.

9. Click Next to begin using the Restore Wizard.

10. In the Restore Wizard What To Restore page (see Figure 11.10), expand the media type that contains the data that you want to restore or click Import File. This can be either tape or file media.

Figure 11.10   Restore Wizard What To Restore page

11. Expand the appropriate media set until the data that you want to restore is visible. You can restore a backup set or specific files and folders.

12. Select the data you want to restore, then click Next.

13. Do one of the following:

   ■ Click Finish to start the restore process. The Restore Wizard requests verification for the source of the restore media and then performs the restore. During the restore, the Restore Wizard displays status information about the restore.

   ■ Click Advanced to specify advanced restore options.

Specifying Advanced Restore Settings

The Advanced settings in the Restore Wizard vary, depending on the type of backup media from which you are restoring. Table 11.10 describes the advanced restore options.

Table 11.10   Advanced Restore Options

Advanced Settings Page	Option	Description
Where To Restore	Restore Files To	The target location for the data that you are restoring. The choices in the list are: *Original Location*—replaces corrupted or lost data *Alternate Location*—restores an older version of a file to a folder you designate *Single Folder*—consolidates the files from a tree structure into a single folder. For example, use this option if you want copies of specific files but do not want to restore the hierarchical structure of the files. If you select either an alternate location or a single folder, you must also provide the path.
How To Restore	When Restoring Files That Already Exist	Whether or not to overwrite existing files. The choices are: *Do Not Replace The File On My Disk*—prevents accidental overwriting of existing data. This is the default *Replace The File On Disk Only If It Is Older Than The Backup Copy*—verifies that the most recent copy exists on the computer *Always Replace The File On Disk*—Windows Backup does not provide a confirmation message if it encounters a duplicate file name during the restore operation.
Advanced Restore Options	Select The Special Restore Options You Want To Use	Whether or not to restore security or special system files. The choices are: *Restore Security*—applies the original permissions to files that you are restoring to a Windows NTFS volume. Security settings include access permisions, audit entries, and ownership. This option is only available if you have backed up data from an NTFS volume and are restoring to an NTFS volume *Restore Removable Storage Database*—restores the configuration database for removable storage management (RSM) devices and the media pool settings. The database is located in *systemroot* system32\Ntmsdata *Restore Junction Points, Not The Folders And File Data They Reference*—restores junction points on your hard disk as well as the data that the junction points refer to. If you have any mounted drives and you want to restore the data that the mounted drives point to, you should select this check box. If you do not select this check box, the junction point will be restored but the data your junction point refers to may not be accessible.

After you have finished the Restore Wizard, Windows Backup does the following:

- Prompts you to verify your selection of the source media to use to restore data. After the verification, Windows Backup starts the restore process.
- Displays status information about the restore process. As with a backup process, you can choose to view the report (restore log) of the restore. It contains information about the restore, such as the number of files that have been restored and the duration of the restore process.

Performing an Authoritative Restore

An authoritative restore occurs after a nonauthoritative restore and designates the entire directory, a subtree, or individual objects to be recognized as authoritative with respect to replica domain controllers in the forest. The NTDSUTIL utility allows you to mark objects as authoritative so that they are propagated through replication, thereby updating existing copies of those objects throughout the forest.

▶ **To authoritatively restore Active Directory**

1. Perform a nonauthoritative restore as described previously.
2. Restart the computer.
3. During the phase of startup where the operating system is normally selected, press F8.
4. On the Windows 2000 Advanced Startup Options Menu, select Directory Services Restore Mode and press Enter. This ensures that the domain controller is offline and is not connected to the network.
5. Select Windows 2000 Server.
6. Log on as Administrator.

Note   When you restart the computer in Directory Services Restore Mode, you must log on as an Administrator by using a valid SAM account name and password, *not* the Active Directory Administrator's name and password. This is because Active Directory is offline and account verification cannot occur. Rather, the SAM accounts database is used to control access to Active Directory while it is offline.

---

7. On the Desktop message box that warns you that Windows is running in Safe Mode, click OK.
8. Point to Start, point to Programs, point to Accessories, then select Command Prompt.
9. At the command prompt, type **ntdsutil** and press Enter.
10. At the NTDSUTIL prompt, type **authoritative restore** and press Enter.

11. At the authoritative restore prompt:

- To authoritatively restore the entire directory, type **restore database** and press Enter.

- To authoritatively restore a portion or subtree of the directory, such as an OU, use the OU's distinguished name, type **restore subtree** <*subtree distinguished name*> and press Enter.

For example, to restore the Security1 OU in the Microsoft.com domain, the commands would be:

```
ntdsutil
authoritative restore
restore subtree OU=Security1,DC=Microsoft,DC=COM
```

- To authoritatively restore the entire directory *and* override the version increase, type **restore database verinc** <*version increase*> and press Enter.

- To authoritatively restore a subtree of the directory *and* override the version increase, type **restore subtree** <*subtree distinguished name*>**verinc** <*version increase*> and press Enter.

The authoritative restore opens the NTDS.DIT, increases version numbers, counts the records that need updating, verifies the number of records updated, and reports completion. If a version number increase is not specified, one is automatically calculated.

12. Type **quit** and press Enter to exit the NTDSUTIL utility, then close the Command Prompt window.

13. Restart the domain controller in normal mode and connect the restored domain controller to the network.

When the restored domain controller is online and connected to the network, normal replication brings the restored domain controller up to date with any changes from the additional domain controllers that were not overridden by the authoritative restore. Replication also propagates the authoritatively restored object(s) to other domain controllers in the forest. The deleted objects that were marked as authoritative are replicated from the restored domain controller to the additional domain controllers. Because the objects that are restored have the same object GUID and object SID, security remains intact, and object dependencies are maintained.

Additional Tasks for Authoritatively Restoring the Entire Active Directory Database

When you authoritatively restore the entire Active Directory database, you also must perform an additional procedure involving the SYSVOL directory. This is necessary to ensure the integrity of the computer's group policy. To ensure the proper elements are authoritatively restored, you must also:

- Copy the SYSVOL directory on the alternate location over the existing one *after* the SYSVOL share is published.

When you authoritatively restore a portion of the Active Directory database (including policy objects), you also must perform an additional procedure involving the SYSVOL directory. To ensure the proper elements are authoritatively restored, you must also:

- Copy only policy folders (identified by the GUID) corresponding to the restored Policy objects from the alternate location *after* the SYSVOL share is published. Then, copy them over the existing ones.

When authoritatively restoring either the entire Active Directory database or selected objects, it is important that you copy the SYSVOL and policy data from the alternate location *after* the SYSVOL share is published. If the computer is in a replicated domain, it may take several minutes before the SYSVOL share is published because it needs to synchronize with its replication partners. If all computers in the domain are authoritatively restored and restarted at the same time, then each will be waiting (indefinitely) to synchronize with each other. In this case, restore one of the domain controllers first so that its SYSVOL share can be published; then restore the other computers nonauthoritatively.

Lesson Summary

In this lesson you learned how to restore Active Directory using nonauthoritative and authoritative restore. You learned that you must choose whether to restore in nonauthoritative or authoritative mode. In nonauthoritative restore mode, any component of the System State data that is replicated with another domain controller, such as Active Directory directory service, will be brought up to date by replication after you restore the data. In authoritative mode, changes that have been made, subsequent to the last backup operation are not restored; the deleted objects are recovered and replicated.

To restore the System State data on a domain controller, you must first start your computer in a special safe mode called Directory Services Restore Mode. This allows you to restore the SYSVOL directory and Active Directory directory services database. You can only restore System State data on a local computer. You cannot restore the System State data on a remote computer.

When performing a nonauthoritative restore, the Restore Wizard helps you restore data. When performing an authoritative restore, you first perform a nonauthoritative restore and then use the NTDSUTIL utility to mark objects as authoritative so that they are propagated through replication.

Lesson 8: Troubleshooting Active Directory

This lesson describes some problems you may encounter that relate to Active Directory and possible solutions.

After this lesson, you will be able to

- Troubleshoot Active Directory

Estimated lesson time: 10 minutes

Troubleshooting Active Directory

Table 11.11 describes Active Directory troubleshooting scenarios.

Table 11.11   Active Directory Troubleshooting Scenarios

Symptom: Cannot add or remove a domain

Cause	Solution
The domain naming master is not available. This may be caused by a network connectivity problem. It may also be due to a failure of the computer holding the domain naming master role.	Resolve the network connectivity problem. Or, repair or replace the domain naming master computer. It may be necessary to seize the domain naming master role.

Symptom: Cannot create objects in Active Directory

Cause	Solution
The relative ID master is not available. This may be caused by a network connectivity problem. It may also be due to a failure of the computer holding the relative ID master role.	Resolve the network connectivity problem. Or, repair or replace the computer holding the relative ID master role. It may be necessary to seize the relative ID master role.

Symptom: Cannot modify the schema

Cause	Solution
The schema master is not available. This may be caused by a network connectivity problem. It may also be due to a failure of the computer holding the schema master role.	Resolve the network connectivity problem. Or, repair or replace the computer holding the schema master role. It may be necessary to seize the schema master role.

Table 11.11   Active Directory Troubleshooting Scenarios *(continued)*

Symptom: Changes to group memberships are not taking effect

Cause	Solution
The infrastructure master is not available. This may be caused by a network connectivity problem. It may also be due to a failure of the computer holding the infrastructure master role.	Resolve the network connectivity problem. Or, repair or replace the computer holding the infrastructure master role. It may be necessary to seize the infrastructure master role.

Symptom: Clients without Active Directory client software installed cannot log on

Cause	Solution
The primary domain controller emulator is not available. This may be caused by a network connectivity problem. It may also be due to a failure of the computer holding the primary domain controller emulator role.	Resolve the network connectivity problem. Or, repair or replace the computer holding the primary domain controller emulator role. It may be necessary to seize the primary domain controller emulator role.

Symptom: Clients are unable to access resources in another domain

Cause	Solution
There has been a failure of the trust between the domains.	Reset and verify the trust between the domains. The PDC emulator must be available for a trust to be successfully reset.

Lesson Summary

In this lesson you examined some problems you may encounter with Active Directory and possible solutions.

Review

Here are some questions to help you determine if you have learned enough to move on to the next chapter. If you have difficulty answering these questions, please go back and review the material in this chapter before beginning the next chapter. The answers for these questions are located in Appendix A, "Questions and Answers."

1. How does the global catalog help users locate Active Directory objects?

2. You want to allow the manager of the Sales department to create, modify, and delete only user accounts for sales personnel. How can you accomplish this?

3. What happens to the permissions of an object when you move it from one OU to another OU?

4. The Delegation Of Control Wizard allows you to set administrative control at what level?

5. When backing up Active Directory, what type of data must you specify to be backed up? What is included in this data type?

6. When you restart the computer in Directory Services Restore Mode, what logon must you use? Why?

CHAPTER 12

Administering Group Policy

About This Chapter

Administrators use group policy to manage desktop configurations for groups of computers and users. Group policy is very flexible and includes options for registry-based policy settings, security settings, application management, scripts, computer startup and shutdown, logon and logoff, and folder redirection. Microsoft Windows 2000 Server includes hundreds of group policy settings you can configure. By allowing administrators to enhance and control user's desktops, group policy allows an organization to reduce total cost of ownership (TCO).

Before You Begin

To complete this chapter, you must have

- Completed the Setup procedures located in "About This Book"
- Configured the computer as a domain controller in a domain
- Completed the exercises and obtained the knowledge and skills covered in Chapter 8, "Group Account Administration," and Chapter 11, "Administering Active Directory"

Lesson 1: Group Policy Concepts

Before attempting to implement group policy you must be familiar with concepts that affect group policy operations. This lesson defines group policy, explains how group policy is administered, and provides an overview of the group policy settings. It also introduces you to how group policy affects startup and logon, how it is processed, and how security groups are used to filter group policy.

After this lesson, you will be able to

- Explain the purpose and function of group policy
- Explain how to delegate administrative control of group policy
- Identify group policy settings
- Explain how group policy affects startup and logon
- Describe how group policy is processed
- Explain how security groups can be used to filter group policy

Estimated lesson time: 35 minutes

What Is Group Policy?

Group policies are collections of user and computer configuration settings that can be linked to computers, sites, domains, and organizational units (OUs) to specify the behavior of users' desktops. For example, using group policies, you can determine the programs that are available to users, the programs that appear on the user's desktop, and Start menu options.

Group Policy Objects

To create a specific desktop configuration for a particular group of users, you create *group policy objects* (GPOs). GPOs are collections of group policy settings. Each Windows 2000 computer has one *local* GPO, and may in addition be subject to any number of *nonlocal* (Active Directory-based) GPOs.

One local GPO is stored on each computer whether or not the computer is part of an Active Directory environment or a networked environment. However, as the local GPO settings can be overridden by nonlocal GPOs, the local GPO is the least influential if the computer is in an Active Directory environment. In a non-networked environment (or in a networked environment lacking a Windows 2000 domain controller), the local GPO's settings are more important because they are not overwritten by nonlocal GPOs.

Nonlocal GPOs are linked to Active Directory objects (sites, domains, or OUs) and can be applied to either users or computers. To use nonlocal GPOs, you must have a Windows 2000 domain controller installed. Following the properties of

Active Directory, nonlocal GPOs are applied hierarchically from the least restrictive group (site) to the most restrictive group (OU) and are cumulative.

This lesson discusses nonlocal GPOs unless otherwise specified.

Delegating Control of Group Policy

You can determine which administrative groups can administer (create, modify, delete) GPOs by defining access permissions for each GPO. By assigning Read and Write permissions to a GPO for an administrative group, the group can delegate control of the GPO.

The Group Policy Snap-In

A Microsoft Management Console (MMC) snap-in is used to organize and manage the many group policy settings in each GPO. The snap-in for the Default Domain Controllers Policy GPO is shown in Figure 12.1.

Figure 12.1   Group Policy snap-in

Ways to Open the Group Policy Snap-In

You can open the Group Policy snap-in in several ways, as shown in Table 12.1, depending on what action you want to perform.

Table 12.1   Ways to Open the Group Policy Snap-In

To Apply Group Policy To	Do This
The local computer (local GPO)	Open the local GPO that is stored on the local computer, as described in "To open the local Group Policy snap-in," then set the group policy setting in the Group Policy snap-in. Local security settings only are available by selecting Local Security Policy from the Administrative Tools menu.
Another computer (local GPO)	Open the local GPO that is stored on the Windows 2000 network computer, as described in "To open the local Group Policy snap-in," and then browse to the network computer. You must be an administrator of the network computer.
A site	Open a GPO as described in "To open the Group Policy snap-in from Active Directory Sites and Services," and then link a GPO to the intended site.
A domain	Open a GPO as described in "To open the Group Policy snap-in from Active Directory Users and Computers," and then link a GPO to the intended domain.
An organizational unit	Open a GPO as described in "To open the Group Policy snap-in from Active Directory Users and Computers," and then link a GPO to the intended OU. You can also link a GPO to an OU higher in the Active Directory hierarchy, so that the OU can inherit group policy settings.
Any existing GPO or set of GPOs	Create and save your own custom MMC console.

▶ **To open the local Group Policy snap-in**

1. Open Microsoft Management Console.

2. On the MMC console's menu bar, click Console, and then click Add/Remove Snap-In.

3. In the Add/Remove Snap-In dialog box, on the Standalone tab, click Add.

4. In the Add Standalone Snap-In dialog box, click Group Policy, and then click Add.

5. In the Select Group Policy Object dialog box, ensure that Local Computer appears in the Group Policy Object box.

6. Click Finish, then click Close on the Add Standalone Snap-In dialog box.

7. In the Add/Remove Snap-In dialog box click OK.

   The Group Policy snap-in for the local computer is now available.

▶ **To open the Group Policy snap-in from Active Directory Sites and Services**

1. Open Active Directory Sites and Services.

2. In the console tree, right-click the site you want to set group policy for, then click Properties.

3. Click the Group Policy tab, click an entry in the Group Policy Object Links list to select an existing GPO, then click Edit. (Or, click New to create a new GPO, and then click Edit.)

   The Group Policy snap-in for the site is now available.

▶ **To open the Group Policy snap-in
from Active Directory Users and Computers**

1. Open Active Directory Users and Computers.

2. In the console tree, right-click the domain or OU you want to set group policy for, then click Properties.

3. Click the Group Policy tab, click an entry in the Group Policy Object Links list to select an existing GPO, then click Edit. (Or, click New to create a new GPO, and then click Edit.)

   The Group Policy snap-in for the domain or OU is now available.

Group Policy Settings

Group policy settings are contained in a GPO and determine the user's desktop environment. There are two types of group policy settings: computer configuration settings and user configuration settings.

Computer and User Configuration Settings

Computer configuration settings are used to set group policies applied to computers, regardless of who logs on to them. Computer configuration settings are applied when the operating system initializes.

User configuration settings are used to set group policies applied to users, regardless of which computer the user logs on to. User configuration settings are applied when users log on to the computer.

Note Although some settings are user interface settings—for example, the background bitmap or the ability to use the Run command on the Start menu—they can be applied to computers using computer configuration settings.

Both computer configuration settings and user configuration settings include Software Settings, Windows Settings, and Administrative Templates.

Software Settings

For both the computer configuration and user configuration, Software Settings (see Figure 12.2) contains only Software Installation settings by default. Software Installation settings help you specify how applications are installed and maintained within your organization. Software Installation settings also provide a place for independent software vendors to add settings.

You manage an application within a GPO that, in turn, is associated with a particular Active Directory container—a site, domain, or OU. Applications can be managed in one of two modes: assigned or published. You assign an application to a computer when you want computers or people managed by the GPO to have the application. You publish an application when you want the application to be available to people managed by the GPO, should a person want the application. You cannot publish an application to computers. More information on setting software installation using group policy is provided in Lesson 4.

Figure 12.2   Software settings

Windows Settings

For both the computer configuration and user configuration, Windows Settings (see Figure 12.3) holds Scripts and Security Settings.

Scripts allow you to specify two types of scripts: startup/shutdown and logon/logoff. Startup/shutdown scripts run at computer startup or shutdown. Logon/logoff scripts run when a user logs on or off the computer. When you assign multiple logon/logoff or startup/shutdown scripts to a user or computer, Windows 2000 executes the scripts from top to bottom. You can determine the order of execution for multiple scripts in the Properties dialog box. When a computer is shut down, Windows 2000 first processes logoff scripts followed by shutdown scripts. By default, the timeout value for processing scripts is 10 minutes. If the logoff and shutdown scripts require more than 10 minutes to process, you must adjust the timeout value with a software policy.

Administrators can use any ActiveX scripting language they are comfortable with. Some possibilities include VBScript, JScript, Perl, and MS-DOS style batch files (.bat and .cmd).

Security Settings allows a security administrator to manually configure security levels assigned to a local or nonlocal GPO. This can be done after, or instead of, using a security template to set system security. For details on system security, see Chapter 13, "Administering a Security Configuration."

For the user configuration only, Windows Settings holds additional group policy settings for Internet Explorer Maintenance, Remote Installation Services, and Folder Redirection. Internet Explorer Maintenance allows you to administer and customize Microsoft Internet Explorer on Windows 2000 computers. Remote Installation Services is used to control the behavior of remote operating system installation. Optionally, this can be used to provide customized packages for non-Windows 2000 clients of Active Directory. (Group policy requires a genuine Windows 2000 client, not merely a pre-Windows 2000 client of Active Directory, however.) Folder Redirection allows you to redirect Windows 2000 special folders (My Documents, Application Data, Desktop, and Start menu) from their default user profile location to an alternate location on the network, where they can be centrally managed. More information on redirecting special folders using group policy is provided in Lesson 5.

Figure 12.3   Windows settings

Administrative Templates

For both the computer and user configurations, Administrative Templates (see Figure 12.4) contains all registry-based group policy settings, including settings for Windows Components, System, and Network. Windows Components allows you to administer Windows 2000 components including NetMeeting, Internet Explorer, Windows Explorer, Microsoft Management Console, Task Scheduler, and Windows Installer. System is used to control logon and logoff functions and group policy itself. Network allows you to control settings for Offline Files and Network and Dial-Up Connections.

For the computer configuration only, Administrative Templates contains additional group policy settings for Printers. Additionally, System Settings contains Disk Quotas, and Domain Name System (DNS) Client and Windows File Protection.

For the user configuration only, Administrative Templates contains additional registry-based group policy settings, including settings for Start Menu & Taskbar, Desktop, and Control Panel. Start Menu & Taskbar settings control a user's start menu and taskbar, and desktop settings control the appearance of a user's desktop. Control Panel settings determine the Control Panel options available to a user.

In Administrative Templates there are more than 450 of these settings available for configuring the user environment. In the registry, computer configurations are saved in HKEY_LOCAL_MACHINE (HKLM) and user configurations are saved in HKEY_CURRENT_USER (HKCU).

Figure 12.4   Administrative templates

Note   You can display administrative template settings by clicking the Administrative Templates node, clicking View, then clicking Show Policies Only to show all settings, or Show Configured Policies Only to show only those settings that have been configured.

The MMC Snap-In Model

The nodes of the Group Policy snap-in are themselves MMC snap-in extensions. By default, all the available Group Policy snap-in extensions are loaded when you start the Group Policy snap-in. You can modify this default behavior by using the MMC method of creating custom consoles and by using policy settings to control the behavior of MMC itself. Use the Administrative Templates node to configure these policy settings.

Using this extension model, developers can create an MMC extension to the Group Policy snap-in to provide additional policies. These snap-in extensions may in turn be extended. An example of such a snap-in is the Security Settings snap-in, which itself includes several snap-in extensions.

Group Policy Snap-In Namespace

The root node of the Group Policy snap-in is displayed as the name of the GPO and the domain to which it belongs, in the following format:

```
GPO Name [DomainName] Policy
```

For example: Default Domain Controllers Policy [server1.microsoft.com] Policy

How Group Policy Affects Startup and Logon

The following sequence shows the order in which computer configuration and user configuration settings are applied when a computer starts and a user logs on:

1. The network starts. Remote Procedure Call System Service (RPCSS) and Multiple Universal Naming Convention Provider (MUP) are started.

2. An ordered list of GPOs is obtained for the computer. The list contents may depend on these factors:

   ■ Whether the computer is part of a Windows 2000 domain, and is therefore subject to group policy through Active Directory.

   ■ The location of the computer in Active Directory.

   ■ If the list of GPOs has not changed, then no processing is done. You can use a group policy setting to change this behavior.

3. Computer configuration settings are processed. This occurs synchronously by default, and in the following order: local GPO, site GPOs, domain GPOs, OU GPOs, and so on. No user interface is displayed while computer configuration settings are being processed. See the section "How Group Policy Is Processed" for details about GPO processing.

4. Startup scripts run. This is hidden and synchronous by default; each script must complete or time out before the next one starts. The default timeout is 600 seconds (10 minutes). You can use several group policy settings to modify this behavior.

5. The user presses Ctrl+Alt+Delete to log on.

6. After the user is validated, the user profile is loaded, governed by the group policy settings in effect.

7. An ordered list of GPOs is obtained for the user. The list contents may depend on these factors:

   ■ Whether the user is part of a Windows 2000 domain, and is therefore subject to group policy through Active Directory.

- Whether loopback is enabled, and the state (Merge or Replace) of the loopback policy setting. Refer to the section "How Group Policy Is Processed" for more information about loopback.

- The location of the user in Active Directory.

- If the list of GPOs to be applied has not changed, then no processing is done. You can use a policy setting to change this behavior.

8. User configuration settings are processed. This occurs synchronously by default, and in the following order: local GPOs, site GPOs, domain GPOs, OU GPOs, and so on. No user interface is displayed while user policies are being processed. See the section "How Group Policy Is Processed" for details about GPO processing.

9. Logon scripts run. Unlike Windows NT 4.0 scripts, group policy-based logon scripts are run hidden and asynchronously by default. The user object script runs last.

10. The operating system user interface prescribed by group policy appears.

How Group Policy Is Processed

Group policy settings are processed in the following order:

1. **Local GPO.**   Each Windows 2000 computer has exactly one GPO stored locally.

2. **Site GPOs.**   Any GPOs that have been linked to the site are processed next. Processing is synchronous; the administrator specifies the order of GPOs linked to a site.

3. **Domain GPOs.**   Multiple domain-linked GPOs are processed synchronously; the administrator specifies the order of GPOs linked to a domain.

4. **OU GPOs.**   GPOs linked to the OU highest in the Active Directory hierarchy are processed first, followed by GPOs linked to its child OU, and so on. Finally, the GPOs linked to the OU that contains the user or computer are processed. At the level of each OU in the Active Directory hierarchy, one, many, or no GPOs can be linked. If several group policies are linked to an OU, then they are processed synchronously in an order specified by the administrator.

This order means that the local GPO is processed first, and GPOs linked to the OU of which the computer or user is a direct member are processed last, over-writing the earlier GPOs. For example, you set up a domain GPO to allow anyone to log on interactively. However, an OU GPO, set up for the domain controller, prevents everyone from logging on except for certain administrative groups. Figure 12.5 shows the relationship of group policy and Active Directory.

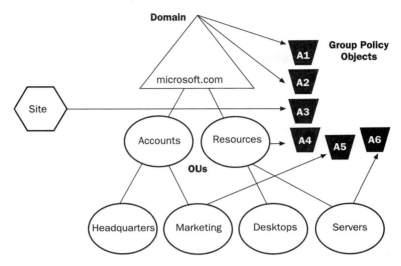

Group policy processing order for the Marketing OU = A3, A1, A2, A5
Group policy processing order for the Servers OU = A3, A1, A2, A4, A6

Figure 12.5   Group Policy and the Active Directory

Exceptions to the Processing Order

The default order of processing group policy settings is subject to the following exceptions:

- **A computer that is a member of a workgroup processes only the local GPO.**

- **No Override.**   Any GPO linked to a site, domain, or OU (not the local GPO) can be set to No Override with respect to that site, domain, or OU, so that none of its policy settings can be overridden. When more than one GPO has been set to No Override, the one highest in the Active Directory hierarchy (or higher in the hierarchy specified by the administrator at each fixed level in Active Directory) takes precedence. No Override is applied to the GPO link.

- **Block Policy Inheritance.**   At any site, domain, or OU, group policy inheritance can be selectively marked as Block Policy Inheritance. However, GPO links set to No Override are always applied and cannot be blocked.

  Block Policy Inheritance is applied directly to the site, domain, or OU. It is not applied to GPOs, nor is it applied to GPO links. Thus, Block Policy Inheritance deflects *all* group policy settings that reach the site, domain, or OU from above (by way of linkage to parents in the Active Directory hierarchy) no matter what GPOs those settings originate from.

- **Loopback setting.**   Loopback is an advanced group policy setting that is useful on computers in certain closely managed environments such as kiosks, laboratories, classrooms, and reception areas. Loopback provides alternatives to the default method of obtaining the ordered list of GPOs whose user configuration settings affect a user. By default, a user's settings come from a GPO list that depends on the user's location in Active Directory. The ordered list goes from site-linked to domain-linked to OU-linked GPOs, with inheritance determined by the location of the user in Active Directory and in an order specified by the administrator at each level.

Loopback can be Not Configured, Enabled, or Disabled, as can any other group policy setting. In the Enabled state, loopback can be set to Merge or Replace mode.

- **Replace.** In this case, the GPO list for the user is replaced in its entirety by the GPO list already obtained for the computer at computer startup (during Step 2 in "How Group Policy Affects Startup and Logon"). The computer's GPOs replace the user GPOs normally applied to the user.

- **Merge.** In this case, the GPO list is concatenated. The GPO list obtained for the computer at computer startup (Step 2 in "How Group Policy Affects Startup and Logon") is appended to the GPO list obtained for the user at logon (Step 7). Because the GPO list obtained for the computer is applied later, it has precedence if it conflicts with settings in the user's list.

Group Policy Inheritance

In general, group policy is passed down from parent to child containers. If you have assigned a separate group policy to a parent container, that group policy applies to all containers beneath the parent container, including the user and computer objects in the container. However, if you specify a group policy setting for a child container, the child container's group policy setting overrides the setting inherited from the parent container.

If a parent OU has policy settings that are not configured, the child OU doesn't inherit them. Policy settings that are disabled are inherited as disabled. Also, if a policy is configured for a parent OU, and the same policy is not configured for a child OU, the child inherits the parent's policy setting.

If a parent policy and a child policy are compatible, the child inherits the parent policy, and the child's setting is also applied. Policies are inherited as long as they are compatible. For example, if the parent's policy causes a certain folder to be placed on the desktop and the child's setting calls for an additional folder, the user sees both folders.

If a policy configured for a parent OU is incompatible with the same policy configured for a child OU, the child does not inherit the policy setting from the parent. The setting in the child is applied.

Using Security Groups to Filter Group Policy

Because you can link more than one GPO to a site, domain, or OU, you may need to link GPOs associated with other directory objects. By setting the appropriate permissions for security groups, you can filter group policy to influence only the computers and users you specify.

Lesson Summary

In this lesson you learned that group policies are collections of user and computer configuration settings that can be linked to computers, sites, domains, and OUs to define settings of various components that make up the users' desktop environment. To create a specific desktop configuration for a particular group of users, you create GPOs, which are collections of group policy settings. You learned that you can determine which administrative groups can administer (create, modify, delete) GPOs by defining access permissions for each GPO.

You walked through the various group policy settings. There are two types of group policy settings: computer configuration settings and user configuration settings. Both computer configuration settings and user configuration settings include Software Settings, Windows Settings, and Administrative Templates.

You examined in detail how group policy affects startup and logon and how it is processed. Computer configuration settings are processed first, followed by user configuration settings. The settings are processed synchronously by default in the following order: local GPO, site GPOs, domain GPOs, and OU GPOs. Exceptions to this processing order include the No Override and Block Policy Inheritance options and the Loopback group policy setting.

Finally, you learned that by setting the appropriate permissions for security groups, you can filter group policy to influence only the computers and users you specify.

Lesson 2: Group Policy Implementation Planning

Before implementing group policies, you should create a plan to manage them. You can plan your GPO settings and GPO implementation methods to provide the most efficient group policy management for your organization. This lesson examines GPO settings and GPO implementation strategies.

After this lesson, you will be able to
- Recognize management options for group policies

Estimated lesson time: 15 minutes

Designing GPOs by Setting Type

You can create GPOs based on the type of settings they contain. There are three main GPO setting designs:

- **Single Policy Type** includes GPOs that deliver a single type of group policy setting—for example, a GPO that includes only security settings.
- **Multiple Policy Type** includes GPOs that deliver multiple types of group policy settings—for example, a GPO that includes both software settings and application deployment, or a GPO that includes security and scripts settings.
- **Dedicated Policy Type** includes GPOs dedicated to either computer configuration or user configuration group policies.

Figure 12.6 illustrates these GPO setting types.

Figure 12.6   GPO setting types

Single Policy Type

With this approach, the goal is to separate each type of group policy setting into a separate GPO. To do this, create a GPO for software management settings, a GPO for user documents and settings, a GPO for software policies, and so on. Give Read/Write access only to the user or users who need to administer a GPO.

This model is best suited for organizations in which administrative responsibilities are delegated among several individuals.

Multiple Policy Type

With this approach, the goal is to include multiple types of group policy settings in a single GPO.

This model is best suited for organizations in which administrative responsibilities are centralized and an administrator may need to perform many or all types of group policy administration.

Dedicated Policy Type

With this approach, the goal is to include all user configuration group policy settings in one GPO and all computer configuration group policy settings in a separate GPO. This model increases the number of GPOs that must be processed at logon, thereby lengthening logon time, but it can aid in troubleshooting. For example, if a problem with computer configuration policy is suspected, an administrator can log on as a user who has no user configuration policy assigned so user policy can be eliminated as a factor.

GPO Implementation Strategies

When planning an Active Directory structure, consider how group policy will be implemented for the organization. Delegation of authority, separation of administrative duties, central versus decentralized administration, and design flexibility are important factors to be considered when designing group policy and selecting which scenarios to adapt for an organization.

The group policy implementation strategies described in this section are samples that illustrate principles of design for group policy. Most organizations will combine several of these strategies to create custom solutions.

Layered vs. Monolithic GPO Design

These design strategies provide decentralized (layered) and centralized (monolithic) locations for policy settings within GPOs.

Layered GPO Design

With a layered GPO approach (see Figure 12.7), the goal is to include a specific policy setting in as few GPOs as possible. When a change is required, only one (or few) GPO(s) has to be changed to enforce the change. Administration is simplified at the expense of a somewhat longer logon time (due to multiple GPO processing).

To achieve this goal, create a base GPO to be applied to the domain that contains policy settings for as many users and computers in the domain as possible. For example, the base GPO could contain corporate- or group-wide security settings such as account and password restrictions.

Next, create additional GPOs tailored to the common requirements of each corporate group, such as engineering, sales, marketing, executives, and administrative assistants, and apply them to the appropriate OUs.

This model is best suited for environments in which different groups in the organization have common security concerns and changes to group policy are frequent.

Monolithic GPO Design

With a monolithic GPO approach (see Figure 12.7), the goal is to use very few GPOs (ideally only one) for any given user or computer. All of the policy settings required for a given site, domain, or OU should be implemented within a single GPO. If the site, domain, or OU has groups of users or computers with different policy requirements, consider subdividing the container into OUs and applying separate GPOs to each OU rather than to the parent.

A change in the monolithic design involves more administration than the layered approach because the settings may need to be changed in multiple GPOs, but logon time will be shorter.

This model is best suited for environments in which users and computers can be classified into a small number of groups for policy assignment.

Figure 12.7   Layered vs. monolithic design

Functional Roles vs. Team Design

Active Directory's OU structure was designed to facilitate ease of administration and delegation of authority. The OU structure may represent the functional roles within the organization or it may not. When designing group policy for an organization with a functional role OU structure, design the group policy by delegating control to the OU levels. If the OU architecture does not represent group organization, then use OU delegation of control, but also choose to use groups as a filtering mechanism for applying group policy.

Functional Roles Design

With this approach (see Figure 12.8), the goal is to use an OU structure that reflects the functional roles within the organization for applying group policy. A minimum number of GPOs is used, with each tailored to a group's specific needs.

To do this, create a GPO for each OU. Network administrators can set access control list (ACL) permissions for GPO administration either at the domain administrator level or at each OU administrator level.

This model is best suited for organizations designed according to functional roles—groups of users organized according to users' occupations such as engineering, sales, marketing, and so on. Each functional role requires specific group policies. The OU architecture reflects the functional roles within the organization.

Team Design

With this approach (see Figure 12.8), the goal is to use groups as a filtering mechanism in applying group policy in an organization that uses the virtual team concept. Individuals within the organization form teams to perform a task or project and each individual is a member of multiple teams. Each team has specific group policy requirements.

To do this, create GPOs for each virtual team. As users can exist in only one OU at a time, it is best to create a single GPO at the top of the hierarchy that filters down to each OU. Then, create GPOs for each team as necessary. This approach eliminates complexity by strategically applying the GPOs at only one location, allowing administrators to centrally administer the GPOs and minimizing the GPO-to-OU assignments.

This model is best suited for organizations that need an efficient and flexible method of managing group policy in a dynamic environment with an OU architecture that does not reflect the team structure.

Figure 12.8   Functional roles vs. team design

OU Delegation with Central or Distributed Control

The administration of OUs can be delegated and OU administrators may need to be allowed to block group policies that have been assigned to their OUs at higher organizational levels. However, certain policies may need to be enforced and OU administrators will not be allowed to block them. This can be accomplished using a central or distributed control design.

Central Control Design

With this approach (see Figure 12.9), administration is delegated to OU administrators, yet there is also centralized control.

To do this, use the No Override option on OUs. For example, create a GPO including only security settings for a domain, and then set the No Override option so that all child OUs are affected by the security options specified at the domain level. For all other types of policy, control of those GPOs could be delegated to the specific OU administrators.

This model is best suited for organizations that choose to delegate administration of OUs, but would like to enforce certain group policies throughout the domain (for example, specific security policies).

Distributed Control Design

With this approach (see Figure 12.9), administrators of OUs are allowed to block group policies from being applied to their OU. However, the administrator cannot block group policies that are marked as No Override.

To do this, create GPOs for each OU. Set ACL permission allowing OU administrators full control over GPOs. Then, set the Block Policy Inheritance option for each OU.

This model is best suited for organizations that choose to minimize the number of domains but do not want to sacrifice autonomous administration of OUs. It allows administrators to enforce certain group policies throughout the domain.

Figure 12.9   Central vs. distributed control

Lesson Summary

In this lesson you learned that GPOs that deliver a single type or multiple types of group policy settings can be created. GPOs can also be dedicated to either computer configuration or user configuration group policies.

You also learned various strategies for implementing group policy. The layered GPO design model is best suited for environments in which different groups in the organization have common security concerns and changes to group policy are frequent. The monolithic GPO design model is best suited for environments in which users and computers can be classified into a small number of groups for policy assignment.

The functional role design model is best suited for organizations designed according to functional roles—groups of users organized according to users' occupations such as engineering, sales, marketing, and so on. The team design model is best suited for organizations that need an efficient and flexible method of managing group policy in a dynamic environment with an OU architecture that does not reflect the team structure.

The central control design model is best suited for organizations that choose to delegate administration of OUs, but would like to enforce certain group policies throughout the domain. The distributed control design model is best suited for organizations that choose to minimize the number of domains but do not want to sacrifice autonomous administration of OUs.

Lesson 3: Implementing Group Policy

You can use group policy to establish configuration settings for your organization. This lesson guides you through the steps of implementing a group policy using the Group Policy tab and the Group Policy snap-in. You also learn how to modify a group policy.

After this lesson, you will be able to
- Implement a group policy
- Modify a group policy

Estimated lesson time: 60 minutes

Implementing Group Policy

The tasks for implementing group policy are

1. Creating a GPO
2. Creating a console for the GPO
3. Delegating administrative control of the GPO
4. Specifying group policy settings for the GPO
5. Disabling unused group policy settings
6. Indicating any GPO processing exceptions
7. Filtering the scope of the GPO
8. Linking the GPO to a site, domain, or OU

Creating a GPO

The first step in implementing a group policy is to create a GPO. Recall that a GPO is a collection of group policy settings.

▶ **To create a GPO**

1. Determine the type of GPO you want to create.
   - To create a GPO linked to a domain or an OU, open Active Directory Users and Computers.
   - To create a GPO linked to a site, open Active Directory Sites and Services.
2. Right-click the site, domain, or OU for which you want to create a GPO, click Properties, and select the Group Policy tab (see Figure 12.10).
3. Click New, then type the name you would like to use for this GPO.

   By default, the new GPO is linked to the site, domain, or OU that was selected in the MMC when it was created and its settings apply to that site, domain, or OU.
4. Click Close.

Figure 12.10   Group Policy tab

Creating a GPO Console

After you create a GPO, you should add the Group Policy snap-in to an MMC and create a stand-alone GPO console. After saving the console, you can open it whenever necessary from the Administrative Tools menu.

▶ **To create a GPO console**

1. Click Start, then point to Run.

2. In the Run dialog box, type **mmc** in the Open box and click OK.

3. In the new MMC console, from the Console menu, click Add/Remove Snap-In.

4. In the Add/Remove Snap-In dialog box, click Add.

5. In the Add Standalone Snap-In dialog box, select Group Policy, then click Add.

6. In the Select Group Policy Object page, click Browse to find the GPO for which you want to create a snap-in.

7. In the Browse For A Group Policy Object dialog box, click the All tab, click the GPO name, then click OK.

8. In the Select Group Policy Object page, click Finish, then click Close in the Add Standalone Snap-In dialog box.

9. Click OK in the Add/Remove Snap-In dialog box.

10. On the Console menu, click Save As.

11. In the Save As dialog box, type the GPO name in the File Name box and click Save. The GPO is now available on the Administrative Tools menu.

Delegating Administrative Control of a GPO

After you create a GPO, it is important to determine which groups of administrators have access permissions to the GPO. The default permissions on GPOs are shown in Table 12.2.

Table 12.2   Default GPO Permissions

Security Group	Default Settings
Authenticated Users	Read, Apply Group Policy, Special Permissions
CREATOR OWNER	Special Permissions
Domain Administrators	Read, Write, Create All Child Objects, Delete All Child Objects, Special Permissions
Enterprise Administrators	Read, Write, Create All Child Objects, Delete All Child Objects, Special Permissions
SYSTEM	Read, Write, Create All Child Objects, Delete All Child Objects, Special Permissions

By default, the Default Domain Policy GPO cannot be deleted by any administrator. This prevents the accidental deletion of this GPO, which contains important required settings for the domain.

If you are working with a GPO from a pre-built console, such as the Active Directory Users and Computers, the Delegation Of Control Wizard is not available for use in delegating administrative control of a GPO; it only controls security of an object.

▶ **To delegate administrative control of a GPO**

1. Access the Group Policy snap-in for the GPO.

2. Right-click the root node of the console and click Properties

3. Click the Security tab (see Figure 12.11), then click the security group for which you want to allow or deny administrative access to the GPO.

   If you need to change the list of security groups for which you want to allow or deny administrative access to the GPO, you can add or remove security groups using Add and Remove.

4. To provide administrative control of all aspects of the GPO, set the Read permission to Allow and set the Write permission to Allow.

   A user or administrator who has Read access but does not have Write access to a GPO cannot use the Group Policy snap-in to see the settings that it contains. All extensions to the Group Policy snap-in require Write access to open a GPO.

5. Click OK.

Figure 12.11   GPO Properties Security tab

Specifying Group Policy Settings

After you create a GPO and determine the administrators who have access
permissions to the GPO, you can specify the group policy settings.

▶ **To specify group policy settings for a GPO**

1. Access the Group Policy snap-in for the GPO (see Figure 12.12).

Figure 12.12   Group Policy snap-in

2. In the console tree, expand the item that represents the particular policy you want to set.

For example, in Figure 12.12, User Configuration, Administrative Templates, and Control Panel were expanded, and then Display was expanded.

3. In the details pane, right-click the policy that you want to set, then click Properties. In Figure 12.13, the Hide Screen Saver Tab policy was selected in the details pane.

Figure 12.13   Hide Screen Saver Tab Properties dialog box

4. Click Enabled to apply the policy to users or computers that are subject to this GPO, then click OK.

Not Configured indicates that no change will be made to the registry regarding this setting. Disabled indicates that the registry will indicate that the policy does not apply to users or computers that are subject to this GPO.

Disabling Unused Group Policy Settings

If a GPO has, under the Computer Configuration or User Configuration node of the console, only settings that are Not Configured, then you can avoid processing those settings by disabling the node. This action expedites startup and logon for those users and computers subject to the GPO.

▶ **To disable the Computer Configuration
or User Configuration settings for a GPO**

1. Access the Group Policy snap-in for the GPO.

2. Right-click the root node of the console and click Properties.

3. In the General tab in the Properties dialog box:

- To disable the Computer Configuration settings, click the Disable Computer Configuration Settings check box.

- To disable the User Configuration settings, click the Disable User Configuration Settings check box.

4. Click OK.

Indicating GPO Processing Exceptions

GPOs are processed according to the Active Directory hierarchy: local GPO, site GPOs, domain GPOs, and OU GPOs. However, the default order of processing group policy settings may be changed by modifying the order of GPOs for an object, specifying the Block Policy Inheritance option, specifying the No Override option, or by enabling the Loopback setting.

▶ **To modify the order of GPOs for an object**

1. Open Active Directory Users and Computers to set the order of GPOs for a domain or OU, or open Active Directory Sites and Services to modify the order of GPOs for a site.

2. In the console tree, right-click the site, domain, or OU for which you want to modify the GPO order, click Properties, then click the Group Policy tab.

3. In the Group Policy Object Links list, select the GPO and click the Up button (as shown in Figure 12.14) or the Down button to change the priority for a GPO for this site, domain, or OU. Windows 2000 processes GPOs from the bottom of the list to the top of the list.

Figure 12.14 Modifying the order of GPOs

▶ **To specify the Block Policy Inheritance option**

1. Open Active Directory Users and Computers to specify the Block Policy Inheritance option for a domain or OU, or open Active Directory Sites and Services to specify the Block Policy Inheritance option for a site.

2. In the console tree, right-click the site, domain, or OU for which you want to specify the Block Policy Inheritance option, click Properties, then click the Group Policy tab.

3. Select the Block Policy Inheritance check box to specify that all GPOs linked to higher level sites, domains, or OUs should be blocked from linking to this site, domain, or OU. You cannot block GPOs that use the No Override option (see later).

▶ **To specify the No Override option**

1. Open Active Directory Users and Computers to specify the No Override option for a domain or OU, or open Active Directory Sites and Services to specify the No Override option for a site.

2. In the console, right-click the site, domain, or OU to which the GPO is linked, click Properties, then click the Group Policy tab.

3. Select the GPO, click Options, select the No Override check box in the Options dialog box (see Figure 12.15) to specify that other GPOs should be prevented from overriding settings in this GPO, then click OK.

Figure 12.15   Options dialog box

▶ **To enable the Loopback setting**

1. Access the Group Policy snap-in for the GPO.

2. In the console tree, expand Computer Configuration, Administrative Templates, System, and Group Policy.

3. In the details pane, double-click User Group Policy Loopback Processing Mode.

4. In the User Group Policy Loopback Processing Mode Properties dialog box, click Enabled.

5. Select one of the following modes in the Mode list:

   ▪ **Replace** to replace the GPO list for the user with the GPO list already obtained for the computer at computer startup.

   ▪ **Merge** to append the GPO list obtained for the user at logon with the GPO list already obtained for the computer at computer startup.

6. Click OK.

Filtering GPO Scope

The policies in a GPO apply only to users who have Read permission for that GPO. You can filter the scope of a GPO by creating security groups and then assigning Read permission to the selected groups. Thus, you can prevent a policy from applying to a specific group by denying that group Read permission to the GPO.

▶ **To filter the scope of a GPO**

1. Access the Group Policy snap-in for the GPO.

2. Right-click the root node of the console, then click Properties.

3. Click the Security tab (see Figure 12.11), and then click the security group through which to filter this GPO.

   If you need to change the list of security groups through which to filter this GPO, you can add or remove security groups using Add and Remove.

4. Set the permissions as shown in Table 12.3, then click OK.

Table 12.3   Permissions for GPO Scopes

GPO Scope	Set These Permissions	Result
Members of this security group should have this GPO applied to them.	Set Apply Group-Policy (AGP) to Allow. Set Read to Allow.	This GPO applies to members of this security group unless they are members of at least one other security group that has AGP set to Deny, or Read set to Deny, or both.
Members of this security group are exempt from this GPO.	Set AGP to Deny. Set Read to Deny.	This GPO never applies to members of this security group regardless of the permissions those members have in other security groups.
Membership in this security group is irrelevant to whether the GPO should be applied.	Set AGP to neither Allow nor Deny. Set Read to neither Allow nor Deny.	This GPO applies to members of this security group only if they have both AGP and Read set to Allow as members of at least one other security group. They also must not have AGP or Read set to Deny as members of any other security group.

Linking a GPO

By default, a new GPO is linked to the site, domain, or OU that was selected in the MMC when it was created. Therefore, its settings apply to that site, domain, or OU. Use the Group Policy tab for the site, domain, or OU properties to link a GPO to additional sites, domains, or OUs.

▶ **To link a GPO to a site, domain, or OU**

1. Open Active Directory Users and Computers to link a GPO to a domain or OU, or open Active Directory Sites and Services to link a GPO to a site.

2. In the console, right-click the site, domain, or OU to which the GPO should be linked.

3. Click Properties, then click the Group Policy tab.

4. If the GPO already appears in the Group Policy Object Links list, then click Cancel. If the GPO does not appear in the Group Policy Object Links list, then click Add.

5. In the Add A Group Policy Object Link dialog box (see Figure 12.16), click the All tab, click the desired GPO, then click OK.

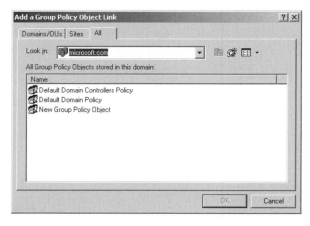

Figure 12.16   Add A Group Policy Object Link dialog box

6. In the Properties dialog box for the site, domain, or OU, click OK.

Modifying Group Policy

The tasks for modifying group policy are

1. Removing a GPO link

2. Deleting a GPO

3. Editing a GPO and GPO settings

Removing a GPO Link

Removing a GPO link simply unlinks the GPO from the specified site, domain, or OU. The GPO remains in Active Directory until it is deleted.

▶ **To remove a GPO link**

1. Open Active Directory Users and Computers to unlink a GPO from a domain or OU, or open Active Directory Sites and Services to unlink a GPO from a site.

2. In the console, right-click the site, domain, or OU from which the GPO should be unlinked.

3. Click Properties, then click the Group Policy tab.

4. In the Group Policy tab, select the GPO that you want to unlink, then click Delete.

5. In the Delete dialog box, click Remove The Link From The List.

   The GPO remains in Active Directory but is no longer linked.

Deleting a GPO

If you delete a GPO, it is removed from Active Directory, and any sites, domains, or OUs to which it is linked will no longer be affected by it. You may wish to take the less drastic step of removing the GPO link, which disassociates the GPO from its OU but leaves the GPO intact in Active Directory.

▶ **To delete a GPO**

1. Open Active Directory Users and Computers to delete a GPO from a domain or OU, or open Active Directory Sites and Services to delete a GPO from a site.

2. In the console, right-click the site, domain, or OU from which the GPO should be deleted.

3. Click Properties, then click the Group Policy tab.

4. In the Group Policy tab, select the GPO that you want to delete, then click Delete.

5. In the Delete dialog box, click Remove The Link And Delete The Group Policy Object Permanently, then click OK.

   The GPO is removed from Active Directory.

Editing a GPO and GPO Settings

To edit a GPO or its settings, follow the procedures outlined earlier in this lesson for creating a GPO and for specifying group policy settings.

Practice: Implementing a Group Policy

In this practice you implement a group policy for your domain. In Exercises 1 through 8 you create a GPO, create a GPO console, delegate administrative control of the GPO, specify group policy settings for the GPO, disable unused group policy settings, indicate a GPO processing exception, filter the scope of the GPO, and link the GPO to an additional OU. In Exercise 9 you test the group policy.

Exercise 1: Creating a GPO

In this exercise you create a GPO at the OU level.

▶ **To create a GPO for your OU**

1. Log on to the domain as Administrator.
2. Click Start, point to Programs, point to Administrative Tools, then click Active Directory Users And Computers.
3. Double-click microsoft.com (or the name of the domain you have created).
4. Create a new OU called Dispatch.
5. Right-click the Dispatch OU, click Properties, then select the Group Policy tab.
6. Click New, then type **DispatchPolicy** to name this GPO.
7. Click Close.

Exercise 2: Creating a GPO Console

In this exercise you create a console for the DispatchPolicy GPO. After saving it, you can open it whenever necessary from the Administrative Tools menu.

▶ **To create a DispatchPolicy GPO console**

1. Click Start, then point to Run.

   The Run dialog box appears.
2. Type **mmc** in the Open box, then click OK.

   A new MMC appears.
3. From the Console menu, click Add/Remove Snap-In.

   The Add/Remove Snap-In dialog box appears.
4. Click Add.

   The Add Standalone Snap-In dialog box appears.
5. Select Group Policy, then click Add.

   The Select Group Policy Object page appears.
6. Click Browse to find the DispatchPolicy GPO.

   The Browse For A Group Policy Object dialog box appears.

7. Click the All tab, click the DispatchPolicy GPO, then click OK.

   The Select Group Policy Object page appears with DispatchPolicy in the Group Policy Object box.

8. Click Finish, then click Close on the Add Standalone Snap-In dialog box.

9. Click OK on the Add/Remove Snap-In dialog box.

10. On the Console menu, click Save As.

    The Save As dialog box appears.

11. Type **DispatchPolicy GPO** in the File Name box, then click Save.

    The DispatchPolicy GPO is now available on the Administrative Tools menu.

Exercise 3: Delegating Administrative Control of a GPO

In this exercise you delegate administrative control for the DispatchPolicy GPO to the Administrators group.

▶ **To delegate administrative control for your GPO**

1. Access the DispatchPolicy GPO console.

2. Right-click the root node of the console, DispatchPolicy [server1.microsoft.com] Policy, click Properties, then click the Security tab.

   The DispatchPolicy [server1.microsoft.com] Policy Properties dialog box appears.

   What security groups already have administrative control of the DispatchPolicy GPO?

3. Add the Administrators group using the Add button.

4. To provide administrative control of all aspects of the GPO to the Administrators group, set Read, Write, Create All Child Objects, and Delete All Child Objects to Allow for the group.

5. Click OK.

Exercise 4: Specifying Group Policy Settings

In this exercise you specify some group policy settings for the Dispatch Policy GPO.

▶ **To specify group policy settings for your GPO**

1. In the DispatchPolicy GPO console, in the console tree, expand the root node of the console.

2. Click User Configuration, then click Administrative Templates.

3. In the console tree, click Start Menu & Task Bar.

   What appears in the details pane?

4. In the details pane, double-click Remove Search Menu From Start Menu.

   The Remove Search Menu From Start Menu Properties dialog box appears.

5. Click Enabled, then click OK.

   How can you tell at a glance that this setting is enabled?

6. Repeat Steps 4 and 5 to enable the Remove Run Menu From Start Menu policy (still under User Configuration).

7. In the console tree, double-click System, then click Logon/Logoff.

   The policies available for this category appear in the details pane.

8. In the details pane, enable the Disable Lock Computer policy and click OK.

Exercise 5: Disabling Unused Group Policy Settings

In this exercise you disable the Computer Configuration node of the console, as this node contains only settings that are not configured. This action expedites startup for those users and computers subject to the GPO.

▶ **To disable the Computer Configuration settings for your GPO**

1. On the DispatchPolicy GPO console, right-click the root node of the console, then click Properties.

   The DispatchPolicy [server1.microsoft.com] Policy Properties dialog box appears.

2. In the General tab, click Disable Computer Configuration Settings.

   The Confirm Disable message box appears, asking you to confirm that you want to disable the Computer Configuration settings.

3. Click Yes, then click OK.

Exercise 6: Indicating GPO Processing Exceptions

In this exercise you set the No Override option to prevent other GPOs from overriding the policies set in the DispatchPolicy GPO.

▶ **To set the No Override option for your GPO**

1. Click Start, point to Programs, point to Administrative Tools, then click Active Directory Users And Computers.

2. Right-click the Dispatch OU, then click Properties.

   The Dispatch Properties dialog box appears.

3. Click the Group Policy tab, click the DispatchPolicy GPO, then click Options.

   The DispatchPolicy Options dialog box appears.

4. Select the No Override check box, then click OK.

5. In the Dispatch Properties dialog box, click OK.

Exercise 7: Filtering GPO Scope

In this exercise you prevent a policy from applying to the Sales security group by denying that group Read permission to the GPO. You created the Sales group and its members in Chapter 8.

▶ **To filter the scope of your GPO**

1. In the DispatchPolicy GPO console, right-click the root node of the console, then click Properties.

   The DispatchPolicy [server1.microsoft.com] Policy Properties dialog box appears.

2. Click the Security tab, then click the Sales security group. You will need to add the Sales group using the Add button.

3. For the Sales group, set Apply Group Policy to Deny and set Read to Deny, then click OK.

   The Security message box appears, asking you to confirm that you want to prevent the DispatchPolicy from applying to the Sales group.

4. Click Yes.

Exercise 8: Linking a GPO

By default, the DispatchPolicy GPO is linked and its settings apply to the Dispatch OU. In this exercise you will link the DispatchPolicy GPO to the Security1 OU you created in Chapter 11.

▶ **To link your GPO to an additional OU**

1. Click Start, point to Programs, point to Administrative Tools, then click Active Directory Users And Computers.

2. Right-click the Security1 OU, then click Properties.

   The Security1 Properties dialog box appears.

3. Click the Group Policy tab, then click Add.

   The Add A Group Policy Object Link dialog box appears.

4. Click the All tab, click the DispatchPolicy GPO, then click OK.

5. In the Security1 Properties dialog box, click OK.

Exercise 9: Testing a GPO

In this exercise you view the effects of the group policy implemented in the previous exercises.

▶ **To test the DispatchPolicy GPO**

1. Log on as Assistant1, a member of the Security1 OU.

2. Press Ctrl+Alt+Delete.

   The Windows Security dialog box appears.

   Are you able to lock the workstation? Why?

3. Click Cancel, then click Start.

   Does the Search command appear on the Start menu?

   Does the Run command appear on the Start menu?

4. Log off as Assistant1, then log on as Administrator.

5. Make Assistant1 a member of the Sales security group.

6. Log off as Administrator, then log on as Assistant1.

7. Press Ctrl+Alt+Delete.

   Are you able to lock the workstation? Why?

8. Log off the computer.

Lesson Summary

In this lesson you learned the tasks involved with implementing group policy. The tasks are: create a GPO, create a GPO console, delegate administrative control of the GPO, specify group policy settings for the GPO, disable unused group policy settings, indicate GPO processing exceptions, filter the scope of the GPO, and link the GPO to a site, domain, or OU.

In the practice portion of this lesson you implemented a group policy for your domain. You created a GPO, created a console for the GPO, delegated administrative control of the GPO, specified group policy settings for the GPO, disabled unused group policy settings, set the No Override option for the GPO, filtered the scope of the GPO, and linked the GPO to an additional OU. Finally, you tested the effects of the GPO.

Lesson 4: Managing Software Using Group Policy

The Software Installation extension, a software management feature of Windows 2000, is the administrator's primary tool for managing software within an organization. Managing software using Software Installation provides your users with immediate access to the software they need to perform their jobs and ensures that users have an easy and consistent experience when working with software throughout its life cycle. Users no longer need to look for a network share, use a CD-ROM, or install, fix, and upgrade software themselves. This lesson walks you through the steps for implementing Software Installation.

After this lesson, you will be able to
- Deploy software using group policy
- Configure deployment options
- Maintain software using group policy

Estimated lesson time: 75 minutes

Software Management Tools

Three tools are provided with Windows 2000 Server for software installation and maintenance. Table 12.4 describes these tools.

Table 12.4   Windows 2000 Software Installation and Maintenance Tools

Tool	Role
The Software Installation extension of the Group Policy snap-in	Used by administrators to manage software
Windows Installer	Installs software packaged in Windows Installer files
Add/Remove Programs in Control Panel	Used by users to manage software on their own computers

The Software Installation Extension

The Software Installation extension is the administrator's primary tool for managing software within an organization. Software Installation works in conjunction with group policy and Active Directory, establishing a group policy-based software management system that allows you to centrally manage

- Initial deployment of software.
- Mandatory and nonmandatory upgrades, patches, and quick fixes for software. You can update a version of the software or replace it. You can even upgrade the operating system using service packs.
- Removal of software.

Using Software Installation, you can centrally manage the installation of software on a client computer by assigning applications to users or computers or by publishing applications for users. *Assign* required or mandatory software to users or to computers. *Publish* software that users might find useful to perform their jobs.

Assigning Applications

When you assign an application to a user, the application is advertised to the user the next time he or she logs on to a workstation. The application advertisement follows the user regardless of which physical computer he or she actually uses. This application is installed the first time the user activates the application on the computer, either by selecting the application on the Start menu or by activating a document associated with the application.

When you assign an application to the computer, the application is advertised and the installation is performed when it is safe to do so. Typically this happens when the computer starts up so that there are no competing processes on the computer.

Publishing Applications

When you publish the application to users, the application does not appear installed on the users' computers. No shortcuts are visible on the desktop or Start menu, and no changes are made to the local registry on the users' computers. Instead, published applications store their advertisement attributes in Active Directory. Then, information such as the application's name and file associations is exposed to the users in the Active Directory container. The application is then available for the user to install using Add/Remove Programs in Control Panel or by clicking a file associated with the application (such as an .xls file for Microsoft Excel).

How Software Installation Works

The Software Installation extension uses Windows Installer technology to systematically maintain software. Windows Installer is a service that allows the operating system to manage the installation process. Windows Installer is composed of three key parts:

- An operating system service that performs the installation, modification, and removal of the software in accordance with the information in the Windows Installer package.

- The Windows Installer package, a database containing information that describes the installed state of the application.

- An application programming interface (API) that allows applications to interact with Windows Installer to install or remove additional features of the application after the initial installation is complete.

Because Software Installation leverages Windows Installer, users can take advantage of self-repairing applications. Windows Installer notes when a program file is missing and immediately reinstalls the damaged or missing files, thereby fixing the application.

The Windows Installer package is a file that contains explicit instructions on the installation and removal of specific applications. The developer who produces the application provides the Windows Installer package .msi file and ships it with the application. If a Windows Installer package does not come with an application, you might need to create a Windows Installer package, or repackage the application, using a third-party tool.

You can only deploy software using the Software Installation extension if the file type fits one of the following categories:

- Native Windows Installer package (.msi) files are developed as a part of the application and take full advantage of the Windows Installer.

- Repackaged application (.msi) files allow you to repackage applications that do not have a native Windows Installer package in much the same way that you repackage software today to customize installations.

- An existing setup program—an application (.zap) file—installs an application by using its original SETUP.EXE program.

In addition, you can make modifications to customize the installation of a Windows Installer package at the time of assignment or publication. Modifications are saved with the .mst file extension.

Other files you may encounter during Software Installation are

- Patch (.msp) files, which are used for bug fixes, service packs, and similar files

- Application assignment scripts (.aas files), which contain instructions associated with the assignment or publication of a package

Customizing Windows Installer Packages

You can customize Windows Installer applications by using *modifications*, also called *transforms*. The Windows Installer package format provides for customization by allowing you to "transform" the original package using authoring and repackaging tools. Some applications also provide wizards or templates that permit a user to create modifications.

For example, Microsoft Office 2000 supplies a Customization Wizard that builds modifications. Using the Microsoft Office 2000 Customization Wizard, you can create a modification that allows you to manage the configuration of Microsoft Office 2000 that is deployed to users. A modification might be designed to accommodate Microsoft Word as a key feature, installing it during the first installation. Less popular features, such as revision support or document translators, could install on first usage, and other features, such as clip art, might not install at all. You might have another modification that provides all of the features of Word and does not install Microsoft PowerPoint. The exact mix of which features to install and when to install them varies based on the audience for the application and how they use the software.

Implementing Software Installation

The tasks for implementing software installation are

1. Planning and preparing the software installation
2. Setting up a software distribution point
3. Specifying software installation defaults
4. Deploying software applications
5. Setting automatic installation options
6. Setting up application categories
7. Setting software application properties
8. Maintaining software applications

Planning and Preparing a Software Installation

When planning a software installation

- Review your organization's software requirements on the basis of your overall organizational structure within Active Directory and your available GPOs
- Determine how you want to deploy your applications
- Create a pilot to test how you want to assign or publish software to users or computers
- Prepare your software using a format that allows you to manage it based on what your organization requires, and test all of the Windows Installer packages or repackaged software

Table 12.5 describes strategies and considerations for implementing a software installation. Some of these strategies might seem contradictory, but select the strategies that meet your business goals.

Table 12.5   Strategies and Considerations for Implementing Software Installation

Strategy	Considerations
Create OUs based on software management needs.	Allows you to target applications to the appropriate set of users. Group policy security settings are not required to target the appropriate set of users.

Strategy	Considerations
Deploy software close to the root in the Active Directory tree.	Makes it easy to provide all users in an organization with access to an application. This reduces administration because you can deploy a single GPO rather than having to re-create that object in multiple containers deep in the Active Directory tree.
Deploy multiple applications with a single GPO.	Reduces administration overhead by allowing you to create and manage a single GPO rather than multiple GPOs. The logon process is faster because a single GPO deploying 10 applications processes faster than 10 GPOs each deploying one application. This is appropriate in organizations where users share the same core set of applications.
Publish or assign one application only once in the same GPO or in a series of GPOs that might apply to a single user or computer.	Makes it easier to determine which instance of the application applies to the user or computer.

Software licenses are required for software written by independent software vendors and distributed using software distribution points (SDPs). It is your responsibility to match the number of users who can access software to the number of licenses you have on hand. It is also your responsibility to verify that you are working within the guidelines provided by each independent software vendor with the software.

Gather the package formats for the software and perform any necessary modifications to the packages.

Setting Up an SDP

After you have planned and prepared for software management, the next step is to copy the software to one or more SDPs, network locations from which people are able to get the software that they need.

▶ **To set up a software distribution point**

1. Create the folders for the software on the file server that will be the SDP and make the folders network shares. For example: *server**share*

2. Replicate the software to the SDPs by placing or copying the software, packages, modifications, all necessary files, and components to a distribution share(s). Place all software (the package and all related installation files) in a separate folder on the SDP.

3. Set the appropriate permissions on the folders so that only administrators can change the files (Read and Write), and users can only read the files from the SDP folders and shares. Use group policy to manage the software within the appropriate GPO.

Note Some software supports special commands to facilitate the creation of an SDP. For example, Microsoft Office 2000 should be prepared by running SETUP /A from a command prompt. This allows you to enter the software key once for all users, and the network share (SDP) location to copy the files to. Other software might have other ways to expand any compressed files from the distribution media and transfer the files to the appropriate location.

Specifying Software Installation Defaults

A GPO can contain several settings that affect how an application is installed, managed, and removed. You can globally define the default settings for the new packages within the GPO in the General tab of the Software Installation Properties dialog box. Some of these settings can be changed later by editing the package properties in the Software Installation extension.

▶ **To specify software installation defaults**

1. Open the Group Policy snap-in, then in Computer or User Configuration open Software Settings.

2. Right-click the Software Installation node, then click Properties.

3. In the General tab of the Software Installation Properties dialog box (see Figure 12.17), type the path to the default SDP for packages (.msi files) in the Default Package Location box.

Figure 12.17 General tab of the Software Installation Properties dialog box

4. In the New Packages section, select one of the following:

- **Display The Deploy Software Dialog Box** to specify that when you add a new package, the Deploy Software dialog box will display, allowing you to assign, publish, or configure package properties.

- **Publish** to specify that when you add a new package, by default you want it published with standard package properties. Packages can only be published to users, not computers. If this is an installation under the Computer Configuration node of the Group Policy snap-in, the Publish choice appears dimmed.

- **Assign** to specify that when you add a new package by default, you want it assigned with standard package properties. Packages can be assigned to users and computers.

- **Advanced Published Or Assigned** to specify that when you add a new package, the Configure Package Properties form should appear.

5. In the Installation User Interface Options section, select one of the following:

- **Basic** to provide only a basic display of the install process.

- **Maximum** to provide all installation messages and screens during the package installation.

6. Check the Uninstall The Applications When They Fall Out Of The Scope Of Management check box to specify that the package should be removed when the GPO no longer applies to users or computers.

7. Click OK.

Deploying Software Applications

Given that software can be either assigned or published, and targeted to users or computers, you can establish a workable combination to meet your software management goals. Table 12.6 details the different approaches.

Table 12.6   Software Deployment Approaches

	Publish (User Only)	Assign (User)	Assign (Computer)
After deployment the software is available for installation after:	The next logon	The next logon	The next time the computer starts
Typically the user installs the software from:	Add/Remove Programs in Control Panel	Start menu or Desktop shortcut	The software is already installed (the software automatically installs when the computer reboots)

Table 12.6   Software Deployment Approaches *(continued)*

	Publish (User Only)	Assign (User)	Assign (Computer)
If the software is not installed, and the user opens a file associated with the software, does the software install?	Yes (if auto-install is turned on)	Yes	Does not apply; the software is already installed
Can the user remove the software using Add/Remove Programs in Control Panel?	Yes, and the user can choose to install it again from Add/Remove Programs in Control Panel	Yes, and the software is available for installation again from the typical install points	No. Only the local administrator can remove the software; a user can run a repair on the software
Supported installation files:	Windows Installer packages, .zap files	Windows Installer packages	Windows Installer packages

Modifications, or .mst files, are customizations applied to Windows Installer packages. A modification must be applied at the time of assignment or publication, not at the time of installation.

Assigning Applications

Assign an application when you want everyone to have the application on his or her computer. An application can be assigned to both computers and users.

▶   **To assign applications**

1. Open the Group Policy snap-in, then, in Computer or User Configuration, open Software Settings.

2. Right-click the Software Installation node, click New, and click Package.

    The File Name list in the Open dialog box shows those Windows Installer packages located at the SDP you specified as the default. If the Windows Installer package is located on a different network share, you can browse to find the SDP for the package.

3. In the File Name list in the Open dialog box, select the Windows Installer package to be assigned, then click Open.

4. In the Deploy Software dialog box (see Figure 12.18), click Assigned, then click OK. If this is an application under the Computer Configuration node of the Group Policy snap-in, the Published choice appears dimmed, because packages can only be assigned to computers, not published.

Figure 12.18   Deploy Software dialog box

Publishing Applications

Publish an application when you want the application to be available to people managed by the GPO, should they want the application. With published applications it is up to each person to decide whether or not to install the published application. An application can only be published to users.

▶ **To publish applications**

1. Open the Group Policy snap-in, then, in User Configuration, open Software Settings.

2. Right-click the Software Installation node, click New, then click Package.

   The File Name list in the Open dialog box shows those packages located at the SDP you specified as the default. If the Windows Installer package is located on a different network share, you can browse to find the SDP for the package.

3. In the File Name list in the Open dialog box, select the Windows Installer package to be published, then click Open.

4. In the Deploy Software dialog box (see Figure 12.18), click Published, then click OK.

   The application is available for users to install either by using Add/Remove Programs in Control Panel or by opening a file with a file name extension that you have associated with the application.

Deploying Applications with Modifications

Modifications are associated with the Windows Installer package at deployment time rather than when the Windows Installer is actually using the package to install or modify the application. Modifications (.mst files) are applied to

Windows Installer packages (which have the .msi extension) in an order specified by the administrator. This order must be determined before the application is assigned or published.

▶ **To add or remove modifications for applications**

1. Open the Group Policy snap-in, then, in Computer or User Configuration, open Software Settings.

2. Right-click the Software Installation node, click New, then click Package.

3. In the File Name list in the Open dialog box, select the Windows Installer package to be published, then click Open.

4. In the Deploy Software dialog box, click Advanced Published Or Assigned, then click OK.

5. In the Properties dialog box for the package, click the Modifications tab (see Figure 12.19).

Figure 12.19   Modifications tab of the Properties dialog box

- To add modifications, click Add. In the Open dialog box, browse to find the modification file (.mst), then click Open. You can add multiple modifications.

- To remove modifications, click the modification you want to remove, then click Remove. Repeat until each unwanted modification has been removed.

- To set the order of modifications, select a modification and then click Move Up or Move Down. Modifications are applied according to the order specified in the list.

6. Make sure that the modifications are configured exactly the way you want them, then click OK.

Important   Do not click OK until you have finished configuring the modifications. When you click OK, the package is assigned or published immediately. If the modifications are not properly configured you will have to uninstall the package or upgrade the package with a correctly configured version.

Setting Automatic Installation Options

To determine which application users install when they select a file, you can select a file extension and configure a priority for installing applications associated with the file extension using the File Extensions tab in the Software Installation Properties dialog box. The first application listed is the application installed in association with the file extension.

For example, if you use a GPO to deploy both Microsoft Word 2000 and Microsoft FrontPage 2000, both of these applications can edit HyperText Markup Language (HTML) documents, files with the .htm extension. To configure the file extension priority so that users who are managed by this GPO always install Microsoft FrontPage, set FrontPage as the application with the highest priority for the .htm extension. When users managed by this GPO who have installed neither Microsoft Word 2000 nor Microsoft FrontPage 2000 receive an .htm file (by e-mail or other means) and they double-click on the .htm file, Software Installation installs FrontPage 2000 and opens the .htm file for editing. Without Software Installation, the user would see the Open With dialog box and be asked to select the best alternative from the software already present on his or her computer.

File extension associations are managed on a per-GPO basis. Changing the priority order in a GPO affects only those users who have that GPO applied to them.

▶ **To set automatic installation options based on file name extension**

1. Open the Group Policy snap-in, then, in Computer or User Configuration, open Software Settings.

2. Right-click the Software Installation node, then click Properties.

3. In the File Extensions tab of the Software Installation Properties dialog box (see Figure 12.20), select the file extension for which you want to specify an automatic software installation from the Select File Extension list.

4. In the Application Precedence list box, move the application with the highest precedence by default to the top of the list using the Up or Down buttons. The application at the top of the list is automatically installed if a document with the selected file name extension is invoked before the application has been installed.

5. Click OK.

Figure 12.20   File Extensions tab of the Software Installation Properties dialog box

Setting Up Application Categories

You can organize assigned and published applications into logical categories to make it easier for users to locate the appropriate application from within Add/Remove Programs in Control Panel. Windows 2000 does not ship with any predefined categories.

The categories that you establish are per domain, not per GPO. You only need to define them once for the whole domain.

▶ **To set up categories for applications to be managed**

1. Open the Group Policy snap-in, then, in Computer or User Configuration, open Software Settings.

2. Right-click the Software Installation node, then click Properties.

3. In the Categories tab of the Software Installation Properties dialog box (see Figure 12.21), click Add.

4. In the Enter New Category dialog box, type the name of the application category in the Category box and click OK.

5. On the Software Installation Properties dialog box, click OK.

Figure 12.21   Categories tab of the Software Installation Properties dialog box

Setting Software Application Properties

You can fine-tune each application by editing installation options, specifying application categories to be used, and setting permissions for the software installation.

Editing Installation Options for Applications

Although you may have globally defined the default settings for new packages within the GPO in the General tab of the Software Installation Properties dialog box, some of these same settings can be changed later by editing the package properties. Installation options affect how an application is installed, managed, and removed.

▶ **To edit installation options for applications**

1. Open the Group Policy snap-in, then, in Computer or User Configuration, open Software Settings.

2. Click the Software Installation node.

3. In the details pane, right-click the application for which you want to edit installation options, then click Properties.

4. In the Deployment tab of the Properties dialog box for the application (see Figure 12.22), select one of the following in the Deployment Type area:

- **Published** to allow users in the selected site, domain, or OU to install the application using either Add/Remove Programs in Control Panel or the application installation by file activation.

- **Assigned** to allow users in the selected site, domain, or OU to receive this application the next time they log on (for assignment to users) or when the computer restarts (for assignment to computers).

Figure 12.22 Deployment tab of the Properties dialog box

5. In the Deployment Options area, select one of the following:

- **Auto-Install This Application By File Extension Activation** to use the application precedence for the file name extension as determined in the File Extensions tab of the Software Installation Properties dialog box. If this is an application under the Computer Configuration node of the Group Policy snap-in, the check box appears dimmed and selected, because by default the application is installed automatically.

- **Uninstall This Application When It Falls Out Of The Scope Of Management** to remove the application at logon (for users) or startup (for computers) if they move to a site, domain, or OU for which the application is not deployed.

- **Do Not Display This Package In The Add/Remove Programs Control Panel** to specify that this package should not be displayed in Add/Remove Programs in Control Panel.

6. In the Installation User Interface Options area, select one of the following:

  ▪ **Basic** to provide only a basic display to users during the install process.

  ▪ **Maximum** to provide all installation messages and screens to users during the package installation.

7. Click Advanced to display the Advanced Deployment Options dialog box. In the Advanced Deployment Options area, select either of the following check boxes:

  ▪ **Ignore Language When Deploying This Package** to specify whether to deploy the package even if it is in a different language.

  ▪ **Remove Previous Installs Of This Product From** (Users/Computers) **If Product Was Not Installed By Group Policy-Based Software Installation** to specify whether to remove previous installs of this product from users or computers if product was not installed by group policy-based Software Installation.

8. Click OK.

9. On the Properties dialog box, click OK.

Specifying Application Categories

You must associate applications with existing categories. Categories you set generally pertain to published applications only, as assigned applications do not appear in Add/Remove Programs in Control Panel. The application appears in the selected categories in Add/Remove Programs, which the user can use to install the application.

▶ **To specify application categories for Add/Remove Programs in Control Panel**

1. Open the Group Policy snap-in, then, in Computer or User Configuration, open Software Settings.

2. Click the Software Installation node.

3. In the details pane, right-click the application for which you want to specify application categories, then click Properties.

4. In the Categories tab of the Properties dialog box for the application (see Figure 12.23), click the category you want to specify from the Available Categories list, then click Select.

5. Repeat Step 4 to specify additional categories. Click OK when you finish selecting categories.

Figure 12.23   Categories tab of the Properties dialog box

Setting Permissions for Software Installation

Permissions set for software installation pertain only to the application installation.

▶ **To set permissions for software installation**

1. Open the Group Policy snap-in, then, in Computer or User Configuration, open Software Settings.

2. Click the Software Installation node.

3. In the details pane, right-click the application for which you want to specify software installation permissions, then click Properties.

4. In the Security tab of the application's Properties dialog box, click the security group on which to set permissions.

   Administrators who manage the application installation should have the Full Control permission set to Allow. Users who use the software assigned or published by the application should have the Read permission set to Allow.

5. Click OK.

Maintaining Software Applications

After the deployment of software applications it may be necessary to upgrade or remove them at some point in the software life cycle.

Upgrading Applications

Several events in the life cycle of the software can trigger an upgrade, including the following:

- The original developer of the software might release a new version with new and improved features
- The organization might choose to use a different vendor's application

Upgrades typically involve major changes to the software and normally have new version numbers. Usually a substantial number of files change for an upgrade. You can use the Software Installation extension to establish the procedure to upgrade an existing application to the current release.

▶ **To upgrade applications**

1. Open the Group Policy snap-in, then, in Computer or User Configuration, open Software Settings.

2. Click the Software Installation node.

3. In the details pane, right-click the Windows Installer package that will function as the upgrade (not the package to be upgraded), then click Properties. You will have previously assigned or published this package.

4. In the Upgrades tab of the application's Properties dialog box, click Add to create or add to the list of packages that are to be upgraded by the current package.

5. In the Add Upgrade Package dialog box (see Figure 12.24), specify either Current Group Policy Object or A Specific GPO as the source of the package to be upgraded. In the latter case, click Browse, click the GPO you want, and then in the Browse For A Group Policy Object dialog box, click OK.

   A list of all the other packages assigned to be published within the selected GPO appears under the heading Package To Upgrade. Depending on the GPO, this list may have zero or more entries.

6. Click the package to upgrade.

7. Click either Uninstall The Existing Package, Then Install The Upgrade Package, or Package Can Upgrade Over The Existing Package, then click OK. Typically, the uninstall option is for replacing an application with a completely different one (perhaps from a different vendor). The upgrade option is for installing a newer version of the same product while retaining the user's application preferences, document type associations, and so on.

8. On the Upgrades tab in the Properties dialog box, enable the Required Upgrade For Existing Packages check box if you want the upgrade to be mandatory, then click OK.

   If this is an upgrade under the Computer Configuration node of the Group Policy snap-in, the check box appears dimmed and selected, because packages can only be assigned to computers, not published.

Figure 12.24   Add Upgrade Package dialog box

Removing Applications

At some point, users may no longer require an application, so you may need to remove it. The following two scenarios are addressed through the removal choices set within the Software Installation extension:

- **A version of a software application is no longer supported.**   Administrators can remove the software version from Software Installation without forcing the (physical) removal of the software from the computers of users who are still using the software. Users can continue to use the software until they remove it themselves. No user is able to install the software version (from the Start menu, from Add/Remove Programs in Control Panel, or by document invocation).

- **A software application is no longer used.**   Administrators can force the removal of the software. The software is automatically deleted from a computer, either the next time the computer is turned on (when the software is assigned to the computer), or the next time the user logs on (when the software is assigned to the user). Users cannot install or run the software.

Note   When you originally deploy the software, if you want the application to be removed when a GPO no longer applies, select the Uninstall This Application When It Falls Out Of The Scope of Management option.

▶   **To remove applications**

1. Open the Group Policy snap-in, then in Computer or User Configuration, open Software Settings.

2. Click the Software Installation node.

3. In the details pane, right-click the application you want to remove, click All Tasks, then click Remove.

4. In the Remove Software Dialog box, select one of the following removal options:

   ■ **Immediately Uninstall The Software From Users And Computers.**   Select this option to specify that the application be removed the next time a user logs on or restarts the computer.

   ■ **Allow Users To Continue To Use The Software, But Prevent New Installations.**   Select this option to specify that users can continue to use the application if they have already installed it. If they remove the application or have never installed it, they will not be able to install it.

5. Click OK.

Lesson Summary

In this lesson you learned how the Software Installation extension helps you specify how applications are installed and maintained in your organization. You can centrally manage the installation of software on a client computer by assigning applications to users or computers or by publishing applications for users. *Assign* required or mandatory software to users or to computers. *Publish* software that users might find useful to perform their jobs.

The Software Installation extension uses Windows Installer technology to systematically maintain software. The Windows Installer package is a file that contains explicit instructions on installing and removing specific applications.

You also walked through the tasks for implementing software installation, which are: planning and preparing, setting up an SDP, specifying software installation defaults, deploying software applications, setting automatic installation options, setting up application categories, setting software application properties, and maintaining software applications.

Lesson 5: Managing Special Folders Using Group Policy

Microsoft Windows 2000 allows you to redirect the folders containing a user's profile to a location on the network using the Folder Redirection extension in the Group Policy snap-in. This lesson introduces special folder redirection and walks you through the steps for setting up folder redirection using group policy.

After this lesson, you will be able to

- Redirect special folders

Estimated lesson time: 15 minutes

Folder Redirection

You use the Folder Redirection extension to the Group Policy snap-in to redirect certain Windows 2000 special folders to network locations. Special folders such as My Documents and My Pictures are located in C:\Documents and Settings (where C:\ is the name of your system drive).

Windows 2000 allows the following special folders to be redirected:

- Application Data
- Desktop
- My Documents
- My Pictures
- Start Menu

The Folder Redirection extension is located under User Configuration, Windows Settings in the Group Policy snap-in.

Advantages of Redirecting the My Documents Folder

The following benefits pertain to redirecting any folder, but redirecting My Documents can be particularly advantageous because this folder tends to become large over time.

- Even if a user logs on to various computers on the network, his or her documents are always available.
- When roaming user profiles are used, only the network path to the My Documents folder is part of the roaming user profile, not the My Documents folder itself. Therefore, its contents do not have to be copied back and forth between the client computer and the server each time the user logs on or off, and the process of logging on or off can be much faster than it was in Windows NT 4.0.
- Data stored on a shared network server can be backed up as part of routine system administration. This is safer because it requires no action on the part of the user.

- The system administrator can use group policy to set disk quotas, limiting the amount of space taken up by users' special folders.

- Data specific to a user can be redirected to a different hard disk on the user's local computer from the hard disk holding the operating system files. This makes the user's data safer if the operating system needs to be reinstalled.

Default Special Folder Locations

The default locations for special folders that have not been redirected depend on the operating system that was in place previously (see Table 12.7).

Table 12.7   Default Locations for Special Folders

Operating System	Location of Special Folders
Windows 2000 new installation (no previous operating system), Windows 2000 upgrade of Windows 95, or Windows 98 with user profiles disabled	C:\Documents and Settings (where C:\ is the name of your system drive); for example, C:\Documents and Settings
Windows 2000 upgrade of Windows NT 4.0 or Windows NT 3.51	*systemroot*\Profiles; for example, C:\WinNT\Profiles
Windows 2000 upgrade of Windows 95 or Windows 98 with user profiles enabled	*systemroot*\Profiles; for example, C:\Windows\System\Profiles

Setting Up Folder Redirection

There are two ways to set up folder redirection:

1. Redirect special folders to a location according to security group membership.

2. Redirect special folders to one location for everyone in the site, domain, or OU.

In addition, you can also direct the My Pictures folder to follow the redirection of the My Documents folder (to remain as its subfolder whenever My Documents is redirected, as it does by default).

Note The default (My Pictures following My Documents) is recommended unless you have a specific reason (such as file share scalability) for separating My Pictures from My Documents. If they are separated, a shortcut takes the place of the My Pictures folder in My Documents.

▶ **To redirect special folders to a location according to security group membership**

1. Open a GPO linked to the site, domain, or OU containing the users whose special folders you want to redirect to a network location.

2. In User Configuration, open Windows Settings, then double-click the Folder Redirection node to show the folder you want to redirect.

3. Right-click the folder you want (such as Desktop, My Documents, and so on), then click Properties.

4. In the Target tab in the Properties dialog box for the folder (see Figure 12.25), in the Setting list, select Advanced-Specify Locations For Various User Groups, then click Add.

Figure 12.25   Target tab in the Properties dialog box

5. In the Specify Group And Location dialog box (see Figure 12.26), in the Security Group Membership box, click Browse.

6. In the Select Group dialog box, click the security group for which you want to redirect the folder, then click OK.

7. In the Specify Group And Location dialog box, in the Target Folder Location box, click Browse.

8. On the Browse For Folder dialog box, select the redirect location you want for this security group, then click OK.

If you enter a drive letter, such as D:\, then this must represent a valid path on the user's local computer. It is recommended that you enter a full universal naming convention (UNC) path.

If you want each user in the specified security group to have his or her own subfolder at this location, then you can incorporate %username% into the UNC path, such as \\server\share\%username%. Including %username% in the path is recommended. For example, SecUser, member of the Users security group could have My Documents redirected to \\server1\share\secuser \My Documents when using \\server1\share\%username%\My Documents.

Figure 12.26 Specify Group And Location dialog box

9. In the Specify Group And Location dialog box, click OK.

10. If you want to redirect folders for members of other security groups, repeat Steps 4 through 9 until all the groups have been entered.

11. In the Properties dialog box for the folder, click the Settings tab (see Figure 12.27), and then set each of the following options (the default setting is recommended):

   ▪ **Grant The User Exclusive Rights To** (the special folder type) to allow the user and the local system full rights to the folder, and no one else, not even administrators, has any rights. If this setting is disabled, no changes are made to the permissions on the folder. The permissions that apply by default remain in effect. Enabled by default.

   ▪ **Move The Contents Of** (the user's current special folder) **To The New Location** to redirect the contents of the folder to the new location. Enabled by default.

12. Choose one of the following options in the Policy Removal area (the default setting is recommended):

   ▪ **Leave The Folder In The New Location When Policy Is Removed** to leave the folder it its new location even though the GPO no longer applies. Enabled by default.

   ▪ **Redirect The Folder Back To The Local User Profile Location When Policy Is Removed** to move the folder back to its local user profile location when the GPO no longer applies.

Figure 12.27   Settings tab of the Properties dialog box

Important   See the section on Policy Removal Considerations for details on selecting a policy removal option.

---

13. Available for the My Documents folder only, choose one of the following options in the My Pictures Preferences area:

   ▪ **Make My Pictures A Subfolder Of My Documents** to redirect My Pictures automatically to remain a subfolder of My Documents.

   ▪ **Do Not Specify Administrative Policy For My Pictures** to remove My Pictures as a subfolder of My Documents and have the user profile determine the location of My Pictures.

Note   You can also specify if you want the My Pictures folder to follow the My Documents folder by setting the folder redirection properties for My Pictures. See the "To direct the My Pictures folder to follow the redirection of the My Documents folder" procedure for details.

---

14. Click OK.

▶ **To redirect special folders to one location**
for everyone in the site, domain, or OU

   1. Open a GPO linked to the site, domain, or OU containing the users whose special folders you want to redirect to a network location.

   2. In User Configuration, open Windows Settings, then double-click the Folder Redirection node to show the folder you want to redirect.

3. Right-click the folder you want (such as Desktop, My Documents, and so on), then click Properties.

4. In the Target tab in the Properties dialog box for the folder (see Figure 12.25), in the Setting list, select Basic-Redirect Everyone's Folder To The Same Location, then click Browse.

5. On the Browse For Folder dialog box, select the redirect location you want for this GPO.

   If you enter a drive letter, such as D:\, then this must represent a valid path on the user's local computer. It is recommended that you enter a full UNC path.

   If you want each user in the site, domain, or organizational unit to have his or her own subfolder at this location, then you can incorporate %username% into the UNC path, such as \\server\share\%username%. Including %username% in the path is recommended. For example, SecUser, member of the Users security group could have My Documents redirected to \\server1\share\secuser\My Documents when using \\server1\share\%username%\My Documents.

6. In the Browse For Folder dialog box, click OK.

7. In the Properties dialog box for the folder, click the Settings tab (see Figure 12.27), and then set each of the following options (the default setting is recommended):

   ▪ **Grant The User Exclusive Rights To** (the special folder type) to allow the user and the local system full rights to the folder, and no one else, not even administrators, has any rights. If this setting is disabled, no changes are made to the permissions on the folder. The permissions that apply by default remain in effect. Enabled by default.

   ▪ **Move The Contents Of** (the user's current special folder) **To The New Location** to redirect the contents of the folder to the new location. Enabled by default.

8. Choose one of the following options in the Policy Removal area (the default setting is recommended):

   ▪ **Leave The Folder In The New Location When Policy Is Removed** to leave the folder it its new location even though the GPO no longer applies. Enabled by default.

   ▪ **Redirect The Folder Back To The Local User Profile Location When Policy Is Removed** to move the folder back to its local user profile location when the GPO no longer applies.

Important See the section on Policy Removal Considerations for details on selecting a policy removal option.

---

9. Available for the My Documents folder only, choose one of the following options in the My Pictures Preferences area:

- **Make My Pictures A Subfolder Of My Documents** to redirect My Pictures automatically to remain a subfolder of My Documents.

- **Do Not Specify Administrative Policy For My Pictures** to remove My Pictures as a subfolder of My Documents and have the user profile determine the location of My Pictures.

Note   You can also specify if you want the My Pictures folder to follow the My Documents folder by setting the folder redirection properties for My Pictures. See the "To direct the My Pictures folder to follow the redirection of the My Documents folder" procedure for details.

---

10. Click OK.

▶ **To direct the My Pictures folder
to follow the redirection of the My Documents folder**

1. Open a GPO linked to the site, domain, or OU containing the users whose My Pictures folders you want to direct.

2. In User Configuration, open Windows Settings, then double-click the Folder Redirection node.

3. Right-click My Pictures (a folder located in My Documents), then click Properties.

4. In the My Pictures Properties dialog box, in the Setting list, select Follow The My Documents Folder, then click OK.

Policy Removal Considerations

Table 12.8 summarizes what happens to redirected folders and their contents when the group policy object no longer applies.

Table 12.8   Policy Removal Considerations

When the Move The Contents Of (special folder type) To The New Location Setting Is	And the Policy Removal Option Is	Results When Policy Is Removed Are
Enabled	Redirect The Folder Back To The User Profile Location When Policy Is Removed	The special folder returns to its user profile location. The contents are copied, not moved, back to the user profile location. The contents are not deleted from the redirected location. The user continues to have access to the contents, but only on the local computer.

When the Move The Contents Of (special folder type) To The New Location Setting Is	And the Policy Removal Option Is	Results When Policy Is Removed Are
Disabled	Redirect The Folder Back To The User Profile Location When Policy Is Removed	The special folder returns to its user profile location. The contents are not copied or moved to the user profile location. *Caution* If the contents of a folder are not copied to the user profile location, the user can no longer see them.
Either Enabled or Disabled	Leave The Folder In The New Location When Policy Is Removed	The special folder remains at its redirected location. The contents remain at the redirected location. The user continues to have access to the contents at the redirected folder.

Lesson Summary

In this lesson you learned how to redirect the folders containing a user's profile to a location on the network. Windows 2000 allows the following special folders to be redirected: Application Data, Desktop, My Documents, My Pictures, and Start Menu. You also learned that the Folder Redirection extension in the Group Policy snap-in is used to redirect special folders. Folder redirection can be set up to redirect special folders to a location according to security group membership, or redirect special folders to one location for everyone in the site, domain, or OU.

Lesson 6: Troubleshooting Group Policy

This lesson describes problems you may encounter that relate to group policy. It also describes some best practices you should employ to keep group policy troubleshooting activities to a minimum.

After this lesson, you will be able to

- Troubleshoot group policy
- Employ best practices for group policy

Estimated lesson time: 10 minutes

Troubleshooting Group Policy

An important part of troubleshooting group policy problems is to consider dependencies between components. For example, Software Installation relies on group policy, and group policy relies on Active Directory. Active Directory relies on proper configuration of network services. When trying to fix problems that appear in one component, it is generally helpful to check whether components, services, and resources on which it relies are working correctly. Event logs are useful for tracking down problems caused by this type of hierarchical dependency.

Table 12.9 describes scenarios in which there are problems using the Group Policy snap-in.

Table 12.9   Group Policy Snap-In Problems and Solutions

Symptom: The user cannot open a GPO even though he or she has Read access to it

Cause	Solution
An administrator must have both Read permission and Write permission for the GPO to open it in the Group Policy snap-in.	Be a member of a security group with Read and Write permission for the GPO. For example, a domain administrator can manage nonlocal GPOs. An administrator for a computer can edit the local GPO on that computer.

Symptom: When the user tries to edit a GPO, the "Failed To Open The Group Policy Object" message appears

Cause	Solution
A networking problem, specifically a problem with the domain name system (DNS) configuration.	Make sure DNS is working properly.

Table 12.10 describes scenarios where group policy settings are not taking effect.

Table 12.10   Group Policy Settings Problems and Solutions

**Symptom: Group policy is not being applied to users
and computers in a security group that contains those users and
computers, even though a GPO is linked to an OU containing that security group**

Cause	Solution
This is correct behavior. Group policy affects only users and computers contained in sites, domains, and OUs. GPOs are not applied to security groups.	Link GPOs to sites, domains, and OUs only. Keep in mind that the location of a security group in Active Directory is unrelated to whether group policy applies to the users and computers in that security group.

**Symptom: Group policy is not affecting
users and computers in a site, domain, or OU**

Cause	Solution
Group policy settings can be prevented, intentionally or inadvertently, from taking effect on users and computers in several ways. A GPO can be disabled from affecting users, computers, or both. It also needs to be linked either directly to an OU containing the users and computers or linked to a parent domain or OU so that the group policy settings apply through inheritance. When multiple GPOs apply, they are processed in this order: local, site, domain, OU. By default, settings applied later have precedence. In addition, group policy can be blocked at the level of any OU, or enforced through a setting of No Override applied to a particular GPO link. Finally, the user or computer must belong to one or more security groups with appropriate permissions set.	Make sure that the intended policy is not being blocked. Make sure no policy set at a higher level of Active Directory has been set to No Override. If Block Policy Inheritance and No Override are both used, keep in mind that No Override takes precedence. Verify that the user or computer is not a member of any security group for which the AGP permission is set to Deny. Verify that the user or computer is a member of at least one security group for which the AGP permission is set to Allow. Verify that the user or computer is a member of at least one security group for which the Read permission is set to Allow.

**Symptom: Group policy is not affecting
users and computers in an Active Directory container**

Cause	Solution
GPOs cannot be linked to Active Directory containers other than sites, domains, and OUs.	Link a GPO to an OU that is a parent to the Active Directory container. Then, by default, those settings are applied to the users and computers in the container through inheritance.

Table 12.10   Group Policy Settings Problems and Solutions *(continued)*

Symptom: Group policy is not taking effect on the local computer

Cause	Symptom
Local policies are the weakest. Any nonlocal GPO can overwrite them.	Check to see what GPOs are being applied through Active Directory and if those GPOs have settings that are in conflict with the local settings.

Table 12.11 describes scenarios in which there are problems using the Software Installation extension.

Table 12.11   Software Installation Extension Problems and Solutions

Symptom: Published applications do not appear in Add/Remove Programs in Control Panel

Cause	Solution
Several causes are possible: Group policy was not applied. Active Directory cannot be accessed. User does not have any published applications in the GPOs that apply to him or her. Client is running Terminal Server.	Investigate each possibility. Note that Software Installation is not supported for Terminal Server clients.

Symptom: Document activation of a published application does not cause the application to install

Cause	Solution
The administrator did not set auto-install.	Ensure that Auto-Install This Application By File Extension Activation is checked in the Deployment tab in the application's properties sheet.

Symptom: The user receives an error message such as "The feature you are trying to install cannot be found in the source directory"

Cause	Solution
Network or permissions problems.	Make sure the network is working correctly. Ensure that the user has Read and AGP permission for the GPO. Ensure that the user has Read permission for the SDP. Ensure that the user has Read permission for the application.

Symptom: After removal of an application, the shortcuts for the application still appear on the user's desktop

Cause	Solution
The user has created shortcuts and Windows Installer has no knowledge of them.	The user must remove the shortcuts manually.

Symptom: The user receives an error message such as "Another Installation Is Already In Progress"

Cause	Solution
An uninstallation might be taking place in the background with no user interface presented to the user, or perhaps the user has inadvertently triggered two installations simultaneously (which is not supported).	The user can try again later.

Symptom: The user opens an already installed application, and the Windows Installer starts

Cause	Solution
An application might be undergoing automatic repair or a user-required feature is being added.	No action is required.

Symptom: The user receives error messages such as "Active Directory Will Not Allow The Package To Be Deployed" or "Cannot Prepare Package For Deployment"

Cause	Solution
The package might be corrupted or there might be a networking problem.	Investigate and take appropriate action.

Group Policy Best Practices

The following best practices may minimize your need to troubleshoot group policy.

General Group Policy Practices

- **Disable unused parts of a GPO.**   If a GPO has, under the User Configuration or Computer Configuration node of the console, only settings that are Not Configured, you can avoid processing those settings by disabling the node. This expedites startup and logon for those users and computers subject to the GPO.

- **Use the Block Policy Inheritance and No Override features sparingly.**   Routine use of these features makes it difficult to troubleshoot group policy.

- **Minimize the number of GPOs associated with users or computers in domains or OUs.**   The more GPOs applied to a user, the longer it takes to start up and log on.

- **Filter policy based on security group membership.**   Users who do not have permissions directing that a particular GPO be applied to them can avoid the associated logon delay, because the GPO will not be processed for those users.

- **Use loopback only when necessary.** Use loopback only if you need the desktop configuration to be the same regardless of who logs on.

- **Avoid cross-domain GPO assignments.** The processing of GPOs will slow logon and startup if group policy is obtained from another domain.

Software Installation Practices

- **Specify application categories for your organization.** Using categories makes it easier for users to find an application in Add/Remove Programs in Control Panel. For example, you could define categories such as Sales Applications, Accounting Applications, and so on.

- **Make sure Windows Installer packages include modifications before they are published or assigned.** Remember that modifications are applied to packages at the time of assignment or publication. In practical terms, this means that you should make sure the Modifications tab of the package Properties dialog box is set up as you intend before you click OK. If you neglect to do this, and assign or publish a modified package before you have completely configured it, you can either remove the software and republish or reassign it or upgrade the software with a completely modified version.

- **Assign or publish just once per GPO.** A Windows Installer package should be assigned or published no more than once in the same GPO. For example, if you assign Microsoft Office to the computers affected by a GPO, then do not assign or publish it to users affected by the GPO.

- **Take advantage of authoring tools.** Developers familiar with the files, registry entries, and other requirements for an application to work properly can author native Windows Installer packages using tools available from various software vendors.

- **Repackage existing software.** You can use commercially available tools to create Windows Installer packages for software that does not include natively authored .msi files. These work by comparing a computer's state before and after installation. For best results, install onto a computer free of other application software (clean install).

- **Use SMS and Dfs.** Microsoft Systems Management Server (SMS) and the Windows 2000 Distributed File System (Dfs) are helpful in managing the SDPs (the network shares from which users install their managed software).

- **Assign or publish close to the root in the Active Directory hierarchy.** Because group policy settings apply by default to child Active Directory containers, it is efficient to assign or publish by linking a GPO to a parent OU or domain. Use security descriptors (ACEs) on the GPO for finer control over who receives the software.

- **Use Software Installation properties for widely scoped control.** This spares administrative keystrokes when assigning or publishing a large number of packages with similar properties in a single GPO—for example, when all the software is published and it all comes from the same SDP.

- **Use Windows Installer package properties for fine control.**   Use the package properties for assigning or publishing a single package.

Folder Redirection Practices

- **Incorporating %username% into fully qualified UNC paths.**   This allows users to have their own folders. For example, \\server\share\%username%\ My Documents

- **Having My Pictures follow My Documents.**   This is advisable unless there is a compelling reason not to, such as file share scalability.

- **Policy removal considerations.**   Keep in mind the behavior your Folder Redirection policies will have upon policy removal, as described in "Policy Removal Considerations."

- **Accepting defaults.**   In general, accept the default Folder Redirection settings.

Lesson Summary

In this lesson you examined some group policy problems that you may encounter and possible solutions. You also learned some best practices for handling group policy.

Review

The following questions are intended to reinforce key information presented in the chapter. If you are unable to answer a question, review the appropriate lesson and then try the question again. Answers to the questions can be found in Appendix A, "Questions and Answers."

1. What is a GPO?

2. What are the two types of group policy settings and how are they used?

3. In what order is group policy implemented through the Active Directory structure?

4. Name the tasks for implementing group policy.

5. What is the difference between Block Policy Inheritance and No Override?

6. What is the difference between assigning software and publishing software?

7. What folders can be redirected?

C H A P T E R   1 3

Administering a Security Configuration

About This Chapter

Security settings define the security-relevant behavior of the system. Through the use of group policy objects (GPOs) in Active Directory, administrators can centrally apply the security levels required to protect enterprise systems. Local GPOs can also be used to apply security to nonenterprise and workgroup systems. This chapter provides details on using security settings to determine a system's security configuration.

Before You Begin

To complete this chapter, you must have

- Completed the Setup procedures located in "About This Book"
- Configured the computer as a domain controller in a domain
- Obtained the knowledge and skills covered in Chapter 12, "Administering Group Policy"

Lesson 1: Security Configuration Overview

You use the Security Settings extension in the Group Policy snap-in to define security configurations for computers and groups. This lesson introduces the security configuration settings.

After this lesson, you will be able to

- Recognize security configuration settings in a GPO

Estimated lesson time: 10 minutes

Security Configuration Settings

A *security configuration* consists of security settings applied to each security area supported by Microsoft Windows 2000. Using the Security Settings extension in the Group Policy snap-in, the following security areas may be configured for a nonlocal GPO:

- Account policies
- Local policies
- Event log
- Restricted groups
- System services
- Registry
- File system
- Public key policies
- IP security policies

Account Policies

Account policies apply to user accounts. This security area contains attributes for

- **Password Policy.**   For domain or local user accounts, determines settings for passwords such as enforcement and lifetimes.
- **Account Lockout Policy.**   For domain or local user accounts, determines when and for whom an account will be locked out of the system.

- **Kerberos Policy.**   For domain user accounts, determines Kerberos-related settings, such as ticket lifetimes and enforcement.

Important   Account policies should not be configured for organizational units (OUs) that do not contain any computers, as OUs that contain only users will always receive account policy from the domain.

When setting account policies in Active Directory, keep in mind that Windows 2000 only allows one domain account policy: the account policy applied to the root domain of the domain tree. The domain account policy will become the default account policy of any Windows 2000 workstation or server that is a member of the domain. The only exception to this rule is when another account policy is defined for an OU. The account policy settings for the OU will affect the local policy on any computers contained in the OU, as is the case with a Domain Controllers OU.

Local Policies

These policies pertain to the security settings on the computer used by an application or user. Local policies are based on the computer you are logged on to and the rights you have on that particular computer. This security area contains attributes for

- **Audit Policy.**   Determines which security events are logged into the security log on the computer (successful attempts, failed attempts, or both). (The security log is a part of the Event Viewer console.)
- **User Rights Assignment.**   Determines which users or groups have logon or task privileges on the computer.
- **Security Options.**   Enables or disables security settings for the computer, such as digital signing of data, Administrator and Guest account names, floppy drive and CD-ROM access, driver installation, and logon prompts.

Local policies, by definition, are local to a computer. When these settings are imported to a GPO in Active Directory, they will affect the local security settings of any computer accounts to which that GPO is applied.

Event Log

The event log security area defines attributes related to the Application, Security, and System event logs: maximum log size, access rights for each log, and retention settings and methods (see Figure 13.1).

Event log size and log wrapping should be defined to match your business and security requirements. You may consider implementing these event log settings at the site, domain, or OU level, to take advantage of group policy settings.

Figure 13.1   Event log settings

Restricted Groups

The Restricted Groups security area provides an important new security feature that acts as a governor for group membership. Restricted Groups automatically provides security memberships for default Windows 2000 groups that have predefined capabilities, such as Administrators, Power Users, Print Operators, Server Operators, and Domain Admins. You can later add any groups that you consider sensitive or privileged to the Restricted Groups security list.

For example, the Power Users group is automatically part of Restricted Groups, since it is a default Windows 2000 group. Assume it contains two users: Alice and Bob. Bob adds Charles to the group, through the Active Directory Users and Computers console, to cover for him while he is on vacation. However, no one remembers to remove Charles from the group when Bob comes back from vacation. In actual deployments, over time, these situations can add up, resulting in extra members in various groups who should no longer have these rights. Configuring security through Restricted Groups can prevent this situation. Because only Alice and Bob are listed in the Restricted Groups node for Power Users, when group policy settings are applied, Charles is removed from the group automatically.

Configuring Restricted Groups ensures that group memberships are set as specified. Groups and users not specified in Restricted Groups are removed from the specific group. In addition, the reverse membership configuration option ensures that each Restricted Group is a member of only those groups specified in the Member Of column. For these reasons, Restricted Groups should be used primarily to configure membership of local groups on workstation or member servers.

System Services

The system services area is used to configure security and startup settings for services running on a computer.

The Security properties for the service determine what user or group accounts have permission to read/write/delete/execute, as well as inheritance settings, auditing, and ownership permission.

The startup settings are

- **Automatic.**   Starts a service automatically at system start time.
- **Manual.**   Starts a service only if manually started.
- **Disabled.**   The service is disabled so it cannot be started.

If you choose to set system service startup to Automatic, perform adequate testing to verify that the services can start without user intervention. You should track the system services used on a computer. For performance optimization, set unnecessary or unused services to Manual.

Registry and File System Areas

The registry area is used to configure security on registry keys. The file system area is used to configure security on specific file paths. You can edit the Security properties of the registry key or file path: what user or group accounts have permission to read/write/delete/execute, as well as inheritance settings, auditing, and ownership permission.

Public Key Policies

The public key policies area is used to configure encrypted data recovery agents, domain roots, and trusted certificate authorities.

IP Security Policies

The IP security policies area is used to configure network Internet Protocol (IP) security.

Lesson Summary

In this lesson you were introduced to the security configuration settings in a nonlocal GPO.

Lesson 2: Auditing

In this lesson you will learn about Windows 2000 auditing, which is a tool for maintaining network security. Auditing allows you to track user activities and system-wide events. You will learn about audit policies and what you need to consider before you set one up. You also will learn how to set up auditing on resources.

After this lesson, you will be able to

- Describe the purpose of auditing
- Plan an audit strategy and determine which events to audit
- Set up an audit policy
- Set up auditing on files and folders
- Set up auditing on Active Directory objects
- Set up auditing on printers

Estimated lesson time: 60 minutes

Understanding Auditing

Auditing in Microsoft Windows 2000 is the process of tracking both user activities and Windows 2000 activities, which are called *events,* on a computer. Through auditing, you can specify which events are written to the security log. For example, the security log can maintain a record of valid and invalid logon attempts and events relating to creating, opening, or deleting files or other objects. An audit entry in the security log contains the following information:

- The action that was performed
- The user who performed the action
- The success or failure of the event and when the event occurred

Using an Audit Policy

An *audit policy* defines the categories of events that Windows 2000 records in the security log on each computer. The security log allows you to track the events that you specify.

Windows 2000 writes events to the security log on the computer where the event occurs. For example, any time someone tries to log on to the domain using a domain user account and the logon attempt fails, Windows 2000 writes an event to the security log on the domain controller. The event is recorded on the domain controller rather than on the computer at which the logon attempt was made because it is the domain controller that attempted to and could not authenticate the logon attempt.

You can set up an audit policy for a computer to do the following:

- Track the success and failure of events, such as logon attempts by users, an attempt by a particular user to read a specific file, changes to a user account or to group memberships, and changes to your security settings
- Eliminate or minimize the risk of unauthorized use of resources

You use Event Viewer to view events that Windows 2000 has recorded in the security log. You can also archive log files to track trends over time—for example, to determine the use of printers or files or to verify attempts at unauthorized use of resources.

Audit Policy Guidelines

When you plan an audit policy you must determine the computers on which to set up auditing. Auditing is turned off by default. As you are determining which computers to audit, you must also plan the events to audit on each computer. Windows 2000 records audited events on each computer separately.

After you have determined the events to audit, you must determine whether to audit the success of events, failure of events, or both. Tracking successful events can tell you how often Windows 2000 or users gain access to specific files, printers, or other objects. You can use this information for resource planning. Tracking failed events can alert you to possible security breaches. For example, if you notice several failed logon attempts by a certain user account, especially if these attempts are occurring outside normal business hours, you can assume that an unauthorized person is attempting to break into your system.

Other guidelines in determining your audit policy include the following:

- **Determine if you need to track trends of system usage.**   If so, plan to archive event logs. Archiving these logs will allow you to view how usage changes over time and to plan to increase system resources before they become a problem.
- **Review security logs frequently.**   You should set a schedule and regularly review security logs because configuring auditing alone does not alert you to security breaches.
- **Define an audit policy that is useful and manageable.**   Always audit sensitive and confidential data. Audit only those events that will provide you with meaningful information about your network environment. This will minimize usage of server resources and make essential information easier to locate. Auditing too many types of events can create excess overhead for Windows 2000.
- **Audit resource access by the Everyone group instead of the Users group.**   This will ensure that you audit anyone who can connect to the

network, not just the users for whom you create user accounts in the domain. Also audit resource access failures by the Everyone group.

- **Audit all administrative tasks by the administrative groups.** This will ensure that you audit any additions or changes made by administrators.

Configuring Auditing

You implement an audit policy based on the role of the computer in the Windows 2000 network. Auditing is configured differently for the following types of computers running Windows 2000:

- For member or stand-alone servers, or computers running Windows 2000 Professional, an audit policy is set for each individual computer. To audit events that occur on a local computer, you configure a local group policy for that computer, which applies to that computer only.

- For domain controllers, an audit policy is set for all domain controllers in the domain. To audit events that occur on domain controllers, you configure the audit policy in a nonlocal GPO for the domain, which applies to all domain controllers and is accessible through the Domain Controllers OU.

The event categories on a domain controller are identical to those on a computer that is not a domain controller.

Auditing Requirements

The requirements to set up and administer auditing are as follows:

- You must have the Manage Auditing And Security Log user right for the computer where you want to configure an audit policy or review an audit log. By default, Windows 2000 grants these rights to the Administrators group. For information about user rights, see Lesson 4.

- The files and folders to be audited must be on Microsoft Windows NT file system (NTFS) volumes.

Setting Up Auditing

Setting up auditing is a two-part process:

1. **Set the audit policy.** The audit policy enables auditing of objects but does not activate auditing of specific objects.

2. **Enable auditing of specific resources.** You specify the specific events to audit for files, folders, printers, and Active Directory objects. Windows 2000 then tracks and logs the specified events.

Setting Up an Audit Policy

The first step in implementing an audit GPO is selecting the categories of events that Windows 2000 audits. For each event category that you can audit, the configuration settings indicate whether to track successful or failed attempts. You set audit policies in the Group Policy snap-in. The security log is limited in size. Select the events to be audited carefully and consider the amount of disk space you are willing to devote to the security log. Table 13.1 describes the event categories that Windows 2000 can audit.

Table 13.1   Types of Events Audited by Windows 2000

Event Category	Description
Account logon	A domain controller received a request to validate a user account.
Account management	An administrator created, changed, or deleted a user account or group. A user account was renamed, disabled, or enabled, or a password was set or changed.
Directory service access	A user gained access to an Active Directory object. You must configure specific Active Directory objects for auditing to log this type of event.
Logon events	A user logged on or logged off, or a user made or canceled a network connection to the computer.
Object access	A user gained access to a file, folder, or printer. You must configure specific files, folders, or printers for auditing. Directory service access is auditing a user's access to specific Active Directory objects. Object access is auditing a user's access to files, folders, and printers.
Policy change	A change was made to the user security options, user rights, or audit policies.
Privilege use	A user exercised a right, such as changing the system time (this does not include rights that are related to logging on and logging off).
Process tracking	A program performed an action. This information is generally useful only for programmers who want to track details of program execution.
System events	A user restarted or shut down the computer, or an event occurred that affects Windows 2000 security or the security log (for example, the audit log is full and Windows 2000 discards entries).

▶ **To set an audit policy for a domain controller**

1. Open Active Directory Users and Computers.

2. In the console tree, right-click Domain Controllers, then click Properties.

3. In the Group Policy tab, click the policy in which you want set the audit policy, then click Edit.

4. In the Group Policy snap-in, in the console tree, click Computer Configuration, double-click Windows Settings, double-click Security Settings, double-click Local Policies, then double-click Audit Policy.

The console displays the current audit policy settings in the details pane, as shown in Figure 13.2.

Figure 13.2   Custom console showing events that Windows 2000 can audit

5. In the details pane, right-click the event category you want to audit, then click Security.

6. In the Security Policy Setting dialog box (see Figure 13.3), click Define These Policy Settings, then click one or both:

   ▪ Success, to audit successful attempts for the event category

   ▪ Failure, to audit failed attempts for the event category

7. Click OK.

8. Because the changes that you make to your computer's audit policy take effect only when the policy is propagated (applied) to your computer, do one of the following to initiate policy propagation:

   ▪ Type **secedit /refreshpolicy machine_policy** at the command prompt, then press Enter.

   ▪ Restart your computer.

   ▪ Wait for automatic policy propagation, which occurs at regular, configurable intervals. By default, policy propagation occurs every 90 minutes for Windows 2000–based computers, and every 5 minutes for the domain controller.

Figure 13.3   The Security Policy Setting dialog box

▶ **To set an audit policy on a computer that does not participate in a domain**

1. Click Start, point to Programs, point to Administrative Tools, then click Local Security Policy.

2. In Local Security Settings, in the console tree, double-click Local Policies, then double-click Audit Policy.

3. In the details pane, right-click the event category you want to audit, then click Security.

4. In the Local Security Policy Setting dialog box (see Figure 13.4), click one or both:

   ▪ Success, to audit successful attempts for the event category

   ▪ Failure, to audit failed attempts for the event category

   The Effective Policy Setting box shows the security setting value currently enforced on the system. If an audit policy has already been set at the domain level or the OU level, it overrides the local audit policy.

5. Click OK.

6. Because the changes that you make to your computer's audit policy take effect only when the policy is propagated (applied) to your computer, do one of the following to initiate policy propagation:

   ▪ Type **secedit /refreshpolicy machine_policy** at the command prompt, then press Enter.

   ▪ Restart your computer.

   ▪ Wait for automatic policy propagation, which occurs at regular, configurable intervals. By default, policy propagation occurs every 90 minutes for Windows 2000–based computers, and every 5 minutes for the domain controller.

Figure 13.4   The Local Security Policy Setting dialog box

▶ **To set an audit policy on a member server or workstation**

1. Create an OU for the remote computer(s) and add the desired machine account(s) to the OU.

2. Using Active Directory Users and Computers, as in the "To set an audit policy for a domain controller" procedure described earlier, create an audit policy to enable security auditing.

Note   Security auditing for workstations, member servers, and domain controllers can be enabled remotely only by domain and enterprise administrators.

Auditing Access to Files and Folders

If security breaches are an issue for your organization, you can set up auditing for files and folders on NTFS partitions. To audit user access to files and folders, you must first set the Audit Object Access event category, which includes files and folders, in the audit policy.

Once you have set Audit Object Access in your audit policy, you enable auditing for specific files and folders and specify which types of access, by which users or groups, to audit.

▶ **To set up auditing for specific files and folders**

1. In Windows Explorer, right-click the file or folder you want to audit, then click Properties.

2. In the Security tab in the Properties dialog box for a file or folder, click Advanced.

3. In the Access Control Settings For dialog box for the file or folder, in the Auditing tab, click Add, select the users and groups for whom you want to audit file and folder access, then click OK.

4. In the Auditing Entry For dialog box for the file or folder (see Figure 13.5), select the Successful check box, the Failed check box, or both check boxes for the events that you want to audit.

Figure 13.5   The Auditing Entry For dialog box for the Command Prompt file

Table 13.2 describes the events that can be audited for files and folders and explains what action triggers the event to occur.

Table 13.2   User Events and What Triggers Them

Event	User Activity that Triggers the Event
Traverse Folder/ Execute File	Moving through folders to reach other files or folders, even if the user has no permissions to for traversed folders (folders only) or running program files (files only)
List Folder/Read Data	Viewing filenames and subfolder names within a folder (folders only) or viewing data in files (files only)
Read Attributes and Read Extended Attributes	Displaying the attributes of a file or folder
Create Files/Write Data	Creating files within a folder (folders only) or changing the contents of a file (files only)
Create Folders/ Append Data	Creating folders within a folder (folders only) or making changes to the end of the file but not changing, deleting, or overwriting existing data (files only)

Table 13.2   User Events and What Triggers Them *(continued)*

Event	User Activity that Triggers the Event
Write Attributes and Write Extended Attributes	Changing attributes of a file or folder
Delete Subfolders And Files	Deleting a file or subfolder in a folder
Delete	Deleting a file or folder
Read Permissions	Viewing permissions or the file owner for a file or folder
Change Permissions	Changing permissions for a file or folder
Take Ownership	Taking ownership of a file or folder

5. In the Apply Onto list (available only for folders), specify where objects are audited. By default, this box is set to This Folder, Subfolders And Files, so any auditing changes that you make to a parent folder also apply to all child folders and all files in the parent and child folders. Where objects are audited depends on the selection in the Apply Onto list and whether the Apply These Auditing Entries To Objects And/Or Containers Within This Container Only check box is selected as shown in Table 13.3.

Table 13.3   Results When the Apply These Auditing Entries To Objects And/Or Containers Within This Container Only Check Box Is Cleared

Apply Onto	Audits Current Folder	Audits Sub-folders in the Current Folder	Audits Files in the Current Folder	Audits All Subsequent Folders	Audits Files in all Subsequent Subfolders
This folder only	X				
This folder, subfolders, and files	X	X	X	X	X
This folder and subfolders	X	X		X	
This folder and files	X		X		X
Subfolders and files only		X	X	X	X
Subfolders only		X		X	
Files only			X		X

When the Apply These Auditing Entries To Objects And/Or Containers Within This Container Only check box is selected, auditing is applied to the selection in the Apply Onto box and all applicable child objects within the tree.

6. Click OK to return to the Access Control Settings For dialog box for the file or folder.

7. To prevent changes that are made to a parent folder from applying to the currently selected file or folder, clear the Allow Inheritable Auditing Entries From Parent To Propagate To This Object check box.

   If the check boxes under Access are shaded in the Auditing Entry For dialog box for the file or folder, or if the Remove button is unavailable in the Access Control Settings For dialog box for the file or folder, then auditing has been inherited from the parent folder.

8. Click OK.

Auditing Access to Active Directory Objects

Similar to auditing file and folder access, to audit Active Directory object access, you have to configure an audit policy and then set auditing for specific objects, such as users, computers, OUs, or groups, by specifying which types of access and access by which users to audit. You audit Active Directory objects to track access to Active Directory objects, such as changing the properties on a user account. To enable auditing of user access to Active Directory objects, set the Audit Directory Service Access event category in the audit policy.

▶ **To set up auditing for specific Active Directory objects**

1. In Active Directory Users and Computers, click View, then click Advanced Features.

2. Select the object that you want to audit, click Properties on the Action menu, click the Security tab, then click the Advanced button.

3. In the Access Control Settings For dialog box for the object, in the Auditing tab, click Add, select the users or groups for whom you want to audit file and folder access, then click OK.

4. In the Auditing Entry For dialog box for the object (see Figure 13.6), select the Successful check box, the Failed check box, or both check boxes for the events that you want to audit.

   Table 13.4 describes some of the audit events for Active Directory objects and explains what action triggers the event to occur.

Table 13.4 Some Active Directory Object Events and What Triggers Them

Event	User Activity that Triggers the Event
Full Control	Performing any type of access to the audited object
List Contents	Viewing the objects within the audited object
Read All Properties	Viewing any attribute of the audited object
Write All Properties	Changing any attribute of the audited object
Create All Child Objects	Creating any object within the audited object
Delete All Child Objects	Deleting any object within the audited object

Table 13.4   Some Active Directory Object Events and What Triggers Them *(continued)*

Event	User Activity that Triggers the Event
Read Permissions	Viewing the permissions for the audited object
Modify Permissions	Changing the permissions for the audited object
Modify Owner	Taking ownership of the audited object

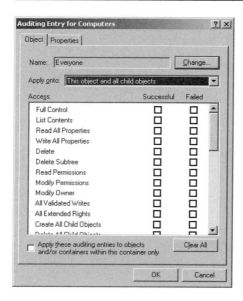

Figure 13.6   The Auditing Entry For dialog box for the Computers folder

5. In the Apply Onto list, specify where objects are audited. By default, this box is set to This Object And All Child Objects, so any auditing changes that you make to a parent object also apply to all child objects. Where objects are audited depends on the selection in the Apply Onto list and whether the Apply These Auditing Entries To Objects And/Or Containers Within This Container Only check box is selected. These two features are only enabled for objects that act as containers.

6. Click OK to return to the Access Control Settings For dialog box for the object.

7. To prevent changes that are made to a parent folder from applying to the currently selected file or folder, clear the Allow Inheritable Auditing Entries From Parent To Propagate To This Object check box.

   If the check boxes under Access are shaded in the Auditing Entry For dialog box for the object, or if the Remove button is unavailable in the Access Control Settings For dialog box for the object, then auditing has been inherited from the parent folder.

8. Click OK.

Auditing Access to Printers

Audit access to printers to track access to sensitive printers. To audit access to printers, set the Audit Object Access event category in your audit policy, which includes printers. Then, enable auditing for specific printers and specify which types of access and access by which users to audit. After you select the printer, you use the same steps that you use to set up auditing on files and folders.

▶ **To set up auditing on a printer**

1. Click Start, point to Settings, then click Printers.

2. In the Printers system folder, right-click the printer you want to audit, then click Properties.

3. In the Properties dialog box for the printer, click the Security tab, then click Advanced.

4. In the Access Control Settings For dialog box for the printer, in the Auditing tab, click Add, select the appropriate users or groups for whom you want to audit printer access, click Add, then click OK.

5. In the Auditing Entry For dialog box for the printer (see Figure 13.7), select the Successful check box, the Failed check box, or both check boxes for the events that you want to audit.

Figure 13.7   The Auditing Entry For dialog box for a printer

Table 13.5 describes audit events for printers and explains what action triggers the event to occur.

Table 13.5 Printer Events and What Triggers Them

Event	User Activity that Triggers the Event
Print	Printing a file
Manage Printers	Changing printer settings, pausing a printer, sharing a printer, or removing a printer
Manage Documents	Changing job settings; pausing, restarting, moving, or deleting documents; sharing a printer; or changing printer properties
Read Permissions	Viewing printer permissions
Change Permissions	Changing printer permissions
Take Ownership	Taking printer ownership

6. In the Apply Onto list, select where the auditing setting applies.
7. Click OK in the appropriate dialog boxes to exit.

Auditing Practices

Table 13.6 lists various events that you should audit, as well as the specific security threat that the audit event monitors.

Table 13.6 Recommended Audit Events

Audit Event	Potential Threat
Failure audit for logon/logoff.	Random password hack
Success audit for logon/logoff.	Stolen password break-in
Success audit for user rights, user and group management, security change policies, restart, shutdown, and system events.	Misuse of privileges
Success and failure audit for file-access and object-access events. File Manager success and failure audit of Read/Write access by suspect users or groups for the sensitive files.	Improper access to sensitive files
Success and failure audit for file-access printers and object-access events. Print Manager success and failure audit of print access by suspect users or groups for the printers.	Improper access to printers
Success and failure write access auditing for program files (.exe and .dll extensions). Success and failure auditing for process tracking. Run suspect programs; examine security log for unexpected attempts to modify program files or create unexpected processes. Run only when actively monitoring the system log.	Virus outbreak

Practice: Auditing Resources and Events

In this practice you plan a domain audit policy. Then you set up an audit policy for a domain controller by enabling auditing of certain events. You set up auditing of a file, a printer, and an Active Directory object.

Exercise 1: Planning a Domain Audit Policy

In this exercise you plan an audit policy for your server. You need to determine the following:

- Which types of events to audit
- Whether to audit the success or failure of an event, or both

Use the following criteria to make your decisions:

- Record unsuccessful attempts to gain access to the network.
- Record unauthorized access to the files that make up the Customer database.
- For billing purposes, track color printer usage.
- Track whenever someone tries to tamper with the server hardware.
- Keep a record of actions that an administrator performs to track unauthorized changes.
- Track backup procedures to prevent data theft.
- Track unauthorized access to sensitive Active Directory objects.

Record your decisions to audit successful events, failed events, or both for the actions listed in Table 13.7.

Table 13.7   Audit Policy Plan for Exercise 1

Action to Audit	Successful	Failed
Account logon events	☐	☐
Account management	☐	☐
Directory service access	☐	☐
Logon events	☐	☐
Object access	☐	☐
Policy change	☐	☐
Privilege use	☐	☐
Process tracking	☐	☐
System events	☐	☐

Exercise 2: Setting Up an Audit Policy

In this exercise you enable auditing for selected event categories.

▶ **To set up an audit policy**

1. Open Active Directory Users and Computers.
2. In the console tree, right-click Domain Controllers, then click Properties.
3. In the Properties dialog box, in the Group Policy tab, select the Default Domain Controllers Policy group policy, then click Edit.
4. In the Group Policy snap-in, in the console tree, click Computer Configuration, double-click Windows Settings, double-click Security Settings, double-click Local Policies, then double-click Audit Policy.
5. To set the audit policy, in the details pane, double-click each event category, then select either Success or Failure as listed in Table 13.8.

Table 13.8   Audit Policy Settings for Exercise 2

Event Category	Success	Failure
Account logon events		
Account management	X	
Directory service access		X
Logon events		X
Object access	X	X
Policy change	X	
Privilege use	X	
Process tracking		
System events	X	X

6. Close the Group Policy snap-in.
7. Close the Domain Controllers Properties dialog box.
8. Start a command prompt.
9. At the command prompt, type **secedit /refreshpolicy machine_policy**, then press Enter.

   The policy changes take effect in a few moments.
10. Close the command prompt.

Exercise 3: Setting Up Auditing of Files

In this exercise you set up auditing for a file.

▶ **To set up auditing of files**

1. In Windows Explorer, locate a file such as a simple text file.

2. Right-click the filename, then click Properties.

3. In the Properties dialog box, click the Security tab, then click Advanced.

4. In the Access Control Settings For dialog box for the text file, click the Auditing tab.

5. Click Add.

6. In the Select User, Computer, Or Group dialog box, double-click Everyone in the list of user accounts and groups.

7. In the Auditing Entry For dialog box for the text file, select the Successful check box and the Failed check box for each of the following events:

   ■ Create Files/Write Data

   ■ Delete

   ■ Change Permissions

   ■ Take Ownership

8. Click OK.

   Windows 2000 displays the Everyone group in the Access Control Settings For dialog box for the text file.

9. Click OK to apply your changes.

▶ **To change file permissions**

1. In the Properties dialog box, on the Security tab, add the Everyone group.

2. Change the NTFS permissions for the Everyone group to only the Read permission for the file, and clear the Allow Inheritable Permissions From Parent To Propagate To This Object check box.

   The Security message box appears asking you to confirm that you want to clear the Allow Inheritable Permissions From Parent To Propagate To This Object check box.

3. On the Security message box, click Remove, then click OK.

   Any other permissions are removed.

4. Click OK to close the Properties dialog box, then close Windows Explorer.

Exercise 4: Setting Up Auditing of a Printer

In this exercise you set up auditing of a printer.

Important   As in Chapter 11, you need to have a local printer installed on your computer. However, you do *not* need a printing device connected to the computer. If you do not have a local printer installed, create one now. Remember that *printing device* refers to the physical machine that prints and that *local printer* refers to the software that Windows 2000 needs to send data to the printing device.

▶ **To set up auditing of a printer**

1. Click Start, point to Settings, then click Printers.

2. In the Printers system folder, right-click a printer associated with your computer, then click Properties.

3. Click the Security tab, then click Advanced.

4. In the Access Control Settings For dialog box for the printer, click the Auditing tab, then click Add.

5. In the Select User, Computer, Or Group dialog box, double-click Everyone in the list box.

6. In the Auditing Entry For dialog box for the printer, select the Successful check box for all types of access.

7. Click OK.

   Windows 2000 displays the Everyone group in the Access Control Settings For dialog box for the printer.

8. In the Access Control Settings For dialog box for the printer, click OK to apply your changes.

9. Click OK to close the printer Properties dialog box.

10. Close the Printers system folder.

Exercise 5: Setting Up Auditing of an Active Directory Object

In this exercise you set up auditing of an Active Directory object.

▶ **To review auditing of an Active Directory object**

1. Start Active Directory Users and Computers.

2. On the View menu, click Advanced Features.

3. In the console tree, click your domain.

4. In the details pane, click Users, and then on the Action menu, click Properties.

5. In the Users Properties dialog box, click the Security tab, then click Advanced.

6. In the Access Control Settings For Users dialog box, click the Auditing tab, then double-click Everyone.

   The Auditing Entry For Users dialog box appears.

   Review the default audit settings for object access by members of the Everyone group. How do the audited types of access differ from the types of access that are not audited?

7. Click OK three times to close the Auditing Entry For Users, the Access Control Settings For Users, and the Users Properties dialog boxes.

   At which computer or computers does Windows 2000 record log entries for Active Directory access? Will you be able to review them?

8. Close Active Directory Users and Computers.

Lesson Summary

In this lesson you learned how to set up an audit policy. The first step in implementing an audit policy is selecting the event categories that Windows 2000 audits. For each event that you can audit, the configuration settings indicate whether to track successful or failed attempts.

For member or stand-alone servers, or computers running Windows 2000 Professional, an audit policy is set for each individual computer. To audit events that occur on a local computer, you configure a local group policy for that computer, which applies to that computer only.

For domain controllers, an audit policy is set for all domain controllers in the domain. To audit events that occur on domain controllers, you configure a nonlocal group policy for the domain, which applies to all domain controllers.

In the practice portion of this lesson you planned a domain audit policy, set up an audit policy for a domain controller, and set up auditing of a file, a printer, and an Active Directory object.

Lesson 3: Using Security Logs

The security log contains information on security events that are specified in the audit policy. To view the security log, you use the Event Viewer console. Event Viewer also allows you to find specific events within log files, filter the events shown in log files, and archive security log files.

After this lesson, you will be able to

- View a log
- Locate events in a log
- Filter events in a log
- Configure the size of audit logs
- Archive security logs

Estimated lesson time: 25 minutes

Understanding Windows 2000 Logs

You use the Event Viewer console to view information contained in Windows 2000 logs. By default, there are three logs available to view in Event Viewer. These logs are described in Table 13.9.

Table 13.9   Logs Maintained by Windows 2000

Log	Description
Application log	Contains errors, warnings, or information that programs, such as a database program or an e-mail program, generate. The program developer presets which events to record.
Security log	Contains information about the success or failure of audited events. The events that Windows 2000 records are a result of your audit policy.
System log	Contains errors, warnings, and information that Windows 2000 generates. Windows 2000 presets which events to record.

Application and system logs can be viewed by all users. Security logs are accessible only to system administrators. By default, security logging is turned off. To enable security logging, you must use group policy at the appropriate level to set up an audit policy.

Note   If additional services are installed, they might add their own event log. For example, the Domain Name System (DNS) Service logs events that this service generates in the DNS server log.

Viewing Security Logs

The security log contains information about events that are monitored by an audit policy, such as failed and successful logon attempts.

▶ **To view the security log**

1. Click Start, point to Programs, point to Administrative Tools, then click Event Viewer.

2. In the console tree, select Security Log.

   In the details pane, Event Viewer displays a list of log entries and summary information for each item, as shown in Figure 13.8.

   Successful events appear with a key icon and unsuccessful events appear with a lock icon. Other important information includes the date and time that the event occurred, the category of the event, and the user who generated the event.

   The category indicates the event category, such as object access, account management, directory service access, or logon events.

Figure 13.8   Event Viewer displaying a sample security log

3. To view additional information for any event, double-click the event.

Windows 2000 records events in the security log on the computer at which the event occurred. You can view these events from any computer as long as you have administrative privileges for the computer where the events occurred.

▶ **To view the security log on a remote computer**

1. Ensure that security auditing has been enabled on a remote machine. (Refer to Lesson 2 for details.)

2. Click Start, point to Programs, point to Administrative Tools, then click Event Viewer.

3. Right-click the Event Viewer (Local) node and select Connect To Another Computer.

4. In the Select Computer dialog box, click Another Computer and type the network name, IP address, or DNS address for the computer for which Event Viewer will display a security log. You can also browse for the computer name.

5. Click OK.

Locating Events

When you first start Event Viewer, it automatically displays all events that are recorded in the security log. You can search for specific events by using the Find command.

▶ **To find events**

1. Start Event Viewer, click the security log, then click Find on the View menu.

2. On the Find In dialog box for the security log, configure the options shown in Figure 13.9 and described in Table 13.10.

   Table 13.10   Options on the Find In Dialog Box

Option	Description
Event Types	Check boxes that indicate the types of events to find. In the security log you can only find audit events, because others are not recorded.
Event Source	A list that indicates the software or component driver that logged the event.
Category	A list that indicates the event category, such as a logon or logoff attempt or a system event.
Event ID	An event number to identify the event. This number helps product support representatives track events.
User	A user logon name.
Computer	A computer name.
Description	Text that is in the description of the event.
Search Direction	The direction in which to search the log (up or down).
Find Next	Finds and selects the next occurrence defined by the Find settings.

Figure 13.9 The Find In dialog box for a security log

Filtering Events

To show specific events that appear in the security log—for example, attempting to write to a text file without the necessary permissions—you can narrow down the events to display by using the Filter command.

▶ **To filter events**

1. Start Event Viewer, click the security log, then click Filter on the View menu.
2. In the Security Log Properties dialog box, in the Filter tab, configure the options shown in Figure 13.10 and described in Table 13.11.

Table 13.11 Options on the Filter Tab of the Security Log Properties Dialog Box

Option	Description
Event Types	Check boxes that indicate the types of events to filter. In the security log you can only filter using audit events, because others are not recorded.
Event Source	A list that indicates the software or component driver that logged the event.
Category	A list that indicates the type of event, such as a logon or logoff attempt or a system event.
Event ID	An event number to identify the event. This number helps product support representatives track events.
User	A user logon name.
Computer	A computer name.

**Table 13.11   Options on the Filter Tab
of the Security Log Properties Dialog Box** *(continued)*

Option	Description
From	The beginning of the range of events that you want to filter. In the list under From, select First Event to see events starting with the first event in the log. Select Events On to see events that occurred starting at a specific time and date.
To	The end of the range of events that you want to filter. In the list under To, select Last Event to see events ending with the last event in the log. Select Events On to see events that occurred ending at a specific time and date.

Figure 13.10   The Filter tab of the Security Log Properties dialog box

Configuring Security Logs

Security logging begins when you set an audit policy for the domain controller or local computer. Logging stops when the security log becomes full and cannot overwrite itself, either because it has been set for manual clearing or because the first event in the log is not old enough. When security logging stops, an error may be written to the application log. You can avoid a full security log by logging only key events. You can configure the properties of each individual audit log.

▶   **To configure the settings for security logs**

1. Open Event Viewer.

2. Right-click the security log in the console tree, then click Properties.

3. In the Security Log Properties dialog box, in the General tab, configure the options shown in Figure 13.11 and described in Table 13.12.

Table 13.12   Options on the General Tab of the Security Log Properties Dialog Box

Option	Description
Display Name	The name of the log view. You can change the name to distinguish different views of the same log on one computer or to distinguish logs on different computers.
Log Name	The name and location of the log file.
Maximum Log Size	The size of each log, which can be from 64 KB to 4,194,240 KB (4 GB). The default size is 512 KB.
Overwrite Events As Needed	Specifies whether all new events will be written to the log, even when the log is full. When the log is full, each new event replaces the oldest event. Use this option with caution; it can be used to hide undesirable events.
Overwrite Events Older Than X Days	Specifies the number of days (1-365) a log file will be retained before writing over it. New events will not be added if the maximum log size is reached and there are no events older than this period.
Do Not Overwrite Events (Clear Log Manually)	Specifies whether existing events will be retained when the log is full. If the maximum log size is reached, new events are discarded. This option requires you to manually clear the log.
Using A Low Speed Connection	Specifies whether the log file is located on another computer, and whether your computer is connected to it by a low speed device, such as a modem.

Figure 13.11   The General tab of the Security Log Properties dialog box

When the log is full and no more events can be logged, you can free the log by manually clearing it. Clearing the log erases all events permanently. Reducing the amount of time you keep an event also frees the log if it allows the next record to be overwritten.

▶ **To manually clear the security log**

1. Open Event Viewer.

2. Right-click the security log in the console tree, then click Clear All Events.

3. On the Event Viewer message box

   ▪ Click Yes to archive the log before clearing

   ▪ Click No to permanently discard the current event records and start recording new events

4. If you clicked Yes, in the Save As dialog box, in the File Name list, enter a name for the log file to be archived.

5. In the Save As Type list, click a file format, then click Save.

Archiving Security Logs

Archiving security logs allows you to maintain a history of security-related events. Many organizations have policies on keeping archive logs for a specified period to track security-related information over time. When you archive a log file, the entire log is saved, regardless of filtering options.

▶ **To archive a security log**

1. Open Event Viewer.

2. Right-click the security log in the console tree, then click Save Log File As.

3. In the Save As dialog box, in the File Name list, enter a name for the log file to be archived.

4. In the Save As Type list, click a file format, then click Save.

If you archive a log in log-file format you can reopen it in Event Viewer. Logs saved as event log files (*.evt) retain the binary data for each event recorded. If you archive a log in text or comma-delimited format (*.txt and *.csv, respectively), you can reopen the log in other programs such as word processing or spreadsheet programs. Logs saved in text or comma-delimited format do not retain the binary data.

▶ **To view an archived security log**

1. Open Event Viewer.

2. Right-click the security log in the console tree, then click Open Log File.

3. In the Open dialog box, click the file you want to open. You may need to search for the drive or folder that contains the document.

4. In the Log Type list, select Security for the type of log to be opened.

5. In the Display Name box, enter the name of the file as you want it to appear in the console tree, then click Open.

To remove an archived log file from your system, delete the file in Windows Explorer.

Practice: Using the Security Log

In this practice you view the security log file and configure Event Viewer to overwrite events when the log file is filled. Then you clear and archive a security log file.

Important   Before attempting the exercises in this practice, you must first complete all exercises in Lesson 2.

Exercise 1: Viewing the Security Log

In this exercise you view the security log for your computer. Then, you use Event Viewer to filter events and to search for potential security breaches.

▶ **To view the security log for your computer**

1. Click Start, click Programs, click Administrative Tools, then click Event Viewer.

2. In the console tree, click the security log and view the contents. As you scroll through the log, double-click a couple of events to view a description.

Exercise 2: Managing the Security Log

In this exercise you configure Event Viewer to overwrite events when the log file gets full.

▶ **To configure the size and contents of the security log file**

1. Right-click the security log in the console tree, then click Properties.

2. In the Security Log Properties dialog box, click Overwrite Events As Needed.

3. In the Maximum Log Size box, change the maximum log size to 2048 KB, then click OK.

   Windows 2000 will now allow the log to grow to 2048 KB, and will then overwrite older events with new events as necessary.

Exercise 3: Clearing and Archiving the Security Log

In this exercise you clear the security log, archive a security log, and view the archived security log.

▶ **To clear and archive the security log**

1. Open Event Viewer.

2. Right-click the security log in the console tree, then click Clear All Events.

3. In the Event Viewer message box, click Yes to archive the log before clearing.

4. In the Save As dialog box, in the File Name list, type **archive** to name the log file to be archived.

5. In the Save As Type list, ensure that the Event Log (*.evt) file type is selected, then click Save.

▶ **To view the archived security log**

1. Right-click the security log in the console tree, then click Open Log File.

2. On the Open dialog box, click the ARCHIVE.EVT file (or the name of the file you archived).

3. In the Log Type list, select Security for the type of log to be opened.

4. In the Display Name box, ensure that Saved Security Log appears, then click Open.

   The Saved Security Log appears in Event Viewer. You cannot click Refresh or Clear All Events to update the display or to clear an archived log.

5. Close Event Viewer.

Lesson Summary

In this lesson you learned about the Windows 2000 security log. You learned how to use Event Viewer to view the contents of the Windows 2000 security logs, to locate and display specific events in security logs, to configure log size, and to archive security logs.

In the practice portion of this lesson you viewed the security log file and configured Event Viewer to overwrite events when the log file is filled. Then you cleared and archived a security log file.

Lesson 4: User Rights

Although access to Windows 2000 objects such as files, folders, and printers is controlled by permissions, user rights grant other privileges and logon rights to users and groups in your computing environment.

After this lesson, you will be able to

- Explain the purpose of user rights
- Explain the purpose of privileges and logon rights
- Assign user rights to users and groups

Estimated lesson time: 10 minutes

User Rights

Administrators can assign specific rights to group accounts or to individual user accounts. These rights authorize users to perform specific actions, such as logging on to a system interactively or backing up files and directories. *User rights* are different from permissions because user rights apply to user accounts, and permissions are attached to objects. Additionally, because user rights are part of a GPO, user rights can be overridden depending on the GPO affecting the user.

User rights define capabilities at the local level. Although user rights can apply to individual user accounts, user rights are best administered on a group account basis. This ensures that a user logging on as a member of a group automatically inherits the rights associated with that group. By assigning user rights to groups rather than individual users, you simplify the task of user account administration. When users in a group all require the same user rights, you can assign the set of user rights once to the group, rather than repeatedly assigning the same set of user rights to each individual user account.

User rights that are assigned to a group are applied to all members of the group while they remain members. If a user is a member of multiple groups, the user's rights are cumulative, which means that the user has more than one set of rights. The only time that rights assigned to one group might conflict with those assigned to another is in the case of certain logon rights. In general, however, user rights assigned to one group do not conflict with the rights assigned to another group. To remove rights from a user, the administrator simply removes the user from the group. In this case, the user no longer has the rights assigned to that group.

There are two types of user rights: privileges and logon rights.

Privileges

Privileges specify allowable user actions on the network. Table 13.13 describes the privileges that can be assigned to a user.

Table 13.13   Privileges

Privilege	Description
Act As Part Of The Operating System	Allows a process to authenticate as any user, and therefore gain access to the same resources as any user. Only low-level authentication services should require this privilege. The potential access is not limited to what is associated with the user by default, because the calling process may request that arbitrary additional accesses be put in the access token. Of even more concern is that the calling process can build an anonymous token that can provide any and all accesses. Additionally, this token does not provide a primary identity for tracking events in the audit log. Processes that require this privilege should use the LocalSystem account, which already includes this privilege, rather than using a separate user account with this privilege specially assigned.
Add Workstations To Domain	Allows the user to add a computer to a specific domain. The user specifies the domain through an administrative user interface on the computer being added, creating an object in the Computer container of Active Directory. The behavior of this privilege is duplicated in Windows 2000 by another access control mechanism (permissions attached to the Computer container or OU).
Back Up Files And Directories	Allows the user to circumvent file and directory permissions to back up the system. Specifically, the privilege is similar to granting the following permissions on all files and folders on the local computer: Traverse Folder/Execute File, List Folder/Read Data, Read Attributes, Read Extended Attributes, and Read Permissions. See also the Restore Files And Directories privilege.
Bypass Traverse Checking	Allows the user to pass through directories to which the user otherwise has no access, while navigating an object path in any Windows file system or in the registry. This privilege does not allow the user to list the contents of a directory, only to traverse directories.
Change The System Time	Allows the user to set the time for the internal clock of the computer.
Create A Pagefile	Allows the user to create and change the size of a pagefile by specifying a paging file size for a given drive in the System Properties Performance Options.
Create A Token Object	Allows a process to create a token that it can then use to get access to any local resources when the process uses NtCreateToken() or other token-creation application programming interfaces (APIs). It is recommended that processes requiring this privilege use the LocalSystem account, which already includes this privilege, rather than using a separate user account with this privilege specially assigned.

Privilege	Description
Create Permanent Shared Objects	Allows a process to create a directory object in the Windows 2000 object manager. This privilege is useful to kernel-mode components that plan to extend the Windows 2000 object namespace. Because components running in kernel mode already have this privilege assigned to them, it is not necessary to specifically assign this privilege.
Debug Programs	Allows the user to attach a debugger to any process, providing powerful access to sensitive and critical system operating components.
Enable Computer And User Accounts To Be Trusted For Delegation	Allows the user to set the Trusted For Delegation setting on a user or computer object. The user or object that is granted this privilege must have write access to the account control flags on the user or computer object. A server process either running on a computer that is trusted for delegation or run by a user that is trusted for delegation can access resources on another computer. This uses a client's delegated credentials, as long as the client account does not have the Account Cannot Be Delegated account control flag set. Misuse of this privilege or of the Trusted For Delegation settings could make the network vulnerable to sophisticated attacks using Trojan horse programs that impersonate incoming clients and use their credentials to gain access to network resources.
Force Shutdown From A Remote System	Allows a user to shut down a computer from a remote location on the network. See also the Shut Down The System privilege.
Generate Security Audits	Allows a process to make entries in the security log for object access auditing. The process can also generate other security audits. The security log is used to trace unauthorized system access. See also the Manage Auditing And Security Log privilege.
Increase Quotas	Allows a process with write property access to another process to increase the processor quota assigned to that other process. This privilege is useful for system tuning, but can be abused, as in a denial-of-service attack.
Increase Scheduling Priority	Allows a process with write property access to another process to increase the execution priority of that other process. A user with this privilege can change the scheduling priority of a process through the Task Manager user interface.
Load and Unload Device Drivers	Allows a user to install and uninstall Plug and Play device drivers. Device drivers that are not Plug and Play are not affected by this privilege and can only be installed by administrators. Because device drivers run as trusted (highly privileged) programs, this privilege could be misused to install hostile programs and give these programs destructive access to resources.

Table 13.13   Privileges *(continued)*

Privilege	Description
Lock Pages In Memory	Allows a process to keep data in physical memory, preventing the system from paging the data to virtual memory on disk. Exercising this privilege could significantly affect system performance. This privilege is obsolete and is therefore never checked.
Manage Auditing And Security Log	Allows a user to specify object access auditing options for individual resources such as files, Active Directory objects, and registry keys. Object access auditing is not actually performed unless you have enabled it in the computer-wide audit policy settings under group policy or under group policy defined in Active Directory; this privilege does not grant access to the computer-wide audit policy. A user with this privilege can also view and clear the security log from the Event Viewer.
Modify Firmware Environment Values	Allows modification of the system environment variables, either by a user through the System Properties or by a process.
Profile Single Process	Allows a user to use Windows NT and Windows 2000 performance-monitoring tools to monitor the performance of nonsystem processes.
Profile System Performance	Allows a user to use Windows NT and Windows 2000 performance-monitoring tools to monitor the performance of system processes.
Remove Computer From Docking Station	Allows a user to undock a computer using the Windows 2000 user interface.
Replace A Process Level Token	Allows a process to replace the default token associated with a subprocess that has been started.
Restore Files And Directories	Allows a user to circumvent file and directory permissions when restoring backed up files and directories, and to set any valid security principal as the owner of an object. See also the Back Up Files And Directories privilege.
Shut Down The System	Allows a user to shut down the local computer.
Synchronize Directory Service Data	Allows a process to provide directory synchronization services; relevant only on domain controllers. By default, this privilege is assigned to the Administrator and LocalSystem accounts on domain controllers.
Take Ownership Of Files Or Other Objects	Allows a user to take ownership of any securable object in the system, including Active Directory objects, files and folders, printers, registry keys, processes, and threads.

Some of these privileges can override permissions set on an object. For example, a user logged on to a domain account as a member of the Backup Operators group has the right to perform backup operations for all domain servers. However, this requires the ability to read all files on those servers, even files on which their owners have set permissions that explicitly deny access to all users, including members of the Backup Operators group. A user right, in this case the right to perform a backup, takes precedence over all file and directory permissions.

Logon Rights

Logon rights specify the ways in which a user can log on to a system. Table 13.14 describes the logon rights that can be assigned to a user.

Table 13.14   Logon Rights

Logon Right	Description
Access This Computer From The Network	Allows a user to connect to the computer over the network. By default, this privilege is granted to Administrators, Everyone, and Power Users.
Deny Access To This Computer From The Network	Prohibits a user or group from connecting to the computer from the network. By default, no one is denied this right.
Deny Logon As A Batch Job	Prohibits a user or group from logging on through a batch-queue facility. By default, no one is denied this right.
Deny Logon As A Service	Prohibits a user or group from logging on as a service. By default, no one is denied this right.
Deny Logon Locally	Prohibits a user or group from logging on locally. By default, no one is denied this right.
Log On As A Batch Job	Allows a user to log on using a batch-queue facility. By default, this privilege is granted to Administrators.
Log On As A Service	Allows a security principal to log on as a service, as a way of establishing a security context. The LocalSystem account always retains the right to log on as a service. Any service that runs under a separate account must be granted this right. By default, this right is not granted to anyone.
Log On Locally	Allows a user to log on at the computer's keyboard. By default, this right is granted to Administrators, Account Operators, Backup Operators, Print Operators, and Server Operators.

The special user account LocalSystem has almost all privileges and logon rights assigned to it because all processes that are running as part of the operating system are associated with this account, and these processes require a complete set of user rights.

Assigning User Rights

To ease the task of user account administration, you should assign user rights primarily to group accounts, rather than to individual user accounts. When you assign privileges to a group account, users are automatically assigned those privileges when they become a member of that group.

▶ **To assign user rights**

1. Access the Group Policy snap-in for a GPO.

2. In the Group Policy snap-in, click Computer Configuration, double-click Windows Settings, double-click Security Settings, double-click Local Policies, then double-click User Rights Assignment.

3. In the details pane, right-click the user right that you want to set, then click Security.

4. In the Security Policy Setting dialog box (see Figure 13.12), click the Define These Policy Settings check box, then click Add.

Figure 13.12   The Security Policy Setting dialog box

5. In the Add User Or Group dialog box, add the users and/or groups you want to be affected by this user right, then click OK.

6. Click OK twice when you have finished adding users and/or groups.

   A list of users and/or groups appears in the Computer Setting column in the details pane.

Lesson Summary

In this lesson you learned how user rights grant specific privileges and logon rights to users and groups in your computing environment. Privileges specify allowable user actions on the network. Logon rights specify the ways in which a user can log on to a system. To ease the task of user account administration, you should assign user rights primarily to group accounts, rather than to individual user accounts. User rights are assigned using the Group Policy snap-in.

Lesson 5: Using Security Templates

Windows 2000 provides a centralized method of defining security using security templates. This lesson explains how to use security templates.

After this lesson, you will be able to

- Explain the purpose of security templates
- Explain the purpose of the predefined security templates
- Manage security templates

Estimated lesson time: 25 minutes

Security Templates Overview

A *security template* is a physical representation of a security configuration, a single file where a group of security settings is stored. Locating all security settings in one place streamlines security administration. Each template is saved as a text-based .inf file. This allows you to copy, paste, import, or export some or all of the template attributes. With the exceptions of IP Security and Public Key policies, all security attributes can be contained in a security template.

Security Template Uses

You can import (apply) a security template file to a local or nonlocal GPO. Any computer or user accounts in the site, domain, or OU to which the GPO is applied will receive the security template settings. Importing a security template to a GPO eases domain administration by configuring security for multiple computers at once.

The security settings in the local GPO are the initial settings applied to a computer. You can export the local security settings to a security template file to preserve initial system security settings. This enables the restoration of the initial security settings at any later point.

Predefined Security Templates

Windows 2000 includes a set of predefined security templates, each based on the role of a computer and common security scenarios: from security settings for low-security domain clients to highly secure domain controllers. These templates can be used as provided, they can be modified, or they can serve as a basis for creating custom security templates. Do not apply predefined security templates to production systems without testing to ensure that the right level of application functionality is maintained for your network and system architecture.

The predefined security templates are

- Default domain controller security settings (BASICDC.INF)
- Default server security settings (BASICSV.INF)
- Default workstation security settings (BASICWK.INF)
- Compatible workstation or server security settings (COMPATWS.INF)
- Default security settings updated for domain controllers (DC SECURITY.INF)
- Highly secure domain controller security settings (HISECDC.INF)
- Highly secure workstation or server security settings (HISECWS.INF)
- Removes the Terminal Server User SID from Windows 2000 server (NOTSSID.INF)
- Optional Component File Security for server (OCFILESS.INF)
- Optional Component File Security for workstation (OCFILESW.INF)
- Secure domain controller security settings (SECUREDC.INF)
- Secure workstation or server security settings (SECUREWS.INF)
- Out of the box default security settings (SETUP SECURITY.INF)

By default, these templates are stored in the *systemroot*\Security\Templates folder.

Security Levels

The predefined security templates are designed to cover common requirements for security:

- **Basic (BASIC*.INF).**   The basic configuration templates are provided as a means to reverse the application of a different security configuration. The basic configurations apply the Windows 2000 default security settings to all security areas except those pertaining to user rights. These are not modified in the basic templates because application setup programs commonly modify user rights to enable successful use of the application. It is not the intent of the basic configuration files to undo such modifications.

- **Compatible (COMPAT*.INF).**   By default, Windows 2000 security is configured such that members of the local users group have ideal security settings and members of the local Power Users group have security settings that are compatible with Windows NT 4.0 users. This default configuration enables development of applications to a standard definition of a secure Windows environment, while still allowing existing applications to run successfully under the less secure Power User configuration. By default, all users that are authenticated by Windows 2000 are members of the Power Users group. This may be too unsecured for some environments, where it would be preferable to have users, by default, only be members of the Users group, and decrease the security on the Users group to the level where the applications run successfully. The compatible templates are designed for such environments. By lowering the security levels on specific files, folders, and registry keys that are commonly accessed by applications, the compatible templates allow most applications to run successfully. In addition, as it is assumed that the administrator applying the compatible template does not want users to be Power Users, all members of the Power Users group are removed.

- **Secure (SECURE*.INF).** The secure templates implement recommended security settings for all security areas except files, folders, and registry keys. These are not modified because file system and registry permissions are configured securely by default.

- **Highly Secure (HISEC*.INF).** The highly secure templates define security settings for Windows 2000 network communications. The security areas are set to require maximum protection for network traffic and protocols used between computers running Windows 2000. As a result, such computers configured with a highly secure template can only communicate with other Windows 2000 computers. They will not be able to communicate with computers running Windows 95, Windows 98, or Windows NT.

Managing Security Templates

The tasks for managing security templates are

1. Accessing the Security Templates console
2. Customizing a predefined security template
3. Defining a new security template
4. Importing a security template to a local and nonlocal GPO
5. Exporting security settings to a security template

Accessing the Security Templates Console

The Security Templates console is the main tool for managing security templates.

▶ **To access the Security Templates console**

1. Decide whether to add the Security Templates console to an existing console or create a new console.
    - To create a new console, click Start, click Run, type **mmc**, then click OK.
    - To add the Security Templates console to an existing console, open the console, then proceed to Step 2.

2. On the Console menu, click Add/Remove Snap-In, then click Add.

3. In the Add Standalone Snap-In dialog box, select Security Templates, click Add, click Close, then click OK.

4. On the Console menu, click Save.

5. Enter the name to assign to this console and click Save.

    The console appears on the Administrative Tools menu.

Customizing a Predefined Security Template

Customizing a predefined security template allows you to save the predefined template as a new template (to preserve the original predefined template) and then make edits to security settings to create a new template.

▶ **To customize a predefined security template**

1. In the Security Templates console (see Figure 13.13), double-click Security Templates.

Figure 13.13   The Security Templates console

2. Double-click the default path folder (*systemroot*\Security\Templates), right-click the predefined template you want to modify, then click Save As.

3. In the Save As dialog box, in the File Name box, specify a filename for the new security template, then click Save.

4. In the console tree, right-click the new security template, then select Set Description.

5. In the Security Template Description dialog box, enter a description for the new security template, then click OK.

6. In the console tree, double-click the new security template to display the security policies, and double-click the security policy (such as Account Policies) you want to modify.

7. Click the security policy you want to customize (such as Password Policy), then double-click the security setting to modify (such as Minimum Password Length).

8. On the Template Security Policy Setting dialog box, click the Define This Policy Setting In The Template check box to allow configuration, then configure the security setting.

9. Click OK.

10. Configure other security settings as needed.

11. Close the Security Templates console.

12. In the Save Security Templates dialog box, click Yes to save the new security template file.

Defining a New Security Template

You can define a new security template and then modify the default settings to meet your requirements.

▶ **To define a new security template**

1. In the Security Templates console, double-click Security Templates.

2. Right-click the template path folder where you want to store the new template and click New Template.

3. In the dialog box for the templates folder, enter the name and description for your new security template, then click OK.

4. In the console tree, right-click the new security template, then select Set Description.

5. In the Security Template Description dialog box, enter a description for the new security template, then click OK.

6. In the console tree, double-click the new security template to display the security policies, and double-click the security policy (such as Account Policies) you want to define.

7. Click the security policy you want to define (such as Password Policy), then double-click the security setting to define (such as Minimum Password Length).

8. In the Template Security Policy Setting dialog box, click the Define This Policy Setting In The Template check box to allow configuration, then configure the security setting.

9. Click OK.

10. Configure other security settings as needed.

11. Close the Security Templates console.

12. In the Save Security Templates dialog box, click Yes to save the new security template file.

Importing a Security Template to a GPO

You can import a security template to local or nonlocal GPOs. Importing security templates make administration easier because security is configured in one step for multiple objects.

► **To import a security template to a local and nonlocal GPO**

1. In a console from which you manage local or nonlocal group policy settings, click the GPO to which you want to import the security template.

2. In the console tree, right-click Security Settings, then click Import Policy.

3. In the Import Policy From dialog box (see Figure 13.14), click the security template you want to import, then click Open.

Figure 13.14   The Import Policy From dialog box

4. Because the security settings are applied when the group policy is propagated (applied) to your computer, do one of the following to initiate policy propagation:

   ▪ Type **secedit /refreshpolicy machine_policy** at the command prompt, then press Enter.

   ▪ Restart your computer.

   ▪ Wait for automatic policy propagation, which occurs at regular, configurable intervals. By default, policy propagation occurs every eight hours.

Exporting Security Settings to a Security Template

You can export both local and effective security settings to a security template. By exporting the local settings to a security template, you can preserve initial system settings. Because the local GPO is overridden by domain-based GPOs, the local security settings are available for restoration later, if necessary. By exporting the effective security settings to a security template, you can then import the settings into a security database (discussed in the next lesson), overlay new templates, and analyze potential conflicts.

▶ **To export security settings to a security template**

1. Click Start, point to Programs, point to Administrative Tools, then click Local Security Policy.

2. In the console tree, right-click Security Settings, click Export Policy, and select Local Policy or Effective Policy.

3. In the Export Policy To dialog box (see Figure 13.15), enter the name of the security template to which you want to export security settings, then click Save.

Figure 13.15   The Export Policy To dialog box

Practice: Managing Security Templates

In this practice you access the Security Templates console and customize a predefined security template.

Exercise 1: Accessing the Security Templates Console

In this exercise you access the Security Templates console, the main tool for managing security templates.

▶ **To access the Security Templates console**

1. Click Start, click Run, type **mmc**, then click OK.

2. On the Console menu, click Add/Remove Snap-In, then click Add.

3. In the Add Standalone Snap-In dialog box, select Security Templates, click Add, click Close, then click OK.

4. On the Console menu, click Save.

5. In the File Name list, type **Security Templates** to name this console, then click Save. The console appears on the Administrative Tools menu.

Exercise 2: Customizing a Predefined Security Template

In this exercise you customize a predefined security template by saving the predefined template as a new template (to preserve the original predefined template) and then making edits to security settings to create a new template.

▶ **To customize a predefined security template**

1. In the Security Templates console, double-click Security Templates.

2. Double-click the default path folder (*systemroot*\Security\Templates), right-click the basicdc template, then click Save As.

3. In the Save As dialog box, in the File Name box, type **new template**, then click Save.

4. In the console tree, right-click New Template, then select Set Description.

5. In the Security Template Description dialog box, type the description **New domain controller template**, then click OK.

6. In the console tree, double-click the new security template to display the security policies.

7. Double-click Account Policies, click Password Policy, then double-click Minimum Password Length.

8. In the Template Security Policy Setting dialog box, click the Define This Policy Setting In The Template check box to allow configuration, then set the password to be at least 10 characters.

9. Click OK.

10. Close the Security Templates console and save the console settings.

11. In the Save Security Templates dialog box, click Yes to save the NEW TEMPLATE.INF security template file.

Lesson Summary

In this lesson you learned that a security template is a physical representation of a security configuration, a single file where a group of security settings is stored. Locating all security settings in one place streamlines security administration.

You learned that the tasks for managing security templates are accessing the Security Templates console, customizing a predefined security template, defining a new security template, importing a security template to a local and nonlocal GPO, and exporting security settings to a security template.

In the practice portion of this lesson you accessed the Security Templates console, the main tool for managing security templates, and customized a predefined security template.

Lesson 6: Security Configuration and Analysis

Security Configuration and Analysis is a tool that offers the ability to configure security, analyze security, view results, and resolve any discrepancies revealed by analysis. This tool is located on the Security Configuration and Analysis console. This lesson shows you how to use the Security Configuration and Analysis console.

After this lesson, you will be able to

- Explain how the Security Configuration and Analysis console works
- Use the Security Configuration and Analysis console to perform security configuration and analysis tasks

Estimated lesson time: 25 minutes

How the Security Configuration and Analysis Console Works

The Security Configuration and Analysis console uses a database to perform configuration and analysis functions. The security configuration and analysis database is a computer-specific data store. The database architecture allows the use of personal databases, security template import and export, and the combination of multiple security templates into one composite security template that can be used for analysis or configuration. New security templates can be incrementally added to the database to create a composite security template; overwriting a template is also an option. You can also create personal databases for storing your own customized security templates.

Security Configuration

The Security Configuration and Analysis console can be used to configure local system security. Through its use of personal databases, you can import security templates created with the Security Templates console and apply these templates to the GPO for the local computer. This immediately configures the system security with the levels specified in the template.

Security Analysis

The state of the operating system and applications on a computer is dynamic. For example, to enable immediate resolution of an administration or network issue, security levels may occasionally be required to change temporarily. After this security requirement is finished, the temporary change may not be reversed. This means that a computer may no longer meet the requirements for enterprise security.

The Security Configuration and Analysis console allows administrators to perform a quick security analysis. In the analysis, recommendations are presented alongside current system settings, and icons or remarks are used to highlight any areas where the current settings do not match the proposed level of security. Security Configuration and Analysis also offers the ability to resolve any discrepancies revealed by analysis.

Regular analysis enables an administrator to track and ensure an adequate level of security on each computer as part of an enterprise risk management program. Analysis is highly specified and information about all system aspects related to security is provided in the results. This enables an administrator to tune the security levels, and most important, to detect any security flaws that may occur in the system over time.

Using Security Configuration and Analysis

The tasks for using Security Configuration and Analysis are

1. Accessing the Security Configuration and Analysis console
2. Setting a working security database
3. Importing a security template into a security database
4. Analyzing system security
5. Viewing security analysis results
6. Configuring system security
7. Exporting security database settings to a security template

Accessing the Security Configuration and Analysis Console

The Security Configuration and Analysis console is the main tool for using the security configuration and analysis tool.

▶   **To access the Security Configuration and Analysis console**

1. Do one of the following:
    - To add the Security Configuration and Analysis console to a new console, click Start, click Run, type **mmc**, then click OK.
    - To add the Security Configuration and Analysis console to an existing console, go directly to Step 2.
2. On the Console menu, click Add/Remove Snap-In, then click Add.
3. In the Add Standalone Snap-In dialog box, select Security Configuration And Analysis and click Add.
4. Click Close, then click OK.
5. On the Console menu, click Save.
6. Enter the name to assign to this console and click Save.

    The console appears on the Administrative Tools menu.

Setting a Working Security Database

The Security Configuration and Analysis console uses a database to perform configuration and analysis functions. Before you can configure or analyze security you must determine the working security database to use.

▶ **To set a working security database**

1. In the Security Configuration and Analysis console (see Figure 13.16), right-click Security Configuration And Analysis.

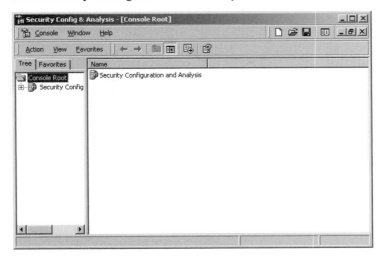

Figure 13.16   The Security Configuration and Analysis console

2. Click Open Database.

3. In the Open Database dialog box, choose an existing personal database or type a filename to create a new personal database, then click Open.

   ▪ If you chose an existing personal database, this database is now the working security database.

   ▪ If you created a new personal database, the Import Template dialog box appears.

4. Select the security template to load into the security database, then click Open.

   This database is now the working security database.

Importing a Security Template into a Security Database

In Lesson 5 you learned to import a security template directly into a GPO. In this lesson you import a security template into the security database used in the Security Configuration and Analysis console.

You can merge several different templates into one composite template that then can be used for analysis or configuration of a system, by importing each template into a working database. The database will merge the various templates to create one composite template, resolving conflicts in order of import; the last one imported takes precedence when there is contention. Only if you chose to overwrite will they not be merged into a composite template (stored configuration). Once the templates are imported to the selected database, you can analyze or configure the system.

▶ **To import a security template into a security database**

1. In the Security Configuration and Analysis console, right-click Security Configuration And Analysis.

2. Open or create a working security database.

3. Select Import Template.

4. Select a security template file, then click Open.

5. Repeat the previous step for each template you want to merge with previous templates into the database.

Note If you want to replace the template rather than merge it into the stored template, click the Clear This Database Before Importing check box in the Import Template dialog box.

Analyzing System Security

Security Configuration and Analysis performs security analysis by comparing the current state of system security against a security template that you have imported to a personal database. This template is the database configuration, and it is the template that contains your preferred or recommended security settings for that system.

Security Configuration and Analysis queries the system's security settings for all security areas in the database configuration. Values found are compared to the database configuration. If the current system settings match the database configuration settings, they are assumed to be correct. If not, the policies in question are displayed as potential problems that need investigation.

▶ **To analyze system security**

1. In the Security Configuration and Analysis console, set a working database (if one is not currently set).

2. Right-click Security Configuration And Analysis, then click Analyze Computer Now.

3. In the Perform Analysis dialog box, verify the path for the log file location, then click OK.

   The different security areas are displayed as they are analyzed. Once this is complete, you can check the log file or review the results.

Note   To check the log file, right-click Security Configuration And Analysis, then click View Log File.

Viewing Security Analysis Results

The Security Configuration and Analysis console displays the analysis results organized by security area with visual flags to indicate problems. For each security policy in the security area, the current database and computer configuration settings are displayed.

▶ **To view security analysis results**

1. In the Security Configuration and Analysis console, click Security Configuration And Analysis.

2. Double-click a security policies node (such as Account Policies), then click the security area (such as Password Policy) for which you want to view results.

3. In the details pane (see Figure 13.17), the Policy column indicates the policy name for the analysis results, the Database Setting column indicates the security value in your template, and the Computer Setting column indicates the current security level in the system.

   ▪ A red X indicates a difference from the database configuration.

   ▪ A green check mark indicates consistency with the database configuration.

   ▪ No icon indicates that the security policy was not included in your template and therefore not analyzed.

Figure 13.17   Analysis results for Password Policy

Configuring System Security

Security Configuration and Analysis offers the ability to resolve any discrepancies revealed by analysis, including the following:

- Accepting or changing some or all of the values flagged or not included in the configuration if you determine the local system security levels are valid due to the context (role) of that computer

- Configuring the system to the original database configuration values if you determine the system is not in compliance with valid security levels

- Importing a more appropriate template, for the role of that computer, into the database as the new database configuration and applying it to the system

You can repeat the import process and load multiple templates. The database will merge the various templates to create one composite template, resolving conflicts in order of import; the last one imported takes precedence when there is contention. Once the templates are imported to the database, you can choose Configure System Now to apply the stored template (database configuration) to the system.

Important   These changes are made to the stored template in the database, not to the security template file. The security template file will only be modified if you either return to Security Templates and edit that template or export the stored configuration to the same template file.

Using the Security Configuration and Analysis console is not recommended when you are analyzing security for domain-based clients, as you would have to go to each client individually. In this case, you should return to the Security Templates console, modify the template, and reapply it to the appropriate GPO.

▶ **To configure system security**

1. In the Security Configuration and Analysis console, set a working database (if one is not currently set).

2. Right-click Security Configuration And Analysis, then click Configure Computer Now.

3. In the Configure System dialog box, click OK to use the default analysis log or enter a filename and valid path.

    The different security areas are displayed as they are configured. Once this is complete, you can check the log file or analyze system security and view the results.

▶ **To edit the database security configuration**

1. In the Security Configuration and Analysis console, click Security Configuration And Analysis.

2. Double-click a security policies node (such as Account Policies), then click a security area (such as Password Policy).

3. In the details pane, double-click the security attribute you want to edit.

4. Click the Define This Policy In The Database check box to allow editing.

5. Enter a new value for the security policy, then click OK.

6. Repeat the previous four steps for each security policy you want to edit.

▶ **To view security configuration results**

1. In the console from which you manage group policy, double-click the GPO.

2. In the console tree, click Security Settings.

3. Double-click a security policy node (such as Account Policies), then click a security area (such as Password Policy).

4. Double-click the security attribute you want to view (such as Minimum Password Length).

Exporting Security Templates

The export feature provides the ability to save a security database configuration as a new template file that can be imported into other databases, used as is to analyze or configure a system, or even redefined with the Security Templates console.

▶ **To export security database settings to a security template**

1. In the Security Configuration and Analysis console, right-click Security Configuration and Analysis.

2. If you have created a composite security template by importing multiple templates into one database and you want to save the composite template as a separate template file, click Export Template.

3. In the Export Template To dialog box, type a valid filename in the File Name box, type a path to where your template should be saved in the Save In list, and select the type of file you want to save in the Save As Type list, then click Save.

Practice: Using Security Configuration and Analysis

In this practice you access the Security Configuration and Analysis console, set a working security database, analyze system security, and then view the results.

Exercise 1: Accessing the Security Configuration and Analysis Console

In this exercise you access the Security Configuration and Analysis console, the main tool for using the Security Configuration and Analysis tool.

▶ **To access the Security Configuration and Analysis console**

1. Click Run, type **mmc**, then click OK.

2. On the Console menu, click Add/Remove Snap-In, then click Add.

3. In the Add Standalone Snap-In dialog box, select Security Configuration And Analysis, then click Add.

4. Click Close, then click OK.

5. On the Console menu, click Save.

6. In the File Name box, type **security config & analysis** to name this console and click Save.

   The console appears on the Administrative Tools menu.

Exercise 2: Setting a Working Security Database

In this exercise you determine the working security database to use.

▶ **To set a working security database**

1. In the Security Configuration and Analysis console, right-click Security Configuration And Analysis.

2. Click Open Database.

3. In the Open Database dialog box, in the File Name box, type **new** for the new personal database file name, then click Open.

4. In the Import Template dialog box, select the securedc security template to load into the security database, then click Open.

   The *new* database is now the working security database, and it contains the *securedc* security template.

Exercise 3: Analyzing System Security

In this exercise you analyze system security, comparing the settings in the security template *securedc* with the security settings currently running on your system.

▶ **To analyze system security**

1. Right-click Security Configuration And Analysis, then click Analyze Computer Now.

2. In the Perform Analysis dialog box, verify the path for the log file location, then click OK.

   The different security areas are displayed as they are analyzed.

Exercise 4: Viewing Security Analysis Results

In this exercise you view the security analysis results.

▶ **To view security analysis results**

1. In the Security Configuration and Analysis console, click Security Configuration And Analysis.

2. Double-click the Account Policies node, then click the Password Policy security area.

In the details pane, what is indicated in the Policy column? In the Database Setting column? In the Computer Setting column?

In the Policy column, what does the red X indicate? What does the green check mark indicate?

Lesson Summary

In this lesson you learned how the Security Configuration and Analysis console uses a database to perform configuration and analysis functions.

You learned that when you configure system security using the Security Configuration and Analysis console, changes are made to the stored template in the database, not to the security template file. The security template file will only be modified if you either return to Security Templates and edit that template or export the stored configuration to the same template file.

You also learned that Security Configuration and Analysis performs security analysis by comparing the current state of system security against a security template that you have imported to a personal database. This template is the database configuration, and it is the template that contains your preferred or recommended security settings for that system.

In the practice portion of this lesson you accessed the Security Configuration and Analysis console, set a working security database, analyzed system security, and then viewed the results.

Lesson 7: Troubleshooting a Security Configuration

This lesson describes problems you may encounter that relate to security configuration.

After this lesson, you will be able to

■ Troubleshoot a security configuration

Estimated lesson time: 5 minutes

Troubleshooting a Security Configuration

Table 13.15 describes scenarios in which there are problems using a security configuration.

Table 13.15   Security Configuration Troubleshooting Scenarios

**Symptom: Received error message: Event message: Event ID 1202,
Event source: scecli, Warning (0x%x) occurs to apply security policies**

Cause	Solution
Group policy was not refreshed after changes were made.	Trigger another application of group policy settings or local policy refresh by using the Secedit command-line tool to refresh security settings.

Symptom: Received error message: Failed to open the Group Policy Object

Cause	Solution
The most likely causes for this error are network-related.	Check the DNS configuration for the following: Make sure that there are no stale entries in the DNS database. Resolve local DNS servers and Internet service provider (ISP) DNS server entries. For example, the DNS settings for a local LAN network adapter points to two DNS servers: the local DNS server (possibly the same computer) and the DNS server of an ISP. If you try to ping your domain, a message may indicate that this is an unknown host. Even with correct local DNS entries, the ISP DNS server cannot identify your domain, so there is a difference in their databases. To resolve this error, remove the second and add the ISP DNS server *IPAddress* to the forwarders in the local DNS server.

Symptom: Modified security settings are not taking effect

Cause	Solution
Any policies configured locally may be overridden by like policies specified in the domain. If your setting shows up in local policy but not in effective policy, it implies that there is a policy from the domain that is overriding your setting. Also, as group policy changes are applied periodically, it is likely that the policy changes made in the directory have not yet been refreshed in your computer.	Manually do a policy refresh by typing the following at the command line: **secedit / refreshpolicy machine_policy**

Symptom: Policies do not migrate from Windows NT 4.0 to Windows 2000

Cause	Solution
Windows NT 4.0 policies cannot be migrated to Windows 2000. In Windows NT 4.0, system policies were stored in one .pol file with group information embedded; no method is available to translate that information to the Windows 2000 Active Directory structure. Groups are handled very differently in Windows 2000.	Windows NT 4.0 clients accessing a Windows 2000 Server computer and Windows 2000 Professional clients accessing a Windows NT 4.0 Server computer will use the Netlogon share (the Windows NT 4.0 model). With Windows 2000 Server, when a Windows NT 4.0 client is upgraded to Windows 2000, it will get only Active Directory-based group policy settings and not Windows NT 4.0-style policies. Although Windows NT 4.0-style policies may be enabled (using a group policy setting) if the administrator chooses to do so, this practice is strongly discouraged. Windows NT 4.0-style policies are applied only during the logon process. This means that both computer and user settings are processed. This is not optimal behavior for the following reasons: The Windows NT 4.0-style computer settings override the group policy settings that have already been applied to the computer during startup. During the group policy settings refresh cycle, the group policy settings change any conflicting settings back. This creates an indeterminate state. Windows NT 4.0-style policies result in persistent settings in the registry (tattooing). Note also that Terminal Server cannot allow computer settings to be set based on a user logon.

Lesson Summary

In this lesson you examined some security problems that you may encounter and possible solutions.

Review

The following questions are intended to reinforce key information presented in the chapter. If you are unable to answer a question, review the appropriate lesson and then try the question again. Answers to the questions can be found in Appendix A, "Questions and Answers."

1. On which computer do you set an audit policy to audit a folder that is located on a member server that belongs to a domain?

2. What is the difference between what the audit policy settings track for directory service access and object access?

3. When you view a security log, how do you determine if an event failed or was successful?

4. How are user rights different from permissions?

5. What is a security template and why is it useful?

6. Where does the Security Configuration and Analysis console store information for performing configuration and analysis functions?

C H A P T E R   1 4

Managing Active Directory Performance

About This Chapter

In this chapter you learn how performance monitoring tools, diagnostic tools, and shared folder monitoring help you to manage Active Directory performance.

Before You Begin

To complete this chapter, you must have

- Completed the Setup procedures located in "About This Book"
- Obtained the knowledge and skills necessary to set up MMCs
- Configured the computer as a domain controller in a domain

Lesson 1: Active Directory Performance Monitoring Tools

Monitoring Active Directory performance is an important part of maintaining and administering your Microsoft Windows 2000 installation. You use Active Directory performance data to

- Understand Active Directory performance and the corresponding effect on your system's resources
- Observe changes and trends in performance and resource usage so you can plan for future upgrades
- Test configuration changes or other tuning efforts by monitoring the results
- Diagnose problems and target components or processes for optimization

This lesson introduces you to the Active Directory performance monitoring tools and guides you through the steps required to set up Active Directory performance monitoring.

After this lesson, you will be able to

- Describe the purpose of the Event Viewer console
- Use the Event Viewer console to view event logs
- Describe the components of the Performance console
- Describe the purpose of the System Monitor
- Use the System Monitor to monitor performance counters
- Describe the purpose of counter logs, trace logs, and alerts
- Use Performance Logs and Alerts to create counter logs, trace logs, and alerts

Estimated lesson time: 50 minutes

Performance Monitoring Tools

Windows 2000 provides several tools for monitoring Active Directory performance. On the Administrative Tools menu, the Event Viewer console allows you to view log files and error messages sent by applications. The Performance console provides a graphical way to view performance of Active Directory according to measurements, or counters, that you select. The Performance console also provides a means to log activity or send alerts according to those measurements and view the logs either printed or online.

The Event Viewer Console

Windows 2000 provides the Event Viewer console as a way to monitor Windows-wide events such as application, system, and security events, and service-specific events such as directory service events. These events are recorded in event logs. For example, if you need detailed information about when directory partitions are being replicated, you would study the File Replication Service log in the Event Viewer.

Also, if you experience problems with Active Directory, it is recommended that the directory service event logs be the *first* item that you use to investigate the causes of the problem. By using information from the event log, you can better understand the sequence and types of events that led up to a particular performance problem.

In Chapter 13, you learned about using Event Viewer to view, locate, filter, and archive information contained in Windows 2000 security logs and to configure security logs. The procedures for each of these tasks are similar for the event logs used to monitor Active Directory performance. These logs are described in Table 14.1.

Table 14.1   Event Logs for Monitoring Active Directory Performance

Log	Description
Application	Contains errors, warnings, or information that applications, such as a database server or an e-mail program, generate. The application developer presets which events to record.
Directory Service	Contains errors, warnings, and information that Active Directory generates (see Figure 14.1).
File Replication Service	Contains errors, warnings, and information that the File Replication service generates.
System	Contains errors, warnings, and information that Windows 2000 generates. Windows 2000 presets which events to record.

Figure 14.1   The Directory Service log

The Performance Console

The Performance console allows you to monitor conditions within local and remote computers anywhere in your network and to summarize performance at selected intervals. The Performance console can use various counters for monitoring real-time resource usage. It can log results into a file so that you can view and diagnose historical performance problems. With appropriate permissions, it can monitor resource usage of other computers that run server services on the network. The Performance console can also be used for collecting baseline performance data, then configured to send alerts to the Event Log or other locations about exceptions to the baseline.

The Performance console contains two snap-ins: System Monitor (an ActiveX control) and Performance Logs and Alerts.

System Monitor

With System Monitor, you can measure Active Directory performance on your own computer or other computers on a network:

- Collect and view real-time performance data on a local computer or from several remote computers.
- View data collected either currently or previously recorded in a counter log.
- Present data in a printable graph, histogram, or report view.
- Incorporate System Monitor functionality into Microsoft Word or other applications in the Microsoft Office suite by means of Automation.
- Create HTML pages from performance views.
- Create reusable monitoring configurations that can be installed on other computers using Microsoft Management Console (MMC).

A sample System Monitor is shown in Figure 14.2.

You can define the Active Directory data you want to collect in the following ways:

- **Type of data.**   To select the data to be collected, you specify performance objects and performance counters.
- **Source of data.**   System Monitor can collect data from your local computer or from other computers on the network where you have permission. (By default, administrative permission associated with the task is required.) In addition, you can include real-time data or data collected previously using counter logs.
- **Sampling parameters.**   System Monitor supports manual, on-demand sampling or automatic sampling based on a time interval you specify. When viewing logged data, you can also choose starting and stopping times so that you can view data spanning a specific time range.

Figure 14.2   A sample System Monitor

In addition to options for defining data content, you have considerable flexibility in designing the appearance of your System Monitor views:

- **Type of display.**   System Monitor supports chart, histogram, and report views.
- **Display characteristics.**   For any of the three display types, you can define the characteristics, colors, and fonts for the display.

Defining Data for Monitoring

To begin monitoring data, you specify performance objects and performance counters. A *performance object* is a logical connection of counters that is associated with a resource or service that can be monitored. For the purposes of monitoring Active Directory, you monitor the activity of the NTDS (NT Directory Service) performance object. By using System Monitor, you can track the activity of performance objects through the use of counters. *Performance counters* refer to the multitude of conditions that can apply to a performance object. For example, if you need to find out the number of connected Lightweight Directory Access Protocol (LDAP) client sessions, you can select the LDAP Client Sessions counter under the NTDS performance object and then view the current activity by using System Monitor.

The NTDS Performance Object Counters

The NTDS performance object contains many performance counters that provide statistics about Active Directory performance. After determining the statistics you want to monitor you must find the matching performance counters.

Performance counters can provide some baseline analysis information for capacity and performance planning. Typically, counters that are suited for capacity planning contain the word "total" in their name. These counters fall into three types: statistic counters, ratio counters, and accumulative counters. *Statistic counters* show totals per second, for example: DRA (Directory Replication Agent) Inbound Properties Total/Sec, which is the total number of object properties received from inbound replication partners. *Ratio counters* show percentage of total, for example: DS (Directory Service) % Writes From LDAP, which is the percentage of directory writes coming from LDAP query. *Accumulative counters* show totals since Active Directory was last started, for example: DRA Inbound Bytes Total Since Boot, which is the total number of bytes replicated in, the sum of the number of uncompressed bytes (never compressed) and the number of compressed bytes (after compression).

Each counter has its own guidelines and limits. The counters in Table 14.2 are of special interest for the reasons described.

Table 14.2   Important Active Directory System Monitor Counters on the NTDS Performance Object

Counter	Description
DRA Inbound Bytes Compressed (Between Sites, After Compression)/Sec	The compressed size (in bytes) of inbound compressed replication data (size after compression, from Directory System Agents [DSAs] in other sites).
DRA Inbound Bytes Compressed (Between Sites, Before Compression)/Sec	The original size (in bytes) of inbound compressed replication data (size before compression, from DSAs in other sites).
DRA Inbound Bytes Not Compressed (Within Site)/Sec	The number of bytes received through inbound replication that were not compressed at the source—that is, from other DSAs in the same site.
DRA Inbound Bytes Total/Sec	The total number of bytes received through replication, per second. It is the sum of the number of uncompressed bytes (never compressed) and the number of compressed bytes (after compression).
DRA Inbound Full Sync Objects Remaining	The number of objects remaining until the full synchronization process is completed, or set.
DRA Inbound Objects/Sec	The number of objects received, per second, from replication partners through inbound replication.
DRA Inbound Objects Applied/Sec	The rate, per second, at which replication updates are received from replication partners and applied by the local directory service. This count excludes changes that are received but not applied (for example, when the change is already present). This indicates how much replication update activity is occurring on the server as a result of changes generated on other servers.
DRA Inbound Objects Filtered/Sec	The number of objects received per second from inbound replication partners that contained no updates that needed to be applied.

Counter	Description
DRA Inbound Object Updates Remaining in Packet	The number of object updates received in the current directory replication update packet that have not yet been applied to the local server. This tells you whether the monitored server is receiving changes but taking a long time applying them to the database.
DRA Inbound Properties Applied/Sec	The number of properties that are applied through inbound replication as a result of reconciliation logic.
DRA Inbound Properties Filtered/Sec	The number of property changes that are already known received during the replication.
DRA Inbound Properties Total/Sec	The total number of object properties received per second from inbound replication partners.
DRA Inbound Values (DNs Only)/Sec	The number of object property values received from inbound replication partners that are Distinguished Names (DNs), per second. This includes objects that reference other objects. Distinguished Names values, such as group or distribution list memberships, are more expensive to apply than other kinds of values because group or distribution list objects can include hundreds and thousands of members and therefore are much bigger than a simple object with only one or two attributes. This counter might explain why inbound changes are slow to be applied to the database.
DRA Inbound Values Total/Sec	The total number of object property values received from inbound replication partners per second. Each inbound object has one or more properties, and each property has zero or more values. Zero values indicate property removal.
DRA Outbound Bytes Compressed (Between Sites, After Compression)/Sec	The compressed size (in bytes) of outbound compressed replication data, after compression, from DSAs in other sites.
DRA Outbound Bytes Compressed (Between Sites, Before Compression)/Sec	The original size (in bytes) of outbound compressed replication data, before compression, from DSAs in other sites.
DRA Outbound Bytes Not Compressed (Within Site)/Sec	The number of bytes replicated out that were not compressed; that is, from DSAs in the same site.
DRA Outbound Bytes Total/Sec	The total number of bytes replicated out per second. The sum of the number of uncompressed bytes (never compressed) and the number of compressed bytes (after compression).
DRA Outbound Objects/Sec	The number of objects replicated out per second.
DRA Outbound Objects Filtered/Sec	The number of objects acknowledged by outbound replication that required no updates. They also represent objects that the outbound partner did not already have.

Table 14.2   Important Active Directory System Monitor Counters on the NTDS Performance Object *(continued)*

Counter	Description
DRA Outbound Properties/Sec	The number of properties replicated out per second. This tells you whether a source server is returning objects or not.
DRA Outbound Values (DNs Only)/Sec	The number of object property values containing Distinguished Names sent to outbound replication partners. Distinguished Name values, such as group or distribution list memberships, are more expensive to read than other kinds of values because group or distribution list objects can include hundreds and thousands of members and therefore are much bigger than a simple object with only one or two attributes.
DRA Outbound Values Total/Sec	The number of object property values sent to outbound replication partners per second.
DRA Pending Replication Synchronizations	The number of directory synchronizations that are queued for this server but not yet processed. This helps in determining replication backlog; the larger the number, the larger the backlog.
DRA Sync Requests Made	The number of synchronization requests made to replication partners.
DS Directory Reads/Sec	The number of directory reads per second.
DS Directory Writes/Sec	The number of directory writes per second.
DS Security Descriptor Suboperations/Sec	The number of Security Descriptor Propagation suboperations per second. One Security Descriptor Propagation operation is made up of many suboperations. A suboperation roughly corresponds to an object the propagation causes the propagator to examine.
DS Security Descriptor Propagations Events	The number of Security Descriptor Propagation events that are queued but not yet processed.
DS Threads in Use	The current number of threads in use by the directory service (different than the number of threads in the directory service process). Threads in Use is the number of threads currently servicing client application programming interface (API) calls and can be used to indicate whether additional processors can be of benefit.
Kerberos Authentications/Sec	The number of times per second that clients use a ticket to this domain controller to authenticate this domain controller.
LDAP Bind Time	The time (in milliseconds) taken for the last successful LDAP binding.
LDAP Client Sessions	The number of connected LDAP client sessions.
LDAP Searches/Sec	The number of search operations per second performed by LDAP clients.

Counter	Description
LDAP Successful Binds/Sec	The number of successful LDAP binds per second.
NTLM Authentications	The number of NT LAN Manager (NTLM) authentications per second serviced by this domain controller.
XDS Client Sessions	The number of connected Extended Directory Service (XDS) client sessions. This indicates the number of connections from other Windows NT services and the Windows NT Administrator program.

Monitoring Performance Counters

You can select the performance counters to monitor and then view them graphically in the System Monitor as a chart, histogram, or log file data display.

▶ **To monitor Active Directory performance counters**

1. From the Start menu, select Programs, point to Administrative Tools, then click Performance.

2. Right-click the System Monitor details pane and click Add Counters.

3. In the Add Counters dialog box (see Figure 14.3):

   ▪ To monitor any computer on which the monitoring console is run, click Use Local Computer Counters.

   ▪ To monitor a specific computer, regardless of where the monitoring console is run, click Select Counters From Computer and select a computer name from the list (the name of the local computer is selected by default).

Figure 14.3 The Add Counters dialog box

4. In the Performance Object list, select the NTDS performance object.

Note For a description of a particular counter (see Figure 14.3), click the name of the counter from the list, then click Explain.

---

5. Select the counters to monitor.

- To monitor all counters for the NTDS performance object, click All Counters.

Note Because there are many counters, monitoring all counters will affect processing time and is not a practical solution.

- To monitor only selected counters, click Select Counters From List and select the counters you want to monitor. You can select multiple counters by clicking on a counter and holding the Ctrl key.

6. Click Add.

7. When you are finished adding counters, click Close.

The counters that you selected appear in the lower part of the screen; each counter is represented by its own color. Choose either the chart, histogram, or report display view by clicking the appropriate toolbar button.

Note When creating a System Monitor snap-in for export, make sure to select Use Local Computer Counters on the Select Counters dialog box. Otherwise, System Monitor obtains data from the computer named in the text box, regardless of where the snap-in is installed.

Performance Logs and Alerts

The Performance Logs and Alerts snap-in provides you with the ability to create counter logs, trace logs, and system alerts automatically from local or remote computers.

Counter Logs

Similar to System Monitor, counter logs support the definition of performance objects and performance counters and setting sampling intervals for monitoring data about hardware resources and system services. Counter logs collect performance counter data in a comma-separated or tab-separated format for easy import to spreadsheet or database programs. You can view logged counter data using System Monitor or export the data to a file for analysis and report generation.

Trace Logs

Using the default system data provider or another nonsystem provider, trace logs record data when certain activities such as a disk I/O operation or a page fault occur. When the event occurs, the provider sends the data to the Performance Logs and Alerts service. This differs from the operation of counter logs; when counter logs are in use, the service obtains data from the system when the update interval has elapsed, rather than waiting for a specific event.

Active Directory nonsystem providers include those for NetLogon, Kerberos, Security Accounts Manager (SAM), and Windows NT Active Directory Service. These providers generate trace log files containing messages that may be used to track the operations performed.

A parsing tool is required to interpret the trace log output. Developers can create such a tool using APIs provided on the Microsoft Developer Web site (*http://msdn.microsoft.com/*).

Logging Options

For both counter and trace logs you can

- Define start and stop times, filenames, file types, file sizes, and other parameters for automatic log generation and manage multiple logging sessions from a single console window.

- Start and stop logging either manually on demand or automatically based on a user-defined schedule.

- Configure additional settings for automatic logging, such as automatic file renaming, and set parameters for stopping and starting a log based on the elapsed time or the file size.

- Define a program that runs when a log is stopped.

- View logs during collection as well as after collection has stopped. Because logging runs as a service, data collection occurs regardless of whether any user is logged on to the computer being monitored.

Counter and Trace Logging Requirements

To create or modify a log, you must have Full Control permission for the following registry key, which controls the Performance Logs and Alerts service:

HKEY_LOCAL_MACHINE\SYSTEM\CurrentControlSet\Services\SysmonLog \Log Queries

Administrators usually have this permission by default. Administrators can grant permission to users by using the Security menu in REGEDT32.EXE.

To run the Performance Logs and Alerts service (which runs in the background when you configure a log), you must have permission to start or otherwise configure services on the system. Administrators have this right by default and can grant it to users by using group policy. To log data on a remote computer, the Performance Logs and Alerts service must run under an account that has access to the remote system.

Creating a Counter Log

To create a counter log you first define the counters you want to log and then set log file and scheduling parameters.

▶ **To create a counter log**

1. From the Start menu, select Programs, point to Administrative Tools, then click Performance.

2. Double-click Performance Logs And Alerts, then click Counter Logs.

   Any existing logs will be listed in the details pane. A green icon indicates that a log is running; a red icon indicates that a log has been stopped.

3. Right-click a blank area of the details pane, then click New Log Settings.

4. In the New Log Settings dialog box, in the Name box, type the name of the log, then click OK.

5. In the General tab of the counter log's dialog box, type the name of the path and filename of the log file in the Current Log File Name box, then click Add.

6. In the Select Counters dialog box, choose the computer for which you want to log counters.

   - To log counters from the computer on which the Performance Logs and Alerts service will run, click Use Local Computer Counters.

   - To log counters from a specific computer regardless of where the service is run, click Select Counters From Computer and select the name of the computer you want to monitor from the list.

7. In the Performance Object list, select an object to log.

8. Select the counters you want to log from the list, then click Add.

9. Click Close when you have finished selecting counters to log.

10. In the Log Files tab of the counter log's dialog box, configure the options shown in Figure 14.4 and described in Table 14.3.

Table 14.3   Options on the Log Files Tab

Option	Description
Location	The name of the folder where you want the log file created, or click Browse to search for the folder.
File Name	A partial or base name for the log file. You can use File Name in conjunction with End File Names With if appropriate. Appears on the details pane.
End File Names With	The suffix style you want from the list. Distinguish between individual log files with the same log filename that are in a group of logs that have been automatically generated.
Start Numbering At	The start number for automatic file numbering, when you select nnnnnn as the End File Names With.

Option	Description
Log File Type	The format you want for this log file: *Text File—CSV* defines a comma-delimited log file (with a .csv extension). Use this format to export the log data to a spreadsheet program. *Text File—TSV* defines a tab-delimited log file (with a .tsv extension). Use this format to export the log data to a spreadsheet program. *Binary File* defines a sequential, binary-format log file (with a .blg extension). Use this file format if you want to be able to record data instances that are intermittent—that is, stopping and resuming after the log has begun running. Nonbinary file formats cannot accommodate instances that are not persistent throughout the duration of the log. *Binary Circular File* defines a circular, binary-format log file (with a .blg extension). Use this file format to record data continuously to the same log file, overwriting previous records with new data.
Comment	A comment or description for the log file. Appears in the details pane.
Log File Size	*Maximum Limit.* Data is continuously collected in a log file until it reaches limits set by disk quotas or the operating system. *Limit Of.* The maximum size (in kilobytes, up to two gigabytes) of the log file. Select this option if you want to do circular logging.

Figure 14.4   The Log Files tab of a counter log's dialog box

11. In the Schedule tab of the counter log's dialog box, configure the options shown in Figure 14.5 and described in Table 14.4.

Table 14.4   Options on the Schedule Tab

Option	Description
Start Log	*Manually.* Logging will start manually. *At.* Logging will start according to the time and date parameters you set.
Stop Log	*Manually.* Logging will stop manually. *After.* Logging will stop after the time you specify. *At.* Logging will stop at the time and date parameters you set. *When The Log File Is Full.* Logging will stop when the log file reaches a maximum size.
When A Log File Closes	*Start A New Log File.* Logging will resume in a new file after logging stops for the current log file. *Run This Command.* A command you specify is run when a log file closes.

Figure 14.5   The Schedule tab of a counter log's dialog box

12. Click OK.

Note   When creating a Performance Logs and Alerts snap-in for export, make sure to select Use Local Computer Counters on the Select Counters dialog box. Otherwise, counter logs will obtain data from the computer named in the text box, regardless of where the snap-in is installed.

Creating a Trace Log

To create a trace log you first define how you want events logged and then set log file and scheduling parameters.

▶ **To create a trace log**

1. From the Start menu, select Programs, point to Administrative Tools, then click Performance.

2. Double-click Performance Logs And Alerts, then click Trace Logs.

   Any existing logs will be listed in the details pane. A green icon indicates that a log is running; a red icon indicates that a log has been stopped.

3. Right-click a blank area of the details pane, then click New Log Settings.

4. In the New Log Settings dialog box, in the Name box, type the name of the log, then click OK.

   In the General tab of the trace log's Properties dialog box, the name of the path and filename of the log file is shown in the Current Log File Name box. By default, the log file is created in the PerfLogs folder in the root directory, and a sequence number is appended to the filename you entered and the sequential trace file type with the .etl extension.

5. Select which events you want logged.

   - Select Events Logged By System Provider for the default provider (the Windows kernel trace provider) to monitor processes, threads, and other activity. To define events for logging, click the check boxes as appropriate. This can create some performance overhead for the system.

   - Select Nonsystem Providers to select the trace data providers you want—for example, if you have written your own providers. Use the Add or Remove buttons to select or remove nonsystem providers.

   For a list of the installed providers and their status (enabled or not), click Provider Status.

Note You can have only one trace log that uses the system provider running at a time. In addition, you cannot concurrently run multiple trace logs from the same nonsystem provider. If the system trace provider is enabled, nonsystem providers cannot be enabled, and vice versa. However, you can enable multiple nonsystem providers simultaneously.

---

6. In the Log Files tab of the trace log's Properties dialog box, configure the options as you do for counter logs, except for the options shown in Table 14.5.

Table 14.5   Trace Log-Specific Options in the Log Files Tab

Option	Description
Log File Type	The format you want for this log file: *Circular Trace File.* Defines a circular trace log file (with an .etl extension). Use this file format to record data continuously to the same log file, overwriting previous records with new data. *Sequential Trace File.* Defines a sequential trace log file (with an .etl extension) that collects data until it reaches a user-defined limit and then closes and starts a new file.
Log File Size	*Maximum Limit.* Data is continuously collected in a log file until it reaches limits set by disk quotas or the operating system. *Limit Of.* The maximum size (in megabytes) of the log file. Select this option if you want to do circular logging.

7. In the Schedule tab of the trace log's Properties dialog box, configure the options as shown for counter logs.

8. Click OK.

Note   Trace logging of file details and page faults can generate an extremely large amount of data. It is recommended that you limit trace logging using the file details and page fault options to a maximum of 2 hours.

Alerts

Similar to System Monitor and counter logs, alerts support the use of performance objects and performance counters and setting sampling intervals for monitoring data about hardware resources and system services. Using this data, you can create an alert for a counter, which logs an entry in the application event log, sends a network message to a computer, starts a performance data log, or runs a program when the selected counter's value exceeds or falls below a specified setting.

You can start or stop an alert scan either manually on demand or automatically based on a user-defined schedule.

Creating an Alert

To create an alert you first define the counters you want to monitor for the alert and then set alert triggering and scheduling parameters.

▶   **To create an alert**

1. From the Start menu, select Programs, point to Administrative Tools, then click Performance.

2. Double-click Performance Logs And Alerts, then click Alerts.

   Any existing alerts will be listed in the details pane. A green icon indicates that the alerts are running; a red icon indicates alerts have been stopped.

3. Right-click a blank area of the details pane and click New Alert Settings.

4. In the New Alert Settings dialog box, in the Name box, type the name of the alert, then click OK.

5. In the Comment box on the alert's dialog box, type a comment to describe the alert as needed, then click Add.

6. In the Select Counters dialog box, choose the computer for which you want to create an alert.

   - To create an alert on the computer on which the Performance Logs and Alerts service will run, click Use Local Computer Counters.

   - To create an alert on a specific computer regardless of where the service is run, click Select Counters From Computer and specify the name of the computer.

7. In the Performance Object list, select an object to monitor.

8. Select the counters you want to monitor, then click Add.

9. Click Close when you have finished selecting counters to monitor for the alert.

10. In the Alert When The Value Is list, specify Under or Over, and in the Limit box, specify the value that triggers the alert.

11. In the Sample Data Every section, specify the amount and the unit of measure for the update interval.

12. In the Action tab of the alert's dialog box, select when an alert is triggered as shown in Figure 14.6 and described in Table 14.6.

Table 14.6   Options on the Action Tab

Option	Description
Log An Entry In The Application Event Log	Creates an entry visible in Event Viewer
Send A Network Message To	Triggers the messenger service to send a message to the specified computer
Start Performance Data Log	Runs a specified counter log when an alert occurs
Run This Program	Triggers the service to create a process and run a specified program when an alert occurs
Command Line Arguments	Triggers the service to copy specified command-line arguments when the Run This Program option is used

13. In the Schedule tab of the alert's dialog box, configure the options as shown for counter logs.

14. Click OK.

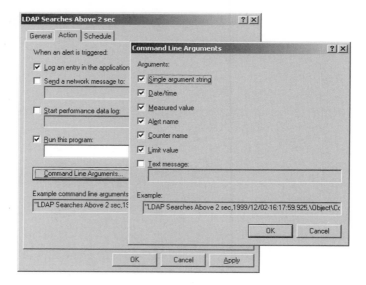

Figure 14.6   The Action tab of an alert's dialog box and the Command Line
Arguments dialog box

Practice: Using System Monitor

In this practice you monitor specified performance counters using System Monitor.
Then you use Performance Logs and Alerts to create a counter log and an alert
for the LDAP Searches/Sec counter.

Exercise 1: Monitoring Performance Counters

In this exercise you select performance counters to monitor and then view them
graphically in the System Monitor as a chart, histogram, or log file data display.

▶ **To monitor Active Directory performance counters**

1. From the Start menu, select Programs, point to Administrative Tools, then
   click Performance.

2. In the console tree, click System Monitor.

3. Right-click the System Monitor details pane and click Add Counters.

4. Click Select Counters From Computer and ensure that the name of the local
   computer is selected.

5. In the Performance Object list, select the NTDS performance object.

6. Click Select Counters From List and select the DRA Pending Replication
   Synchronizations counter to monitor, then click Add.

7. Select the LDAP Searches/Sec counter to monitor, then click Add.

8. Click Close.

The counters that you selected appear in the lower part of the screen; each counter is represented by its own color. Choose either the chart, histogram, or report display view by clicking the appropriate toolbar button.

Exercise 2: Creating a Counter Log

In this exercise you create a counter log by first defining the counters you want to log and then setting log file and scheduling parameters.

▶ **To create a counter log**

1. From the Start menu, select Programs, point to Administrative Tools, then click Performance.

2. Double-click Performance Logs And Alerts, then click Counter Logs.

3. Right-click a blank area of the details pane, then click New Log Settings.

4. In the New Log Settings dialog box, in the Name box, type **LDAP Searches Per Sec**, then click OK.

5. In the General tab of the LDAP Searches Per Sec dialog box, ensure that the default name of the path and filename of the log file in the Current Log File Name box is showing, then click Add.

6. In the Select Counters dialog box, click Select Counters From Computer and ensure that the name of the local computer is selected.

7. In the Performance Object list, select the NTDS performance object to log.

8. Select the LDAP Searches/Sec counter to log, click Add, then click Close.

9. In the Log Files tab, set the following options:

   ▪ Location: C:\PerfLogs (where C:\ is the name of your system drive)

   ▪ File Name: LDAP_Searches_Per_Sec

   ▪ End File Names With: nnnnnn

   ▪ Start Numbering At: 1

   ▪ Log File Type: Text File—CSV

   ▪ Log File Size: Maximum Limit

10. In the Schedule tab, set the following options:

    ▪ Start Log At: a time 3 minutes from now

    ▪ Stop Log After: 2 minutes

11. Click OK.

12. When the log starts in 3 minutes, open Active Directory Users and Computers, open and close various OUs and objects, then close Active Directory Users and Computers.

13. When the log has stopped, you can view the contents of the counter log by opening the file \PERFLOGS\LDAP_SEARCHES_PER_SEC_000001.CSV using a spreadsheet program such as Microsoft Excel.

Exercise 3: Creating an Alert

In this exercise you create an alert by first defining the counters you want to monitor for the alert and then setting alert triggering and scheduling parameters.

▶ **To create an alert**

1. From the Start menu, select Programs, point to Administrative Tools, then click Performance.

2. Double-click Performance Logs And Alerts, then click Alerts.

3. Right-click a blank area of the details pane and click New Alert Settings.

4. In the New Alert Settings dialog box, in the Name box, type **LDAP Searches Above 5 Sec**, then click OK.

5. In the Comment box on the alert's dialog box, type **Alerts when LDAP Searches are more than 5 per second**, then click Add.

6. In the Select Counters dialog box, click Select Counters From Computer and ensure that the name of the local computer is selected.

7. In the Performance Object list, click the NTDS performance object to monitor.

8. Select the LDAP Searches/Sec counter to monitor, click Add, then click Close.

9. In the Alert When The Value Is box, specify Over, and in Limit, specify 5.

10. In the Sample Data Every section, specify the interval of 3 seconds.

11. In the Action tab, select the Log An Entry In The Application Event Log check box.

12. In the Schedule tab, set the following options:
    - Start Scan At: a time 3 minutes from now
    - Stop Scan After: 2 minutes

13. Click OK.

15. When the log starts in 3 minutes, open Active Directory Users and Computers, open and close various OUs and objects, then close Active Directory Users and Computers.

16. When the log has stopped, you can view the alerts in the Application Log in Event Viewer. View the alert information by double-clicking the log entries.

Lesson Summary

In this lesson you learned about the Active Directory performance monitoring tools, the Event Viewer console, and the Performance console.

The Event Viewer console is a tool to monitor events such as application or system errors or the successful starting of a service. If you experience problems with

Active Directory, it is recommended that the directory service event logs be the first item that you use to investigate the causes of the problem.

The Performance console allows you to monitor conditions within local and remote computers anywhere in your network and to summarize performance at selected intervals. The Performance console contains two snap-ins: System Monitor (an ActiveX control) and Performance Logs and Alerts. With System Monitor, you can measure Active Directory performance on your own computer or other computers on a network. The Performance Logs and Alerts snap-in provides you with the ability to create counter logs, trace logs, and system alerts automatically from local or remote computers.

In the practice portion of this lesson you monitored specified performance counters using System Monitor. Then you used Performance Logs and Alerts to create a counter log and an alert for the LDAP Searches/Sec counter.

Lesson 2: Active Directory Support Tools

Some of the Windows 2000 Support Tools included on the Windows 2000 CD-ROM can help you monitor, maintain, and troubleshoot Active Directory. This lesson introduces you to the Windows 2000 Support Tools used to support Active Directory.

After this lesson, you will be able to

- Install the Windows 2000 Support Tools
- Identify the Windows 2000 Support Tools used to support Active Directory

Estimated lesson time: 10 minutes

Active Directory Support Tools

The Windows 2000 Support Tools included on the Windows 2000 CD-ROM are intended for use by Microsoft support personnel and experienced users to assist in diagnosing and resolving computer problems.

Note   See Chapter 3, "Active Directory Administration Tasks and Tools" for instructions on installing the Windows 2000 Support Tools.

The following tools are available for support of Active Directory:

- LDP.EXE: Active Directory Administration Tool
- REPLMON.EXE: Active Directory Replication Monitor
- REPADMIN.EXE: Replication Diagnostics Tool*
- DSASTAT.EXE: Active Directory Diagnostic Tool*
- SDCHECK.EXE: Security Descriptor Check Utility*
- NLTEST.EXE*
- ACLDIAG.EXE: ACL Diagnostics*
- DSACLS.EXE*

*Command-prompt-only tools

LDP.EXE: Active Directory Administration Tool

The Active Directory Administration Tool allows users to perform LDAP operations, such as connect, bind, search, modify, add, and delete, against any LDAP-compatible directory, such as Active Directory. LDAP is an Internet-standard wire protocol used by Active Directory. The Active Directory Administration Tool is a graphical tool located on the Tools menu within Windows 2000 Support Tools.

In troubleshooting, the Administration Tool can be used by administrators to view objects stored in Active Directory along with their metadata, such as security descriptors and replication metadata.

REPLMON.EXE: Active Directory Replication Monitor

The Active Directory Replication Monitor tool enables administrators to view the low-level status of Active Directory replication, force synchronization between domain controllers, view the topology in a graphical format, and monitor the status and performance of domain controller replication through a graphical interface. The Active Directory Replication Monitor is a graphical tool located on the Tools menu within Windows 2000 Support Tools.

Active Directory Replication Monitor Features

Some of the key features of the Active Directory Replication Monitor are

- **Graphic displays.**   Replication Monitor displays whether or not the monitored server is a global catalog server, automatically discovers the directory partitions that the monitored server hosts, graphically displays this breakdown, and shows the replication partners that are used for inbound replication for each directory partition. Replication Monitor distinguishes between direct replication partners, transitive replication partners, bridgehead servers, and servers removed from the network in the user interface. Failures from a specific replication partner are indicated by a change in the icon used for the partner.

- **Replication status history.**   The history of replication status per directory partition, per replication partner is recorded, generating a granular history of what occurred between two domain controllers. This history can be viewed through Replication Monitor's user interface or can be viewed offline or remotely through a text editor.

- **Property pages.**   For direct replication partners, a series of property pages displays the following for each partner: the name of the domain controller, its globally unique identifier (GUID), the directory partition that it replicates to the monitored server, the transport used (remote procedure call [RPC] or Simple Mail Transfer Protocol [SMTP] and distinguishes between intra- and inter-site when RPC is used), the time of the last successful and attempted replication events, update sequence number (USN) values, and any special properties of the connection between the two servers.

- **Status report generation.**   Administrators can generate a status report for the monitored server that includes a listing of the directory partitions for the server, the status of each replication partner (direct and transitive) for each directory partition, detail on which domain controllers the monitored server notifies when changes have been recorded, the status of any group policy objects (GPOs), the domain controllers that hold the Flexible Single Master Operations (FSMO) roles, a snapshot of the performance counters on the computer, and the registry configuration of the server (including parameters for the Knowledge Consistency Checker [KCC], Active Directory, Jet database, and LDAP). Additionally, the administrator can also choose to record (in the same report) the enterprise configuration, which includes each site, site link, site link bridge, subnet, and domain controller (regardless of domain) and the properties of each type of object just mentioned. For example, for the domain controller properties, this records the GUID that makes up the Domain Name System (DNS) record that is used in replication, the location of the computer account in Active Directory, the inter-site mail address (if it exists), the host name of the computer, and any special flags for the server (whether or not it is a global catalog server). This can be extremely helpful when troubleshooting an Active Directory replication problem.

- **Server Wizard.**   With Server Wizard, administrators can either browse for the server to monitor or explicitly enter it. The administrator can also create an .ini file, which predefines the names of the servers to monitor, which is then loaded by Replication Monitor to populate the user interface.

- **Graphical site topology.**   Replication Monitor displays a graphical view of the intra-site topology and, by using the context menu for a given domain controller in the view, allows the administrator to quickly display the properties of the server and any intra- and inter-site connections that exist for that server.

- **Properties display.**   Administrators can display the properties for the monitored server including the server name, the DNS host name of the computer, the location of the computer account in Active Directory, preferred bridgehead status, any special flags for the server (for example, if it is the Primary Domain Controller [PDC] Emulator for its domain or not), which computers it believes to hold the FSMO roles, the replication connections (Replication Monitor differentiates between administrator and automatically generated connection objects) and the reasons they were created, and the Internet Protocol (IP) configuration of the monitored server.

- **Statistics and replication state polling.**   In Automatic Update mode, Replication Monitor polls the server at an administrator-defined interval to get the current statistics and replication state. This feature generates a history of changes for each monitored server and its replication partners and allows the administrator to see topology changes as they occur for each monitored server. In this mode, Replication Monitor also monitors the count of failed replication attempts for each replication partner. If the failure count meets or exceeds an administrator-defined value, it can write to the event log and send an e-mail notification to the administrator.

- **Replication triggering.**   Administrators can trigger replication on a server with a specific replication partner, with all other domain controllers in the site, or all other domain controllers intra- and inter-site.

- **KCC triggering.**   Administrators can trigger the KCC on the monitored server to recalculate the replication topology.

- **Display nonreplicated changes.**   Administrators can display, on demand, Active Directory changes that have not yet replicated from a given replication partner.

REPADMIN.EXE: Replication Diagnostics Tool

REPADMIN.EXE is a command-line tool that assists administrators in diagnosing replication problems between Windows 2000 domain controllers.

During normal operation, the KCC automatically manages the replication topology for each naming context held on domain controllers.

REPADMIN.EXE allows the administrator to view the replication topology as seen from the perspective of each domain controller. In addition, REPADMIN.EXE can be used to manually create the replication topology (although in normal practice this should not be necessary), to force replication events between domain controllers, and to view both the replication metadata and up-to-dateness vectors.

Note   During the normal course of operations, there is no need to manually create the replication topology. Incorrect use of this tool may adversely impact the replication topology. The major use of this tool is to monitor replication so problems such as offline servers or unavailable local area network (LAN)/wide area network (WAN) connections can be identified.

DSASTAT.EXE: Active Directory Diagnostic Tool

DSASTAT.EXE is a command-line tool that compares and detects differences between naming contexts on domain controllers.

DSASTAT.EXE can be used to compare two directory trees across replicas within the same domain or, in the case of a global catalog, across different domains. The tool retrieves capacity statistics, such as MB per server, objects per server, and MB per object class, and performs comparisons of attributes of replicated objects.

The user specifies the targeted domain controllers and additional operational parameters from the command line or from an initialization file. DSASTAT.EXE determines if domain controllers in a domain have a consistent and accurate image of their own domain. In the case of global catalogs, DSASTAT.EXE checks to see if the global catalog has a consistent image with domain controllers in other domains. As a complement to the replication monitoring tools, REPADMIN.EXE and REPLMON.EXE, DSASTAT.EXE can be used to ensure that domain controllers are up to date with one another.

SDCHECK.EXE: Security Descriptor Check Utility

SDCHECK.EXE is a command-line tool that displays the security descriptor for any object stored in the Active Directory. The security descriptor contains the ACLs defining the permissions that users have on objects stored in the Active Directory.

To enable administrators to determine the effective access controls on an object, SDCHECK.EXE also displays the object hierarchy and any ACLs that are inherited by the object from its parent.

As changes are made to the ACLs of an object or its parent, they are propagated automatically by the Active Directory. SDCHECK.EXE displays the security descriptor propagation metadata so that administrators can monitor these changes with respect to propagation of inherited ACLs as well as replication of ACLs from other domain controllers.

As a compliment to the replication monitoring tools, REPADMIN.EXE, REPLMON.EXE, and SDCHECK.EXE can be used to ensure that domain controllers are up to date with one another.

NLTEST.EXE

Nltest.exe is a command-line tool that helps perform network administrative tasks such as the following:

- Testing trust relationships and the state of a domain controller replication in a Windows domain
- Querying and checking on the status of trust
- Forcing a shutdown
- Getting a list of PDCs
- Forcing a user account database into sync on Microsoft Windows NT 4.0 or earlier domain controllers (Windows 2000 domain controllers use a completely different mechanism for maintaining user accounts)

NLTEST.EXE runs only on x86-based computers.

ACLDIAG.EXE: ACL Diagnostics

ACLDIAG.EXE is a command-line tool that helps diagnose and troubleshoot problems with permissions on Active Directory objects. It reads security attributes from ACLs and outputs information in either readable or tab-delimited format. The latter can be uploaded into a text file for searches on particular permissions, users, or groups, or into a spreadsheet or database for reporting. The tool also provides some simple cleanup functionality.

With ACLDIAG.EXE, you can

- Compare the ACL on a directory services object to the permissions defined in the schema defaults
- Check or fix standard delegations performed using templates from the Delegation of Control Wizard in the Active Directory Users and Computers console
- Get effective permissions granted to a specific user or group or to all users and groups that show up in the ACL

ACLDIAG.EXE displays only the permissions of objects the user has the right to view. Because GPOs are virtual objects that have no distinguished name, this tool cannot be used on them.

For general-purpose ACL reporting and setting from the command prompt, you can also use DSACLS.EXE, another Windows 2000 Support tool.

DSACLS.EXE

DSACLS.EXE is a command-line tool that facilitates management of ACLs for directory services. DSACLS.EXE enables you to query and manipulate security attributes on Active Directory objects. It is the command-line equivalent of the Security page on various Active Directory snap-in tools.

Along with ACLDIAG.EXE, another Windows 2000 Support tool, DSACLS.EXE provides security configuration and diagnosis functionality on Active Directory objects from the command prompt.

Lesson Summary

In this lesson you were introduced to the Windows 2000 Support Tools that support Active Directory.

Lesson 3: Monitoring Access to Shared Folders

Microsoft Windows 2000 includes the Shared Folders snap-in so that you can easily monitor access to network resources and send administrative messages to users. You monitor access to network resources to assess and manage current usage on network servers.

After this lesson, you will be able to

- Identify the tool included with Windows 2000 to monitor access to network resources and to send administrative messages
- Identify who can monitor access to network resources
- Determine the shared folders on a computer
- Monitor shared folders
- Monitor open files
- Disconnect users from one or all open files

Estimated lesson time: 20 minutes

Why Monitor Network Resources?

Some of the reasons it is important to assess and manage network resources are the following:

- **Maintenance.**   You should determine which users are currently using a resource so that you can notify them before making the resource temporarily or permanently unavailable.
- **Security.**   You should monitor user access to resources that are confidential or need to be secure to verify that only authorized users are accessing them.
- **Planning.**   You should determine which resources are being used and how much they are being used so that you can plan for future system growth.

Microsoft Windows 2000 includes the Shared Folders snap-in so that you can easily monitor access to network resources and send administrative messages to users. The Shared Folders snap-in is preconfigured in the Computer Management console, allowing you to monitor resources on the local computer. If you add the Shared Folders snap-in to an MMC, you can specify whether you want to monitor the resources on the local computer or a remote computer.

Network Resource Monitoring Requirements

Not all users can monitor access to network resources. Table 14.7 lists the group membership requirements for monitoring access to network resources.

Table 14.7   Groups that Can Access Network Resources

A Member of These Groups	Can Monitor
Administrators or Server Operators for the domain	All computers in the domain
Administrators or Power Users for a member server, stand-alone server, or computer running Microsoft Windows 2000 Workstation	That computer

Monitoring Access to Shared Folders

You use the Shares folder in the Shared Folders snap-in to view a list of all shared folders on the computer and to determine how many users have a connection to each folder. In Figure 14.7, the Shares folder has been selected in the Computer Management console tree and all the shared folders on that computer are shown in the details pane.

Figure 14.7   The Shares folder of the Shared Folders snap-in

Table 14.8 explains the information provided in the details pane shown in Figure 14.7.

Table 14.8   Fields in the Details Pane for the Shares Folder

Column Name	Description
Shared Folder	The name of the shared folders on the computer.
Shared Path	The path to the shared folder.
Type	The operating system that must be running on a computer so that it can be used to gain access to the shared folder.
# Client Redirections	The number of clients who have made a remote connection to the shared folder.
Comment	Descriptive text about the folder. This comment was provided when the folder was shared.

Note Windows 2000 does not update the list of shared folders, open files, and user sessions automatically. To update these lists, on the Action menu, click Refresh.

Determining How Many Users Can Access a Shared Folder Concurrently

You can use the Shared Folders snap-in to determine the maximum number of users that are permitted to gain access to a folder. In the Shared Folders details pane, click the shared folder for which you want to determine the maximum number of concurrent users that can access the folder. On the Action menu, click Properties, and the Properties dialog box for the shared folder appears. The General tab shows you the user limit.

You can also use the Shared Folders snap-in to determine if the maximum number of users that are permitted to gain access to a folder has been reached. This is an easy way to troubleshoot connectivity problems. If a user cannot connect to a share, determine the number of connections to the share and the maximum connections allowed. If the maximum number of connections has already been made, the user cannot connect to the shared resource.

Modifying Shared Folder Properties

You can modify existing shared folders, including shared folder permissions, from the Shares folder. To change a shared folder's properties, click the shared folder, and then on the Action menu, click Properties. The General tab of the Properties dialog box shows you the share name, the path to the shared folder, and any comment that has been entered. The General tab also allows you to view and set a user limit for accessing the shared folder. The Security tab allows you to view and change the shared folders permissions.

Monitoring Open Files

Use the Open Files folder in the Shared Folders snap-in to view a list of open files that are located in shared folders and the users who have a current connection to each file (see Figure 14.8). You can use this information when you need to contact users to notify them that you are shutting down the system. Additionally, you can determine which users have a current connection and should be contacted when another user is trying to gain access to a file that is in use.

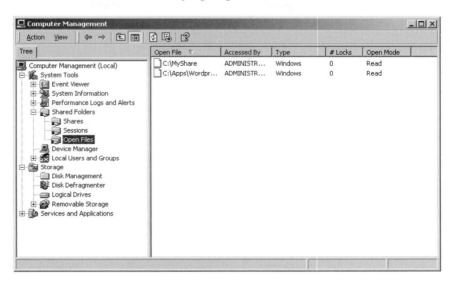

Figure 14.8   The Open Files folder of the Shared Folders snap-in

Table 14.9 describes the information that is available in the Open Files folder.

Table 14.9   Information Available in the Open Files Folder

Column Name	Description
Open File	The name of the open files on the computer.
Accessed By	The logon name of the user who has the file open.
Type	The operating system running on the computer where the user is logged on.
# Locks	The number of locks on the file. Programs can request the operating system to lock a file to gain exclusive access and prevent other programs from making changes to the file.
Open Mode	The type of access that the user's application requested when it opened the file, such as Read or Write.

Disconnecting Users from Open Files

You can disconnect users from one open file or from all open files. If you make changes to Windows NT file system (NTFS) permissions for a file that is currently opened by a user, the new permissions will not affect the user until he or she closes and then attempts to reopen the file.

You can force these changes to take place immediately by doing either of the following:

- Disconnecting all users from all open files. To disconnect all users from all open files, in the Shared Folders snap-in console tree, click Open Files, and then on the Action menu, click Disconnect All Open Files.
- Disconnecting all users from one open file. To disconnect users from one open file, in the Shared Folders snap-in console tree, click Open Files. In the details pane select the open file, and then on the Action menu, click Close Open File.

Caution   Disconnecting users from open files can result in data loss.

Sending Console Messages

To avoid data loss, you can send a message to some or all users who have an active session with the shared folders that you are managing.

▶ **To send a console message to a connected user**

1. Click the Shared Folders snap-in, click the Action menu, select All Tasks, then click Send Console Message.
2. In the Send Console Message dialog box, type the message you want to send to users in the Message box.
3. Select the computer name that will receive the message in the Recipients box, then click Send.

   If a user is logged on to more than one computer, only the computer that has its name in the recipient list will receive the message.

   If any recipients do not successfully receive the message, you are returned to the Send Console Message dialog box. Recipients that did not successfully receive the message are the only computer names remaining in the list. You should check to see if the computer names are valid or if the computers are unavailable.

Practice: Managing Shared Folders

In this practice you use the Shared Folders snap-in to view the shared folders and open files on your server. You will disconnect all users from all open files.

▶ **To view the shared folders on your computer**

1. Click Start, point to Programs, point to Administrative Tools, then click Computer Management.
2. In the console tree of Computer Management, expand System Tools, then expand Shared Folders.

3. In the console tree, click Shares under Shared Folders.

Notice that the details pane shows a list of the existing Shared Folders on your computer.

▶ **To view the open files on your computer**

1. In the console tree, click Open Files under Shared Folders.

If you are working on a computer that is not connected to a network, there will not be any open files because the open files only show connections from a remote computer to a share on your computer.

▶ **To disconnect all users from open files on your computer**

1. In the console tree, select Open Files under Shared Folders, then click Disconnect All Open Files on the Action menu.

If you are not on a network, there will not be any open files to disconnect.

2. Close Computer Management.

Lesson Summary

In this lesson you learned that Windows 2000 includes the Shared Folders snap-in so that you can monitor access to network resources. You can monitor resources on the local computer or on a remote computer. To monitor resources on a remote computer, you specify the computer on which you want to monitor resources when you add the Shared Folders snap-in to an MMC console.

You also learned that you use the Shares folder in the Shared Folders snap-in to view a list of all shared folders on the computer and to determine how many users have a connection to each folder. The General tab of the Properties page for a shared folder shows you the user limit, or maximum number of users that can concurrently connect to that share. You use the Open Files folder in the Shared Folders snap-in to view a list of open files that are located in shared folders and the users who have a current connection to each file.

In the practice portion of this lesson you viewed the shared folders and open files on your server and disconnected all users from all open files.

Review

The following questions are intended to reinforce key information presented in the chapter. If you are unable to answer a question, review the appropriate lesson and then try the question again. Answers to the questions can be found in Appendix A, "Questions and Answers."

1. If you experience problems with Active Directory, what item should you investigate first?

2. What is the difference between a performance object and a performance counter?

3. What is the difference between a counter log and a trace log?

4. What actions can be triggered by an alert?

5. What does the Active Directory Replication Monitor support tool allow an administrator to do and how is this tool accessed?

6. If you want to find out which files are open in a shared folder and the users who have a current connection to those files, what action should you take?

C H A P T E R   1 5

Deploying Windows 2000 Using RIS

About This Chapter

Using Remote Installation Services (RIS), you can set up new client computers remotely without the need to physically visit each client machine. Specifically, you can install operating systems (OSs) on remote boot-enabled client computers by connecting the computer to the network, starting the client computer, and logging on with a valid user account. This chapter introduces you to RIS. Procedures walk you through the steps for implementing and administering RIS. Finally, this chapter provides answers to frequently asked RIS questions and troubleshooting problems.

Before You Begin

There are no special requirements to complete this chapter.

Lesson 1: RIS Overview

This lesson provides an overview of the RIS architecture, components, and Microsoft Windows 2000 services that are required to take advantage of the Remote OS Installation feature. This lesson also describes the client components and services that are required to implement Remote OS Installation in your organization.

After this lesson, you will be able to

- Identify the services and components that make up the Remote OS Installation feature
- Explain how the Remote OS Installation process works
- Identify RIS server and client requirements
- Identify network cards supported by RIS boot disk

Estimated lesson time: 20 minutes

Remote OS Installation Overview

Figure 15.1 illustrates the services and components that make up the Remote OS Installation feature.

Figure 15.1   Remote OS Installation

Remote OS Installation uses some of the existing services that may already be deployed and in use within your organization and it adds some services that you may or may not be familiar with. Remote OS Installation requires Active Directory, an updated Dynamic Host Configuration Protocol (DHCP) server, and a compliant version of DNS.

Remote Install Server Components

When RIS is installed, these additional services are added to the server:

- **Boot Information Negotiation Layer (BINL).**   The BINL service is added during the RIS installation process and provides overall management of the RIS environment. The BINL service is responsible for answering client computer network service requests, querying Active Directory on behalf of the client computer, and ensuring that the correct policy and configuration settings are applied to the client computer during the OS installation. The BINL service makes sure the client is passed the correct files and, in the case of a prestaged client, makes sure it is serviced by the correct RIS server. If the client computer has not been prestaged, BINL creates the client computer account object within Active Directory.

- **Trivial File Transfer Protocol Daemon (TFTPD).**   This server-side TFTP service is responsible for hosting specific file download requests made by the client computer. The TFTPD service is used to download the Client Installation Wizard (CIW) and all client dialog boxes contained within the CIW for a given session.

- **Single Instance Store (SIS).**   SIS is the service responsible for reducing disk space requirements on the volumes used for storing RIS installation images. When you install RIS as an optional component, you are prompted for a drive and directory where you would like to install RIS, known as the RIS volume. The SIS service attaches itself to the RIS volume and looks for any duplicate files that are placed on that volume. If duplicate files are found, SIS creates a link to the duplicates, thus reducing the disk space required.

Remote Install Client Components

There are two types of remote boot-enabled client computers:

- Computers with Pre-Boot eXecution Environment (PXE) DHCP-based remote boot ROMS

- Computers with network cards supported by the RIS Boot Disk

PXE Remote Boot Technology

Remote OS Installation uses the new PXE DHCP-based remote boot technology to initiate the installation of an OS from a remote source to a client hard disk. The remote source—a server that supports RIS—provides the network equivalent of a CD-based installation of Windows 2000 Professional or a preconfigured Remote Installation Preparation (RIPrep) desktop image. The Windows 2000 Professional OS is currently the only installation option supported by RIS.

- **CD-based installation.**   The CD-based option is similar to setting up a workstation directly from the Windows 2000 Professional CD-ROM; however, the source files reside across the network on available RIS servers.

- **RIPrep image format.** The RIPrep imaging option allows a network administrator to clone a standard corporate desktop configuration, complete with OS configurations, desktop customizations, and locally installed applications. After first installing and configuring the Windows 2000 Professional OS, its services, and any standard applications on a computer, the network administrator runs a wizard that prepares the installation image and replicates it to an available RIS server on the network for installation on other clients.

Once the images have been posted on the RIS server(s), end users equipped with PXE-based remote boot-enabled client computers can request to install those images from any available RIS server on the network. The fact that the user can install the OS without administrator assistance means the administrator is free to complete other tasks requiring his or her attention, thus saving both the time and expense normally associated with OS installations.

How the PXE Remote Boot Technology Works

PXE is a new form of remote boot technology that has been created within the computing industry. PXE provides companies with the ability to use their existing Transmission Control Protocol/Internet Protocol (TCP/IP) network infrastructure with DHCP to discover RIS servers on the network. Net PC/PC98-compliant systems can take advantage of the remote boot technology included in the Windows 2000 OS. Net PC/PC98 refers to the annual guide for hardware developers co-authored by Microsoft with Intel, including contributions from Compaq and other industry hardware manufacturers. PC98 is intended to provide standards for hardware development that advance the PC platform and enable Microsoft to include advanced features, like RIS, in the Windows platform.

Figure 15.2 describes the step-by-step process the PXE remote boot ROM goes through during every network service boot request.

When a PXE-enabled client computer is turned on, the PXE-based ROM requests an IP address from a DHCP server using the normal DHCP discovery process. As part of the initial DHCP discover request, the client computer identifies itself as being PXE-enabled, which indicates to the RIS servers on the network that it is looking to be serviced. Any available RIS server on the network can respond by providing the client with its IP address and the name of a boot file the client should request if that client wants service from that server. When the client computer responds to the server indicating that it wants service, the DHCP service sends a message granting service. The client must also request service from the BINL service, which then passes the bootstrap file to the client and ensures that prestaged clients are serviced by the correct RIS server.

After the network bootstrap program is sent to the client by the BINL service, the client-side experience will be different, depending on the remote installation server vendor that is responding to the client request for service. The following section details the implementation of Remote OS Installation that is included in the Windows 2000 Server OS.

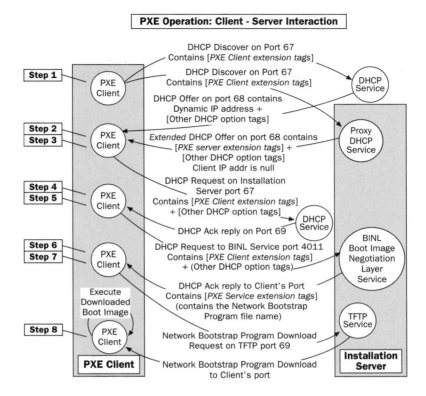

Figure 15.2   PXE remote boot ROM boot process

The RIS Boot Disk

For computers that do not contain a PXE-based remote boot ROM, Windows 2000 provides the administrator with a tool to create a remote boot disk for use with RIS. The RIS remote boot disk can be used with a variety of Peripheral Component Interconnect (PCI)-based network adapter cards. Using the RIS boot disk eliminates the need to retrofit existing client computers with new network cards that contain a PXE-based remote boot ROM to take advantage of the Remote OS Installation feature. The RIS boot disk simulates the PXE remote boot sequence and supports frequently used network cards.

How the Remote OS Installation Process Works

A graphical representation of how the Remote OS Installation process works is shown in Figure 15.3. The process is the same for both the PXE remote boot ROM and the RIS boot disk boot processes. Each step of the process is then discussed in detail.

The process of contacting an RIS server and selecting an OS image is accomplished in a few steps. The following steps outline the sequence of events when a PXE-enabled client computer starts on the network and is serviced by an RIS server.

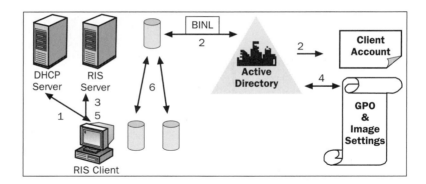

Figure 15.3   RIS architecture

The Remote OS Installation Process

1. An RIS client connected to the network starts, and during the power up, the computer initiates a network service request. As part of the network service request, a DHCP discover packet is sent to the network requesting an IP address from the closest DHCP server, the IP address of an available RIS server. As part of that request, the client sends its globally unique identifier (GUID). The GUID is present in client computers that are PC98- or Net PC-compliant and is found in the system basic input/output system (BIOS) of the computer. The DHCP server responds to the request by providing an IP address to the client. Any available RIS server can respond with its IP address and the name of the boot file the client should request if the client selects that RIS server for service. The user is prompted to press the F12 key to initiate service from that RIS server.

2. The RIS server (using the BINL service) must check in Active Directory for the existence of a prestaged client computer account that matches this client computer. BINL checks for the existence of a client computer by querying Active Directory for a client computer that matches the GUID sent in Step 1.

3. Once the RIS server has checked for the existence of a client computer account, the CIW is downloaded to the client computer. It prompts the user to log on to the network.

4. Once the user logs on, the RIS server checks Active Directory for a corresponding user account, verifying the password. RIS then checks the RIS-specific group policy settings to find out which installation options the user should have access to. RIS also checks to see which OS images the specific user should be offered. The CIW makes those options available to the client (see Figure 15.4).

5. If the user is only allowed a single installation option and OS choice, the user is not prompted to select anything. If the user has more than one installation option and OS image available to him or her for installation, the list of images is displayed for selection. The CIW warns the user that the installation will reformat his or her hard disk and previously stored information will be deleted, and then prompts the user to start the Remote OS Installation.

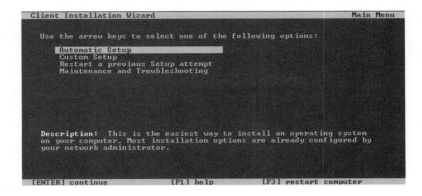

Figure 15.4 CIW installation options

Note   To configure the setup options displayed to users in the CIW, see Lesson 2, "Implementing RIS," for more information.

6. Once the user confirms the installation settings on the summary screen, the OS installation begins. At this point, if a client computer account was not present in Active Directory, the BINL service creates the client computer account, thus automatically providing a name for the computer. The OS is installed locally as an unattended installation, which means the end user is not offered any installation choices during the OS installation phase.

Important   Because the CIW is running in a preboot execution environment, there is no support for extended characters in either the text displayed or the input fields (user name, password, domain, or any custom input parameters). Careful consideration should be taken before creating user or domain names that contain extended characters because they will be not be usable with RIS.

The Remote OS Installation process is straightforward from an end user perspective. The administrator can guide the user through a successful OS installation by predetermining the installation options, if any, an end user has access to. The administrator can also restrict the OS image or images a user has access to, thus ensuring the correct OS installation type is offered to the user for a successful installation.

RIS Server and Client Requirements

Server hardware requirements:

- Pentium or Pentium II 166 MHz (200 MHz or faster processor recommended)
- 64 megabytes (MB) of RAM (96 to 128 MB if additional services such as Active Directory, DHCP, and DNS are installed)

- 2 gigabyte (GB) minimum hard disk or partition dedicated to the RIS directory tree. RIS requires a significant amount of disk space.
- 10 or 100 megabits per second (mbps) network adapter card (100 mbps preferred)

Important   A separate partition from the system's boot partition is required to install the RIS. RIS cannot be installed on the same drive as the system volume. The volume you choose to install RIS onto must be formatted with the Windows NT file system (NTFS).

Server Software Requirements

The following services can be installed either on individual servers or on the same server and must be active and available:

- DNS
- DHCP
- Active Directory

Note   For information on the installation and configuration of DHCP, see Appendix B, "Installing and Configuring the DHCP Service."

Client Hardware Requirements

- Pentium 166 MHz or faster processor Net PC client computer
- 32 MB RAM minimum (64 MB recommended)
- 800 MB hard disk drive
- Supported PCI Plug and Play network adapter card
- Optional: PXE-based remote boot ROM version .99c or later

Network Cards Supported by RIS Boot Disk

The RIS boot disk supports the following network card models. You can also run the RBFG utility at the command prompt, then select Adapter List to see a list of supported network cards.

3Com Network Adapters:

- 3C900 (Combo and TP0)
- 3C900B (Combo, FL, TPC, TP0)
- 3C905 (T4 and TX)
- 3C905B (Combo, TX, FX)
- 3C905C (TX)

AMD Network Adapters:

- AMD PCNet and Fast PCNet

Compaq Network Adapters:

- Netflex 100 (NetIntelligent II)
- Netflex 110 (NetIntelligent III)
- Netflex 3

Digital Equipment Corp (DEC) Network Adapters:

- DE 450
- DE 500

Hewlett-Packard Network Adapters:

- HP Deskdirect 10/100 TX

Intel Corporation Network Adapters:

- Intel Pro 10+
- Intel Pro 100+
- Intel Pro 100B (including the E100 series)

SMC Network Adapters:

- SMC 8432
- SMC 9332
- SMC 9432

Note   The RIS boot disk generator only supports PCI-based network cards. Industry Standard Architecture (ISA), Extended Industry Standard Architecture (EISA), and token ring cards are not supported.

Lesson Summary

In this lesson you learned about RIS architecture and the Windows 2000 services that are required to take advantage of the Remote OS Installation feature. You also learned about the server and client components and services that are required to implement Remote OS Installation in your organization.

Lesson 2: Implementing RIS

This section discusses the tasks necessary to implement RIS, including setting up and configuring RIS, creating an RIPrep image, creating an RIS boot disk, and verifying an RIS configuration.

After this lesson, you will be able to

- Set up RIS
- Configure RIS
- Create an RIPrep image
- Create an RIS boot disk
- Verify an RIS configuration

Estimated lesson time: 30 minutes

Implementing RIS

To implement RIS you must complete the following tasks:

- Set up RIS
- Configure RIS
- Create an RIPrep image
- Create an RIS boot disk (optional)
- Verify the RIS configuration

Setting Up RIS

RIS requires a two-stage setup process: adding the RIS component and installing RIS.

Important   Refer to the "RIS Server and Client Requirements" section in Lesson 1 before attempting to set up RIS.

Adding the RIS Component

The first stage of RIS setup occurs when RIS is added as an optional component. This stage copies the files required for installation to the hard disk drive on the server. You can add the RIS component during Windows 2000 Server installation or after the server installation by using Add/Remove Programs.

▶ **To add the RIS component**

1. Access the Windows Components Wizard in one of the following ways:
   - During Windows 2000 Server installation

- Click Start, point to Settings, point to Control Panel, open Add/Remove Programs, then click Add/Remove Windows Components

2. In the Windows Components Wizard dialog box, shown in Figure 15.5, select the Remote Installation Services check box, then click Next.

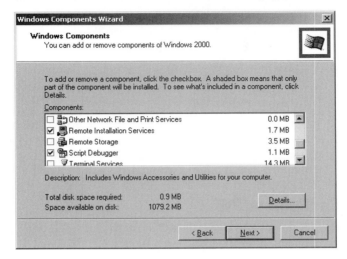

Figure 15.5   Windows Components Wizard dialog box

3. Insert the Windows 2000 Server CD-ROM when prompted.

4. On the Completing The Windows Components Wizard page, click Finish.

5. In the System Settings Change message box, click Yes to restart the server before installing RIS.

Installing RIS

The second stage of RIS setup occurs when RIS is installed. This stage installs RIS on the server.

▶ **To install RIS**

1. Click Start, point to Programs, point to Administrative Tools, then click Configure Your Server.

2. In the Configure Your Server dialog box, click Finish Setup.

3. In the Add/Remove Programs dialog box, in the Configure Remote Installation Services box, click Configure to start the Remote Installation Services Setup Wizard.

4. In the Welcome To The Remote Installation Services Setup Wizard dialog box, click Next.

5. Continue through the prompts provided by the Remote Installation Services Setup Wizard, including:

- A location on the server where the RIS folder will be created

- Whether the RIS server should begin servicing client computers immediately after completing setup

- The location of the Windows 2000 Professional CD-ROM or a location on the network that contains the installation files

- A location on the server where image installation files will be copied

- A friendly description and associated help text that describes the OS image to users of the CIW

After the Remote Installation Services Setup Wizard completes, depending on the settings chosen, the RIS server either begins servicing client computers or pauses while you set RIS configuration options. The next section describes the configuration options available to an RIS administrator.

Configuring RIS

By default, an RIS server is not configured to begin servicing client computers immediately after the installation of RIS is completed. To configure RIS you must complete the following tasks:

- Authorize RIS servers
- Set RIS server properties
- Set RIS client installation options
- Set RIPrep image permissions

Authorizing RIS Servers

By specifying the RIS servers allowed to run on your network, you can prevent unauthorized (often referred to as *rogue*) RIS servers, ensuring that only RIS servers authorized by administrators can service clients. If an attempt is made to start an unauthorized RIS server on the network, it will be automatically shut down and thus unable to service client computers. An RIS server must be authorized before it can service client computers.

▶ **To authorize RIS servers**

1. Click Start, point to Programs, point to Administrative Tools, then click DHCP.

2. In the DHCP console tree, click the DHCP node.

3. On the Action menu, click Manage Authorized Servers.

4. In the Manage Authorized Servers dialog box, click Authorize.

5. In the Authorize DHCP Server dialog box, type the name or IP address of the RIS server to be authorized, then click OK.

6. In the DHCP message box, click Yes.

7. In the Manage Authorized Servers dialog box, select the computer, then click OK.

The authorized RIS server is now listed under the DHCP node.

Setting RIS Server Properties

By setting properties on individual RIS servers, you control how the server supplies RIS to clients requesting service.

▶ **To set RIS server properties**

1. Click Start, point to Programs, point to Administrative Tools, then click Active Directory Users And Computers.

2. In the console tree, click the folder that contains the computer whose configuration you want to verify, such as Computers or Domain Controllers.

3. In the details pane, right-click the applicable RIS server, then click Properties.

4. In the Properties dialog box for the server, click the Remote Install tab.

5. In the Remote Install tab (see Figure 15.6) of the Properties dialog box, set the options described in Table 15.1.

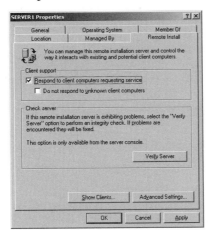

Figure 15.6   Remote Install tab

Table 15.1   Options on the Remote Install Tab of the Properties Dialog Box

Configuration Option	Description
Respond To Client Computers Requesting Service	The RIS server responds to all clients requesting service.
Do Not Respond To Unknown Client Computers	The RIS server does not respond to unknown client computers. This option is available only if the Respond To Client Computers Requesting Service check box is checked.

5. In the Remote Install tab, click Advanced Settings.

6. In the Remote Installation Services Properties dialog box for the server, in the New Clients tab (see Figure 15.7), set the options described in Table 15.2.

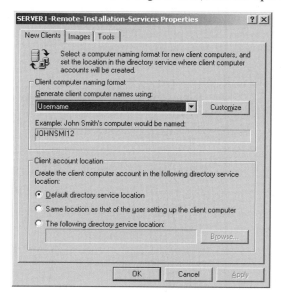

Figure 15.7   New Clients tab on the Remote Installation Services Properties dialog box

Table 15.2   **Options on the New Clients Tab of the Remote Installation Services Dialog Box**

Configuration Option	Description
Generate Client Computer Names Using	When the client computer name is automatically generated, this option determines how the name is formatted. Provides flexibility in naming new client computers during OS installation without the need for end user or administrator involvement.
Customize	Accesses the Computer Account Generation dialog box on which you can create a custom naming format for the client computer.
Client Account Location	The directory service location of the client computer account, either: *Default Directory Service Location.* Specifies that the computer account object for the client computer be created in the Active Directory location where all computer accounts are created by default during the domain join operation. *Same Location As That Of The User Setting Up The Client Computer.* Specifies that the client computer account object be created within the same Active Directory container as the user setting up the machine.

Configuration Option	Description
Client Account Location *(continued)*	*Use The Following Directory Service Location.* Allows the administrator to set a specific Active Directory container where all client computer account objects installing from this server are created. It is assumed that most administrators will select this option and specify a specific container for all remote installation client computer account objects to be created in.

7. In the Remote Installation Services Properties dialog box for the server, in the Images tab (see Figure 15.8), view the images installed on the RIS server. Click Add and follow the directions in the wizard to install additional images on the RIS server. Refer to Lesson 3, "Administering RIS," for details.

Figure 15.8   Images tab on the Remote Installation Services Properties dialog box

8. In the Remote Installation Services Properties dialog box for the server, in the Tools tab (see Figure 15.9), view the maintenance and troubleshooting tools installed on the RIS server.

9. In the Remote Installation Services Properties dialog box, click OK.

10. In the Properties dialog box for the server, click OK.

Administrators wishing to remotely manage their servers from Windows 2000 Professional workstations can access the administrative tools by installing the Windows 2000 Administration Tools package located on the Windows 2000 Server CD-ROM.

Figure 15.9   Tools tab on the Remote Installation Services Properties dialog box

Note   When using Windows 2000 Administration Tools on a system other than the RIS server, the administrator cannot add additional OS images or verify the integrity of the RIS server. All other configuration options are available.

Setting RIS Client Installation Options

By setting the RIS client installation options, you can control the options presented to different groups of users during the CIW. There are four client installation options (see Figure 15.4) that can appear on the CIW:

- Automatic Setup
- Custom Setup
- Restart A Previous Setup Attempt
- Maintenance And Troubleshooting

Automatic Setup

The Automatic Setup option is the client installation option that all users of the Remote OS Installation feature have access to by default. The Automatic Setup option allows you to restrict the OS installation options so that that the user simply logs on and the OS installation starts automatically. The user is not prompted during the OS install, which avoids calls to help desk professionals for assistance and saves the organization additional expenses in support costs.

While restricting installation options, you can still allow users to choose the OS for installation. Remote OS Installation allows you to provide a friendly description and associated help text that describes the OS options so that an end user can choose the most appropriate OS.

By preselecting the Remote OS Installation configuration options, you predefine the automatic machine naming format and the location within Active Directory where client computer accounts will be created.

Custom Setup

The Custom Setup option is very similar to the Automatic Setup option, yet it provides you with the ability to set up a computer for another person within the organization. This option can be used to fully preinstall a client computer or to prestage the client computer by creating a corresponding computer account within the Active Directory service.

The Custom Setup option lets you override the automatic computer naming and location where the computer account is created within Active Directory. By default, the RIS server will generate a computer name based on a format defined by the Remote OS Installation administrator. You can also define where client computer account objects (CAO) will be created in the Active Directory service during the installation. By default, the automatic computer naming policy is set to create computer names based on the person who logs on to the CIW.

Restart A Previous Setup Attempt

The Restart A Previous Setup Attempt option is provided in the event that the installation of the OS fails for any reason. The CIW can be customized to ask a series of questions about the specific OS being installed. When restarting a failed OS setup attempt, the end user is not asked these questions again. Rather, Setup already has this information and simply restarts the file copy operation and completes the OS installation.

Maintenance And Troubleshooting

The Maintenance And Troubleshooting option provides access to third-party hardware and software vendor tools. These tools range from system BIOS flash updates and memory virus scanners to a wide range of computer diagnostic tools that check for hardware-related problems. These tools are available before installing and starting the OS on the client computer.

If the option to display the Maintenance And Troubleshooting menu is enabled, user access to individual tool images is controlled in the same way as OS options, by setting specific end user permissions on the individual answer file (.sif) for that tool. For example, you can allow end users access to only one computer diagnostic tool, yet provide help desk professionals with access to the entire suite of diagnostic tools. When the user calls a help desk professional for assistance, the professional can guide him or her through the diagnostic tool for retrieval of information necessary to diagnose the problem being encountered. If the help desk staff must visit the end user for further investigation, they simply log on to the CIW and, based on their credentials, they can access the tools they need to resolve the problem.

▶ **To set client installation options**

1. Click Start, point to Programs, point to Administrative Tools, then click Active Directory Users And Computers.

2. In the console tree, right-click the applicable OU, such as Computers or Domain Controllers, click Properties, then click the Group Policy tab.

3. In the Properties dialog box for the group policy, click the group policy object (GPO), then click Edit to start group policy.

4. In the Group Policy console tree, click User Configuration, open Windows Settings, then click Remote Installation Services.

5. Double-click the Choice Options object.

   In the Choice Options Properties dialog box (see Figure 15.10), the following installation options affect how the CIW appears to users:

   ▪ Automatic Setup

   ▪ Custom Setup

   ▪ Restart Setup

   ▪ Tools

Figure 15.10 Choice Options Properties dialog box

6. Click one of the following group policy options for each installation option:

- **Allow.** Use this policy option to offer the installation option to users to which this policy applies.

- **Don't Care.** Use this policy option to accept the policy settings of the parent container. For example, if the administrator for the entire domain has set group policy that is specific to RIS, and the administrator of this container has chosen the Don't Care option, the policy that is set on the domain is applied to all users that are affected by that policy. Don't Care is the default setting.

- **Deny.** Use this policy option to deny the users that are affected by this policy access to the installation option.

7. In the Choice Options Properties dialog box, click OK.

8. Close the Group Policy snap-in, and then, in the Properties dialog box for the group policy, click OK.

Note Because the changes that you make to RIS policy take effect only when the policy is propagated (applied) to your computer, do one of the following to initiate policy propagation:

- Type **secedit /refreshpolicy user_policy** at the command prompt, then press Enter.

- Restart your computer.

- Wait for automatic policy propagation, which occurs at regular, configurable intervals. By default, policy propagation occurs every 90 minutes for Windows 2000–based computers, and every 5 minutes for the domain controller.

Setting RIPrep Image Permissions

By specifying which users or groups of users should have access to the RIPrep OS images available on the RIS server, you can guide users through the selection of the unattended OS installation appropriate for their role within the company. By default, when an OS image is added to an RIS server, the image will be available to all users serviced by that RIS server.

▶ **To set RIPrep image permissions**

1. Click Start, point to Programs, point to Accessories, then click Windows Explorer.

2. In the \RemoteInstall\Setup*applicable_language*\Images*applicable_image_name*\i386\templates folder (or the location on the server where you chose to copy image installation files), right-click the appropriate .sif file, then click Properties.

3. In the Properties dialog box for the file, click the Security tab.

4. Set the appropriate permissions to allow users access to images and click OK.

Note   To reduce the work involved in maintaining the security applied to images, where possible, set the security on the Templates folder of the image rather than the individual .sif files. Grant or restrict access to groups rather than individual users.

Create an RIPrep Image

To build and maintain standard desktops, many organizations use disk imaging or cloning software that allows you to configure a client computer exactly how you want it, and then make a copy of that image for installation on client computers on the network. Remote OS Installation supports creation and installation of standard desktop images using RIPrep images.

Before you can create an RIPrep image, you must complete the following tasks:

- Create the source computer
- Configure the workstation

Creating the Source Computer

To create the source computer, use the Remote OS Installation feature to remotely install the base Windows 2000 Professional OS. Once the OS is installed, you can install applications or application suites including in-house line of business (LOB) applications. Then configure the workstation to adhere to company policies. For example, you may choose to define specific screen colors, set the background bitmap to a company-based logo, remove any games installed by the base OS, and set Internet Explorer proxy settings.

Configuring the Workstation

When creating RIPrep images, it is important to understand the relationship of user profiles, the changes made to an RIPrep source computer, and the desired result for users that log on to computers that are installed using the RIPrep image. Applications that carry the "Certified for Windows" logo properly separate user-specific and computer-specific configuration settings and data, and can therefore be installed computer-wide so that they are available to all users of the system. Such applications would also then be available to all users of systems later installed with the resulting RIPrep image. Non-Windows 2000-compliant applications may perform and/or rely on per-user configurations that are specific to the profile of the user actually installing the application prior to running RIPrep (typically a local administrator), rather than to all users of the system. Such configurations remain specific to that user, which may result in the application or configuration setting not being available or not functioning properly for users of computers installed with the RIPrep image. In addition, some non-application configuration changes, such as the wallpaper specified for the user desktop, are by default applied only to the current user's profile and will not be applied to users of systems installed with the RIPrep image.

You must thoroughly test any applications or configuration settings desired for use in an RIPrep image to ensure they will work properly with your organization's implementation of user profiles. To test, make the change as one user (typically a local administrator of the computer), log off, and log on as a user account that is representative of your organization. If the changes you made are applied to the second user, the changes will also apply to users that log on to systems installed with an RIPrep image that contains the same change. To complete the test, create an RIPrep image, restore it to a different computer, and log on as a different representative user. Verify that the changes are applied and fully functional.

Some configuration settings can be copied directly from the profile they were applied to (the local administrator in the preceding example) the All Users profile, such as the desktop wallpaper, some Start menu options, and shortcuts. However, all such changes must be tested carefully to verify that their functionality is not broken by the manual adjustments.

Creating an RIPrep Image

When the workstation is configured exactly to specifications, you are ready to create an RIPrep image.

▶ **To create an RIPrep image**

1. On the client workstation, click Start, click Run, then type the Universal Naming Convention (UNC) path of the RIPrep utility in the Open box and click OK. For example: *Server**Share*\RemoteInstall\Admin\I386\ RIPREP.EXE

2. In the Welcome To The Remote Installation Preparation Wizard dialog box, click Next.

3. Continue through the prompts provided by the Remote Installation Preparation Wizard, including the following:

   ▪ **Server Name.**   The name of the server to which this installation image will be copied. By default this is the server on which you are running the Remote Installation Preparation Wizard.

   ▪ **Folder Name.**   The name of the folder on the RIS server to which this installation image will be copied.

   ▪ **Friendly Description And Help Text.**   A friendly description and associated help text that describes the OS image to users of the CIW.

4. Stop all programs or services on the source computer before proceeding. Review the list of programs or services that are currently running on the source computer, close any running applications, then click Next.

5. Review the settings summary, then click Next.

6. Review the information from Completing The Remote Installation Preparation Wizard and click Next to replicate the source computer installation image onto the RIS server.

Note If the source computer contains a 1 GB disk drive and the destination computer contains a 2 GB disk drive, by default RIS will format the destination computer's drive as a 2 GB partition in the same file system format as the source computer used to create the image.

After the initial image questions have been answered, the wizard configures the workstation to a generic state, removing anything unique to the client installation such as the computer's unique security identifier (SID), computer name, and any registry settings unique to that system. Once the preparation phase is complete, the image is automatically replicated to the RIS server provided. After the image is replicated to the RIS server, it is added to the list of available OS installation choices displayed within the CIW. At this point, any remote boot-enabled or compatible client computers that use the PXE-based remote boot technology can install the image.

7. The source computer shuts down when the image replication process is complete. The abbreviated Setup program automatically runs when you restart the source computer. Complete the setup process to use this client computer to create another installation image.

RIPrep Requirements

- The destination computer (the computer that installs the image posted to the RIS server) is not required to contain hardware identical to that of the source computer that was used to create the image. RIPrep uses the Plug and Play support in the computer running Windows 2000 Professional to detect differences between the source and the destination computers' hardware during image installation. However, the hardware abstraction layer (HAL) drivers must be the same between the source computer and all destination computers that later install the image (for example, they both must be Advanced Configuration and Power Interface (ACPI)-based or both must be non-ACPI-based). In most cases, workstations do not require the unique HAL drivers that servers require.

- The destination computer's disk capacity must be equal to or larger than that of the source computer.

- All copies of Microsoft software made or installed using RIS must be properly licensed. All copies of other software made or installed using RIS must be properly licensed, and it is the licensee's obligation to ensure that it is licensed to make any such copies.

RIPrep Limitations

- RIPrep currently supports replicating a single disk-single partition (C partition only) Windows 2000 Professional installation to an available RIS server. This means that the OS and all of the applications that make up the standard installation must reside on the C partition prior to running the Remote Installation Preparation Wizard.

- The Remote Installation Preparation Wizard currently allows source image replication only to available RIS servers. Source replication to alternate drives or media types is not supported.

- Replication of encrypted files is not supported.

- Changes made in the source computer's registry before running the Remote Installation Preparation Wizard are not maintained in the installation image.

- Modifications to replicated installation images are not supported.

Installation Image Sources

When you use the Remote Installation Preparation Wizard to create an installation image of a client computer that was originally installed using a retail version (rather than a Select or original equipment manufacturer [OEM] version) of Windows 2000 Professional, the RIS unattended setup answer file (RIPREP.SIF) must be modified to include the product identification number (PID). The PID is a unique identification number specific to each copy of Windows 2000 Professional used to identify the OS installation and track the number of copies installed throughout an organization.

Note   If the PID is not entered in the RIPREP.SIF file, the installation process will stop and prompt the user for the PID information during the installation of that RIPrep image.

▶ **To include the PID in the RIPREP.SIF file**

1. Open the RIPREP.SIF file located at \RemoteInstall\Setup*applicable_ language*\Images*applicable_image_name*\I386\Templates\RIPREP.SIF.

2. Type **ProductID = "xxxxx-xxx-xxxxxxx-xxxxx"** (including the dashes and quotation marks, where x is the PID of the retail version of Windows 2000 Professional) into the [UserData] section of the RIPREP.SIF file.

The PID for each client installation is randomly generated using the PID entered in the RIPREP.SIF file.

When the source computer OS is installed from the Select or OEM version of the Windows 2000 Professional CD, the PID does not need to be modified in the RIPREP.SIF file.

Creating an RIS Boot Disk

You must create a boot disk to support existing client computers that do not have a PXE-based remote boot-enabled ROM but do have a supported network adapter. The RIS boot disk works like the PXE boot process: Turn on the computer, boot from the RIS boot disk, press F12 to initiate a network service boot, and the CIW is downloaded and starts. Once the CIW starts, the rest of the RIS process is identical regardless of whether the client was booted using a PXE boot ROM or the RIS remote boot disk.

▶ **To create an RIS boot disk**

1. Click Start, click Run, then type the UNC path of the RBFG utility in the Open box and click OK. For example:
   *server**share*\RemoteInstall\Admin\I386\RBFG.EXE

2. Insert a formatted disk into the disk drive.

3. In the Windows 2000 Remote Boot Disk Generator dialog box (see Figure 15.11), click the appropriate destination drive option (either Drive A or Drive B), and then click Create Disk.

Figure 15.11   Windows 2000 Remote Boot Disk Generator dialog box

4. Click Close when the disk is ready, then remove the disk from the disk drive.

Note   You can use the boot disk only with computers that contain supported PCI-based network adapters. To view the list of supported network adapters, click Adapter List in the Windows 2000 Remote Boot Disk Generator dialog box.

Verifying an RIS Configuration

RIS provides the ability to check the integrity of the RIS-enabled server. You can verify an RIS configuration if you suspect that the server is failing, if you are currently seeing inconsistent behavior, or if you need to restore an RIS volume from backup. The Check Server Wizard checks whether all of the settings, services, and configuration options are correctly set and functioning.

▶ **To verify an RIS configuration**

1. Click Start, point to Programs, point to Administrative Tools, then click Active Directory Users And Computers.

2. In the console tree, click the folder that contains the computer whose configuration you want to verify, such as Computers or Domain Controllers.

3. In the details pane, right-click the applicable RIS server, then click Properties.

4. In the Properties dialog box for the server, in the Remote Install tab, click Verify Server to start the Check Server Wizard.

5. On the Welcome To The Check Server Wizard page, click Next.

6. Read the summary on the Remote Installation Services Verification Complete page, then click Finish.

Note   If you are verifying the server configuration because you need to restore an RIS volume from backup, you must verify the server configuration before you restore the volume.

Lesson Summary

In this lesson you learned about the tasks necessary to implement RIS, including setting up and configuring RIS, creating an RIPrep image, creating an RIS boot disk, and verifying an RIS configuration.

Lesson 3: Administering RIS

This section discusses the tasks necessary to administer RIS, including managing client installation images, managing RIS client computers, and managing RIS security.

After this lesson, you will be able to
- Manage RIS client installation images
- Manage RIS client computers
- Manage RIS security

Estimated lesson time: 20 minutes

Administering RIS

Administering RIS includes the following tasks:

- Managing RIS client installation images
- Managing RIS client computers
- Managing RIS security

Managing RIS Client Installation Images

Managing RIS client installation images includes the following tasks:

- Adding new client OS installation images
- Associating unattended setup answer files

▶ **To add a new client OS installation image**

1. Click Start, point to Programs, point to Administrative Tools, then click Active Directory Users And Computers.

2. In the console tree, right-click the applicable RIS server, then click Properties.

3. In the Properties dialog box for the server, click the Remote Install tab, then click Advanced Settings.

4. In the Remote Installation Services Properties dialog box, click the Images tab.

5. Click Add to start the Add Wizard.

6. On the New Answer File Or Installation Image page, click Add A New Installation Image, then click Next to start the Add Installation Image Wizard.

7. On the Welcome To The Add Installation Image Wizard page, click Next.

8. On the Installation Source Files Location page, type the location of the Windows 2000 Professional installation image, then click Next. The location can be either a CD-ROM or network share.

9. On the Windows Installation Image Folder Name page, type a name for the Windows installation image, then click Next.

10. On the Friendly Description And Help Text page, enter the friendly description and help text for the installation image, then click Next.

11. If a previous set of CIW screens exists, the Previous Client Installation Screens Found page appears. Select the CIW screen you want to use for this image, then click Next.

12. On the Review Settings page, review the installation summary, then click Finish.

The Remote Installation Setup Wizard completes the addition of the new client installation image.

▶ **To associate unattended setup answer files**

1. Click Start, point to Programs, point to Administrative Tools, then click Active Directory Users And Computers.

2. In the console tree, right-click the applicable RIS server, then click Properties.

3. In the Properties dialog box for the server, click the Remote Install tab, then click Advanced Settings.

4. In the Remote Installation Services Properties dialog box, click the Images tab.

5. Click Add to start the Add Wizard.

6. On the New Answer File Or Installation Image page, click Associate A New Answer File To An Existing Image, then click Next.

7. On the Unattended Setup Answer File Source page, click the source that contains the unattended setup file you want to copy:

   ▪ Windows Image Sample Files

   ▪ Another Remote Installation Server

   ▪ An Alternate Location

8. Click Next.

9. On the Select An Installation Image page, select the installation image the answer file will be associated with, then click Next.

10. On the Select A Sample Answer File page, select a sample unattended setup answer file, then click Next.

11. On the Friendly Description And Help Text page, enter the friendly description and help text for the installation image, then click Next.

12. On the Review Settings page, review the settings summary, then click Finish.

Managing RIS Client Computers

Managing RIS client computers includes the following tasks:

▪ Prestaging RIS client computers

▪ Finding RIS client computers

Prestaging RIS Client Computers

Prestaging an RIS client computer is the process of creating a valid client CAO within Active Directory. By prestaging the client computer account in Active Directory, you can configure the RIS servers to only respond to prestaged client computers. This ensures that only those client computers that have been prestaged as authorized users are allowed to install an OS from the RIS server. Prestaging can save time and money by reducing, and in some cases eliminating, the need to fully preinstall the computer.

When you prestage a client computer, you can define a specific computer name and optionally specify the RIS server to service the computer. This information is used to identify and route the client computers during the network service boot request. Make sure you set the appropriate access permissions for users of the prestaged client computer. When prestaging a client computer into a domain with multiple domain controllers, the replication delay of the client CAO information can cause a client computer to be serviced by another RIS server.

▶ **To prestage a client computer**

1. Click Start, point to Programs, point to Administrative Tools, then click Active Directory Users And Computers.

2. In the console tree, right-click the applicable OU that will contain the new client computer, click New, then click Computer.

3. In the New Object-Computer dialog box (see Figure 15.12), type the client computer name, authorize domain join permissions for the user or security group containing the user that will receive the physical computer this computer account represents, then click Next.

Figure 15.12 New Object-Computer dialog box

4. In the Managed dialog box (see Figure 15.13), click This Is A Managed Computer, type the client computer GUID into the text entry field, then click Next. See "Locating the GUID for Client Computers" later in this lesson for details.

Figure 15.13   Managed dialog box

5. In the Host Server dialog box (see Figure 15.14), click one of the following options to determine which server will support this client computer:

■ **Any Available Remote Installation Server.**   Selecting this option indicates this client computer can be serviced by any RIS server.

■ **The Following Remote Installation Server.**   Selecting this option allows you to designate a specific server.

Figure 15.14   Host Server dialog box

You can use the options in the Host Server dialog box to manually set clients across the available RIS servers within your organization and to segment the network traffic, if you know the physical location of the specific RIS server and where this computer will be delivered. For example, if an RIS server was located on the fifth floor of your building, and you are delivering these computers to users on that floor, then you could choose to assign this computer to the RIS server on the fifth floor.

6. Click Next.

7. Review the settings on the New Object-Computer dialog box, then click Finish.

Finding RIS Client Computers

You can search Active Directory for RIS client computer accounts using their computer name or GUID. The Show Clients feature searches for all client computers that are prestaged for this RIS server. The search process can include the entire Active Directory structure or be limited to a specific domain. The search process returns a list of the client computers and displays them by their computer name and GUID.

The Show Clients search process uses a wildcard search attribute appended to the current RIS server computer name. For example, if the RIS server is named RISsvr1, the Show Clients feature will use RISsvr1* for the server name. When you use the Show Clients feature in multiple RIS server environments, the search result might contain client computers from multiple servers. For example, if you have multiple RIS servers with computer names such as RISsvr1, RISsvr10, and RISsvr100, the search will return, from each of the servers, client computers that begin with the same computer name.

Locating the GUID for Client Computers

The computer's GUID appears in the following areas:

- A label on the side of the computer case
- A label within the computer case
- The BIOS of the client computer

The manufacturer supplies the computer's GUID. The GUID must be in the form {*dddddddd-dddd-dddd-dddd-dddddddddddd*}, where *d* is a hexadecimal text digit. For example: 8 hexadecimal text digits, followed by 4, then 4, then 4, then 12, such as the following: {921FB974-ED42-11BE-BACD-00AA0057B223}

Valid entries for the client GUID are restricted to the following:

0 1 2 3 4 5 6 7 8 9 a b c d e f - A B C D E F

Dashes are optional and spaces are ignored. Brackets { } must be included.

▶ **To find RIS client computers**

1. Click Start, point to Programs, point to Administrative Tools, then click Active Directory Users And Computers.

2. In the console tree, right-click the applicable RIS server, then click Properties.

3. In the Properties dialog box for the server, click the Remote Install tab.

4. In the Remote Install dialog box, click Show Clients.

5. In the Find Remote Installation Clients dialog box (see Figure 15.15), in the GUID box, enter the client computer's GUID, then click Find Now.

Figure 15.15   Find Remote Installation Clients dialog box

Note   You can limit the client computer search to a specific RIS server by entering the server name in the RI server box.

---

6. The RIS client computers appear in the Name and GUID columns in the lower portion of the Find Remote Installation Clients dialog box.

7. Close the Find Remote Installation Clients dialog box.

8. Close the Properties dialog box for the server.

Managing RIS Security

Managing RIS security includes the following tasks:

- Setting permissions for creating prestaged and user-created computer accounts

- Setting permissions for joining computers created in the Computers container and OUs to the domain

Setting Permissions for Creating Computer Accounts

To create new computer accounts in Active Directory, users need to have permissions and rights assigned to them. You must determine which users will be creating new client computer accounts and modify the users' rights and privileges accordingly.

▶ **To set permissions for creating prestaged computer accounts**

1. Click Start, point to Programs, point to Administrative Tools, then click Active Directory Users And Computers.

2. On the View menu, enable Users, Groups And Computers As Containers and Advanced Features.

3. In the console tree, right-click the applicable client computer account, then click Properties.

4. In the Properties dialog box, click the Security tab, then click Add.

5. In the Select Users, Computers, Or Groups dialog box, select the user or group from the list, click Add, then click OK.

6. In the Properties dialog box, click the user or group you have added.

7. In the Permissions box, click the Read, Write, Change Password, and Reset Password permissions, then click OK.

   If a group is allowed to have these permissions, remember to add users to that group.

   For client computer accounts that are prestaged in another Active Directory folder location, expand the Active Directory Users and Computer console and select the appropriate client computer account.

▶ **To set permissions for creating user-created computer accounts**

1. Click Start, point to Programs, point to Administrative Tools, then click Active Directory Users And Computers.

2. In the console tree, right-click the applicable domain, then click Delegate Control to start the Delegation Of Control Wizard.

3. On the Welcome To The Delegation Of Control Wizard page, click Next.

4. On the Users Or Groups page, click Add.

5. In the Select Users, Computers, Or Groups dialog box, click the user account or security group (preferred) containing the users you are setting permissions for, click Add, then click OK.

6. On the Users Or Groups page, click Next.

7. On the Tasks To Delegate page, click Delegate The Following Common Tasks, click Join A Computer To The Domain, then click Next.

8. Review the delegation of control summary information, then click Finish.

Setting Permissions for Joining Computer Accounts to a Domain

To join new computer accounts to the domain, users need to have permissions and rights assigned to them. You must determine which users will be joining new client computer accounts to a domain and modify the users' rights and privileges accordingly.

▶ **To set permissions for joining computer accounts created in the Computers container to the domain**

1. Click Start, point to Programs, point to Administrative Tools, then click Active Directory Users And Computers.

2. In the console tree, right-click the applicable domain, then click Delegate Control to start the Delegation Of Control Wizard.

3. On the Welcome To The Delegation Of Control Wizard page, click Next.

4. On the Users Or Groups page, click Add.

5. In the Select Users, Computers, Or Groups dialog box, click the user account or security group (preferred) containing the users that will be joining client computers to the domain, click Add, then click OK.

6. On the Users Or Groups page, click Next.

7. On the Tasks To Delegate page, click Delegate The Following Common Tasks, click Join A Computer To The Domain, then click Next.

8. Review the delegation of control summary information, then click Finish.

▶ **To set permissions for joining computer accounts created in OUs to the domain**

1. Click Start, point to Programs, point to Administrative Tools, then click Active Directory Users And Computers.

2. In the console tree, right-click the applicable OU, then click Properties.

3. In the Properties dialog box for the OU, in the Group Policy tab, click the GPO in the Group Policy Object Links box, then click Edit.

4. In the Group Policy snap-in, open Computer Configuration, click Windows Settings, click Security Settings, click Local Policies, then click User Rights Assignment.

5. Double-click Add Workstations To Domain.

6. In the Security Policy Setting dialog box, click Add.

7. In the Add User Or Group dialog box, type or use the Browse button to enter the names of the user accounts or security groups (preferred) containing the users who will be adding client computers to the domain in the User And Group Names box, then click OK.

8. In the Security Policy Setting dialog box, click OK.

9. Close the Group Policy snap-in.

10. In the Properties dialog box for the OU, click OK.

Note Because the changes that you make to RIS policy take effect only when the policy is propagated (applied) to your computer, do one of the following to initiate policy propagation:

- Type **secedit /refreshpolicy machine_policy** at the command prompt, then press Enter.

- Restart your computer.

- Wait for automatic policy propagation, which occurs at regular, configurable intervals. By default, policy propagation occurs every 90 minutes for Windows 2000–based computers, and every 5 minutes for the domain controller.

Lesson Summary

In this lesson you learned about the tasks necessary to administer RIS, including managing RIS client installation images, managing RIS client computers, and managing RIS security.

Lesson 4: RIS Frequently Asked Questions and Troubleshooting

This lesson provides answers to frequently asked RIS questions. It also describes some RIS problems you may encounter and possible solutions.

After this lesson, you will be able to

- Troubleshoot RIS

Estimated lesson time: 15 minutes

Frequently Asked RIS Questions

This section provides answers to frequently asked RIS questions.

Question 1:   I am not sure whether I have the correct PXE ROM version.

Answer: When the Net PC or client computer containing a remote boot ROM starts, the version of the PXE ROM appears on the screen. RIS supports .99c or greater PXE ROMs. You may be required to obtain a newer version of the PXE-based ROM code from your OEM if you have problems with the existing ROM version installed on a client computer.

Question 2:   I am not sure whether the client computer has received an IP address and has contacted the RIS server.

Answer: When the client computer boots, you will see the PXE boot ROM begin to load and initialize. The following remote boot ROM load sequence occurs with most PC98 and Net PCs, PXE ROM-based computers, and the computers using the RIS boot disk.

Remote Boot ROM Load Sequence

Step 1:   The client computer displays the message "DHCP," which indicates that the client is requesting an IP address from the DHCP server. This can also mean that the client has obtained an IP address from DHCP and is awaiting a response from the RIS server. To verify that the client is receiving an IP address, check the IP leases that have been granted on your DHCP server.

Troubleshooting: If the client does not receive the message, an IP address might not have been received or the BINL server might not be responding. Consider the following:

- Is the DHCP server available and has the service started? DHCP and RIS servers must be authorized in Active Directory for their services to start. Make sure the service has started and that other clients that are not remote boot-enabled are receiving IP addresses on this segment.
- Does the DHCP server have a defined IP address scope and has it been activated?

- Is there a router between the client and the DHCP server that is not allowing DHCP packets through?
- Are there any error messages in the event log under the system log for DHCP?
- Can other client computers—that is, those that are not remote boot-enabled clients—receive an IP address on this network segment?

Step 2:   When the client receives an IP address from the DHCP server, the message may change to "BINL." This indicates that the client successfully leased an IP address and is now waiting to contact the RIS server. The client will eventually time out and post the error message "No Bootfile received from DHCP, BINL, or Bootp."

Troubleshooting: If the client does not receive the BINL message, this indicates the client is not receiving a response from the RIS server. Consider the following:

- Is the RIS server available and has the RIS started? RIS servers must be authorized to start on the network. Use the DHCP console to authorize both DHCP and RIS servers within Active Directory.
- Are other remote boot-enabled clients receiving the CIW? If so, this client computer either is not supported or is having remote boot ROM-related problems. Check the version of the PXE ROM on the client computer. Also, check Active Directory to see whether the administrator has prestaged this client computer to an RIS server that is offline or unavailable to the client computer.
- Is a router between the client and the RIS server not allowing the DHCP-based requests or responses through? The RIS server communicates by way of the DHCP packet type during the initial service request and response sequence. You may need to configure the router to forward the DHCP packets.
- Are there any error messages in the event log under the system or application logs specific to RIS (BINLSVC), DNS, or Active Directory?

Step 3:   The client then changes to TFTP or prompts the user to press F12. This indicates that the client has contacted the RIS server and is waiting to receive the first image file—CIW. You might not see the BINL and TFTP message on some machines because this sequence can occur very rapidly.

Troubleshooting: If the client machine does not get a response from the RIS server, the client will time out and send an error message saying that it did not receive a file from DHCP, BINL, or TFTP. In this case, the RIS server did not answer the client computer. Do the following:

1. Stop and restart the BINLSVC service by clicking Start and pointing to Run.
2. In the Run dialog box, type **Net Stop BINLSVC Net Start BINLSVC** in the text field, then click OK.

3. Unless you have prestaged the client computer in Active Directory prior to starting the client computer, check the RIS server properties to make sure the Respond To Client Computers Requesting Service check box is selected and that the Do Not Respond To Unknown Client Computers check box is cleared.

4. Check the event log in Event Viewer to make sure no errors relating to DHCP, DNS, RIS (BINLSVC), or Active Directory exist.

Step 4: At this point, the client should have downloaded and displayed the CIW Welcome screen.

Question 3: Is the pre-boot portion of the PXE-based remote boot ROM secure?

Answer: No. The entire boot ROM sequence and OS installation or replication process is not secure with regard to packet type encryption, client/server spoofing, or wire sniffer-based mechanisms. As such, use caution when using RIS on your corporate network. Make sure you allow only authorized RIS servers on your network and that you control the number of administrators allowed to install and configure RIS servers.

Question 4: Does RIS preserve the file attributes and security settings defined on the source computer when using the RIPrep image feature?

Answer: Yes. The file attributes and security settings that are defined on the source computer are preserved on the destination computer that installs that image. However, the RIPrep feature does not support the encrypted file system if enabled and used on the source client computer.

Question 5: How do I replicate all of the OS installation images currently located on one RIS server to other RIS servers on the network for consistency across all client installations?

Answer: Currently the RIS feature does not provide a mechanism for replication of OS images from one RIS server to another, but there are several mechanisms you can use to solve this problem. Use the strong replication features of the Systems Management Server product, which provides for scheduled replication, compression, and slow-link features. You can also use other vendor solutions for OS image replication. Make sure the replication mechanism you choose supports maintaining the file attributes and security settings of the source images.

Question 6: Can I have an RIS server and another vendor remote boot server on the network at the same time? If so, what are the implications?

Answer: Yes, you can have multiple vendor remote boot/installation (RB/RI) servers on one physical network. It is important to understand that currently the remote boot PXE ROM code does not know the difference between vendors' RB/RI servers. As such, when a remote boot-enabled client computer starts and requests the IP address of an RB/RI server, all of the available servers will respond to that client; thus, the client has no way to ensure it is serviced by a specific RB/RI server.

RIS gives you the ability to prestage client computers into Active Directory and determine which RIS server will service a client computer. By configuring the RIS server to answer only known client computers (prestaged), you are assured that the correct RIS server will service the client.

Not all of the other RB/RI vendors have implemented the ability to ignore service requests. You might need to isolate the specific vendors' servers on the network so that these vendors' RB/RI servers do not answer clients.

Question 7:   Can I add more network adapters to the RIS boot disk?

Answer: No. The RBFG.EXE utility cannot be modified with regard to the number of supported network adapters for this release of RIS. Microsoft will be adding network card adapters over time and will make the updated RBFG.EXE utility available through normal distribution channels such as the World Wide Web, Windows updates, and future service or feature pack updates.

Question 8:   Can I use the Active Directory object attributes to create a naming format for use with the RIS automatic computer-naming feature?

Answer: No. Currently the existing attributes supported with the automatic computer naming feature use Active Directory. However, not all of the Active Directory object attributes are currently supported.

Troubleshooting RIS

Table 15.3 describes some RIS problems you may encounter and possible solutions.

Table 15.3   Troubleshooting Scenarios for RIS

Symptom: Command settings are not being processed during the unattended installation

Cause	Solution
When using the "OemPreinstall = yes" setting in an .sif file, the correct directory information is required.	Change the directory information to \RemoteInstall\Setup*applicable_language*\ Images*applicable_image_name*\\$oem\$.

Symptom: Language choice options are not displayed during the CIW session

Cause	Solution
By default, RIS uses the WELCOME.OSC file to manage the client installation image choices. For multiple language installation image options, you need to replace the default WELCOME.OSC file with the MULTILNG.OSC file.	The CIW uses the WELCOME.OSC file located in the \RemoteInstall\OSChooser folder to manage client installation image choices. When you remove the WELCOME.OSC file and rename the MULTILNG.OSC file to WELCOME.OSC, the CIW will also offer a menu of multiple language choices to the user. You can edit the WELCOME.OSC file to create custom language options.

**Symptom: The client computer is prestaged
to an RIS server but is being serviced by a different server**

Cause	Solution
When you prestage a client computer into a domain with multiple domain controllers, the replication delay of the CAO information can cause a client computer to be serviced by another RIS server.	You can wait for the computer account information to be propagated during the next scheduled replication session or modify the replication frequency between your domain controllers.

**Symptom: Following the restoration
of a backup of an RIS volume, RIS no longer functions properly**

Cause	Solution
Backup restored the volume without an SIS directory.	Verify the configuration of the RIS volume and then restore the volume again.

Lesson Summary

In this lesson you reviewed frequently asked RIS questions and answers. You also examined some RIS problems you may encounter and possible solutions.

Review

The following questions are intended to reinforce key information presented in the chapter. If you are unable to answer a question, review the appropriate lesson and then try the question again. Answers to the questions can be found in Appendix A, "Questions and Answers."

1. What is RIS? What types of remote booting are supported by RIS?

2. What does PXE remote boot technology provide?

3. What is the RIS boot disk?

4. What is an RIPrep image?

5. What is the CIW?

Preparation for MCP Exam 70-217

Installing and Configuring Active Directory Services

The Installing and Configuring Active Directory Services domain focuses on the implementation of Active Directory services, which includes the installation of Active Directory software, the configuration of your Active Directory site structure, and the administration of Active Directory backups. To carry out the installation of Active Directory services, Microsoft Windows 2000 Server provides the Active Directory Installation Wizard. You can use the wizard to add a domain controller to an existing domain, to create the first domain controller of a new domain, to create a new child domain, and to create a new domain tree. You can configure Active Directory site structure using the Active Directory Sites And Services console. Sites allow administrators to configure Active Directory access and replication topology easily and to take advantage of the physical network. You can use the Backup Wizard to back up System State data, which includes Active Directory services. Scheduling regular backups of Active Directory services ensures that you will be able to recover in the event of a system failure.

Tested Skills and Suggested Practices

The skills that you need to successfully master the Installing and Configuring Active Directory Services domain on the *Implementing and Administering a Microsoft Windows 2000 Directory Services Infrastructure* exam include:

- **Installing Active Directory services.**

    - Practice 1: Create the first domain controller in a new domain. Add a new domain controller to an existing domain. Configure Domain Name System

(DNS) automatically for Active Directory services using the Active Directory Installation Wizard. Examine the types of files created when you install Active Directory—database and database log files and the shared system volume—and the optimum location for these files. Promote your domain from mixed mode to native mode.

- Practice 2: Start the Active Directory Installation Wizard in two different ways. Use the wizard to install Active Directory services on a stand-alone server.

- **Creating a site in a domain.**

  - Practice 1: Use the Active Directory Sites And Services console to create sites in a domain. Notice that the Default-First-Site-Name site is created automatically when Active Directory is installed on the first domain controller in the site.

- **Creating a subnet for a site and associating an existing subnet with a site.**

  - Practice 1: Use the Active Directory Sites And Services console to create subnets and associate subnets with a site.

- **Creating a site link and adding a site to an existing site link.**

  - Practice 1: Determine the purpose of creating site links. Determine whether Internet Protocol (IP) or Simple Mail Transfer Protocol (SMTP) replication is best for your organization.

  - Practice 2: Review site link attributes: site link cost, replication frequency, and replication availability. Enter the site link attributes that suit your organizational needs using the Active Directory Sites And Services console.

  - Practice 3: Use the Active Directory Sites And Services console to create site links and to add sites to existing site links. Notice that the DEFAULTIP-SITELINK site link is created automatically when Active Directory is installed on the first domain controller in the site.

- **Creating site link bridges and understanding when to use site link bridges.**

  - Practice 1: Use the Active Directory Sites And Services console to create site link bridges and to bridge all site links for an intersite transport.

- **Configuring connections manually and forcing replication over a connection.**

  - Practice 1: Use the Active Directory Sites And Services console to configure connections manually. Learn how to force replication over a connection.

- **Moving server objects (member servers and domain controllers) between sites.**

  - Practice 1: Use the Active Directory Sites And Services console to move member servers and domain controllers between sites.

- **Creating global catalog servers.**

  - Practice 1: Use the Active Directory Sites And Services console to enable a global catalog.

- **Verifying Active Directory installation by viewing a domain.**

  - Practice 1: Log on as Administrator and use My Network Places to view a domain and thus verify Active Directory installation.

- **Transferring operations master roles assignments from one domain controller to another.**

  - Practice 1: Use the Active Directory Users And Computers console to transfer the relative ID master, the PDC emulator master, and the infrastructure master role assignments. Use the Active Directory Domains And Trusts console to transfer the domain naming master role assignment. Use the Active Directory Schema snap-in to transfer the schema master role assignment.

- **Implementing an organizational unit (OU) structure.**

  - Practice 1: Use the Active Directory Users And Computers console to create OUs that mirror your organization's functional or business structure. Review the various tabs and data fields of the OU properties sheet. Set properties for the OUs.

Further Reading

This "Further Reading" section provides lists of important readings to supplement your current understanding of the skills tested within this Objective Domain. The lists are delineated into pertinent readings for each objective within this Objective Domain. If you feel that you need additional preparation prior to taking the exam, study these sources thoroughly.

Objective 1.1

Microsoft Corporation. *MCSE Training Kit: Microsoft Windows 2000 Active Directory Services*. Redmond, Washington: Microsoft Press, 2000. Review Lessons 2 through 4 in Chapter 4, "Implementing Active Directory," for instruction and practice on installing Active Directory, transferring operations master roles, verifying Active Directory installation, and implementing an OU structure. Review Lessons 1 through 4 in Chapter 6, "Configuring Sites," for instruction and practice on creating sites, subnets, site links, site link bridges, connection objects, and global catalog servers and on moving server objects between sites.

Microsoft Corporation. *MCSE Training Kit: Microsoft Windows 2000 Server*. Redmond, Washington: Microsoft Press, 2000. Review Lessons 3 and 4 in Chapter 6, "Active Directory Services," for instruction and practice on installing Active Directory services and implementing an OU structure.

Microsoft Corporation. *Microsoft Windows 2000 Server Resource Kit. Volume: Microsoft Windows 2000 Server Distributed Systems Guide*. Redmond, Washington: Microsoft Press, 2000. Review Chapter 1, "Active Directory Logical Structure," for information about global catalog servers. Review Chapter 6, "Active Directory Replication," for information about creating sites, subnets, site links, site link bridges, connection objects, and global catalog servers. Review Chapter 7, "Managing Flexible Single-Master Operations," for detailed information about transferring operations master roles.

Objective 1.2

Microsoft Corporation. *MCSE Training Kit: Microsoft Windows 2000 Active Directory Services*. Redmond, Washington: Microsoft Press, 2000. Review Lessons 6 and 7 in Chapter 11, "Administering Active Directory," for instruction on backing up and restoring Active Directory, including recovering from a system failure.

Microsoft Corporation. *Microsoft Windows 2000 Server Resource Kit. Volume: Microsoft Windows 2000 Server Distributed Systems Guide*. Redmond, Washington: Microsoft Press, 2000. Review Chapter 6, "Active Directory Replication," for detailed information about backing up and restoring Active Directory services, including recovering from a system failure.

O B J E C T I V E   1 . 1

Install, configure, and troubleshoot the components of Active Directory services.

You can install **Active Directory** services by using the Active Directory Installation Wizard. Launch the wizard by running Configure Your Server on the Administrative Tools menu of the Start menu, or by running DCPROMO from the command prompt. When you install Active Directory services using the wizard, you must have the background knowledge and skills to determine:

- Whether to create the first **domain controller** of a new **domain** or add a domain controller to an existing domain

- Whether to create a new **child domain**

- Whether to create a new domain **tree**

- Whether to allow the wizard to install a **DNS server** or to configure **DNS** manually

- The location of the **database**, **database log files**, and the shared **system volume**

Once Active Directory services are installed, you can verify the installation by viewing the new domain using the **Active Directory Users And Computers console**.

Active Directory services supports multimaster replication of the directory data store between all domain controllers in the domain. Some changes are impractical to perform in multimaster fashion, however, so only one domain controller, called the *operations master*, accepts requests for such changes.

After you have completed and verified the installation, you should plan operations master role locations for the domain and **forest**. **Operations master roles** are assigned to one or more domain controllers in a domain for the purpose of performing single-master **replication**. There are five operations master roles; two of the roles must appear in every forest, and the remaining three roles must appear in every domain in the forest. The operations master roles that must appear in every forest are:

- Schema master

- Domain naming master

The operations master roles that must appear in every domain in a forest are:

- **Relative ID master**

- **Primary domain controller (PDC) emulator master**

- **Infrastructure master**

You transfer the schema master role assignment to another domain controller by using the **Active Directory Schema snap-in**. You transfer the domain naming master role assignment to another domain controller by using the **Active Directory Domains And Trusts console**. You transfer the relative ID master, the PDC emulator master, and the infrastructure master role assignments by using the Active Directory Users And Computers console.

The **organizational unit** (OU) structure for your domain should mirror your organization's functional or business structure. You can implement your OU structure by creating OUs and setting OU properties using the Active Directory Users And Computers console. The properties that you set for each OU can be used to perform a search within Active Directory services.

After you determine the logical environment for your organization, you must determine the physical structure. Site structure mirrors the physical environment of your organization and is maintained separately from the logical environment (domain structure). In Active Directory services, a **site** is a combination of one or more Internet Protocol (IP) subnets connected by a fast, reliable link. The way in which sites are configured affects the workstation logon/authentication and directory replication processes. To configure a site, you must first configure the settings for the site and then configure **intersite replication**.

You configure site settings by using the **Active Directory Sites And Services console** to perform the following tasks:

- Creating a site

- Associating a subnet with the site

- Connecting the site using site links

- Selecting a site license server

When you install Active Directory services on the first domain controller at a site, a default site named Default-First-Site-Name is automatically created in the Sites container. **Subnet** information is used to locate a domain controller during workstation logon/authentication and to determine the best routes between domain controllers during Active Directory replication. **Site links** must be created for replication to occur between two sites. Site links can exchange information using one of two replication protocols: IP or SMTP. **IP replication** allows low-speed, point-to-point, synchronous replication between all directory partitions. **SMTP replication** allows low-speed, asynchronous replication between the schema, configuration, and global catalog directory partitions. When you install Active Directory on the first domain controller at a site, a default site link named DEFAULTIPSITELINK is automatically created in the IP container. A **site license server** collects licensing information for a site and allows the site administrator to view the site's licensing history (purchases, deletions, usage).

You configure intersite replication by using the Active Directory Sites And Services console to perform the following tasks:

- Configuring site link attributes

- Creating site link bridges

- Configuring connection objects (optional)

- Designating a preferred bridgehead server (optional)

Site link attributes include site link cost, replication frequency, and replication availability information. Site link cost is a value assigned to each connection used for intersite replication. Because Active Directory services select connections based on cost, the cheapest connection will always be used if available. Replication frequency is the number of minutes Active Directory services should wait before using a connection to check for replication updates. Replication availability is the schedule that determines when a site link is available. A **site link bridge** represents a set of site links whose sites communicate transitively through some transport. A site link bridge can allow connections to be created between two sites that are not connected by an explicit site link.

Because Active Directory services automatically create and delete connections designed to optimize replication, it may not be necessary to configure **connection objects** manually. You should configure connections manually only if you are certain the connection is required.

Although all domain controllers are used to exchange information between sites, you can specify a **preferred bridgehead server** to specify the preferred domain controller for intersite replication. Using **intrasite replication**, the bridgehead server then distributes directory information. If your organization uses a firewall to protect a site, you must establish your firewall proxy server as a preferred bridgehead server to ensure the successful exchange of directory information.

To meet the changing needs of your organization, you may need to maintain server settings for a site. A global catalog is created automatically on the first domain controller in the forest, which becomes the **global catalog server**. Depending on the ability of your network structure to handle replication and query traffic, you can designate additional domain controllers as global catalog servers using the Active Directory Sites And Services console. You can also move member servers and domain controllers between sites using the Active Directory Sites And Services console.

Objective 1.1 Questions

70-217.01.01.001

Replication on part of your network is inefficient due to a slow link between network segments. To solve this problem, you want to configure a new site for part of your network. You have created a site object using the Active Directory Sites And Services console. Which tasks must you complete to configure the site? (Choose all that apply.)

A. Create a new domain.

B. Select a site license server.

C. Configure filters for the link.

D. Assign a DNS server to the site.

E. Associate a subnet with the site.

F. Connect the site using site links.

70-217.01.01.002

You are creating site links and have chosen SMTP replication as the replication protocol. What are the advantages of using this protocol? (Choose all that apply.)

A. SMTP does not require a certificate authority (CA).

B. SMTP can replicate over site links and within a site.

C. SMTP enables uniform high-speed, synchronous replication.

D. SMTP traffic can be secured, monitored, and managed across a WAN environment.

E. SMTP can replicate information over a network backbone that is not based on TCP/IP.

70-217.01.01.003

A segment on your network has a slow and congested link that is made worse by directory replication. You need to create a new site for the network segment to solve this problem. The network segment already has an assigned subnet that you should use when you configure the site. Which object should you configure using the Active Directory Sites And Services console to associate the existing subnet with the new site?

A. The DNS server object

B. The site you are configuring

C. The subnet that you want to associate with the site

D. The NTDS settings object of the server associated with the site

E. The relative ID master for the domain that contains the subnet object

70-217.01.01.004

Which tasks should you complete in the New Object-Site Link Bridge dialog box when creating a site link bridge? (Choose two.)

A. Set the replication schedule.

B. Select the transport protocol.

C. Select two or more sites to connect.

D. Enter a name for the site link bridge.

E. Clear (disable) the Bridge All Site Links check box.

70-217.01.01.005

You are configuring site link costs for a T1, an ISDN, and a dial-up connection. You need to assign a cost for each link. Which cost values would be appropriate?

A. Dial-up=80, ISDN=100, T1=110

B. ISDN=80, dial-up=100, T1=110

C. ISDN=100, T1=110, dial-up=120

D. T1=100, ISDN=110, dial-up=120

70-217.01.01.006

You need to configure a connection manually. You start the Active Directory Sites And Services console by clicking Start, pointing to Programs, pointing to Administrative Tools, and clicking Active Directory Sites And Services. What should you do next?

A. Right-click the Sites folder, and select New Active Directory Connection.

B. Expand the Subnets folder, and select the subnet for one of the sites you want to connect.

C. Navigate to the NTDS settings for the domain controller for which you want to add the connection.

D. Open the Servers folder, right-click the domain controller for which you want to add the connection, and select New Active Directory Connection.

70-217.01.01.007

Your Active Directory network exists in two locations, LON and PAR. Each location is a separate site. The sites are connected via a T1 link, and each site is protected by a proxy server firewall. You created a site link that uses the SMTP-over-IP transport to facilitate replication between the sites. A global catalog server resides at the LON site, but none exists at the PAR site. You want to designate a global catalog server at the PAR site to facilitate the logon process. On which computer should you enable the global catalog server?

A. Workstation

B. Proxy server

C. Member server

D. Domain controller

70-217.01.01.008

You need to install Active Directory services on a Windows 2000 server. In so doing, you want to achieve the following results:

- Install a DNS server

- Install a DHCP server

- Install a certificate server

- Create multiple sites and site links

- Create the shared system volume

- Create the first domain controller of a new domain

- Create the database and database log files for the new domain

Your proposed solution is:

Launch the Active Directory Installation Wizard at the Windows 2000 server and use the wizard to complete the tasks listed above.

Which results does the proposed solution provide? (Choose all that apply.)

A. Install a DNS server.

B. Install a DHCP server.

C. Create multiple sites and site links.

D. Install a certificate server.

E. Create the shared system volume.

F. Create the first domain controller of a new domain.

G. Create the database and database log files for the new domain.

70-217.01.01.009

When you install Active Directory services, you can accept the default locations of the directory database, database log files, and shared system volume, or you can specify an alternate location. Which locations would yield the best performance in a server with two hard disks, assuming both are formatted as NTFS 5.0? (Choose two.)

A. Accept the default locations.

B. Place the shared system volume and database log files on one disk and the directory database on the other.

C. Place the directory database and database log files on one disk and the shared system volume on the other.

D. Place the directory database and shared system volume on one disk and the database log files on the other.

70-217.01.01.010

You need to install Active Directory services on a Windows 2000 server. Which methods can you use to launch the Active Directory Installation Wizard? (Choose two.)

A. Run DCPROMO from the Run dialog box.

B. Run ADSETUP from the Run dialog box.

C. Run Configure Your Server on the Administrative Tools menu of the Start menu.

D. Run Install Active Directory on the Action menu of the Active Directory Sites And Services console.

70-217.01.01.011

You need to move a domain controller from one site to another. You start the Active Directory Sites And Services console and select the domain controller that you want to move. What should you do next?

A. Drag the domain controller to the new site.

B. Right-click the domain controller, select Cut, navigate to the site to which you want to move the domain controller, and click Paste.

C. Click Move on the Action menu, select the site to which you want to move the domain controller in the Move Server dialog box, and click OK.

D. Right-click the domain controller, select Advanced, select the site to which you want to move the domain controller in the Move Server dialog box, and click OK.

70-217.01.01.012

You need to transfer the role of relative ID master for a domain. What should you do first?

A. Open the Active Directory Schema snap-in.

B. Open the Active Directory Sites And Services console.

C. Open the Active Directory Domains And Trusts console.

D. Open the Active Directory Users And Computers console.

70-217.01.01.013

You need to transfer the domain naming master role assignment. What should you do first?

A. Open the Active Directory Schema snap-in.

B. Open the Active Directory Sites And Services console.

C. Open the Active Directory Domains And Trusts console.

D. Open the Active Directory Users And Computers console.

70-217.01.01.014

You need to transfer the schema master role assignment. What should you do first?

A. Open the Active Directory Schema snap-in.

B. Open the Active Directory Sites And Services console.

C. Open the Active Directory Domains And Trusts console.

D. Open the Active Directory Users And Computers console.

70-217.01.01.015

You need to create an organizational unit (OU) for the Sales department of your company. You log on to a Windows 2000 domain controller as Administrator. What should you do next?

A. Open the Active Directory Schema snap-in.

B. Open the Active Directory Sites And Services console.

C. Open the Active Directory Domains And Trusts console.

D. Open the Active Directory Users And Computers console.

70-217.01.01.016

You created an organizational unit (OU) but did not specify any values on the General tab for the OU Properties dialog box. How will this affect the functionality of Active Directory services?

A. The OU cannot link to group policies.

B. You cannot search for the OU by its description.

C. Only the creator of the OU can view the OU.

D. The OU will not replicate across site links.

Objective 1.1 Answers

70-217.01.01.001

▶ **Correct Answers: B, E, and F**

A. **Incorrect:** It is not necessary to create a new domain to configure the site.

B. **Correct:** The site license server contains the Microsoft BackOffice software licensing information for each site. This information is used by the site or site license server administrator to view licensing history for the entire site. By default, the site license server is the first domain controller for the site; however, the site license server does not have to be a domain controller. Selecting a site license server is the final consideration in configuring the site.

C. **Incorrect:** It is not possible to configure filters for a site link.

D. **Incorrect:** DNS servers are assigned not to sites but to domains.

E. **Correct:** A site is a set of one or more subnets. When a computer in a site is authenticated during logon, subnet information is used to find the site's domain controller and to determine the best routes between domain controllers for Active Directory replication. After you create a site object, you must create a subnet and associate the subnet with the site.

F. **Correct:** For replication to occur between two sites, a site link must be established. The Active Directory Installation Wizard automatically creates an object named DEFAULTIPSITELINK, which you can rename to the name you want to use for a site link. After you create a site object and a subnet, and associate a subnet with the site, you must create a site link.

70-217.01.01.002

▶ **Correct Answers: D and E**

A. **Incorrect:** The CA is responsible for ensuring the authenticity of directory updates. SMTP replication requires you to complete the process of installing and configuring a CA.

B. **Incorrect:** SMTP replication is used only for replication over site links (intersite). It is not used for replication within a site (intrasite).

C. **Incorrect:** SMTP enables low-speed, asynchronous replication between the schema, configuration, and global catalog directory partitions.

D. **Correct:** When sites are on opposite ends of a WAN link, it may not be desirable or possible to perform synchronous IP replication. Asynchronous SMTP replication provides store-and-forward transport necessary for the WAN environment.

E. **Correct:** SMTP replication is best used where RPC-over-IP transport is not possible, such as an X.400 network backbone.

70-217.01.01.003

▶ **Correct Answers: C**

A. **Incorrect:** It is not necessary, nor is it possible, to configure the DNS server object using the Active Directory Sites And Services console.

B. **Incorrect:** You have already created a new site. Configuring a site includes associating a subnet with the site, connecting the site using site links, and selecting a site license server. At this point, you want to associate an existing subnet with your site.

C. **Correct:** To associate an existing subnet with your site using the Active Directory Sites And Services console, you must configure that subnet object. In the Active Directory Sites And Services console, open the Subnets folder, right-click the subnet you want to configure, and then click Properties. In the Properties dialog box for the subnet, select the site with which to associate this subnet from the choices available in the Site list, and then click OK.

D. **Incorrect:** It is not necessary to configure the NTDS settings object of the server associated with the site to associate the existing subnet with the new site.

E. **Incorrect:** It is not necessary, nor is it possible, to configure the relative ID master for the domain that contains the subnet object using the Active Directory Sites And Services console.

70-217.01.01.004

▶ **Correct Answers: C and D**

A. **Incorrect:** It is not necessary to set the replication schedule to create a site link bridge. You cannot set the replication schedule in the New Object-Site Link Bridge dialog box.

B. **Incorrect:** You select the replication transport protocol when you create a site link, not when creating a site link bridge. You cannot select the transport protocol in the New Object-Site Link Bridge dialog box.

C. **Correct:** To create a site link bridge, you must select two or more sites to connect in the New Object-Site Link Bridge dialog box.

D. **Correct:** To create a site link bridge, you must enter a name for the site link bridge in the New Object-Site Link Bridge dialog box.

E. **Incorrect:** It is not necessary to clear the Bridge All Site Links check box to create a site link bridge. The New Object-Site Link Bridge dialog box does not have a Bridge All Site Links check box. You can clear the Bridge All Site Links check box in the IP Properties dialog box or the SMTP Properties dialog box.

70-217.01.01.005

▶ **Correct Answers: D**

A. **Incorrect:** Cost values are relative; the lower the cost value, the higher the priority. The fastest link (T1) should have the lowest value, the next fastest link (ISDN) should have a higher value, and the slowest link (dial-up) should have the highest cost value.

B. **Incorrect:** Cost values are relative; the lower the cost value, the higher the priority. The fastest link (T1) should have the lowest value, the next fastest link (ISDN) should have a higher value, and the slowest link (dial-up) should have the highest cost value.

C. **Incorrect:** Cost values are relative; the lower the cost value, the higher the priority. The fastest link (T1) should have the lowest value, the next fastest link (ISDN) should have a higher value, and the slowest link (dial-up) should have the highest cost value.

D. **Correct:** Cost values are relative; the lower the cost value, the higher the priority. The fastest link (T1) has the lowest value of 100, the next fastest link (ISDN) has a higher value of 110, and the slowest link (dial-up) has the highest cost value of 120.

70-217.01.01.006

▶ **Correct Answers: C**

A. **Incorrect:** You cannot select New Active Directory Connection by right-clicking the Sites folder.

B. **Incorrect:** You cannot configure a connection manually using the subnet objects for the sites you want to connect.

C. **Correct:** To navigate to the NTDS settings for the domain controller for which you want to add the connection, you double-click the site that contains the domain controller. Then, open the Servers folder, right-click the domain controller, right-click NTDS Settings, and then click New Active Directory Connection. From this point, in the Find Domain Controllers dialog box, click the domain controller you want to include in the connection object, and click OK. Then in the New Object-Connection dialog box, enter a name for the new connection object in the Name field, and click OK.

D. **Incorrect:** You cannot select New Active Directory Connection by right-clicking the domain controller. The connection object is a child of the NTDS settings object and references the replication source domain controller.

70-217.01.01.007

▶ **Correct Answers: D**

A. **Incorrect:** You cannot designate a workstation as a global catalog server. Only a domain controller can be designated as a global catalog server.

B. **Incorrect:** You cannot designate a proxy server as a global catalog server. Only a domain controller can be designated as a global catalog server.

C. **Incorrect:** You cannot designate a member server as a global catalog server. Only a domain controller can be designated as a global catalog server.

D. **Correct:** Only a domain controller can be designated as a global catalog server.

70-217.01.01.008

▶ **Correct Answers: A, E, F, and G**

A. **Correct:** The Active Directory Installation Wizard configures your Windows 2000 DNS server automatically. If you want to set up a configuration other than the default configuration provided by the wizard, you can configure DNS manually using the DNS console.

B. **Incorrect:** The Active Directory Installation Wizard does not configure your Windows 2000 DHCP server. To install a DHCP server, you must install and configure the DHCP service.

C. **Incorrect:** Although the Active Directory Installation Wizard creates the Default-First-Site-Name default site and the DEFAULTIPSITELINK default site link, you cannot create multiple sites and site links by using the wizard.

D. **Incorrect:** The Active Directory Installation Wizard does not install a certificate server. To install a certificate server; you must install and configure Certificate services.

E. **Correct:** The Active Directory Installation Wizard automatically creates the shared system volume in the default location of *systemroot*\SYSVOL, where *systemroot* is the Windows 2000 directory. The shared system volume is a folder structure on all Windows 2000 domain controllers that stores scripts and some group policy objects for the domain and enterprise.

F. **Correct:** The Active Directory Installation Wizard allows you to choose whether to add the new domain controller to an existing domain or create the first domain controller for a new domain.

G. **Correct:** The Active Directory Installation Wizard automatically creates the database and database log files in the default location of *systemroot*\NTDS, where *systemroot* is the Windows 2000 directory. The database is the directory for the new domain.

70-217.01.01.009

▶ **Correct Answers: B and D**

A. **Incorrect:** The default locations place all three components on the same hard disk. For best performance, you should place the directory database and the log file on separate hard disks.

B. **Correct:** For best performance, you should place the directory database and the log file on separate hard disks. The shared system volume only requires location on a partition or volume formatted with NTFS 5.0.

C. **Incorrect:** For best performance, you should place the directory database and the log file on separate hard disks. The shared system volume only requires location on a partition or volume formatted with NTFS 5.0.

D. **Correct:** For best performance, you should place the directory database and the log file on separate hard disks. The shared system volume only requires location on a partition or volume formatted with NTFS 5.0.

70-217.01.01.010

▶ **Correct Answers: A and C**

A. **Correct:** Running DCPROMO from the Run dialog box is one method of launching the Active Directory Installation Wizard.

B. **Incorrect:** Running ADSETUP from the Run dialog box results in an error message and is not a valid method of launching the Active Directory Installation Wizard.

C. **Correct:** Running Configure Your Server on the Administrative Tools menu of the Start menu is one method of launching the Active Directory Installation Wizard.

D. **Incorrect:** The Run Install Active Directory option is not available on the Action menu of Active Directory Sites And Services.

70-217.01.01.011

▶ **Correct Answers: C**

A. **Incorrect:** It is not possible to drag the domain controller to a new site.

B. **Incorrect:** It is not possible to cut and paste the domain controller to the new site.

C. **Correct:** By clicking Move on the Action menu, selecting the site to which you want to move the domain controller, and then clicking OK, you can successfully move the domain controller to the new site.

D. **Incorrect:** It is not possible to select Advanced when right-clicking the domain controller in the Active Directory Sites And Services console.

70-217.01.01.012

▶ **Correct Answers: D**

   A. **Incorrect:** Use the Active Directory Schema snap-in to transfer the schema master role assignment.

   B. **Incorrect:** You cannot use the Active Directory Sites And Services console to transfer any of the operations master roles.

   C. **Incorrect:** Use the Active Directory Domains And Trusts console to transfer the domain naming master role assignment.

   D. **Correct:** Use the Active Directory Users And Computers console to transfer the relative ID master, the PDC emulator master, or the infrastructure master role assignments.

70-217.01.01.013

▶ **Correct Answers: C**

   A. **Incorrect:** Use the Active Directory Schema snap-in to transfer the schema master role assignment.

   B. **Incorrect:** You cannot use the Active Directory Sites And Services console to transfer any of the operations master roles.

   C. **Correct:** Use the Active Directory Domains And Trusts console to transfer the domain naming master role assignment.

   D. **Incorrect:** Use the Active Directory Users And Computers console to transfer the relative ID master, the PDC emulator master, or the infrastructure master role assignments.

70-217.01.01.014

▶ **Correct Answers: A**

   A. **Correct:** Use the Active Directory Schema snap-in to transfer the schema master role assignment.

   B. **Incorrect:** You cannot use the Active Directory Sites And Services console to transfer any of the operations master roles.

   C. **Incorrect:** Use the Active Directory Domains And Trusts console to transfer the domain naming master role assignment.

   D. **Incorrect:** Use the Active Directory Users And Computers console to transfer the relative ID master, the PDC emulator master, or the infrastructure master role assignments.

70-217.01.01.015

▶ **Correct Answers: D**

   A. **Incorrect:** The Active Directory Schema snap-in allows you to view and modify Active Directory schema. It is not used to create an OU.

   B. **Incorrect:** The Active Directory Sites And Services console is used to manage information about the physical structure of your network (sites). It is not used to create an OU.

   C. **Incorrect:** The Active Directory Domains And Trusts console is used to manage trust relationships between domains. It is not used to create an OU.

   D. **Correct:** The Active Directory Users And Computers console is used to create OUs. Right-click on the location (such as a domain node) where you want to create the OU, point to New from the shortcut menu, and then click Organizational Unit.

70-217.01.01.016

▶ **Correct Answers: B**

   A. **Incorrect:** If you do not specify property values for the OU, the OU will still be able to link to group policies.

   B. **Correct:** If you do not specify property values for the OU in the General tab of the OU properties dialog box, you will not be able to search for the OU by its description. Although there are many fields on the General tab, the "description" criterion is the only searchable property contained in the General tab.

   C. **Incorrect:** If you do not specify property values for the OU, other users may still view the OU.

   D. **Incorrect:** If you do not specify property values for the OU, the OU will still replicate across site links.

O B J E C T I V E   1 . 2

Back up and restore Active Directory services.

When you back up Active Directory services, you must specify that you want to back up **System State data**. In Windows 2000, System State data is comprised of the registry, the COM+ Class Registration database, system boot files, the Certificate Services database (if the server is a certificate server), and Active Directory services and the **SYSVOL** directory (if the server is a domain controller).

When you restore the System State data (including Active Directory services) to a domain controller, you must specify whether you want to perform a **nonauthoritative restore** or an **authoritative restore**. The default restore method is nonauthoritative.

A nonauthoritative restore brings components of the System State data that are replicated with another domain controller (such as Active Directory services) up to date by replication after you restore the data. An authoritative restore recovers the deleted objects and replicates them; changes made after the last backup operation are not restored.

To perform an authoritative restore, you must first start your computer in a special mode called **Directory Services Restore Mode**. This mode takes Active Directory services offline, allowing you to restore the SYSVOL directory and Active Directory database. The next step is to perform a nonauthoritative restore using the Restore Wizard. Restart the computer, but before the computer completes restart, you must again start in Directory Services Restore Mode. Use the **NTDSUTIL utility** to authoritatively restore your choice of Active Directory objects, which will then be propagated through replication.

Objective 1.2 Questions

70-217.01.02.001

While configuring Active Directory services, you erroneously deleted an organizational unit (OU) object. Fortunately, you have a known good Active Directory backup that you can use to restore the object. You want to use the backup to achieve these results:

- Restore the deleted OU object and all objects within the OU

- Retain modifications made to the objects within the OU since the backup was created

- The restore should not affect objects outside of the deleted OU object

- Propagate the restored object to other domain controllers through replication

Your proposed solution is to perform an authoritative restore of the OU. After the authoritative restore is complete, you will then restart the computer in normal mode, verify that the SYSVOL share is published, and copy policy folders corresponding to the restored policy objects from the alternate location over the existing ones.

Which results does the proposed solution provide? (Choose all that apply.)

A. Restore the deleted OU object and all objects within the OU.

B. Retain modifications made to the objects within the OU since the backup was created.

C. The restore should not affect objects outside of the deleted OU object.

D. Propagate the restored object to other domain controllers through replication.

70-217.01.02.002

You are using the NTDSUTIL utility to authoritatively restore an organizational unit (OU) that was mistakenly deleted. The deleted OU is named "orders" and was located in the stsware.com domain. Which command should you enter at the authoritative restore prompt to authoritatively restore the organizational unit?

A. Ntdsutil OU=orders,DC=stsware,DC=com

B. Restore subtree OU=orders,DC=stsware,DC=com

C. Restore database OU=orders,DC=stsware,DC=com

D. Authoritative restore OU=orders,DC=stsware,DC=com

70-217.01.02.003

You need to authoritatively restore a select portion of Active Directory data. What must you do before you can use the NTDSUTIL utility to authoritatively restore the data?

A. Publish the SYSVOL.

B. Perform a Primary restore.

C. Synchronize Active Directory services.

D. Revoke and reissue orphaned certificates.

E. Bring down all domain controllers at the site.

F. Nonauthoritatively restore the System State data.

70-217.01.02.004

The primary disk drive in one of your domain controllers failed. You replaced the disk and successfully restored the file system using a tape backup. You also need to restore Active Directory services from the tape backup, but the Active Directory data stored on the tape is not current. Which type of restore should you perform to restore Active Directory services on the domain controller and allow the Active Directory replication system to update the restored data with newer data from your servers?

A. Verinc

B. Primary

C. Authoritative

D. Nonauthoritative

Objective 1.2 Answers

70-217.01.02.001

▶ **Correct Answers: A, C, and D**

   A. **Correct:** By performing an authoritative restore of the OU, you restore the OU and its objects without any effect on other data and objects.

   B. **Incorrect:** An authoritative restore does not allow you to retain modifications made to the objects within the OU since the last backup was created. You should perform a nonauthoritative restore to update the restored data with newer data from your other servers.

   C. **Correct:** When performing an authoritative restore, you mark only the deleted OU object as authoritative. This action restores only the deleted OU and leaves other objects undisturbed.

   D. **Correct:** When the restored domain controller is online and connected to the network, replication propagates the authoritatively restored OU to other domain controllers in the forest.

70-217.01.02.002

▶ **Correct Answers: B**

   A. **Incorrect:** This is not the command to enter at the authoritative restore prompt to authoritatively restore the OU. You should type **ntdsutil** at the command prompt to invoke the NTDSUTIL utility. You should type the distinguished name of the OU after the RESTORE SUBTREE command to authoritatively restore the OU.

   B. **Correct:** To authoritatively restore the OU, you should type **restore subtree** followed by the OU's distinguished name at the authoritative restore prompt.

   C. **Incorrect:** This is not the command to enter at the authoritative restore prompt to authoritatively restore the OU. You should type **restore database** at the authoritative restore prompt to restore the entire directory. You should type the distinguished name of the OU after the RESTORE SUBTREE command to authoritatively restore the OU.

   D. **Incorrect:** This is not the command to enter at the authoritative restore prompt to authoritatively restore the OU. You should type **authoritative restore** at the NTDSUTIL prompt to invoke the authoritative restore command. You should type the distinguished name of the OU after the RESTORE SUBTREE command to authoritatively restore the OU.

70-217.01.02.003

▶ **Correct Answers: F**

A. **Incorrect:** It is not necessary to publish the SYSVOL before you can use the NTDSUTIL utility to authoritatively restore the data.

B. **Incorrect:** Because primary restore does not exist in Windows 2000, it is not possible to perform a primary restore for Active Directory services.

C. **Incorrect:** It is not necessary to synchronize Active Directory services before you can use the NTD-SUTIL utility to authoritatively restore the data.

D. **Incorrect:** It is not necessary to revoke and reissue orphaned certificates before you can use the NTD-SUTIL utility to authoritatively restore the data.

E. **Incorrect:** It is not necessary to bring down all domain controllers at the site before you can use the NTDSUTIL utility to authoritatively restore the data.

F. **Correct:** To authoritatively restore a select portion of Active Directory data, you must run the NTD-SUTIL utility after you perform a nonauthoritative restore of the System State data but before you restart the server.

70-217.01.02.004

▶ **Correct Answers: D**

A. **Incorrect:** Verinc is not a type of restore. Verinc is part of a command used to authoritatively restore a subtree of the directory and override the version increase.

B. **Incorrect:** Primary is not a type of restore used in Windows 2000.

C. **Incorrect:** An authoritative restore does not allow you to retain modifications made to Active Directory services since the tape backup was created.

D. **Correct:** A nonauthoritative restore will restore Active Directory services on the domain controller and allow the Active Directory replication system to update the restored data with newer data from your servers.

Installing, Configuring, Managing, Monitoring, and Troubleshooting DNS for Active Directory Services

The Installing, Configuring, Managing, Monitoring, and Troubleshooting DNS for Active Directory Services domain examines the issues involved in using Microsoft Windows 2000 Domain Name Service (DNS) for Active Directory. These issues include integrating Active Directory DNS zones with non–Active Directory DNS zones, configuring zones for dynamic updates, and managing the replication of DNS data.

The DNS namespace represents the logical structure of your network, and DNS zones consist of zone database files that contain the resource information associated with one or more DNS domains. Active Directory–integrated DNS zones use Active Directory services to store zone database files and replicate them to other domain controllers. All domain controllers in a domain can modify the zone and replicate the changes to other domain controllers. Standard DNS zones use standard primary zones to store zone database files in text files. A replica of the standard primary zone is stored in a standard secondary zone. Only the primary server for a zone can modify the zone using zone transfer. Windows 2000 DNS provides a dynamic update capability, with which name servers and clients within a network can automatically update the zone database files for both Active Directory–integrated and standard DNS zones. An additional feature called secure dynamic update, in which the authoritative name server accepts updates only from authorized clients and servers, is available only for Active Directory–integrated zones. You can monitor DNS servers by viewing the DNS server log, Event Viewer, and the DNS.LOG trace file. To troubleshoot DNS for Active Directory, you can use the NSLOOKUP command-line utility to verify server responsiveness and zone delegation.

Tested Skills and Suggested Practices

The skills that you need to successfully master the Installing, Configuring, Managing, Monitoring, and Troubleshooting DNS for Active Directory Services domain on the *Implementing and Administering a Microsoft Windows 2000 Directory Services Infrastructure* exam include:

- **Integrating Active Directory DNS zones with non–Active Directory DNS zones.**

  - Practice 1: Plan a DNS zone configuration for your home network: Analyze delegation of management, traffic and performance, and growth needs as reasons for creating zones. Recognize the benefits of using Active Directory–integrated zones. Analyze your needs for integration with existing DNS servers.

  - Practice 2: Create new forward and reverse Active Directory–integrated, standard primary, and standard secondary lookup zones using the New Zone Wizard. Observe that the zone filename is required for the standard primary forward and reverse lookup zones. In addition, note that you must first copy the zone file to the destination computer when migrating a standard primary zone from another server. Observe that the primary DNS server IP address is required for standard secondary forward and reverse lookup zones.

  - Practice 3: Identify the various resource records and their function. Note the resource records that were created automatically for the zones you created. Use the DNS console tree to view resource records for a zone. Add a resource record to one of your zones.

- **Configuring zones for dynamic updates.**

  - Practice 1: Use the General tab in the Properties dialog box for a zone to configure dynamic updates for one of the Active Directory–integrated and one of the standard zones you created. Observe that the secure dynamic updates option can be used only for Active Directory–integrated zones.

- **Managing replication of DNS data.**

  - Practice 1: Review the benefits of delegating zones. Familiarize yourself with using the New Delegation Wizard to create a zone delegation.

  - Practice 2: Review the benefits of using additional DNS servers for zone replication. Distinguish between incremental zone transfer used for Windows 2000 DNS and full zone transfer used for earlier DNS implementations. Identify the steps in the zone transfer process. Use the Zone Transfers tab in the Properties dialog box for a zone to specify servers allowed to participate in zone transfers. Then use the Notify button in the Properties dialog box to specify the servers to be notified when a zone is updated.

- Practice 3: Use Event Viewer to view the DNS server log. Set all of the DNS server debug options, add a new zone, and then pause and restart the server. View the DNS.LOG file stored in the *systemroot*\System32\Dns folder. Be sure to go back and delete all of the debug options and the new zone.

- Practice 4: Familiarize yourself with the NSLOOKUP command-line utility. Use NSLOOKUP to verify DNS server responsiveness and verify a zone delegation.

Further Reading

This "Further Reading" section provides lists of important readings to supplement your current understanding of the skills tested within this Objective Domain. The lists are delineated into pertinent readings for each objective within this Objective Domain. If you feel that you need additional preparation prior to taking the exam, study these sources thoroughly.

Objective 2.1

Microsoft Corporation. *MCSE Training Kit: Microsoft Windows 2000 Active Directory Services*. Redmond, Washington: Microsoft Press, 2000. Review Lesson 2 in Chapter 5, "DNS and Active Directory Integration," for instruction and practice on understanding and configuring zones, including zone planning, selecting zone types, zone delegation, and configuring dynamic updates for a zone. Review Lesson 4 for instruction on monitoring and troubleshooting DNS for Active Directory.

Microsoft Corporation. *Microsoft Windows 2000 Server Resource Kit. Volume: Microsoft Windows 2000 Server TCP/IP Core Networking Guide*. Redmond, Washington: Microsoft Press, 2000. Review Chapter 5, "Introduction to DNS," for information about DNS concepts, including zones, DNS servers, resource records, zone transfer, DNS notify, and dynamic updates. Review Chapter 6, "Windows 2000 DNS," for more detailed information on installing, configuring, managing, monitoring, and troubleshooting Windows 2000 DNS for Active Directory.

"Windows 2000 DNS White Paper." (Free download available at *http://www.microsoft.com/windows2000/library/howitworks/communications/nameadrmgmt/w2kdns.asp*. You can find this paper by searching on the title.) Review the sections on the structure of DNS, replicating the DNS database, Active Directory storage and replication integration, and dynamic updates.

Albitz, Paul, and Cricket Liu. *DNS and BIND*. 3rd ed. Sebastopol, California: O'Reilly & Associates, 1998. ISBN 1-56592-512-2. This book is an excellent guide to DNS and the Berkeley Internet Name Domain (BIND) software, the UNIX implementation of DNS.

Objective 2.2

Microsoft Corporation. *MCSE Training Kit: Microsoft Windows 2000 Active Directory Services*. Redmond, Washington: Microsoft Press, 2000. Review Lesson 3 in Chapter 5, "DNS and Active Directory Integration," for instruction and practice on zone replication and transfer, including specifying servers allowed to participate in zone transfers and specifying servers to be notified. Review Lesson 4 for instruction on monitoring and troubleshooting DNS for Active Directory services including problems related to zone transfers and zone delegation.

Microsoft Corporation. *Microsoft Windows 2000 Server Resource Kit. Volume: Microsoft Windows 2000 Server TCP/IP Core Networking Guide*. Redmond, Washington: Microsoft Press, 2000. Review Chapter 6, "Windows 2000 DNS," for an excellent section about DNS troubleshooting tools, including NSLOOKUP.

OBJECTIVE 2.1

Install, configure, and troubleshoot DNS for Active Directory services.

Active Directory services uses DNS as its domain naming and location service, enabling clients to find the location of domain controllers. To find a domain controller in a domain, the client queries DNS for **resource records** that provide the names and **IP addresses** of the servers for the domain. A Windows 2000 DNS name server is required and is installed automatically when you install Active Directory. You do not need to configure DNS manually to support Active Directory services unless your organization uses a non–Windows 2000 DNS server or requires a special configuration.

The DNS service allows you to divide the DNS **namespace** into **zones**, also known as zone database files. A zone is a contiguous portion of the DNS namespace and contains resource records. Resource records contain information that is used to process client queries; some resource records also define the domain. There are two zone lookup types: forward lookup zones and reverse lookup zones. Forward lookup zones contain information needed to perform **forward lookup queries**, in which the friendly DNS name of a host computer is searched to find its IP address. When you install Active Directory services and allow the Active Directory Installation Wizard to install your DNS server, a forward lookup zone based on the server DNS name is automatically created. Reverse lookup zones contain information needed to perform **reverse lookup queries**, in which an IP address is mapped to a name.

Depending on the zone's type, zones can be stored, distributed, and replicated to other DNS servers. Both forward and reverse lookup zones can be one of three zone types:

- Active Directory–integrated. An Active Directory–integrated zone uses Active Directory services to store and replicate zone database files. This zone type contains the master copy of a zone.

- Standard primary. A standard primary zone stores zone database files in a standard text file on the **primary server** on which you create the zone. Replication is accomplished through **zone transfer** of database files to a standard secondary zone. This zone type contains the master copy of a zone.

- Standard secondary. A standard secondary zone is a replica of an existing zone stored in a standard, read-only text file on the **secondary server** on which you create the zone. A standard primary zone must be configured before you can create a secondary zone. When configuring a standard secondary zone, you must specify the primary DNS server from which standard primary zone database information will be transferred.

The DNS service includes a feature called **dynamic update**, which automatically updates the zone database files between name servers and clients within a network. You can choose to allow dynamic updates for Active Directory–integrated, standard primary, and standard secondary zone types. Additionally, if the zone type is Active Directory–integrated, you can choose to allow only dynamic DNS updates that use secure DNS. You can configure zones for dynamic updates on the General tab of the Properties dialog box for a zone.

You can create a temporary DNS trace log, which allows you to monitor DNS server activity such as the queries received by the server and the notification messages received by the server. The log is generated when you set various DNS server debug options on the Logging tab of the Properties dialog box for the DNS server. By default, these debug options are disabled. When an option is enabled, a DNS.LOG file is created and stored in the *systemroot*\System32\Dns folder.

Objective 2.1 Questions

70-217.02.01.001

You need to enable dynamic updates for a forward lookup zone named stsware.com. You start the DNS console, double-click the server hosting the zone, and highlight the stsware.com zone. What should you do next?

A. Right-click, select Properties, mark Enable Dynamic Updates on the Zone Transfers tab, and then click OK.

B. Right-click, select Options, select Yes in the Allow Dynamic Updates? list on the General tab, and then click OK.

C. Right-click, select Properties, select Yes in the Allow Dynamic Updates? list on the General tab, and then click OK.

D. Right-click, select Options, mark Allow Dynamic Updates, select either Only Secure Updates or Allow Unsecured Updates, and then click OK.

70-217.02.01.002

You are implementing DNS on your network. You have configured a forward lookup zone, and you are now configuring a reverse lookup zone to speed DNS lookup requests and to aid in troubleshooting. You need to map the IP address of your intranet servers to their host names. Which type of records should you create for each intranet server in the reverse lookup zone?

A. Host (A)

B. Service (SRV)

C. Pointer (PTR)

D. Name Server (NS)

E. Mail Exchanger (MX)

F. Start of Authority (SOA)

70-217.02.01.003

You are implementing DNS on your Active Directory network. You are configuring zones, and you need to identify in DNS those servers that can validate logon requests. Which type of records should you create for these servers?

A. Service (SRV)

B. Pointer (PTR)

C. Alias (CNAME)

D. Name Server (NS)

E. Mail Exchanger (MX)

F. Start of Authority (SOA)

70-217.02.01.004

Each department in your company has its own intranet server. Each intranet server hosts the Web server for its respective department. The Human Resources department's intranet server, however, hosts both a Web server and an FTP server. You need to identify the Human Resources department's intranet server as the host for both the FTP and Web server in DNS. Which type of records should you create for the server?

A. Service (SRV)

B. Pointer (PTR)

C. Alias (CNAME)

D. Name Server (NS)

E. Mail Exchanger (MX)

F. Start of Authority (SOA)

70-217.02.01.005

When creating a new DNS zone, you selected Active Directory–integrated as the zone type. What are the advantages of creating zones that are Active Directory–integrated? (Choose four.)

A. Directory replication is faster and more efficient than standard DNS replication.

B. Dynamic updates to DNS are conducted based on a multimaster update model, whereas standard zones use a single-master model.

C. Active Directory–integrated zones index the zone database by IP address rather than by host name, which dramatically decreases the time required to perform lookup queries.

D. Active Directory–integrated zones are replicated and synchronized automatically with new domain controllers, which are running the DNS server service, whenever a new zone is added to Active Directory.

E. DNS updates in an Active Directory–integrated zone can use dynamic updates, whereas in a standard zone you must manually update the zone database file on the primary name server.

F. Unified storage and replication for both DNS and Active Directory information offers simplified planning and administration in Active Directory–integrated zones, as opposed to standard zones.

70-217.02.01.006

You are troubleshooting a problem with DNS for Active Directory. You want to log information in the DNS server activity log and use this information to trace the problem. You would like to log the following information:

- Queries received by the DNS server service from clients

- Contents of the question section and answer section for each DNS query message processed by the DNS server service

- Number of DNS query messages sent and received by the DNS server service

- Notification messages received by the DNS server service from other servers

Your proposed solution is to start the DNS console at your DNS server, right-click the name server, click Properties, click the Logging tab, select the Questions, Answers, Send, Receive, UDP, and TCP debug logging options, and then click OK.

Which results does the proposed solution provide? (Choose all that apply.)

A. The queries received by the DNS server service from clients

B. The contents of the question sections and answer sections for each DNS query message processed by the DNS server service

C. The number of DNS query messages sent and received by the DNS server service

D. Notification messages received by the DNS server service from other servers

70-217.02.01.007

You installed a Windows 2000 server into a domain with Windows NT 4.0 servers. One of the Windows NT servers is running DNS. The Windows 2000 server is also running DNS and hosts an Active Directory–integrated zone. You have configured the zone on the Windows 2000 server to use dynamic updates, but dynamic synchronization is not occurring. No other network problems have been noted. What is the most likely cause of the problem?

A. Network connectivity problems.

B. Interoperability-related problems.

C. The DNS server service is stopped or the zone is paused.

D. You failed to grant proper permissions to the zone database folder on the Windows NT 4.0 server.

70-217.02.01.008

You need to create a reverse lookup zone to enable reverse lookup queries. You open the DNS console and expand the DNS server. What should you do next?

A. Right-click the DNS server and click Properties.

B. Right-click the DNS server and select New Domain.

C. Right-click the Reverse Lookup Zone folder and click New Zone.

D. Right-click the Reverse Lookup Zone folder and click Advanced.

70-217.02.01.009

You need to create a new DNS zone. You plan to create a standard primary forward lookup zone using the DNS console. However, before launching the New Zone Wizard to create the zone, you need to gather the information required to create the zone. Which information must you supply when creating the zone using the New Zone Wizard? (Choose two.)

A. The zone name

B. The zone filename

C. The master DNS server(s)

D. The Start-of-Authority (SOA) resource record for the new zone

Objective 2.1 Answers

70-217.02.01.001

▶ **Correct Answers: C**

A. **Incorrect:** The Zone Transfers tab is not used to enable dynamic updates for a forward lookup zone. In addition, the Enable Dynamic Updates list does not exist on the Zone Transfers tab.

B. **Incorrect:** It is not possible to right-click the stsware.com zone and select Options.

C. **Correct:** You configure the DNS service to enable dynamic updates for the stsware.com forward lookup zone by right-clicking the zone, selecting Properties, selecting Yes in the Allow Dynamic Updates? list on the General tab, and then clicking OK.

D. **Incorrect:** It is not possible to right-click the stsware.com zone and select Options.

70-217.02.01.002

▶ **Correct Answers: C**

A. **Incorrect:** The Host (A) resource record type lists the host-name-to-IP-address mappings for a forward lookup zone.

B. **Incorrect:** The Service (SRV) resource record type identifies which servers are hosting a particular service.

C. **Correct:** The Pointer (PTR) resource record points from the DNS domain name that owns the record (the same name as that of the console tree node where the PTR record is located) to a specified DNS domain name location. This resource record is often used in a special domain, such as the in-addr.arpa domain, to provide reverse lookups of address-to-name mappings. If you create Pointer resource records for each intranet server in the reverse lookup zone, these Pointer resource records list the IP-address-to-host-name mappings.

D. **Incorrect:** The Name Server (NS) resource record lists the name servers that are assigned to a particular domain.

E. **Incorrect:** The Mail Exchanger (MX) resource record identifies which mail exchanger to contact for a specified domain and in what order to use each mail host.

F. **Incorrect:** The Start-of-Authority (SOA) resource record identifies which name server is the authoritative source of information for data within this domain.

70-217.02.01.003

▶ **Correct Answers: A**

A. **Correct:** Because the Service (SRV) resource record type identifies which servers are hosting a particular service, you should create Service resource records for the servers. To identify the servers that can validate logon requests, you can then send a query to the DNS server to obtain a list of domain controllers.

B. **Incorrect:** The Pointer (PTR) resource record points from the DNS domain name that owns the record (the same name as that of the console tree node where the PTR record is located) to a specified DNS domain name location. This resource record is often used in a special domain, such as the in-addr.arpa domain, to provide reverse lookups of address-to-name mappings.

C. **Incorrect:** The Alias (CNAME) resource record type creates an alias, or alternate name, for the specified host name.

D. **Incorrect:** The Name Server (NS) resource record lists the name servers that are assigned to a particular domain.

E. **Incorrect:** The Mail Exchanger (MX) resource record identifies which mail exchanger to contact for a specified domain and in what order to use each mail host.

F. **Incorrect:** The Start-of-Authority (SOA) resource record identifies which name server is the authoritative source of information for data within this domain.

70-217.02.01.004

▶ **Correct Answers: C**

A. **Incorrect:** The Service (SRV) resource record type identifies which servers are hosting a particular service.

B. **Incorrect:** The Pointer (PTR) resource record points from the DNS domain name that owns the record (the same name as that of the console tree node where the PTR record is located) to a specified DNS domain name location. This resource record is often used in a special domain, such as the in-addr.arpa domain, to provide reverse lookups of address-to-name mappings.

C. **Correct:** Because the Alias (CNAME) resource record type creates an alias, or alternate name, for the specified host name, you can use a CNAME record to point two names to a single IP address. This allows you to host an FTP server, such as ftp.microsoft.com, and a Web server, such as www.microsoft.com, on the same computer.

D. **Incorrect:** The Name Server (NS) resource record lists the name servers that are assigned to a particular domain.

E. **Incorrect:** The Mail Exchanger (MX) resource record identifies which mail exchanger to contact for a specified domain and in what order to use each mail host.

F. **Incorrect:** The Start-of-Authority (SOA) resource record identifies which name server is the authoritative source of information for data within this domain.

70-217.02.01.005

▶ **Correct Answers: A, B, D, and F**

A. **Correct:** Active Directory replication processing is performed on a per-property basis, which propagates only the relevant changes. This means that less data is used in updates for directory-stored zones, resulting in faster and more efficient replication.

B. **Correct:** Active Directory–integrated zones use the multimaster update model, which ensures that any of the primary servers for the zone can process update requests from DNS clients as long as the domain controller is available on the network. Standard zones use the single-master update model, which designates only one authoritative DNS server as the primary server for the zone. If this primary server is not available, update requests from DNS clients cannot be processed for the zone.

C. **Incorrect:** Active Directory–integrated zones are not indexed by IP address, but are named after the highest domain in the hierarchy that the domain encompasses—the root domain for the zone.

D. **Correct:** Active Directory–integrated zones are stored at each domain controller, so it is not necessary to employ transfer or management procedures. Standard zones can require transfer of the entire zone to synchronize a domain controller added to a domain.

E. **Incorrect:** Dynamic updates are available for both Active Directory–integrated zones and standard zones.

F. **Correct:** Planning and administration are simplified when you unify the storage of your DNS namespace within Active Directory. Additional planning and maintenance are necessary when you store and replicate DNS and Active Directory namespaces separately.

70-217.02.01.006

▶ **Correct Answers: B and C**

A. **Incorrect:** The Query debug logging option logs queries received by the DNS server service from clients. You have not selected the Query debug logging option.

B. **Correct:** The Questions and Answers debug logging options log the contents of the question and answer sections (respectively) for each DNS query message processed by the DNS server service.

C. **Correct:** The Send and Receive debug logging options log the number of DNS query messages sent and received (respectively) by the DNS server service.

D. **Incorrect:** The Notify debug logging option logs notification messages received by the DNS server service from other servers. You have not selected the Notify debug logging option.

70-217.02.01.007

▶ **Correct Answers: B**

A. **Incorrect:** Because the only symptom noted is that dynamic synchronization is not occurring, it is unlikely that network connectivity is the cause of the problem.

B. **Correct:** One of the causes of dynamic synchronization not occurring is a lack of interoperability between Windows 2000 DNS servers and Windows NT 4.0 DNS servers. Only Windows 2000 DNS servers support dynamic updates. The DNS server provided with Windows NT 4.0 does not support dynamic updates.

C. **Incorrect:** If the DNS server service is stopped or the zone is paused, you will experience other network problems, such as failure to connect to network resources.

D. **Incorrect:** It is not necessary to grant permissions to the zone database folder on the Windows NT 4.0 server to perform dynamic updates. Because the DNS server provided with Windows NT 4.0 does not support dynamic updates, it must be upgraded to Windows 2000.

70-217.02.01.008

▶ **Correct Answers: C**

A. **Incorrect:** Right-clicking the DNS server and clicking Properties allows you to set properties for the DNS server, not create a reverse lookup zone.

B. **Incorrect:** It is not possible to right-click the DNS server and select New Domain.

C. **Correct:** The next step in creating a reverse lookup zone is to right-click the Reverse Lookup Zone folder and click New Zone. This action starts the New Zone Wizard, which guides you through the process of setting up a reverse lookup zone. The wizard prompts you to configure the Zone Type, Reverse Lookup Zone name, Zone File (standard primary zone type only), and Master DNS Servers (standard secondary zone type only).

D. **Incorrect:** It is not possible to right-click the Reverse Lookup Zone folder and click Advanced.

70-217.02.01.009

▶ **Correct Answers: A**

A. **Correct:** When you create a standard primary forward lookup zone, the New Zone Wizard requires you to name the zone. A zone is usually named after the root domain for the zone—the highest domain in the hierarchy that the domain encompasses.

B. **Incorrect:** When you create a standard primary forward lookup zone, the New Zone Wizard does not require you to specify a name for the zone database filename. The zone database filename defaults to the zone name with a .dns extension. If you are migrating a standard primary forward lookup zone from another server, you must first copy the zone database file to the systemroot\system32\dns folder on the target server.

C. **Incorrect:** When you create a standard primary forward lookup zone, it is not necessary to specify the master DNS server from which you want to copy the zone. It is only necessary to specify the master DNS server when you create a standard secondary forward or secondary reverse lookup zone.

D. **Incorrect:** When you create a standard primary forward lookup zone, it is not necessary to specify a Start-of-Authority (SOA) resource record for the new zone. The SOA resource record is automatically added when you create the zone.

OBJECTIVE 2.2

Manage, monitor, and troubleshoot DNS

After you configure DNS zones as discussed in Objective 2.1, you must be able to manage the replication of DNS data. You can manage replication by delegating zones and configuring zones for zone transfer.

If subdomains are added below a domain used to create a zone, you must either include the subdomain in the zone or delegate the subdomain to a new zone that supports the subdomain. Delegating a subdomain into a separate new zone is called zone **delegation**. For each new zone, you must create resource records in the parent zone that point to the authoritative DNS servers for the new, delegated zone. These resource records include:

- A **Name Server (NS) resource record**, to advertise the authoritative server for the delegated subdomain

- A **Host (A) resource record**, to resolve the name of the server in the NS resource record to its IP address

The New Delegation Wizard provides assistance in the delegation of zones.

Zone transfer is the interaction of DNS primary and secondary servers for the purpose of maintaining and synchronizing zone database files. For standard primary and standard secondary zone types, you must set up and maintain zone transfers to replicate zone database files between primary and secondary servers. For Active Directory–integrated zone types, you do not need to set up and maintain zone transfers because Active Directory performs replication automatically. However, it is also possible to set up standard zone transfers to secondary servers for Active Directory–integrated zones. This action may be useful if you need to implement zone transfer to non–Windows 2000 DNS servers or previous versions of Microsoft DNS servers. You may also need to create a second copy of an Active Directory–integrated zone if you have a remote site from which your users need to be able to resolve names, but you do not want to increase your network traffic by adding a domain controller.

There are two types of zone transfer: **full zone transfer** and **incremental zone transfer**. In a full zone transfer, the primary server transmits a full copy of the zone database to the secondary server for the zone. In an incremental zone transfer, the primary server transmits only the part of the zone database that has been modified. When a new secondary DNS server is added to the network or for earlier DNS implementations, a full zone transfer is performed. In **Windows 2000 Server**, incremental zone transfers can also be performed. In both types of zone transfer, the secondary server for the zone initiates the zone transfer process by polling the primary server for its **Start-of-Authority (SOA) resource record**. Incremental zone transfers consume less network bandwidth and provide a more efficient method of zone replication.

To configure zones for zone transfer, you can specify the servers allowed to participate in zone transfers and specify the secondary servers to be notified when a zone is updated. You can accomplish these tasks on the Zone Transfers tab in the Properties dialog box for the zone in question.

The DNS Server log in Event Viewer allows you to monitor DNS server events such as when the server starts and stops. Error and warning messages are also provided. You can also use Event Viewer on clients to view and monitor client-related DNS events.

When troubleshooting DNS, use the **NSLOOKUP** command-line utility to verify server responsiveness and zone delegation. Use the **PING** command to verify IP-level connectivity.

Objective 2.2 Questions

70-217.02.02.001

In order to increase security, you want to specify which servers are allowed to participate in zone transfers with a standard primary zone. You start the DNS console from the Administrative Tools menu and highlight the zone for which you want to set up zone transfers. What should you do next?

A. Right-click the zone and then click Other New Records.

B. Right-click the zone and then click Properties.

C. Right-click the zone and then click New Delegation.

D. Right-click the zone and then click Update Server Data File.

70-217.02.02.002

You need to use NSLOOKUP to confirm that a zone delegation was successful. At the command prompt on your DNS server, you type the NSLOOKUP 10.0.0.25 command. What should you do next?

A. Type **Q=NS**

B. Type **SET Q=A**

C. Type **VERIFY ZONE**

D. Type **SET NORECURSION**

70-217.02.02.003

You want to use NSLOOKUP to verify DNS server responsiveness for a DNS server whose IP address is 10.0.0.25. On the DNS server computer, you open a command prompt. What should you do next at the command prompt on your DNS server?

A. Type **SET Q=A**

B. Type **VERIFY ZONE**

C. Type **SET NO RECURSION**

D. Type **NSLOOKUP 10.0.0.25:80**

E. Type **NSLOOKUP 10.0.0.25 127.0.0.1**

70-217.02.02.004

You are troubleshooting a problem with your DNS servers that appears to be related to problems with zone transfers between primary and secondary DNS servers. Which actions should you take to solve the problem? (Choose three.)

A. Make sure the serial numbers for the zones involved in the transfer are not the same.

B. Make sure a bridgehead server is properly configured between each zone.

C. Delete the secondary DNS server from the primary zone's Notify list.

D. Use the PING command to ping each DNS server by its IP address from its remote counterpart.

E. Verify that the DNS servers involved in the transfer are both started and that the zone is not paused.

Objective 2.2 Answers

70-217.02.02.001

▶ **Correct Answers: B**

A. **Incorrect:** Right-clicking the zone and selecting Other New Records opens the Resource Record Type dialog box, from which you can add resource records for the zone.

B. **Correct:** Right-clicking the zone and selecting Properties opens the Properties dialog box for the zone. You can then specify the servers allowed to participate in zone transfers for the zone on the Zone Transfers tab.

C. **Incorrect:** Right-clicking the zone and selecting New Delegation opens the New Delegation Wizard, from which you can delegate authority for a subdomain to a different zone.

D. **Incorrect:** Right-clicking the zone and selecting Update Server Data File causes the DNS server to immediately write its in-memory changes out to disk for storage with the zone database file. These changes are usually written only at predefined intervals and when the DNS server is shut down.

70-217.02.02.002

▶ **Correct Answers: D**

A. **Incorrect:** Q=NS is not a command used with the NSLOOKUP command-line utility.

B. **Incorrect:** Although SET Q=A is a command used with the NSLOOKUP command-line utility to verify that a zone delegation is successful, it is typed in after the SET NORECURSION command completes.

C. **Incorrect:** VERIFY ZONE is not a command used with the NSLOOKUP command-line utility.

D. **Correct:** After you type **NSLOOKUP** followed by the IP address for the root server, the next step in using NSLOOKUP to confirm a zone delegation is to type **SET NORECURSION**. Then type **SET Q=rr_type**, where *rr_type* is the type of resource record used by the failed name for which you are attempting to verify a zone delegation. Finally, type the fully qualified domain name (FQDN) for the failed name followed by a trailing period (**.**). If zone delegations are set correctly, a list of name server (NS) resource records for delegated servers should be returned in the response.

70-217.02.02.003

▶ **Correct Answers: E**

A. **Incorrect:** SET Q=A is a command used with the NSLOOKUP command-line utility to verify that a zone delegation is successful, not to verify DNS server responsiveness.

B. **Incorrect:** VERIFY ZONE is not a command used with the NSLOOKUP command-line utility.

C. **Incorrect:** SET NO RECURSION is a command used with the NSLOOKUP command-line utility to verify that a zone delegation is successful, not to verify DNS server responsiveness.

D. **Incorrect:** Typing NSLOOKUP 10.0.0.25:80 will not provide the necessary result to verify DNS server responsiveness.

E. **Correct:** Typing NSLOOKUP followed by the server IP address of 10.0.0.25 followed by 127.0.0.1 will provide the necessary result to verify DNS server responsiveness. If the server is responsive, the server name "localhost" is returned.

70-217.02.02.004

▶ **Correct Answers: A, D, and E**

A. **Correct:** If the serial numbers for the zones involved in the zone transfer are the same, zone transfer cannot occur between the servers. To solve this problem, start the DNS console, and on the master Start of Authority (SOA) tab, increase the value of the serial number for the zone at the primary server (source) to a number greater than the value at the secondary server (destination). Then initiate zone transfer at the secondary server.

B. **Incorrect:** Bridgehead servers are configured between sites, not zones. Configuring a bridgehead server cannot solve problems with zone transfers.

C. **Incorrect:** By deleting the secondary DNS server from the primary zone's Notify list, you are no longer notifying the selected secondary servers for the zone when a zone is updated. The selected secondary servers will no longer know when to initiate the zone transfer process and pull changes from the notifying server to update the zone. This action could cause even more zone transfer problems.

D. **Correct:** Using the PING command eliminates the possibility of a basic network connectivity problem between the two servers. If you are able to successfully ping each DNS server by its IP address from its remote counterpart, the servers are connected. If not, you must investigate and resolve network connectivity issues.

E. **Correct:** You can verify that the primary (source) and secondary (destination) DNS servers involved in completing transfer of the zone are both started by right-clicking on the name server, clicking All Tasks, and then looking to see that both the Start and Resume options are not available. If the server is started, these options are not available. You can verify that the zone is not paused at either server by looking at the Status field on the General tab of the Properties dialog box for the zone.

Installing, Configuring, Managing, Monitoring, Optimizing, and Troubleshooting Change and Configuration Management

This Installing, Configuring, Managing, Monitoring, Optimizing, and Troubleshooting Change and Configuration Management domain focuses on using group policy–based change and configuration management to simplify basic tasks such as user data and settings management, software installation, network configuration management, and remote OS installation. The goal of change and configuration management is to ensure the availability of computer resources to users and reduce the overall cost of supporting Microsoft Windows 2000 users. Group policy is a collection of user and computer settings that can be linked to Active Directory computers, sites, domains, or OUs to specify the behavior of users' desktops. Group policy is the main tool used in change and configuration management. You can specify the user data and settings to follow the user whether the user is online (connected to the network) or offline by using the Administrative Templates and Scripts group policy extensions. You can manage the installation, configuration, repair, and removal of software for groups of users and computers by using the Software Installation extension. You can redirect the special folders containing a user's profile to a location on the network by using the Folder Redirection extension. Remote OS Installation allows you to simplify the task of setting up new Windows 2000 Professional client computers remotely by using Active Directory, group policy, Dynamic Host Configuration Protocol (DHCP), Domain Name System (DNS), PXE-based remote boot technology, and Remote Installation Services (RIS).

Tested Skills and Suggested Practices

The skills that you need to successfully master the Installing, Configuring, Managing, Monitoring, Optimizing, and Troubleshooting Change and Configuration Management domain on the *Implementing and Administering a Microsoft Windows 2000 Directory Services Infrastructure* exam include:

- **Implementing and troubleshooting group policy for a domain.**

  - Practice 1: Implement a group policy for a domain. Plan your group policy object (GPO) implementation strategy. Create a GPO, create a GPO console, delegate administrative control of the GPO, specify group policy settings for the GPO, and disable any unused group policy settings. Search Windows 2000 Help for information about the GPO processing exceptions and then indicate any GPO processing exceptions for the GPO. Search Windows 2000 Help for information about filtering GPO scope and then filter the scope of the GPO. Link the GPO to an additional OU and test the GPO.

  - Practice 2: Use Windows 2000 Help to identify the problems and solutions associated with the Group Policy snap-in. Use Windows 2000 Help to identify the problems and solutions associated with group policy settings.

- **Managing and troubleshooting user environments by using group policy.**

  - Practice 1: Examine the registry-based group policy settings contained in Administrative Templates for both the computer and the user configuration. Note the additional registry-based group policy settings contained in the user configuration that are used to control user environments, such as Start Menu & Taskbar, Desktop, and Control Panel. Practice invoking these settings.

  - Practice 2: Identify whether and exactly when startup and logon scripts run when a computer starts and a user logs on. Use the Windows Settings folder under Computer Configuration of the Group Policy snap-in to assign startup/shutdown scripts to computers. Use the Windows Settings folder under User Configuration of the Group Policy snap-in to assign logon/logoff scripts to users.

  - Practice 3: Use Windows 2000 Help to identify the problems and solutions associated with Administrative Templates settings and startup and logon scripts configured in GPOs.

- **Managing and troubleshooting software by using group policy.**

  - Practice 1: Identify the tools provided with Windows 2000 Server for software installation and maintenance. Distinguish between assigning and publishing software. Examine how the software installation process works.

- Practice 2: Implement a software installation. Plan and prepare the installation, set up a software distribution point, and specify software installation defaults that define how an application is installed. Deploy software applications by assigning or publishing applications. Set automatic installation options and application categories. Set additional software application properties by editing installation options, specifying application categories to be used, and setting permissions for the software installation.

- Practice 3: Practice upgrading and removing applications.

- Practice 4: Use Windows 2000 Help to identify the problems and solutions associated with the Software Installation extension.

- **Managing network configuration by using group policy.**

  - Practice 1: Determine the purpose and advantages of folder redirection. Identify the special folders that Windows 2000 allows to be redirected.

  - Practice 2: Redirect special folders to a location according to security group membership. Redirect special folders to one location for everyone in the site, domain, or OU. Direct the My Pictures folder to follow the redirection of the My Documents Folder.

- **Deploying Windows 2000 by using Remote Installation Services (RIS).**

  - Practice 1: Identify the services and components that make up the Remote OS Installation feature. Examine how the Remote OS Installation process works. Familiarize yourself with the RIS server and client requirements and the network cards supported by RIS.

  - Practice 2: Implement RIS. Set up RIS by adding the RIS component to the RIS server and installing RIS. Configure RIS by authorizing RIS servers, setting RIS server properties, setting RIS client installation options, and setting RIPrep image permissions. Create an RIPrep image after first creating the source computer and configuring the workstation. Create an RIS boot disk, and then verify the RIS configuration.

  - Practice 3: Add a new client OS installation image and associate an unattended setup answer file.

  - Practice 4: Use Windows 2000 Help to identify the frequently asked questions, problems, and solutions associated with RIS.

- **Configuring RIS security.**

  - Practice 1: Set permissions for creating prestaged and user-created computer accounts. Set permissions for joining computers created in the Computers container and OUs to the domain. Practice prestaging RIS client computers and finding RIS client computers.

Further Reading

This "Further Reading" section provides lists of important readings to supplement your current understanding of the skills tested within this Objective Domain. The lists are delineated into pertinent readings for each objective within this Objective Domain. If you feel that you need additional preparation prior to taking the exam, study these sources thoroughly.

Objective 3.1

Microsoft Corporation. *MCSE Training Kit: Microsoft Windows 2000 Active Directory Services*. Redmond, Washington: Microsoft Press, 2000. Review Lesson 3 in Chapter 12, "Administering Group Policy," for instruction and practice on the tasks for implementing group policy. Review Lesson 6 for information on troubleshooting group policy implementation.

Microsoft Corporation. *Microsoft Windows 2000 Server Resource Kit*. Volume: *Microsoft Windows 2000 Server Distributed Systems Guide*. Redmond, Washington: Microsoft Press, 2000. Review Chapter 22, "Group Policy," for detailed information about implementing group policy. Review the section on "Group Policy Issues" in Chapter 25, "Troubleshooting Change and Configuration Management," for information about troubleshooting group policy implementation.

Microsoft Corporation. *Microsoft Windows 2000 Server Resource Kit*. Volume: *Microsoft Windows 2000 Server Deployment Planning Guide*. Redmond, Washington: Microsoft Press, 2000. Review the section on "Setting Uniform Security Policies" in Chapter 21, "Planning Distributed Security," for a discussion on deploying the security settings of group policy.

Objective 3.2

Microsoft Corporation. *MCSE Training Kit: Microsoft Windows 2000 Active Directory Services*. Redmond, Washington: Microsoft Press, 2000. Review Lesson 1 in Chapter 12, "Administering Group Policy," for instruction on the tasks for managing user environments by using group policy. Review Lesson 6 for information on troubleshooting user environments by using group policy.

Microsoft Corporation. *Microsoft Windows 2000 Server Resource Kit*. Volume: *Microsoft Windows 2000 Server Distributed Systems Guide*. Redmond, Washington: Microsoft Press, 2000. Review Chapter 22, "Group Policy," for detailed information about managing user environments using group policy. Review the section on "Group Policy Issues" in Chapter 25, "Troubleshooting Change and Configuration Management," for information about troubleshooting Administrative Templates and Scripts problems.

Microsoft Corporation. *Microsoft Windows 2000 Server Resource Kit.* Volume: *Microsoft Windows 2000 Server Deployment Planning Guide.* Redmond, Washington: Microsoft Press, 2000. Review the section on "Using Group Policy to Administer Clients" in Chapter 23, "Defining Client Administration and Configuration Standards," for detailed information about deploying group policy in user environments.

Objective 3.3

Microsoft Corporation. *MCSE Training Kit: Microsoft Windows 2000 Active Directory Services.* Redmond, Washington: Microsoft Press, 2000. Review Lesson 4 in Chapter 12, "Administering Group Policy," for instruction on the tasks for managing software by using group policy. Review Lesson 6 for information on troubleshooting software managed by using group policy.

Microsoft Corporation. *Microsoft Windows 2000 Server Resource Kit.* Volume: *Microsoft Windows 2000 Server Distributed Systems Guide.* Redmond, Washington: Microsoft Press, 2000. Review Chapter 23, "Software Installation and Maintenance," for detailed information about managing software using group policy. Review the section on "Software Installation and Maintenance Issues" in Chapter 25, "Troubleshooting Change and Configuration Management," for information about troubleshooting software managed by using group policy.

Microsoft Corporation. *Microsoft Windows 2000 Server Resource Kit.* Volume: *Microsoft Windows 2000 Server Deployment Planning Guide.* Redmond, Washington: Microsoft Press, 2000. Review the section on "Using Group Policy to Improve Software Management" in Chapter 24, "Applying Change and Configuration Management," for detailed information about managing software deployment.

Objective 3.4

Microsoft Corporation. *MCSE Training Kit: Microsoft Windows 2000 Active Directory Services.* Redmond, Washington: Microsoft Press, 2000. Review Lesson 5 in Chapter 12, "Administering Group Policy," for instruction on the tasks for redirecting special folders to network locations.

Microsoft Corporation. *Microsoft Windows 2000 Server Resource Kit.* Volume: *Microsoft Windows 2000 Server Distributed Systems Guide.* Redmond, Washington: Microsoft Press, 2000. Review the section on "User Data Management Issues" in Chapter 25, "Troubleshooting Change and Configuration Management," for detailed information about troubleshooting folder redirection.

Objective 3.5

Microsoft Corporation. *MCSE Training Kit: Microsoft Windows 2000 Active Directory Services*. Redmond, Washington: Microsoft Press, 2000. Review Lesson 2 in Chapter 15, "Deploying Windows 2000 Using RIS," for instruction on the tasks for implementing RIS. Review Lesson 3 for instruction on the tasks for administering RIS. Review Lesson 4 for instruction on RIS troubleshooting.

Microsoft Corporation. *Microsoft Windows 2000 Server Resource Kit*. Volume: *Microsoft Windows 2000 Server Distributed Systems Guide*. Redmond, Washington: Microsoft Press, 2000. Review Chapter 24, "Remote OS Installation," for detailed information about deploying Windows 2000 RIS. Review the section on "Remote OS Installation Issues" in Chapter 25, "Troubleshooting Change and Configuration Management," for detailed information about troubleshooting remote OS installation issues.

Microsoft Corporation. *Microsoft Windows 2000 Server Resource Kit*. Volume: *Microsoft Windows 2000 Server Deployment Planning Guide*. Redmond, Washington: Microsoft Press, 2000. Review the section on "Enabling Remote OS Installation" in Chapter 24, "Applying Change and Configuration Management," for an overview of remote OS installation deployment.

Minasi, Mark. *Mastering Windows 2000 Server*. Sybex Inc., 1999. ISBN 0-7821-2774-6. Read the section on "Installing Windows 2000 on Workstations with Remote Installation Services" from Chapter 3 for an excellent description of using RIS. (Available online at *http://www.microsoft.com/technet/win2000/ris.asp*)

Objective 3.6

Microsoft Corporation. *MCSE Training Kit: Microsoft Windows 2000 Active Directory Services*. Redmond, Washington: Microsoft Press, 2000. Review Lesson 2 in Chapter 15, "Deploying Windows 2000 Using RIS," for instruction on the tasks for implementing RIS. Review Lesson 3 for instruction on the tasks for administering RIS. Review Lesson 4 for instruction on RIS troubleshooting.

Microsoft Corporation. *Microsoft Windows 2000 Server Resource Kit*. Volume: *Microsoft Windows 2000 Server Distributed Systems Guide*. Redmond, Washington: Microsoft Press, 2000. Review Chapter 24, "Remote OS Installation," for detailed information about deploying Windows 2000 RIS. Review the section on "Remote OS Installation Issues" in Chapter 25, "Troubleshooting Change and Configuration Management," for detailed information about troubleshooting remote OS installation issues.

O B J E C T I V E   3 . 1

Implement and troubleshoot group policy.

A **group policy** is a collection of user and computer configuration settings for defining and controlling how programs, network resources, and the operating system work for users and computers in an organization. A group policy can be linked to computers, sites, domains, and OUs. To create these configuration settings for a group of users, you must create **group policy objects** (GPOs). A GPO is a collection of group policy settings. Each Windows 2000 computer has one group of settings stored locally in a **local GPO** and may also be subject to settings stored in any number of **nonlocal** (Active Directory–based) **GPOs**. The settings stored in nonlocal GPOs override the settings stored in the local GPO.

You use the Group Policy snap-in to organize and manage the many group policy settings in each GPO. There are two types of group policy settings: Computer Configuration settings and User Configuration settings. Computer Configuration settings are applied when the operating system initializes, and they affect the group policies applied to computers, regardless of which user is logged on. User Configuration settings are applied when users log on to the computer and affect the group policies applied to users, regardless of which computer a user logs on to.

The Computer Configuration settings and the User Configuration settings each contain three types of settings: Software Settings, Windows Settings, and Administrative Templates. Software Settings contains the **Software Installation** extension, where you can specify how applications are installed and maintained within your organization. Windows Settings contains the Scripts and Security Settings extensions, where you can specify startup/shutdown and logon/logoff scripts and manually configure security levels assigned to a local or nonlocal GPO. For the User Configuration settings only, Windows Settings holds additional settings for Internet Explorer Maintenance, **Remote Installation Services (RIS)**, and **Folder Redirection**.

The tasks for implementing group policy are: creating a GPO, creating a console for the GPO, delegating administrative control of the GPO, specifying group policy settings for the GPO, disabling unused group policy settings, indicating any GPO processing exceptions, filtering the scope of the GPO, and linking the GPO to a site, domain, or OU. If you need to modify any of the group policy settings, you should follow the procedures for creating a GPO and specifying group policy settings.

To troubleshoot Group Policy snap-in problems, be aware that an administrator must have both Read and Write **permission** for a GPO to open it in the Group Policy snap-in. To troubleshoot group policy settings problems, recall that GPOs can only be applied to sites, domains, and OUs. Be aware of GPO processing exceptions, such as GPO processing order, the Block Policy Inheritance option, the No Override option, and the Loopback setting. Examine the **security group** or groups of which the user or computer is a member.

Objective 3.1 Questions

70-217.03.01.001

You need to create a group policy object (GPO) linked to a domain. The GPO will be applied to all users in the domain. What should you do first?

A. Open the DispatchPolicy GPO console.

B. Add the Group Policy snap-in to an MMC console.

C. Open Active Directory Sites And Services.

D. Open Active Directory Users And Computers.

70-217.03.01.002

You need to create a group policy object (GPO) linked to a site. The GPO will be applied to all users in the domain. What should you do first?

A. Open the DispatchPolicy GPO console.

B. Add the Group Policy snap-in to an MMC console.

C. Open Active Directory Sites And Services.

D. Open Active Directory Users And Computers.

70-217.03.01.003

You are implementing a group policy for your Active Directory network. You have created a group policy object (GPO) and now need to add the Group Policy snap-in to an MMC and create a GPO console. How should you proceed?

A. Enter **MMC** in the Run dialog box, and select Add/Remove Snap-In on the Console menu.

B. Open Active Directory Sites And Services, and select Install Snap-Ins on the Action menu.

C. Open Active Directory Sites And Services, right-click the GPO, click Properties, select the Group Policy tab, and check the Install GPO Snap-In box.

D. Open Control Panel, click Add/Remove Programs, click Add/Remove Windows Components, mark MMC Snap-Ins, and click Next.

Objective 3.1 Answers

70-217.03.01.001

▶ **Correct Answers: D**

A. **Incorrect:** The DispatchPolicy GPO console exists on your system only if you created a GPO named DispatchPolicy and then created a console for the DispatchPolicy GPO. Opening the DispatchPolicy GPO console or any other existing GPO console is not the first step in creating a GPO linked to a domain.

B. **Incorrect:** By adding the Group Policy snap-in to an MMC console, you create a stand-alone GPO console. Creating a stand-alone GPO console is not the first step in creating a GPO linked to a domain.

C. **Incorrect:** You should open Active Directory Sites And Services to create a GPO linked to a site. Opening Active Directory Sites And Services is not the first step in creating a GPO linked to a domain.

D. **Correct:** Opening Active Directory Users And Computers is the first step in creating a GPO linked to a domain. To finish creating the GPO, you should right-click the domain for which you want to create the GPO, click Properties, and select the Group Policy tab. Then click New and type the name you would like to use for the GPO. Click Close. By default, the GPO is linked to the domain that you selected, and its settings apply to that domain.

70-217.03.01.002

▶ **Correct Answers: C**

A. **Incorrect:** The DispatchPolicy GPO console exists on your system only if you created a GPO named DispatchPolicy and then created a console for the DispatchPolicy GPO. Opening the DispatchPolicy GPO console or any other existing GPO console is not the first step in creating a GPO linked to a site.

B. **Incorrect:** By adding the Group Policy snap-in to an MMC console, you create a stand-alone GPO console. Creating a stand-alone GPO console is not the first step in creating a GPO linked to a site.

C. **Correct:** Opening Active Directory Sites And Services is the first step in creating a GPO linked to a site. To finish creating the GPO, you should right-click the site for which you want to create the GPO, click Properties, and select the Group Policy tab. Then click New and type the name you would like to use for the GPO. Click Close. By default, the GPO is linked to the site that you selected, and its settings apply to that site.

D. **Incorrect:** You should open Active Directory Users And Computers to create a GPO linked to a domain or OU. Opening Active Directory Sites And Services is not the first step in creating a GPO linked to a site.

70-217.03.01.003

► **Correct Answers: A**

A. **Correct:** Entering MMC in the Run dialog box and selecting Add/Remove Snap-In on the Console menu is the first step in creating a GPO console.

B. **Incorrect:** It is not possible to select Install Snap-Ins on the Action menu of the Active Directory Sites And Services console.

C. **Incorrect:** The GPO is not accessible from Active Directory Sites And Services.

D. **Incorrect:** You cannot create a GPO console using Add/Remove Programs on the Control Panel.

OBJECTIVE 3.2

Manage and troubleshoot user environments by using group policy.

You manage user environments to ensure that a user's computing environment and files are always accessible and available. The group policy **Administrative Templates extensions** under both **Computer Configuration** and **User Configuration** contains over 450 registry-based group policy settings for configuring the user's environment, which are saved in HKEY_LOCAL_MACHINE (HKLM) and HKEY_CURRENT_USER (HKCU). Included are settings for Windows Components, System, and Network. The settings in Windows Components allow you to administer Windows 2000 components including NetMeeting, Internet Explorer, Windows Explorer, Microsoft Management Console (MMC), Task Scheduler, and Windows Installer. The settings in System are used to control logon and logoff functions and group policy functions. The settings in Network are used to control settings for offline files and network and dial-up connections.

In Computer Configuration, Administrative Templates also contains settings for Printers, and settings in System are provided for Disk Quotas, Domain Name System (DNS) Client, and Windows File Protection. In User Configuration, Administrative Templates also contains settings for Start Menu & Taskbar, Desktop, and Control Panel.

The **Scripts extensions** allow you to specify the logon/logoff scripts that run when a user logs on or off the computer and the startup/shutdown scripts that run at computer startup or shutdown. These extensions are located in Windows Settings in both Computer Configuration and User Configuration. Windows 2000 supports any scripting language that can use Microsoft ActiveX, including VBScript, JScript, Perl, and MS-DOS-style batch files (.bat and .cmd). You can control how scripts are run by using the group policy settings in the Administrative Templates/System/Logon or Logon/Logoff folders under Computer Configuration and User Configuration, respectively.

To troubleshoot problems with settings in Administrative Templates or with scripts configured in a GPO, confirm that the group policy settings are applied to the user's computer by running GPRESULT.EXE, a tool available on the Windows 2000 Server Resource Kit CD. Use NETDIAG.EXE, available on the Windows 2000 Operating System CD, to check the network configuration and confirm that DNS is working and configured. Run GPTOOL.EXE, available on the Windows 2000 Server Resource Kit CD, to check domain controller replication status. For script problems, you can also run GPTOOL.EXE to determine whether there is a synchronization problem with the Sysvol on the domain controller in use.

Objective 3.2 Questions

70-217.03.02.001

Company policy requires all Windows computers to display the company logo as the background wallpaper. You want to use the group policy object (GPO) shown in the exhibit to specify the bitmap file used for wallpaper throughout the company. You have opened the GPO console to make the required changes. What should you do next?

Examine the GPO shown in the figure below.

A. Under User Configuration\Administrative Templates, click System.

B. Under User Configuration\Administrative Templates, click Desktop.

C. Under Computer Configuration\Administrative Templates, click System.

D. Under Computer Configuration\Administrative Templates, click Network.

E. Under User Configuration\Administrative Templates, click Windows Components.

F. Under Computer Configuration\Administrative Templates, click Windows Components.

70-217.03.02.002

You created a script written in JScript that should run whenever a user in the Active Directory domain logs on to a Windows 2000 computer, and another that should run whenever a user logs off. You want to configure script policies in the group policy object (GPO) linked to the domain to accomplish this goal. To that end, you open the GPO console for the GPO linked to your domain as shown in the exhibit. What should you do next?

Examine the GPO shown in the figure below.

A. Expand the Windows Settings folder under User Configuration.

B. Expand the Software Settings folder under User Configuration.

C. Expand the Windows Settings folder under Computer Configuration.

D. Expand the Software Settings folder under Computer Configuration.

E. Expand the Administrative Templates folder under User Configuration.

F. Expand the Administrative Templates folder under Computer Configuration.

70-217.03.02.003

You want to establish disk quotas to prevent your hard disks from running out of disk space. You want to use the group policy object (GPO) shown in the exhibit to specify the maximum amount of disk space each user is allowed to use on each of the NTFS file system volumes within the domain linked to the GPO and to enforce the disk space limit. You have opened the GPO console to make the required changes. What should you do next?

Examine the GPO shown in the figure below.

A. Under User Configuration\Administrative Templates, click System.

B. Under User Configuration\Administrative Templates, click Desktop.

C. Under Computer Configuration\Administrative Templates, click System.

D. Under Computer Configuration\Administrative Templates, click Network.

E. Under User Configuration\Administrative Templates, click Windows Components.

F. Under Computer Configuration\Administrative Templates, click Windows Components.

70-217.03.02.004

You want to maintain version control of the Internet Explorer software on the Windows 2000 computers in the domain you administer. To accomplish this, you open the group policy object (GPO) console for the GPO linked to your domain and enable the Disable Periodic Check For Internet Explorer Software Updates setting under Computer Configuration/Administrative Templates/Windows Components/Internet Explorer. Where in each Windows 2000 computer's registry will this change be written when the new policy is read?

A. HKEY_USERS

B. HKEY_CURRENT_USER

C. HKEY_CLASSES_ROOT

D. HKEY_LOCAL_MACHINE

70-217.03.02.005

You created a script written in JScript to run at logon, and another to run when users log off. You then assigned script policies in the group policy object (GPO) linked to the domain to accomplish this goal. The script works properly when users in the Active Directory domain log on and log off on Windows 2000 and Windows 98 clients, but the scripts fail to run properly when they log on and log off Windows 95 and Windows NT 4.0 clients. What could you do to solve this problem? (Choose two.)

A. Run the logon scripts synchronously.

B. Embed the scripts in batch files.

C. Run the scripts in a minimized window.

D. Decrease the default wait time for group policy scripts.

E. Install Windows Script Host on the Windows 95 and Windows NT clients.

70-217.03.02.006

You are configuring group policies for computers and users in your Active Directory domain. The domain contains the Sales, Engineering, and Production OUs. The Production OU contains mostly Windows 2000 Terminal Services clients, whereas the Engineering and Sales OUs contain only Windows 2000 Professional clients. Because you would like to use the same global scripts for all computers within the domain, you configured startup and shutdown scripts for the group policy object (GPO) linked to the domain. You also used administrative templates to further configure the environments for those computers and users who are in the Active Directory domain. However, one of the settings (Disable The Command Prompt) is preventing the scripts from running properly on the Terminal Services clients. You need to make sure that the Disable The Command Prompt setting in the domain GPO does not affect the Terminal Services clients in the Production OU. How can you accomplish this if No Override is applied to the domain GPO link?

A. Apply the Block Policy Inheritance exception to the Production OU, and configure a GPO linked to the Production OU that disables the Disable The Command Prompt setting.

B. Remove the No Override exception from the domain GPO, and configure a GPO for the Production OU that disables the Disable The Command Prompt setting.

C. Remove the No Override exception from the domain GPO, and configure a local GPO for each Terminal Services computer that disables the Disable The Command Prompt setting.

D. Apply the Block Policy Inheritance exception to the local GPO for each Terminal Services computer, and configure a GPO linked to the Production OU that disables the Disable The Command Prompt setting.

Objective 3.2 Answers

70-217.03.02.001

▶ **Correct Answers: B**

A. **Incorrect:** The user configuration settings in the System folder are used to control logon and logoff functions and group policy itself. There are no settings in the System folder that allow you to specify the bitmap file used for background wallpaper.

B. **Correct:** The user configuration settings in the Desktop folder are used to control the appearance of a user's desktop. The Active Desktop Wallpaper setting allows you to specify the desktop background displayed on all users' desktops and prevents users from changing the image or its presentation. You can also use this setting to specify that the wallpaper image be centered, tiled, or stretched. If the image is unavailable when the user logs on, no image is displayed.

C. **Incorrect:** The computer configuration settings in the System folder are used to control logon functions, disk quotas, DNS clients, Windows File Protection, and group policy itself. There are no settings in the System folder that allow you to specify the bitmap file used for background wallpaper.

D. **Incorrect:** The computer configuration policy settings in the Network folder are used to control settings for Offline Files and for Network and Dial-Up Connections. There are no settings in the Network folder that allow you to specify the bitmap file used for background wallpaper.

E. **Incorrect:** The user configuration policy settings in the Windows Components folder are used to administer Windows 2000 components including NetMeeting, Internet Explorer, Windows Explorer, Microsoft Management Console, Task Scheduler, and Windows Installer. There are no settings in the Windows Components folder that allow you to specify the bitmap file used for background wallpaper.

F. **Incorrect:** The computer configuration policy settings in the Windows Components folder are used to administer Windows 2000 components including NetMeeting, Internet Explorer, Task Scheduler, and Windows Installer. There are no settings in the Windows Components folder that allow you to specify the bitmap file used for background wallpaper.

70-217.03.02.002

▶ **Correct Answers: A**

A. **Correct:** To configure script policies to run a script when a user logs on or off a Windows 2000 computer, you must expand the Windows Settings folder under User Configuration and then double-click the Scripts (Logon/Logoff) extension. To specify the script to run during logon and logoff, double-click Logon or Logoff and then specify the script or scripts that are to run when the user logs on or off the computer.

B. **Incorrect:** The user configuration policy settings in the Software Settings folder contain only the Software Installation settings, which help you specify how applications are installed and maintained for all users within your organization, regardless of which computer they log on to. You cannot use the Software Installation settings to configure script policies to run a script when a user logs on or off a Windows 2000 computer.

C. **Incorrect:** The computer configuration policy settings in the Windows Settings folder contain the Scripts (Startup/Shutdown) extension, which allows you to specify the script or scripts that are to run at computer startup or shutdown. You cannot use this extension to configure script policies to run a script when a user logs on or off a Windows 2000 computer.

D. **Incorrect:** The computer configuration policy settings in the Software Settings folder contain only the Software Installation settings, which help you specify how applications are installed and maintained for all users within your organization who log on to the computer. You cannot use the Software Installation settings to configure script policies to run a script when a user logs on or off a Windows 2000 computer.

E. **Incorrect:** The user configuration policy settings in the Administrative Templates folder contain all registry-based group policy settings, including settings for Windows Components, Start Menu & Taskbar, Desktop, Control Panel, Network, and System. Although the System settings folder contains logon and logoff settings that control how logon and logoff scripts are run, you cannot use any of these settings to specify the script that runs when a user logs on or off a Windows 2000 computer.

F. **Incorrect:** The computer configuration policy settings in the Administrative Templates folder contain all registry-based group policy settings, including settings for Windows Components, System, Network, and Printers. Although the System settings folder contains logon settings that control how logon scripts are run, you cannot use any of these settings to specify the script that runs when a user logs on or off a Windows 2000 computer.

70-217.03.02.003

▶ **Correct Answers: C**

A. **Incorrect:** The user configuration settings in the System folder are used to control logon and logoff functions and group policy itself. There are no settings in the System folder that allow you to specify the maximum amount of disk space each user is allowed to use on each NTFS system volume and to enforce the disk space limit.

B. **Incorrect:** The user configuration settings in the Desktop folder are used to control the appearance of a user's desktop. There are no settings in the Desktop folder that allow you to specify the maximum amount of disk space each user is allowed to use on each NTFS system volume and to enforce the disk space limit.

C. **Correct:** The computer configuration settings in the System folder are used to control logon functions, disk quotas, DNS clients, Windows File Protection, and group policy itself. The Default Quota Limit And Warning Level setting allows you to specify the maximum amount of disk space each user is allowed to use on each NTFS system volume. The Enforce Disk Quota Limit setting allows you to enforce disk quota limits and prevent users from changing the setting.

D. **Incorrect:** The computer configuration policy settings in the Network folder are used to control settings for Offline Files and for Network and Dial-Up Connections. There are no settings in the Network folder that allow you to specify the maximum amount of disk space each user is allowed to use on each NTFS system volume and to enforce the disk space limit.

E. **Incorrect:** The user configuration policy settings in the Windows Components folder are used to administer Windows 2000 components including NetMeeting, Internet Explorer, Windows Explorer, Microsoft Management Console, Task Scheduler, and Windows Installer. There are no settings in the Windows Components folder that allow you to specify the maximum amount of disk space each user is allowed to use on each NTFS system volume and to enforce the disk space limit.

F. **Incorrect:** The computer configuration policy settings in the Windows Components folder are used to administer Windows 2000 components including NetMeeting, Internet Explorer, Task Scheduler, and Windows Installer. There are no settings in the Windows Components folder that allow you to specify the maximum amount of disk space each user is allowed to use on each NTFS system volume and to enforce the disk space limit.

70-217.03.02.004

▶ **Correct Answers: D**

A. **Incorrect:** HKEY_USERS contains information about actively loaded user profiles. Changes to settings for Computer Configuration are not written to HKEY_USERS.

B. **Incorrect:** Changes to settings for User Configuration are written to the registry in HKEY_CURRENT_USER. You made changes to settings in Computer Configuration.

C. **Incorrect:** HKEY_CLASSES_ROOT contains information used by various OLE technologies and file-class association data. Changes to settings for Computer Configuration are not written to HKEY_CLASSES_ROOT.

D. **Correct:** Changes to settings for Computer Configuration are written to the registry in HKEY_LOCAL_MACHINE.

70-217.03.02.005

▶ **Correct Answers: B and E**

A. **Incorrect:** Running the logon scripts synchronously ensures that Windows Explorer does not start until the logon scripts have finished running. Although logon scripts are run hidden and asynchronously by default, running logon scripts synchronously will not allow Windows 95 and Windows NT 4.0 clients to run the scripts properly.

B. **Correct:** One of the solutions for running the scripts properly on Windows 95 and Windows NT 4.0 clients is to embed the scripts in batch (.bat) files. After you take this action, the scripts continue to run in a normal window.

C. **Incorrect:** If you run the scripts in a minimized window, you can stop the scripts from processing by normalizing the window. However, this action does not allow Windows 95 and Windows NT 4.0 clients to run the scripts properly.

D. **Incorrect:** By decreasing the default wait time for the group policy scripts, you allow less time for the scripts to run. This action does not allow Windows 95 and Windows NT 4.0 clients to run the scripts properly.

E. **Correct:** One of the solutions for running the scripts properly on Windows 95 and Windows NT 4.0 clients is to install Windows Script Host to run embedded scripts. The names of the scripts and their command lines are stored in a .pol file in the form of registry keys and values.

70-217.03.02.006

▶ **Correct Answers: B**

A. **Incorrect:** By applying the Block Policy Inheritance exception to the Production OU, you would deflect *all* group policy settings that reach the Production OU, including the global scripts. Thus, you would not achieve your goal of using the same global scripts for all computers in the domain.

B. **Correct:** The Disable The Command Prompt setting should not be used for Terminal Services clients. Although this setting prevents users from running the interactive command prompt, it also prevents the Application Compatibility scripts from running. Removing the No Override exception from the domain GPO and then creating a new GPO linked to the Production OU that disables the Disable The Command Prompt setting will allow scripts to run properly on the Terminal Services clients while not affecting the Windows 2000 Professional clients.

C. **Incorrect:** Although the No Override exception is removed from the domain GPO, the local GPOs are overwritten by the domain GPO. Thus, the Disable The Command Prompt setting, which is enabled in the domain GPO, remains in effect. The Disable The Command Prompt setting should not be used for Terminal Services clients. Although this setting prevents users from running the interactive command prompt, it also prevents the Application Compatibility scripts from running.

D. **Incorrect:** The Block Policy Inheritance exception is applied to a site, domain, or OU and cannot be applied to a GPO. And, although the Production OU disables the Disable The Command Prompt setting, the domain GPO, which contains the enabled Disable The Command Prompt setting, is processed first. The Disable The Command Prompt setting should not be used for Terminal Services clients. Although this setting prevents users from running the interactive command prompt, it also prevents the Application Compatibility scripts from running.

OBJECTIVE 3.3

Manage and troubleshoot software by using group policy.

Windows 2000 provides the **Software Installation** group policy extension as the administrator's primary tool for managing software within an organization. By using the Software Installation extension, you can deploy, update, and remove software.

To install software on client computers, you can **assign** applications to both users and computers, or you can **publish** applications to users. When you assign applications to users, an application advertisement appears on the user's computer regardless of the physical location of the computer. When the user selects the application from the Start menu or by activating a document associated with the application, the application is installed. When you assign applications to computers, the application is installed when the computer is turned on. When you publish applications to users, the application is not advertised, and the user decides whether or not to install the application by using Add/Remove Programs in Control Panel. You should assign required or mandatory software to users or computers, and publish software to users for on-demand availability.

The Software Installation extension uses the **Windows Installer** service, which allows Windows 2000 to manage the installation process by installing software packaged in files called **Windows Installer packages**. A Windows Installer package is a file (.msi) shipped with the application that contains explicit instructions on the installation and removal of the application. To deploy software using the Software Installation extension, the application must have either a native Windows Installer package (.msi) file, a repackaged application (.msi) file, or a text file that contains instructions about how to publish an application (from setup.exe or install.exe files) defined into a .zap file. You can customize a Windows Installer package by using **modifications** (also called **transforms**) to set the configuration of the application deployed to users.

The tasks for deploying software installation are: planning and preparing, setting up a **software distribution point**, specifying software installation defaults, deploying software applications, setting automatic installation options, setting up application categories, and setting software application properties. After software deployment, it may be necessary to upgrade or remove applications. When you're upgrading, the Software

Installation extension allows you to upgrade an existing application to a newer version and to uninstall an application and replace it with a completely different one. When you're removing an application, the Software Installation extension allows you to immediately uninstall the application or to allow users to continue to use the software but prevent new installations.

To troubleshoot software installation, view the "Troubleshooting" topic for "Group Policy" in Windows 2000 online help or the "Software Installation and Maintenance Issues" topic in Chapter 25, "Troubleshooting Change and Configuration Management," in the *Microsoft Windows 2000 Server Resource Kit*. Use these topics to find software installation problem descriptions and suggestions for resolution.

Objective 3.3 Questions

70-217.03.03.001

You are implementing Software Installation services to deploy applications to users. You plan to create organizational units (OUs) based on software management needs to aid in deployment. What are the advantages of using this strategy to implement Software Installation? (Choose all that apply.)

A. Fewer software distribution points (SDPs) are needed.

B. Applications can be targeted to the appropriate set of users.

C. Group policy security settings are not required to target the appropriate set of users.

D. Administration overhead is reduced because it allows you to create and manage a single GPO.

E. The logon process and setup process are faster than if you use GPOs higher in the Active Directory tree.

70-217.03.03.002

You want to use Software Installation to distribute common applications to all computers in the portion of the network that you administer. The portion of the network for which you are responsible is a mixed-mode Active Directory domain with Windows 95, Windows 98, Windows NT 4.0, and Windows 2000 Professional clients. The domain is further divided into the Sales, Engineering, and Production OUs. The Production OU contains Windows 95 and Windows 98 clients. The Engineering OU contains Windows 2000 Professional and Windows NT 4.0 clients, and the Sales OU contains Windows 95 and Windows 98 clients. You want to use Software Installation and a GPO linked to the domain to distribute and maintain common applications to all clients in the domain. On which clients are you able to distribute and maintain software using this method?

A. All clients in the domain

B. Only the clients in the Engineering OU

C. Only the Windows 2000 Professional clients

D. All clients in the domain except the Windows 95 computers in the Sales and Production OUs

70-217.03.03.003

You want to deploy Microsoft Office 2000 to Windows 2000 Professional clients using Software Installation and group policy objects. You also need to customize the applications so that unnecessary features are removed and other features are customized for the company, such as adding templates. Which files should you create to modify the Office 2000 Windows Installer package?

A. .msp files

B. .zap files

C. .mst files

D. .msi files

70-217.03.03.004

You want to deploy an application to Windows 2000 clients using Software Installation and a group policy object (GPO) linked to the OU that you administer. A file with a .zap extension already exists for the application due to successful deployment by another OU administrator. You would like to use the existing file, but you are concerned that there might be some drawbacks to using the file. What are the potential drawbacks to using the existing file? (Choose all that apply.)

A. You cannot force the application to install.

B. You cannot customize the install with the GPO.

C. You cannot use the .zap file until file ownership is transferred to you.

D. You cannot publish the application to Active Directory Users, only computers.

E. You cannot change the administrative privileges required to install the application using the GPO.

70-217.03.03.005

You are the network administrator for a company that is deploying Windows 2000 and Active Directory into its existing network. Most of the Windows NT servers have been upgraded or replaced with Windows 2000 and Active Directory. Approximately 33 percent of the clients have been upgraded to Windows 2000 Professional and all new client installations will run the Windows 2000 Professional operating system. The percentage of Windows 2000 clients on the network should climb to 40 percent within the next six months, but because of hardware incompatibilities and budget constraints, the majority of network clients will remain pre-Windows 2000 Professional clients—most of which are Windows 95 clients.

You have used Systems Management Server for some time to manage software on your clients. However, you are considering dismantling your Systems Management Server infrastructure and using Windows 2000 Software Installation and Active Directory exclusively to deploy and manage software maintenance and installation on your clients.

Why is this not a good idea? (Choose all that apply.)

A. You will not be able to schedule software deployments.

B. You will not be able to centrally manage software for the clients that are not Windows 2000 based.

C. You will not be able to use the self-repairing capabilities of the Windows Installer on any clients.

D. You will not be able to deploy and manage software to clients over slow network or dial-up connections.

E. You will not be able to license or meter software using Windows 2000 Software Installation and Active Directory.

70-217.03.03.006

You want to use the Software Installation feature of Windows 2000 to distribute an application to all Windows 2000 users in the Active Directory domain that you administer. Because the application is necessary for all users in the domain to do their work, you must make sure that all Windows 2000 users have access to the application. You also want to make sure that users are not able to remove the application. You have created a Windows Installer package for the application and are ready to configure deployment options for the software package. How should you deploy the application?

A. Assign the software package to deploy to users.

B. Publish the software package to deploy to users.

C. Assign the software package to deploy to computers.

D. Publish the software package to deploy to computers.

70-217.03.03.007

You used Windows Installer and a group policy object (GPO) linked to an Active Directory organizational unit (OU) named Research to distribute a 1.0 release of an application to all users in the linked Research OU. Your company recently purchased version 2.0 of the application. You need to update the application from version 1.0 to 2.0 for all users in the Research OU who use the application.

The early version (1.0) of the software was supplied to you in a native Windows Installer package file. You used the native Windows Installer package file to create a software installation package named SearchApp. The 2.0 release also has a native Windows Installer package file, which should simplify the upgrade.

You copied the native Windows Installer package file for version 2.0 of the software to the software distribution point. You have also opened the Group Policy snap-in for the GPO linked to the Research OU and navigated to the Software Installation node under User Configuration.

What should you do next?

A. Open the SearchApp software package's properties, click the Upgrades tab, add the Windows Installer package for release 2.0 of the application, and then click the Apply button.

B. Open the SearchApp software package's properties, click the Modifications tab, add the Windows Installer package for release 2.0 of the application, and then click the Apply button.

C. Create a software installation package for the 2.0 release using the Windows Installer package, access the Upgrades tab for the software package you created, add SearchApp to the list on the Upgrades tab, and then click the Apply button.

D. Create a software installation package for the 2.0 release using the Windows Installer package, access the Modifications tab for the software package you created, add SearchApp to the list on the Modifications tab, and then click the Apply button.

70-217.03.03.008

You are using the Software Installation feature of Windows 2000 to distribute an application to all Windows 2000 users in the Active Directory organizational unit (OU) that you administer. You have created a Windows Installer package for the application and configured deployment options for the software package so that it is published to all users in the OU. However, published applications do not appear in Add/Remove Programs in Control Panel. What could cause this to happen? (Choose all that apply.)

A. Active Directory cannot be accessed.

B. The application is already installed.

C. Clients are running Terminal Services.

D. You did not enable the application to autoinstall by file extension.

E. Users have local group policies that conflict with the GPO linked to the OU.

70-217.03.03.009

You are using the Software Installation feature of Windows 2000 to distribute an application to all Windows 2000 users in the Active Directory domain that you administer. You have copied the application's .msi file to the software distribution point (SDP), created the software installation package, and set deployment options for the application package in the Group Policy snap-in for the GPO linked to the domain that you administer. However, when users log in, they receive this message: "The feature you are trying to install cannot be found in the source directory." You have ruled out the possibility of network failure and are now checking for permissions problems.

You first check the permissions at the GPO linked to the domain. You find that Authenticated Users have Read permissions to the GPO. Next you check the application package and find that Authenticated Users have Read permission to the application package. Finally, you check the SDP and again find that only Read permissions apply.

What should you do to solve this problem?

A. Assign Write permissions at the GPO.

B. Assign Apply Group Policy permissions at the GPO.

C. Assign Write permissions at the application package.

D. Assign Full Control permissions at the application package.

E. Assign Write permissions at the SDP.

F. Assign Read and Execute permissions at the SDP.

70-217.03.03.010

You configured deployment options for a software package so that when a user in the Active Directory domain double-clicks a file with the .htm or .html extension, Microsoft FrontPage 2000 is automatically delivered to the user and installed if an application associated with the file type is not already installed. However, the application is not being deployed as planned. Users who double-click an .htm or .html file and do not already have an application associated with the file type consistently receive the error message "Cannot Prepare Package For Deployment." What is the most likely cause of this problem?

A. The package is corrupt.

B. You did not enable the autoinstall for the application.

C. Another application might be undergoing automatic repair.

D. There are insufficient permissions at the software distribution point (SDP).

70-217.03.03.011

You are using Software Installation and Active Directory to deploy applications to users in your Active Directory domain. The first application you deployed was Microsoft Word 2000. You published the application to users in the domain and configured deployment options so that it would autoinstall when a user double-clicks a file with the .doc, .htm, or .html extension and an application associated with the file type is not already installed. The deployment has worked well.

You now want to deploy FrontPage 2000 in the same manner. For the FrontPage 2000 software package, you again published the application to users in the domain and configured deployment options so that it would autoinstall. However, you want the autoinstall to run only when a user double-clicks a file with the .htm or .html extension and an application associated with the file type is not already installed.

After configuring deployment options, you test the software deployment by logging in to the Active Directory domain from a Windows 2000 Professional client that has not yet had any applications installed. You find that FrontPage 2000 appears in Add/Remove Programs in Control Panel, but double-clicking an .htm or .html file starts the Word 2000 autoinstall, not the FrontPage 2000 install.

What should you do to solve this problem?

A. Publish FrontPage 2000 to computers, and make sure that Word 2000 is published only to users.

B. Create Application Categories and make sure the category that contains FrontPage 2000 is at the top of the Categories list for the domain.

C. Move FrontPage 2000 to the top of the Application Precedence list box at the appropriate Software Installation node for the .htm and .html file extensions.

D. Enable Loopback for the appropriate Software Installation node and specify a higher priority for the FrontPage 2000 software package than for the Word 2000 software package.

70-217.03.03.012

You have an application that you want to deploy using group policy. You need to create a .zap file so that you can use the application's setup program (SETUP.EXE) to deploy the application. Which application should you use to create the .zap file?

A. WinZip

B. Notepad

C. VERITAS WinINSTALL LE

D. Microsoft Management Console

Objective 3.3 Answers

70-217.03.03.001

▶ **Correct Answers: B and C**

A. **Incorrect:** Only one SDP is needed to implement Software Installation. Creating OUs based on software management needs has no effect on SDPs.

B. **Correct:** The users are contained within the OU because they have common software management needs. As a result, you can target applications to the appropriate set of users.

C. **Correct:** The users are already contained within the OU because they have common software management needs. As a result, there is no need to deploy separate group policy security settings to target the users.

D. **Incorrect:** Because the users are contained within OUs specific to their software usage needs, a single GPO may not be feasible or possible. Administration overhead may not be reduced because, depending on software management needs, there may be multiple GPOs.

E. **Incorrect:** Because the users are contained within OUs specific to their software needs, a smaller number of GPOs located higher in the Active Directory tree may not be feasible or possible. The logon and setup process may not be faster because, depending on software management needs, there may be multiple GPOs.

70-217.03.03.002

▶ **Correct Answers: C**

A. **Incorrect:** To take advantage of the Software Installation feature in Windows 2000, you must be running Windows 2000 Server with Active Directory and group policy on the server computer and Windows 2000 Professional on the client computers. You can deploy software to the Windows 95, Windows 98, and Windows NT 4.0 clients using the advanced change and configuration management tools provided with Microsoft Systems Management Server 2.0.

B. **Incorrect:** Although you can distribute software to the Windows 2000 Professional clients in the Engineering OU using the Software Installation feature in Windows 2000, you cannot distribute software to the Windows NT 4.0 clients in the OU. You can deploy software to the Windows NT 4.0 clients using the advanced change and configuration management tools provided with Microsoft Systems Management Server 2.0.

C. **Correct:** To take advantage of the Software Installation feature in Windows 2000, you must be running Windows 2000 Server with Active Directory and group policy on the server computer and Windows 2000 Professional on the client computers.

D. **Incorrect:** To take advantage of the Software Installation feature in Windows 2000, you must be running Windows 2000 Server with Active Directory and group policy on the server computer and Windows 2000 Professional on the client computers. You can deploy software to the Windows 95, Windows 98, and Windows NT 4.0 clients using the advanced change and configuration management tools provided with Microsoft Systems Management Server 2.0.

70-217.03.03.003

▶ **Correct Answers: C**

A. **Incorrect:** Patch (.msp) files are used for bug fixes, service packs, and similar files and are not used to modify the Office 2000 Windows Installer package.

B. **Incorrect:** Application (.zap) files are used to install an application by using its original SETUP.EXE or INSTALL.EXE program and are not used to modify the Office 2000 Windows Installer package.

C. **Correct:** You use .mst files to make modifications or to customize the installation of a Windows Installer package at the time of assignment or publication. The modifications are saved in a file with the .mst extension.

D. **Incorrect:** Package (.msi) files are used by Windows Installer to store all the instructions and data required to install (and uninstall) programs. They are not used to modify Windows Installer packages.

70-217.03.03.004

▶ **Correct Answers: A, B, and E**

   A. **Correct:** Because .zap files can only be published, users must install the application on their own by using Add/Remove Programs in Control Panel. You cannot force the application to install.

   B. **Correct:** When you deploy an application by using a .zap file, the application is installed by using its original SETUP.EXE program. No customization is available; the existing setup is published and the user's experience is the same as the existing setup.

   C. **Incorrect:** Ownership of the .zap file is not required to use the .zap file. The privileges required to prepare and publish the .zap file are the same as those originally required to install it.

   D. **Incorrect:** A .zap file can only be published (not assigned) to users.

   E. **Correct:** The administrative privileges required to prepare and publish the .zap file are the same as those originally required to install it and are not changeable.

70-217.03.03.005

▶ **Correct Answers: A, B, D, and E**

   A. **Correct:** Software Installation supports the management of software, including software deployment scheduling, on Windows 2000 Professional only. Without Systems Management Server, you will not be able to schedule software deployments for nearly 60 percent of your clients. The features of Systems Management Server and Software Installation are designed to complement each other.

   B. **Correct:** Software Installation supports the central management of software on Windows 2000 Professional only. Without Systems Management Server, you will not be able to centrally manage software for the non–Windows 2000 clients. The features of Systems Management Server and Software Installation are designed to complement each other.

   C. **Incorrect:** Because Software Installation uses Windows Installer technology, you will be able to use the self-repairing capabilities of Windows Installer on the Windows 2000 Professional clients. The self-repairing capabilities perform functions such as noting when a file is missing and immediately reinstalling the damaged or missing files to fix the application.

   D. **Correct:** Software Installation does not operate over slow network or dial-up connections. Systems Management Server is required to provide options for deploying software over slow network links. The features of Systems Management Server and Software Installation are designed to complement each other.

   E. **Correct:** Software Installation does not have the capability to license or meter software. Systems Management Server is required to provide software licensing and metering. The features of Systems Management Server and Software Installation are designed to complement each other.

70-217.03.03.006

▶ **Correct Answers: C**

   A. **Incorrect:** When you assign the software package to users, the application is advertised the next time the user logs on to a workstation. The application is installed the first time the user activates it on the computer, either by selecting the application from the Start menu or by activating a document associated with the application. However, assigning the software package to users allows them to remove the application by using Add/Remove Programs in Control Panel. Although the software is then reapplied to the user, the user must select the software from the Start menu or a desktop shortcut to reinstall it.

   B. **Incorrect:** When you publish the software package to users, the application does not appear installed on the users' computers. The application stores its advertisement attributes in Active Directory. Then, information such as the application's name and file associations is exposed to the users in the Active Directory container. The application is then ready for the user to install by using Add/Remove Programs in Control Panel or by clicking a file associated with the application. However, publishing the software package to users allows them to remove the application using Add/Remove Programs in Control Panel.

   C. **Correct:** When you assign the software package to computers, the application is advertised and the installation is performed when it is safe to do so, such as when the computer starts up and there are no competing processes on the computer. The software is automatically installed when the computer reboots. The user cannot remove the software; however, he or she can run a repair on the software.

   D. **Incorrect:** You cannot publish a software package to computers.

70-217.03.03.007

▶ **Correct Answers: C**

   A. **Incorrect:** You should open the software package properties for the 2.0 release, not the SearchApp software package's properties. Then in the Upgrades tab you must specify the package to be upgraded, SearchApp, not the package that will function as the upgrade.

   B. **Incorrect:** You should open the software package properties for the 2.0 release, not the SearchApp software package's properties. Then in the Upgrades tab you must specify the package to be upgraded, SearchApp, not the package that will function as the upgrade.

C. **Correct:** You should open the software package properties for the 2.0 release and then in the Upgrades tab, you must specify SearchApp, the package to be upgraded.

D. **Incorrect:** You should open the software package properties for the 2.0 release and then in the Upgrades tab, not the Modifications tab, you must specify SearchApp, the package to be upgraded. The Modifications tab is used to specify the modifications or transforms files to be applied to the software package and the order in which the files are applied.

70-217.03.03.008

▶ **Correct Answers: A and C**

A. **Correct:** If a published software package does not appear in Add/Remove Programs in Control Panel, a possible cause is that the user cannot access Active Directory. You can check to see that the user can access Active Directory by determining whether the user is validated by a Windows 2000 domain controller. If the user is validated, he or she can access Active Directory.

B. **Incorrect:** If a published software package does not appear in Add/Remove Programs in Control Panel, a possible cause is not that the application is already installed. If the software was already installed, it would still appear in Add/Remove Programs.

C. **Correct:** If a published software package does not appear in Add/Remove Programs in Control Panel, a possible cause is that the user is running Terminal Services on the desktop. Software Installation is not supported for Terminal Server clients. You can check to see whether the user is running Terminal Services by using the ADDIAG.EXE utility.

D. **Incorrect:** It is not necessary to enable the application to autoinstall by file extension for it to appear in Add/Remove Programs in Control Panel. If the package is published properly, it automatically appears in Add/Remove Programs.

E. **Incorrect:** Because the local GPOs are overwritten by the organizational unit GPO, the presence of conflicting local GPOs cannot be the reason why the published software package does not appear in Add/Remove Programs in Control Panel. However, if the GPO linked to the OU does not manage the user due to the user being filtered out or due to another domain or OU GPO, Add/Remove Programs will not appear in Control Panel.

70-217.03.03.009

▶ **Correct Answers: B**

A. **Incorrect:** It is not necessary for the user to have Write permission for the GPO to be able to access the software application. It is sufficient for the user to have both the Read and Apply Group Policy permissions for the GPO.

B. **Correct:** The user must have both the Read and Apply Group Policy permissions for the GPO to be able to access the software application.

C. **Incorrect:** The user does not need Write permission for the application package to be able to access the software application. It is sufficient for the user to have Read permission for the application.

D. **Incorrect:** It is not necessary for the user to have Full Control permission for the application package to be able to access the software application. It is sufficient for the user to have Read permission for the application.

E. **Incorrect:** It is not necessary for the user to have Write permission at the SDP to be able to access the software application. It is sufficient for the user to have Read permission at the SDP.

F. **Incorrect:** It is not necessary for the user to have Read and Execute permission at the SDP to be able to access the software application. It is sufficient for the user to have Read permission at the SDP.

70-217.03.03.010

▶ **Correct Answers: A**

A. **Correct:** If users consistently receive the error message, a possible cause is that the software package is corrupt. You can test the package by installing it on another computer with the same configuration. To do this, start Windows Installer from the command line and type **C:>msiexec /i** *PackageName*. Then make sure that the package can be opened.

B. **Incorrect:** If you did not enable the autoinstall for the application, the users would not receive the error message. Instead, the application would simply not install when the users activated the document of the published application.

C. **Incorrect:** If another application were undergoing automatic repair, users would not receive the error message. When a user starts an application that requires automatic repair, Windows Installer automatically repairs the application, returning to the application source for files if necessary.

D. **Incorrect:** If the users do not have Read permissions at the SDP, the users would not receive the "Cannot Prepare Package For Deployment" error message. Instead, they would receive the error message "The feature you are trying to install cannot be found in the source directory."

70-217.03.03.011

▶ **Correct Answers: C**

A. **Incorrect:** You cannot publish a software package to computers.

B. **Incorrect:** Application categories are a means for organizing assigned and published applications to make it easier for users to locate the appropriate application from within Add/Remove Programs in Control Panel. You cannot use categories to determine which application users install when they select a file.

C. **Correct:** Use the File Extensions tab of the Software Installation Properties dialog box to configure the file extension priority in the Application Precedence list box so that users who are managed by this GPO always install FrontPage first when they open files with the .htm or .html extension.

D. **Incorrect:** Enabling Loopback for a GPO affects the order of processing group policy settings, not software packages. You cannot use the Loopback setting to determine which application users install when they select a file.

70-217.03.03.012

▶ **Correct Answers: B**

A. **Incorrect:** WinZip is a file compression program used to create .zip files. It cannot be used to create .zap files.

B. **Correct:** You can create or modify a .zap file by using a text editor such as Notepad. Be sure that the filenames of .zap files created with Notepad use the .zap extension. Notepad may automatically add the .txt extension to a .zap file.

C. **Incorrect:** The VERITAS WinINSTALL LE program is a tool included with Windows 2000 Server that is used to view existing .msi packages and to repackage applications. It cannot be used to create .zap files.

D. **Incorrect:** The Microsoft Management Console is a tool used to create, save, and open collections of administrative tools, called consoles. It cannot be used to create .zap files.

Manage network configuration by using group policy.

Windows 2000 provides the **Folder Redirection** group policy extension as an administrative tool for redirecting the special local folders containing a **user's profile** to a specified network server location. Folder Redirection allows users to work with individual or shared files on a secure server as if the folders were on the local drive. The following special folders can be redirected: Application Data, Desktop, My Documents (including My Pictures), and Start Menu. The Folder Redirection extension is located under User Configuration/Windows Settings in the Group Policy snap-in.

You can redirect special folders to a location according to security group membership or redirect special folders to one location for everyone in the site, domain, or OU. You can also direct the My Pictures folder to follow the redirection of the My Documents folder, which it does by default. To redirect special folders, you must enter the full **Universal Naming Convention (UNC)** path to the new location, such as \\<*servername*> \<*sharename*>. If you want each user in the security group, site, domain, or OU to have his or her own folder in the new location (recommended), you must add *%username%* to the end of the UNC path.

When a group policy object that redirects special folders is removed, the folders are affected in various ways, depending on how the Move The Folder Contents and Policy Removal options settings within the Folder Redirection are set up.

To troubleshoot folder redirection, view the "User Data Management Issues" topic in Chapter 25, "Troubleshooting Change and Configuration Management," in the *Microsoft Windows 2000 Server Resource Kit*. Use this topic to find folder redirection problem descriptions and suggestions for resolution.

Objective 3.4 Questions

70-217.03.04.001

You want to use group policy to redirect the My Documents and My Pictures special folders to a location on a network server according to security group membership. Which group policy folder should you access to configure the redirection options?

Examine the GPO shown in the figure below.

A. Computer Configuration\Software Settings

B. Computer Configuration\Windows Settings

C. Computer Configuration\Administrative Templates

D. User Configuration\Software Settings

E. User Configuration\Windows Settings

F. User Configuration\Administrative Templates

70-217.03.04.002

You want to use a group policy object (GPO) linked to an Active Directory domain to redirect everyone's My Documents and My Pictures folder to a location on the network. You configured the My Documents folder properties as shown in the exhibit and clicked the Apply button. You did not change any of the options on the Settings tab; therefore, the default settings were applied when you clicked the Apply button.

To test the redirection, you create a user named Mowgli in the Active Directory domain, and log in to a Windows 2000 client as Mowgli. You then copy a .jpg file to the My Pictures folder. If the redirection is working properly, where should you find the .jpg file you copied to the My Pictures folder?

Examine the My Documents Properties dialog box shown below.

A. \\fs1\data\mowgli pictures

B. \\fs1\data\mowgli\my pictures

C. \\fs1\data\mowgli documents\my pictures

D. \\fs1\data\mowgli\my documents\my pictures.

70-217.03.04.003

You want to use group policy to redirect Windows 2000 special folders to locations on network servers. Your main goals in doing so are to improve the availability of documents for users who log in from different computers and to decrease the chances of losing data. Which Windows 2000 folders will you be able to redirect using group policy? (Choose all that apply.)

A. Desktop

B. Start Menu

C. My Pictures

D. Recycle Bin

E. My Documents

F. Application Data

G. My Network Places

70-217.03.04.004

You are configuring options to redirect My Documents to a location on the network for everyone in an Active Directory organizational unit (OU) named Orders. You have configured the options on the Target tab and now need to configure the Settings options. You want to achieve these results:

- The My Pictures folder should not be redirected.

- When the GPO no longer applies, the My Documents folder returns to its user profile location.

- When the GPO no longer applies, the contents of My Documents are copied back to the user profile location and deleted from the redirected location.

- Allow only the user and the local file system to have full rights to the redirected folder, and no one else, not even administrators, should have any rights.

To achieve these results, you propose to apply the Settings options as shown in the exhibit.

Which results does the proposed solution provide? (Choose all that apply.)

Examine the My Documents Properties dialog box shown below.

A. The My Pictures folder is not redirected.

B. When the GPO no longer applies, the My Documents folder returns to its user profile location.

C. When the GPO no longer applies, the contents of My Documents are copied back to the user profile location and deleted from the redirected location.

D. Only the user and the local file system have full rights to the redirected folder, and no one else, not even administrators, has any rights.

Objective 3.4 Answers

70-217.03.04.001

▶ **Correct Answers: E**

A. **Incorrect:** The computer configuration policy settings in the Software Settings folder contain only the Software Installation settings, which help you specify how applications are installed and maintained within your organization. You cannot use the Software Installation settings to configure folder redirection options.

B. **Incorrect:** The computer configuration policy settings in the Windows Settings folder include the Scripts (Startup/Shutdown) extension, which allows you to specify the script or scripts that are to run at computer startup or shutdown, and the Security Settings folder, which allows a security administrator to manually configure security levels assigned to a local or nonlocal GPO. You cannot use these settings to configure folder redirection options.

C. **Incorrect:** The computer configuration policy settings in the Administrative Templates folder contain all registry-based group policy settings, including settings for Windows Components, System, Network, and Printers. You cannot use any of these settings to configure folder redirection options.

D. **Incorrect:** The user configuration policy settings in the Software Settings folder contain only the Software Installation settings, which help you specify how applications are installed and maintained within your organization. You cannot use the Software Installation settings to configure folder redirection options.

E. **Correct:** The user configuration policy settings in the Windows Settings folder include the Folder Redirection settings. Use the settings in the Folder Redirection folder to redirect Windows 2000 special folders (My Documents, Application Data, Desktop, and Start Menu) from their default user profile location to an alternate location on the network where they can be centrally managed.

F. **Incorrect:** The user configuration policy settings in the Administrative Templates folder contain all registry-based group policy settings, including settings for Windows Components, Start Menu & Taskbar, Desktop, Control Panel, Network, and System. You cannot use any of these settings to configure folder redirection options.

70-217.03.04.002

▶ **Correct Answers: B**

A. **Incorrect:** Because you did not change any default settings on the Settings tab of the My Documents Properties dialog box, the My Pictures folder remains a subfolder of My Documents. Therefore, My Pictures follows My Documents to the redirection target specified on the Target tab of the My Documents Properties dialog box, which is \\fs1\data\%username%. The path suggested in this answer choice does not contain the My Documents folder, nor does it properly label the My Pictures folder.

B. **Correct:** Because you did not change any default settings on the Settings tab of the My Documents Properties dialog box, the My Pictures folder remains a subfolder of My Documents. Therefore, My Pictures follows My Documents to the redirection target specified on the Target tab of the My Documents Properties dialog box, which is \\fs1\data\%username%. The path suggested in this answer choice correctly shows the My Pictures folder as a subfolder of \\fs1\data\%username%, which is the My Documents folder.

C. **Incorrect:** Because you did not change any default settings on the Settings tab of the My Documents Properties dialog box, the My Pictures folder remains a subfolder of My Documents. Therefore, My Pictures follows My Documents to the redirection target specified on the Target tab of the My Documents Properties dialog box, which is \\fs1\data\%username%. The path suggested in this answer choice does not properly label the My Documents folder.

D. **Incorrect:** Folder Redirection does not create a subfolder called "My Documents" under \\fs1\data\%username%. \\fs1\data\%username% is the redirected My Documents folder. Therefore, the answer is incorrect.

70-217.03.04.003

▶ **Correct Answers: A, B, C, E, and F**

A. **Correct:** Using the Folder Redirection settings in group policy, you can redirect the Desktop special folder to an alternate location on the network, where it can be centrally managed.

B. **Correct:** Using the Folder Redirection settings in group policy, you can redirect the Start Menu folder to an alternate location on the network, where it can be centrally managed.

C. **Correct:** Using the folder redirection settings in group policy, you can redirect the My Pictures special folder to an alternate location on the network, where it can be centrally managed. By default, the My Pictures folder follows the redirection of the My Documents folder (remaining as its subfolder whenever My Documents is redirected). You can also remove the My Pictures folder as a subfolder of My Documents and have the user profile determine the location of My Pictures. This action is recommended only if there is a specific reason (such as file share scalability) for separating My Pictures from My Documents. If the folders are separated, a shortcut representing the My Pictures folder appears in My Documents.

D. **Incorrect:** Using the Folder Redirection settings in group policy, you cannot redirect the Recycle Bin to an alternate location on the network.

E. **Correct:** Using the Folder Redirection settings in group policy, you can redirect the My Documents folder to an alternate location on the network, where it can be centrally managed.

F. **Correct:** Using the Folder Redirection settings in group policy, you can redirect the Application Data folder to an alternate location on the network, where it can be centrally managed.

G. **Incorrect:** Using the Folder Redirection settings in group policy, you cannot redirect the My Network Places folder to an alternate location on the network.

70-217.03.04.004

▶ **Correct Answers: B and D**

A. **Incorrect:** Because Make My Pictures A Subfolder Of My Documents is selected under My Pictures Preferences in the My Documents Properties dialog box, the My Pictures folder remains a subfolder of My Documents and follows the redirection of the My Documents folder.

B. **Correct:** Because the Move The Contents Of My Documents To The New Location check box and the Redirect The Folder Back To The Local Userprofile Location When Policy Is Removed option are selected in the My Documents Properties dialog box, the My Documents folder returns to its user profile location when the GPO no longer applies.

C. **Incorrect:** Because the Move The Contents Of My Documents To The New Location check box and the Redirect The Folder Back To The Local Userprofile Location When Policy Is Removed option are selected in the My Documents Properties dialog box, the My Documents folder is copied to its user profile location when the GPO no longer applies. Although the contents of My Documents return to the user profile location, they are not deleted from the redirected location.

D. **Correct:** Because the Grant The User Exclusive Rights To My Documents check box is checked in the My Documents Properties dialog box, the user and the local system have full rights to the folder, and no one else, not even administrators, has any rights.

O B J E C T I V E   3 . 5

Deploy Windows 2000 by using Remote Installation Services (RIS).

The **Remote OS Installation** feature of Windows 2000 uses **Remote Installation Services (RIS)** technology to customize and enable automated installation of **Windows 2000 Professional** on new or replacement **remote boot**-enabled **client** computers. To perform Remote OS Installation, you must install an RIS server on a Windows 2000 server that has access to: Active Directory, a compliant version of DNS, and an updated **Dynamic Host Configuration Protocol (DHCP)** server. Recommended hardware for an RIS server includes: a Pentium II 200-MHz or faster processor, 96 to 128 MB RAM, a 2-GB minimum hard disk or partition dedicated to the RIS directory tree, and a 100-Mbps **network adapter card**. Recommended hardware for the client includes: a Pentium 166-MHz or faster processor, 64 MB RAM, an 800-MB disk drive, and a DHCP **PXE**-based remote boot ROM version .99c or a network adapter supported by the **RIS book disk**.

The tasks for implementing RIS are: setting up RIS, configuring RIS, creating an **RIPrep image**, creating an RIS boot disk (for non-PXE-capable computers), and verifying the RIS configuration. To set up RIS, you must first add the RIS component from the Windows Components Wizard dialog box and then install RIS on the server using the Remote Installation Services Wizard. To configure RIS, you must: authorize the RIS servers allowed to run on your network using the DHCP console, set properties that control how the server supplies RIS to clients using the Active Directory Users And Computers console, set options presented to different groups of users during installation in the **Client Installation Wizard** using the Active Directory Users And Computers console, and specify the users or groups who have access to the RIPrep OS images available on the RIS server by setting permissions for the image installation files. Before you can create an RIPrep image, you must create and configure the source workstation and then test the workstation configuration. When the workstation is configured to specifications, you can create an RIPrep image on the workstation using the

Remote Installation Preparation Wizard. If your client computers do not have a **PXE**-based remote boot-enabled **ROM** but do have a supported network adapter, you must also create an RIS boot disk using the RBFG.EXE tool on the RIS server. Finally, you can verify and check the integrity of an RIS-enabled server using the Active Directory Users And Computers console.

After you implement RIS, it may be necessary to maintain and manage client installation images by adding new client OS installation images and associating unattended setup **answer files** with an image (CD-based images only) using the Images tab in the Remote Installation Services Properties dialog box.

To troubleshoot RIS, view the "Troubleshooting Remote Installation Services" topic in Windows 2000 online help, the "Troubleshooting RIS" topic in Chapter 24, "Remote Installation," or the "Remote OS Installation Issues" topic in Chapter 25, "Troubleshooting Change and Configuration Management," in the *Microsoft Windows 2000 Server Resource Kit*. Use these topics to find RIS problem descriptions and suggestions for resolution.

Objective 3.5 Questions

70-217.03.05.001

You are the administrator for your Windows 2000 domain. You have set up a Remote Installation Services (RIS) server and properly authorized and configured the server. You set up the RIPrep image and are ready for deployment to your client systems.

Before deploying, you realize that there could be a problem with the display settings. Some clients must have a higher display resolution than the one used on the RIPrep source computer. You want to resolve this issue with as little administrative overhead as possible.

What should you do?

A. Contact the users who need the higher display resolution, and instruct them on how to change the display settings after the RIPrep image has been installed.

B. Open the HKEY_CLASSES_ROOT on Local Machine registry key in the Registry Editor. Change the .osc\Display entry to Yes. Create a new file named Display.osc, and edit accordingly. Update the appropriate answer files.

C. Create another source computer configured with the higher display resolution. Create a second RIPrep image using the new source computer. Give access to the new image only to those needing the higher display resolution.

D. Create a new file named Display.osc, and edit it accordingly. Enable the display of the new screen by modifying the OSChoice.osc file to display the new Display.osc when the user presses Enter. Update the appropriate answer files.

70-217.03.05.002

You are the administrator for your Windows 2000 network, which contains a Remote Installation Services (RIS) server. You have several images residing on this RIS server.

You no longer need one of the RIPrep images located on the RIS server. You decide you want to remove it. You want to accomplish complete removal of the image with as little administrative overhead as possible.

What should you do?

A. Use the Remove option found on the Images tab of the Advanced Settings property page.

B. Use Windows Explorer to delete the directory and subdirectories containing the image you want to remove.

C. Temporarily disable the RIS server. Delete the image file directory. Then reset the RIS service to Automatic.

D. Edit the RIS Client Installation options, and deny access to all menu options for all group policies that have access to the RIPrep image. Then delete the image file directory.

70-217.03.05.003

You are setting up new computers for your company's network. The network is one domain consisting of one Windows 2000 DNS server. There are no other Windows 2000 servers on your TCP/IP network. The 50 client machines you want to add to the network contain the same hardware configuration. Each client machine is configured with an RIS-supported PCI Plug and Play network adapter and PXE-based remote boot ROM version .99c.

You want to accomplish the following goals:

- You want to use Remote Installation Services (RIS) to install Windows 2000 Professional on the 50 new computers.

- You want to provide all members of the Information Technology (IT) OU with access to all of the installation options on the Client Installation Wizard (CIW).

- You want to restrict all members of the General Users OU to only the Automatic Setup option and the Maintenance and Troubleshooting installation option on the CIW.

- You want all clients to be prestaged for security.

You take the following actions. On your DNS server, you install the DHCP Server service and properly configure all options. On that same server, you set up and authorize RIS. You create the RIPrep image, and set the client support properties to "Respond To Client Computers Requesting Service." You set the Client Account Location to "Default Directory Service Location." You then set up a group policy object setting for the IT OU, allowing these users access to all installation options. You then set up a group policy object setting for the General Users OU and allow access to only the Automatic Setup and Tools installation options.

The 50 client computers start, and then initiate a network service request from the RIS server.

Which goals do these actions accomplish? (Choose all that apply.)

A. RIS is used to install Windows 2000 Professional on the 50 new computers.

B. Members of the IT OU have access to all of the installation options on the CIW.

C. Members of the General Users OU are restricted to the Automatic Setup option and the Maintenance and Troubleshooting installation option on the CIW.

D. All clients are prestaged for security.

70-217.03.05.004

You are the administrator for your Windows 2000 network. You have decided to deploy Remote Installation Services (RIS). You set up, configure, and authorize an RIS server. After creating the source computer, you create an RIPrep image and store it on the RIS server. You notify the users about what they will need to do the next morning.

The next morning, Steve, a user, contacts you. He states that he didn't receive any of the special messages you told him about. He does not think that the image installed on his computer. When you go to Steve's system, you discover that it does not have a PXE-based ROM.

You want Steve's computer to be able to install the RIPrep image on the RIS server. You want to accomplish this task with as little administrative overhead as possible.

Which steps should you take? (Choose three.)

A. Create an RIS boot disk using the RBFG utility on the RIS server.

B. Create an RIS boot disk using the MAKEDISK utility on the RIS server.

C. Create an RIS boot disk using the RBFG utility on the Windows 2000 Professional CD.

D. Create an RIS boot disk using the MAKEDISK utility on the Windows 2000 Professional CD.

E. Make sure the network adapter in Steve's system is included in the Hardware Compatibility List (HCL).

F. Make sure the network adapter in Steve's system is included in the adapter list of the utility you used.

G. Boot Steve's computer using the disk you created using the RBFG utility. Press F12 to initiate a network service boot.

H. Boot Steve's computer using the disk you created using the MAKEDISK utility. Press F12 to initiate a network service boot.

70-217.03.05.005

You are the administrator for your Windows 2000 domain. You have set up a Windows 2000 Server computer to act as your Remote Installation Services (RIS) server. You set up, authorize, and configure the RIS server to deliver an RIPrep image to your Windows 2000 Professional systems.

When users at the systems start the Client Installation Wizard, they are prompted to enter the product identification (PID) number. The users have contacted you requesting the PID.

You want to prevent the users from having to type in the PID during installation. You want to accomplish this with as little administrative overhead as possible.

What should you do?

A. On the RIS server, reconfigure the image to include the PID.

B. Make a copy of the RIPREP.SIF file for each user. Tell the users to copy the file to their C: drive and reboot their system.

C. On the RIS server, open the RIPREP.SIF file. In the [User Data] section of the file, type **ProductID =** "*xxxxx-xxx-xxxxxxx-xxxxx*" (including the dashes and quotation marks, where the *x*es are the PID of the retail version of Windows 2000 Professional). Ask the users to restart their systems.

D. On the RIS server, open the RIPREP.SIF file. In the [Product Data] section of the file, type **ProductID =** "*xxxxx-xxx-xxxxxxx-xxxxx*" (including the dashes and quotation marks, where the *x*es are the PID of the retail version of Windows 2000 Professional). Ask the users to restart their systems.

E. On the RIS server, open the Registry Editor. In the HKEY_LOCAL_MACHINE on the Local Machine\Software\Policies\Microsoft\RIS key, change the PID key value to *xxxxx-xxx-xxxxxxx-xxxxx* where the *x*es are the PID of the retail version of Windows 2000 Professional. Ask the users to restart their systems.

70-217.03.05.006

You are the administrator for your company's Windows 2000 domain. Srv1 is your company's Windows 2000 DHCP server. You have decided to implement Remote Installation Services (RIS) on a Windows 2000 Server computer named Srv2.

Currently Srv2 has a 10-gigabyte (GB) hard drive installed. One NTFS partition of 5 GB has been set up as a C: drive. The C: drive currently has 3 GB of free space. The rest of the hard drive is unformatted.

You want to install RIS on Srv2. You do not want to purchase any more hardware than is absolutely necessary. You want to leave as much unformatted space as possible for future expansion. You want to accomplish these goals with as little administrative overhead as possible.

What should you do?

A. Install RIS on the partition that already exists on Srv2.

B. Create a second NTFS partition of 1 GB. Make sure the new drive is a separate volume from the C: drive. Install RIS on this partition.

C. Create a second NTFS partition of 2 GB. Make sure that the new drive is a separate volume from the C: drive. Install RIS on this partition.

D. Purchase a second 10-GB hard drive. Create a 2-GB NTFS partition. Make sure that the new drive is a separate volume from the C: drive. Install RIS on this partition.

E. Create a 1-GB FAT partition on the 10-GB hard drive already installed. Make sure that the new drive is a separate volume from the C: drive. Install RIS on this partition.

F. Create a 2-GB FAT partition on the 10-GB hard drive already installed. Make sure that the new drive is a separate volume from the C: drive. Install RIS on this partition.

70-217.03.05.007

You administer your company's Windows 2000 domain, which contains an RIS server that manages several RIPrep images.

You want to install one of your images on three older computers, which do not have a PXE-based ROM. Although the adapter used in the three computers is the same, it is not listed in the RIS boot disk adapter list.

You want to be able to use the RIS boot disk on these three computers to install the RIPrep image with as little administrative overhead as possible.

What should you do?

A. Download the appropriate driver for the network adapter from Microsoft. Add the driver to the RBFG.EXE utility.

B. Download the appropriate driver for the network adapter from Microsoft. Add the driver to each computer's hard drive.

C. Download the appropriate driver for the network adapter from the network adapter vendor. Add the driver to the RBFG.EXE utility.

D. Download the appropriate driver for the network adapter from the network adapter vendor. Add the driver to each computer's hard drive.

E. For these three computers, purchase an adapter that is on the RIS boot disk adapter list. Install the adapters in the computers, and use the RIS boot disk.

70-217.03.05.008

You are the administrator for your Windows 2000 domain. You have an RIS server named RIS1 that has been properly configured and authorized.

You have installed the operating system and desktop applications on the source computer, named Source1. You want to run the Remote Installation Preparation Wizard to create the image.

What should you do?

A. From Source1's Start menu, click Run and type **\\RIS1\Reminst\i386\RBFG.EXE**

B. From RIS1's Start menu, click Run and type **\\Source1\Reminst\i386\RBFG.exe**

C. From Source1's Start menu, click Run and type **\\RIS1\Reminst\i386\RIPrep.exe**

D. From RIS1's Start menu, click Run and type **\\Source1\Reminst\i386\RIPrep.exe**

E. From Source1's Start menu, click Run and type **\\RIS1\Reminst\Admin\i386\RBFG.exe**

F. From RIS1's Start menu, click Run and type **\\Source1\Reminst\Admin\i386\RBFG.exe**

G. From Source1's Start menu, click Run and type **\\RIS1\Reminst\Admin\i386\RIPrep.exe**

H. From RIS1's Start menu, click Run and type **\\Source1\Reminst\Admin\i386\RIPrep.exe**

Objective 3.5 Answers

70-217.03.05.001

▶ **Correct Answers: D**

A. **Incorrect:** Although contacting each of the users who need the higher display resolution and instructing them on how to change the display settings after the RIPrep image has been installed would solve the problem, this is not the solution with the least amount of administrative overhead.

B. **Incorrect:** There is no .osc\Display entry in HKEY_CLASSES_ROOT on the Local Machine registry key in the Registry Editor. In addition, Microsoft recommends that you not use the Registry Editor to edit the registry directly unless you have no alternative.

C. **Incorrect:** Although creating another source computer configured with the higher display resolution, creating a second RIPrep image from the source computer, and providing access to users needing higher display resolution would solve the problem, this is not the solution with the least amount of administrative overhead.

D. **Correct:** By creating a new file named Display.osc, you create a new screen in the Client Installation Wizard that allows the user to change the default video display settings to be used on the client. By modifying the OSChoice.osc file, you allow the Operating System Choice screen in the Client Installation Wizard to display the new Display.osc screen rather than the default Warning.osc screen. By updating the answer files, you allow the answer files to accept the new variables that specify the display resolution. When these actions are complete, the user is prompted to adjust the default video display settings, and the input is incorporated into the answer file used during the remote installation.

70-217.03.05.002

▶ **Correct Answers: B**

A. **Incorrect:** The Remove option found on the Images tab of the Advanced Settings property page removes only the unattended setup answer file (.sif) associated with the operating system image.

B. **Correct:** To completely remove an RIPrep image from the RIS server, use Windows Explorer to delete the directory and subdirectories that contain the image you want to remove. You can delete the directories from the server console or by browsing the Reminst share on the RIS server.

C. **Incorrect:** It is not necessary to temporarily disable the RIS server and reset the RIS service. Although deleting the image file directory would solve the problem, this is not the solution with the least amount of administrative overhead.

D. **Incorrect:** It is not necessary to edit the RIS Client Installation options and deny access to all menu options for all group policies who have access to the RIPrep image. Although deleting the image file directory would solve the problem, this is not the solution with the least amount of administrative overhead.

70-217.03.05.003

▶ **Correct Answers: A, B, and C**

A. **Correct:** By installing the DHCP Server service on your DNS server, setting up and authorizing RIS, creating an RIPrep image, and configuring the appropriate GPO settings for the IT OU general users, you have used RIS to install Windows 2000 Professional on the 50 new computers.

B. **Correct:** Members of the IT OU have access to all of the installation options on the CIW because you set up a GPO for the IT OU allowing its members access to all client installation options. To do this, access the Group Policy console tree, click User Configuration, open Windows Settings, and then click Remote Installation Services. Then you must open the Choice Options dialog box and select Allow for the Automatic Setup, Custom Setup, Restart Setup, and Tools options.

C. **Correct:** Members of the General Users OU have access to only the Automatic Setup and the Mainte-nance and Troubleshooting installation options on the CIW because you set up a GPO for the General Users OU allowing them access to only these installation options. To do this, access the Group Policy console tree, click User Configuration, open Windows Settings, and then click Remote Installation Services. Then you must open the Choice Options dialog box, select Allow for the Automatic Setup and Tools options, and select Deny for the Custom Setup and Restart Setup options.

D. **Incorrect:** You have taken no action to prestage clients for security. To prestage client computers, you must access the New Object-Computer dialog box from the Active Directory Users And Com-puters console to define a specific computer name and to optionally specify the RIS server to service the client.

70-217.03.05.004

▶ **Correct Answers: A, F, and G**

A. **Correct:** To support existing client computers that do not have a PXE-based remote boot-enabled ROM but do have a supported network adapter, you must create an RIS boot disk. One of the ways to create an RIS boot disk is to use the remote boot floppy disk generator tool, RBFG.EXE, found on every RIS server.

B. **Incorrect:** You cannot use the MAKEDISK utility to create an RIS boot disk. To create an RIS boot disk, you must use the RBFG utility, which can be found on every RIS server and in the Administra-tive Tools Windows Installer (adminpak.msi) package included with Windows 2000 Server.

C. **Incorrect:** The RBFG utility can be found on every RIS server and in the Administrative Tools Win-dows Installer (adminpak.msi) package included with Windows 2000 Server. The RBFG utility is not included on the Windows 2000 Professional CD.

D. **Incorrect:** You cannot use the MAKEDISK utility to create an RIS boot disk. To create an RIS boot disk, you must use the RBFG utility, which can be found on every RIS server and in the Administra-tive Tools Windows Installer (adminpak.msi) package included with Windows 2000 Server.

E. **Incorrect:** The HCL does not contain a list of PCI-based network adapters supported by the RIS boot disk.

F. **Correct:** Because you can use an RIS boot disk only with computers that contain supported PCI-based network adapters, you should verify that the network adapter installed in Steve's system is included in the adapter list supported by the RBFG utility. To view the adapter list, run the RBFG utility and then click the Adapter List button at the bottom of the Windows 2000 Remote Boot Disk Generator dialog box.

G. **Correct:** After you verify that the network adapter installed in Steve's system is included in the adapter list supported by the RBFG utility and create an RIS boot disk using the RBFG utility, the next step is to turn on Steve's computer, boot from the RIS boot disk, and press F12 to initiate a network service boot. This action downloads and starts the Client Installation Wizard. The rest of the RIS process is identical to the PXE boot ROM installation process.

H. **Incorrect:** You cannot use the MAKEDISK utility to create an RIS boot disk. To create an RIS boot disk, you must use the RBFG utility, which can be found on every RIS server and in the Administrative Tools Windows Installer (adminpak.msi) package included with Windows 2000 Server.

70-217.03.05.005

▶ **Correct Answers: C**

A. **Incorrect:** You cannot reconfigure the image to include the PID. You must include the PID in RIPREP.SIF, the RIS unattended setup answer file.

B. **Incorrect:** Copying the RIPREP.SIF file for each user and asking the users to copy the file to their C: drive and reboot will have no effect on the users having to type in the PID during installation. You must include the PID in RIPREP.SIF, the RIS unattended setup answer file.

C. **Correct:** To prevent the users from having to type in the PID during installation, you must include the PID in RIPREP.SIF, the RIS unattended setup answer file. To include the PID, open the RIPREP.SIF file, and type **ProductID** = "*xxxxx-xxx-xxxxxxx-xxxxx*" (including the dashes and quotation marks, where the *x*es are the PID of the retail version of Windows 2000 Professional) into the [User Data] section of the RIPREP.SIF file. Have the users restart their systems.

D. **Incorrect:** To prevent the users from having to type in the PID during installation, you must include the PID in RIPREP.SIF, the RIS unattended setup answer file. However, to include the PID, you need to type **ProductID** = "*xxxxx-xxx-xxxxxxx-xxxxx*" (including the dashes and quotation marks) in the [User Data] section of the file, not the [Product Data] section. The [Product Data] section does not exist in RIPREP.SIF.

E. **Incorrect:** There is no RIS key in HKEY_LOCAL_MACHINE on Local Machine\Software\Policies\Microsoft in the Registry Editor. In addition, Microsoft recommends that you not use the Registry Editor to edit the registry directly unless you have no alternative.

70-217.03.05.006

▶ **Correct Answers: C**

   A. **Incorrect:** A separate, 2-GB minimum NTFS-formatted hard disk or partition dedicated to the RIS directory tree is required for installation of the RIS server. You cannot install RIS on the existing partition.

   B. **Incorrect:** A separate, 2-GB minimum NTFS-formatted hard disk or partition dedicated to the RIS directory tree is required for installation of the RIS server. You cannot install RIS on a 1-GB partition.

   C. **Correct:** A separate, 2-GB minimum NTFS-formatted hard disk or partition dedicated to the RIS directory tree is required for installation of the RIS server. This installation meets the established criteria; you do not need to purchase any more hardware than necessary, you are leaving as much unformatted space as possible (3 GB) for future expansion, and you have accomplished these goals with as little administrative overhead as possible.

   D. **Incorrect:** Although this solution allows you to successfully install the RIS server, it does not meet the established criteria. It is not necessary to purchase a second 10-GB hard drive when there are 5 unformatted GB remaining on the existing 10-GB hard drive on Srv2.

   E. **Incorrect:** A separate, 2-GB minimum NTFS-formatted hard disk or partition dedicated to the RIS directory tree is required for installation of the RIS server. You cannot install RIS on a 1-GB FAT partition.

   F. **Incorrect:** A separate, 2-GB minimum NTFS-formatted hard disk or partition dedicated to the RIS directory tree is required for installation of the RIS server. You cannot install RIS on a FAT partition.

70-217.03.05.007

▶ **Correct Answers: E**

A. **Incorrect:** You can use an RIS boot disk only with computers that contain supported Peripheral Component Interconnect (PCI)-based network adapters, listed in the adapter list supported by the RBFG utility. To view the adapter list, run the RBFG utility, and then click the Adapter List button at the bottom of the Windows 2000 Remote Boot Disk Generator dialog box. If the network adapter does not appear on the adapter list, you must purchase supported network adapters. There are no drivers for unsupported network adapters available from Microsoft, and you cannot add a driver to the RBFG utility.

B. **Incorrect:** You can use an RIS boot disk only with computers that contain supported PCI-based network adapters, listed in the adapter list supported by the RBFG utility. To view the adapter list, run the RBFG utility and then click the Adapter List button at the bottom of the Windows 2000 Remote Boot Disk Generator dialog box. If the network adapter does not appear on the adapter list, you must purchase supported network adapters. There are no drivers for unsupported network adapters available from Microsoft.

C. **Incorrect:** You can use an RIS boot disk only with computers that contain supported PCI-based network adapters, listed in the adapter list supported by the RBFG utility. To view the adapter list, run the RBFG utility, and then click the Adapter List button at the bottom of the Windows 2000 Remote Boot Disk Generator dialog box. If the network adapter does not appear on the adapter list, you must purchase supported network adapters. There are no drivers for unsupported network adapters, and you cannot add a driver to the RBFG utility.

D. **Incorrect:** You can use an RIS boot disk only with computers that contain supported PCI-based network adapters, listed in the adapter list supported by the RBFG utility. To view the adapter list, run the RBFG utility, and then click the Adapter List button at the bottom of the Windows 2000 Remote Boot Disk Generator dialog box. If the network adapter does not appear on the adapter list, you must purchase supported network adapters. There are no drivers for unsupported network adapters.

E. **Correct:** You can use an RIS boot disk only with computers that contain supported PCI-based network adapters, listed in the adapter list supported by the RBFG utility. To view the adapter list, run the RBFG utility, and then click the Adapter List button at the bottom of the Windows 2000 Remote Boot Disk Generator dialog box. If the network adapter used in the three computers does not appear on the adapter list, the easiest solution is to purchase new, supported network adapters.

70-217.03.05.008

▶ **Correct Answers: G**

A. **Incorrect:** This solution attempts to invoke the RBFG utility, used to create an RIS boot disk, from the client source computer. From Source1's Start menu, you should click Run, type the Universal Naming Convention (UNC) path of the RIPrep utility in the Open box (for example, \\RIS1\Reminst \Admin\i386\RIPrep.exe), and click OK.

B. **Incorrect:** This solution attempts to invoke the RBFG utility, used to create an RIS boot disk, from the RIS server. From Source1's Start menu, you should click Run, type the Universal Naming Convention (UNC) path of the RIPrep utility in the Open box (for example, \\RIS1\Reminst\Admin\i386 \RIPrep.exe), and click OK.

C. **Incorrect:** This solution does not use the correct Universal Naming Convention (UNC) path of the RIPrep utility. From Source1's Start menu, you should click Run, type the UNC path of the RIPrep utility in the Open box (for example, \\RIS1\Reminst\Admin\i386\RIPrep.exe), and click OK.

D. **Incorrect:** This solution attempts to invoke the RIPrep utility from the RIS server and does not use the correct Universal Naming Convention (UNC) path of the RIPrep utility. From Source1's Start menu, you should click Run, type the UNC path of the RIPrep utility in the Open box (for example, \\RIS1\Reminst\Admin\i386\RIPrep.exe), and click OK.

E. **Incorrect:** This solution attempts to invoke the RBFG utility, used to create an RIS boot disk, from the client source computer. From Source1's Start menu, you should click Run, type the Universal Naming Convention (UNC) path of the RIPrep utility in the Open box (for example, \\RIS1\Reminst \Admin\i386\RIPrep.exe), and click OK.

F. **Incorrect:** This solution attempts to invoke the RBFG utility, used to create an RIS boot disk, from the RIS server. From Source1's Start menu, you should click Run, type the Universal Naming Convention (UNC) path of the RIPrep utility in the Open box (for example, \\RIS1\Reminst\Admin \i386\RIPrep.exe), and click OK.

G. **Correct:** To run the Remote Installation Preparation Wizard and create the RIPrep image, you must access the client source computer's Start menu, click Run, type the Universal Naming Convention (UNC) path of the RIPrep utility in the Open box, and click OK.

H. **Incorrect:** This solution attempts to invoke the RIPrep utility from the RIS server. From Source1's Start menu, you should click Run, type the Universal Naming Convention (UNC) path of the RIPrep utility in the Open box (for example, \\RIS1\Reminst\Admin\i386\RIPrep.exe), and click OK.

O B J E C T I V E 3 . 6

Configure RIS security.

Security for RIS is configured in four tasks: **authorizing** an RIS server, setting computer account creation and domain joining permissions, setting RIPrep image permissions, and **prestaging** client computers. By authorizing an RIS server, you ensure that only RIS servers authorized by administrators can service clients. You authorize RIS servers during RIS implementation using the DHCP console. By setting the appropriate permissions, you ensure that only authorized users are allowed to create client computer accounts and to join client computer accounts to a domain. By specifying the users or groups who have access to RIPrep images, you can ensure that the image is available to authorized users or groups. By default, images are available to all users serviced by an RIS server. During RIS implementation, you set RIPrep image permissions on the folder containing the image installation files. Prestaging an RIS client computer creates a client account object within Active Directory, which can ensure that only authorized client computers are allowed to install an OS from the RIS server if the server is also configured to respond only to prestaged client computers. You prestage a client computer by accessing the New Object-Computer dialog box from the Active Directory Users And Computers console.

Objective 3.6 Questions

70-217.03.06.001

A small section of servers and a workstation on your Windows 2000 network are shown in the exhibit. You are the administrator of Computer B and have local administrative rights to it. Computer B is authorized in Active Directory.

You must install RIS services on Computer B.

You must authorize the RIS service in Active Directory services.

You must apply the changes immediately so that you can remotely install Windows 2000 Professional on 50 Windows 2000 computers.

You plan to take the following actions. You install RIS on Computer B using the RIS Installation Services Setup Wizard, and run the following command from Computer D:

secedit /refreshpolicy MACHINE_POLICY

What does the proposed solution provide? (Choose all that apply.)

Examine the figure shown below.

A. RIS services are installed on the server.

B. The proposed actions do not meet any of the desired results.

C. The RIS server is authorized in Active Directory services.

D. The changes are applied immediately, and the RIS server is available to install Windows 2000 Professional.

70-217.03.06.002

Your network has a combination of Windows NT 4.0 File and Print server computers and Windows 2000 Server computers. The Windows 2000 servers are configured as follows: a domain controller with Windows 2000 Advanced Server and Active Directory installed on it; a Windows 2000 Server computer with DHCP, DNS, and RIS installed on it; a Windows 2000 Server computer that serves as the RAS server; and two Windows 2000 SQL Server 7.0 database servers.

All clients on the network are either new machines purchased for the Windows 2000 Professional implementation, or they are Windows NT 4.0 Workstation computers. As the network administrator, you have decided to use the Windows 2000 RIS server to install Windows 2000 Professional on the workstations. You want to implement the most secure setting for the RIS server, and you want to enable only prestaged clients to use the RIS server. How should you configure the RIS server? (Choose all that apply.)

A. Select the Do Not Respond To Unknown Client Computers check box.

B. Clear the Respond To Client Computers Requesting Service check box.

C. Select the Respond To Client Computers Requesting Service check box.

D. Clear the Do Not Respond To Unknown Client Computers check box.

70-217.03.06.003

A small section of servers and a workstation on your Windows 2000 network are shown in the exhibit. You are the administrator of Computer A and have local administrative rights to it.

You must install RIS services on Computer A.

You must authorize the RIS service in Active Directory services.

You must apply the changes immediately so that you can remotely install Windows 2000 Professional on 50 Windows 2000 computers.

You plan to take the following actions. You install RIS on Computer A using the RIS Installation Services Setup Wizard, and run the following command from Computer D:

secedit /refreshpolicy MACHINE_POLICY

What does the proposed solution provide?

Examine the figure shown below.

A. RIS services are installed on the server.

B. The RIS server is authorized in Active Directory services.

C. The changes are applied immediately, and the RIS server is available to install Windows 2000 Professional.

D. The proposed actions do not meet any of the results.

70-217.03.06.004

You are the administrator of your company's Windows 2000 domain. The domain contains a domain controller running Windows 2000 DHCP server, two Windows 2000 Server computers configured as member servers, and 100 Windows 2000 Professional computers.

You want all client computers to use Remote Installation Services (RIS) to deploy a company-wide installation of Windows 2000 Professional. You take one of your Windows 2000 member servers and promote it to be a domain controller and install the RIS component.

You want this computer to be the only RIS server on your network. You also want the changes to the RIS policy to be propagated immediately.

What should you do? (Choose two.)

A. First, go to the DHCP server's Start menu. Click Run, and type: **authorize /RISserverIP**

B. First, open the DHCP console. Right-click the DHCP root node, and click Manage Authorized Servers. Click Authorize, and enter the IP address or name of the RIS server.

C. Second, at the command prompt on the RIS server, type: **secedit refresh MACHINE_POLICY**

D. Second, at the command prompt on the DHCP server, type: **secedit /refresh MACHINE_POLICY**

E. Second, at the command prompt on the DHCP server, type: **secedit /refreshpolicy MACHINE_POLICY**

F. Second, at the command prompt on the RIS server, type: **secedit /refreshpolicy MACHINE_POLICY**

70-217.03.06.005

A small section of servers and a workstation on your Windows 2000 network are shown in the exhibit. You are the administrator of Computer B and have local administrative rights to it and Computer E. Computer B is not authorized in Active Directory.

You must install RIS services on Computer B.

You must authorize the RIS service in Active Directory services.

You must apply the changes immediately so that you can remotely install Windows 2000 Professional on 50 Windows 2000 computers.

You plan to take the following actions. You install RIS on Computer B using the RIS Installation Services Setup Wizard, authorize the RIS server from Computer E, and run the following command from Computer D:

secedit /refreshpolicy MACHINE_POLICY

What does the proposed solution provide?

Examine the figure shown below.

A. RIS services are installed on the server.

B. The RIS server is authorized in Active Directory services.

C. The changes are applied immediately, and the RIS server is available to install Windows 2000 Professional.

D. The proposed actions do not meet any of the results.

70-217.03.06.006

You are setting up an additional 35 Windows 2000 Professional workstations on your network using RIS. Your RIS configuration is set up so that only prestaged clients can install Windows 2000 Professional. Due to the strict security policies of the company, none of the users who use RIS to install Windows 2000 Professional can have rights to anything but a specific computer object. Using the most restrictive permissions, which permissions must a user have to the computer object so that RIS is still available to her? (Choose all that apply.)

A. Read

B. Write

C. Full Control

D. Create All Child Objects

E. Delete All Child Objects

70-217.03.06.007

Your Windows 2000 Server's RIS configuration is set to respond only to prestaged clients. The RIS server resides on the same server as the DHCP server, and the DHCP server was authorized in Active Directory before the RIS server was installed. While attempting to install Windows 2000 Professional on a workstation, you receive only IP information and no servers are listed to support the client's boot process. What is the most likely cause?

A. The RIS server is not authorized.

B. The Active Directory service is stopped.

C. The Active Directory service is corrupt.

D. The computer object is not in Active Directory.

70-217.03.06.008

A small section of servers and a workstation on your Windows 2000 network are shown in the exhibit. You are the administrator of Computer B and have local administrative rights to it and Computer E. Computer B is not authorized in Active Directory services.

You must install RIS services on Computer B.

You must authorize the RIS service in Active Directory services.

You must apply the changes immediately so that you can remotely install Windows 2000 Professional on 50 Windows 2000 computers.

You plan to take the following actions. You install RIS on Computer B using the RIS Installation Services Setup Wizard, have a member of the Enterprise Admins group authorize the RIS server from Computer E, and run the following command from Computer D:

secedit /refreshpolicy MACHINE_POLICY

What does the proposed solution provide? (Choose all that apply.)

Examine the figure shown below.

A. RIS services are installed on the server.

B. The RIS server is authorized in Active Directory.

C. The changes are applied immediately, and the RIS server is available to install Windows 2000 Professional.

D. The proposed actions do not meet any of the results.

Objective 3.6 Answers

70-217.03.06.001

▶ **Correct Answers: A, C, and D**

A. **Correct:** By installing RIS on Computer B using the RIS Installation Services Setup Wizard, you have successfully installed RIS services on the server.

B. **Incorrect:** The proposed actions meet all of the desired results.

C. **Correct:** Because you installed RIS on Computer B, which is a DHCP server that is already authorized in Active Directory services, you do not need to perform separate authorization steps using the DHCP console.

D. **Correct:** Because you ran the secedit /refreshpolicy MACHINE_POLICY command from Computer D, the domain controller from which you set the user rights, the new RIS policy is applied immediately, and the RIS server is available to install Windows 2000 Professional.

70-217.03.06.002

▶ **Correct Answers: A and C**

   A. **Correct:** By selecting the Do Not Respond To Unknown Client Computers check box when you set up RIS server properties on the Remote Install tab of the Properties dialog box for the server, you ensure that the RIS server responds only to prestaged clients. This option is available only if the Respond To Client Computers Requesting Service check box is selected.

   B. **Incorrect:** Clearing the Respond To Client Computers Requesting Service check box when you set up RIS server properties on the Remote Install tab of the Properties dialog box for the server would prevent all clients from establishing a connection with the server.

   C. **Correct:** By selecting the Respond To Client Computers Requesting Service check box when you set up RIS server properties on the Remote Install tab of the Properties dialog box for the server, you allow the RIS server to respond to all clients requesting service. This check box must be selected in order to select the Do Not Respond To Unknown Client Computers check box.

   D. **Incorrect:** Clearing the Do Not Respond To Unknown Client Computers check box when you set up RIS server properties on the Remote Install tab of the Properties dialog box for the server would allow the RIS server to respond to unknown client computers.

70-217.03.06.003

▶ **Correct Answers: A**

   A. **Correct:** By installing RIS on Computer A using the RIS Installation Services Setup Wizard, you have successfully installed RIS services on the server.

   B. **Incorrect:** The RIS server is not authorized in Active Directory services. To authorize an RIS server in Active Directory services, you must log on to the domain where the RIS server resides and access the DHCP console. Then click the DHCP node, select Manage Authorized Servers on the Action menu, and click Authorize in the Manage Authorized Servers dialog box. In the Authorize DHCP Server dialog box, type the name or IP address of the RIS server to be authorized, and click OK. In the DHCP message box, click Yes. Finally, in the Manage Authorized Servers dialog box, click OK. The authorized RIS server is listed under the DHCP node.

   C. **Incorrect:** An RIS server must be authorized before it can service client computers. The RIS server is not authorized in Active Directory services.

   D. **Incorrect:** By installing RIS on Computer A using the RIS Installation Services Setup Wizard, you have successfully installed RIS services on the server.

70-217.03.06.004

▶ **Correct Answers: B and F**

A. **Incorrect:** The first action to take after installing RIS on the Windows 2000 member server is to authorize the RIS server. To authorize an RIS server in Active Directory, you must log on to the domain where the RIS server resides and access the DHCP console. Then click the DHCP node, select Manage Authorized Servers on the Action menu, and click Authorize in the Manage Authorized Servers dialog box. In the Authorize DHCP Server dialog box, type the name or IP address of the RIS server to be authorized, and then click OK. In the DHCP message box, click Yes. Finally, in the Manage Authorized Servers dialog box, click OK. The authorized RIS server is listed under the DHCP node.

B. **Correct:** The first action to take after installing RIS on the Windows 2000 member server is to authorize the RIS server. To authorize an RIS server in Active Directory, you must log on to the domain where the RIS server resides and access the DHCP console. Then click the DHCP node, select Manage Authorized Servers on the Action menu, and click Authorize in the Manage Authorized Servers dialog box. In the Authorize DHCP Server dialog box, type the name or IP address of the RIS server to be authorized, and then click OK. In the DHCP message box, click Yes. Finally, in the Manage Authorized Servers dialog box, click OK. The authorized RIS server is listed under the DHCP node.

C. **Incorrect:** The second action to take after authorizing the RIS server in Active Directory is to run the secedit /refreshpolicy MACHINE_POLICY command on the RIS server, the domain controller from which you set the user rights. This is not the correct command.

D. **Incorrect:** The second action to take after authorizing the RIS server in Active Directory is to run the secedit /refreshpolicy MACHINE_POLICY command on the RIS server, the domain controller from which you set the user rights. This is not the correct command, and the correct command must be run on the RIS server.

E. **Incorrect:** The second action to take after authorizing the RIS server in Active Directory is to run the secedit /refreshpolicy MACHINE_POLICY command on the RIS server, the domain controller from which you set the user rights. This is the correct command, but it must be run on the RIS server.

F. **Correct:** The second action to take after authorizing the RIS server in Active Directory is to run the secedit /refreshpolicy MACHINE_POLICY command on the RIS server, the domain controller from which you set the user rights. The new RIS policy is applied immediately, and the RIS server is available to install Windows 2000 Professional.

70-217.03.06.005

▶ **Correct Answers: A**

A. **Correct:** By installing RIS on Computer B using the RIS Installation Services Setup Wizard, you have successfully installed RIS services on the server.

B. **Incorrect:** Although Computer E is a Windows 2000 Professional computer with Administrative Tools, you cannot authorize the RIS server in Active Directory from Computer E logged on as a local administrator. To authorize a DHCP server, you must login as either a member of the Enterprise Administrators Group or Domain Adminisrators groups. You have only local administrative rights to Computer E.

C. **Incorrect:** An RIS server must be authorized before it can service client computers. The RIS server is not authorized in Active Directory services.

D. **Incorrect:** By installing RIS on Computer B using the RIS Installation Services Setup Wizard, you have successfully installed RIS services on the server.

70-217.03.06.006

▶ **Correct Answers: A and B**

A. **Correct:** To be able to turn on their system, connect to the RIS server, log on with their domain account, and install an operating system image without assistance, users need the Read and Write permissions to the computer object created when the client was prestaged.

B. **Correct:** To be able to turn on their system, connect to the RIS server, log on with their domain account, and install an operating system image without assistance, users need the Read and Write permissions to the computer object created when the client was prestaged.

C. **Incorrect:** Full Control permission for the computer object is not necessary. To be able to turn on their system, connect to the RIS server, log on with their domain account, and install an operating system image without assistance, users need the Read and Write permissions to the computer object created when the client was prestaged.

D. **Incorrect:** Create All Child Objects permission for the computer object is not necessary. To be able to turn on their system, connect to the RIS server, log on with their domain account, and install an operating system image without assistance, users need the Read and Write permissions to the computer object created when the client was prestaged.

E. **Incorrect:** Delete All Child Objects permission for the computer object is not necessary. To be able to turn on their system, connect to the RIS server, log on with their domain account, and install an operating system image without assistance, users need the Read and Write permissions to the computer object created when the client was prestaged.

70-217.03.06.007

▶ **Correct Answers: D**

   A. **Incorrect:** The DHCP server was authorized in Active Directory before the RIS server was installed. You do not need to additionally authorize the RIS server using the DHCP console.

   B. **Incorrect:** Because you have received IP information, Active Directory service cannot be stopped.

   C. **Incorrect:** Because you have received IP information, Active Directory service cannot be corrupt.

   D. **Correct:** Because the RIS server is configured to respond only to known clients, the RIS server fails to respond to the client's DHCP request because the computer object is not located in Active Directory. Because the RIS server and the DHCP server are on the same computer, the DHCP offer from the DHCP/RIS server contains only IP information and no information about available servers to support the client's network boot process.

70-217.03.06.008

▶ **Correct Answers: A, B, and C**

   A. **Correct:** By installing RIS on Computer B using the RIS Installation Services Setup Wizard, you have successfully installed RIS services on the server.

   B. **Correct:** To authorize an RIS server in Active Directory from a Windows 2000 Professional computer with Administrative Tools, you must log on with an account that is a member of the Enterprise Admins group. By having a member of the Enterprise Admins group authorize the RIS server from Computer E, you have successfully authorized the RIS server in Active Directory.

   C. **Correct:** Because you ran the secedit /refreshpolicy MACHINE_POLICY command from Computer D, the domain controller from which you set the user rights, the new RIS policy is applied immediately and the RIS server is available to install Windows 2000 Professional.

   D. **Incorrect:** The proposed actions meet all of the desired results.

Managing, Monitoring, and Optimizing the Components of Active Directory

The Managing, Monitoring, and Optimizing the Components of Active Directory domain focuses on Active Directory administration, including the management of objects, performance, and replication. Objects represent resources in the Active Directory directory service. Effective object management ensures that resources are available to authorized users when the users need them. Object management tasks include moving objects within and between domains, publishing objects and services, locating objects, creating and managing user and group accounts, controlling access to objects, and delegating administrative control of objects. Performance monitoring and diagnostic tools are provided for managing Active Directory performance. Event Viewer allows you to view log files and error messages sent by applications. System Monitor allows you to specify the real-time Active Directory data you want to monitor. The Performance Logs And Alerts snap-in allows you to specify criteria for creating counter logs, trace logs, and system alerts. The Shared Folders snap-in allows you to monitor access to network resources and send administrative messages to users. Support tools specific to Active Directory are provided in the Windows 2000 Support Tools included on the Microsoft Windows 2000 CD-ROM. These tools are provided for experienced users to assist in the diagnosis and resolution of Active Directory problems. Active Directory manages and generates replication links within and between sites. Although the links within sites are generated automatically, links between sites must be specified and configured. By creating site links and configuring cost, replication frequency, replication availability, site link bridges, and bridgehead servers according to your needs, you can optimize Active Directory replication for your organization.

Tested Skills and Suggested Practices

The skills that you need to successfully master the Managing, Monitoring, and Optimizing the Components of Active Directory domain on the *Implementing and Administering a Microsoft Windows 2000 Directory Services Infrastructure* exam include:

- **Managing Active Directory objects.**

  - Practice 1: Move Active Directory objects within your home network: use Active Directory Users And Computers to move objects within a domain, use the MOVETREE command-line utility to move objects between domains, use the NETDOM support tool to move a workstation or member server between domains, and use Active Directory Sites And Services to move domain controllers between sites.

  - Practice 2: Use Active Directory Users And Computers to publish users, computers, printers, and folders in Active Directory. Review the types of service information that are useful to publish in the directory. Use the MSDN Online Library to review how to publish services with service connection points.

  - Practice 3: Identify the common object types found in Active Directory. Use the Find dialog box to search the global catalog to locate various Active Directory objects in your home network. Use the Find Printers dialog box in Active Directory Users And Computers to locate printers in your network.

  - Practice 4: Create accounts and set properties for user accounts in your home network. Configure local and roaming user profiles. Create and manage home directories. Disable, enable, rename, and delete user accounts; reset user passwords, and unlock user accounts. Distinguish between the various group types and group scopes. Create groups for users in your home network. Add users to the groups. Describe the four types of default groups and identify their capabilities. Use Run As to start a program as an administrator.

  - Practice 5: Set standard permissions on Active Directory objects in your home network to control user access. Review how a user's effective permissions are a combination of his or her user and group permissions. Review the special permissions and identify how they provide a finer degree of control than standard permissions. Identify how, by default, permissions inheritance propagates permissions from parent objects to their child objects. Identify how to prevent permissions inheritance.

- Practice 6: Use the Delegation Of Control Wizard to delegate administrative control of Active Directory objects in your home network: assign a user the permissions to change properties on a particular container; assign a user the permissions to create, modify, or delete objects of a specific type in a specific OU or container; and assign a user the permissions to modify specific properties on objects of a specific type in a specific OU or container.

- **Managing Active Directory performance.**

  - Practice 1: Use Active Directory monitoring tools, including the Event Viewer to view event logs, the System Monitor to monitor performance counters, and Performance Logs and Alerts to create counter logs, trace logs, and alerts. Use the Shared Folders snap-in to monitor access to network resources and send administrative messages to users.

  - Practice 2: Install Active Directory Support Tools. Familiarize yourself with the support tools. Use the LDP.EXE, REPADMIN.EXE, DSASTAT.EXE, ACLDIAG.EXE, and DSACLS.EXE tools to troubleshoot various aspects of Active Directory. Use the REPLMON.EXE tool to monitor Active Directory replication. Use the SDCHECK.EXE tool to display the security descriptor for objects stored in Active Directory. Use the NLTEST.EXE tool to perform various network administration tasks.

  - Practice 3: Familiarize yourself with the problems and solutions associated with Active Directory.

- **Managing and troubleshooting Active Directory replication.**

  - Practice 1: Analyze how site links and replication protocols affect intersite replication. Analyze how the following site link attributes affect intersite replication: site link cost, replication frequency, and replication availability. Analyze how site link bridges and bridgehead servers affect intersite replication. Analyze how reciprocal replication allows sites with only one-way replication capabilities to achieve the results of two-way replication. Analyze how change notification allows a domain controller to notify a replication partner that it has changes. Review the events that trigger urgent replication.

Further Reading

This "Further Reading" section provides lists of important readings to supplement your current understanding of the skills tested within this Objective Domain. The lists are delineated into pertinent readings for each objective within this Objective Domain. If you feel that you need additional preparation prior to taking the exam, study these sources thoroughly.

Objective 4.1

Microsoft Corporation. *MCSE Training Kit: Microsoft Windows 2000 Active Directory Services*. Redmond, Washington: Microsoft Press, 2000. Review Lessons 1 through 6 in Chapter 7, "User Account Administration," for instruction and practice on planning and creating user accounts, creating user profiles and home directories, and maintaining user accounts. Review Lessons 1 through 5 in Chapter 8, "Group Account Administration," for instruction and practice on creating and maintaining group accounts. Review Lessons 1 through 5 in Chapter 11, "Administering Active Directory," for instruction and practice on the tasks for locating objects, assigning permissions to objects, publishing resources, moving objects within and between domains, and delegating administrative control to organizational units (OUs). Review Lesson 4 in Chapter 13, "Administering a Security Configuration," for information on assigning user rights to users and groups.

Microsoft Corporation. *Microsoft Windows 2000 Server Resource Kit*. Volume: *Microsoft Windows 2000 Server Distributed Systems Guide*. Redmond, Washington: Microsoft Press, 2000. Review the section on "Directory Infrastructure for Service Publication" in Chapter 5, "Service Publication in Active Directory," for information on publishing services in Active Directory. Review the section on "Rights" in Chapter 12, "Access Control," for details about using permissions and user rights to control access to Active Directory objects.

Use the Microsoft MSDN Online Library (available at *http://msdn.microsoft.com/ library/default.asp*) to find information about publishing services. To find this information, click Platform SDK; Networking and Directory Services; Active Directory, ADSI, and Directory Services; Active Directory; Using Active Directory; Service Publication.

Iseminger, David. *Active Directory Services for Windows 2000 Technical Reference*. Microsoft Press, 2000. Review Chapter 13, "Making Postdeployment Organizational Changes," for information on making structural changes to a network using MOVE-TREE and other methods.

Use the Microsoft MSDN Online Library (available at *http://msdn.microsoft.com/ library/default.asp*) to find information about using scripting and ADSI to set up and maintain users and groups of users. To find this information, click Platform SDK; Networking and Directory Services; Active Directory, ADSI, and Directory Services; Active Directory Service Interfaces; ADSI Tutorial; Users and Groups.

Lowe-Norris, Alistair G. *Windows 2000 Active Directory Services*. Sebastopol, California: O'Reilly & Associates, 2000. Chapters 14 through 21 cover the details of scripting Active Directory with ADSI. In particular, Chapter 14 introduces scripting with ADSI, and Chapter 16 provides details about scripts for creating user accounts.

Objective 4.2

Microsoft Corporation. *MCSE Training Kit: Microsoft Windows 2000 Active Directory Services*. Redmond, Washington: Microsoft Press, 2000. Review Lesson 8 in Chapter 11, "Administering Active Directory," for a basic list of Active Directory–related problems you may encounter and possible solutions. Review Lessons 1 through 3 in Chapter 14, "Managing Active Directory Performance," for instruction and practice using the tools for monitoring Active Directory performance, for information about the Windows 2000 Support Tools used to support Active Directory services, and for details on monitoring access to shared folders and instruction and practice on the tasks for managing shared folders.

Microsoft Corporation. *Microsoft Windows 2000 Server Resource Kit*. Volume: *Microsoft Windows 2000 Server Distributed Systems Guide*. Redmond, Washington: Microsoft Press, 2000. Review Chapter 8, "Monitoring Performance in Active Directory," for information on the performance tools and system monitor counters used to monitor Active Directory performance. Review Chapter 10, "Active Directory Diagnostics, Troubleshooting, and Recovery," for detailed information about troubleshooting domain controller performance and Active Directory components.

Microsoft Corporation. *Microsoft Windows 2000 Server Resource Kit*. Volume: *Microsoft Windows 2000 Server Operations Guide*. Redmond, Washington: Microsoft Press, 2000. Review Chapter 5, "Overview of Performance Monitoring," for general information on performance monitoring using Windows 2000 Server.

Objective 4.3

Microsoft Corporation. *MCSE Training Kit: Microsoft Windows 2000 Active Directory Services*. Redmond, Washington: Microsoft Press, 2000. Review Lessons 1 and 2 in Chapter 6, "Configuring Sites," for instruction and practice on the tasks for managing Active Directory replication. Review Lesson 3 for information on troubleshooting replication.

Microsoft Corporation. *Microsoft Windows 2000 Server Resource Kit*. Volume: *Microsoft Windows 2000 Server Distributed Systems Guide*. Redmond, Washington: Microsoft Press, 2000. Review Chapter 6, "Active Directory Replication," for detailed information about managing Active Directory replication.

O B J E C T I V E   4 . 1

Manage Active Directory objects.

An **object** is a distinct named set of attributes that represents a resource stored in the Active Directory directory service, such as a **user**, **group**, organizational unit (OU), printer, **computer**, or server. **Attributes** are characteristics of objects that are stored in the directory. Some objects, called **containers**, are used to organize and store other objects. For example, an OU can contain user accounts, groups, computers, printers, and other OUs. To make the information in Active Directory available and useful, you must be able to manage objects. Object management includes moving objects within and between domains, publishing resources, locating objects, creating accounts, assigning permissions to objects, and delegating administrative control to objects.

From time to time, you may be required to move objects from one location to another due to changes in organizational or administrative functions. In the logical environment, which refers to a network's nonphysical components of organizational units, domains, trees, and forests, you can move objects within and between both domains and OUs. Use the Move dialog box in Active Directory Users And Computers to move objects within domains. Use the MOVETREE command-line utility to move objects such as users, groups, and organizational units between domains in a single forest, with some exceptions. Use the Windows 2000 Domain Manager support tool, NETDOM, to move a **workstation** or **member server** between domains. In the physical environment, which refers to sites and domain controllers, you can only move domain controllers between sites. Use the Move Server dialog box in Active Directory Sites And Services to move domain controllers between sites.

As an administrator, you must provide for the secure publication of network resources while also allowing users easy access to the information they need to do their jobs. By **publishing** objects in the directory, you can integrate Windows 2000 security mechanisms and provide users with access to objects such as users, computers, printers, folders, files, and network services. When users and computers are added to the directory using Active Directory Users And Computers, information that is useful to other network users is published automatically. Windows 2000 network printers are also published automatically, though pre–Windows 2000 printers must be published manually by using the New Object-Printer dialog box in Active Directory Users And Computers.

Shared folders allow authorized users to make connections to folders containing network files. When you publish a shared folder using the New Object-Shared Folder dialog box in Active Directory Users And Computers, users can easily access the folder and files on the network. When you publish **services** in Active Directory, information about one or more instances of a service is created and maintained so that administrators and clients can find and use the service. Services publish their existence in Active Directory by using objects, called **connection point objects**, which contain **binding information**. When a client wants to use a service, it queries Active Directory for the service's connection point object and then uses the binding information to connect to the service. The location in which you publish services varies, depending on the type of service.

The Active Directory directory service uses object attributes to provide information to queries about objects from both users and programs. The Find dialog box in Active Directory Users And Computers allows you to search the **global catalog** to locate Active Directory objects in two ways. You can perform a search for an object based on attributes you specify. You can perform a more detailed search based on a set of conditions and values that you specify.

User accounts allow the user to log on to the domain and gain access to network resources. Using Active Directory Users And Computers, you can create user accounts, set their properties, and set up user profiles and **home directories**. Group accounts are collections of user accounts that simplify the administration of permissions and **user rights**. **Global groups** are often used to organize users who share similar network access requirements. **Domain local groups** are often used to assign permissions to resources. **Universal groups** are often used to assign permissions to related resources in multiple domains. **Default groups** are automatically created and have a predetermined set of user rights and group membership. Administrators should not log on as an administrator or a member of an administrative group. Instead, administrators should assign themselves to the Users or Power Users group and log on using the **Run As program** only when they need to run administrative tools. This action minimizes the risk of **Trojan horse** attacks and other security risks. When you are creating and managing large quantities of user accounts and user accounts within groups, it is recommended that you write **scripts** that use **Active Directory Services Interface** (**ADSI**) to perform these functions. Scripting provides a more efficient method of creating and managing users in organizations with hundreds or thousands of user accounts.

To control access to objects in Active Directory, you can apply **permissions to users or groups**. Administrators or the object owner must specify permissions before users or groups can gain access. The type of object determines the permissions that you can set. Permissions can be set to Allow or Deny on the Security tab in the Properties dialog box for the object. The standard permissions usually available on the Security tab are Full Control, Write, Read, Create All Child Objects, and Delete All Child Objects.

Special permissions provide a finer degree of access control and are available by clicking the Advanced button on the Security tab. By default, permissions applied to **parent objects** are inherited by **child objects**. You can also prevent **permissions inheritance**.

To control administrative tasks performed on objects in Active Directory, you can **delegate** administrative responsibility to users and groups at the container level. Containers include domains, OUs, and sites. The Delegation Of Control Wizard simplifies the process of delegating administration. For the container you select, the Delegation Of Control Wizard allows you to select the user or group to which you want to delegate control and the administrative tasks you want the user or group to delegate. For example, a user can be given the control to reset passwords on user accounts in an OU you specify.

Objective 4.1 Questions

70-217.04.01.001

The first computer installed into your Active Directory forest just met the minimum hardware requirements. To increase performance, you purchased a more powerful server to replace the server. You want to demote the initial server to a Windows 2000 member server, but first you need to transfer all operations master roles to the new Windows 2000 server. You want to achieve these results:

- Transfer the relative ID master role

- Transfer the schema master role

- Transfer the PDC emulator role

- Transfer the domain naming master role

- Transfer the infrastructure master role

Your proposed solution is to open the Active Directory Users And Computers console on the initial server. Right-click the domain node that you want to transfer the roles to, and then click Connect To Domain. In the Connect To Domain dialog box, click Browse and select the domain from the list, and then click OK. In the console tree, right-click the Active Directory Users And Computers node, and then click Operations Masters. In the Operations Master dialog box, perform the following tasks:

1. Click the RID tab, and then click Change.

2. Click the Schema tab, and then click Change.

3. Click the PDC tab, and then click Change.

4. Click the Domain Naming tab, and then click Change.

5. Click the Infrastructure tab, and then click Change.

6. Click OK to close the Operations Master dialog box.

Which results does the proposed solution provide? (Choose all that apply.)

A. Transfer the relative ID master.

B. Transfer the schema master role.

C. Transfer the PDC emulator master role.

D. Transfer the domain naming master role.

E. Transfer the infrastructure master role.

70-217.04.01.002

Your organization wants to make its Dispatch OU subordinate to its Sales OU. You move the Dispatch OU into the Sales OU. User SallyC is a subadministrator for the Sales OU and was previously able to read all user information only for users in the Sales OU. Now she is able to read all user information for users in both the Sales OU and the Dispatch OU. What could cause this to happen?

A. User SallyC was previously delegated administrative control for the Sales OU, which has now been inherited by the Dispatch OU.

B. Because you moved the Dispatch OU using the MOVETREE command, user SallyC gained permissions through group memberships.

C. As a result of the move, user SallyC is now a member of the Dispatch OU and receives permissions for the Dispatch OU.

D. A user object named SallyC already existed in the Dispatch OU before the move operation, so the two objects were merged during the move, producing unpredictable results.

70-217.04.01.003

Your company is in the process of restructuring its operations. You need to modify the company's Active Directory structure to reflect the new organizational structure. This restructuring will require you to move user objects, OUs, groups, and other Active Directory objects between domains in the same forest. You need to move the following items to different domains:

- Objects and nonempty containers

- Domain local and global groups that contain members

- Users and their associated data such as user profiles, logon scripts, and public key certificates

- Universal groups with members

- Domain controllers

You propose using the MOVETREE command-line utility to perform the above actions.

What does your proposed solution provide?

A. Move domain controllers to different domains.

B. Move universal groups with members to different domains.

C. Move objects and nonempty containers to different domains.

D. Move domain local and global groups that contain members to different domains.

E. Move users and their associated data such as user profiles, logon scripts, and public key certificates to different domains.

70-217.04.01.004

You are using the MOVETREE utility to move an OU and its contents to a different domain. You successfully move the OU to the destination domain, but several objects that were previously in the OU are no longer contained in the OU. You search the source domain but fail to find the missing objects. What happened to the objects?

A. They were placed in the LostAndFound container in the source domain.

B. They were moved into the Orphaned container in the destination domain.

C. They were renamed and placed in the moved OU in the destination domain.

D. They were deleted because of error conditions or operation restrictions.

70-217.04.01.005

You want to publish the Microsoft NetMeeting service to Active Directory. The service, which is not strongly tied to any one computer, will be used primarily by members of the Management OU. However, other users throughout the domain will occasionally use the service. Where should you publish the service?

A. At the root of the domain

B. In the Management OU

C. In the System container

D. In the Computers container

70-217.04.01.006

You want to publish a printer running on a Microsoft Windows NT server to Active Directory. You launch Active Directory Users And Computers, double-click the domain node, and right-click the organizational unit where you want to publish the printer. You are then presented with several menu options. Which option should you select next to publish the printer?

Examine the menu shown below.

A. Delegate Control

B. Move

C. New

D. All Tasks

E. Properties

70-217.04.01.007

You need to perform a search for computers in your Active Directory domain. You know that you can perform searches on information entered in each computer's description field. Which other criteria could you use to search for computers in your Active Directory domain? (Choose three.)

A. Password

B. Logon status

C. Computer name

D. Operating system

E. Person administering the computer

70-217.04.01.008

You are creating a new user object using the Active Directory Users And Computers console for a new employee who will start work in a few days. You want to achieve these results:

- No one should be able to use the user object to log on until the user actually starts work.

- The user should be the only person who knows the password.

- The password must be at least seven characters in length.

- The user should be forced to re-create the password every 30 days.

To achieve these results, you configure password settings as shown in the exhibit.

Which desired results are achieved? (Choose all that apply.)

Examine the New Object-User dialog box shown below.

A. No one should be able to use the user object to log on until the user actually starts work.

B. The user should be the only person who knows the password.

C. The password must be at least seven characters in length.

D. The user should be forced to re-create the password every 30 days.

70-217.04.01.009

You are creating a new user object using the Active Directory Users And Computers console for a new employee who will start work in a few days. You want to ensure that only administrators are allowed to control passwords for the object. Which password option in the New Object-User dialog box should you check?

A. User Must Change Password At Next Logon

B. User Cannot Change Password

C. Password Never Expires

D. Account Is Disabled

70-217.04.01.010

You need to restrict the workstations that a user can log on to. You start Active Directory Users And Computers and navigate to the appropriate user account. You then right-click the user account and click Properties. Which tab should you click next to specify the workstations that the user can log on to?

A. General

B. Address

C. Account

D. Profile

E. Sessions

70-217.04.01.011

Several users in your Active Directory domain often log on to the network from different Windows 2000 computers. Currently, the users do not have access to files stored in their home directory when they log on to the network away from their main computer. You want to provide users in your domain with the same desktop environment no matter which computer they log on to. You want to achieve these results:

- Changes users make to their desktops are retained for subsequent logons.

- Users have access to files stored in their home directory no matter which computer they log on to.

- Users have the same desktop environment no matter which Windows 2000 computer they log on to.

- Authentication should not be adversely affected.

Your proposed solution is to create a shared folder named Profiles on a domain controller named FS1. Then, on the Profile tab in the Properties dialog box for each user account, type **\\FS1\Profiles**%*user-name*% in the Profile Path box, and click the Apply button.

Which results does the proposed solution achieve? (Choose all that apply.)

A. Changes users make to their desktops are retained for subsequent logons.

B. Users have access to files stored in their home directory no matter which computer they log on to.

C. Users have the same desktop environment no matter which Windows 2000 computer they log on to.

D. Authentication should not be adversely affected.

70-217.04.01.012

Several users in your Active Directory domain often log on to the network from different Windows 2000 computers. Currently, the users do not have access to files stored in their home directory when they log on to the network away from their main computer. You want to provide users in your domain with the same desktop environment no matter which computer they log on to. You want to achieve these results:

- Changes users make to their desktops are retained for subsequent logons.

- Users have access to files stored in their home directory no matter which computer they log on to.

- Users have the same desktop environment no matter which Windows 2000 computer they log on to.

- Authentication should not be adversely affected.

Your proposed solution is to create a shared folder named Users on a domain controller named FS1, removing the default permission Full Control from the Everyone group and assigning Full Control to the Users group. Then, configure the Profile tab in the Properties dialog box for each user account as shown in the exhibit and click the Apply button.

Which results does the proposed solution achieve? (Choose all that apply.)

Examine the User1 Properties dialog box below.

A. Changes users make to their desktops are retained for subsequent logons.

B. Users have access to files stored in their home directory no matter which computer they log on to.

C. Users have the same desktop environment no matter which Windows 2000 computer they log on to.

D. Authentication should not be adversely affected.

70-217.04.01.013

You need to create a group. You want to achieve these results:

- Users should be able to use the group to send e-mail to a collection of users.

- Administrators should be able to use the group to define permissions on resources.

- Pre–Windows 2000 users should be able to use the group.

- Group members can come from any domain in the forest.

You start Active Directory Users And Computers, click the stsware.com domain, right-click the Users container, point to New, and click Group. You then configure the New Object-Group dialog box as shown in the exhibit and click the OK button.

Which results did you achieve? (Choose all that apply.)

Examine the New Object-Group dialog box shown below.

A. Users should be able to use the group to send e-mail to a collection of users.

B. Administrators should be able to use the group to define permissions on resources.

C. Pre–Windows 2000 users will be included in the group.

D. Group members can come from any domain in the forest.

70-217.04.01.014

Your Windows 2000 network contains five domains that you need to administer. To increase security, you created a new account that you want to use to administer the entire network. To which group should you add the account so that you can use the account to administer the entire network?

A. Interactive

B. Domain Admins

C. Administrators

D. Enterprise Admins

70-217.04.01.015

You are logged in to a Windows 2000 computer as a nonadministrative user. You need to launch Active Directory Users And Computers to create a group account. How can you complete the task without logging out and logging back on using an administrator account?

A. Use the NLTEST.EXE command-line tool.

B. Create a remote session to a domain controller and log on as an administrator.

C. Use the Run As program to start Active Directory Users And Computers as an administrator.

D. Assign the nonadministrative user account temporary rights to Active Directory Users And Computers.

70-217.04.01.016

You created a new user account using Active Directory Users And Computers. After creating the user account, you checked the Security tab in the user account properties and found several shaded check boxes in the Allow column for most of the permissions for the Administrators group. What does this mean?

Examine the User1 Properties dialog box shown below.

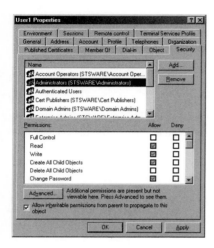

A. The permissions are inherited.

B. The permissions do not apply if logged on locally.

C. The user account is a member of the Administrators group.

D. The Administrators group receives the permissions from multiple sources.

70-217.04.01.017

Your network contains the seabreezecruises.com and oceanbreezecruises.com domains. Both domains are running in native mode. Members of the oceanbreezecruises.com domain need access to resources in the Caribbean organizational unit (OU) in the seabreezecruises.com domain. Members of the seabreeze-cruises.com domain receive permissions to the Caribbean OU through membership in a domain local group named CaribbeanUsers. What action can you take to allow users in the oceanbreezecruises.com domain to access the Caribbean OU in the seabreezecruises.com domain? (Choose three.)

A. Add the users from the oceanbreezecruises.com domain to the CaribbeanUsers domain local group.

B. Change the CaribbeanUsers domain local group to a global group, and add the users from the ocean-breezecruises.com domain.

C. Change the CaribbeanUsers group to a universal group, and add the users from the oceanbreeze-cruises.com domain.

D. Create a new global group in the oceanbreezecruises.com domain that grants access to the Caribbean OU, and add users from the oceanbreezecruises.com domain.

E. Create a new domain local group in the oceanbreezecruises.com domain that grants access to the Caribbean OU, and add users from the oceanbreezecruises.com domain.

70-217.04.01.018

Your company recently hired a Directory Engineer to oversee the different directory services running on your network. You need to give the Directory Engineer permissions to perform the following tasks in your Active Directory domain:

- Create and manage sites, site links, subnets, and intersite transports.

- Create and manage user accounts in Active Directory.

- Back up and restore Active Directory.

- Manage DNS and Active Directory integration.

- Extend the schema.

You created a user object for the Directory Engineer and granted membership in the Replicator, Account Operators, and Backup Operators built-in domain local groups.

You have not changed any of the default permissions assigned to built-in local groups.

Which tasks can the Directory Engineer perform? (Choose all that apply.)

A. Create and manage sites, site links, subnets, and intersite transports.

B. Create and manage user accounts in Active Directory.

C. Back up and restore Active Directory.

D. Manage DNS and Active Directory integration.

E. Extend the schema.

Objective 4.1 Answers

70-217.04.01.001

▶ **Correct Answers: A, C, and E**

A. **Correct:** The proposed solution uses the Active Directory Users And Computers console to transfer the roles. The RID tab is used to transfer the relative ID master role assignment.

B. **Incorrect:** You must use the Active Directory Schema snap-in to transfer the schema master role assignment.

C. **Correct:** The proposed solution uses the Active Directory Users And Computers console to transfer the roles. The PDC tab is used to transfer the PDC emulator master role assignment.

D. **Incorrect:** You must use the Active Directory Domains And Trusts console to transfer the domain naming master role assignment.

E. **Correct:** The proposed solution uses the Active Directory Users And Computers console to transfer the roles. The Infrastructure tab is used to transfer the infrastructure master role assignment.

70-217.04.01.002

▶ **Correct Answers: A**

A. **Correct:** Because you moved the Dispatch OU into the Sales OU, the administrative responsibilities delegated to user SallyC for the Sales OU are inherited by Dispatch OU.

B. **Incorrect:** First, you probably have not used MOVETREE because it is unnecessarily difficult to do so compared to using the Move dialog box in Active Directory Users And Computers. MOVETREE is normally used for moving objects between domains, not within a domain. Second, regardless of whether you have used MOVETREE, group memberships are native to domains, not to OUs. For this reason, a user does not gain group-based permissions when you move an OU into another OU within the same domain.

C. **Incorrect:** Because OUs are not security principals, they cannot have members, and they cannot grant or deny access to resources. As a result of the move, the user object SallyC is not contained in the Dispatch OU.

D. **Incorrect:** The user logon name, SallyC, must be unique in the directory for that domain. Therefore, a user object named SallyC could not have existed in the Dispatch OU before the move operation, and the two objects were not merged during the move operation.

70-217.04.01.003

▶ **Correct Answers: C**

A. **Incorrect:** Domain controllers cannot be moved between domains. To move a computer acting as a domain controller from one domain to another, first demote the computer to a member server and then move the computer using the NETDOM command-line utility, not the MOVETREE command-line utility. In addition, you can move domain controllers between sites within a domain by using Active Directory Sites And Services, not the MOVETREE command-line utility.

B. **Incorrect:** Because universal groups are, by definition, forestwide and not attached to a specific domain, it is not necessary to move the universal groups between domains in this forest.

C. **Correct:** The MOVETREE command-line utility supports moving an object or a nonempty container to a different domain within the same forest.

D. **Incorrect:** Domain local and global groups that contain members cannot be moved *between* domains by using the MOVETREE command-line utility. However, domain local and global groups that contain members can be moved *within* domains by using the MOVETREE command-line utility.

E. **Incorrect:** Although users can be moved between domains by using the MOVETREE command-line utility, the data associated with user objects, such as user profiles, logon scripts, users' personal data, encrypted files, smart cards, and public key certificates, cannot be moved between domains.

70-217.04.01.004

▶ **Correct Answers: A**

A. **Correct:** Objects that are not moved during a MOVETREE operation are classified as orphaned objects and are placed in an "orphan" container in the LostAndFound container in the source domain. You can view the LostAndFound container in the Active Directory Users And Computers console in Advanced View. The orphan container is named by using the globally unique identifier (GUID) of the parent container being moved.

B. **Incorrect:** There is no Orphaned container in the destination domain. Objects that are not moved during a MOVETREE operation are classified as orphaned objects and are placed in an "orphan" container in the LostAndFound container in the source domain. You can view the LostAndFound container in the Active Directory Users And Computers console in Advanced View. The orphan container is named by using the globally unique identifier (GUID) of the parent container being moved.

C. **Incorrect:** The objects are not in the moved OU in the destination domain. Objects that are not moved during a MOVETREE operation are classified as orphaned objects and are placed in an "orphan" container in the LostAndFound container in the source domain. You can view the LostAndFound container in the Active Directory Users And Computers console in Advanced View. The orphan container is named by using the globally unique identifier (GUID) of the parent container being moved.

D. **Incorrect:** Objects that are not moved are never deleted during a move operation. Objects that are not moved during a MOVETREE operation are classified as orphaned objects and are placed in an "orphan" container in the LostAndFound container in the source domain. You can view the LostAndFound container in the Active Directory Users And Computers console in Advanced View. The orphan container is named by using the globally unique identifier (GUID) of the parent container being moved.

70-217.04.01.005

▶ **Correct Answers: C**

A. **Incorrect:** Although you could publish the NetMeeting service to the root of the domain, this location would not provide convenient administration and maintenance of the service. Publishing services to the root of the domain would not allow you to control access to them using policy and inherited access permissions. In addition, the root of the domain is not a logical container that will help you organize and find services easily. Recommended places to publish services include a specific computer, a specific OU, and a container within the System container.

B. **Incorrect:** The Management OU is used to group together objects for administrative purposes. Although you could use the Management OU to group service-specific objects together for administrative purposes, the OU is not used for publishing services, such as NetMeeting.

C. **Correct:** Operational information, organized by domain, is stored in the System container. When a service, such as NetMeeting, is not strongly tied to a single computer, you should publish services in a container that is a child of the System container.

D. **Incorrect:** Computer objects are stored in the Computers container. You should not move service-specific objects directly into or create new containers in the Computers container.

70-217.04.01.006

▶ **Correct Answers: C**

A. **Incorrect:** Selecting the Delegate Control option starts the Delegation Of Control Wizard, which allows you to delegate control of the organizational unit. You cannot publish the printer to Active Directory by using the Delegation Of Control Wizard.

B. **Incorrect:** Selecting the Move option opens the Move dialog box, which allows you to move the organizational unit to another location within the domain. You cannot publish the printer to Active Directory by using the Move dialog box.

C. **Correct:** Selecting the New option and then clicking Printer opens the New Object-Printer dialog box. You can publish the printer to Active Directory by typing the Universal Naming Convention (UNC) name of the printer in the Network Path Of The Pre-Windows 2000 Print Share box, and then clicking OK.

D. **Incorrect:** Selecting the All Tasks option is a means for selecting the Delegate Control, Add Members To A Group, Move, and Find options from a secondary menu. None of these options allow you to publish the printer to Active Directory.

E. **Incorrect:** Selecting the Properties option opens the OU Properties dialog box, which allows you to set general, management, or group policy properties for the organizational unit. You cannot publish the printer to Active Directory by using the OU Properties dialog box.

70-217.04.01.007

▶ **Correct Answers: C, D, and E**

A. **Incorrect:** Password is not a valid search criteria for computers or any other Active Directory object.

B. **Incorrect:** Logon status is not a valid search criteria for computers or any other Active Directory object.

C. **Correct:** You can search for computers by entering the Computer Name in the Find Computers dialog box.

D. **Correct:** You can search for computers by selecting the Operating System attribute in the Field list on the Advanced tab in the Find Computers dialog box.

E. **Correct:** You can search for computers by selecting the Managed By attribute in the Field list on the Advanced tab in the Find Computers dialog box.

70-217.04.01.008

▶ **Correct Answers: A and B**

   A. **Correct:** Because the Account Is Disabled check box is checked, use of the new user object is prevented. When the user actually starts work, the Account Is Disabled check box must be cleared.

   B. **Correct:** Because the User Must Change Password At Next Logon check box is checked, the user is required to change his or her password the first time he or she logs on. This action ensures that the user is the only person who knows the password.

   C. **Incorrect:** None of the settings in the New Object-User dialog box can ensure that the user's password will be at least seven characters in length.

   D. **Incorrect:** None of the settings in the New Object-User dialog box can force the user to re-create the password every 30 days.

70-217.04.01.009

▶ **Correct Answers: B**

   A. **Incorrect:** If you check the User Must Change Password At Next Logon check box, the user is required to change his or her password the first time he or she logs on. This action ensures that the user is the only person who knows the password and prevents administrators from controlling the password.

   B. **Correct:** If you check the User Cannot Change Password check box, only administrators will be able to control the password for the user. The user cannot change the password.

   C. **Incorrect:** If you check the Password Never Expires check box, Windows 2000 will never require the password to be changed. This action does not prevent a user from changing the password.

   D. **Incorrect:** The Account Is Disabled check box is not a password option and does not allow administrators to control the password. If you check the Account Is Disabled check box, use of the new user object is prevented.

70-217.04.01.010

▶ **Correct Answers: C**

   A. **Incorrect:** The General tab in the Properties dialog box for the user documents the user's first name, last name, display name, description, office location, telephone number or numbers, e-mail address, home page, and additional Web pages. You cannot specify the workstations that the user can log on to on the General tab.

B. **Incorrect:** The Address tab in the Properties dialog box for the user documents the user's street address; post office box; city, state or province; zip or postal code; and country or region. You cannot specify the workstations that the user can log on to on the Address tab.

C. **Correct:** The Account tab in the Properties dialog box for the user documents the user's account properties, including the computers the user is permitted to log on to. You can specify the workstations that the user can log on to in the Logon Workstations dialog box, which is accessed by selecting the Log On To button on the Account tab.

D. **Incorrect:** The Profile tab in the Properties dialog box for the user sets the profile path, logon script path, home directory, and shared document folder. You cannot specify the workstations that the user can log on to on the Profile tab.

E. **Incorrect:** The Sessions tab in the Properties dialog box for the user sets the Terminal Services time-out and reconnection settings. You cannot specify the workstations that the user can log on to on the Sessions tab.

70-217.04.01.011

▶ **Correct Answers: A and C**

A. **Correct:** The proposed solution sets up a roaming user profile. When a user logs off, changes that were made to the local copy of the roaming user profile, including changes users make to their desktops, are copied back to the server, where the roaming user profile is stored and retained for subsequent logons.

B. **Incorrect:** You have not created a home directory on the network file server, which is required to allow users to access files stored in their home directory. To create a home directory on a network file server, you must first create and share a folder in which to store all home directories. Then you must remove the default permission Full Control from the Everyone group and assign Full Control to the Users group. Finally, you must provide the path to the user's home directory folder in the shared home directory folder on the Profile tab of the Properties dialog box for the user account.

C. **Correct:** The proposed solution sets up a roaming user profile, which provides a standard desktop environment for each user no matter which computer the user logs on to.

D. **Incorrect:** Because the copying of roaming user profiles between server and client computers can require a great deal of system resources, you should place the roaming user profile folder on a member server rather than a domain controller whenever possible. In this solution, the roaming user profiles are stored on the domain controller; thus, the authentication of users may be delayed.

70-217.04.01.012

▶ **Correct Answers: A, B, and C**

A. **Correct:** The proposed solution sets up a roaming user profile. When a user logs off, changes that were made to the local copy of the roaming user profile, including changes users make to their desktops, are copied back to the server, where the roaming user profile is stored and retained for subsequent logons.

B. **Correct:** By creating a Users share and then providing a network path to it in the Home Folder section on the Profile tab of the Properties dialog box for the user account, you have provided a home directory for User1 that will be accessible anywhere on the network.

C. **Correct:** The proposed solution sets up a roaming user profile, which provides a standard desktop environment for each user, no matter which computer the user logs on to.

D. **Incorrect:** Because the copying of roaming user profiles between server and client computers can require a great deal of system resources, you should place the roaming user profile folder on a member server rather than a domain controller whenever possible. In this solution, the roaming user profiles are stored on the domain controller; thus, the authentication of users may be delayed.

70-217.04.01.013

▶ **Correct Answers: A and C**

A. **Correct:** Because the group type you've selected is Distribution, users are able to use the group to send e-mail to a collection of users. The Security group type also allows users to use the group to send e-mail to a collection of users.

B. **Incorrect:** Because the group type you've selected is Distribution, you cannot assign permissions to the group. Distribution groups are used to list users for non-security-related functions, such as sending e-mail messages.

C. **Correct:** Because the Group Name (Pre–Windows 2000) box contains the name Group3, the users in the pre–Windows 2000 group named Group3 will be included in the new group.

D. **Incorrect:** Because the group scope you've selected is Global, group members come only from the stsware.com domain.

70-217.04.01.014

▶ **Correct Answers: D**

A. **Incorrect:** Members of the Interactive special identity group can gain access to resources on the computer at which they are physically located. These group members can log on and gain access to resources by "interacting" with the computer. The Interactive group does not allow you to administer the entire network, which contains five domains.

B. **Incorrect:** Members of the Domain Admins predefined global group can perform administrative tasks on any computer anywhere within a domain. By default, the Domain Admins group is a member of the Administrators built-in domain local group. The Domain Admins group does not allow you to administer the entire network, which contains five domains.

C. **Incorrect:** Members of the Administrators built-in domain local group can perform all administrative tasks on all domain controllers and the domain itself. The Administrators group does not allow you to administer the entire network, which contains five domains.

D. **Correct:** Members of the Enterprise Admins predefined group have administrative control of the entire network. By default, the Administrator account is a member of the Enterprise Admins group.

70-217.04.01.015

▶ **Correct Answers: C**

A. **Incorrect:** The NLTEST.EXE command-line tool helps perform network administrative tasks and cannot be used to run Active Directory Users And Computers with administrative rights and permissions while logged on as a normal user.

B. **Incorrect:** A nonadministrative user cannot create a remote session to a domain controller and log on as an administrator.

C. **Correct:** The Run As program allows you to run Active Directory Users And Computers with administrative rights and permissions while logged on as a nonadministrative user, provided that the following conditions are met: you provide the correct administrative account and password information, the administrative account has the ability to log on to the computer, and Active Directory Users And Computers is available on the system and to the administrative account.

D. **Incorrect:** To assign administrative rights to a nonadministrative account, you would need to sign off and on again as an administrator. In addition, running a nonadministrative account with the ability to access Active Directory Users And Computers makes the network vulnerable to Trojan horse attacks and other security risks. You should not assign administrative rights to a nonadministrative user account.

70-217.04.01.016

▶ **Correct Answers: A**

A. **Correct:** If the check boxes in the Allow column are shaded, the Administrators group has inherited permissions for the user account from its parent folder.

B. **Incorrect:** If the check boxes in the Allow column are shaded, the Administrators group has inherited permissions for the user account from its parent folder.

C. **Incorrect:** In the User1 Properties dialog box, the permissions checked in the Permissions list indicate the permissions for the user account, group, or special entity highlighted in the Name list. If a check box in the Permissions list is shaded, the permission is inherited. In this case, the Administrators group has inherited the Read, Write, Create All Child Objects, and Change Password permissions.

D. **Incorrect:** If the check boxes in the Allow column are shaded, the Administrators group has inherited permissions for the user account from its parent folder. Because all check boxes are shaded, the Administrators group receives permissions from only one source, its parent folder.

70-217.04.01.017

▶ **Correct Answers: A, C, and D**

A. **Correct:** You can add members from any domain in the forest to the CaribbeanUsers domain local group. By adding the users from the oceanbreezecruises.com domain to the CaribbeanUsers domain local group, you allow users to access resources in the Caribbean OU in the seabreezecruises.com domain.

B. **Incorrect:** When you change the CaribbeanUsers domain local group in the seabreezecruises.com domain to a global group, you can add members only from the domain in which the global group is created. Therefore, you are not able to add the users from the oceanbreezecruises.com domain to the CaribbeanUsers global group, and users cannot access resources in the Caribbean OU in the seabreezecruises.com domain.

C. **Correct:** You can add members from any domain in the forest to the CaribbeanUsers universal group. By adding the users from the oceanbreezecruises.com domain to the CaribbeanUsers universal group, you allow users to access resources in the Caribbean OU in the seabreezecruises.com domain.

D. **Correct:** You can use a global group to assign permissions to gain access to resources located in any domain in the forest. By adding the users from the oceanbreezecruises.com domain to the new global group, you allow users to access resources in the Caribbean OU in the seabreezecruises.com domain.

E. **Incorrect:** When you create a new domain local group in the oceanbreezes.com domain, you can assign permissions to gain access only to resources located in the domain in which the new domain local group is created. Therefore, the users in the new domain local group in the oceanbreeze-cruises.com domain are unable to access resources in the Caribbean OU, which is located in the seabreezecruises.com domain.

70-217.04.01.018

▶ **Correct Answers: B and C**

A. **Incorrect:** The permissions provided with the Replicator, Account Operators, and Backup Operators built-in domain local groups do not allow the Directory Engineer to create and manage sites, site links, subnets, and intersite transports. The Administrators built-in domain local group allows a group member to perform these actions.

B. **Correct:** The permissions provided with the Account Operators built-in domain local group allow the Directory Engineer to create and manage user accounts in Active Directory.

C. **Correct:** The permissions provided with the Backup Operators built-in domain local group allow the Directory Engineer to back up and restore Active Directory.

D. **Incorrect:** The permissions provided with the Replicator, Account Operators, and Backup Operators built-in domain local groups do not allow the Directory Engineer to manage DNS and Active Directory integration. The DnsAdmins built-in domain local group allows a group member to perform this action.

E. **Incorrect:** The permissions provided with the Replicator, Account Operators, and Backup Operators built-in domain local groups do not allow the Directory Engineer to extend the schema. The Schema Admins predefined global group allows a group member to perform this action.

OBJECTIVE 4.2

Manage Active Directory performance.

To ensure that the Active Directory directory service is meeting your business and networking goals, you must manage Active Directory performance. Performance management includes monitoring, maintaining, and troubleshooting the performance of the domain controller and Active Directory components.

You use **Event Viewer**, **System Monitor**, and **Performance Logs and Alerts** to monitor the performance of the domain controller and Active Directory components. Event Viewer allows you to monitor Microsoft Windows–wide events and Active Directory events by viewing **event logs**. The Directory Service event log contains errors, warnings, and information generated by Active Directory. You should check the Directory Service event log first when investigating the cause of an Active Directory problem. System Monitor allows you to measure Active Directory performance on your own computer or other computers on a network. By selecting **performance objects** and **performance counters**, you can view statistics about Active Directory performance as a chart, **histogram**, or **log file** data display. Performance Logs and Alerts allows you to create **counter logs**, **trace logs**, and **performance alerts** from local or remote computers. Counter logs collect performance counter data for a specific time period in a comma-separated or tab-separated format for importing into database programs and viewing using System Monitor. Trace logs record data when a specific event, such as disk I/O operation, occurs. A parsing tool is required to view the trace log output. You can create a system alert for a counter, which logs an entry on the application event log, sends a network message to a computer, starts a performance data log, or runs a program when the selected counter's value exceeds or falls below a specified setting.

The Shared Folders snap-in is provided so that you can easily monitor access to network resources and send administrative messages to users. The Shares folder allows you to view a list of all shared folders on the computer and the users connected to each folder. The Open Files folder allows you to view a list of open files in shared folders and the users connected to each file.

The following Windows 2000 **Support Tools** are included on the Windows 2000 CD-ROM and are intended for use in troubleshooting and maintaining Active Directory:

- LDP.EXE: Active Directory Administration Tool
  A graphical interface used to perform **Lightweight Directory Access Protocol (LDAP)** functions, such as binding and unbinding, adding objects to and deleting objects from the directory, modifying object attributes, and searching against any LDAP-compatible directory service, such as Active Directory.

- REPLMON.EXE: Active Directory Replication Monitor
  A graphical interface used to view the topology in a graphical format, view the low-level status of Active Directory replication, force synchronization between domain controllers, and monitor the status and performance of domain controller replication.

- REPADMIN.EXE: Replication Diagnostics Tool
  A command-line tool that helps diagnose replication problems between domain controllers.

- DSASTAT.EXE: Active Directory Diagnostic Tool
  A command-line tool that compares and detects differences between directory information on domain controllers.

- SDCHECK.EXE: Security Descriptor Check Utility
  A command-line tool used to verify that ACL entries are being propagated correctly through parent-child relationships and that changes are being replicated from one domain controller to another.

- NLTEST.EXE
  A command-line tool that helps perform network administration tasks.

- ACLDIAG.EXE: ACL Diagnostics
  A command-line tool that helps diagnose and troubleshoot problems with permissions on Active Directory objects.

- DSACLS.EXE
  A command-line tool that facilitates management of access control lists (ACLs) for directory services.

To troubleshoot Active Directory, view the "Troubleshooting" topic for "Active Directory" in Windows 2000 Server online help or Chapter 10, "Active Directory Diagnostics, Troubleshooting, and Recovery" in the Distributed Systems Guide in the *Microsoft Windows 2000 Server Resource Kit*. Use these topics to find Active Directory problem descriptions and suggestions for resolution.

70-217.04.02.001

You are experiencing problems with Active Directory replication. For some reason, changes to Active Directory are not replicating to one of your domain controllers. What should you do first to try to identify the problem?

A. Check the directory service event logs.

B. Audit port 135 using a packet analyzer.

C. Run NLTEST.EXE at the domain controller.

D. Collect replication traffic data in System Monitor.

70-217.04.02.002

You are viewing event logs in Event Viewer to identify a problem at a Windows 2000 domain controller. You find several warnings in the Directory Service log. What generated the warnings that appear in the log?

A. Windows 2000

B. Active Directory

C. File Replication Service

D. E-mail program or other application running on the server

70-217.04.02.003

You are troubleshooting a replication problem with Active Directory. The biggest impediment to solving the problem is a lack of documentation for the replication topology. You need a record of the enterprise configuration, including each site, site links, site link bridges, subnets and domain controllers, and the GUID for each object. If you had this information, troubleshooting the problem would be much easier. Which Active Directory support tool should you use to record the information you need to troubleshoot the problem?

A. ACLDIAG.EXE: ACL Diagnostics

B. REPADMIN.EXE: Replication Diagnostic Tool

C. DSASTAT.EXE: Active Directory Diagnostic Tool

D. LDP.EXE: Active Directory Administration Tool

E. SDCHECK.EXE: Security Descriptor Check Utility

F. REPLMON.EXE: Active Directory Replication Monitor

70-217.04.02.004

You are troubleshooting a problem with Active Directory. You need to ensure that the global catalog contains an accurate replica with domain controllers in other domains and that each domain controller is up to date with other domain controllers. Which Active Directory support tool should you use?

A. ACLDIAG.EXE: ACL Diagnostics

B. REPADMIN.EXE: Replication Diagnostic Tool

C. DSASTAT.EXE: Active Directory Diagnostic Tool

D. LDP.EXE: Active Directory Administration Tool

E. SDCHECK.EXE: Security Descriptor Check Utility

F. REPLMON.EXE: Active Directory Replication Monitor

70-217.04.02.005

Your company's CEO needs to access a file but cannot because the file is open. Only the CEO and Vice President of Accounting are supposed to have access to the file, but neither of them is currently accessing the file. You need to determine who is accessing the file. What should you do?

A. Use the Connections tab in Internet Explorer to view a list of open files in the shared folders and the users who have a current connection to each file.

B. Use the Open Files folder in System Monitor to view a list of open files in the shared folders and the users who have a current connection to each file.

C. Use the Open Files folder in the Shared Folders snap-in to view a list of open files in the shared folders and the users who have a current connection to each file.

D. Use the Open Files folder in Active Directory Users And Computers to view a list of open files in the shared folders and the users who have a current connection to each file.

70-217.04.02.006

You are experiencing slow replication on your network that you suspect is caused by an overloaded domain controller. You want to log the synchronization requests and the number of directory synchronizations that are queued for the domain controller over time to determine the extent of the replication backlog. Which tool could you use to accomplish this task?

A. System Monitor

B. Replication Diagnostic Tool

C. Active Directory Administration Tool

D. Active Directory Replication Monitor

Objective 4.2 Answers

70-217.04.02.001

▶ **Correct Answers: A**

    A. **Correct:** If you experience a problem with Active Directory, the first item that you use to try to identify the cause should be the directory service event logs. You can use the Application, Directory Service, File Replication Service, and System logs in Event Viewer to investigate the problem.

    B. **Incorrect:** Allowing access to RPC port 135 permits remote client access to Active Directory. Auditing the port using a packet analyzer is not the first action you should take to identify a problem with Active Directory replication.

    C. **Incorrect:** NLTEST.EXE is a command-line tool that can be used to test the logical connection between a Windows 2000 Professional computer and a Windows 2000 or Windows NT domain controller. Although this may be an appropriate tool to use while troubleshooting, it is not the first action you should take to identify a problem with Active Directory replication.

    D. **Incorrect:** Although the collection of replication traffic data using the various Directory Replication Agent (DRA) counters could be useful, it is not the first action you should take to identify a problem with Active Directory replication.

70-217.04.02.002

▶ **Correct Answers: B**

    A. **Incorrect:** Warnings generated by Windows 2000 are contained in the System log in Event Viewer.

    B. **Correct:** Warnings generated by Active Directory are contained in the Directory Service log.

    C. **Incorrect:** Warnings generated by the File Replication Service are contained in the File Replication Service log.

    D. **Incorrect:** Warnings generated by an e-mail program or other application running on the server are contained in the Application log.

70-217.04.02.003

▶ **Correct Answers: F**

A. **Incorrect:** ACLDIAG.EXE is a command-line tool that helps diagnose and troubleshoot problems with permissions on Active Directory objects. You cannot use ACLDIAG.EXE to provide a record of the enterprise configuration (including each site, site links, site link bridges, subnets, and domain controllers) and the GUID for each object.

B. **Incorrect:** Although REPADMIN.EXE is a command-line tool that allows administrators to view the replication topology as seen from the perspective of each Windows 2000 domain controller, this tool cannot provide a general record of the enterprise configuration (including each site, site links, site link bridges, subnets, and domain controllers) and the GUID for each object.

C. **Incorrect:** DSASTAT.EXE is a command-line tool that compares and detects differences between directory information on domain controllers. You cannot use DSASTAT.EXE to provide a record of the enterprise configuration (including each site, site links, site link bridges, subnets, and domain controllers) and the GUID for each object.

D. **Incorrect:** LDP.EXE is a graphical administration tool used to perform LDAP functions (such as binding and unbinding, adding objects to and deleting objects from the directory, modifying object attributes, and searching against any LDAP-compatible directory service such as Active Directory). You cannot use LDP.EXE to provide a record of the enterprise configuration (including each site, site links, site link bridges, subnets, and domain controllers) and the GUID for each object.

E. **Incorrect:** SDCHECK.EXE is a command-line tool used to verify that ACL entries are being propagated correctly through parent-child relationships and that changes are being replicated from one domain controller to another. You cannot use SDCHECK.EXE to provide a record of the enterprise configuration (including each site, site links, site link bridges, subnets, and domain controllers) and the GUID for each object.

F. **Correct:** REPLMON.EXE is a graphical administration tool used to view the replication topology, view the low-level status of Active Directory replication, force synchronization between domain controllers, and monitor the status and performance of domain controllers. The status reporting feature of REPLMON.EXE allows administrators to generate a record of the enterprise configuration (including each site, site link, site link bridge, subnet, and domain controller) and the GUID for each object.

70-217.04.02.004

► **Correct Answers: C**

A. **Incorrect:** ACLDIAG.EXE is a command-line tool that helps diagnose and troubleshoot problems with permissions on Active Directory objects. You cannot use ACLDIAG.EXE to ensure that the global catalog has a consistent image with domain controllers in other domains and that each domain controller is up to date with other domain controllers.

B. **Incorrect:** REPADMIN.EXE is a command-line tool that allows administrators to view the replication topology as seen from the perspective of each Windows 2000 domain controller. You cannot use REPADMIN.EXE to ensure that the global catalog has a consistent image with domain controllers in other domains and that each domain controller is up to date with other domain controllers.

C. **Correct:** DSASTAT.EXE is a command-line tool that compares and detects differences between directory information on domain controllers. This tool is used to compare directory trees across replicas within the same domain, or, as in the case of a global catalog, across different domains.

D. **Incorrect:** LDP.EXE is a graphical administration tool used to perform LDAP functions, such as binding and unbinding, adding objects to and deleting objects from the directory, modifying object attributes, and searching against any LDAP-compatible directory service such as Active Directory. You cannot use LDP.EXE to ensure that the global catalog has a consistent image with domain controllers in other domains and that each domain controller is up to date with other domain controllers.

E. **Incorrect:** SDCHECK.EXE is a command-line tool used to verify that ACL entries are being propagated correctly through parent-child relationships and that changes are being replicated from one domain controller to another. You cannot use SDCHECK.EXE to ensure that the global catalog has a consistent image with domain controllers in other domains and that each domain controller is up to date with other domain controllers.

F. **Incorrect:** REPLMON.EXE is a graphical administration tool used to view the replication topology, view the low-level status of Active Directory replication, force synchronization between domain controllers, and monitor the status and performance of the domain controller. You cannot use REPLMON.EXE to ensure that the global catalog has a consistent image with domain controllers in other domains and that each domain controller is up to date with other domain controllers.

70-217.04.02.005

▶ **Correct Answers: C**

A. **Incorrect:** The Connections tab in Internet Explorer does not contain a list of open files in the shared folders and the users who have a current connection to each file. The Connections tab is used to specify the settings for connecting your computer to the Internet.

B. **Incorrect:** System Monitor does not contain the Open Files folder. System Monitor uses performance objects and performance counters to graphically display performance data.

C. **Correct:** To view a list of open files that are located in shared folders and the users who have a current connection to each file, click the Open Files folder in the Shared Folders snap-in.

D. **Incorrect:** Active Directory Users And Computers does not contain the Open Files folder. Active Directory Users And Computers allows you to add, modify, delete, and organize Windows 2000 user accounts, computer accounts, security and distribution groups, and published resources in your organization's directory. It also allows you to manage domain controllers and OUs.

70-217.04.02.006

▶ **Correct Answers: A**

A. **Correct:** By indicating the name of the suspected domain controller and specifying that you want to monitor the DRA Sync Requests Made and DRA Pending Replication Synchronizations counters on the NTDS Performance object, you can log the synchronization requests and the number of directory synchronizations queued for the domain controller.

B. **Incorrect:** Although the Replication Diagnostic Tool, REPADMIN.EXE, is a command-line tool that allows administrators to view the replication topology as seen from the perspective of each Windows 2000 domain controller, you cannot use this tool to log the synchronization requests and the number of directory synchronizations queued for the domain controller.

C. **Incorrect:** The Active Directory Administration Tool, DSASTAT.EXE, is a command-line tool that compares and detects differences between directory information on domain controllers. You cannot use this tool to log the synchronization requests and the number of directory synchronizations queued for the domain controller.

D. **Incorrect:** Although the Active Directory Replication Monitor, REPLMON.EXE, is a graphical administration tool used to display the replication topology, display the low-level status of Active Directory replication, force synchronization between domain controllers, and monitor the status and performance of domain controllers, you cannot use this tool to log the synchronization requests and the number of directory synchronizations queued for the domain controller.

O B J E C T I V E 4 . 3

Manage and troubleshoot Active Directory replication.

In Active Directory, **replication** is the process of copying data from the directory database to multiple domain controllers in order to synchronize the data. Directory information can be replicated to domain controllers both within sites (**intrasite replication**) and among sites (intersite replication).

For intrasite replication, the Windows 2000 **Knowledge Consistency Checker (KCC)** service automatically generates replication links between domain controllers, forming the **replication topology**. These links are checked by default every 15 minutes; if a domain controller is added or removed, the topology is reconfigured to reflect the change. A separate automatic notification process is used in intrasite replication to announce when changes to directory information have occurred. There are few intrasite replication management activities that must be performed by a system administrator.

For intersite replication to occur, an administrator must customize how Active Directory replicates information by setting up **site links**. The KCC will then automatically generate the replication topology. To ensure efficient replication and fault tolerance, you must provide site link configuration information, including:

- **Replication transport protocol**
  The protocol used for replication, either Directory Service Remote Procedure Call (DS-RPC, designated in Windows 2000 as IP) or **Simple Mail Transport Protocol (SMTP).**

- Site link cost
  A value assigned to the site link that indicates the cost of the connection in relation to the speed of the link. Higher costs are used for slow links, and lower costs are used for fast links.

- Replication frequency
  A value assigned to the site link that indicates the number of minutes Active Directory should wait before using a connection to check for replication updates.

- Replication availability
  A schedule assigned to the site link that indicates when the link is available for replication.

- **Site link bridges**
  Links that indicate that replication can take place between two sites that are not directly linked.

- Preferred **bridgehead server**
  A preferred contact point for the exchange of directory information between sites.

In addition, you can perform the special fine-tuning operations of **reciprocal replication** and **change notification** by modifying the options attribute value on the site link object. Reciprocal replication provides the effect of two-way replication over a one-way connection such as a dial-up connection through an Internet service provider (ISP). Change notification allows a domain controller to notify a replication partner that it has changes. You configure change notification on site links only for special circumstances when you want to propagate changes to the remote site with the same frequency that they are propagated within the source site.

Objective 4.3 Questions

70-217.04.03.001

Your domain contains the San Diego, Los Angeles, and Phoenix sites. The San Diego and Los Angeles sites are connected by a T1 link. The Phoenix site is connected to the San Diego site by a permanent 128-Kbps link and to the Los Angeles site by a dial-up ISDN line. The network is fully routed. You created site links between San Diego and Los Angeles, San Diego and Phoenix, and Los Angeles and Phoenix. Replication is occurring properly, but the replication traffic across the Phoenix–Los Angeles site is costing your company a great deal of money in extra connection and usage fees. To save money, you want to force the Phoenix replication traffic across the permanent 128-Kbps link whenever possible. Which action should you take to solve the problem?

A. Use the Simple Mail Transport Protocol (SMTP) between the Phoenix and San Diego sites.

B. Configure preferred bridgehead servers for the Phoenix and San Diego sites.

C. Increase the default replication period for the Phoenix–Los Angeles site link.

D. Assign cost factors to the site links to favor the Phoenix–San Diego site link.

70-217.04.03.002

Your company has several branch offices that each contain at least one domain controller. Each branch office is configured as a separate site. When a domain controller in one of the branch sites needs to replicate changes to the main office, it dials an Internet service provider (ISP) and establishes a tunneled connection with the main office. However, this results in a one-way replication, because domain controllers at the main office cannot initiate a connection to any of the branch offices. What should you do to ensure two-way replication between the branch offices and the main office?

A. Lower the cost factor on the site links.

B. Enable change notification on all site links.

C. Enable reciprocal replication on all site links.

D. Create a preferred bridgehead server at each site.

70-217.04.03.003

Your domain contains the two sites, which are connected by a permanent 128-Kbps WAN link. The WAN link is operating correctly, but replication is occurring slowly between the two sites. Which action should you take to solve the problem?

A. Assign a lower cost to the site link.

B. Place a global catalog server at each site.

C. Configure bridgehead servers at each site.

D. Decrease the replication frequency setting.

Objective 4.3 Answers

70-217.04.03.001

► **Correct Answers: D**

A. **Incorrect:** SMTP enables low-speed, asynchronous replication between the schema, configuration, and global catalog directory partitions, but not between domain directory partitions. Changing the transport protocol on the 128-Kbps link between Phoenix and San Diego to SMTP will not force Phoenix replication traffic to this link. If you change the transport protocol between the Phoenix and San Diego sites to SMTP, not only will the Phoenix–San Diego link be slower, but the domain will be forced to use the Phoenix–Los Angeles link (which uses IP transport protocol) even more often for domain replication between Phoenix and San Diego. Therefore, changing the transport protocol between Phoenix and San Diego will cost your company even more money.

B. **Incorrect:** Bridgehead servers provide criteria for choosing which domain controllers should be preferred as the recipients for intersite replication. Establishing preferred bridgehead servers for the Phoenix and San Diego sites will not force Phoenix replication traffic across the 128-Kbps link between Phoenix and San Diego.

C. **Incorrect:** The replication period tells Active Directory how many minutes it should wait before using a connection to check for replication updates. If you increase the number of minutes between replication updates, replication will occur less often, and you will simply reduce the number of connections between the Phoenix and Los Angeles sites. Although this may save some money in connection costs, by increasing the replication frequency on the Phoenix–Los Angeles link, you will not force Phoenix replication traffic across the 128-Kbps link between Phoenix and San Diego.

D. **Correct:** The cost values assigned to site links determine the connection used for Active Directory replication. The cheapest connections are used if they are available. By assigning a higher cost value to the Phoenix–Los Angeles dial-up ISDN link, you can force Phoenix–to–Los Angeles replication traffic across the 128-Kbps link between Phoenix and San Diego whenever possible. The Phoenix–Los Angeles link is used only if the Phoenix–San Diego link is unavailable. This action will save your company money in connection and usage fees.

70-217.04.03.002

▶ **Correct Answers: C**

A. **Incorrect:** The cost values assigned to site links determine the connection used for Active Directory replication. The cheapest connections are used if they are available. Lowering the cost value does not ensure two-way replication between the branch offices and the main office when the sites connect through an ISP.

B. **Incorrect:** By default, changes are replicated between sites according to a schedule. When change notification is enabled, a domain controller notifies a replication partner that it has changes. You configure change notification on all site links only for special circumstances in which you want to propagate changes to the remote site with the same frequency that they are propagated within the source site. Enabling change notification on all site links does not ensure two-way replication between the branch offices and the main office when the sites connect through an ISP.

C. **Correct:** When reciprocal replication is enabled, a flag is set on the connection object to implement two-way replication between the branch site and the main office in the following manner: The domain controller at the branch site opens a connection and initiates replication (requests changes from the main office). After the domain controller at the branch site receives the changes from the domain controller at the main office, it responds by sending a change notification. The change notification prompts the domain controller at the main office to request changes from the domain controller at the branch site, which the branch site domain controller then sends. Because all directory information is current, the ISP connection is then closed.

D. **Incorrect:** Bridgehead servers provide criteria for choosing which domain controllers should be preferred as the recipients for intersite replication. Creating a preferred bridgehead server at each site does not ensure two-way replication between the branch offices and the main office when the sites connect through an ISP.

70-217.04.03.003

▶ **Correct Answers: D**

A. **Incorrect:** The cost values assigned to site links determine the connection used for Active Directory replication. The cheapest connections are used if they are available. Because there is only one site link, there is no other connection available. Lowering the cost value does not change the replication speed between the two sites.

B. **Incorrect:** The global catalog server is a domain controller that contains a partial replica of every domain directory partition in a forest, a full replica of its own domain directory partition, and the schema and configuration directory partitions. Although you could place global catalog servers at each site to provide fault tolerance and faster responses to user inquiries, they cannot change the replication speed between the two sites.

C. **Incorrect:** Bridgehead servers provide criteria for choosing which domain controllers should be preferred as the recipients for intersite replication. Configuring bridgehead servers at each site does not change the replication speed between the two sites.

D. **Correct:** Replication frequency tells Active Directory how many minutes it should wait before using a connection to check for replication updates. If you decrease the number of minutes between replication updates, replication will occur more often between the two sites.

Configuring, Managing, Monitoring, and Troubleshooting Security in a Directory Services Infrastructure

The Configuring, Managing, Monitoring, and Troubleshooting Security in a Directory Services Infrastructure domain focuses on administering a security configuration, including the configuration and troubleshooting of a security policy and the monitoring and analysis of security events. A security configuration consists of security settings you apply to the security areas supported by Microsoft Windows 2000 by using group policy objects (GPOs) in Active Directory directory service. A centralized method for defining a security configuration is provided by Windows 2000 through the use of security templates. Predefined security templates based on common security scenarios can be modified, be used without modification, or serve as the basis for creating custom security templates. The Security Configuration and Analysis tool provides a simulated security environment to help you configure and analyze security, view results, and resolve any discrepancies revealed in the analysis.

To maintain network security, you can track user activities and Windows 2000 activities, called events, by setting up an auditing strategy. You set up this strategy by defining an audit policy, which tracks the events you specify in the security log in each computer. To view the security log, you open the Event Viewer console, which also allows you to locate and filter events in the log and to archive security log files.

Tested Skills and Suggested Practices

The skills that you need to successfully master the Configuring, Managing, Monitoring, and Troubleshooting Security in a Directory Services Infrastructure domain on the *Implementing and Administering a Microsoft Windows 2000 Directory Services Infrastructure* exam include:

- **Configuring and troubleshooting security in a directory services infrastructure.**

  - Practice 1: Identify the security areas in the Security Settings extension of the Group Policy snap-in. Analyze the effects of the settings in each security area. Practice configuring security settings and applying security policies to computers and groups in your home network.

  - Practice 2: Identify the predefined security templates. Analyze the effects of each predefined security template. Practice customizing a predefined security template, defining a new security template, importing a security template to a GPO, and exporting security settings to a security template.

  - Practice 3: Review how the Security Configuration and Analysis tool works. Practice using the Security Configuration and Analysis tool to set a working security database, import a security template into a security database, analyze system security, view security analysis results, configure system security, and export security database settings to a security template.

  - Practice 4: Identify the types of events that can be audited by Windows 2000. Practice setting up policies that audit access to files and folders, Active Directory objects, and printers.

  - Practice 5: Use Windows 2000 Help to identify the problems and solutions associated with a security configuration by searching and reading entries under "Troubleshooting security."

- **Monitoring and analyzing security events.**

  - Practice 1: View a security log for your home network. Practice locating and filtering events in the log. Configure the settings for the security log size, overwrite behavior, and connection speed. Archive the security log using event log, text, and comma-delimited formats.

Further Reading

This "Further Reading" section provides lists of important readings to supplement your current understanding of the skills tested within this Objective Domain. The lists are delineated into pertinent readings for each objective within this Objective Domain. If you feel that you need additional preparation prior to taking the exam, study these sources thoroughly.

Objective 5.1

Microsoft Corporation. *MCSE Training Kit: Microsoft Windows 2000 Active Directory Services*. Redmond, Washington: Microsoft Press, 2000. Review Lessons 1 through 7 in Chapter 13, "Administering a Security Configuration," for instruction and practice on using security settings to define a security configuration.

Microsoft Corporation. *Microsoft Windows 2000 Server Resource Kit*. Volume: *Microsoft Windows 2000 Server Distributed Systems Guide*. Redmond, Washington: Microsoft Press, 2000. Review the "Configuring Group Policy" section in Chapter 22, "Group Policy," for information about defining a security configuration using security settings.

Microsoft Corporation. *Microsoft Windows 2000 Server Resource Kit*. Volume: *Microsoft Windows 2000 Server Deployment Planning Guide*. Redmond, Washington: Microsoft Press, 2000. Review the section on "Setting Uniform Security Policies" in Chapter 21, "Planning Distributed Security," for a discussion on deploying the security settings of group policy.

Microsoft Corporation. *MCSE Training Kit: Microsoft Windows 2000 Server*. Redmond, Washington: Microsoft Press, 2000. Review Lesson 4 in Chapter 11, "Microsoft Windows 2000 Security," for instruction and practice on using security configuration tools.

Objective 5.2

Microsoft Corporation. *MCSE Training Kit: Microsoft Windows 2000 Active Directory Services*. Redmond, Washington: Microsoft Press, 2000. Review Lesson 3 in Chapter 13, "Administering a Security Configuration," for instruction and practice on the tasks for using security logs.

Microsoft Corporation. *Microsoft Windows 2000 Server Resource Kit*. Volume: *Microsoft Windows 2000 Server Operations Guide*. Redmond, Washington: Microsoft Press, 2000. Review the section on "Event Viewer" in "Troubleshooting Options" in Chapter 14, "Troubleshooting Strategies," for detailed information about using Event Viewer.

Microsoft Corporation. *MCSE Training Kit: Microsoft Windows 2000 Server*. Redmond, Washington: Microsoft Press, 2000. Review Lesson 5 in Chapter 11, "Microsoft Windows 2000 Security," for instruction and practice on using audit policies and Event Viewer.

OBJECTIVE 5.1

Configure and troubleshoot security in a directory services infrastructure.

To configure network security, you can apply security settings by using the Security Settings extension in the Group Policy snap-in. You apply security settings to the following security areas supported by Windows 2000: Account Policies, Local Policies, Event Log, Restricted Groups, System Services, Registry, File System, Public Key Policies, and IP Security Policies On Active Directory. Account policies pertain to user accounts and contain settings for passwords, account lockout, and Kerberos information. Local policies apply to security settings on computers used by applications or users and contain settings for determining the **audit policy**, **user rights**, and computer security. The **Event Log** security area defines how the application, security, and system event logs are maintained. The Restricted Groups security area controls the users and groups allowed to be members of security-sensitive groups. The System Services area controls the startup mode and access permissions for services running on a computer. The Registry area controls security settings for registry keys, and the File System area controls access to file system objects. The Public Key Policies area is used to configure encrypted data recovery agents and automatic certificate requests and to manage lists of trusted certification authorities. The IP Security Policies On Active Directory security area configures the server to respond to IPSec communication requests. As an administrator, you must be able to recognize the effects of the settings in each security area so that you can design and apply an effective **security policy**.

Security templates provide a centralized method for defining a **security configuration**. Designed to cover common security requirements, four categories of predefined security templates have been defined: basic, compatible, secure, and highly secure. Basic security templates apply default Windows 2000 access control settings to all security areas except user rights. The basic templates are a means for reversing the application of other security configurations such as those encountered after upgrading a Microsoft Windows NT computer to Windows 2000. Compatible security templates apply the compatible security settings, relaxing the default permissions for the Users group so that older applications are more likely to run, and removing all members of the Power Users Group. Compatible templates do not establish a secure environment.

Secure security templates apply recommended security settings for all security areas except files, folders, and registry keys, which are configured securely by default. Highly secure security templates apply increased security settings for maximum protection of network traffic and protocols. You can modify the predefined security templates, use them without modification, or use them to create your own custom security templates.

To help you configure and analyze security, view results, and resolve any discrepancies revealed in the analysis, you can use the **Security Configuration And Analysis** console. This console uses a database to perform configuration and analysis functions in a simulated security environment. Security is analyzed by comparing your current system security settings to a security template containing your preferred security settings that you have imported to the database. If the settings match, they are assumed to be correct. If the settings do not match, they are displayed on the console as potential problems. The console allows you to resolve discrepancies by accepting or changing settings, configuring the system to its original settings, or importing a more appropriate template.

By setting up Windows 2000 **auditing**, you can track user activities and Windows 2000 activities, called **events**. You set up auditing by defining an **audit policy**, which tracks the events you specify in the **security log** in each computer. To set up an audit policy, you must select the event categories for audit in the Local Policies security area in the Security Settings extension in the Group Policy snap-in. The event categories include: account logon, account management, directory service access, logon events, object access, policy change, privilege use, process tracking, and system events. Events logged in the security log contain a record of the action that was performed, the user who performed the action, the success or failure of the event, and the time at which the event occurred. As an administrator, you must be able to recognize the items audited by each event category and determine the computers on which to set up auditing so that you audit the appropriate events to maintain an effective network security policy.

Objective 5.1 Questions

70-217.05.01.001

You are concerned that someone is trying to hack into your network by guessing passwords. To combat this problem, you want to configure security settings for your domain group policy so that an account is locked after three unsuccessful logon attempts, and both successful and unsuccessful logon attempts are logged into the security log. You open the Group Policy snap-in for the domain GPO and expand the Security Settings node as shown in the exhibit. Which security settings must you configure to enable the system to lock accounts after three unsuccessful logon attempts, and log both successful and unsuccessful logon attempts into the security log? (Choose two.)

Examine the GPO shown below.

A. Account Policies

B. Local Policies

C. Event Log

D. Restricted Groups

E. System Services

F. Registry

G. File System

70-217.05.01.002

You want to log successful and unsuccessful directory access attempts. You also want to specify that the security log cannot be overwritten. You open the Group Policy snap-in for the domain GPO and expand the Security Settings node as shown in the exhibit. Which security settings must you configure to log successful and unsuccessful directory service access attempts and specify that the log cannot be overwritten? (Choose two.)

Examine the GPO shown below.

A. Account Policies

B. Local Policies

C. Event Log

D. Restricted Groups

E. System Services

F. Registry

G. File System

70-217.05.01.003

You recently implemented a smart card system on your domain. Each user was assigned a smart card, which he or she uses to log on to computers in the domain. The smart card system is working properly for logging on to the system, but logging off is inconsistent. You need to ensure that a user is logged off when the user removes his or her smart card. You open the Group Policy snap-in for the domain GPO and expand the Security Settings node as shown in the exhibit. Which security settings must you configure to force a logoff when a user removes his or her smart card?

Examine the GPO shown below.

A. Account Policies

B. Local Policies

C. Event Log

D. Restricted Groups

E. System Services

F. Registry

G. File System

70-217.05.01.004

You are configuring security settings in the Group Policy snap-in for a GPO that you want to apply to an OU named Domain Controllers. You want to ensure that only members of a domain local group named Registry Editors are able to edit the registry for all domain controllers in the Domain Controllers OU. How should you configure the security settings for the GPO?

A. Remove the Registry Editors group from the Restricted Groups security area.

B. Add the Registry Editors group to the Edit Registry subfolder under the Restricted Groups security area.

C. Under the Registry security area, add the Registry Editors group to the security list for each registry key and allow all permissions, and then remove the Everyone group from the security list for each registry key.

D. Expand the Local Policies security area, click the User Rights Assignment area, right-click the Edit Registry setting and select Security, mark the Define These Policies Settings In The Template option, and add the Registry Editors group to the list.

70-217.05.01.005

You are configuring Event Log settings for a GPO linked to an OU named Domain Controllers. You want to achieve these results for all domain controllers in the Domain Controllers OU:

- The maximum security log file size should be limited to 4 MB.

- When the security log file size exceeds 2 MB, the log file should be stored on a specified member server.

- Security log access should be limited to Administrators.

- The system should not overwrite entries in the security log.

- Domain controllers should shut down when the security log is full.

You propose to open the Group Policy snap-in for the GPO and configure policies contained in the Event Log security area to achieve the wanted results.

Which results are achieved? (Choose all that apply.)

A. The maximum security log file size should be limited to 4 MB.

B. When the security log file size exceeds 2 MB, the log file should be stored on a specified member server.

C. Security log access should be limited to Administrators.

D. The system should not overwrite entries in the security logs.

E. Domain controllers should shut down when the security log is full.

70-217.05.01.006

You were recently assigned the task of administering an Active Directory domain in your company's network. The domain contains an OU named Domain Controllers that contains all the domain controllers in the domain. You are configuring settings for event logs in the Group Policy snap-in for a GPO linked to the Domain Controllers OU. You configured the event log settings as shown in the exhibit. How will these settings affect the security logs for domain controllers in the Domain Controllers OU when the GPO is applied?

Examine the event log settings in the GPO shown below.

A. When the log file exceeds 2 MB, the system will stop adding entries to the security log file for seven days.

B. When the log file exceeds 2 MB, the system will delete all entries in the log file that are seven days old or older.

C. When the log file exceeds 2 MB, the system will start a new security log file and retain the old log file for seven days.

D. When the log file entries are seven days old or older, the system will begin overwriting entries in the log file, but if the log file exceeds 2 MB before the log file entries are seven days old, new events will not be added to the log.

70-217.05.01.007

You were recently assigned the task of administering an Active Directory domain in your company's network. You are configuring user rights assignments settings in a GPO associated with an OU named Member Servers. You assigned a user account named User1 the Bypass Traverse Checking privilege in the User Rights Assignment security area. What does this give User1 the ability to do?

A. Shut down member servers remotely

B. Manually replace the default token associated with a subprocess that has been started

C. Authenticate to access all member servers by authenticating to only one member server

D. Pass through directories on the member servers to which the user otherwise has no access

70-217.05.01.008

You made changes to the account policies for a GPO applied to an OU named Computers. However, the changes are not propagating correctly to all computers in the OU. What action can you take to troubleshoot this problem?

A. Use the SECEDIT command-line tool to refresh security settings.

B. Make sure that the No Override option is enabled for the GPO.

C. Check the DNS configuration to make sure there are no stale entries in the DNS database, and resolve local DNS servers and Internet service provider (ISP) DNS server entries.

D. Look for specific errors that occur during policy propagation in the Winlogon.log file located in the systemroot\Security\Logs folder.

70-217.05.01.009

You upgraded all servers and workstations in your network to Windows 2000. You performed a clean install of Windows 2000 on all of the servers in the network, but only about 20 percent of the workstations were clean-installed. The majority of the workstations were upgraded to Windows 2000 from a previous version of Windows. This has caused problems with network security because the upgraded computers do not have the same security settings as the Windows 2000 workstations that were clean-installed. You need to ensure that the upgraded Windows 2000 computers have the same default security settings that were applied to the clean-installed computers. You want to use a predefined security template to ensure that all workstations have the same Windows 2000 default security settings. Which predefined security template should you apply?

A. BASICWK.INF

B. HISECWS.INF

C. NOTSSID.INF

D. COMPATWS.INF

E. SECUREWS.INF

F. OCFILESW.INF

70-217.05.01.010

You upgraded all servers and workstations in your network to Windows 2000. You performed a clean install of Windows 2000 on all the servers in the network, but only about 20 percent of the workstations were clean-installed. The majority of the workstations were upgraded to Windows 2000 from a previous version of Windows. After the computers were upgraded, you removed end users from the Power Users group to increase the security of your network. However, after you removed end users from the Power Users group, some users were not able to run Microsoft Office 97 applications on their workstations. A closer inspection of the problem revealed that users could successfully run Microsoft Office 97 applications on clean-installed workstations but were not able to run the applications on upgraded workstations. To solve this problem, you want to apply a predefined security template at the domain level to ensure that users can successfully run Microsoft Office 97 applications from any Windows 2000 computer in the domain. Which predefined security template should you apply?

A. BASICWK.INF

B. HISECWS.INF

C. NOTSSID.INF

D. COMPATWS.INF

E. SECUREWS.INF

F. OCFILESW.INF

70-217.05.01.011

You want to use security templates to streamline security in your Windows 2000 network. You want to define all security areas possible in security templates and apply them to OUs in your domain. Which security areas will you not be able to configure with security templates? (Choose all that apply.)

A. IP Security Policies

B. Account Policies

C. Restricted Groups

D. Registry

E. File System

F. Public Key Policies

70-217.05.01.012

You want to use security templates to streamline security in your Windows 2000 network. You want to define all security areas possible in security templates and apply them to OUs in your domain. Which methods can you use to create your security templates? (Choose all that apply.)

A. Define a new security template in the Security Templates console.

B. Customize a predefined security template in the Security Templates console.

C. Import a security template to a console from which you manage your group policy settings.

D. Convert existing Windows NT profiles to Windows 2000 security templates in the Security Templates console.

70-217.05.01.013

You used security templates to apply security policies to your Windows 2000 network. Since the policies were first applied, you have had to temporarily change security levels to troubleshoot a network problem. You are concerned that the temporarily changed security levels might not have been changed back, and you want to use the Security Configuration And Analysis tool to determine whether this is indeed the case. What should you do before you use the Security Configuration And Analysis tool to analyze the security settings on your domain controllers? (Choose two.)

A. Create a counter log.

B. Set a working security database.

C. Import a security template into a security database.

D. Type **secedit /refreshpolicy machine policy** at the command prompt.

E. Set an audit policy to log successful and unsuccessful directory service access attempts.

70-217.05.01.014

You need to set up and administer auditing on a Windows 2000 network. To simplify the process, you want to configure auditing on your domain controllers using a nonlocal GPO. You want to audit several events including account logons, account management, directory service access, and file and folder access. What are the requirements for setting up auditing? (Choose two.)

A. The domain must be operating in native mode.

B. The files and folders to be audited must be on NTFS volumes.

C. Make sure that you have a home directory with adequate free space to store the audit logs.

D. The SECUREDC.INF predefined security template must be applied to the domain controllers prior to setting up auditing.

E. To set up auditing, you must be a member of the Administrators group or have the Manage Auditing And Security Log user right for the computers on which you want to configure an audit policy.

70-217.05.01.015

You want to set up auditing for your Windows 2000 domain controllers. The domain controllers are in an OU named Domain Controllers. You want to audit these events:

- Domain controller requests to validate a user account

- Modifications to user and group accounts, such as creating, deleting, or renaming system time changes

- Modifications to user security options

- System restarts and shutdowns

You propose to configure an auditing policy in a nonlocal group policy object (GPO) for the domain. You will set the auditing policy for the GPO and enable the auditing for successes and failures for the following events:

- Account logon

- Directory service access

- Policy change

- Process tracking

- System events

Which events will you successfully audit when the proposed solution is implemented? (Choose all that apply.)

A. Domain controller requests to validate a user account

B. Modifications to user and group accounts, such as creating, deleting, or renaming

C. System time changes

D. Modifications to user security options

E. System restarts and shutdowns

70-217.05.01.016

You want to audit user access to files and folders located on your Windows 2000 domain controllers. You open the Group Policy snap-in for your GPO, and expand the Audit Policy security area as shown in the exhibit. Which audit policy setting should you set to audit user access to files and folders on your domain controllers?

Examine the audit policy settings in the GPO shown below.

A. Account logon

B. Account management

C. Directory service access

D. Object access

E. Policy change

F. Privilege use

G. Process tracking

70-217.05.01.017

Your network contains one Active Directory domain. The domain contains four OUs: Domain Controllers, Member Servers, Computers, and Users. The Domain Controllers OU contains only domain controllers. The Member Servers OU contains Windows 2000 member servers. The Computers OU contains Windows 2000 workstations, Windows NT workstations, and Windows 98 workstations. You want to enable auditing of printers attached to your Windows 2000 member servers. You open the Group Policy snap-in for the GPO associated with the Member Servers OU and expand the Audit Policy security area as shown in the exhibit. Which audit policy setting should you set to audit printers on your member servers?

Examine the audit policy settings in the GPO shown below.

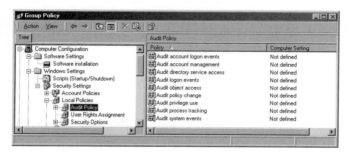

A. Account logon

B. Account management

C. Directory service access

D. Object access

E. Policy change

F. Privilege use

G. Process tracking

70-217.05.01.018

You are concerned that someone might be trying to remotely gain access into your Windows 2000 network using a random password hack. You need to define an audit policy to help you combat this threat to network security. Because all of your domain controllers are located in the Domain Controllers OU, you can implement an audit policy once at the OU to audit all your domain controllers. Which event should you audit to combat this threat?

A. Success audit for logon events

B. Failure audit for account logon events

C. Success and failure audit of system events

D. Failure audit of directory service access events

70-217.05.01.019

You are concerned that someone might have stolen a user name and password for a user account and is using that user name and password to remotely access your Windows 2000 network during off hours. You need to define an audit policy to help you combat this threat to network security. Because all of your domain controllers are located in the Domain Controllers OU, you can implement an audit policy once at the OU to audit all your domain controllers. Which event should you audit to combat this threat?

A. Success audit for logon events

B. Failure audit for account logon events

C. Success and failure audit of system events

D. Success audit of directory service access events

70-217.05.01.020

You are concerned that someone inside your company might have stolen a user name and password for an administrative account and is using that account to grant certain user rights to accounts that should not have them. You need to define an audit policy to help you combat this threat to network security. Because all of your domain controllers are located in the Domain Controllers OU, you can implement an audit policy once at the OU to audit all your domain controllers. Which event should you audit to combat this threat?

A. Successful audit of system events

B. Successful audit for object access events

C. Successful audit for policy change events

D. Successful audit of directory service access events

70-217.05.01.021

You are setting up auditing to track access to printers. You have set the object access event category in your audit policy, and now need to specify the types of access and the groups to audit for the Lexmark Optra Color 1200n printer attached to a member server, as shown in the exhibit. You want to audit this printer to determine who is changing the printer's settings. Which events should you audit?

Examine the Auditing Entry For Lexmark Optra Color 1200n dialog box shown below.

A. Successful print

B. Successful manage printers

C. Successful manage documents

D. Successful read permissions

E. Successful change permissions

F. Successful take ownership

Objective 5.1 Answers

70-217.05.01.001

▶ **Correct Answers: A and B**

A. **Correct:** You can set the Account Lockout Threshold setting in the Account Lockout Policy extension in Account Policies to 3 to enable the system to lock accounts after three unsuccessful logon attempts.

B. **Correct:** You can use the settings in the Audit Policy extension in Local Policies to log successful and unsuccessful logon attempts into the security log in the Event Viewer console. Although the log reflects events on only the computer used by an application or user, because the settings are imported to the domain GPO, they affect the local security settings of all computers in the domain. As a result, logon events for the entire domain are reflected in the security log.

C. **Incorrect:** You can use the Event Log security area to define the characteristics of the Application, Security, and System event logs. You cannot use the settings in the Event Log area to provide account lockout or to log successful and unsuccessful logon attempts into the security log.

D. **Incorrect:** You can use the Restricted Groups security area to govern the membership of Windows 2000 groups that have predefined capabilities, such as Administrators, Power Users, and Print Operators. You cannot use the settings in the Restricted Groups area to provide account lockout or to log successful and unsuccessful logon attempts into the security log.

E. **Incorrect:** You can use the System Services security area to configure security and startup settings for services running on a computer. You cannot use the settings in the System Services area to provide account lockout or to log successful and unsuccessful logon attempts into the security log.

F. **Incorrect:** You can use the Registry security area to configure security on registry keys. You cannot use the settings in the Registry area to provide account lockout or to log successful and unsuccessful logon attempts into the security log.

G. **Incorrect:** You can use the File System security area to configure security and auditing policies on files and folders. You cannot use the settings in the File System area to provide account lockout or to log successful and unsuccessful logon attempts into the security log.

70-217.05.01.002

▶ **Correct Answers: B and C**

A. **Incorrect:** You can use the settings in the Account Policies security area to set password policies, account lockout policies, and Kerberos policies. You cannot use the settings in the Account Policies area to log successful and unsuccessful directory service access attempts or to specify that the security log cannot be overwritten.

B. **Correct:** You can use the Audit Directory Service Access settings in the Audit Policy extension in Local Policies to log successful and unsuccessful directory service access attempts into the security log in the Event Viewer console. Although the log reflects events on only the computer used by an application or user, because the settings are imported to the domain GPO, they affect the local security settings of all computers in the domain. As a result, successful and unsuccessful directory service access attempts for the entire domain are reflected in the security log.

C. **Correct:** You can use the Event Log security area to define the characteristics of the Application, Security, and System event logs. By opening the Settings For Event Logs extension and setting the Retention Method For Security Log setting to Do Not Overwrite Events, you can specify that the security log cannot be overwritten.

D. **Incorrect:** You can use the Restricted Groups security area to govern the membership of Windows 2000 groups that have predefined capabilities, such as Administrators, Power Users, and Print Operators. You cannot use the settings in the Restricted Groups area to log successful and unsuccessful directory service access attempts or to specify that the security log cannot be overwritten.

E. **Incorrect:** You can use the System Services security area to configure security and startup settings for services running on a computer. You cannot use the settings in the System Services area to log successful and unsuccessful directory service access attempts or to specify that the security log cannot be overwritten.

F. **Incorrect:** You can use the Registry security area to configure security on registry keys. You cannot use the settings in the Registry area to log successful and unsuccessful directory service access attempts or to specify that the security log cannot be overwritten.

G. **Incorrect:** You can use the File System security area to configure security and auditing policies on files and folders. You cannot use the settings in the File System area to log successful and unsuccessful directory service access attempts or to specify that the security log cannot be overwritten.

70-217.05.01.003

▶ **Correct Answers: B**

A. **Incorrect:** You can use the settings in the Account Policies security area to set password policies, account lockout policies, and Kerberos policies. You cannot use the settings in the Account Policies area to force a logoff when a user removes his or her smart card.

B. **Correct:** You can set the Smart Card Removal Behavior in the Security Options extension in Local Policies to force a logoff when a user removes his or her smart card. Although the behavior setting reflects events on only the computer used by an application or user, because the settings are imported to the domain GPO, they affect the local security settings of all computers in the domain. As a result, logoffs are forced when a user removes his or her smart card for the entire domain.

C. **Incorrect:** You can use the Event Log security area to define the characteristics of the Application, Security, and System event logs. You cannot use the settings in the Event Log area to force a logoff when a user removes his or her smart card.

D. **Incorrect:** You can use the Restricted Groups security area to govern the membership of Windows 2000 groups that have predefined capabilities, such as Administrators, Power Users, and Print Operators. You cannot use the settings in the Restricted Groups area to force a logoff when a user removes his or her smart card.

E. **Incorrect:** You can use the System Services security area to configure security and startup settings for services running on a computer. You cannot use the settings in the System Services area to force a logoff when a user removes his or her smart card.

F. **Incorrect:** You can use the Registry security area to configure security on registry keys. You cannot use the settings in the Registry area to force a logoff when a user removes his or her smart card.

G. **Incorrect:** You can use the File System security area to configure security and auditing policies on files and folders. You cannot use the settings in the File System area to force a logoff when a user removes his or her smart card.

70-217.05.01.004

▶ **Correct Answers: C**

  A. **Incorrect:** You can use the Restricted Groups security area to control the membership of security-sensitive groups and to control the groups to which a security-sensitive group belongs. Removing the Registry Editors group from the Restricted Groups security area will not ensure that only members of the Registry Editors domain local group are able to edit the registry for all domain controllers in the Domain Controllers OU.

  B. **Incorrect:** There is no Edit Registry subfolder under the Restricted Groups security area.

  C. **Correct:** By adding the Registry Editors group to the security list for each registry key in the Registry security area and allowing all permissions, and then removing the Everyone group from the security list for each registry key, you ensure that only members of the Registry Editors domain local group are able to edit the registry for all domain controllers in the Domain Controllers OU.

  D. **Incorrect:** There is no Edit Registry setting in the User Rights Assignment area.

70-217.05.01.005

▶ **Correct Answers: A, D, and E**

  A. **Correct:** By opening the Settings For Event Logs extension and setting the Maximum Security Log Size setting to 4096 kilobytes, you can specify that the maximum security log file size should be limited to 4 MB.

  B. **Incorrect:** There is no setting in the Settings For Event Logs extension that allows you to specify that when the security log file size exceeds 2 MB, the log file should be stored on a specified member server.

  C. **Incorrect:** Although there is a setting that allows you to restrict guest access to the security log, there is no setting in the Settings For Event Logs extension that allows you to specify that security log access should be limited to Administrators.

  D. **Correct:** By opening the Settings For Event Logs extension and setting the Retention Method For Security Log setting to Do Not Overwrite Events, you can specify that the system should not overwrite entries in the security logs.

  E. **Correct:** By opening the Settings For Event Logs extension and setting the Shut Down The Computer When The Security Audit Log Is Full setting to Enabled, you can specify that domain controllers should shut down when the security log is full.

70-217.05.01.006

▶ **Correct Answers: D**

A. **Incorrect:** Although the Maximum Security Log Size setting indicates that the maximum security log size is 2048 kilobytes, and although the Retain Security Log setting indicates that security log entries should be kept for seven days, there is no setting to stop the system from adding entries to the log for seven days when the log file exceeds 2 MB.

B. **Incorrect:** Although the Maximum Security Log Size setting indicates that the maximum security log size is 2048 kilobytes, and although the Retain Security Log setting indicates that security log entries should be kept for seven days, there is no setting to delete all entries in the log file that are seven days old or older when the log file exceeds 2 MB.

C. **Incorrect:** Although the Maximum Security Log Size setting indicates that the maximum security log size is 2048 kilobytes, and although the Retain Security Log setting indicates that security log entries should be kept for seven days, there is no setting that will start a new security log file and retain the old log file for seven days when the log file exceeds 2 MB.

D. **Correct:** The Maximum Security Log Size setting indicates that the maximum security log size is 2048 kilobytes, and the Retain Security Log setting indicates that the system will begin overwriting entries in the log file that are seven days old or older. Therefore, the system will begin overwriting entries in the log file when the entries are seven days or older, but if the maximum size of the log file is reached before then, new events will simply not be added to the log (nothing will be overwritten).

70-217.05.01.007

▶ **Correct Answers: D**

A. **Incorrect:** The Force Shutdown From A Remote System privilege allows a user to shut down a computer from a remote location on the network.

B. **Incorrect:** The Replace A Process Level Token privilege allows a process to manually replace the default token associated with a subprocess that has been started.

C. **Incorrect:** There is no privilege that allows the user to authenticate to access all member servers by authenticating to only one member server.

D. **Correct:** The Bypass Traverse Checking privilege allows the user to pass through directories to which the user otherwise has no access, while navigating an object path in any Windows file system or in the registry.

70-217.05.01.008

▶ **Correct Answers: D**

A. **Incorrect:** The SECEDIT command refreshes system security by reapplying the security settings to the GPO. Because the policy changes are propagating to some of the computers in the OU, the security settings are already being applied and the problem cannot be corrected by using the SECEDIT command to perform a manual policy refresh.

B. **Incorrect:** The No Override option prevents any child GPOs for the OU from overriding the policies set in the GPO, even if these policies conflict with the child OU's policies. Because the policy changes are propagating to some of the computers in the OU, the policies in the GPO are not being overridden and the problem cannot be corrected by enabling the No Override option.

C. **Incorrect:** You should check the DNS configuration if you have a network-related problem and are unable to open the GPO. Because the policy changes are propagating to some of the computers in the OU, and you have not experienced problems opening the GPO, there is no network connectivity problem.

D. **Correct:** The Winlogon.log file is created during policy propagation. This file allows you to identify errors that occur during policy propagation.

70-217.05.01.009

▶ **Correct Answers: A**

A. **Correct:** The BASICWK.INF predefined security template applies default settings for Windows 2000 Professional–based computers for all areas except user rights and group membership. User rights and group memberships are not modified in this template because these assignments have usually been customized to suit specific network needs.

B. **Incorrect:** The HISECWS.INF predefined security template applies highly secure workstation or server settings, providing maximum protection for network traffic and protocols used between computers running Windows 2000. Computers configured with this template cannot communicate with other computers running Windows 95, Windows 98, or Windows NT. Because your goal is to use a predefined security template to ensure that all workstations have the same Windows 2000 default security settings, it is not necessary to apply the HISECWS.INF template.

C. **Incorrect:** The NOTSSID.INF predefined security template removes the Terminal Server User SID from Windows 2000 Server. Because your goal is to use a predefined security template to ensure that all workstations have the same Windows 2000 default security settings, it is not necessary to apply the NOTSSID.INF template.

D. **Incorrect:** The COMPATWS.INF predefined security template applies the compatible workstation or server security settings, which relaxes the default permissions for the Users group so that older applications are more likely to run. The COMPATWS.INF template does not provide a secure environment. Because your goal is to use a predefined security template to ensure that all workstations have the same Windows 2000 default security settings, it is not advisable to apply the COMPATWS.INF template.

E. **Incorrect:** The SECUREWS.INF predefined security template applies secure workstation or server settings for all security areas except files, folders, and most registry keys, which are secured by the default access control permissions. Because your goal is to use a predefined security template to ensure that all workstations have the same Windows 2000 default security settings, it is not necessary to apply the SECUREWS.INF template.

F. **Incorrect:** The OCFILESW.INF predefined security template applies security settings for files installed by optional components on the workstation. Because your goal is to use a predefined security template to ensure that all workstations have the same Windows 2000 default security settings, it is not necessary to apply the OCFILESW.INF template.

70-217.05.01.010

▶ **Correct Answers: D**

A. **Incorrect:** The BASICWK.INF predefined security template applies default settings for Windows 2000 Professional–based computers for all areas except user rights and group membership. User rights and group memberships are not modified in this template because these assignments have usually been customized to suit specific network needs. Applying the BASICWK.INF template will not ensure that users can successfully run Microsoft Office 97 applications from any Windows 2000 computer in the domain.

B. **Incorrect:** The HISECWS.INF predefined security template applies highly secure workstation or server settings, providing maximum protection for network traffic and protocols used between computers running Windows 2000. Computers configured with this template cannot communicate with other computers running Windows 95, Windows 98, or Windows NT. Applying the HISECWS.INF template will not ensure that users can successfully run Microsoft Office 97 applications from any Windows 2000 computer in the domain.

C. **Incorrect:** The NOTSSID.INF predefined security template removes the Terminal Server User SID from Windows 2000 Server. Applying the NOTSSID.INF template will not ensure that users can successfully run Microsoft Office 97 applications from any Windows 2000 computer in the domain.

D. **Correct:** The COMPATWS.INF predefined security template applies the compatible workstation or server security settings, which relaxes the default permissions for the Users group so that older applications are more likely to run. Although the COMPATWS.INF template does not provide a secure environment, by applying this template, you ensure that users can successfully run Microsoft Office 97 applications from any Windows 2000 computer in the domain.

E. **Incorrect:** The SECUREWS.INF predefined security template applies secure workstation or server settings for all security areas except files, folders, and most registry keys, which are secured by the default access control permissions. Applying the SECUREWS.INF template will not ensure that users can successfully run Microsoft Office 97 applications from any Windows 2000 computer in the domain.

F. **Incorrect:** The OCFILESW.INF predefined security template applies security settings for files installed by optional components on the workstation. Applying the OCFILESW.INF template will not ensure that users can successfully run Microsoft Office 97 applications from any Windows 2000 computer in the domain.

70-217.05.01.011

▶ **Correct Answers: A and F**

A. **Correct:** A security template is a file where a group of security settings is stored, designed to streamline security administration. The IP Security Policies security area cannot be contained in a security template.

B. **Incorrect:** A security template is a file where a group of security settings is stored, designed to streamline security administration. The Account Policies security area can be contained in a security template.

C. **Incorrect:** A security template is a file where a group of security settings is stored, designed to streamline security administration. The Restricted Groups security area can be contained in a security template.

D. **Incorrect:** A security template is a file where a group of security settings is stored, designed to streamline security administration. The Registry security area can be contained in a security template.

E. **Incorrect:** A security template is a file where a group of security settings is stored, designed to streamline security administration. The File System security area can be contained in a security template.

F. **Correct:** A security template is a file where a group of security settings is stored, designed to streamline security administration. The Public Key Policies security area cannot be contained in a security template.

70-217.05.01.012

▶ **Correct Answers: A, B, and C**

A. **Correct:** When you define a new security template, you modify the default template settings to meet your requirements and create a new template.

B. **Correct:** When you customize a predefined security template, you save the predefined template as a new template to avoid modifying the original predefined template. Then you can make edits to the security settings on the new template to create a new template.

C. **Correct:** When you import a security template, you select a security template to copy to a GPO. A new template exists for that GPO.

D. **Incorrect:** It is not possible to convert Windows NT profiles to Windows 2000 security templates.

70-217.05.01.013

▶ **Correct Answers: B and C**

   A. **Incorrect:** A counter log collects performance counter data in a comma-separated or tab-separated format for input into database or spreadsheet programs. It is not necessary to create a counter log before you use the Security Configuration And Analysis tool to analyze the security settings on your domain controllers.

   B. **Correct:** Because the Security Configuration And Analysis tool uses a database to perform configuration and analysis functions, you must determine the working security database to use for the analysis. To set a working security database, open the Security Configuration And Analysis console and right-click Security Configuration And Analysis. Then select Open Database. In the Open Database dialog box, choose an existing database or type a file name to create a new database, and then select Open. Finally, select the security template to load into the security database, and select Open.

   C. **Correct:** By importing the original security templates and the templates that include the temporary security level changes you made to troubleshoot the network problem into a security database, you can reconstruct the security settings in your system. To import a security template into a working security database, open the Security Configuration And Analysis console and right-click Security Configuration And Analysis. Then open or create a working security database and select Import Template. Select a template to import, and then click Open. You can repeat the previous step for each template you want to merge with previous templates into the database.

   D. **Incorrect:** The SECEDIT command refreshes system security by reapplying the security settings to the GPO. It is not necessary to type **secedit /refreshpolicy machine policy** at the command prompt before you use the Security Configuration And Analysis tool to analyze the security settings on your domain controllers.

   E. **Incorrect:** An audit policy defines the categories of events that Windows 2000 records in the security log in the Event Viewer console. It is not necessary to set an audit policy to log successful and unsuccessful directory service access attempts before you use the Security Configuration And Analysis tool to analyze the security settings on your domain controllers.

70-217.05.01.014

▶ **Correct Answers: B and E**

A. **Incorrect:** Operating the domain in native mode is not a requirement for setting up or administering auditing.

B. **Correct:** The files and folders to be audited must be on Microsoft Windows NT File System volumes.

C. **Incorrect:** It is not necessary or advisable to store the audit logs in a home directory, which is associated with a particular user or group of users. By default, event logs are stored in the systemroot and not in a home directory for any user or users.

D. **Incorrect:** The SECUREDC.INF predefined security template applies secure domain controller security settings to domain controllers. It is not necessary to apply the SECUREDC.INF security template to domain controllers prior to setting up auditing.

E. **Correct:** One of the requirements for setting up and administering auditing is to have the Manage Auditing And Security Log user right for the computer where you configure the audit policy. By default, the Administrators group is granted this user right.

70-217.05.01.015

▶ **Correct Answers: A, D, and E**

A. **Correct:** Because you have set the account logon event category for auditing, requests received by a domain controller to validate a user account are audited.

B. **Incorrect:** To audit modifications to user and group accounts, such as creating, deleting, or renaming, you must set the account management event category for auditing. You have not set the account management category for auditing.

C. **Incorrect:** You must set the privilege use event category for auditing to audit users who exercise rights, such as changing the system time.

D. **Correct:** Because you have set the policy change event category for auditing, changes made to user security options, user rights, or audit policies are audited.

E. **Correct:** Because you have set the system events event category for auditing, the following events are audited: computer restarts or shutdowns, events that affect Windows 2000 security, and events that affect the security log.

70-217.05.01.016

▶ **Correct Answers: D**

A. **Incorrect:** The account logon event category allows you to audit a request received by a domain controller to validate a user account.

B. **Incorrect:** The account management event category allows you to audit an administrator's creation, modification, or deletion of a user account or group and the renaming, disabling, or enabling of a user account or a password set or change.

C. **Incorrect:** The directory service access event category allows you to audit user access to an Active Directory object, such as users, computers, OUs, or groups. You must specify the Active Directory objects to be audited for this event category.

D. **Correct:** The object access event category allows you to audit user access to files, folders, or printers. You must specify the files for auditing for this event category.

E. **Incorrect:** The policy change event category allows you to audit changes made to user security options, user rights, or audit policies.

F. **Incorrect:** The privilege use event category allows you to audit users who exercise rights, such as changing the system time.

G. **Incorrect:** The process tracking event category allows you to audit programs performing a specific action.

70-217.05.01.017

▶ **Correct Answers: D**

A. **Incorrect:** The account logon event category allows you to audit a request received by a domain controller to validate a user account.

B. **Incorrect:** The account management event category allows you to audit an administrator's creation, modification, or deletion of a user account or group and the renaming, disabling, or enabling of a user account or a password set or change.

C. **Incorrect:** The directory service access event category allows you to audit user access to Active Directory objects, such as users, computers, OUs, or groups. You must specify the Active Directory objects to be audited for this event category.

D. **Correct:** The object access event category allows you to audit user access to files, folders, or printers. You must specify the files for auditing for this event category.

E. **Incorrect:** The policy change event category allows you to audit changes made to user security options, user rights, or audit policies.

F. **Incorrect:** The privilege use event category allows you to audit users who exercise rights, such as changing the system time.

G. **Incorrect:** The process tracking event category allows you to audit programs performing a specific action.

70-217.05.01.018

▶ **Correct Answers: B**

A. **Incorrect:** The logon events event category allows you to audit user logon and logoff or user network connection and disconnection. By auditing successful logon events, you track only successful user logons. A random password hack requires many unsuccessful logon attempts before a successful logon is attained; therefore, auditing successful logon events will not help you combat the threat of a random password hack.

B. **Correct:** The account logon event category allows you to audit a request received by a domain controller to validate a user account. A random password hack requires many unsuccessful requests for validation before a successful logon is attained. Therefore, auditing unsuccessful account logon events can help you combat the threat of a random password hack.

C. **Incorrect:** The system events event category allows you to audit computer restarts or shutdowns, events that affect Windows 2000 security, and events that affect the security log. Auditing successful and unsuccessful system events will not help you combat the threat of a random password hack.

D. **Incorrect:** The directory service access event category allows you to audit user access to Active Directory objects, such as users, computers, OUs, or groups. Auditing unsuccessful directory service access attempts will not help you combat the threat of a random password hack.

70-217.05.01.019

▶ **Correct Answers: A**

A. **Correct:** The logon events event category allows you to audit user logon and logoff or user network connection and disconnection. By auditing successful logon events, you can track successful user logons that occurred during off hours and locate the account being used to hack into your network.

B. **Incorrect:** The account logon event category allows you to audit a request received by a domain controller to validate a user account. Because you suspect that someone may have stolen a user name and password for a user account and is using that user name and password to remotely log on to your Windows 2000 network during off hours, user logons are most likely to be successful. Therefore, auditing unsuccessful account logon events cannot help you combat the threat of an unauthorized logon during off hours.

C. **Incorrect:** The system events event category allows you to audit computer restarts or shutdowns, events that affect Windows 2000 security, and events that affect the security log. Auditing successful and unsuccessful system events will not help you combat the threat of an unauthorized logon during off hours.

D. **Incorrect:** The directory service access event category allows you to audit user access to Active Directory objects, such as users, computers, OUs, or groups. Auditing successful directory service access attempts will not help you combat the threat of an unauthorized logon during off hours.

70-217.05.01.020

▶ **Correct Answers: C**

A. **Incorrect:** The system events event category allows you to audit computer restarts or shutdowns, events that affect Windows 2000 security, and events that affect the security log. Auditing successful and unsuccessful system events will not help you combat the threat of an unauthorized administrative account.

B. **Incorrect:** The object access event category allows you to audit user access to files, folders, or printers. Auditing successful object access events will not help you combat the threat of an unauthorized administrative account.

C. **Correct:** The policy change event category allows you to audit changes made to user security options, user rights, or audit policies. By auditing successful policy change events, you can track changes made to user rights and locate the administrative account being used to make the changes.

D. **Incorrect:** The directory service access event category allows you to audit user access to Active Directory objects, such as users, computers, OUs, or groups. Auditing successful directory service access attempts will not help you combat the threat of an unauthorized administrative account.

70-217.05.01.021

▶ **Correct Answers: B**

  A. **Incorrect:** The successful print event allows you to audit users who successfully print a file on the Lexmark Optra Color 1200n. Auditing successful print events will not help you determine who is changing the printer's settings.

  B. **Correct:** The successful manage printers event allows you to audit users who successfully change printer settings, including: pausing a printer, sharing a printer, or removing a printer. By auditing successful manage printers events, you can determine who is changing the printer's settings.

  C. **Incorrect:** The successful manage documents event allows you to audit users who successfully change print job settings, including: pausing, restarting, moving or deleting documents, sharing a printer, or changing printer properties. Auditing successful manage documents events will not help you determine who is changing the printer's settings.

  D. **Incorrect:** The successful read permissions event allows you to audit users who successfully view printer permissions on the Lexmark Optra Color 1200n. Auditing successful read permissions events will not help you determine who is changing the printer's settings.

  E. **Incorrect:** The successful change permissions event allows you to audit users who successfully change printer permissions on the Lexmark Optra Color 1200n. Auditing successful change permissions events will not help you determine who is changing the printer's settings.

  F. **Incorrect:** The successful take ownership event allows you to audit users who successfully take ownership of the Lexmark Optra Color 1200n. Auditing successful take ownership events will not help you determine who is changing the printer's settings.

O B J E C T I V E   5 . 2

Monitor and analyze security events.

Security events are Windows 2000 and user security activities. After you set event categories for auditing in the **audit policy**, you can monitor and analyze security events using the **security log**. Only system administrators have access to security logs. To view the security log, you open the **Event Viewer** console, which also allows you to locate and filter events in the log and to archive security log files. By specifying the events to locate or filter, you can narrow down the events displayed in the log. By archiving security logs, you can maintain a history of security-related events in event log (*.evt), text (*.txt), or comma-delimited (*.csv) file formats for later viewing in Event Viewer or in word processing or spreadsheet programs. To assist in your analysis of the security events logged in the security log, double-click the event to view the event description in the Properties dialog box for the event.

Objective 5.2 Questions

70-217.05.02.001

You suspect that several users are accessing secure files and folders on a member server that they should not have access to. To confirm your suspicions, you set up auditing to track access to folders and files on the member server. The system has been logging accesses to the secure files and folders for the past 36 hours. You now need to view the log file to determine whether there has been improper access to the folder and files during the log period. You start Event Viewer at the member server. Which log should you view to determine which user accounts are accessing the secure files and folders?

A. Application log

B. Security log

C. System log

D. Directory service log

E. DNS server log

F. File replication service log

70-217.05.02.002

You recently became concerned that someone might be trying to access your Windows 2000 network during off hours using a stolen user name and password. To combat this threat, you defined an audit policy and applied it to your domain controllers. You now need to view the security log to determine whether someone was able to access your system using the stolen user name and password. However, you only want to view the information relevant to this problem. How should you filter the events in the security log?

A. Filter by successful audit and failed audit event types and the name of the stolen user account.

B. Filter by warning event type and the name of the stolen user account.

C. Filter by Network Dynamic Data Exchange (NetDDE) object event source and the name of the stolen user account.

D. Filter by error event type and the name of the stolen user account.

70-217.05.02.003

You are auditing your domain controller to track trends of system usage. You are concerned that the domain controllers might soon become overloaded. You need to archive the security log files and import them into a spreadsheet program so that you can more easily track the system usage trends. Which file format should you use when archiving the log files?

A. *.evt

B. *.txt

C. *.csv

D. *.ocx

Objective 5.2 Answers

70-217.05.02.001

▶ **Correct Answers: B**

A. **Incorrect:** The application log contains errors, warnings, and information generated by programs. The program developer determines the events that appear in the log. You cannot use the application log to view events monitored by your audit policy.

B. **Correct:** The security log contains information about the success or failure of events monitored by your audit policy, such as access to secure files and folders. To view the security log, open the Event Viewer console and view the list of log entries and summary information in the details pane.

C. **Incorrect:** The system log contains errors, warnings, and information generated by Windows 2000. Windows 2000 determines the events that appear in the log. You cannot use the system log to view events monitored by your audit policy.

D. **Incorrect:** The directory service log appears when Active Directory is installed and contains events generated by Active Directory. Active Directory determines the events that appear in the log. You cannot use the directory service log to view events monitored by your audit policy.

E. **Incorrect:** The DNS server log appears when Domain Name System (DNS) service is installed and contains events generated by the DNS service. DNS determines the events that appear in the log. You cannot use the DNS server log to view events monitored by your audit policy.

F. **Incorrect:** The file replication service log appears when the File Replication Service (FRS) is installed and contains events generated by FRS. FRS determines the events that appear in the log. You cannot use the file replication service log to view events monitored by your audit policy.

70-217.05.02.002

▶ **Correct Answers: A**

A. **Correct:** To audit information relevant to this problem, you must first audit successful and unsuccessful logon events in your audit policy. To filter events that appear in the security log to include only those events relevant to this problem, you must open Event Viewer, select the security log, and then select Filter on the View menu. Then check the Successful Audit and Failed Audit check boxes. Finally, type the user logon name for the stolen account in the User box and click OK.

B. **Incorrect:** To audit information relevant to this problem, you must first audit successful and unsuccessful logon events in your audit policy. Because the logon events event category allows you to audit only success and failure of user logon and logoff or user network connection and disconnection, filtering by warning event type will yield no results in the security log. You cannot audit warning events for the stolen user account.

C. **Incorrect:** To audit information relevant to this problem, you must first audit successful and unsuccessful logon events in your audit policy. The logon events event category allows you to audit only success and failure of user logon and logoff or user network connection and disconnection. Because the NetDDE object event source does not log computer logon events, this solution does not allow you to view only the information relevant to this problem in the security log.

D. **Incorrect:** To audit information relevant to this problem, you must first audit successful and unsuccessful logon events in your audit policy. Because the logon events event category allows you to audit only success and failure of user logon and logoff or user network connection and disconnection, filtering by error event type will yield no results in the security log. You cannot audit error events for the stolen user account.

70-217.05.02.003

▶ **Correct Answers: C**

A. **Incorrect:** The *.evt extension indicates that the security log files were saved in event log format. Because these files retain the binary data for each event recorded, you can reopen them only by using Event Viewer. Because you want to import the log files into a spreadsheet program, you should not archive the logs using the *.evt file format.

B. **Incorrect:** The *.txt extension indicates that the security log files were saved in text format. You can reopen these files only by using a word processing program. Because you want to import the log files into a spreadsheet program, you should not archive the logs using the *.txt file format.

C. **Correct:** The *.csv extension indicates that the security log files were saved in comma-delimited format. You can reopen these files only by using a spreadsheet program or flat-file database. Therefore, you should archive the logs using the *.csv file format.

D. **Incorrect:** You cannot archive the security log files using the *.ocx file format.

Questions and Answers

The following questions and answers are for Part 1 of this book.

Chapter 1

Review Questions

1. What is the primary difference between Windows 2000 Professional and Windows 2000 Server?

   Windows 2000 Professional is optimized for use alone as a desktop oper-ating system, as a networked computer in a peer-to-peer workgroup environment, or as a workstation in a Windows 2000 Server domain environment. Windows 2000 Server is optimized for use as a file, print, and application server, as well as a Web-server platform.

2. What is the major difference between a workgroup and a domain?

   The major difference between a workgroup and a domain is where the user account information resides for user logon authentication. For a workgroup, user account information resides in the local security database on each computer in the workgroup. For the domain, the user account information resides in the Active Directory database.

3. Which of the integral subsystems is responsible for running Active Directory?

   The Security subsystem.

4. What is the purpose of Active Directory?

   Active Directory is the directory service included in Windows 2000 Server. It stores information about objects on a network and makes this information available to users and network administrators. Active Directory gives network users access to permitted resources anywhere on the network using a single logon process. It provides network administra-tors with an intuitive hierarchical view of the network and a single point of administration for all network objects.

5. What happens when a user logs on to a domain?

Windows 2000 sends the logon information to a domain controller, which compares it to the user's information in the directory. If the information matches, the domain controller authenticates the user and issues an access token for the user.

6. How would you use the Windows Security dialog box?

The Windows 2000 Security dialog box provides easy access to important security options, including the ability to lock a computer, change a password, stop programs that are not responding, log off a computer, and shut down the computer. You can also determine the domains to which you are logged on and the user account that you used to log on.

Chapter 2

Review Questions

1. What is the Active Directory schema?

The schema contains a formal definition of the contents and structure of Active Directory, including all attributes, classes, and class properties.

2. What is the purpose of an organizational unit (OU)?

An OU is a container used to organize objects within a domain into logical administrative groups that mirror your organization's functional or business structure. An OU can contain objects such as user accounts, contacts, groups, computers, printers, applications, file shares, and other OUs from the same domain.

3. What are sites and domains and how are they different?

A site is a combination of one or more IP subnets that should be connected by a high-speed link. A domain is a logical grouping of servers and other network resources organized under a single name. A site is a component of Active Directory's physical structure, whereas a domain is a component of the logical structure.

4. What is the difference between implicit two-way transitive trusts and explicit one-way nontransitive trusts?

An implicit two-way transitive trust is a trust between domains that are part of the Windows 2000 scalable namespace, for example, between parent and child domains within a tree and between the top-level domains in a forest. These trust relationships make all objects in all the domains of the tree available to all other domains in the tree.

An explicit one-way nontransitive trust is a relationship between domains that are not part of the same tree. One-way trusts support connections to existing pre-Windows 2000 domains to allow the configuration of trust relationships with domains in other trees.

Chapter 3

Practice Questions

Lesson 3: Using Microsoft Management Consoles

Practice: Using Microsoft Management Console

Exercise 1: Using a Preconfigured MMC

▶ **To use a preconfigured MMC**

2. Click Start, point to Programs, point to Administrative Tools, and then click Event Viewer.

   Windows 2000 displays the Event Viewer console, which gives you access to the contents of the event log files on your computer. You use Event Viewer to monitor various hardware and software activities.

   Looking at the console tree, what three logs are listed?

   Application Log, Security Log, System Log.

   Can you add snap-ins to this console? Why or why not?

   No. This is a preconfigured console and therefore it was saved in User mode. You cannot modify consoles that are saved in User mode.

Exercise 2: Creating a Custom Microsoft Management Console

▶ **To create a custom MMC**

5. To view the currently configured options, click Options on the Console menu.

   MMC displays the Options dialog box with the Console tab active. The Console tab allows you to configure the console mode.

   How does a console that is saved in User mode differ from one that is saved in Author mode?

   You can modify consoles that are saved in Author mode. You can't modify consoles that are saved in User mode after they have been saved. Different levels of User mode restrict the degree of user access.

▶ **To remove extensions from a snap-in**

12. Click Computer Management (Local), and then click the Extensions tab.

    MMC displays a list of available extensions for the Computer Management snap-in.

    What determines which extensions MMC displays in this dialog box?

    The available extensions depend on the snap-in you select.

15. Expand Computer Management and then expand System Tools to confirm that System Information and Device Manager have been removed.

Note   Do not use any of the tools at this point.

When should you remove extensions from a console?

To customize the console for limited administrative tasks. This allows you to include only those extensions that are relevant to the computer that you are administering. You should also remove extensions when you create consoles for administrators who perform only limited tasks.

Review Questions

1. What are the functions of the Active Directory Domains and Trusts, the Active Directory Sites and Services, and the Active Directory Users and Computers consoles?

    The Active Directory Domains and Trusts console manages the trust relationships between domains. The Active Directory Sites and Services console creates sites to manage the replication of Active Directory information. The Active Directory Users and Computers console manages users, computers, security groups, and other objects in Active Directory.

2. What is the purpose of creating custom MMCs?

    Create custom MMCs to meet your administrative requirements. Combine snap-ins that you use together to perform common administrative tasks. Creating custom MMCs allows you to perform most administrative tasks with one MMC. You do not have to switch between different programs or MMC files because all of the snap-ins that you need to use are located in the same MMC file.

3. When and why would you use an extension?

    When specific snap-ins need additional functionality. Extensions are snap-ins that provide additional administrative functionality to another snap-in. A standalone snap-in provides one function or a related set of functions.

4. You need to create a custom MMC for an administrator who only needs to use the Computer Management and Active Directory Users and Computers consoles. The administrator

    ■ Must not be able to add any additional consoles or snap-ins

    ■ Needs full access to both consoles

    ■ Must be able to navigate between consoles

    What console mode would you use to configure the custom MMC?

    User Mode, Full Access.

5. What do you need to do to remotely administer a computer running Windows 2000 Server from a computer running Windows 2000 Professional?

Windows 2000 Professional does not include all snap-ins that are included in Windows 2000 Server. To enable remote administration of many Windows 2000 Server components from a computer running Windows 2000 Professional, you need to add the required snap-ins on the computer running Windows 2000 Professional. This is done by executing the *systemroot*\system32\adminpak.msi file on the Windows 2000 Server using My Network Places from the Windows 2000 Professional desktop.

6. You need to schedule a maintenance utility to run once a week on a computer running Windows 2000 Server. What do you use to accomplish this?

    Use Task Scheduler to schedule the necessary maintenance utilities to run at specific times.

Chapter 4

Practice Questions

Lesson 2: Installing Active Directory

Practice: Installing Active Directory

Exercise 1: Promoting a Standalone Server to a Domain Controller

▶ **To install the Active Directory service on a standalone server**

12. Ensure that the Sysvol folder location is *systemroot*\SYSVOL. (If you did not install Windows 2000 in the WINNT directory, the Sysvol location should default to a SYSVOL folder in the folder where you installed Windows 2000.)

    What is the one Sysvol location requirement?

    Sysvol must be located on a Windows 2000 partition that is formatted as NTFS 5.0.

    What is the function of Sysvol?

    Sysvol is a system volume hosted on all Windows 2000 domain controllers. It stores scripts and part of the group policy objects for both the current domain and the enterprise. *systemroot*\SYSVOL\SYSVOL stores domain public files.

Exercise 2: Viewing Your Domain Using My Network Places

▶ **To view a domain using My Network Places**

1. Double-click My Network Places.

    The My Network Places window appears.

What selections do you see?

Add Network Place and Entire Network.

4. Double-click Entire Network, and then double-click Microsoft Windows Network.

What do you see?

Your domain set up in the previous exercise, Microsoft. Answer may vary depending on your domain name.

Exercise 3: Viewing a Domain Using the Active Directory Users and Computers Console

▶ **To view a domain using the Active Directory Users and Computers console**

2. In the console tree, double-click microsoft.com (or the name of your domain).

What selections are listed under microsoft.com?

Builtin, Computers, Domain Controllers, and Users.

Lesson 4: Implementing an Organizational Unit Structure

Practice: Creating an OU

▶ **To create an OU**

3. Expand the microsoft.com domain (or the domain you set up).

The OUs appear as folders with a directory book icon under the domain. Plain folders are specialized containers.

What are the default OUs in your domain?

Domain Controllers. The Builtin, Computers, and Users folders are container objects.

Review Questions

1. What are some reasons for creating more than one domain?

Some reasons for creating more than one domain are decentralized network administration, replication control, different password requirements between organizations, massive numbers of objects, different Internet domain names, international requirements, and internal political requirements.

2. Your company has an external Internet namespace reserved with a DNS registration authority. As you plan the Active Directory implementation for your company, you decide to recommend extending the namespace for the internal network. What benefits does this option provide?

Extending an existing namespace provides consistent tree names for internal and external resources. In addition, this plan allows your company to

use the same logon and user account names for internal and external resources. Finally, you do not have to reserve an additional DNS namespace.

3. In what two ways does your site configuration affect Windows 2000?

Workstation logon and authentication. When a user logs on, Windows 2000 will try to find a domain controller in the same site as the user's computer to service the user's logon request and subsequent requests for network information.

Directory replication. You can configure the schedule and path for replication of a domain's directory differently for intersite replication, as opposed to replication within a site. Generally, you should set replication between sites to be less frequent than replication within a site.

4. What is the shared system volume, what purpose does it serve, where is it located, and what is its name?

The shared system volume is a folder structure that exists on all Windows 2000 domain controllers. It stores scripts and some of the group policy objects for both the current domain and the enterprise. The default location and name for the shared system volume is *systemroot*\Sysvol. The shared system volume must be located on a partition or volume formatted with NTFS 5.0.

5. What is the purpose of the operations master roles?

Because some changes are impractical to perform in multimaster fashion, one or more domain controllers can be assigned to perform operations that are single-master (not permitted to occur at different places in a network at the same time). Operations master roles are assigned to domain controllers to perform single-master operations.

6. What administrative tool is used to create OUs?

Use the Active Directory Users and Computers console to create OUs.

Chapter 5

Practice Questions

Lesson 2: Understanding and Configuring Zones

Practice: Configuring Zones

Exercise 3: Adding a Resource Record

▶ **To add a PTR resource record for a zone**

2. Click 10.10.1.x Subnet. (If you did not use 10.10.1.1 as the static IP address for your server name, click the appropriate subnet.)

What types of resource records exist in the reverse lookup zone?

Start of Authority and Name Server.

Review Questions

1. What is the function of a forward lookup query? A reverse lookup query?

   A forward lookup query resolves a name to an IP address. A reverse lookup query resolves an IP address to a name.

2. What are the advantages of using the Active Directory-integrated zone type?

   Multimaster update and enhanced security are based on the capabilities of Active Directory. Zones are replicated and synchronized to new domain controllers automatically whenever a new zone is added to an Active Directory domain. By integrating storage of your DNS namespace in Active Directory, you simplify planning and administration for both DNS and Active Directory. Directory replication is faster and more efficient than standard DNS replication.

3. What is the purpose of the SOA resource record?

   The SOA resource record identifies which name server is the authoritative source of information for data within this domain. The first record in the zone database file must be the SOA record. The SOA resource record also stores properties such as version information and timings that affect zone renewal or expiration. These properties affect how often transfers of the zone are done between servers authoritative for the zone.

4. What must be done when you delegate zones within a namespace?

   When you delegate zones within a namespace, you must also create SOA resource records to point to the authoritative DNS server for the new zone. This is necessary both to transfer authority and to provide correct referral to other DNS servers and clients of the new servers being made authoritative for the new zone.

5. Why is an IXFR query more efficient than an AXFR query?

   An IXFR query allows the secondary server to pull only those zone changes it needs to synchronize its copy of the zone with its source, either a primary or secondary copy of the zone maintained by another DNS server. An AXFR query provides a full transfer of the entire zone database.

Chapter 6

Practice Questions

Lesson 1: Configuring Site Settings

Practice: Configuring a Site

▶ **To rename a site**

2. Click on the Sites folder.

What objects appear in the details pane?

Default-First-Site-Name (the default site created by the Active Directory Installation Wizard), the Inter-Site Transports container, and the Subnets container.

▶ **To create a site link**

1. Open the Inter-Site Transports folder and click the IP folder.

   What object appears in the details pane?

   DEFAULTIPSITELINK, the default site link created by the Active Directory Installation Wizard.

Review Questions

1. What four tasks must be completed to configure a site?

   Create a site, associate a subnet with the site, connect the site using site links, and select a licensing computer for the site.

2. What two site configuration objects does the Active Directory Installation Wizard create automatically?

   The Active Directory Installation Wizard automatically creates an object named Default-First-Site-Name in the Sites container and an object named DEFAULTIPSITELINK in the IP container.

3. Which replication protocol uses RPCs for replication over site links (inter-site) and within a site (intra-site)?

   IP replication protocol.

4. What three tasks must be completed to configure inter-site replication?

   Create site links, configure site link attributes (such as site link cost, replication frequency, and replication availability), and create site link bridges.

5. What is the difference between replication frequency and replication availability?

   Replication frequency is the duration between replications on a site link. Replication availability is when a site link is available to replicate directory information.

6. What is the function of a bridgehead server?

   A bridgehead server provides some ranking or criteria for choosing which domain controller should be preferred as the recipient for inter-site replication. The bridgehead server then distributes the directory information via inter-site replication.

Chapter 7

Practice Questions

Lesson 2: Planning New User Accounts

Practice: Planning New User Accounts

Complete Table 7.3 to determine a naming convention for the users in the new hire list by considering the information that is provided in the sections "Scenario," "Criteria," and "New Hire List" in this practice.

Answers may vary. The sample answers use a full name with the department name for duplicate names and a user logon name with the first name and last initial and additional characters from the last name for duplicate names. All user logon names and full names must be unique.

Complete Table 7.4 to determine logon hours and computer use for the users in the new hire list by considering the information that is provided in the sections "Scenario," "Criteria," and "New Hire List" in this practice.

Permanent employees can log on 24 hours a day, seven days a week from any computer on the network. Temporary employees share Temp1 and Temp2. Only two temporary workers are able to log on during a shift, so you must share two computers between four employees.

Select the appropriate password setting for each user in Table 7.5 to determine who controls the user's password.

Temporary employees cannot change their passwords. Permanent employees can change their passwords and must change them the next time they log on.

Lesson 3: Creating User Accounts

Practice: Creating Domain User Accounts

▶   **To create a domain user account**

3. Expand microsoft.com (if you did not use Microsoft as your domain name, expand your domain), and then double-click Users.

In the details pane, notice the default user accounts.

Which user accounts does the Active Directory Installation Wizard create by default?

Administrator, Cert Publishers, DHCP Administrators, DHCP Users, DnsAdmins, DnsUpdateProxy, Domain Admins, Domain Computers, Domain Controllers, Domain Guests, Domain Users, Enterprise Admins, Group Policy Creator Owners, Guest, IUSR_SERVER1, IWAM_SERVER1, krbtgt, RAS and IAS Servers, SchemaAdmins, and TsInternet User. (Answers may vary).

4. Right-click Users, point to New, then click User.

   Windows 2000 displays the New Object-User dialog box.

   Where in the Active Directory will the new user account be created?

   Microsoft.com/Users. (Answer may vary if your domain name is not microsoft.com.)

8. In the list to the right of the User Logon Name box, select @microsoft.com. (The domain name will vary if you did not use microsoft.com as your DNS domain name.)

   The user logon name, combined with the domain name in the box that appears to the right of the User Logon Name box is the user's full Internet logon name. This name uniquely identifies the user throughout the directory (for example, user1@microsoft.com).

   Notice that Windows 2000 completes the pre-Windows 2000 logon name box for you. When is the pre-Windows 2000 logon name used?

   The user's pre-Windows 2000 logon name is used to log on to the Windows 2000 domain from a computer running a previous version of Microsoft Windows.

11. Specify whether or not the user can change his or her password.

    What are the results of selecting both the User Must Change Password At Next Logon check box and the User Cannot Change Password check box? Explain.

    Windows 2000 displays an Active Directory message box with the following message:

    ```
    You cannot check both User must change password at next logon and
    User cannot change password for the same user.
    ```

    The next time that the user attempts to log on, the user would be prompted to change his or her password and would not be able to log on until the password has been changed. However, Windows 2000 will not allow the user to change his or her password, so the user would not be able to log on successfully.

    Under what circumstances would you select the Account Is Disabled check box when creating a new user account?

    Some possible answers include: If the account is for a user who has not yet started at the company. If a user is taking a leave of absence.

Practice: Modifying User Account Properties

Exercise 1: Configuring Logon Hours and Account Expiration

▶ **To specify logon hours**

2. In the details pane, right-click User Three, then click Properties.

Windows 2000 displays the User Three Properties dialog box with the General tab active.

In the General tab, what information can you specify for the user account in addition to the first and last name? How would this information be useful?

Display Name, Description, Office, Telephone Number, E-mail, and Web Page. Active Directory can store user information that might otherwise require a separate application or book. Also, user information that is entered here can be used to locate the user when you search Active Directory.

3. Click the Account tab, and then click Logon Hours.

Windows 2000 displays the Logon Hours for User Three dialog box.

Currently, when can User Three log on?

All hours on all days are allowed by default.

▶ **To set account expiration for a user account**

3. Click the Account tab.

When will the account expire?

Never.

Exercise 2: Testing User Accounts

▶ **To test logon capabilities of user accounts**

3. Click OK to close the Change Password message box.

Were you able to successfully log on? Why or why not?

No. By default administrators have the right to log on to a domain controller, but regular users, like User1, do not.

▶ **To test restrictions on logon hours**

1. Attempt to log on as User1 with a password of student.

Were you able to successfully log on? Why or why not?

Yes, because User1 has access to the network 24 hours a day, seven days a week, and now has the user right to log on interactively.

3. When prompted, change the password to student.

Were you able to successfully log on? Why or why not?

No, because User3 is only allowed to log on between 6 PM and 6 AM. (The answer is Yes if the reader is logging on between 6 PM and 6 AM.)

► **To test password restrictions**

1. Attempt to log on as User7 with no password.

   Were you able to successfully log on? Why or why not?

   No, because User7 was assigned a password when the user accounts were created.

3. When prompted, change the password to student.

   Were you able to log on? Why or why not?

   Yes, because User7 is the correct password for the User7 user account.

5. Attempt to log on as User9 with a password of User9.

   Were you able to successfully log on? Why or why not?

   Yes, because User9 is the correct password for the User9 user account.

► **To test password restrictions by attempting to change a password**

3. In the Old Password box, type the password for the User9 user account; in the New Password and Confirm New Password boxes, type **student,** then click OK.

   Were you able to change the password? Why or why not?

   No, because User9 has been restricted from changing passwords.

► **To test account expiration**

2. When prompted, change your password to student.

   Were you successful? Why or why not?

   Yes, because the account for User5 does not expire until the end of the day today.

Lesson 4: Creating User Profiles

Practice: Managing User Profiles

Exercise 1: Configuring a Local User Profile

► **To view existing profiles**

3. Click the User Profiles tab.

   Which users' profiles are stored on your computer?

   MICROSOFT\administrator, MICROSOFT\puser, and users who have logged on to the computer.

▶ **To define and test a local profile**

5. Log off and log on as the same user, puser.

   Were screen colors saved? Why or why not?

   Yes, because the screen colors are saved in the puser's profile.

Exercise 2: Defining a Standard Roaming User Profile

▶ **To test the roaming profile**

1. Log off and log on as User2.

   Are the screen colors and desktop the same or different from those set in the Profile Template? Why or why not?

   The screen colors are the same as the screen colors set in the Profile Template because the roaming profile for the User2 account was downloaded from the shared folder on the network server and applied to whatever computer User2 logs on to.

▶ **To determine the type of profile assigned to a user**

2. Double-click System, then click the User Profiles tab.

   What type of profile is listed for the User2 account?

   A roaming user profile.

Lesson 6: Maintaining User Accounts

Practice: Administering User Accounts

Exercise 1: Enabling a User Account

▶ **To disable a user account**

6. In the details pane of the Active Directory Users and Computers console, right-click the user account that you just disabled to display the shortcut menu.

   How can you tell that the user account is disabled?

   The Enable Account option appears on the shortcut menu, and a red X appears on the user icon in the details pane.

8. Attempt to log on as puser.

   Were you successful? Why or why not?

   No, because the account is disabled.

▶ **To enable a user account**

6. In the details pane of the Active Directory Users and Computers console, right-click the user account that you just enabled to display the shortcut menu.

How can you tell that the user account is enabled?

The Disable Account option appears on the shortcut menu, and the red X is removed from the user icon in the details pane.

▶ **To test account enabling and to change the password for a user account**

1. Log on as puser.

   Were you successful? Why or why not?

   Yes, because the account is enabled.

Exercise 2: Resetting the Password for a User Account

▶ **To test password resetting**

1. Log on as puser and type **password** as the password.

   Were you successful? Why or why not?

   Not immediately. Because User Must Change Password At Next Logon was selected, the Logon Message appears, stating that the password has expired and must be changed. Then the Change Password dialog box appears where a new password known only to the user must be chosen and confirmed. Only then is puser allowed to log on.

Review Questions

1. What different capabilities do local user accounts and domain user accounts provide to users?

   A local user account allows the user to log on at and gain access to resources on only the computer where you create the local user account. A domain user account allows a user to log on to the domain from any computer in the network and to gain access to resources anywhere in the domain, provided the user has permission to access these resources.

2. What should you consider when you plan new user accounts?

   ■ **A naming convention that ensures unique but consistent user account names**

   ■ **Whether you or the user will determine the user account password**

   ■ **The hours when users need to have access to the network or be restricted from using the network**

   ■ **Whether the user account should be disabled**

   ■ **The type of user profile to use**

   ■ **Whether My Documents or home directories will be used**

3. What information is required to create a domain user account?

   A first or last name, logon name, and pre-Windows 2000 logon name.

4. A user wants to gain access to network resources remotely from home. The user does not want to pay the long-distance charges for the telephone call. How would you set up the user account to accomplish this?

In the Dial-In tab of the Properties dialog box for the user account, click the Set By Caller (Routing and Remote Access Service Only) option to have the RAS server call the user back at a telephone number that he or she specifies. You can also click the Always Callback To option to have the RAS server use a specified telephone number to call back the user. However, the user must be at the specified telephone number to make a connection to the server.

5. What is the difference between a local user profile and a roaming user profile?

A local user profile is stored on the computer where the user logs on. A roaming user profile is stored on a domain server and is copied to the client computer where the user logs on.

6. What do you do to ensure that a user on a client computer running Windows 2000 has a roaming user profile?

First, create a shared folder on a network server. Second, for each user account, in the Properties dialog box for each user, provide a path to the shared folder on the server. The next time that the user logs on, the roaming user profile is created.

7. How can you ensure that a user has a centrally located home directory?

First, create and share a parent folder on a server. Second, change the permission for the folder to Full Control for the Users group. Third, provide a path to the shared folder, including the name of the individual user's home directory (\\server_name\shared_folder_name\ user_logon_name).

8. Why would you rename a user account and what is the advantage of doing so?

Rename a user account if you want a new user to have all of the properties of a former user, including permissions, desktop settings, and group membership. The advantage of renaming an account is that you do not have to rebuild all of the properties as you do for a new user account.

Chapter 8

Practice Questions

Lesson 2: Planning a Group strategy

Practice: Planning New Group Accounts

Record your planning strategies on the Group Planning Worksheet. Follow these instructions to complete the worksheet. This sample presents only one set of possible answers. You may have planned your accounts differently.

Group Accounts Planning Worksheet

Group Name	Type and Scope	Members
Testers	Security, global	All product testers
Customer Service Reps	Security, global	All customer service representatives
Maint Workers	Security, global	All maintenance workers
Managers	Security, global	All managers
Sales Reps	Security, global	All sales reps
Network Admin	Security, global	All network administrators
All Employees	Security, global	All employees
Topics Employees	Security, global	Employees interested in manufacturing topics
Customer database	Security, domain local	Customer service reps, managers, sales reps
Company policies	Security, domain local	All employees
Microsoft Office	Security, domain local	Testers, customer service reps, managers, sales reps, network administrators
Sales reports	Security, domain local	Sales reps
E-mail announcements	Distribution, domain local	All employees
E-mail manufacturing topics	Distribution, domain local	Topics employees

1. Does your network require local groups?

   No. The scenario presents no need to create local groups, which you can only use on a single computer.

2. Does your network require universal groups?

   No. The scenario presents no need to create universal groups. Your domain has no groups that need to have access to resources in multiple domains and also need to have members from multiple domains.

3. Sales representatives at the company frequently visit the company headquarters and other divisions. Therefore, you need to give sales representatives with user accounts in other domains the same permissions for resources that sales representatives in your domain have. You also want to make it easy for administrators in other domains to assign permissions to sales representatives in your domain. How can you accomplish this?

   Create global groups for sales representatives in all other domains. Add these global groups to the appropriate domain local groups in your domain. Tell administrators in other domains about the global group that

represents sales representatives in your domain. Have the administrators add the sales representatives group from your domain to the appropriate domain local groups in their domains.

Review Questions

1. Why should you use groups?

   Use groups to simplify administration by granting rights and assigning permissions once to the group rather than multiple times to each individual member.

2. What is the purpose of adding a group to another group?

   Adding groups to other groups (nesting) creates a consolidated group and can reduce the number of times that you need to assign permissions.

3. When should you use security groups instead of distribution groups?

   Use security groups to assign permissions. Use distribution groups when the only function of the group is not security related, such as an e-mail distribution list. You cannot use distribution groups to assign permissions.

4. What strategy should you apply when you use domain local and global groups?

   Place user accounts into global groups, place global groups into domain local groups, and then assign permissions to the domain local group.

5. Why should you not use local groups on a computer after it becomes a member of a domain?

   Local groups do not appear in Active Directory, and you must administer local groups separately for each computer.

6. What is the easiest way to give a user complete control over all computers in a domain?

   Add his or her user account to the Domain Admins predefined global group. Then he or she can perform all administrative tasks on all domain computers and in Active Directory. The user receives administrative control because Windows 2000 makes the Domain Admins predefined global group a member of both the Administrators built-in domain local group and the Administrators built-in local group on each member server and computer running Windows 2000 Professional. The Administrators built-in domain local group has complete control over all domain controllers and Active Directory. Each Administrators built-in local group has complete control over the computer on which it exists.

7. Why shouldn't you run your computer as an administrator? What action should you take instead?

   Running Windows 2000 as an administrator makes the system vulnerable to Trojan horse attacks and other security risks. For most computer activity, you should assign yourself to the Users or Power Users group.

Then, if you need to perform an administrator-only task, you should log on as an administrator, perform the task, and then log off. If you frequently need to log on as an administrator, you can use **Run As** to start a program as an administrator.

8. Suppose the headquarters for this chapter's imaginary manufacturing company has a single domain that is located in Paris. The company has managers who need to access the inventory database to perform their jobs. What would you do to ensure that the managers have the required access to the inventory database?

Place all of the managers into a global group. Create a domain local group for inventory database access. Make the managers global group a member of the inventory database domain local group and assign permissions to gain access to the inventory database to the domain local group.

9. Now suppose the company has a three-domain environment with the root domain in Paris and the other two domains in Australia and North America. Managers from all three domains need access to the inventory database in Paris to perform their jobs. What would you do to ensure that the managers have the required access and that there is a minimum of administration?

In each domain, create a global group and add user accounts for the managers in that domain to the global group. Create a domain local group for the inventory database access in the domain where the database is located (Paris). Add the managers global groups from each of the domains to the inventory database domain local group. Then, assign permissions to gain access to the inventory database to the domain local group.

Chapter 9

Practice Questions

Lesson 2: Assigning NTFS Permissions

Practice: Planning and Assigning NTFS Permissions

Exercise 1: Planning NTFS Permissions

When you apply custom permissions to a folder or file, which default permission entry should you remove?

The Full Control permission for the Everyone group at the volume level.

Complete Table 9.5 to plan and record your permissions.

Table 9.5 **Permissions Planning Table for Exercise 1**

Path	User Account or Group	NTFS Permissions	Block Inheritance (Yes/No)
Apps	Administrators	Full Control	No
Apps\WordProc	Users	Read & Execute	No
Apps\Spreadsh	Accounting	Read & Execute	No
	Managers	Read & Execute	
	Executives	Read & Execute	
Apps\Database	Accounting	Read & Execute	No
	Managers	Read & Execute	
	Executives	Read & Execute	
Public	Administrators	Full Control	No
	Creator Owner	Full Control	
	Users	Write	
Public\Library	Administrators	Full Control	
	Users	Read & Execute	Yes
Public\Manuals	Administrators	Full Control	Yes
	Users	Read & Execute	
	User81	Full Control	

Exercise 2: Assigning NTFS Permissions for the Data Folder

▶ **To remove permissions from the Everyone group**

4. Click the Security tab to display the permissions for the Data folder.

   Windows 2000 displays the Data Properties dialog box with the Security tab active.

   What are the existing folder permissions?

   The Everyone group has Full Control.

5. Under Name, select the Everyone group, then click Remove.

   What do you see?

   Windows 2000 displays a message box, indicating that the folder is inheriting the permissions for Everyone from its parent folder. To change permissions for Everyone, you must first block inheritance.

8. Click Remove.

   What are the existing folder permissions?

   No permissions are currently assigned.

▶ **To assign permissions to the Users group for the Data folder**

4. Click OK to return to the Data Properties dialog box.

   What are the existing allowed folder permissions?

The Users group has the following permissions: Read & Execute, List Folder Contents, and Read. These are the default permissions that Windows 2000 assigns when you add a user account or group to the list of permissions.

▶ **To assign permissions to the CREATOR OWNER group for the Data folder**

4. Click OK to return to the Data Properties dialog box.

What are the existing allowed folder permissions?

The Users group has the following permissions: Read & Execute, List Folder Contents, Read, and Write. The Creator Owner group has no permissions.

5. Make sure that CREATOR OWNER is selected, and next to Full Control, select the Allow check box, then click Apply to save your changes.

What do you see?

For the Creator Owner group, none of the Allow check boxes are checked for any permissions. A note appears next to the Advanced button stating: "Additional permissions are present but not viewable here. Press Advanced to see them."

7. Under Name, select CREATOR OWNER.

What permissions are assigned to the CREATOR OWNER group and where do these permissions apply? Why?

The Creator Owner group has Full Control permission. These permissions apply to subfolders and files only. Permissions that are assigned to the Creator Owner group are not applied to the folder but only to new files and folders that are created within the folder. The user who creates the new file or folder receives the permissions that are assigned to Creator Owner for the parent folder and must belong to other groups that are capable of writing to the new files and folders.

▶ **To test the folder permissions that you assigned for the Data folder**

3. In the Data folder, attempt to create a text file named user81.txt.

Were you successful? Why or why not?

Yes, because the Users group (of which User81 is a member) is assigned the Write permission for the Data folder.

4. Attempt to perform the following tasks for the file that you just created, and then record those tasks that you are able to complete.

   ▪ Open the file

   ▪ Modify the file

   ▪ Delete the file

The tasks that you can complete are opening, modifying, and deleting the file because Creator Owner has been assigned the NTFS Full Control permission for the Data folder.

Exercise 4: Testing NTFS Permissions

▶ **To test permissions for the Reports folder while logged on as User81**

3. Attempt to create a file in the Reports folder.

   Were you successful? Why or why not?

   No, because only User82, Managers, and Administrator have permissions to create and modify files in the Reports folder.

▶ **To test permissions for the Reports folder while logged on as User82**

3. Attempt to create a file in the Reports folder.

   Were you successful? Why or why not?

   Yes, because User82 has the Modify permission for the folder.

▶ **To test permissions for the Sales folder while logged on as Administrator**

3. Attempt to create a file in the Sales folder.

   Were you successful? Why or why not?

   Yes, because the Administrators group has the Full Control permission for the Sales folder.

▶ **To test permissions for the Sales folder while logged on as User81**

3. Attempt to create a file in the Sales folder.

   Were you successful? Why or why not?

   No, because only the Sales group has NTFS permissions to create and modify files in the Sales folder. User 81 is not a member of the Sales group.

▶ **To test permissions for the Sales folder while logged on as User82**

3. Attempt to create a file in the Sales folder.

   Were you successful? Why or why not?

   Yes, because User82 is a member of the Sales group, which has been assigned Modify permission for the Sales folder.

Lesson 3: Assigning Special Permissions

Practice: Taking Ownership of a File

▶ **To determine the permissions for a file**

4. Click the Security tab to display the permissions for the OWNER.TXT file.

   What are the current allowed permissions for OWNER.TXT?

   The Administrators group has the Full Control permission. The Users group has the Read & Execute permission.

6. Click the Owner tab.

   Who is the current owner of the OWNER.TXT file?

   The Administrators group.

▶ **To take ownership of a file**

6. Click Advanced to display the Access Control Settings For OWNER.TXT dialog box, then click the Owner tab.

   Who is the current owner of OWNER.TXT?

   The Administrators group.

7. Under Name, select User83, then click Apply.

   Who is the current owner of OWNER.TXT?

   User83.

▶ **To test permissions for a file as the owner**

3. In the Security dialog box, click Remove to remove permissions from the Users group and the Administrators group for the OWNER.TXT file.

   Were you successful? Why or why not?

   Yes, because User83 is the owner of OWNER.TXT, and the owner of a folder or file can always change the permissions on folders and files that he or she owns.

Lesson 4: Copying and Moving Folders and Files

Practice: Copying and Moving Folders

▶ **To create a folder while logged on as a user**

1. While you are logged on as User83, in Windows Explorer, in C:\ (where C:\ is the name of your system drive), create a folder named Temp1.

   What are the permissions that are assigned to the folder?

   The Everyone group has Full Control.

Who is the owner? Why?

User83 is the owner because the person who creates a folder or file is the owner.

▶ **To create a folder while logged on as Administrator**

2. In C:\ (where C:\ is the name of your system drive), create the following two folders: Temp2 and Temp3.

What are the permissions for the folders that you just created?

The Everyone group has Full Control.

Who is the owner of the Temp2 and Temp3 folders? Why?

The Administrators group is the owner of Temp2 and Temp3 because a member of the Administrators group created these folders.

▶ **To copy a folder to another folder within a Windows 2000 NTFS volume**

2. Select C:\Temp1\Temp2, then compare the permissions and ownership with C:\Temp2.

Who is the owner of C:\Temp1\Temp2 and what are the permissions? Why?

The owner is still the Administrators group because you are logged on as Administrator. When a folder or file is copied within an NTFS volume, the person who copies the folder or file becomes the owner.

The Everyone group has the Full Control permission because when a folder or file is copied within an NTFS volume, the folder or file inherits the permissions of the folder into which it is copied.

▶ **To move a folder within the same NTFS volume**

2. Select C:\Temp3, then move it to C:\Temp1.

What happens to the permissions and ownership for C:\Temp1\Temp3? Why?

C:\Temp1\Temp3 retains the same permissions and owner (the Administrators group) as C:\Temp3. This is because when a folder or file is moved within the same NTFS volume, the folder or file retains its original permissions and owner.

Lesson 5: Troubleshooting Permissions Problems

Practice: Deleting a File with All Permissions Denied

▶ **To view the result of denying the Full Control permission for a folder**

1. In Windows Explorer, double-click NOACCESS.TXT in C:\Fullaccess to open the file.

Were you successful? Why or why not?

No. The Everyone group has been denied the Full Control permission for C:\Fullaccess\noaccess.txt. The Administrator user account is a member of the Everyone group.

4. Delete NOACCESS.TXT by typing **del noaccess.txt**

   Were you successful? Why or why not?

   Yes, because the Full Control permission includes the Delete Subfolders and Files special permission for POSIX compliance. This special permission allows a user to delete files in the root of a folder to which the user has been assigned the Full Control permission. This permission overrides the file permissions.

   How would you prevent users with Full Control permission for a folder from deleting a file in that folder for which they have been denied the Full Control permission?

   Allow users all of the individual permissions, and then deny users the Delete Subfolders and Files special permission.

Review Questions

1. What is the default permission when a volume is formatted with NTFS? Who has access to the volume?

   The default permission is Full Control. The Everyone group has access to the volume.

2. If a user has Write permission for a folder and is also a member of a group with Read permission for the folder, what are the user's effective permissions for the folder?

   The user has both Read permission and Write permission for the folder because NTFS permissions are cumulative.

3. If you assign the Modify permission to a user account for a folder and the Read permission for a file, and then copy the file to that folder, what permission does the user have for the file?

   The user can modify the file because the file inherits the Modify permission from the folder.

4. What happens to permissions that are assigned to a file when the file is moved from one folder to another folder on the same NTFS volume? What happens when the file is moved to a folder on another NTFS volume?

   When the file is moved from one folder to another folder on the same NTFS volume, the file retains its permissions. When the file is moved to a folder on a different NTFS volume, the file inherits the permissions of the destination folder.

5. If an employee leaves the company, what must you do to transfer ownership of his or her files and folders to another employee?

You must be logged on as Administrator to take ownership of the employee's files and folders. Assign the Take Ownership special permission to another employee to allow that employee to take ownership of the folders and files. Notify the employee to whom you assigned Take Ownership to take ownership of the files and folders.

6. What three things should you check when a user cannot gain access to a resource?

   Check the permissions that are assigned to the user account and to groups of which the user is a member.

   Check whether the user account, or a group of which the user is a member, has been denied permission for the file or folder.

   Check whether the folder or file has been copied to any other file or folder or moved to another volume. If it has, the permissions will have changed.

Chapter 10

Practice Questions

Lesson 1: Understanding Shared Folders

Practice: Applied Permissions

1. User1 is a member of Group1, Group2, and Group3. Group1 has Read permission and Group3 has Full Control permission for FolderA. Group2 has no permissions for FolderA. What are User1's effective permissions for FolderA?

   Because User1 has permissions of all groups, User1's effective permission for FolderA is Full Control, which also includes all capabilities of the Read permission.

2. User1 is also a member of the Sales group, which has Read permission for FolderB. User1 has been denied the shared folder permission Full Control for FolderB as an individual user. What are User1's effective permissions for FolderB?

   User 1 has no access to FolderB. Even though User1 is a member of the Sales group, which has Read permission for FolderB, User1 has been denied Full Control access to FolderB. Denied permissions override all other permissions.

Lesson 4: Combining Shared Folder Permissions and NTFS Permissions

Practice: Managing Shared Folders

Exercise 1: Combining Permissions

1. In the first example, the Data folder is shared. The Sales group has the shared folder Read permission for the Data folder and the NTFS Full Control permission for the Sales subfolder.

What are the Sales group's effective permissions for the Sales subfolder when Sales group members gain access to the Sales subfolder by making a connection to the Data shared folder?

The Sales group has Read permission for the Sales subfolder because when shared folder permissions are combined with NTFS permissions, the more restrictive permission applies.

2. In the second example, the Users folder contains user home folders. Each user home folder contains data that is only accessible to the user for whom the folder is named. The Users folder has been shared, and the Users group has the shared folder Full Control permission for the Users folder. User1 and User2 have the NTFS Full Control permission for only their home folder and no NTFS permissions for other folders. These users are all members of the Users group.

What permissions does User1 have when he or she accesses the User1 subfolder by making a connection to the Users shared folder? What are User1's permissions for the User2 subfolder?

User1 has the Full Control permission for the User1 subfolder because both the shared folder permission and the NTFS permission allow full control. User1 cannot access the User2 subfolder because he or she has no NTFS permissions to gain access to it. The storage of private files on the file server is a common scenario.

Exercise 2: Planning Shared Folders

Shared Folders and Permissions for Exercise 2

Record your answers in Table 10.6.

You have two choices for permissions. You can rely entirely on NTFS permissions and assign Full Control for all shared folders to the Everyone group, or you can use shared folder permissions according to resource needs. The following suggested shared folders include required permissions if you decide to assign shared folder permissions.

Share the Management Guidelines folder as MgmtGd. Assign the Full Control permission to the Managers group.

Share the Data folder as Data. Assign the Full Control permission to the Administrators built-in group.

Share the Data\Customer Service folder as CustServ. Assign the Change permission to the Customer Service group.

Share the Data\Public folder as Public. Assign the Change permission to the Users built-in group and the Full Control permission to the Administrators built-in group.

Share the Applications folder as Apps. Assign the Read permission to the Users built-in group and the Full Control permission to the Administrators built-in group.

Share the Project Management folder as ProjMan. Assign the Change permission to the Managers group and the Full Control permission to the Administrators built-in group.

Share the Database\Customers folder as CustDB. Assign the Change permission to the CustomerDBFull group, the Read permission to the CustomerDBRead group, and the Full Control permission to the Administrators built-in group.

Share the Users folder as Users. Create a folder for every employee below this folder. Assign the Full Control permission to each employee for his or her own folder. Preferably, have Windows 2000 create the folder and assign permissions automatically when you create each user account.

Exercise 3: Sharing Folders

▶ **To share a folder**

4. In the Comment box, type **shared productivity applications,** then click OK.

How does Windows Explorer change the appearance of the Apps folder to indicate that it is a shared folder?

Windows Explorer shows a hand icon holding the Apps folder. The hand indicates that the folder is shared.

Exercise 4: Assigning Shared Folder Permissions

▶ **To determine the current permissions for the Apps shared folder**

1. In the Apps Properties dialog box, click the Sharing tab, then click Permissions.

Windows 2000 displays the Permissions For Apps dialog box.

What are the default permissions for the Apps shared folder?

The Everyone group has Full Control.

▶ **To assign Full Control to the Administrators group**

3. Click OK.

Windows 2000 adds Administrators to the list of names with permissions.

What type of access does Windows 2000 assign to Administrators by default?

The Read permission.

2. In the Permissions box, under Allow, click Full Control.

Why did Windows Explorer also select the Change permission for you?

Full Control includes all permissions.

Optional Exercise 5: Connecting to a Shared Folder

▶ **To connect to a network drive using the Run command**

3. In the Open box, type **\\server1** (if you did not use SERVER1 as the name of your domain controller, use the appropriate name here and in the following steps), then click OK.

   Windows 2000 displays the Server1 window.

   Notice that only the folders that are shared appear.

   Which shared folders are currently available?

   In addition to the folders that you shared on your domain controller, the following folders are also shared: Printers, Scheduled Tasks, NETLOG-ON, and SYSVOL. Any printers that you have shared also appear.

▶ **To connect a network drive to a shared folder using the Map Network Drive command**

7. To confirm that Windows Explorer has successfully completed the drive mapping, on your desktop, double-click My Computer.

   Notice that Windows 2000 has added drive P as Apps On Server1 (P:).

   How does Windows Explorer indicate that this drive points to a remote shared folder?

   Windows Explorer uses an icon that shows a network cable attached to the drive. The network cable icon indicates a mapped network drive.

▶ **To attempt to connect to a shared folder on your domain controller**

3. In the Open box, type **\\server1\apps** (if you did not use SERVER1 as the name of your domain controller, use the appropriate name), then click OK.

   Windows 2000 displays a message stating that access is denied.

   Why were you denied access to the Apps shared folder?

   Because User81, the user account that you used to log on, does not have the required permissions to gain access to the shared folder. Only the Administrators group can gain access to the Apps shared folder.

▶ **To connect to a shared folder using another user account**

4. Click the link labeled Connect Using A Different User Name.

   The Connect As dialog box appears. This dialog box lets you specify a different user account to use to make a connection to the shared folder. It may also be a way to connect to other domains on the network (pre-Windows 2000). When would you use this option?

   Choose to connect as a different user when the user account that you are currently using does not have the necessary permissions for a shared

folder and you have another user account that does. In this situation, you do not have to log off and log on again to gain access to the shared folder.

7. Confirm that the Reconnect At Logon check box is cleared, then click Finish.

   In Windows Explorer, can you gain access to drive J? Why or why not?

   Yes. The administrator account has appropriate permissions to gain access to the shared folder.

Optional Exercise 8: Testing NTFS and Shared Folder Permissions

▶ **To test permissions for the Manuals folder when a user logs on locally as User82**

3. In the Manuals folder, attempt to create a file.

   Were you successful? Why or why not?

   No. Only the Administrators group and User83 have the NTFS permission to create and modify files in the Manuals folder.

▶ **To test permissions for the Manuals folder when a user makes a connection over the network**

5. In the Manuals folder on your domain controller, attempt to create a file.

   Were you successful? Why or why not?

   No. Although the Users group has the Full Control shared folder permission for \\server1\public, only the Administrators group and User83 have the NTFS permission to create and modify files in the Manuals folder.

▶ **To test permissions for the Manuals folder when a user logs on locally as User83**

3. In the Manuals folder, attempt to create a file.

   Were you successful? Why or why not?

   Yes. User83 has the Full Control NTFS permission for the folder.

▶ **To test permissions for the Manuals folder when a user logs on as User83 and connects over the network**

4. In the Manuals folder on your domain controller, attempt to create a file.

   Were you successful? Why or why not?

   Yes. The Users group has Full Control for the Public shared folder. User83 also has the Full Control NTFS permission for the Manuals folder.

Lesson 5: Configuring Dfs to Gain Access to Network Resources

Practice: Using Dfs

▶ **To gain access to a Dfs root**

2. Double-click SERVER1.

Windows Explorer displays a list of all shared folders on your domain controller. Notice that one of the shared folders is Shared Apps, your Dfs root.

Does Windows 2000 provide an indication that Shared Apps is a Dfs root and not an ordinary shared folder?

Windows 2000 does not indicate that the share is a Dfs root.

3. To view the Dfs links, double-click Shared Apps.

Windows Explorer displays the Shared Apps On Server1 window, which shows all the links of Shared Apps.

Does Windows 2000 indicate that the folders inside Shared Apps are Dfs links and not ordinary folders?

Windows 2000 does not indicate that the folders are Dfs links.

Review Questions

1. When a folder is shared on a FAT volume, what does a user with the Full Control shared folder permissions for the folder have access to?

   All folders and files in the shared folder.

2. What are the shared folder permissions?

   Full Control, Change, and Read.

3. By default, what are the permissions that are assigned to a shared folder?

   The Everyone group is assigned the Full Control permission.

4. When a folder is shared on an NTFS volume, what does a user with the Full Control shared folder permission for the folder have access to?

   Only the folder, not necessarily any of the folder's contents. The user would also need NTFS permissions for each file and subfolder in the shared folder to gain access to those files and subfolders.

5. When you share a public folder, why should you use centralized data folders?

   Centralized data folders enable data to be backed up easily.

6. What is the best way to secure files and folders that you share on NTFS partitions?

   Put the files that you want to share in a shared folder and keep the default shared folder permission (the Everyone group with the Full Control

permission for the shared folder). Assign NTFS permissions to users and groups to control access to all contents in the shared folder or to individual files.

7. How does Dfs facilitate network navigation for users?

A user who navigates a Dfs-managed shared folder does not need to know the name of the server where the folder is actually shared. After connecting to the Dfs root, users can browse for and gain access to all of the resources that are contained within each link, regardless of the location of the server on which the resource is located.

Chapter 11

Practice Questions

Lesson 1: Locating Active Directory Objects

Practice: Searching Active Directory

▶ **To find user accounts in the domain**

1. In the console tree, right-click your domain, then click Find.

Windows 2000 displays the Find dialog box.

In the Find dialog box, what object type can you select for a search?

Users, Contacts, and Groups; Computers; Printers; Shared Folders; Organizational Units; Custom Search, and Remote Installation Clients (if Remote Installation Services (RIS) is installed).

2. Ensure that Users, Contacts, And Groups is selected in the Find box, then click Find Now. What do you see?

The list of users and groups in the domain.

Lesson 2: Controlling Access to Active Directory Objects

Practice: Controlling Access to Active Directory Objects

▶ **To view default Active Directory permissions for an OU**

4. In Table 11.5, list the groups that have permissions for the Security1 OU. You will need to refer to these permissions in Lesson 5.

Table 11.5   Groups that Have Permissions for the Security1 OU

User Account or Group	Assigned Permissions
Account Operators	Advanced permissions
Administrators	Inherits the Read, Write, and Create All Child Objects permissions and also has advanced permissions

User Account or Group	Assigned Permissions
Authenticated Users	Read
Domain Admins	Full Control
Enterprise Admins	Inherits Full Control
Pre-Windows 2000 Compatible Access	Advanced permissions
Print Operators	Advanced permissions
SYSTEM	Full Control

How can you tell if any of the default permissions are inherited from the domain, which is the parent object?

The permissions that are assigned to Administrators are inherited from the parent object. The check boxes for inherited permissions are shown as shaded.

▶ **To view special permissions for an OU**

2. To view special permissions for Account Operators, in the Permission Entries box, click each entry for Account Operators, then click View/Edit.

The Permission Entry For Security1 dialog box appears.

What object permissions are assigned to Account Operators? What can Account Operators do in this OU? (Hint: Check each permission entry for Account Operators in the Permission Entries box in the Access Control Settings For Security1 dialog box.)

The permissions that are assigned to Account Operators are Create User Objects, Delete User Objects, Create Group Objects, Delete Group Objects, Create Computer Objects, and Delete Computer Objects. Account operators can only create and delete user accounts, groups, and computers.

Do any objects within this OU inherit the permissions assigned to the Account Operators group? Why or why not?

No. Objects within this OU do not inherit these permissions. The Apply To column in the Permission Entries list in the Access Control Settings For Security1 dialog box shows that permissions granted to Account Operators are applied to This Object Only.

▶ **To view the default Active Directory permissions for a user object**

4. In Table 11.6, list the groups that have permissions for the Secretary1 user account. You will need to refer to these permissions in Lesson 5. If the dialog box indicates that special permissions are present for a group, do not list the special permissions to which you can gain access through the Advanced button.

Table 11.6   Permissions for the Secretary1 User Account

Group	Assigned Permissions
Account Operators	Full Control
Administrators	Inherits all permissions, except the Full Control and Delete All Child Objects permissions, and also has advanced permissions
Authenticated Users	Read permission for General, Personal, Public, and Web Information
Cert Publishers	Advanced
Domain Admins	Full Control
Enterprise Admins	Inherits Full Control
Everyone	Change Password
Pre-Windows 2000 Compatible Access	Inherits Read, Read Phone and Mail Options, Read General Information, Read Group Membership, Read Personal, Public, Remote Access, Logon, and Web Information, and Read Account Restrictions
RAS and IAS Servers	Read permission for Group Membership, Remote Access Information, Account Restrictions, and Logon Information
SELF	Read, Change Password, Receive As, Send As; Read permission for Phone and Mail Options, General Information, Group Membership, Personal Information, Public Information, Remote Access Information, Account Restrictions, Logon Information, and Web Information; Write permission for Phone and Mail Options, Personal Information, and Web Information
SYSTEM	Full Control

Are the standard permissions for a user object the same as those for an OU object? Why or why not?

No. Standard permissions for each type of object are different. The reason for the differences is that different object types are used for different tasks, and therefore the security needs for each object type differ.

Are any of the standard permissions inherited from Security1, the parent object? How can you tell?

Only the standard permissions that are assigned to Administrators, and Enterprise Admins are inherited from the parent object. The check boxes for inherited permissions are shown as shaded.

What do the permissions of the Account Operators group allow its members to do with the user object?

Account Operators have Full Control. A member of the group can make any changes to a user object, including deleting it.

Lesson 4: Moving Active Directory Objects

Practice: Moving Objects Within a Domain

▶ **To log on as a user in a nonstandard OU**

1. Log on to your domain by using the User21 account.

    Did Windows 2000 require you to specify the OU in which your user account is located as part of the logon process? Why or why not?

    No. Windows 2000 automatically locates the user object in Active Directory, independent of its exact location.

Lesson 5: Delegating Administrative Control of Active Directory Objects

Practice: Delegating Administrative Control in Active Directory

▶ **To test current permissions**

3. In the console tree, expand your domain, then click Security1.

    What user objects are visible in the Security1 OU?

    The Secretary1 and Assistant1 user accounts, also User20, User 21, and User22.

    Which permissions allow you to see these objects? (Hint: Refer to your answers in Lesson 2.)

    The Assistant1 user account automatically belongs to the Authenticated Users built-in group, which has Read permission for the OU.

    For the user account with the logon name Secretary1, change the logon hours. Were you successful? Why or why not?

    No. The Assistant1 user account does not have Write permission for the Secretary1 object.

    For the Assistant1 user account, under which you are currently logged on, change the logon hours. Were you successful? Why or why not?

    No. The Assistant1 user account does not have Write permission for the Assistant 1 object.

▶ **To test delegated permissions**

4. Attempt to change the logon hours for the Assistant1 and Secretary1 user accounts in the Security1 OU.

    Were you successful? Why or why not?

    Yes. The Assistant1 user account has been assigned Full Control permission for all user objects in the OU. This includes the permission to change the logon hours.

5. Attempt to change the logon hours for a user account in the Users container.

Were you successful? Why or why not?

No. The Assistant1 user account has not been assigned any permissions for the Users container.

Review Questions

1. How does the global catalog help users locate Active Directory objects?

   The global catalog contains a partial replica of the entire directory, so it stores information about every object in a domain tree or forest. Because the global catalog contains information about every object, a user can find information regardless of which domain in the tree or forest contains the data. Active Directory automatically generates the contents of the global catalog from the domains that make up the directory.

2. You want to allow the manager of the Sales department to create, modify, and delete only user accounts for sales personnel. How can you accomplish this?

   Place all of the sales personnel user accounts in an OU, and then delegate control of the OU to the manager of the Sales department.

3. What happens to the permissions of an object when you move it from one OU to another OU?

   Permissions assigned directly to the object remain the same. The object also inherits permissions from the new OU. Any permissions previously inherited from the old OU no longer affect the object.

4. The Delegation Of Control Wizard allows you to set administrative control at what level?

   OU or container.

5. When backing up Active Directory, what type of data must you specify to be backed up? What is included in this data type?

   You must indicate that you need to back up System State data. For Windows 2000 Server operating systems, the System State data comprises the registry, COM+ Class Registration database, system boot files, and the Certificate Services database (if the server is a certificate server). If the server is a domain controller, Active Directory and the SYSVOL directory are also contained in the System State data.

6. When you restart the computer in Directory Services Restore Mode, what logon must you use? Why?

   When you restart the computer in Directory Services Restore Mode, you must log on as an Administrator by using a valid Security Accounts Manager (SAM) account name and password, *not* the Active Directory Administrator's name and password. This is because Active Directory is offline, and account verification cannot occur. Rather, the SAM accounts database is used to control access to Active Directory while it is offline. You specified this password when you set up Active Directory.

Chapter 12

Practice Questions

Lesson 3: Implementing Group Policy

Practice: Implementing a Group Policy

Exercise 3: Delegating Administrative Control of a GPO

▶ **To delegate administrative control for your GPO**

2. Right-click the root node of the console, DispatchPolicy [server1.microsoft.com] Policy, click Properties, then click the Security tab.

   The DispatchPolicy [server1.microsoft.com] Policy Properties dialog box appears.

   What security groups already have administrative control of the DispatchPolicy GPO?

   Domain Admins, Enterprise Admins, and SYSTEM.

Exercise 4: Specifying Group Policy Settings

▶ **To specify group policy settings for your GPO**

3. In the console tree, click Start Menu & Task Bar.

   What appears in the details pane?

   The policies available for the Start Menu & Task Bar category appear in the details pane.

2. Click Enabled, then click OK.

   How can you tell at a glance that this setting is enabled?

   The setting is listed as enabled in the details pane.

Exercise 9: Testing a GPO

▶ **To test the DispatchPolicy GPO**

2. Press Ctrl+Alt+Delete.

   The Windows Security dialog box appears.

   Are you able to lock the workstation? Why?

   No, the Lock Computer option is not available. Assistant1 is unable to lock the workstation because the DispatchPolicy GPO was linked to the Security1 OU in Exercise 8.

3. Click Cancel, then click Start.

   Does the Search command appear on the Start menu?

   No.

Does the Run command appear on the Start menu?

No.

7. Press Ctrl+Alt+Delete.

Are you able to lock the workstation? Why?

Yes, the Lock Computer option is available. Assistant1 is able to lock the computer because the Sales group was filtered from the DispatchPolicy GPO scope in Exercise 7.

Review Questions

1. What is a GPO?

   A GPO is a group policy object. Group policy configuration settings are contained within a GPO. Each Windows 2000 computer has one local GPO, and may in addition be subject to any number of nonlocal (Active Directory-based) GPOs.

   One local GPO is stored on each computer whether or not the computer is part of an Active Directory environment or a networked environment. Local GPO settings can be overridden by nonlocal GPOs.

   Nonlocal GPOs are linked to Active Directory objects (sites, domains, or OUs) and can be applied to either users or computers. To use nonlocal GPOs, you must have a Windows 2000 domain controller installed. Following the properties of Active Directory, nonlocal GPOs are applied hierarchically from the least restrictive group (site) to the most restrictive group (OU) and are cumulative.

2. What are the two types of group policy settings and how are they used?

   The two types of group policy settings are computer configuration settings and user configuration settings. Computer configuration settings are used to set group policies applied to computers, regardless of who logs onto them. Computer configuration settings are applied when the operating system initializes. User configuration settings are used to set group policies applied to users, regardless of which computer the user logs on to. User configuration settings are applied when users log on to the computer.

3. In what order is group policy implemented through the Active Directory structure?

   Group policy is implemented in the following order: site, domain, and then OU.

4. Name the tasks for implementing group policy.

   The tasks for implementing group policy are: creating a GPO, creating a snap-in for the GPO, delegating administrative control of the GPO, specifying group policy settings for the GPO, disabling unused group policy settings, indicating any GPO processing exceptions, filtering the scope of the GPO, and linking the GPO to a site, domain, or OU.

5. What is the difference between Block Policy Inheritance and No Override?

   Block Policy Inheritance is applied directly to the site, domain, or OU. It is not applied to GPOs, nor is it applied to GPO links. Thus Block Policy Inheritance deflects *all* group policy settings that reach the site, domain, or OU from above (by way of linkage to parents in the Active Directory hierarchy) no matter what GPOs those settings originate from. GPO links set to No Override are always applied and cannot be blocked using the Block Policy Inheritance option.

   Any GPO linked to a site, domain, or OU (not the local GPO) can be set to No Override with respect to that site, domain, or OU, so that none of its policy settings can be overwritten. When more than one GPO has been set to No Override, the one highest in the Active Directory hierarchy (or higher in the hierarchy specified by the administrator at each fixed level in Active Directory) takes precedence. No Override is applied to the GPO link.

6. What is the difference between assigning software and publishing software?

   Assign a software application when you want everyone to have the application on his or her computer. An application can be assigned to both computers and users.

   Publish a software application when you want the application to be available to people managed by the GPO, should the person want the application. With published applications it is up to each person to decide whether or not to install the published application. An application can only be published to users.

7. What folders can be redirected?

   Application Data, Desktop, My Documents, My Pictures, and Start Menu.

Chapter 13

Practice Questions

Lesson 2: Auditing

Practice: Auditing Resources and Events

Exercise 1: Planning a Domain Audit Policy

Record your decisions to audit successful events, failed events, or both for the actions listed in Table 13.7.

Answers may vary. Possible answers include the following:
Account logon events: Failed (for network access attempts)
Account management: Successful (for administrator actions)
Directory service access: Failed (for unauthorized access)

Logon events: Failed (for network access attempts)
Object access: Successful (for printer use) and Failed (for unauthorized access)
Policy change: Successful (for administrator actions)
Privilege use: Successful (for administrator actions and backup procedures)
Process tracking: Nothing (useful primarily for developers)
System events: Successful and Failed (for attempts to breach the server)

Exercise 5: Setting Up Auditing of an Active Directory Object

▶ **To review auditing of an Active Directory object**

6. In the Access Control Settings For Users dialog box, click the Auditing tab, then double-click Everyone.

   The Auditing Entry For Users dialog box appears.

   Review the default audit settings for object access by members of the Everyone group. How do the audited types of access differ from the types of access that are not audited?

   All types of access that result in a change of the object are audited; types of access that do not result in a change of the object are not audited.

7. Click OK three times to close the Auditing Entry For Users, the Access Control Settings For Users, and the Users Properties dialog boxes.

   At which computer or computers does Windows 2000 record log entries for Active Directory access? Will you be able to review them?

   Windows 2000 records auditing events for Active Directory access at domain controllers, at the OU level. Because you configured auditing for a domain controller, you will be able to view auditing events for Active Directory access. If you had configured auditing for the Local Computer, or the Default Domain Policy, you would not be able to view auditing events for Active Directory access.

Lesson 6: Security Configuration and Analysis

Practice: Using Security Configuration and Analysis

Exercise 4: Viewing Security Analysis Results

▶ **To view security analysis results**

1. Double-click the Account Policies node, then click the Password Policy security area.

   In the details pane, what is indicated in the Policy column? In the Database Setting column? In the Computer Setting column?

   The Policy column indicates the policy name for the analysis results. The Database Setting column indicates the security value in your template. The Computer Setting column indicates the current security level in the system.

In the Policy column, what does the red X indicate? What does the green check mark indicate?

A red X indicates a difference from the database configuration. A green check mark indicates consistency with the database configuration.

Review Questions

1. On which computer do you set an audit policy to audit a folder that is located on a member server that belongs to a domain?

   You set the audit policy on the member server; the audit policy must be set on the computer where the folder is located.

2. What is the difference between what the audit policy settings track for directory service access and object access?

   Directory service access tracks if a user gained access to an Active Directory object. Object access tracks if a user gained access to a file, folder, or printer.

3. When you view a security log, how do you determine if an event failed or was successful?

   Successful events appear with a key icon. Unsuccessful events appear with a lock icon.

4. How are user rights different from permissions?

   User rights are different from permissions because user rights apply to user accounts and permissions are attached to objects.

5. What is a security template and why is it useful?

   A security template is a physical representation of a security configuration, a single file where a group of security settings is stored. Locating all security settings in one place streamlines security administration.

6. Where does the Security Configuration and Analysis console store information for performing configuration and analysis functions?

   The Security Configuration and Analysis console uses a database to perform configuration and analysis functions.

Chapter 14

Review Questions

1. If you experience problems with Active Directory, what item should you investigate first?

   You should examine the directory service event logs in Event Viewer.

2. What is the difference between a performance object and a performance counter?

A performance object is a logical connection of performance counters associated with a resource or service that can be monitored. A performance counter is a condition that applies to a performance object.

3. What is the difference between a counter log and a trace log?

   Counter logs collect performance counter data for a specified interval. Trace logs record data collected by the operating system provider or one or more nonsystem providers when certain activities such as a disk I/O operation or a page fault occur. When counter logs are in use, the Performance Logs and Alerts service obtains data from the system when the update interval has elapsed, rather than waiting for a specific event, as for trace logs.

4. What actions can be triggered by an alert?

   Alerts can log an entry in the application event log, send a network message to a computer, start a performance data log, or run a program when the alert counter's value exceeds or falls below a specified setting.

5. What does the Active Directory Replication Monitor support tool allow an administrator to do and how is this tool accessed?

   The Active Directory Replication Monitor tool enables administrators to view the low-level status of Active Directory replication, force synchronization between domain controllers, view the topology in a graphical format, and monitor the status and performance of domain controller replication through a graphical interface. The Active Directory Replication Monitor is a graphical tool accessed on the Tools menu within Windows 2000 Support Tools.

6. If you want to find out which files are open in a shared folder and the users who have a current connection to those files, what action should you take?

   Click Start, point to Programs, point to Administrative Tools, then click Computer Management. In the console tree of Computer Management, expand System Tools, then expand Shared Folders. In the console tree, click Open Files under Shared Folders.

Chapter 15

Review Questions

1. What is RIS? What types of remote booting are supported by RIS?

   Remote Installation Services (RIS) are software services that allow an administrator to set up new client computers remotely without having to visit each client. The target clients must support remote booting. There are two types of remote boot-enabled client computers: Computers with Pre-Boot eXecution Environment (PXE) DHCP-based remote boot ROMS and computers with network cards supported by the RIS Boot Disk.

2. What does PXE remote boot technology provide?

   Pre-Boot eXecution Environment (PXE) is a new form of remote boot technology that has been created within the computing industry. PXE provides companies with the ability to use their existing TCP/IP network infrastructure with DHCP to discover RIS servers on the network. Net PC/PC98-compliant systems can take advantage of the remote boot technology included in the Windows 2000 OS. Net PC/PC98 refers to the annual guide for hardware developers co-authored by Microsoft with Intel, including contributions from Compaq and other industry hardware manufacturers. PC98 is intended to provide standards for hardware development that advance the PC platform and enable Microsoft to include advanced features, like RIS, in the Windows platform.

3. What is the RIS boot disk?

   For computers that do not contain a PXE-based remote boot ROM, Windows 2000 provides the administrator with a tool to create a remote boot disk for use with RIS. The RIS remote boot disk can be used with a variety of PCI-based network adapter cards. Using the RIS boot disk eliminates the need to retrofit existing client computers with new network cards that contain a PXE-based remote boot ROM to take advantage of the Remote OS Installation feature. The RIS boot disk simulates the PXE remote boot sequence and supports frequently used network cards.

4. What is an RIPrep image?

   The Remote Installation Preparation (RIPrep) imaging option allows a network administrator to clone a standard corporate desktop configuration, complete with OS configurations, desktop customizations, and locally installed applications. After first installing and configuring the Windows 2000 Professional OS, its services, and any standard applications on a computer, the network administrator runs a wizard that prepares the installation image and replicates it to an available RIS server on the network for installation on other clients.

5. What is the CIW?

   Users of a remote boot-enabled client use the Client Installation Wizard (CIW) to select installation options, OSs, and maintenance and troubleshooting tools. The wizard prompts the user for his or her user name, password, and domain name. After the user's credentials have been validated, the wizard displays the installation options that are available for the user. After the user selects an option, the selected OS installation image is copied to the client computer's local hard disk.

Installing and Configuring the DHCP Service

Using Remote Installation Services (RIS) requires the installation and configuration of the Dynamic Host Configuration Protocol (DHCP) service on either individual servers or on the same server. To install and configure DHCP, complete the following procedures.

Note   This appendix contains only basic instructions for installing and configuring the DHCP service. Installing and configuring DHCP is beyond the scope of this course. For detailed instruction and practice, refer to the *MCSE Training Kit— Microsoft Windows 2000 Network Infrastructure Administration*.

Installing the DHCP Service

The first step in implementing DHCP is to install the DHCP service. Before you install the DHCP service, you should specify a static Internet Protocol (IP) address, subnet mask, and default gateway address for the network adapter bound to Transmission Control Protocol/Internet Protocol (TCP/IP) in the computer designated as the DHCP server.

▶ **To install the DHCP service**

1. Click Start, point to Settings, open Control Panel, open Add/Remove Programs, then click Add/Remove Windows Components. Click the Components button.
2. In the Windows Components Wizard dialog box, select Networking Services, then click Details.
3. In the Networking Services dialog box, in the Subcomponents Of Networking Services list, click to place a check mark in the box to the left of Dynamic Host Configuration Protocol (DHCP), then click OK.
4. Click Next to install the required components.
5. Insert the Windows 2000 Server CD-ROM when prompted.
6. On the Completing The Windows Components Wizard page, click Finish.
7. Close the Add/Remove Programs dialog box.
8. Close Control Panel and remove the Windows 2000 Server CD-ROM from the drive.

Note   The DHCP service starts automatically during installation and must be running to communicate with DHCP clients.

Configuring the DHCP Service

The basic tasks for configuring the DHCP service are creating a DHCP scope, configuring a DHCP scope, and configuring a client reservation.

Creating a DHCP Scope

Before a DHCP server can lease an address to DHCP clients, you must create a scope. A *scope* is a pool of valid IP addresses available for lease to DHCP clients. After you have installed the DHCP service and it is running, the next step is to create a scope.

When creating a DHCP scope, consider the following points:

- You must create at least one scope for every DHCP server.
- You must exclude static IP addresses from the scope.
- You can create multiple scopes on a DHCP server to centralize administration and to assign IP addresses specific to a subnet. You can assign only one scope to a specific subnet.
- DHCP servers do not share scope information. As a result, when you create scopes on multiple DHCP servers, ensure that the same IP addresses do not exist in more than one scope to prevent duplicate IP addressing.

▶   **To create a DHCP scope**

1. Click Start, point to Programs, point to Administrative Tools, then click DHCP.
2. In the DHCP console, right-click the entry for the DHCP server, then click New Scope to start the New Scope Wizard.
3. On the Welcome To The New Scope Wizard page, click Next.
4. On the Scope Name page, specify a name for the scope in the Name box. You can also specify a description for the scope in the Description box. Click Next.
5. On the IP Address Range page, specify the range of IP addresses included in the scope. You can also specify the subnet mask by length or as an IP address. Click Next.
6. On the Add Exclusions page, specify any addresses to be excluded from the scope, then click Next.

Note   An exclusion is an address or range of addresses that the server should not distribute. You can exclude multiple ranges of addresses.

7. On the Lease Duration page, specify how long a client can use an IP address from this scope as issued by the DHCP server, then click Next.

8. On the Configure DHCP Options page, specify if you want to configure common DHCP options now or later, then click Next.

9. If you specified that you want to configure common DHCP options later, skip to Step 12.

10. If you specified that you want to configure common DHCP options now:

    ■ On the Router (Default Gateway) page, specify the routers, or default gateways, to be distributed by this scope, then click Next.

    ■ On the Domain Name And DNS Servers page, specify the parent domain name you want client computers to use for Domain Name System (DNS) name resolution. If you want to configure scope clients to use DNS servers on your network, enter the server name and IP addresses for those servers. Click Next.

    ■ On the WINS Servers page, specify the server name and IP address to enable clients to query Windows Internet Name Service (WINS) before they use broadcasts to register and resolve NetBIOS names, then click Next.

11. On the Activate Scope page, specify if you want to activate the scope now or later, then click Next.

Note   Once you have created the scope, you must activate it to make it available for lease assignments.

---

12. On the Completing The New Scope Wizard page, click Finish.

Important   You must delete and recreate a scope to specify a new subnet mask or range of IP addresses.

Configuring a DHCP Scope

Once you have created the DHCP scope, you can configure options for DHCP clients. There are two main levels of scope options—global and scope.

Global Options

Global options are available to all DHCP clients. Use global options when all clients on all subnets require the same configuration information. For example, you might want all clients configured to use the same WINS server. Global options are always used, unless scope or client options are configured.

▶ **To configure DHCP global options**

1. In the DHCP console, right-click the Server Options icon, then click Configure Options.

2. In the Server Options dialog box, in the Available Options list, select the DHCP option to configure, enter the appropriate value in the Data Entry box, then click OK.

Scope Options

Scope options are available only to clients who lease an address from the scope. For example, if you have a different scope for each subnet, you can define a unique default gateway address for each subnet. Scope options override global options.

▶ **To configure DHCP scope options**

1. In the DHCP console, expand the scope entry if necessary.

2. Right-click the Scope Options icon, then click Configure Options.

3. In the Scope Options dialog box, in the Available Options list, select the DHCP option to configure, enter the appropriate value in the Data Entry box, then click OK.

Configuring a Client Reservation

For some DHCP clients, it is important that the same IP address be reassigned when their lease expires. For these clients, you can set up a client reservation, which configures the DHCP service so that it always assigns the same IP address to them. For example, if the server known as SRV187 is on a network that contains clients that are not WINS-enabled, SRV187 should be set up with a client reservation. Setting up the reservation ensures that SRV187 always leases the same IP address from the DHCP server. The clients that are on that network and are not WINS-enabled must use the LMHOSTS file to resolve NetBIOS computer names. Because the LMHOSTS file is a static file containing NetBIOS name-to-IP-address mappings, name resolution using the LMHOSTS file will fail if the IP address of SRV187 changes.

▶ **To configure a client reservation**

1. In the DHCP console, open the scope entry, right-click Reservations, then click New Reservation.

2. In the New Reservation dialog box, in the Reservation Name box, type a name to identify the client. The DHCP console uses a name associated with the hardware address of the network adapter card to identify a client.

3. In the IP Address box, type the IP address that you want to reserve for a specific client.

4. In the MAC Address box, type the hardware address (media access control address) of the host's network adapter card. Do not use dashes in the hardware address.

Important   If you type the value for the MAC Address incorrectly, it will not match the value sent by the DHCP client, and the DHCP service will assign the client any available IP address instead of the IP address reserved for that client.

5. In the Description box, type an optional description for the client.

6. Under Supported Types, click to specify which method the client uses:

   ▪ **Both.**   Specifies that either DHCP or BOOTP clients are allowed for this client reservation.

   ▪ **DHCP Only.**   Specifies that only DHCP clients are allowed for this client reservation.

   ▪ **BOOTP Only.**   Specifies that only BOOTP clients are allowed for this client reservation.

7. To add the reservation to the database, click Add.

Glossary

A

access control list (ACL) The mechanisms for limiting access to certain items of information or certain controls based on users' identity and their membership in various predefined groups. Access control is typically used by system administrators for controlling user access to network resources such as servers, directories, and files and is typically implemented by granting permissions to users and groups for access to specific objects.

access token The user's identification for the computers in the domain or for that local computer. The access token contains the user's security settings, including the user's security ID (SID).

account lockout A Windows 2000 security feature that locks a user account if a number of failed logon attempts occur within a specified amount of time, based on security policy lockout settings. Locked accounts cannot log on.

ACL *See* access control list (ACL).

ACPI *See* Advanced Configuration and Power Interface (ACPI).

active The window or icon that you are currently using or that is currently selected. Windows 2000 always applies the next keystroke or command you choose to the active window. Windows or icons on the desktop that are not selected are *inactive.*

Active Directory The directory service included with Microsoft Windows 2000 Server. It stores information about objects on a network and makes this information available to users and network administrators. Active Directory gives network users access to permitted resources anywhere on the network using a single logon process. It

provides network administrators with an intuitive hierarchical view of the network and a single point of administration for all network objects.

Active Directory Domains and Trusts console An administrative tool that allows you to manage trust relationships between domains. These domains can be Microsoft Windows 2000 domains in the same forest, Windows 2000 domains in different forests, pre-Windows 2000 domains, and even Kerberos V5 realms.

Active Directory schema A description of the object classes and attributes stored in Active Directory. For each object class, the schema defines the attributes an object class must have, the additional attributes it may have, and the object class that can be its parent. The Active Directory schema can be updated dynamically by creating or modifying the schema objects stored in Active Directory. Like every object in Active Directory, schema objects have an access control list, so only authorized users may alter the schema.

Active Directory Schema console An administrative tool that allows you to view and modify Active Directory schema. You must install the Active Directory Schema console from the Microsoft Windows 2000 Administration tools on the Windows 2000 Server compact disc.

Active Directory Service Interfaces (ADSI) A directory service model and a set of COM interfaces. Active Directory Service Interfaces enables Microsoft Windows 95, Windows 98, Windows NT, and Windows 2000 applications to access several network directory services, including Active Directory.

Active Directory Sites and Services console An administrative tool that contains information about the physical structure of your network. Active Directory uses this information to determine how to replicate directory information and handle service requests.

Active Directory Support Tools Additional administrative tools that can be used to configure, manage, and debug Active Directory; included in Microsoft Windows 2000 Support Tools. The Windows 2000 Support Tools are included on the Windows 2000 CD in the \Support\tools folder. These tools are intended for use by Microsoft support personnel and experienced users to assist in diagnosing and resolving computer problems.

Active Directory Users and Computers console An administrative tool designed to perform day-to-day Active Directory administration tasks. These tasks include creating, deleting, modifying, moving, and setting permissions on objects stored in the directory. These objects include organizational units, users, contacts, groups, computers, printers, and shared file objects.

ActiveX A set of technologies that allows software components to interact with one another in a networked environment, regardless of the language in which the components were created. Certain ActiveX controls may act as snap-ins for MMC.

ActiveX control A reusable software component that can be used to incorporate ActiveX technology.

adapter card *See* network adapter card.

administrative alerts Messages that notify users about problems in areas such as security and access, user sessions, server shutdown due to power loss (when a uninterruptible power supply is available), directory replication, and printing. When a computer generates an administrative alert, a message is sent to a predefined list of users and computers.

administrator A person responsible for setting up and managing domain controllers or local computers and their user and group accounts, assigning passwords and permissions, and helping users with networking issues.

ADSI *See* Active Directory Service Interfaces (ADSI).

Advanced Configuration and Power Interface (ACPI) An open industry specification that defines power management for a wide range of mobile, desktop, and server computers and peripherals. ACPI is the foundation for the OnNow industry initiative that allows system manufacturers to deliver computers that will start at the touch of a keyboard. ACPI design is essential to take full advantage of power management and Plug and Play in Windows 2000.

American Standard Code for Information Interchange (ASCII) file Also called a *text file,* a *text-only file,* or an *ASCII text file,* refers to a file in the universally recognized text format called *ASCII* (American Standard Code for Information Interchange). An ASCII file contains characters, spaces, punctuation, carriage returns, and sometimes tabs and an end-of-file marker, but it contains no formatting information. This generic format is useful for transferring files between programs that could not otherwise understand each other's documents.

API *See* application programming interface (API).

application A complete, self-contained set of computer instructions that you use to perform a specific task, such as word processing, accounting, or data management. An application is also called a *program.*

application assignment A process that uses Software Installation (an extension of group policy) to assign programs to groups of users. The programs appear to be installed and available on the users' desktops when they log on. You assign programs to a particular group policy object (GPO), which in turn is associated with a selected directory object (site, domain, or organizational unit). When you assign programs, they are advertised to every user managed by the GPO. Advertising the program installs only enough infor-mation about the program to make program shortcuts appear on the Start menu and the necessary file associations appear in the registry. When users managed by the GPO log on to a computer running Microsoft Windows 2000, the program appears on their Start menu. When users select the program from the Start menu for the first time, the program is installed. You can also install advertised programs by clicking a document managed by the program (either by file extension or by COM-based activation).

application programming interface (API) A set of routines that a program uses to request and carry out lower level services performed by another component, such as the computer's operating system or a service running on a network computer. These maintenance chores are performed by the computer's operating system, and an API provides the program with a means of communicating with the system, telling it which system-level task to perform and when.

ASCII file *See* American Standard Code for Information Interchange (ASCII) file.

Asynchronous Transfer Mode (ATM) A high-speed, connection-oriented protocol to transport multiple types of traffic across a network. ATM packages data in a 53-byte, fixed-length cell that can be switched quickly between logical connections on a network.

ATM *See* Asynchronous Transfer Mode (ATM).

attribute Information that indicates whether a file is read-only, hidden, ready for archiving (backing up), compressed, or encrypted, and whether the file contents should be indexed for fast file searching.

audit policy A policy that determines the security events to be reported to the network administrator.

auditing The process that tracks the activities of users by recording selected types of events in the security log of a server or a workstation.

authentication The process by which the system validates the user's logon information. A user's name and password are compared against an authorized list. If the system detects a match, access is granted to the extent specified in the permissions list for that user. When a user logs on to an account on a computer running Microsoft Windows 2000 Professional, the authentication is performed by the workstation. When a user logs on to an account on a Windows 2000 Server domain, any server in that domain may perform authentication.

author mode A console mode that enables full access to all Microsoft Management Console (MMC) functionality, including adding or removing snap-ins, creating new windows, viewing all portions of the console tree, and saving MMCs.

authoritative restore A type of restore operation on a Microsoft Windows 2000 domain controller in which the objects in the restored directory are treated as authoritative, replacing (through replication) all existing copies of those objects. Authoritative restore is applicable only to replicated System State data such as Active Directory data and File Replication service data. You must use the NTDSUTIL.EXE utility to perform an authoritative restore.

authorization A process that verifies that the user has the correct rights or permissions to access a resource in a domain.

AXFR *See* full zone transfer (AXFR).

B

backup domain controller (BDC) In Microsoft Windows NT Server 4.0 or earlier, a computer running Windows NT Server that receives a copy of the domain's directory database (which contains all account and security policy information for the domain). The copy is synchronized periodically and automatically with the master copy on the primary domain controller (PDC). BDCs also authenticate user logon information and can be promoted to function as PDCs as needed. Multiple BDCs can exist in a domain. Windows NT 3.51 and 4.0 BDCs can participate in a Windows 2000 domain when the domain is configured in mixed mode.

backup set A collection of files, folders, and other data that have been backed up and stored in a file or on one or more tapes.

backup types Determine which data is backed up and how it is backed up. There are five backup types: copy, daily, differential, incremental, and normal.

basic input/output system (BIOS) On PC-compatible computers, the set of essential software routines that test hardware at startup, start the operating system, and support the transfer of data among hardware devices. The BIOS is stored in read-only memory (ROM) so that it can be executed when the computer is turned on. Although critical to performance, the BIOS is usually invisible to computer users.

BDC *See* backup domain controller (BDC).

BINL *See* Boot Information Negotiation Layer (BINL).

BIOS *See* basic input/output system (BIOS).

boot The process of starting or resetting a computer. When first turned on (cold boot) or reset (warm boot), the computer executes the software that loads and starts the computer's operating system, preparing it for use.

boot disk A floppy disk that contains key system files. You use a boot disk to start a computer that does not have a bootable CD-ROM drive and is unable to start from the hard disk.

boot files The system files needed to start Microsoft Windows 2000. For Intel-based computers, this includes NTLDR and NTDETECT.COM. For Compaq Alpha-based systems, this is OSLOADER.EXE.

Boot Information Negotiation Layer (BINL) A service that runs on the Microsoft Windows 2000 Server and acts on client boot requests.

boot logging A process in which a computer that is starting (booting) creates a log file that records the loading of each device and service. In Microsoft Windows 2000, this log file is called NTBTLOG.TXT and is saved in the system root directory.

boot partition The partition that contains the Microsoft Windows 2000 operating system and its support files. The boot partition can be, but does not have to be, the same as the system partition.

boot volume The volume that contains the Microsoft Windows 2000 operating system and its support files. The boot volume can be, but does not have to be, the same as the system volume.

bridgehead server The contact point for exchange of directory information between sites. You can specify a preferred bridgehead server if you have a computer with appropriate bandwidth to transmit and receive information. If there is typically a high level of directory information exchange, a computer with more bandwidth can ensure these exchanges are handled promptly.

built-in groups The default groups provided with Microsoft Windows 2000 Professional and Windows 2000 Server. Built-in groups have been granted useful collections of rights and built-in abilities. In most cases, built-in groups provide all the capabilities needed by a particular user.

built-in user account Used to perform administrative tasks or to gain access to network resources.

C

cache For Domain Name System (DNS) and Windows Internet Name Service (WINS), a local information store of resource records for recently resolved names of remote hosts. Typically, the cache is built dynamically as the computer queries and resolves names. It also helps optimize the time required to resolve queried names.

certificate services Software services that provide authentication support, including secure e-mail, Web-based authentication, and smart card authentication. These services contrast with Internet Authentication Services (IAS), which provide authentication for dial-in users.

check box A small box in a dialog box or property page that can be selected or cleared. Check boxes represent an option that you can turn on or off. When a check box is selected, an X or a check mark appears in the box.

child domain For Domain Name System (DNS), domains located in the namespace tree directly beneath another domain name (the parent domain). For example, example.microsoft.com would be a child domain of the parent domain, microsoft.com. A child domain is also called a *subdomain.*

child object An object that resides in another object. For example, a file is a child object that resides in a folder, which is the parent object.

CIW *See* Client Installation Wizard (CIW).

clear To turn off an option by removing the X or check mark from a check box. To clear a check box, you can click it or you can select it and then press Spacebar.

click To press and release a mouse button quickly.

client Any computer or program connecting to, or requesting the services of, another computer or program. For example, Microsoft Windows 2000 Professional is an Active Directory client. Client can also refer to the software that enables the computer or program to establish the connection. For example, to connect a Windows 95-based computer to Windows 2000 Active Directory, you must install the Windows 95 Active Directory client on the computer running Windows 95.

Client Installation Wizard (CIW) In Remote Installation Services (RIS), the CIW makes installation options available to the client.

close Remove a window or dialog box, or quit a program. To close a window, you can click the close button icon in the upper right corner of the dialog box. When you close an application window, you quit the program.

command A word or phrase, usually found on a menu, that you click to carry out an action. You click a command on a menu or type a command at the command prompt. You can also type a command in the Run dialog box, which you open by clicking Run in the Start menu.

Command Prompt window A window displayed on the desktop used to interface with the MS-DOS operating system. MS-DOS commands are typed at an entry point identified by a blinking cursor.

common groups Groups that appear in the program list on the Start menu for all users who log on to the computer. Only administrators can create or change common groups.

computer account An account that is created by a domain administrator and uniquely identifies the computer on the domain. The Microsoft Windows 2000 computer account matches the name of the computer joining the domain.

console Collections of administrative tools.

console mode Determines the Microsoft Management Console (MMC) functionality for the person who is using a saved MMC. The two available console modes are Author mode and User mode.

console tree The left pane in a Microsoft Management Console (MMC) that displays the items contained in the console. By default it is the left pane of a console window, but it can be hidden. The items in the console tree and their hierarchical organization determine the capabilities of a console.

contact Information about a person with a connection to the organization.

container object An object that can logically contain other objects. For example, a folder is a container object.

copy backup Copies all selected files, but does not mark each file as having been backed up. Copying is useful if you want to back up files between normal and incremental backups, because copying will not invalidate these other backup operations.

counter log Collects performance counter data in a comma-separated or tab-separated format for easy import to spreadsheet programs. You can view logged counter data using System Monitor or by exporting the data to spreadsheet programs or databases for analysis and report generation.

D

DACL *See* Discretionary Access Control List (DACL).

daily backup Copies all selected files that have been modified the day that the daily backup is performed.

data store (the database file NTDS.DIT) The directory database.

database layer An architectural layer of Active Directory that isolates the upper layers of the directory service from the underlying database system by exposing application programming interfaces (APIs) to the Directory System Agent (DSA) layer so that no calls are made directly to the Extensible Storage Engine (ESE).

DDNS *See* Dynamic DNS (DDNS).

default groups Groups that have a predetermined set of user rights or group membership. Microsoft Windows 2000 has four categories of default groups: predefined, built-in, built-in local, and special identity.

default user profile The profile that serves as a basis for all user profiles. Every user profile begins as a copy of the default user profile, which is stored on each computer running Microsoft Windows 2000 Professional or Windows 2000 Server.

defragmentation The process of rewriting parts of a file to contiguous sectors on a hard disk to increase the speed of access and retrieval. When files are updated, the computer tends to save these updates on the largest continuous space on the hard disk, which is often on a different sector than the other parts of the file. When files are thus fragmented, the computer must search the hard disk each time the file is opened to find all of the file's parts, which slows down response time.

delegation The ability to assign responsibility for management and administration of a portion of the namespace to another user, group, or organization.

dependency A relationship of reliance between two resources that makes it necessary for them to run in the same group on the same node. For example, an application is dependent on the disks that contain its data resources.

desktop The on-screen work area on which windows, icons, menus, and dialog boxes appear.

details pane The pane in the Microsoft Management Console (MMC) that displays the details for the selected item in the console tree. The details can be a list of items or they can be administrative properties, services, and events that are acted on by a console or snap-in.

device driver A program that allows a specific device, such as a modem, network card, or printer, to communicate with Microsoft Windows 2000. For example, without serial port drivers, network connections cannot use a modem to connect to a network. Although a device may be installed on your system, Windows 2000 cannot use the device until you have installed and configured the appropriate driver. If a device is listed in the Hardware Compatibility List (HCL), a driver is usually included with Windows 2000. Device drivers load automatically (for all enabled devices) when a computer is started, and thereafter run invisibly.

Dfs *See* distributed file system (Dfs).

Dfs link A link from a Dfs root to one or more shared files, another Dfs root, or a domain-based volume.

Dfs replication The process of copying data from a data store or file system to multiple computers to synchronize the data. Active Directory provides multimaster replication of the directory between domain controllers within a given domain. The replicas of the directory on each domain controller are writeable. This allows updates to be applied to any replica of a given domain. The replication service automatically copies the changes from a given replica to all other replicas.

Dfs root A container for files and Dfs links.

DHCP *See* Dynamic Host Configuration Protocol (DHCP).

DHCP client Any network-enabled device that supports the ability to communicate with a DHCP server for the purpose of obtaining dynamic leased Internet Protocol (IP) configuration and related optional parameters information.

DHCP scope A range of Internet Protocol (IP) addresses that are available to be leased or assigned to DHCP clients by the DHCP service.

DHCP server In Microsoft Windows 2000 Server, a computer running the Microsoft DHCP service that offers dynamic configuration of Internet Protocol (IP) addresses and related information to DHCP-enabled clients.

dial-up connection The connection to your network if you are using a device that uses the telephone network. This includes modems with a standard phone line, ISDN cards with high-speed ISDN lines, or X.25 networks. If you are a typical user, you may have one or two dial-up connections, perhaps to the Internet and to your corporate network. In a more complex server situation, multiple network modem connections might be used to implement advanced routing.

dialog box A window that is displayed to request or supply information. Many dialog boxes have options that you must select before Microsoft Windows 2000 can carry out a command.

differential backup Copies files created or changed since the last normal (or incremental) backup. It does not mark files as having been backed up.

digital signature A means for originators of a message, file, or other digitally encoded information to bind their identity to the information. The process of signing information entails transforming the information, as well as some secret information held by the sender, into a tag called a *signature.*

directory An information source (for example, a telephone directory) that contains information about people, computer files, or other objects. In a file system, a directory stores information about files. In a distributed computing environment (such as a Microsoft Windows 2000 domain), the directory stores information about objects such as printers, fax servers, applications, databases, and other users.

directory database The physical storage for each replica of Active Directory. Directory database is also called the *data store.*

directory service Provides the methods for storing directory data and making this data available to network users and administrators. For example, Active Directory stores information about user accounts, such as names, passwords, phone numbers, and so on, and enables other authorized users on the same network to access this information.

directory services restore mode A special safe mode that allows you to restore the System State data on a domain controller. When your computer is started in this mode you can restore the SYSVOL directory and Active Directory directory services database. You can only restore System State data on a local computer. You cannot restore the System State data on a remote computer.

Directory System Agent (DSA) Builds a hierarchy from the parent-child relationships stored in the directory. Provides application programming interfaces (APIs) for directory access calls.

disable To make a device nonfunctional. For example, if you disable a device in a hardware configuration, you will not be able to use the device when your computer uses that hardware configuration. Disabling a device frees the resources that were allocated to the device.

Discretionary Access Control List (DACL) A list that represents part of an object's security descriptor that allows or denies permissions to specific users and groups.

disk A physical data storage device attached to a computer.

distinguished name (DN) A name that uniquely identifies an object by using the relative distin-guished name for the object, plus the names of container objects and domains that contain the object. The distinguished name identifies the object as well as its location in a tree. Every object in Active Directory has a distinguished name. A typical distinguished name might be: CN=MyName,CN=Users,DC=Microsoft,DC=Com This identifies the MyName user object in the microsoft.com domain.

distributed file system (Dfs) A service used to build a logical structure of file shares from sepa-rate computers and presented to users and admin-istrators in a single directory tree.

distribution group A group that is used solely for e-mail distribution and is not security-enabled. Distribution groups cannot be listed in discretionary access control lists (DACLs) used to define permissions on resources and objects. Distribution groups can be used only with e-mail applications (such as Microsoft Exchange) to send e-mail to collections of users. If you do not need a group for security purposes, create a distribution group instead of a security group.

DLL *See* dynamic link library (DLL).

DN *See* distinguished name (DN).

DNS *See* Domain Name System (DNS).

DNS name server In the DNS client/server model, the server containing information about a portion of the DNS database that makes computer names available to client resolvers querying for name resolution across the Internet.

domain In Microsoft Windows 2000 and Active Directory, a collection of computers defined by the administrator of a Windows 2000 Server net-work that share a common directory database. A domain has a unique name and provides access to the centralized user accounts and group accounts maintained by the domain administrator. Each domain has its own security policies and security relationships with other domains and represents a single security boundary of a Windows 2000 computer network. Active Directory is made up of one or more domains, each of which can span more than one physical location. For Domain Name System (DNS), a domain is any tree or subtree within the DNS namespace. Although the names for DNS domains often correspond to Active Directory domains, DNS domains should not be confused with Windows 2000 and Active Directory networking domains.

domain controller In a Microsoft Windows 2000 Server domain, a computer running Windows 2000 Server that manages user access to a network, which includes logging on, authentication, and access to the directory and shared resources.

domain local group A security or distribution group that can contain universal groups, global groups, and accounts from any domain in the domain tree or forest. A domain local group can also contain other domain local groups from its own domain. Rights and permissions can be assigned only at the domain containing the group.

domain model A grouping of one or more domains with administration and communication links between them that is arranged for the purpose of user and resource management.

domain name In Microsoft Windows 2000 and Active Directory, the name given by an administrator to a collection of networked computers that share a common directory. For Domain Name System (DNS), domain names are specific node names in the DNS namespace tree. DNS domain names use singular node names, joined together by periods (.) that indicate each node level in the namespace.

Domain Name System (DNS) A static, hierarchical name service for Transmission Control Protocol/Internet Protocol (TCP/IP) hosts. The network administrator configures the DNS with a list of host names and IP addresses, allowing users of workstations configured to query the DNS to specify remote systems by host names rather than IP addresses. DNS domains should not be confused with Microsoft Windows 2000 networking domains.

domain namespace The database structure used by the Domain Name System (DNS).

domain naming master The domain controller assigned to control the addition or removal of domains in the forest. At any time, there can be only one domain naming master in the forest.

domain user account Allows a user to log on to the domain to gain access to network resources.

double-click To rapidly press and release a mouse button twice without moving the mouse. Double-clicking carries out an action, such as starting a program.

drag To move an item on the screen by selecting the item and then pressing and holding down the mouse button while moving the mouse.

DSA *See* Directory System Agent (DSA).

Dynamic DNS (DDNS) Enables clients with dynamically assigned addresses to register directly with a server running the DNS service and update the DNS table dynamically. DDNS eliminates the need for other Internet naming services, such as Windows Internet Name Service (WINS), in a homogeneous environment.

Dynamic Host Configuration Protocol (DHCP) A Transmission Control Protocol/Internet Protocol (TCP/IP) service protocol that offers dynamic leased configuration of host IP addresses and distributes other configuration parameters to eligible network clients. DHCP provides safe, reliable, and simple TCP/IP network configuration, prevents address conflicts, and helps conserve the use of client IP addresses on the network. DHCP uses a client/server model where the DHCP server maintains centralized management of IP addresses that are used on the network. DHCP-supporting clients can then request and obtain lease of an IP address from a DHCP server as part of their network boot process.

dynamic link library An operating system feature that allows executable routines (generally serving a specific function or set of functions) to be stored separately as files with .dll extensions. These routines are loaded only when needed by the program that calls them.

dynamic volume A logical volume that is created using Disk Management. Dynamic volumes include simple, spanned, striped, mirrored, and RAID-5. You must create dynamic volumes on dynamic disks.

E

enable To make a device functional. For example, if you enable a device in your hardware configuration settings you will be able to use the device when your computer uses that hardware configuration.

environment subsystems One of the components of the Microsoft Windows 2000 User mode; emulate different operating systems by presenting the application programming interfaces (APIs) that the applications expect to be available. The environment subsystems accept the API calls made by the application, convert the API calls into a format understood by Windows 2000, and then pass the converted API to the Executive Services for processing.

ESE *See* Extensible Storage Engine (ESE).

event Any significant occurrence in the system, or an application that requires users to be notified or an entry to be added to a log.

Event Log service A service that records events in the system, security, and application logs. The Event Log service is located in Event Viewer.

event logging The Microsoft Windows 2000 process of recording an audit entry in the audit trail whenever certain events occur, such as services starting and stopping or users logging on and off and accessing resources. You can use Event Viewer to review AppleTalk network integration (formerly Services for Macintosh) events as well as Windows 2000 events.

Event Viewer Maintains logs about application, security, and system events on your computer.

Everyone group In Microsoft Windows NT, includes all local and remote users who have connected to the computer, including those who connect as guests. You cannot control who becomes a member of the Everyone group; however, you can assign permissions and rights.

expand To show hidden directory levels in the directory tree.

explicit one-way nontransitive trust A type of trust relationship in which only one of the two domains trusts the other domain. For example, Domain A trusts Domain B and Domain B does not trust Domain A. All one-way trusts are nontransitive.

Extensible Storage Engine (ESE) The Active Directory database engine. ESE (ESENT.DLL) is an improved version of the Jet database that is used in Microsoft Exchange Server versions 4.x and 5.5. It implements a transacted database system, which means that it uses log files to ensure that committed transactions are safe.

extension snap-ins Usually referred to simply as *extensions*. They are snap-ins that provide additional administrative functionality to another snap-in.

F

fault tolerance The ability of a computer or operating system to ensure data integrity when hardware failures occur.

file A collection of information that has been given a name and is stored on a disk. This information can be a document or a program.

file replication service A service used by the Microsoft distributed file system (Dfs) to automatically synchronize content between assigned replicas, and by Active Directory Sites and Services to replicate topological and global catalog information across domain controllers.

file sharing The ability of a computer running Microsoft Windows 2000 to share parts (or all) of its local file system(s) with remote computers.

file system In an operating system, the overall structure in which files are named, stored, and organized. NTFS, FAT, and FAT32 are types of file systems.

firewall A combination of hardware and software that provides a security system, usually to prevent unauthorized access from outside to an internal network or intranet. A firewall prevents direct communication between network and external computers by routing communication through a proxy server outside of the network. The proxy server determines whether it is safe to let a file pass through to the network.

folder A grouping of files or other folders, graphically represented by a folder icon, in both Microsoft Windows 2000 and Macintosh environments. A folder is analogous to a PC's file system directory, and many folders are, in fact, directories.

folder redirection An extension within group policy that allows you to redirect the following Windows 2000 special folders to network locations: Application Data, Desktop, My Documents, My Pictures, and Start Menu.

forest A collection of one or more Microsoft Windows 2000 domains that share a common schema, configuration, and global catalog, and are linked with two-way transitive trusts.

forward lookup In Domain Name System (DNS), a query process in which the friendly DNS domain name of a host computer is searched to find its Internet Protocol (IP) address.

FQDN *See* fully qualified domain name (FQDN).

full zone transfer (AXFR) The standard query type supported by all Domain Name System (DNS) servers to update and synchronize zone data when the zone has been changed. When a DNS query is made using AXFR as the specified query type, the entire zone is transferred as the response.

fully qualified domain name (FQDN) A Domain Name System (DNS) domain name that has been stated unambiguously so as to indicate with absolute certainty its location in the domain namespace tree. Fully qualified domain names differ from relative names in that they are typically stated with a trailing period (.), for example, host.example.microsoft.com., to qualify their position to the root of the namespace.

G

global account For Microsoft Windows 2000 Server, a normal user account in a user's domain. Most user accounts are global accounts. If there are multiple domains in the network, it is best if each user in the network has only one user account in only one domain, and each user's access to other domains is accomplished through the establishment of domain trust relationships.

global catalog A domain controller that contains a partial replica of every domain in Active Directory. A global catalog holds a replica of every object in Active Directory, but with a limited number of each object's attributes. The global catalog stores those attributes most frequently used in search operations (such as a user's first and last name) and those attributes required to locate a full replica of the object. The Active Directory replication system builds the global catalog automatically. The attributes replicated into the global catalog include a base set defined by Microsoft. Administrators can specify additional properties to meet the needs of their installation.

global catalog server A Microsoft Windows 2000 domain controller that holds a copy of the global catalog for the forest.

global group For Microsoft Windows 2000 Server, a group that can be granted rights and permissions and can become a member of local groups in its own domain, the member servers and workstations thereof, and trusting domains. However, a global group can contain user accounts only from its own domain. Global groups provide a way to create sets of users from inside the domain, available for use both in and out of the domain. Global groups cannot be created or maintained on computers running Windows 2000 Professional. However, for Windows 2000 Professional computers that participate in a domain, domain global groups can be granted rights and permissions at those workstations and can become members of local groups at those workstations.

globally unique identifier (GUID) A 128-bit number that is guaranteed to be unique. GUIDs are assigned to objects when the objects are created. The GUID never changes, even if you move or rename the object. Applications can store the GUID of an object and use the GUID to retrieve that object regardless of its current distinguished name.

GPO *See* group policy object (GPO).

group A collection of users, computers, contacts, and other groups. Groups can be used as security or as e-mail distribution collections. Distribution groups are used only for e-mail. Security groups are used to grant access to resources.

group account A collection of user accounts. By making a user account a member of a group, you give the related user all the rights and permissions granted to the group.

group memberships The groups to which a user account belongs. Permissions and rights granted to a group are also provided to its members. In most cases, the actions a user can perform in Microsoft Windows 2000 are determined by the group memberships of the user account that has been logged on to.

group policy The Microsoft Windows 2000 Microsoft Management Console (MMC) snap-in used to specify the behavior of users' desktops. A group policy object (GPO), which an administrator creates using the Group Policy snap-in, is the mechanism for configuring desktop settings.

group policy object (GPO) A collection of group policy settings. GPOs are essentially the documents created by the Group Policy snap-in. GPOs are stored at the domain level and they affect users and computers contained in sites, domains, and organizational units. In addition, each Microsoft

Windows 2000 computer has exactly one group of settings stored locally, called the *local GPO*.

group scopes Allow you to use groups in different ways to assign permissions. The scope of a group determines where in the network you are able to use the group to assign permissions to the group. The three group scopes are global, domain local, and universal.

guest account A built-in account used to log on to a computer running Microsoft Windows 2000 when a user does not have an account on the computer or domain or in any of the domains trusted by the computer's domain.

GUID *See* globally unique identifier (GUID).

H

HAL *See* Hardware Abstraction Layer (HAL).

Hardware Abstraction Layer (HAL) Virtualizes, or hides, the hardware interface details, making Microsoft Windows 2000 more portable across different hardware architectures. The HAL contains the hardware-specific code that handles input/output (I/O) interfaces, interrupt controllers, and multiprocessor communication mechanisms. This layer allows Windows 2000 to run on both Intel-based and Alpha-based systems without having to maintain two separate versions of Windows 2000 Executive.

Hardware Compatibility List (HCL) A list of the devices supported by Microsoft Windows 2000. The latest version of the HCL can be downloaded from the Hardware Compatibility List Web page at *http://www.microsoft.com/hwtest/hcl/*.

HCL *See* Hardware Compatibility List (HCL).

hierarchical namespace A namespace, such as the Domain Name System (DNS) namespace and the Active Directory namespace, that is hierarchically structured and provides rules that allow the namespace to be partitioned.

histogram A chart consisting of horizontal or vertical bars, the widths or heights of which represent the values of certain data.

home directory Specified in Active Directory Users and Computers or Local Users and Groups, the home directory is a folder that is accessible to the user and can contain files and programs for that user. A home directory can be assigned to an individual user or can be shared by many users. Some programs use the home directory as the default folder for the Open and Save As dialog boxes. Other programs use My Documents.

host name The name of a device on a network. For a device on a Microsoft Windows NT or Windows 2000 network, this can be the same as the computer name, but it may not be. The host name must be in the Hosts file, or it must be known by a Domain Name System (DNS) server, for that host to be found by another computer attempting to communicate with it.

HTTP *See* Hypertext Transfer Protocol (HTTP).

HTTP Uniform Resource Locator (URL) Takes the form of *http://domain/path-to-page* and is familiar to users with Web browsers.

Hypertext Transfer Protocol (HTTP) The standard protocol for displaying pages on the World Wide Web.

I

IETF *See* Internet Engineering Task Force (IETF).

IIS *See* Internet Information Services (IIS).

implicit two-way transitive trust A type of trust relationship in which both of the domains in the relationship trust each other. In a two-way trust relationship, each domain has established a one-way trust with the other domain. For example, Domain A trusts Domain B and Domain B trusts Domain A. Two-way trusts can be transitive or nontransitive. All two-way trusts between

Microsoft Windows 2000 domains in the same domain tree or forest are transitive.

in-addr.arpa domain A special top-level Domain Name System (DNS) domain reserved for reverse mapping of Internet Protocol (IP) addresses to DNS host names.

incremental backup Backs up only the files created or changed since the last normal (or incremental) backup, marking the files as having been backed up.

incremental zone transfer (IXFR) An alternate query type that can be used by some Domain Name System (DNS) servers to update and synchronize zone data when a zone is changed. When IXFR is supported between DNS servers, servers can keep track of and transfer only those incremental resource record changes between each version of the zone.

Indexing service Software that provides search functions for documents stored on disk, allowing users to search for specific document text or properties.

infrastructure master The domain controller assigned to update group-to-user references whenever group memberships are changed, and to replicate these changes to any other domain controllers in the domain. At any time, there can be only one infrastructure master in a particular domain.

initial master A shared folder whose existing files and folders are replicated to other shared folders when replication is initially configured. After replication is complete, there is no initial master, as any of the replicas can accept changes and propagate them to the other replicas. The initial master then becomes another replica.

integral subsystems One of the components of the Microsoft Windows 2000 User mode; perform essential operating system functions, such as security, workstation service, and server service.

IntelliMirror A set of powerful features native to Microsoft Windows 2000 for desktop change and configuration management technology. Intelli-Mirror combines the advantages of centralized computing with the performance and flexibility of distributed computing.

interactive logon A network logon from a computer keyboard, when the user types information in the Log On To Windows dialog box displayed by the computer's operating system.

Internet The global network of networks.

Internet Engineering Task Force (IETF) A large, open community of network designers, operators, vendors, and researchers concerned with the evolution of Internet architecture and the smooth operation of the Internet. Technical work is performed by working groups organized by topic areas (such as routing, transport, and security) and through mailing lists. Internet standards are developed in IETF Requests for Comments (RFCs), which are a series of notes that discuss many aspects of computing and computer communication, focusing on networking protocols, programs, and concepts.

Internet Information Services (IIS) Software services that support Web site creation, configuration, and management, along with other Internet functions. Microsoft Internet Information Services include Network News Transfer Protocol (NNTP), File Transfer Protocol (FTP), and Simple Mail Transfer Protocol (SMTP).

Internet Protocol (IP) The messenger protocol of Transmission Control Protocol/Internet Protocol (TCP/IP) that is responsible for addressing and sending IP packets over the network. IP provides a best-effort, connectionless delivery system that does not guarantee that packets arrive at their destination or in the sequence in which they were sent.

inter-site replication Replication traffic that occurs between sites.

intranet A Transmission Control Protocol/Internet Protocol (TCP/IP) network that uses Internet technology. May be connected to the Internet.

intra-site replication Replication traffic that occurs within a site.

IP *See* Internet Protocol (IP).

IP address A 32-bit address used to identify a node on an Internet Protocol (IP) internetwork. Each node on the IP internetwork must be assigned a unique IP address, which is made up of a network identifier and a host identifier. This address is typically represented in dotted-decimal notation, with the decimal value of each octet separated by a period, for example, 192.168.7.27. In Microsoft Windows 2000, you can configure the IP address statically or dynamically through Dynamic Host Configuration Protocol (DHCP).

IP replication Uses remote procedure calls (RPCs) for replication over site links (inter-site) and within a site (intra-site). By default, inter-site IP replication does adhere to replication schedules, although you may configure Active Directory to ignore schedules.

IXFR *See* Incremental Zone Transfer (IXFR).

K

KCC *See* Knowledge Consistency Checker (KCC).

Kerberos V5 An Internet standard security protocol for handling authentication of user or system identity. With Kerberos V5, passwords that are sent across network lines are encrypted, not sent as plain text. Kerberos V5 also includes other security features.

kernel mode Provides direct access to memory and executes in an isolated memory area. Kernel mode consists of four components: Microsoft Windows 2000 Executive, Device Drivers, the Microkernel, and the Hardware Abstraction Layer (HAL).

Knowledge Consistency Checker (KCC) A built-in service that runs on all domain controllers and automatically establishes connections between individual machines in the same site. These are known as Windows 2000 Directory Service *connection objects*. An administrator may establish additional connection objects or remove connection objects. At any point where replication within a site becomes impossible or has a single point of failure, the KCC will step in and establish as many new connection objects as necessary to resume Active Directory replication.

L

L2TP *See* Layer 2 Tunneling Protocol (L2TP).

LAN *See* local area network (LAN).

Layer 2 Tunneling Protocol (L2TP) An industry-standard Internet tunneling protocol. Unlike Point-to-Point Tunneling Protocol (PPTP), L2TP does not require Internet Protocol (IP) connectivity between the client workstation and the server. L2TP requires only that the tunnel medium provide packet-oriented point-to-point connectivity. The protocol can be used over media such as Asynchronous Transfer Mode (ATM), Frame Relay, and X.25. L2TP provides the same functionality as PPTP. Based on Layer 2 Forwarding (L2F) and PPTP specifications, L2TP allows clients to set up tunnels across intervening networks.

LDAP *See* Lightweight Directory Access Protocol (LDAP).

Lightweight Directory Access Protocol (LDAP) The primary access protocol for Active Directory. LDAP version 3 is defined by a set of Proposed Standard documents in Internet Engineering Task Force (IETF) RFC 2251.

list In a dialog box, a type of box that lists available choices. If all the choices do not fit in the box, there is a scroll bar.

load balancing A technique used to scale the performance of a server-based program (such as a Web server) by distributing its client requests across multiple servers within the cluster. Each host can specify the load percentage that it will handle, or the load can be equally distributed across all the hosts. If a host fails, the load is dynamically redistributed among the remaining hosts.

local area network (LAN) A group of computers and other devices dispersed over a relatively limited area and connected by a communications link that allows one device to interact with any other on the network.

local computer A computer that you can access directly without using a communications line or a communications device, such as a network card or a modem.

local group For computers running Microsoft Windows 2000 Professional and member servers, a group that can be granted permissions and rights from its own computer and (if the computer participates in a domain) user accounts and global groups both from its own domain and from trusted domains.

local group policy object One group policy object (GPO) stored on each computer whether or not the computer is part of an Active Directory environment or a networked environment. Local GPO settings can be overridden by nonlocal GPOs and are the least influential if the computer is in an Active Directory environment. In a nonnetworked environment (or in a networked environment lacking a Microsoft Windows 2000 domain controller), the local GPO's settings are more important because they are not overridden by nonlocal GPOs.

local security database A list of user accounts and resource security information for the computer on which the list resides.

local user account For Microsoft Windows 2000 Server, a user account provided in a domain for a user whose global account is not in a trusted domain. A local account is not required where trust relationships exist between domains.

local user profile A user profile that is created automatically on the computer the first time a user logs on to a computer running Microsoft Windows 2000 Professional or Windows 2000 Server.

log file A file that stores messages generated by an application, service, or operating system. These messages are used to track the operations performed. Log files are usually plain text (ASCII) files and often have a .log extension. In Backup, a file that contains a record of the date the tapes were created and the names of files and directories successfully backed up and restored. The Performance Logs and Alerts service also creates log files.

log off To stop using the network and remove your user name from active use until you log on again.

log on To provide a user name and password that identifies you to the network.

logon rights User Rights that are assigned to a user and specify the ways in which a user can log on to a system. An example of a logon right is the right to log on to a system remotely.

logon workstations In Microsoft Windows 2000 Server, the computers from which a user is allowed to log on.

M

mandatory user profile A user profile that is not updated when the user logs off. It is downloaded to the user's desktop each time the user logs on and is created by an administrator and assigned to one or more users to create consistent or job-specific user profiles. Only members of the Administrators group can change profiles.

MAPI *See* Messaging API (MAPI).

master server An authoritative Domain Name System (DNS) server for a zone. Master servers can vary and will be one of two types (either primary or secondary masters), depending on how the server obtains its zone data.

maximize To enlarge a window to its maximum size by using the Maximize button (at the right of the title bar).

member server A computer that runs Microsoft Windows 2000 Server but is not a domain controller of a Windows 2000 domain. Member servers participate in a domain, but do not store a copy of the directory database. For a member server, permissions can be set on resources that allow users to connect to the server and use its resources. Resource permissions can be granted for domain global groups and users as well as for local groups and users.

menu A list of available commands in a program window.

Message Queuing A message queuing and routing system for Microsoft Windows 2000 that enables distributed applications running at different times to communicate across heterogeneous networks and with computers that may be offline. Message Queuing provides guaranteed message delivery, efficient routing, security, and priority-based messaging.

Messaging API (MAPI) The application programming interface (API) for which Active Directory provides support for backward compatibility with Microsoft Exchange applications. New applications should use Active Directory Service Interfaces for accessing Active Directory.

metadata Information about the properties of data, such as the type of data in a column (numeric, text, and so on) or the length of a column. Information about the structure of data. Information that specifies the design of objects such as cubes or dimensions.

Microkernel Manages the microprocessor only. The kernel coordinates all input/output (I/O) functions and synchronizes the activities of the Executive Services.

Microsoft Management Console (MMC) A framework for hosting administrative tools, called *consoles*. A console may contain tools, folders or other containers, World Wide Web pages, and other administrative items. These items are displayed in the left pane of the console, called a *console tree*. A console has one or more windows that can provide views of the console tree. The main MMC window provides commands and tools for authoring consoles. The authoring features of MMC and the console tree itself may be hidden when a console is in User mode.

minimize To reduce a window to a button on the taskbar by using the Minimize button (at the right of the title bar).

mixed mode The default domain mode setting on Microsoft Windows 2000 domain controllers. Mixed mode allows Windows NT and Windows 2000 backup domain controllers to coexist in a domain. Mixed mode does not support the universal and nested group enhancements of Windows 2000. The domain mode setting can be changed to Windows 2000 native mode when all Windows NT domain controllers are removed from a domain.

MMC *See* Microsoft Management Console (MMC).

modifications .mst files that allow you to customize Windows Installer packages (which have the .msi extension). Modifications are also called *transforms*. The Microsoft Windows Installer package format provides for customization by allowing you to "transform" the original package using authoring and repackaging tools. Some applications also provide wizards or templates that permit a user to create modifications.

multimaster replication A replication model in which any domain controller accepts and replicates directory changes to any other domain con-

troller. This differs from other replication models in which one computer stores the single modifiable copy of the directory and other computers store backup copies.

N

name resolution The process of translating a name into some object or information that the name represents. A telephone book forms a namespace in which the names of telephone subscribers can be resolved to telephone numbers. The Microsoft Windows NT file system (NTFS) forms a namespace in which the name of a file can be resolved to the file itself. The Active Directory forms a namespace in which the name of an object in the directory can be resolved to the object itself.

Name Server (NS) resource record A resource record used in a zone to designate the Domain Name System (DNS) domain names for authoritative DNS servers for the zone.

namespace A set of unique names for resources or items used in a shared computing environment. For Microsoft Management Console (MMC), the namespace is represented by the console tree, which displays all of the snap-ins and resources that are accessible to a console. For Domain Name System (DNS), namespace is the vertical or hierarchical structure of the domain name tree.

native mode The condition in which all domain controllers in the domain have been upgraded to Microsoft Windows 2000 and an administrator has enabled native mode operation (through Active Directory Users and Computers).

Net PC/PC98 The annual guide for hardware developers co-authored by Microsoft with Intel, including contributions from Compaq and other industry hardware manufacturers. PC98 is intended to provide standards for hardware development that advance the PC platform and enable Microsoft to include advanced features, like Remote Installation Services (RIS), in the Windows platform.

NetBIOS *See* network basic input/output system (NetBIOS).

network adapter card A printed circuit board that allows a computer to use a peripheral device for which it does not already have the connections or circuit boards. A network adapter card is also called a *network adapter,* an *adapter card,* or a *card.*

network basic input/output system (NetBIOS) An application programming interface (API) that can be used by programs on a local area network (LAN). NetBIOS provides programs with a uniform set of commands for requesting the lower level services required to manage names, conduct sessions, and send datagrams between nodes on a network.

node For tree structures, a location on the tree that can have links to one or more items below it. For local area networks (LANs), a device that is connected to the network and is capable of communicating with other network devices.

nonauthoritative restore A restore of a backup copy of a Microsoft Windows 2000 domain controller in which the objects in the restored directory are not treated as authoritative. The restored objects are updated with changes held in other replicas of the restored domain.

noncontainer object An object that cannot logically contain other objects. For example, a file is a noncontainer object.

nonlocal group policy object A group policy object (GPO) linked to Active Directory objects (sites, domains, or organizational units) that can be applied to either users or computers. To use nonlocal GPOs, you must have a Microsoft Windows 2000 domain controller installed. Following the properties of Active Directory, nonlocal GPOs are applied hierarchically from the least restrictive group (site) to the most restrictive group (organizational unit) and are cumulative.

nontransitive trust *See* explicit one-way nontransitive trust.

normal backup Copies all selected files and marks each as having been backed up. Normal backups give you the ability to restore files quickly because files on the last tape are the most current.

notify list A list maintained by the primary master for a zone of other Domain Name System (DNS) servers that should be notified when zone changes occur. The notify list is made up of Internet Protocol (IP) addresses for DNS servers configured as secondary masters for the zone. When the listed servers are notified of a change to the zone, they will initiate a zone transfer with another DNS server and update the zone.

NSLOOKUP A command-line utility that allows you to make Domain Name System (DNS) queries for testing and troubleshooting your DNS installation.

NTFS *See* NTFS file system.

NTFS file system An advanced file system designed for use specifically within the Microsoft Windows 2000 operating system. It supports file system recovery, extremely large storage media, long filenames, and various features for the Portable Operating System Interface for UNIX (POSIX) subsystem. It also supports object-oriented applications by treating all files as objects with user-defined and system-defined attributes.

O

object An entity such as a file, folder, shared folder, printer, or Active Directory object described by a distinct, named set of attributes. For example, the attributes of a file object include its name, location, and size; the attributes of an Active Directory user object might include the user's first name, last name, and e-mail address.

object class A logical grouping of objects.

object identifier A label that uniquely identifies an object class or attribute. An object identifier is represented as a dotted-decimal string (for example, 1.2.3.4). Object identifiers form a hierarchy with the root object identifier being issued by a national registration authority responsible for issuing object identifiers. In the United States, this is the American National Standards Institute (ANSI). Organizations or individuals obtain a root object identifier from an issuing authority and use it to allocate additional object identifiers as they develop new classes and attributes. For example, Microsoft has been issued the root object identifier of 1.2.840.113556. Microsoft uses one of the branches from this root object identifier to allocate object identifiers for Active Directory classes and another branch for Active Directory attributes.

open To display the contents of a directory, a document, or a data file in a window.

Open Systems Interconnection Model (OSI) A four-layered conceptual model (consisting of Application, Transport, Internet, and Network Interface layers) to which Transmission Control Protocol/Internet Protocol (TCP/IP) protocols map. Each layer in this TCP/IP model corresponds to one or more layers of the International Standards Organization (ISO) seven-layer OSI model consisting of Application, Presentation, Session, Transport, Network, Data-link, and Physical.

operations master roles A domain controller that has been assigned one or more special roles in an Active Directory domain. The domain controllers assigned these roles perform operations that are single master (not permitted to occur at different places on the network at the same time). Examples of these operations include resource identifier allocation, schema modification, primary domain controller (PDC) election, and certain infrastructure changes. The domain controller that controls the particular operation owns the operations master role for that operation. The ownership of

these operations master roles can be transferred to other domain controllers.

optimize To improve performance.

organizational unit (OU) An Active Directory container object used within domains. OUs are logical containers into which you can place users, groups, computers, and other OUs. It can contain objects only from its parent domain. An OU is the smallest scope to which you can apply a group policy or delegate authority.

OS/2 subsystem Provides a set of application programming interfaces (APIs) for 16-bit, character mode OS/2 applications.

OSI *See* Open Systems Interconnection Model (OSI).

OU *See* organizational unit (OU).

owner In Microsoft Windows 2000, the person who controls how permissions are set on objects and can grant permissions to others.

P

packet An Open Systems Interconnection (OSI) network layer transmission unit that consists of binary information representing both data and a header containing an identification number, source and destination addresses, and error-control data.

parent domain For Domain Name System (DNS), a domain that is located in the namespace tree directly above other derivative domain names (child domains). For example, microsoft.com would be the parent domain for example.microsoft.com, a child domain.

parent object The object in which another object resides. A parent object implies relation. For example, a folder is a parent object in which a file, or child object, resides. An object can be both a parent and a child object. For example, a subfolder that contains files is both the child of the parent folder and the parent folder of the files.

partition A portion of a physical disk that functions as though it were a physically separate disk. Partitions can be created only on basic disks.

password A security measure used to restrict logon names to user accounts and access to computer systems and resources. A password is a unique string of characters that must be provided before a logon name or an access is authorized. For Microsoft Windows 2000, a password for a user account can be up to 14 characters and is case-sensitive.

path A sequence of directory (or folder) names that specifies the location of a directory, file, or folder within the directory tree. Each directory name and filename within the path (except for the first) must be preceded by a backslash (\).

PDC *See* primary domain controller (PDC).

PDC emulator master The domain controller assigned to act as a Microsoft Windows NT 4.0 primary domain controller (PDC) to service network clients that do not have Active Directory client software installed, and to replicate directory changes to any Windows NT backup domain controllers (BDCs) in the domain. For a Windows 2000 domain operating in native mode, the PDC emulator master receives preferential replication of password changes performed by other domain controllers in the domain and handles any password authentication requests that fail at the local domain controller. At any time, there can be only one PDC emulator in a particular domain.

peer Any of the devices on a layered communications network that operate on the same protocol level.

per seat licensing A licensing mode that requires a separate client access license for each client computer that accesses Microsoft Windows 2000 Server, regardless of whether all the clients access the server at the same time.

per server licensing A licensing mode that requires a separate client access license for each concurrent connection to the server, regardless of whether there are other client computers on the network that do not happen to connect concurrently.

performance alert A feature that detects when a predefined counter value rises above or falls below the configured threshold, and notifies a user by means of the Messenger service.

performance counter In System Monitor, a data item associated with a performance object. For each counter selected, System Monitor presents a value corresponding to a particular aspect of the performance defined for the performance object.

Performance Logs and Alerts A tool that provides you with the ability to create counter logs, trace logs, and system alerts automatically from local or remote computers.

performance object In System Monitor, a logical collection of counters that is associated with a resource or service that can be monitored.

performance object instance In System Monitor, a term used to distinguish between multiple performance objects of the same type on a computer.

permission A rule associated with an object to regulate which users can gain access to the object and in what manner.

permissions inheritance A mechanism that allows a given access control entry (ACE) to be copied from the container where it was applied to all children of the container. Inheritance can be combined with delegation to grant administrative rights to a whole subtree of the directory in a single update operation.

PKI *See* public key infrastructure (PKI).

Plug and Play A set of specifications developed by Intel that allows a computer to automatically detect and configure a device and install the appropriate device drivers.

Point-to-Point Tunneling Protocol (PPTP) Networking technology that supports multiprotocol virtual private networks (VPNs), enabling remote users to access corporate networks securely across the Internet or other networks by dialing into an Internet service provider (ISP) or by connecting directly to the Internet. The PPTP tunnels, or encapsulates, Internet Protocol (IP), IPX, or NetBEUI traffic inside of IP packets. This means that users can remotely run applications that are dependent on particular network protocols.

pointer The arrow-shaped cursor on the screen that follows the movement of a mouse (or other pointing device) and indicates which area of the screen will be affected when you press the mouse button. The pointer changes shape during certain tasks.

pointer (PTR) resource record A resource record used in a reverse lookup zone created within the in-addr.arpa domain to designate a reverse mapping of a host Internet Protocol (IP) address to a host Domain Name System (DNS) domain name.

policy The mechanism by which desktop settings are configured automatically, as defined by the administrator. Depending on context, this can refer to Microsoft Windows 2000 group policy, Windows NT 4.0 system policy, or a specific setting in a group policy object (GPO).

Portable Operating System Interface for UNIX (POSIX) An Institute of Electrical and Electronics Engineers (IEEE) standard that defines a set of operating system services. Programs that adhere to the POSIX standard can be easily ported from one system to another. POSIX was based on UNIX system services, but was created in a way that allows it to be implemented by other operating systems.

POSIX *See* Portable Operating System Interface for UNIX (POSIX).

PPTP *See* Point-to-Point Tunneling Protocol (PPTP).

Pre-Boot eXecution Environment (PXE) A new form of remote boot technology that has been created within the computing industry. PXE provides companies with the ability to use their existing Transmission Control Protocol/Internet Protocol (TCP/IP) network infrastructure with Dynamic Host Configuration Protocol (DHCP) to discover Remote Installation Services (RIS) servers on the network. Net PC/PC98-compliant systems can take advantage of the remote boot technology included in the Microsoft Windows 2000 operating system.

prestage To predetermine a specific client computer network account identification for the purpose of identifying and routing a client computer during the network service boot request.

primary domain controller (PDC) In a Microsoft Windows NT Server 4.0 or earlier domain, the computer running Windows NT Server that authenticates domain logons and maintains the directory database for a domain. The PDC tracks changes made to accounts of all computers on a domain. It is the only computer to receive these changes directly. A domain has only one PDC. In Windows 2000, one of the domain controllers in each domain is identified as the PDC for compatibility with Windows NT 4.0 and earlier versions of Windows NT.

primary master An authoritative Domain Name System (DNS) server for a zone that can be used as a point of update for the zone. Only primary masters have the ability to be updated directly to process zone updates, which include adding, removing, or modifying resource records that are stored as zone data. Primary masters are also used as the first sources for replicating the zone to other DNS servers.

primary zone database file The master zone database file. Changes to a zone, such as adding domains or hosts, are performed on the server that contains the primary zone database file.

privileges A user right that is assigned to a user and specifies allowable actions on the network. An example of a privilege is the right to shut down a system.

program A complete, self-contained set of computer instructions that you use to perform a specific task, such as word processing, accounting, or data management. A program is also called an *application.*

protocol A set of rules and conventions for sending information over a network. These rules govern the content, format, timing, sequencing, and error control of messages exchanged among network devices.

public key infrastructure (PKI) The term generally used to describe the laws, policies, standards, and software that regulate or manipulate certificates and public and private keys. In practice, it is a system of digital certificates, certification authorities, and other registration authorities that verify and authenticate the validity of each party involved in an electronic transaction. Standards for PKI are still evolving, even though they are being widely implemented as a necessary element of electronic commerce.

publish To make data available for replication.

PXE *See* Pre-Boot eXecution Environment (PXE).

Q

QoS *See* Quality of Service (QoS).

Quality of Service (QoS) A set of quality assurance standards and mechanisms for data transmission, implemented in Microsoft Windows 2000.

query A specific request for data retrieval, modification, or deletion.

R

RAM *See* random access memory (RAM).

random access memory (RAM) Memory that can be read from or written to by a computer or other devices. Information stored in RAM is lost when you turn off the computer.

RAS *See* Remote Access Server (RAS).

RDN *See* relative distinguished name (RDN).

read-only memory (ROM) A semiconductor circuit that contains information that cannot be modified.

refresh To update displayed information with current data.

refresh interval An interval of time used by secondary masters of a zone to determine how often to check if their zone data needs to be refreshed. When the refresh interval expires, the secondary master checks with its source for the zone to see if its zone data is still current or if it needs to be updated using a zone transfer. This interval is set in the SOA (start-of-authority) resource record for each zone.

relative distinguished name (RDN) The part of an object's distinguished name that is an attribute of the object itself. For most objects this is the Common Name attribute. For security principals, the default common name is the security principal name, also referred to as the *SAM account name.* For the distinguished name CN=MyName,CN=Users,DC=Microsoft,DC=Com the relative distinguished name of the MyName user object is CN=MyName. The relative distinguished name of the parent object is CN=Users.

relative ID An identifier assigned by domain controllers to security principals (user, group, or computer objects) created by that domain controller. The relative ID is combined with the domain security ID to create a security ID that is unique in the forest. A series of relative IDs is assigned (by the relative ID master) to each domain controller in the forest. When a domain controller uses most of the relative IDs assigned to it, it requests additional relative IDs from the domain controller that is the relative ID master.

relative ID master The domain controller assigned to allocate sequences of relative IDs to each domain controller in its domain. Whenever a domain controller creates a security principal (user, group, or computer object), the domain controller assigns the object a unique security ID. The security ID consists of a domain security ID that is the same for all security IDs created in a particular domain, and a relative ID that is unique for each security ID created in the domain. At any time, there can be only one relative ID master in a particular domain.

relative name The partial Domain Name System (DNS) domain name configured in individual resource records to locate and qualify the record within a zone. The relative name is joined to the front of the parent domain (domain of origin) for each resource record to form a fully qualified domain name (FQDN) within the zone.

remote access Part of the integrated Routing and Remote Access service that provides remote networking for telecommuters, mobile workers, and system administrators who monitor and manage servers at multiple branch offices. Users with a computer running Microsoft Windows 2000 and Network and Dial-up Connections can dial in to remotely access their networks for services such as file and printer sharing, electronic mail, scheduling, and SQL database access.

Remote Access Server (RAS) Any Microsoft Windows 2000-based computer configured to accept remote access connections.

remote administration The management of one computer by an administrator working at another computer connected to the first computer across a network.

remote computer A computer that you can access only by using a communications line or a communications device, such as a network card or a modem.

Remote Installation Services (RIS) Software services that allow an administrator to set up new client computers remotely, without having to visit each client. The target clients must support remote booting.

remote procedure call (RPC) A message-passing facility that allows a distributed application to call services available on various computers on a network. Used during remote administration of computers.

replication The process of copying data from a data store or file system to multiple computers to synchronize the data. Active Directory provides multimaster replication of the directory between domain controllers within a given domain. The replicas of the directory on each domain controller are writeable. This allows updates to be applied to any replica of a given domain. The replication service automatically copies the changes from a given replica to all other replicas.

replication policy Rules that define how and when replication is performed.

replication topology A description of the physical connections between replicas and sites. In contrast, Dfs topologies describe the logical connections.

Request for Comments (RFC) The official documents of the Internet Engineering Task Force (IETF) that specify the details for protocols included in the Transmission Control Protocol/ Internet Protocol (TCP/IP) family.

reservation A specific Internet Protocol (IP) address within a scope permanently reserved for leased use to a specific Dynamic Host Configuration Protocol (DHCP) client. Client reservations are made in the DHCP database using the DHCP console and based on a unique client device identifier for each reserved entry.

resolver   Domain Name System (DNS) client programs used to look up DNS name information.

resource   Any part of a computer system or a network, such as a disk drive, printer, or memory, that can be allotted to a program or a process while it is running or shared over a local area network.

resource record   Standard database record types used in zones to associate Domain Name System (DNS) domain names to related data for a given type of network resource, such as a host Internet Protocol (IP) address. Most of the basic resource record types are defined in RFC 1035, but additional resource record types have been defined in other Requests for Comments (RFCs) and approved for use with DNS.

reverse lookup   In Domain Name System (DNS), a query process by which the Internet Protocol (IP) address of a host computer is searched to find its friendly DNS domain name.

RFC   *See* Request for Comments (RFC).

RIPrep image   A clone of a standard corporate desktop configuration, complete with operating system configurations, desktop customizations, and locally installed applications. After first installing and configuring the Microsoft Windows 2000 Professional operating system, its services, and any standard applications on a computer, the network administrator runs a wizard that prepares the RIPrep installation image and replicates it to an available Remote Installation Services (RIS) server on the network for installation on other clients.

RIS   *See* Remote Installation Services (RIS).

RIS boot disk   Simulates the Pre-Boot eXecution Environment (PXE) remote boot sequence and

supports frequently used network cards for computers that do not contain a PXE-based remote boot ROM. The RIS boot disk can be used with a variety of Peripheral Component Interconnect (PCI)-based network adapter cards. Using the RIS boot disk eliminates the need to retrofit existing client computers with new network cards that contain a PXE-based remote boot ROM to take advantage of the Remote Operating System Installation feature.

roaming user profile   A server-based user profile that is downloaded to the local computer when a user logs on, and is updated both locally and on the server when the user logs off. A roaming user profile is available from the server when logging on to any computer running Microsoft Windows 2000 Professional or Windows 2000 Server. When logging on, the user can use the local user profile if it is more current than the copy on the server.

ROM   *See* read-only memory (ROM).

root domain   The domain at the top of the hierarchy, represented as a period (.). The Internet root domain is managed by several organizations, including Network Solutions, Inc.

RPC   *See* remote procedure call (RPC).

Run As program   Allows you to run administrative tools with either local or domain administrator rights and permissions while logged on as a normal user.

S

safe mode   A method of starting Microsoft Windows 2000 using basic files and drivers only, without networking. Safe mode is available by pressing the F8 key when prompted during startup. This allows you to start your computer when a problem prevents it from starting normally.

SAM   *See* Security Accounts Manager (SAM).

scalability A measure of how well a computer, service, or application can grow to meet increasing performance demands.

schema master The domain controller assigned to control all updates to the schema within a forest. At any time, there can be only one schema master in the forest.

scroll To move through text or graphics (up, down, left, or right) to see parts of the file that cannot fit on the screen.

scroll bar A bar that appears at the right and/or bottom edge of a window or list whose contents are not completely visible. Each scroll bar contains two scroll arrows and a scroll box, which enable you to scroll through the contents of the window or list.

SDK *See* Software Development Kit (SDK).

second-level domains Domain names that are rooted hierarchically at the second tier of the domain namespace directly beneath the top-level domain names such as .com and .org. When Domain Name System (DNS) is used on the Internet, second-level domains are names such as microsoft.com that are registered and delegated to individual organizations and businesses according to their top-level classification. The organization then assumes further responsibility for parenting management and growth of its name into additional subdomains.

secondary master An authoritative Domain Name System (DNS) server for a zone that is used as a source for replication of the zone to other servers. Secondary masters update their zone data only by transferring zone data from other DNS servers. They do not have the ability to perform zone updates.

Security Accounts Manager (SAM) A Microsoft Windows 2000 service used during the logon process. SAM maintains user account information, including groups to which a user belongs.

Security Configuration and Analysis A console that uses a database to perform security configuration and analysis functions.

security group Used to assign permissions to gain access to resources. Programs that are designed to search Active Directory can also use security groups for nonsecurity-related purposes, such as retrieving user information for use in a Web application. A security group also has all the capabilities of a distribution group. Microsoft Windows 2000 uses only security groups.

security ID *See* security identifier (SID).

security identifier (SID) A unique number that identifies user, group, and computer accounts. Every account on your network is issued a unique SID when the account is first created. Internal processes in Microsoft Windows 2000 refer to an account's SID rather than the account's user or group name. If you create an account, delete it, and then create an account with the same user name, the new account will not have the rights or permissions previously granted to the old account because the accounts have different SID numbers.

security log An event log containing information on security events that are specified in the audit policy.

security template A physical representation of a security configuration; a single file where a group of security settings is stored. Locating all security settings in one place eases security administration. Each template is saved as a text-based .inf file. This allows you to copy, paste, import, or export some or all of the template attributes.

select To mark an item so that a subsequent action can be carried out on that item. You usually select an item by clicking it with a mouse or pressing a key. After selecting an item, you choose the action that you want to affect the item.

server In general, a computer that provides shared resources to network users.

service A program, routine, or process that performs a specific system function to support other programs, particularly at a low (close to the hardware) level. When services are provided over a network, they can be published in Active Directory, facilitating service-centric administration and usage. Some examples of Microsoft Windows 2000 services are Security Accounts Manager service, File Replication service, and Routing and Remote Access service.

service (SRV) resource record A resource record used in a zone to register and locate well-known Transmission Control Protocol/Internet Protocol (TCP/IP) services. The SRV resource record is specified in RFC 2052 and is used in Microsoft Windows 2000 or later to locate domain controllers for Active Directory service.

share To make resources, such as folders and printers, available to others.

shared folder A folder on another computer that has been made available for others to use on the network.

shared folder permissions Permissions that restrict a shared resource's availability over the network to only certain users.

shared resource Any device, data, or program that is used by more than one other device or program. For Microsoft Windows 2000, shared resources refer to any resource that is made available to network users, such as folders, files, printers, and named pipes. A shared resource can also refer to a resource on a server that is available to network users.

shortcut A link to any item accessible on your computer or on a network, such as a program, file, folder, disk drive, Web page, printer, or another computer. You can put shortcuts in various areas, such as on the desktop, on the Start menu, or in specific folders.

SID *See* security identifier (SID).

Simple Mail Transport Protocol (SMTP) replication Used only for replication over site links (inter-site) and not for replication within a site (intra-site). Because SMTP is asynchronous, it typically ignores all schedules.

Single Instance Store (SIS) The service responsible for reducing disk space requirements on the volumes used for storing Remote Installation Services (RIS) installation images. When you install RIS as an optional component, you are prompted for a drive and directory where you would like to install RIS: This is the RIS volume. The SIS service attaches itself to the RIS volume and looks for any duplicate files that are placed on that volume. If duplicate files are found, SIS creates a link to the duplicates, thus reducing the disk space required.

SIS *See* Single Instance Store (SIS).

site One or more well-connected (highly reliable and fast) Transmission Control Protocol/Internet Protocol (TCP/IP) subnets. A site allows administrators to configure Active Directory access and replication topology quickly and easily to take advantage of the physical network. When users log on, Active Directory clients locate Active Directory servers in the same site as the user.

site link A link between two sites that allows replication to occur. Each site link contains the schedule that determines when replication can occur between the sites that it connects.

site link bridge The linking of more than two sites for replication and using the same transport. When site links are bridged, they are *transitive*—that is, all site links for a specific transport implicitly belong to a single site link bridge for that transport. A site link bridge is the equivalent of a disjoint network; all site links within the bridge can route transitively, but they do not route outside of the bridge.

smart card A credit-card-sized device used to securely store public and private keys, passwords, and other types of personal information. To use a smart card, you need a smart card reader attached to the computer and a personal identification number (PIN) for the smart card. In Microsoft Windows 2000, smart cards can be used to enable certificate-based authentication and single sign-on to the enterprise.

SMTP *See* Simple Mail Transport Protocol (SMTP).

snap-in A type of tool you can add to a console supported by Microsoft Management Console (MMC). A stand-alone snap-in can be added by itself; an extension snap-in can only be added to extend the function of another snap-in.

software distribution point In Software Installation, a network location from which users are able to get the software that they need.

Software Installation An extension within group policy that is the administrator's primary tool for managing software within an organization. Software Installation works in conjunction with group policy and Active Directory, establishing a group policy-based software management system that allows you to centrally manage the initial deployment of software, mandatory and nonmandatory upgrades, patches, quick fixes, and the removal of software.

special permissions On Microsoft Windows NT file system (NTFS) volumes, a custom set of permissions. You can customize permissions on files and directories by selecting the individual components of the standard sets of permissions.

stand-alone server A computer that runs Microsoft Windows 2000 Server but does not participate in a domain. A stand-alone server has only its own database of users, and it processes logon requests by itself. It does not share account information with any other computer and cannot provide access to domain accounts.

Start-of-Authority (SOA) resource record A record that indicates the starting point or original point of authority for information stored in a zone. The SOA resource record (RR) is the first RR created when adding a new zone. It also contains several parameters used by other computers that use Domain Name System (DNS) to determine how long they will use information for the zone and how often updates are required.

status bar A line of information related to the program in the window, usually located at the bottom of a window. Not all windows have a status bar.

subdirectory A directory within a directory. Also called a *folder within a folder.*

subdomain A Domain Name System (DNS) domain located directly beneath another domain name (the parent domain) in the namespace tree. For example, example.microsoft.com would be a subdomain of the domain microsoft.com. A subdomain is also called a *child domain.*

subnet A portion of a network, which may be a physically independent network segment, that shares a network address with other portions of the network and is distinguished by a subnet number. A subnet is to a network what a network is to an internet.

subnet mask A 32-bit value that allows the recipient of Internet Protocol (IP) packets to distinguish the network ID portion of the IP address from the host ID.

support tools Additional tools intended for use by Microsoft support personnel and experienced users to assist in diagnosing and resolving computer problems. The Windows 2000 Support Tools are included on the Windows 2000 CD-ROM in the \Support\Tools folder.

subtree Any node within a tree, along with any selection of connected descendant nodes. In the registry structure, subtrees are the primary node and contain keys, subkeys, and value entries.

support tools   Additional tools intended for use by Microsoft support personnel and experienced users to assist in diagnosing and resolving computer problems. The Windows 2000 Support Tools are included on the Windows 2000 CD-ROM in the \Support\Tools folder.

syntax   The order in which you must type a command and the elements that follow the command.

system files   Files used by Microsoft Windows to load, configure, and run the operating system. Generally, system files must never be deleted or moved.

System menu   A menu that contains commands you can use to manipulate a window or close a program. You click the program icon at the left of the title bar to open the System menu.

System Monitor   A tool that allows you to collect and view extensive data about the usage of hardware resources and the activity of system services on computers you administer.

system partition   The partition that contains the hardware-specific files needed to load Microsoft Windows 2000 (for example, NTLDR, OSLOADER, BOOT.INI, NTDETECT.COM). The system partition can be, but does not have to be, the same as the boot partition.

systemroot   The path and folder name where the Microsoft Windows 2000 system files are located. Typically, this is C:\Winnt, although you can designate a different drive or folder when you install Windows 2000. You can use the value %systemroot% to replace the actual location of the folder that contains the Windows 2000 system files. To identify your systemroot folder, click Start, click Run, then type **%systemroot%**.

system volume   The volume that contains the hardware-specific files needed to load Microsoft Windows 2000. The system volume can be, but does not have to be, the same volume as the boot volume.

SYSVOL   A shared directory that stores the server copy of the domain's public files, which are replicated among all domain controllers in the domain.

T

TAPI   *See* Telephony API (TAPI).

Task Manager   A Microsoft Windows 2000 utility that provides information about programs and processes running on the computer. Using Task Manager, you can end or run programs, end processes, and display a dynamic overview of your computer's performance.

Task Scheduler   A tool used to schedule programs and batch files to run once, at regular intervals, or at specific times.

TCO   *See* total cost of ownership (TCO).

TCP/IP   *See* Transmission Control Protocol/Internet Protocol (TCP/IP).

Telephony API (TAPI)   An application programming interface (API) used by communications programs to work with telephony and network services. Communications programs like HyperTerminal and Phone Dialer use TAPI to dial, answer, and route telephone calls on conventional telephony devices, including PBXs, modems, and fax machines. TAPI 3.0 also provides Internet Protocol (IP) telephony support, which Phone Dialer and other programs use to transmit, route, and control real-time audio and video signals over IP-based networks such as the Internet.

Terminal services   Software services that allow client applications to be run on a server so that client computers can function as terminals rather than independent systems. The server provides a multisession environment and runs the Microsoft Windows-based programs being used on the clients.

text file   A file containing text characters (letters, numbers, and symbols) but no formatting information. A text file can be a "plain" ASCII file that most computers can read. A text file can also refer to a word processing file.

TFTPD *See* Trivial File Transfer Protocol Daemon (TFTPD) service.

thread A specific set of commands within a program.

Time-To-Live (TTL) A timer value included in packets sent over Transmission Control Protocol/Internet Protocol(TCP/IP)-based networks that tells the recipients how long to hold or use the packet or any of its included data before expiring and discarding the packet or data. For Domain Name System (DNS), TTL values are used in resource records within a zone to determine how long requesting clients should cache and use this information when it appears in a query response answered by a DNS server for the zone.

title bar The horizontal bar (at the top of a window) that contains the title of the window or dialog box. On many windows, the title bar also contains the program icon and the Maximize, Minimize, and Close buttons.

top-level domain Domain names that are rooted hierarchically at the first tier of the domain namespace directly beneath the root (.) of the Domain Name System (DNS) namespace. On the Internet, top-level domain names such as .com and .org are used to classify and assign second-level domain names (such as microsoft.com) to individual organizations and businesses according to their organizational purpose.

topology In Microsoft Windows, the relationships among a set of network components. In the context of Active Directory replication, topology refers to the set of connections that domain controllers use to replicate information among themselves.

total cost of ownership (TCO) The total amount of money and time associated with purchasing computer hardware and software and deploying, configuring, and maintaining the hardware and

software. TCO includes hardware and software updates, training, maintenance, administration, and technical support.

trace log A type of log generated when the user selects a trace data provider using the Performance console. Trace logs differ from counter logs in that they measure data continuously rather than taking periodic samples.

transforms *See* modifications.

transitive trust *See* implicit two-way transitive trust.

Transmission Control Protocol/Internet Protocol (TCP/IP) A set of networking protocols used on the Internet that provides communications across interconnected networks made up of computers with diverse hardware architectures and various operating systems. TCP/IP includes standards for how computers communicate and conventions for connecting networks and routing traffic.

tree A set of Microsoft Windows 2000 domains connected together via a two-way transitive trust, sharing a common schema, configuration, and global catalog. The domains must form a contiguous hierarchical namespace such that if microsoft.com is the root of the tree, example.microsoft.com is a child of microsoft.com, another.example.microsoft.com is a child of example.microsoft.com, and so on.

Trivial File Transfer Protocol Daemon (TFTPD) service The service responsible for hosting specific file download requests made by the client computer. The TFTPD service is used to download the Client Installation Wizard (CIW) and all client dialog boxes contained within the CIW for a given session.

Trojan horse A program that masquerades as another common program in an attempt to receive information. An example of a Trojan horse is a program that behaves like a system logon to retrieve user names and password information that the writers of the Trojan horse can later use to break into the system.

trust relationship A logical relationship established between domains to allow pass-through authentication, in which a trusting domain honors the logon authentications of a trusted domain. User accounts and global groups defined in a trusted domain can be given rights and permissions in a trusting domain, even though the user accounts or groups do not exist in the trusting domain's directory.

TTL *See* Time-To-Live (TTL).

tunnel A logical connection over which data is encapsulated. Typically, both encapsulation and encryption are performed and the tunnel is a private, secure link between a remote user or host and a private network.

U

UNC *See* Universal Naming Convention (UNC) name.

Unicode A standard encoding scheme used for computer-text-based data. Unicode uses 2 bytes (16 bits) to represent each character, which allows 65,536 possible unique characters to be assigned. This number of possible character values enables almost all of the written languages of the world to be represented using a single character set.

universal group A security or distribution group that can be used anywhere in the domain tree or forest. A universal group can have members from any Microsoft Windows 2000 domain in the domain tree or forest. It can also include other universal groups, global groups, and accounts from any domain in the domain tree or forest. Rights and permissions must be assigned on a per-domain basis, but can be assigned at any domain in the domain tree or forest. Universal groups can be members of domain local groups and other universal groups but cannot be members

of global groups. Universal groups appear in the global catalog and should contain primarily global groups.

Universal Naming Convention (UNC) name The full Microsoft Windows 2000 name of a resource on a network. It conforms to the *servername*\ *sharename* syntax, where servername is the name of the server and sharename is the name of the shared resource. UNC names of directories or files can also include the directory path under the share name, with the following syntax: *servername**sharename**directory**filename*.

UPN *See* user principal name (UPN).

user account A record that consists of all the information that defines a user to Microsoft Windows 2000. This includes the user name and password required for the user to log on, the groups in which the user account has membership, and the rights and permissions the user has for using the computer and network and accessing their resources. For Windows 2000 Professional and member servers, user accounts are managed with the Local Users and Groups console. For Windows 2000 Server domain controllers, user accounts are managed with the Active Directory Users and Computers console.

user mode A console mode that does not enable full access to all Microsoft Management Console (MMC) functionality. There are three types of user modes that allow different levels of access and functionality: Full Access; Limited Access, Multiple Windows; and Limited Access, Single Window.

user name A unique name identifying a user account to Microsoft Windows 2000. An account's user name must be unique among the other group names and user names within its own domain or workgroup.

user principal name (UPN) This consists of a user account name (sometimes referred to as the *user logon name*) and a domain name identifying the domain in which the user account is located. This is the standard usage for logging on to a Microsoft Windows 2000 domain. The format is: user@domain.com (as for an e-mail address).

user profile A profile that defines the Microsoft Windows 2000 environment that is loaded by the system when a user logs on. It includes all the user-specific settings of a user's Windows 2000 environment, such as program items, screen colors, network connections, printer connections, mouse settings, and window size and position.

user rights Tasks a user is permitted to perform on a computer system or domain, such as backing up files and folders, adding or deleting users in a workstation or domain, and shutting down a computer system. Rights can be granted to groups or to user accounts, but are best reserved for use by groups. User rights are set in group policy.

user rights policy Security settings that manage the assignment of rights to groups and user accounts.

V

Virtual Private Networking (VPN) The extension of a private network that encompasses encapsulated, encrypted, and authenticated links across shared or public networks. VPN connections can provide remote access and routed connections to private networks over the Internet.

volume A portion of a physical disk that functions as though it were a physically separate disk. In My Computer and Microsoft Windows Explorer, volumes appear as local disks such as C: or D:.

volume set A partition consisting of disk space on one or more physical disks that was created with Microsoft Windows NT 4.0 or earlier. You can delete volume sets only with Windows 2000. To create new volumes that span multiple disks, use spanned volumes on dynamic disks.

VPN *See* Virtual Private Networking (VPN).

W

WAN *See* wide area network (WAN).

Web server A computer that is maintained by a system administrator or Internet service provider (ISP) and that responds to requests from a user's browser.

well-connected Sufficient connectivity to make your network and Active Directory useful to clients on your network. The precise meaning of it is determined by your particular needs.

wide area network (WAN) The extension of a data network that uses telecommunication links to connect to geographically separated areas.

Windows 2000 Advanced Server A powerful departmental and application server that provides rich network operations system (NOS) and Internet services. Advanced Server supports large physical memories, clustering, and load balancing.

Windows 2000 Datacenter Server The most powerful and functional server operating system in the Microsoft Windows 2000 family. It is optimized for large data warehouses, econometric analysis, large-scale simulations in science and engineering, and server consolidation projects.

Windows 2000 Executive This component performs most of the input/output (I/O) and object management, including security. It does not perform screen and keyboard I/O; the Microsoft Win32 subsystem performs these functions. The Windows 2000 Executive contains the Windows 2000 kernel mode components.

Windows 2000 Professional A high-performance, secure network client computer and corporate desktop operating system that includes the best features of Microsoft Windows 98, significantly extending the manageability, reliability, security, and performance of Windows NT Workstation 4.0. Windows 2000 Professional can be used alone as a desktop operating system, networked in a peer-to-peer workgroup environment, or used as a workstation in a Windows 2000 Server domain environment.

Windows 2000 Server A file, print, and applications server, as well as a Web server platform that contains all of the features of Microsoft Windows 2000 Professional plus many new server-specific functions. This product is ideal for small- to medium-sized enterprise application deployments, Web servers, workgroups, and branch offices.

Windows Installer Installs software packaged in Microsoft Windows Installer files.

Windows Internet Naming Service (WINS) A software service that dynamically maps Internet Protocol (IP) addresses to computer names (NetBIOS names). This allows users to access resources by name instead of requiring them to use IP addresses that are difficult to recognize and remember. WINS servers support clients running Microsoft Windows NT 4.0 and earlier versions of Microsoft operating systems.

WINS *See* Windows Internet Naming Service (WINS).

workgroup A simple grouping of computers, intended only to help users find such things as printers and shared folders within that group. Workgroups in Windows 2000 do not offer the centralized user accounts and authentication offered by domains.

workstation Any networked Macintosh or PC using server resources.

Z

zone In a Domain Name System (DNS) database, a zone is a subtree of the DNS database that is administered as a single separate entity, a DNS server. This administrative unit can consist of a single domain or a domain with subdomains. A DNS zone administrator sets up one or more name servers for the zone.

zone database file The file where name-to-IP-address mappings for a zone are stored.

zone transfer The process by which Domain Name System (DNS) servers interact to maintain and synchronize authoritative name data. When a DNS server is configured as a secondary master for a zone, it periodically queries another DNS server configured as its source for the zone. If the version of the zone kept by the source is different, the secondary master server will pull zone data from its source DNS server to synchronize zone data.

Index

Note to the reader Italics are used to indicate references to illustrations.

Impact Wrench

Wrenches come in a variety of shapes and functions, such as locking, open-end, box, socket, combination, and torque wrenches. One of the most interesting is the **impact wrench**, powered by air, which can tighten nuts or bolts to a predetermined tension. Nuts and bolts tightened by pneumatic impact wrenches produce a clamping force better than that attainable by rivets, and can retain their clamping force for many years. Using impact wrenches during construction is usually far quieter than driving rivets, and the cost of the resulting structure is comparable.*

At Microsoft Press, we use tools to illustrate our books for software developers and IT professionals. Tools very simply and powerfully symbolize human inventiveness. They're a metaphor for people extending their capabilities, precision, and reach. From simple calipers and pliers to digital micrometers and lasers, these stylized illustrations give each book a visual identity, and a personality to the series. With tools and knowledge, there's no limit to creativity and innovation. Our tagline says it all: *the tools you need to put technology to work*.

Your source for
the most complete, accurate,
and up-to-date *networking*
information available.

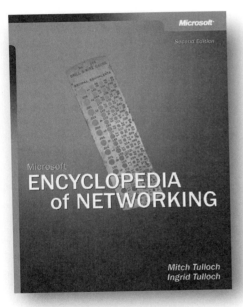

Microsoft® Encyclopedia of Networking

U.S.A. $ 79.99
Canada $115.99
ISBN: 0-7356-1378-8

Get the single resource that defines—and illustrates—the rapidly evolving world of networking. The second edition of the award-winning MICROSOFT ENCYCLOPEDIA OF NETWORKING is fully updated with thousands of entries detailing the latest technologies, standards, products, and services. You get clear, concise explanations, including *hundreds* of new articles and diagrams, that deftly take you from concept to real-world application. You also get the entire encyclopedia on CD-ROM, for definitive answers wherever you need them.

Microsoft®
microsoft.com/mspress

Learn how to use Microsoft
.NET Enterprise Servers
and strategies to solve common e-business problems.

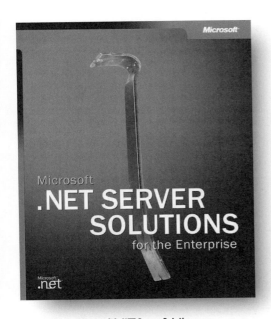

Microsoft® .NET Server Solutions for the Enterprise

U.S.A.	**$49.99**
Canada	$72.99
ISBN: 0-7356-1569-1	

Planning, developing, and deploying enterprise e-business solutions across different platforms can be challenging. MICROSOFT .NET SERVER SOLUTIONS FOR THE ENTERPRISE simplifies the process. This fact-filled guidebook combines a wealth of technical information with real-world scenarios to deliver clear, concrete details on how to solve common e-business integration problems. Each chapter presents a specific e-business problem along with a detailed discussion of the Microsoft .NET Server tools and technologies used to solve it—complete with schematic diagrams and other help. You'll learn how to make Microsoft .NET Servers work together to solve problems—and how to prepare for future Web-based services.

Microsoft
microsoft.com/mspress

Get the *expert guide to*
planning, deploying,
and maintaining
Windows 2000 Server

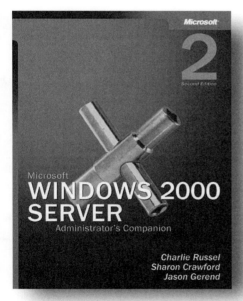

**Microsoft® Windows® 2000 Server
Administrator's Companion, Second Edition**
U.S.A. $ 69.99
Canada $107.99
ISBN: 0-7356-1785-6

The expanded, updated version of this popular operations guide is packed full of practical information to help you plan the installation, deployment, and maintenance of Windows 2000 Server. In addition to updated material on core topics such as security, disaster planning and recovery, and interoperability with NetWare, UNIX, and Linux, it also includes new sections about Microsoft Internet Security and Acceleration Server, scripting, all the features released in Service Pack 3, 128-bit encryption, and other vital topics. Appendices list interface changes, optional components, and support tools.

Microsoft®
microsoft.com/mspress

Get a **Free**
e-mail newsletter, updates,
special offers, links to related books,
and more when you
register on line!

Register your Microsoft Press® title on our Web site and you'll get
a FREE subscription to our e-mail newsletter, *Microsoft Press Book
Connections.* You'll find out about newly released and upcoming books
and learning tools, online events, software downloads, special offers
and coupons for Microsoft Press customers, and information about
major Microsoft® product releases. You can also read useful additional
information about all the titles we publish, such as detailed book
descriptions, tables of contents and indexes, sample chapters, links to
related books and book series, author biographies, and reviews by other
customers.

Registration is easy. Just visit this Web page and fill in your information:

http://www.microsoft.com/mspress/register

Microsoft®

Proof of Purchase

Use this page as proof of purchase if participating in a promotion or rebate offer on
this title. Proof of purchase must be used in conjunction with other proof(s) of
payment such as your dated sales receipt—see offer details.

MCSE Self-Paced Training Kit: Microsoft® Windows® 2000 Active Directory® Services, Exam 70-217, Second Edition
0-7356-1759-7

CUSTOMER NAME

Microsoft Press, PO Box 97017, Redmond, WA 98073-9830

MICROSOFT LICENSE AGREEMENT
Book Companion CD

IMPORTANT—READ CAREFULLY: This Microsoft End-User License Agreement ("EULA") is a legal agreement between you (either an individual or an entity) and Microsoft Corporation for the Microsoft product identified above, which includes computer software and may include associated media, printed materials, and "online" or electronic documentation ("SOFTWARE PRODUCT"). Any component included within the SOFTWARE PRODUCT that is accompanied by a separate End-User License Agreement shall be governed by such agreement and not the terms set forth below. By installing, copying, or otherwise using the SOFTWARE PRODUCT, you agree to be bound by the terms of this EULA. If you do not agree to the terms of this EULA, you are not authorized to install, copy, or otherwise use the SOFTWARE PRODUCT; you may, however, return the SOFTWARE PRODUCT, along with all printed materials and other items that form a part of the Microsoft product that includes the SOFTWARE PRODUCT, to the place you obtained them for a full refund.

SOFTWARE PRODUCT LICENSE

The SOFTWARE PRODUCT is protected by United States copyright laws and international copyright treaties, as well as other intellectual property laws and treaties. The SOFTWARE PRODUCT is licensed, not sold.

1. **GRANT OF LICENSE.** This EULA grants you the following rights:

    a. **Software Product.** You may install and use one copy of the SOFTWARE PRODUCT on a single computer. The primary user of the computer on which the SOFTWARE PRODUCT is installed may make a second copy for his or her exclusive use on a portable computer.

    b. **Storage/Network Use.** You may also store or install a copy of the SOFTWARE PRODUCT on a storage device, such as a network server, used only to install or run the SOFTWARE PRODUCT on your other computers over an internal network; however, you must acquire and dedicate a license for each separate computer on which the SOFTWARE PRODUCT is installed or run from the storage device. A license for the SOFTWARE PRODUCT may not be shared or used concurrently on different computers.

    c. **License Pak.** If you have acquired this EULA in a Microsoft License Pak, you may make the number of additional copies of the computer software portion of the SOFTWARE PRODUCT authorized on the printed copy of this EULA, and you may use each copy in the manner specified above. You are also entitled to make a corresponding number of secondary copies for portable computer use as specified above.

    d. **Sample Code.** Solely with respect to portions, if any, of the SOFTWARE PRODUCT that are identified within the SOFTWARE PRODUCT as sample code (the "SAMPLE CODE"):

    i. **Use and Modification.** Microsoft grants you the right to use and modify the source code version of the SAMPLE CODE, *provided* you comply with subsection (d)(iii) below. You may not distribute the SAMPLE CODE, or any modified version of the SAMPLE CODE, in source code form.

    ii. **Redistributable Files.** Provided you comply with subsection (d)(iii) below, Microsoft grants you a nonexclusive, royalty-free right to reproduce and distribute the object code version of the SAMPLE CODE and of any modified SAMPLE CODE, other than SAMPLE CODE, or any modified version thereof, designated as not redistributable in the Readme file that forms a part of the SOFTWARE PRODUCT (the "Non-Redistributable Sample Code"). All SAMPLE CODE other than the Non-Redistributable Sample Code is collectively referred to as the "REDISTRIBUTABLES."

    iii. **Redistribution Requirements.** If you redistribute the REDISTRIBUTABLES, you agree to: (i) distribute the REDISTRIBUTABLES in object code form only in conjunction with and as a part of your software application product; (ii) not use Microsoft's name, logo, or trademarks to market your software application product; (iii) include a valid copyright notice on your software application product; (iv) indemnify, hold harmless, and defend Microsoft from and against any claims or lawsuits, including attorney's fees, that arise or result from the use or distribution of your software application product; and (v) not permit further distribution of the REDISTRIBUTABLES by your end user. Contact Microsoft for the applicable royalties due and other licensing terms for all other uses and/or distribution of the REDISTRIBUTABLES.

2. **DESCRIPTION OF OTHER RIGHTS AND LIMITATIONS.**

    - **Limitations on Reverse Engineering, Decompilation, and Disassembly.** You may not reverse engineer, decompile, or disassemble the SOFTWARE PRODUCT, except and only to the extent that such activity is expressly permitted by applicable law notwithstanding this limitation.

    - **Separation of Components.** The SOFTWARE PRODUCT is licensed as a single product. Its component parts may not be separated for use on more than one computer.

    - **Rental.** You may not rent, lease, or lend the SOFTWARE PRODUCT.

- **Support Services.** Microsoft may, but is not obligated to, provide you with support services related to the SOFTWARE PRODUCT ("Support Services"). Use of Support Services is governed by the Microsoft policies and programs described in the user manual, in "online" documentation, and/or in other Microsoft-provided materials. Any supplemental software code provided to you as part of the Support Services shall be considered part of the SOFTWARE PRODUCT and subject to the terms and conditions of this EULA. With respect to technical information you provide to Microsoft as part of the Support Services, Microsoft may use such information for its business purposes, including for product support and development. Microsoft will not utilize such technical information in a form that personally identifies you.

- **Software Transfer.** You may permanently transfer all of your rights under this EULA, provided you retain no copies, you transfer all of the SOFTWARE PRODUCT (including all component parts, the media and printed materials, any upgrades, this EULA, and, if applicable, the Certificate of Authenticity), **and** the recipient agrees to the terms of this EULA.

- **Termination.** Without prejudice to any other rights, Microsoft may terminate this EULA if you fail to comply with the terms and conditions of this EULA. In such event, you must destroy all copies of the SOFTWARE PRODUCT and all of its component parts.

3. **COPYRIGHT.** All title and copyrights in and to the SOFTWARE PRODUCT (including but not limited to any images, photographs, animations, video, audio, music, text, SAMPLE CODE, REDISTRIBUTABLES, and "applets" incorporated into the SOFTWARE PRODUCT) and any copies of the SOFTWARE PRODUCT are owned by Microsoft or its suppliers. The SOFT-WARE PRODUCT is protected by copyright laws and international treaty provisions. Therefore, you must treat the SOFTWARE PRODUCT like any other copyrighted material **except** that you may install the SOFTWARE PRODUCT on a single computer provided you keep the original solely for backup or archival purposes. You may not copy the printed materials accompanying the SOFTWARE PRODUCT.

4. **U.S. GOVERNMENT RESTRICTED RIGHTS.** The SOFTWARE PRODUCT and documentation are provided with RESTRICTED RIGHTS. Use, duplication, or disclosure by the Government is subject to restrictions as set forth in subparagraph (c)(1)(ii) of the Rights in Technical Data and Computer Software clause at DFARS 252.227-7013 or subparagraphs (c)(1) and (2) of the Commercial Computer Software—Restricted Rights at 48 CFR 52.227-19, as applicable. Manufacturer is Microsoft Corporation/One Microsoft Way/Redmond, WA 98052-6399.

5. **EXPORT RESTRICTIONS.** You agree that you will not export or re-export the SOFTWARE PRODUCT, any part thereof, or any process or service that is the direct product of the SOFTWARE PRODUCT (the foregoing collectively referred to as the "Restricted Components"), to any country, person, entity, or end user subject to U.S. export restrictions. You specifically agree not to export or re-export any of the Restricted Components (i) to any country to which the U.S. has embargoed or restricted the export of goods or services, which currently include, but are not necessarily limited to, Cuba, Iran, Iraq, Libya, North Korea, Sudan, and Syria, or to any national of any such country, wherever located, who intends to transmit or transport the Restricted Components back to such country; (ii) to any end user who you know or have reason to know will utilize the Restricted Components in the design, development, or production of nuclear, chemical, or biological weapons; or (iii) to any end user who has been prohibited from participating in U.S. export transactions by any federal agency of the U.S. government. You warrant and represent that neither the BXA nor any other U.S. federal agency has suspended, revoked, or denied your export privileges.

DISCLAIMER OF WARRANTY

NO WARRANTIES OR CONDITIONS. MICROSOFT EXPRESSLY DISCLAIMS ANY WARRANTY OR CONDITION FOR THE SOFTWARE PRODUCT. THE SOFTWARE PRODUCT AND ANY RELATED DOCUMENTATION ARE PROVIDED "AS IS" WITHOUT WARRANTY OR CONDITION OF ANY KIND, EITHER EXPRESS OR IMPLIED, INCLUDING, WITHOUT LIMITA-TION, THE IMPLIED WARRANTIES OF MERCHANTABILITY, FITNESS FOR A PARTICULAR PURPOSE, OR NONINFRINGEMENT. THE ENTIRE RISK ARISING OUT OF USE OR PERFORMANCE OF THE SOFTWARE PRODUCT REMAINS WITH YOU.

LIMITATION OF LIABILITY. TO THE MAXIMUM EXTENT PERMITTED BY APPLICABLE LAW, IN NO EVENT SHALL MICROSOFT OR ITS SUPPLIERS BE LIABLE FOR ANY SPECIAL, INCIDENTAL, INDIRECT, OR CONSEQUENTIAL DAM-AGES WHATSOEVER (INCLUDING, WITHOUT LIMITATION, DAMAGES FOR LOSS OF BUSINESS PROFITS, BUSINESS INTERRUPTION, LOSS OF BUSINESS INFORMATION, OR ANY OTHER PECUNIARY LOSS) ARISING OUT OF THE USE OF OR INABILITY TO USE THE SOFTWARE PRODUCT OR THE PROVISION OF OR FAILURE TO PROVIDE SUPPORT SERVICES, EVEN IF MICROSOFT HAS BEEN ADVISED OF THE POSSIBILITY OF SUCH DAMAGES. IN ANY CASE, MICROSOFT'S ENTIRE LIABILITY UNDER ANY PROVISION OF THIS EULA SHALL BE LIMITED TO THE GREATER OF THE AMOUNT ACTUALLY PAID BY YOU FOR THE SOFTWARE PRODUCT OR US$5.00; PROVIDED, HOWEVER, IF YOU HAVE ENTERED INTO A MICROSOFT SUPPORT SERVICES AGREEMENT, MICROSOFT'S ENTIRE LIABILITY REGARDING SUPPORT SERVICES SHALL BE GOVERNED BY THE TERMS OF THAT AGREEMENT. BECAUSE SOME STATES AND JURISDICTIONS DO NOT ALLOW THE EXCLUSION OR LIMITATION OF LIABILITY, THE ABOVE LIMITATION MAY NOT APPLY TO YOU.

MISCELLANEOUS

This EULA is governed by the laws of the State of Washington USA, except and only to the extent that applicable law mandates govern-ing law of a different jurisdiction.

Should you have any questions concerning this EULA, or if you desire to contact Microsoft for any reason, please contact the Microsoft subsidiary serving your country, or write: Microsoft Sales Information Center/One Microsoft Way/Redmond, WA 98052-6399.

System Requirements

To use the online version of this book from the Supplemental Course Materials CD-ROM, you need a computer equipped with the following minimum configuration:

- 133-MHz or higher Pentium-compatible CPU
- Microsoft Windows 95, Windows 98, or Microsoft Windows NT 4.0 or later
- 16 MB of RAM
- 500-MB hard drive with 15 MB of available disk space
- 24X CD-ROM drive
- Microsoft Mouse or compatible pointing device (recommended)
- Microsoft Internet Explorer 5.01 or later

To use the Evaluation Edition of the Microsoft Windows 2000 Server software included with this kit, you need a computer equipped with the following minimum configuration:

- 133-MHz or higher Pentium-compatible CPU
- 256 MB of RAM
- 2-GB hard drive with a minimum of 1.0 GB free space
- 12X CD-ROM drive

To use this book's Readiness Review compact disc, you need a computer equipped with the following minimum configuration:

- Microsoft Windows 95 or Microsoft Windows NT 4 with Service Pack 3 or higher, or Microsoft Windows 98 or Microsoft Windows 2000 Professional
- Microsoft Internet Explorer 5.01 or later
- Multimedia PC with a 75-MHz Pentium or higher processor
- 16 MB RAM for Windows 95 or Windows 98 (minimum)
- 32 MB RAM for Windows NT (minimum)
- 64 MB RAM for Windows 2000 (minimum)
- 17 MB available hard-drive space for installation
- A double-speed CD-ROM drive or better
- Super VGA display with at least 256 colors
- Microsoft Mouse or compatible pointing device